Organizational Theory

TEXT AND CASES

THIRD EDITION

Gareth R. Jones

Texas A & M University

Prentice Hall

Upper Saddle River, New Jersey 07458

Library of Congress Cataloging-in-Publication Data

Jones, Gareth R.
    Organizational theory: text and cases/Gareth R. Jones.—3rd ed.
        p. cm.
    Supplemented by videotape and Powerpoint transparencies packages and an instructor's manual.
    Includes bibliographical references and index.
    ISBN 0-13-018378-4 (alk. paper)
        1. Organizational behavior. 2. Organizational behavior—Case studies. I. Title.

HD58.7. J62 2000
302.3'5—dc2l   00-036319

Senior Editor: David Shafer
Managing Editor (Editorial): Jennifer Glennon
Editorial Assistant: Kim Marsden
Assistant Editor: Michele Foresta
Media Project Manager: Michele Faranda
Executive Marketing Manager: Michael Campbell
Managing Editor (Production): Judy Leale
Production Editor: Lynda P. Hansler/Emma Moore
Production Assistant: Keri Jean
Permissions Coordinator: Suzanne Grappi
Production Manager: Arnold Vila
Manufacturing Buyer: Diane Peirano
Associate Director, Manufacturing: Vincent Scelta
Design Manager: Patricia Smythe
Designer: Steven Frim
Interior Design: Nicola Ferguson
Cover Design: Steven Frim
Cover Art: Eric Vandeville/Liaison Agency
Associate Director, Multimedia Production: Karen Goldsmith
Manager Multimedia Production: Christina Mahon
Composition: Preparè, Inc.

10 9 8 7 6 5 4 3 2 1
ISBN 0-13-018378-4

For Nicholas and Julia

Brief Contents

Contents

Part 3 · THE TECHNOLOGICAL ENVIRONMENT

ORGANIZATIONAL INSIGHTS

9.1 | Progressive Manufacture at Ford, 266 • 9.2 | The Ethics of Mass Production, 272 • 9.3 | The San Diego Zoo Changes Its Stripes, 281 • 9.4 | USAA Improving the Delivery of Intangible Services, 286 • 9.5 | A New Approach at Hewlett-Packard, 289

MANAGERIAL IMPLICATIONS

9.1 | Analyzing Technology, 290

ORGANIZATIONAL INSIGHTS

MANAGERIAL IMPLICATIONS

FOCUS ON NEW INFORMATION TECHNOLOGY:

Part 4 · MANAGING ORGANIZATIONAL PROCESSES

Part 5 · CASES IN ORGANIZATIONAL THEORY

Preface

The wave of organizational change that overtook most large global organizations during the 1990s validates the approach to organizational theory that I have adopted in the last two editions of my book: managers should be responsible for creatively managing their organization's structure and culture and they need to understand the basic building blocks on which they work. Today, a contingency approach to organizational design is not always appropriate because most organizations confront the same or a very similar set of contingency factors. For example, most organizations must manage the same set of forces in the domestic and global environment; managers need to manage the same technological changes brought about by the internet, or they all need to develop low cost and differentiation strategies simultaneously.

The main issue is understanding how organizations work, then understanding how the different contingency factors can affect the choices managers make. This is how my book is organized, and the level of support I have received for my approach from users both in the United States and abroad leads me to believe that my approach is appreciated by the book's adopters. All the main elements that were in the last edition remain because they work. For example, the cases at the end of the book have great teaching value in showing students what the abstract concepts of organizational theory mean in practice. As I emphasized in the last edition, these cases should not be used for student assignments. Their value lies in stimulating class discussion and time has proven their success.

For this edition I have made two main innovations. First, I have incorporated the effects of the Internet on organizational theory and design throughout the book's chapters. For example, I discuss the theoretical implications of the Internet for firm structure and strategy. I have also developed an ongoing case study feature that profiles how Amazon.com has developed an organizational strategy and structure to take advantage of the Internet and outperform its older, more established competitors. This feature can be found in ten of the book's chapters and each part builds systematically on the former.

Second, in response to reviewer and user suggestions, I have streamlined the chapters in order to make the material easier to comprehend and absorb. I have eliminated one idea in each chapter and condensed the number of illustrative examples to provide a more focused learning experience. These ideas have not been lost. They are now to be found in the instructors manual as additional material if so desired. I have also revised and updated all the boxed insights, where relevant to keep the examples as up to date as possible.

Finally, as in the last two editions, I have tried to ensure that (1) it is comprehensive and up-to-date and makes important theories accessible and interesting to students, (2) it maintains a tight, integrated flow between chapters, and (3) it provides direct, clear managerial implications.

COMPREHENSIVE AND UP-TO-DATE COVERAGE

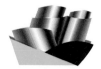

As noted above, each of the chapters has been reorganized both to facilitate students' understanding of organizational theory concepts and to provide expanded coverage of emerging issues such as the Internet. In particular Chapter 10, Managing the New Technological Environments, has been revised to include much greater coverage of Internet technology and its effects on organizational design, such as the flattening of organizational structure.

For new users of *Organizational Theory*, please note that along with other material you will find:

- Detailed coverage of the stakeholder approach to organizations and the implications of this approach for organizational effectiveness.
- Explanations of the most recent developments in organizational structure such as the product team structure, outsourcing, and the network organizations.
- An in-depth look at organizational culture that accounts for the origins of culture and its relationship to organizational effectiveness.
- Discussion of the recent literature on interorganizational linkage mechanisms, and an account of the role of resource dependance theory and transaction cost theory in explaining why organizations choose different types of linkage mechanisms.
- An integrated account of the strategy–structure relationship.
- Comprehensive coverage of international strategy and structure and global organizational design.
- An analysis of new technological developments that is integrated in the traditional concepts used in organizational theory.
- A detailed discussion of both population ecology theory and institutional theory.

INTEGRATED PROGRESSION OF TOPICS

Many textbooks lack a tight, integrated flow of topics from chaper to chapter. In this book students are told from Chapter 1 on how the book's topics are related to each other. Integration has been achieved by organizing the material of earlier ones in a logical fashion.

The book begins with a focus on what an organization is, which stakeholders it serves, and how an organization is constructed to satisfy stakeholder needs—that is, the design of its organizational structure—before turning to contingency factors that effect organizations. In the first four chapters of this book I lay out the central design challenges facing an organization if it is to successfully create value for its stakeholders and achieve a competitive advantage that will allow it to survive. Using examples as diverse as the U.S. Post Office, Kinko's, General Motors, IBM, and the San Diego Zoo, I examine the challenges these organizations have faced in designing their organizational structures to improve their effectiveness. In Chapter 5, I examine the nature and origins of organizational culture and discuss how it affects the way organizations operate and how it impacts organizational effectiveness. By the end of Part 1, students are provided with a clear account of the main components of organizational structure and culture. The issues and challenges facing organizations are discussed in a contemporary context, and the experiences of organizationas such as General Motors, IBM, Digital Equipment, Chrysler, and many others demonstrate the lessons of organizational design and what happens to organizations that do not get it right.

Once students understand what an organization is and the organizational design challenges it confronts in its quest to survive and create value, I then turn to the issues of which contingencies the organization faces in the environment and how it must manage these contingencies—through its structure and its strategy—to gain access to scarce resources. Chapter 6 discusses various organization-environment theories such as contingency theory, resource dependance theory, and transaction cost theory and examines the implications of these theories for the design of organizational structure and the kinds if interorganizational linkage mechanisms organizations must develop to manage the environment. Chapter 7 discusses how organizations develop and use strategies to gain access to resources and to create value for their stakeholders. In this chapter I also examine how different kinds of strategies require different kinks of structures and interorganizational linkage mechanisms if the strategies are to be persued successfully. Chapter 8 focuses on the international environment and the special set of problems that organizations encounter in designing their strategies and structutes to successfully manage the global environment. By the end of Part 2, the way in which environment affects organizations and the organizations can manage the environment through their strategies and structures are clearly outlined.

In Part 3, I move on to technology and innovation. In Chapter 9, I discuss how three dimensions of technology—technical complexity, task nonroutineness, and task interdependence—affect organizational design. I then examine more recent developments in technology in Chapter 10 and discuss how advanced manufacturing technologies, total quality management, and advanced information technologies affect organizational design. Chapter 10 brings the technological concept up to date and demonstrates the continuing importance of this topic in organizational theory and design.

Finally, in Part 4, I discuss the organizational processes that influence the way organizations grow, adapt, and change over time. In Chapter 11, I use population ecology theory to examine the process of organizational birth, I use institutional theory to examine factors affecting organizational growth, and I examine several models of organizational growth and decline. As noted earlier, Chapter 12 then examines the way in which organizations make decisions, how organizational learning can improve the quality of decision making, and the way in which factors such as cognitive biases cause organizational inertia and lower the quality of decision making. Chapter 13 examines the related issues of innovation and change, and Chapter 14 completes this analysis of organizational processes by examining the interrelated issues of conflict, power, and politics. The way in which these processes affect organizational change and development is a major focus of this final chapter.

MANAGERIAL IMPLICATIONS

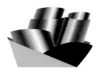

The lessons of organizational theory are clearly articulated for the needs of students who will soon be practicing managers. Each chapter has one or more managerial summaries where the implications of organizational theories and concepts are clearly outlined. In addition, each chapter has several "Organizational Insight" boxes in which the experiences of a real company are tied to the chapter material to highlight the implications of the material, and each chapter begins with a lengthy "Case in Point" that requires a hands-on analysis from students. Other learning features and support material that accompany this book also contribute to the student's learning experience.

LEARNING FEATURES AND SUPPORT MATERIAL

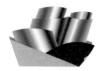

Each chapter ends with a set of experiential exercises designed to facilitate the student's understanding of the text material. The section entitled "Organizational Theory in Action" includes the following hands-on learning exercises/assignments:

- "Practicing Organizational Theory," an experiential exercise designed to give students hands-on experience doing organizational theory. Each exercise takes about 20 minutes of class time. The exercises have been class tested and work very well. Further details on how to use them are found in the instructors manual.
- A "Making the Connection" feature, where students collect examples of companies to illustrate organizational theory concepts.
- A short "Closing Case" with questions, which provides an opportunity for a short class discussion of a chapter-related theme.
- An ongoing "Analyzing the Organization" feature, where students select an organization to study and then complete chapter assignments that lead to an organizational theory analysis and a written case study of their organization. This case study is then presented to the class at the end of the semester. Complete details concerning the use of this and other learning features are in the instructors manual.

In addition to these hands-on learning exercises, I have kept or refined the other learning features that I developed for the first edition:

- Cases. At the end of the book are eighteen cases to be used in conjunction with the book's chapters to enrich students' understanding of organizational theory concepts. I have writted detailed instructor notes for these cases to show how I use these cases in my course in organizational theory. These notes are to be found in the instructor's manual.
- Up-to-date "Organizational Insight" boxes directly related to core chapter concepts.
- "Managerial Implications" sections providing students with lessons from organizational theory.
- Detailed end-of-chapter summaries to facilitate learning.
- Discussion questions with detailed answers in the instructors manual.
- Videotapes. Accompanying the book is a package of videos that illustrate, among other things, the way in which different kinds of technologies—for example, small batch and mass production technologies—operate; problems that organizations encounter managing in the global environment; the nature of interorganizational linkage mechanisms such as keiratsu; and issues in designing the organizational heirarchy. Once again, instructions for using these videos are found in the instructors manual.
- Detailed and comprehensive sets of at least thirty-five multiple-choice questions and ten true/false questions together with short answer and essay questions for each chapter.
- A package of Powerpoint electronic transparencies for all major figures and tables found in the text, and additional and evolving transparencies are provided to adopters.

Acknowledgments

Finding a way to coordinate and integrate the rich and diverse organizational theory literature is no easy task. Nor is it easy to present the material in a way that students can easily understand (and hopefully enjoy) given the plethora of concepts and theories that abound in what is the most abstract and analytical subfield of management. In writing the second edition of *Organizational Theory* I was fortunate to have had the assistance of several people who contributed greatly to the book's final form. Jane Tufts, my developmental editor, helped me decide how to present the material in the chapters on structure and culture, which was my most difficult task. Her efforts can be seen in the integrated flow of material both within and between the chapters. David Shafer and Jennifer Glennon ably coordinated the book's progress and provided me with timely feedback and information from professors and reviewers that allowed me to shape the book to meet the needs of its intended market. Michele Foresta's efforts can be seen in the comprehensiveness of the package materials that constitute *Organizational Theory*. Nancy Marcello, my copy editor, greatly improved the readibility of the text, and Lynda Hansler smoothly coordinated the production process. I thank David Lorree and Susan Peters, who have helped me develop a state-of-the-art supplements package. I am also greatful to the following reviewers and colleagues who provided me with detailed feedback on the chapters in the first, second and third editions of the book:

Ken Bettenhausen, Charles Hill, John Butler, Sara Keck, Tina Dacin, Alan Bluedorn, Pat Feltes, Richard Goodman, Richard Deluca, Gordon Dehler, Janet Barnard, Richard Paulson, Steven Floyd, Marian Clark, John A. Seeger, James Segouis, Arie Lewin, Paul W. Swierez, Bruce H. Johnson, Sonny Ariss, Nate Bennett, Ronald Locke, George Strauss, Ed Conlon, Parthiban David, Lawrence Gales, Mary Jane Saxton, Judi McLean-Parus, Dayle Smith, Janet Near, Tony Buono, John Schaubroeck, Paul Collins, Dave Partridge, Karl Magnusen, Dan Svyantek, Karen Dill Bowerman, Robert Figler, David Loree, and Greg Saltzman.

Finally, I want to thank my wife, Jennifer George, for her continuing encouragement, support, and affection. Once again, it is to our children that I dedicate this book.

G.R.J.

ORGANIZATIONS and ORGANIZATIONAL STAKEHOLDERS

Organizations exist in uncertain environments and continually confront new challenges and problems. Managers must find solutions to these challenges and problems if organizations are to survive and prosper. This chapter begins with an in-depth look at organizations—what they are and why they exist. The purpose of organizational theory and the relationship between organizational theory and organizational design are then considered. Next, the way managers can use organizational theory and design to make organizations more efficient and better able to respond to the problems they encounter in their environments is examined.

The way in which organizations satisfy the needs of various interest groups, or stakeholders, and the concept of organizational effectiveness are then discussed. Finally, several contingency factors that influence the design of organizations are outlined, and the plan of this book is discussed.

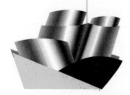

WHAT IS AN ORGANIZATION?

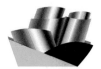

Few things in today's world are as important or as taken for granted as organizations. Although we routinely enjoy the goods and services that organizations provide, we rarely bother to wonder about how these goods and services are produced. We see news film of production lines churning out automobiles or computers, and we read in newspapers that the local schools or hospitals are using new techniques to improve their productivity. Yet we rarely question how or why these organizations go about their business. Most often, we think about organizations only when they fail us in some way—for example, when we are forced to wait two hours in the emergency room to see a doctor, when our new computer crashes, or when we are at the end of a long line in a bank on a Friday afternoon. When such things happen, we wonder why the bank did not anticipate the rush of people and put on more tellers, why the hospital made us spend 30 minutes filling out paperwork in order to obtain service and then kept us waiting for an hour and a half, or why computer companies don't insist on higher-quality hardware from their suppliers.

Most people have a casual attitude toward organizations because organizations are *intangible*. Even though most people in the world today are born, work, and die in organizations, nobody has ever seen or touched an organization. We see the products or services that an organization provides, and sometimes we see the people whom the organization employs as, for example, when we go into a Kinko's store, Kroger's supermarket, or local library. But the reason an organization, such as Kinko's or Kroger's, is motivated to provide goods and services, and the way it controls and influences its members so that it can provide them, are not apparent to most people outside the organization. Nevertheless, grouping people and other resources to produce goods and services is the essence of organizing and of what an organization does.[1]

Organization *A tool used by people to coordinate their actions to obtain something they desire or value.*

An **organization** is a tool used by people to coordinate their actions to obtain something they desire or value—that is, to achieve their goals. People who value security create an organization called a police force, an army, or a bank. People who value entertainment create organizations such as the Walt Disney Company, CBS, or a local club. People who desire spiritual or emotional support create churches, social service organizations, or charities. An organization is a response to and a means of satisfying some human need. New organizations are spawned when new technologies become available and new needs are discovered, and organizations die or are transformed when the needs they satisfied are no longer important or have been replaced by other needs. The need to invent improved drugs, for example, led to the creation of Amgen, Immunex, and other biotechnology organizations. The need to handle increasing amounts of information and the availability of an emerging new computer technology led to the rise of International Business Machines Corporation (IBM), Microsoft, and other computer companies and the shrinking and dying of typewriter companies, such as Smith Corona, whose technology had become outdated. Retail stores such as Wal-Mart, Sears, and Kmart are continually being transformed as they seek to respond to the quickly changing tastes and needs of consumers.

Entrepreneurship *The term used to describe the process by which people recognize opportunities to satisfy needs and then gather and use resources to meet those needs.*

Who creates the organizations that arise to satisfy people's needs? Sometimes an individual or a few people believe they possess the necessary skills and knowledge and set up an organization to produce goods and services. In this way organizations like sandwich shops, Yahoo!, and design studios are created. Sometimes several people form a group to respond to a perceived need by creating an organization. People with a lot of money may invest jointly to build a vacation resort. A group of people with similar beliefs may form a new church, or a nation's citizens may move to establish a new political party. In general, **entrepreneurship** is the term used to describe the process by which people recognize opportunities to satisfy needs and then gather and use resources to meet those needs.[2]

Today, many organizations being founded, and particularly those experiencing the fastest growth, are producing goods and services related in some way to new information technology. The increasing use of computers and new information technologies such as the Internet are revolutionizing the way all organizations operate. This book examines this crucial issue by focusing on one company that has achieved explosive growth, Amazon.com, and in nine chapters of this book the story of this company is used to illustrate the many ways in which the new information technology revolution is affecting the way organizations operate and create value today. We begin this analysis here by examining why and how Amazon.com was founded.

Focus on New Information Technology: Amazon.com, Part 1

In 1994, Jeffrey Bezos, a computer science and electrical engineering graduate from Princeton University, was growing weary of working for a Wall Street investment bank. With his computer science background prompting him, he saw an entrepreneurial opportunity in the fact that usage of the Internet was growing at over 2,300 percent a year as more and more people were becoming aware of its information advantages.[3]

Searching for an opportunity to exploit his skills in the new electronic, virtual marketplace, he decided that the book-selling market would be a good place to invest his personal resources. Deciding to make a break, he packed up his belongings and drove to the West Coast, deciding en route that Seattle, Washington, a new Mecca for high-tech software developers and the hometown of Starbucks coffee shops, would be an ideal place to begin his venture.

What was his vision for his new venture? To build an on-line bookstore that would be customer friendly, easy to navigate, and would offer the broadest possible selection of books. Bezos's mission? "To use the Internet to offer products that would educate, inform and inspire."[4] Bezos realized that compared to a real "bricks and mortar" bookstore, an on-line bookstore would be able to offer a much larger and more diverse selection of books. Moreover, on-line customers would be able to search easily for any book in print on a computerized, on-line catalog, browse different subject areas, read reviews of books, and even ask other shoppers for on-line recommendations—something most people would hesitate to do in a regular bookstore.

With a handful of employees and operating from his garage in Seattle, Bezos launched his venture on-line in July 1995 with $7 million in borrowed capital. Word of his venture spread like wildfire across the Internet and book sales quickly picked up as satisfied customers spread the good word. Within weeks Bezos was forced to relocate to new larger premises and to hire new employees as book sales soared. Bezos's new venture seemed to be poised for success.

How Does an Organization Create Value?

The way in which an organization creates value is depicted in Figure 1.1. Value creation takes place at three stages: input, conversion, and output. Each stage is affected by the environment in which the organization operates.

Inputs include human resources, information and knowledge, raw materials, and money and capital. The way an organization chooses and obtains from its environment the inputs it needs to produce goods and services determines how much value the organization creates at the input stage. For example, Jeff Bezos chose to make the design of the Amazon.com Web site as simple and user friendly as he possibly could, and he only recruited people who could provide high-quality, customer-friendly service who would most appeal to his Internet customers. If he had made poor choices and customers had not liked Amazon.com's Web site or customer service, his company would not have been successful.

The way the organization uses human resources and technology to transform inputs into outputs determines how much value is created at the conversion stage. The amount of value the organization creates is a function of the quality of its skills, including its ability to learn from and respond to the environment. For example, Jeff Bezos had to decide

FIGURE 1.1

How an Organization
Creates Value

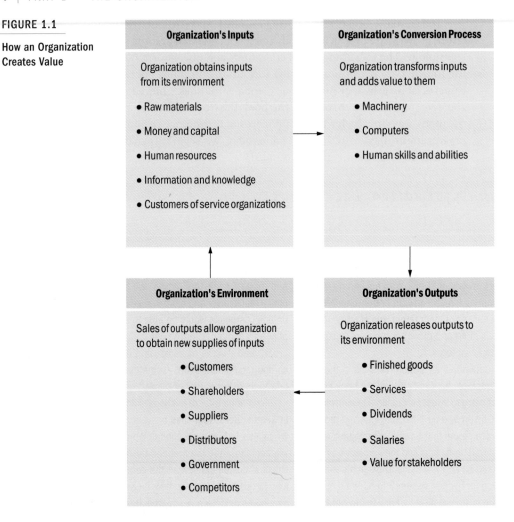

Organization's Inputs

Organization obtains inputs
from its environment

- Raw materials
- Money and capital
- Human resources
- Information and knowledge
- Customers of service organizations

Organization's Conversion Process

Organization transforms inputs
and adds value to them

- Machinery
- Computers
- Human skills and abilities

Organization's Environment

Sales of outputs allow organization
to obtain new supplies of inputs

- Customers
- Shareholders
- Suppliers
- Distributors
- Government
- Competitors

Organization's Outputs

Organization releases outputs to
its environment

- Finished goods
- Services
- Dividends
- Salaries
- Value for stakeholders

how best to sell and market his products to attract customers. His answer was to offer wide choices, low prices, and to ship books quickly to customers. His skill at these activities created the value that customers saw in his concept.

The result of the conversion process is an output of finished goods and services that the organization releases to its environment, where they are purchased and used by customers to satisfy their needs—such as delivered books. The organization uses the money earned from the sale of its output to obtain new supplies of inputs, and the cycle begins again. An organization that continues to satisfy people's needs will be able to obtain increasing amounts of resources over time and will be able to create more and more value as it adds to its stock of skills and capabilities.[5] Amazon.com has grown from strength to strength because satisfied customers have provided the revenues it needs to improve its skills and expand its operations.

A value-creation model can be used to describe the activities of most kinds of organizations. Manufacturing companies, such as General Motors and IBM, take from the environment component parts, skilled or semiskilled labor, and technical knowledge and at the conversion stage create value by using their manufacturing skills to organize and assemble those inputs into outputs, such as cars and computers. Service organizations, such as McDonald's, Amazon.com, the Salvation Army, and your family doctor, interact directly with customers or clients, who are the "inputs" to their operations. Hungry peo-

FIGURE 1.2

How McDonald's Creates Value

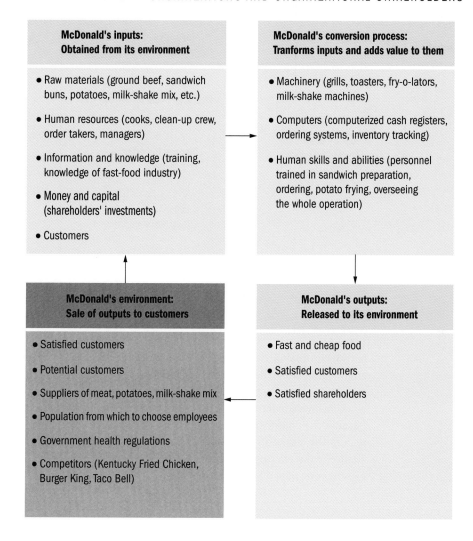

**McDonald's inputs:
Obtained from its environment**

- Raw materials (ground beef, sandwich buns, potatoes, milk-shake mix, etc.)
- Human resources (cooks, clean-up crew, order takers, managers)
- Information and knowledge (training, knowledge of fast-food industry)
- Money and capital (shareholders' investments)
- Customers

**McDonald's conversion process:
Tranforms inputs and adds value to them**

- Machinery (grills, toasters, fry-o-lators, milk-shake machines)
- Computers (computerized cash registers, ordering systems, inventory tracking)
- Human skills and abilities (personnel trained in sandwich preparation, ordering, potato frying, overseeing the whole operation)

**McDonald's environment:
Sale of outputs to customers**

- Satisfied customers
- Potential customers
- Suppliers of meat, potatoes, milk-shake mix
- Population from which to choose employees
- Government health regulations
- Competitors (Kentucky Fried Chicken, Burger King, Taco Bell)

**McDonald's outputs:
Released to its environment**

- Fast and cheap food
- Satisfied customers
- Satisfied shareholders

ple who go to McDonald's for a meal, needy families who go to the Salvation Army for assistance, and sick people who go to a doctor for a cure are all "inputs." In the conversion stage, service organizations create value by applying their skills to yield an output: satisfied hunger, a cared-for family, a cured patient. Figure 1.2 is a simplified model of how McDonald's creates value.

Why Do Organizations Exist?

The production of goods and services most often takes place in an organizational setting because people working together to produce goods and services can usually create more value than people working separately. Figure 1.3 summarizes five reasons for the existence of organizations.

TO INCREASE SPECIALIZATION AND THE DIVISION OF LABOR.   People who work in organizations may become more productive and efficient at what they do than people who work alone. For many kinds of productive work the use of an organization allows the development of specialization and a division of labor. The collective nature of organizations allows individuals to focus on a narrow area of expertise, and this allows them to

FIGURE 1.3

Why Organizations Exist

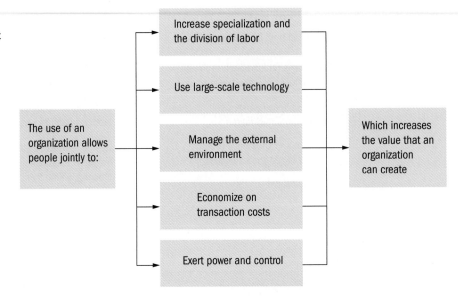

become more skilled or specialized at what they do. For example, engineers working in the engineering design department of a large car manufacturer like GM or Toyota might specialize in improving the design of carburetors or other engine components. An engineer working for a small car manufacturer might be responsible for designing the whole engine. Because the engineer in the small company must do many more things than the engineer in the large company, specialization in the small company is lower and there is less chance of discovering what makes for a great carburetor and, thus, creating more value for someone who desires high speed.

TO USE LARGE-SCALE TECHNOLOGY.   Organizations are able to take advantage of the economies of scale and scope that result from the use of modern automated and computerized technology. **Economies of scale** are cost savings that result when goods and services are produced in large volume on automated production lines. **Economies of scope** are cost savings that result when an organization is able to use underutilized resources more effectively because they can be shared across several different products or tasks. Economies of scope (as well as of scale) can be achieved, for example, when it is possible to design an automated production line to produce several different types of products simultaneously. Toyota and Honda were the first automakers to design assembly lines capable of producing three models of a car instead of just one. Ford and GM have recently followed suit. Multimodel assembly lines give car companies lower manufacturing costs and greater flexibility to change quickly from one model to another to meet customer needs.

TO MANAGE THE EXTERNAL ENVIRONMENT.   Pressures from the environment in which organizations operate also make organizations the favored mode for organizing productive resources. An organization's environment includes not only economic, social, and political factors but also the sources from which the organization obtains inputs and the marketplace into which it releases outputs. Managing complex environments is a task beyond the abilities of most individuals, but an organization has the resources to develop

Economies of scale

Cost savings that result when goods and services are produced in large volume on automated production lines.

Economies of scope

Cost savings that result when an organization is able to use underutilized resources more effectively because they can be shared across different products or tasks.

specialists to anticipate or attempt to influence the many demands from the environment. This specialization allows the organization to create more value for the organization, its members, and its customers. Huge companies like IBM, American Telephone and Telegraph (AT&T), and Ford have whole departments of corporate executives who are responsible for monitoring, responding to, and attempting to manage the external environment, but those activities are just as important for small organizations. Although local stores and restaurants do not have whole departments to scan the environment, their owners and managers need to spot emerging trends and changes so that they can respond to changing customer needs, just as Jeff Bezos did.[6] Indeed, the Internet is helping many small companies to manage their environment since it permits access to huge numbers of potential customers at very low cost.

TO ECONOMIZE ON TRANSACTION COSTS.

When people cooperate to produce goods and services, certain problems arise as they learn what to do and how to work with others to perform a task effectively. People jointly have to decide who will do which tasks (the division of labor), who will get paid what amounts, and how to decide if each worker is doing his or her share of the work. The costs associated with negotiating, monitoring, and governing exchanges between people are called **transaction costs**. Organizations' ability to control the exchanges between people reduces the transaction costs associated with the exchanges. Suppose Intel bought the services of its scientists on a daily basis and thousands of scientists had to spend time every day discussing what to do and who should work with whom. Such a system would be very costly and would waste valuable time and money. The structure and coordination imposed by the Intel organization, however, let managers hire scientists on a long-term basis and assign them to specific tasks and work teams. The resulting stability reduces transaction costs and increases productivity.

Transaction costs The costs associated with negotiating, monitoring, and governing exchanges between people.

TO EXERT POWER AND CONTROL.

Organizations can exert great pressure on individuals to conform to task and production requirements in order to increase production efficiency.[7] To get a job done efficiently, it is important for people to come to work in a predictable fashion, to behave in the interests of the organization, and to accept the authority of the organization and its managers. All these requirements make production less costly and more efficient but put a burden on individuals who must conform to organizational requirements. When individuals work for themselves, they need to address only their own needs. When they work for an organization, however, they must pay attention to the organization's needs as well as their own. Organizations can discipline or fire workers who fail to conform and can reward good performance with promotion and increased rewards. Because employment, promotion, and increased rewards are important and often scarce, organizations can use them to exert power over individuals.

Taken together, these five factors help to explain why often more value can be created when people work together, coordinating their actions in an organized setting, than when they work alone. Over time, the stability created by an organization provides a setting in which the organization and its members can increase their skills and capabilities, and the ability of the organization to create value increases by leaps and bounds. In the last 10 years, for example, Microsoft has grown to become the biggest and most powerful software company in the world because Bill Gates, its founder, created an organizational setting in which people are given the freedom to develop their skills and capabilities to create valuable new products. In contrast, in the last 10 years other software companies like Wordperfect, Novell, and Borland have experienced huge problems because they have not been able to create innovative software at a price that customers will pay. Why does Microsoft's organization allow Microsoft to create more and more value while these other organizations have actually reduced the value they can create? Before we can answer this question, we need to take a close look at organizational theory and design.

WHAT IS ORGANIZATIONAL THEORY?

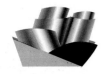

Organizational theory
The study of how organizations function and how they affect and are affected by the environment in which they operate.

Organizational theory is the study of how organizations function and how they affect and are affected by the environment in which they operate. In this book, we examine the principles that underlie the design and operation of effective organizations. Understanding how organizations operate, however, is only the first step in learning how to control and change organizations so that they can effectively create wealth and resources. Thus, the second aim of this book is to equip you, as a student of organizational theory or as a manager in an organization, with the conceptual tools to influence organizational situations in which you find yourself. The lessons of organizational theory are as important at the level of first-line supervisor as they are at the level of chief executive officer, in small or large organizations, and in settings as diverse as a not-for-profit organization or the assembly line of a manufacturing company.

Managers knowledgeable about organizational theory are able to analyze the structure and culture of their organization, diagnose problems, and, utilizing the process of organizational design, make adjustments that help the organization to achieve its goals. Figure 1.4 outlines the relationship among organizational theory and organizational structure, culture, and design.

Organizational Structure

Organizational structure
The formal system of task and authority relationships that control how people coordinate their actions and use resources to achieve organizational goals.

Once a group of people has established an organization to accomplish collective goals, organizational structure evolves to increase the effectiveness of the organization's control of the activities necessary to achieve its goals. **Organizational structure** is the formal system of task and authority relationships that control how people coordinate their actions and use resources to achieve organizational goals.[8] The principal purpose of organizational structure is one of *control*: to control the way people coordinate their actions to achieve organizational goals and to control the means used to motivate people to achieve these goals. At Microsoft, for example, the control problems facing Bill Gates were how to coordinate scientists' activities to make the best use of their talents and how to reward scientists when they developed innovative products. Gates's solution was to place scientists in small, self-contained teams and to reward them with stock in Microsoft based on team performance.

For any organization, an appropriate structure is one that facilitates effective responses to problems of coordination and motivation—problems that can arise for any number of environmental, technological, or human reasons.[9] As organizations grow and differentiate, the structure likewise evolves. Organizational structure can be managed and changed through the process of organizational design.

Organizational Culture

At the same time that organizational structure is evolving, so is organizational culture. **Organizational culture** is the set of shared values and norms that controls organizational members' interactions with each other and with suppliers, customers, and other people

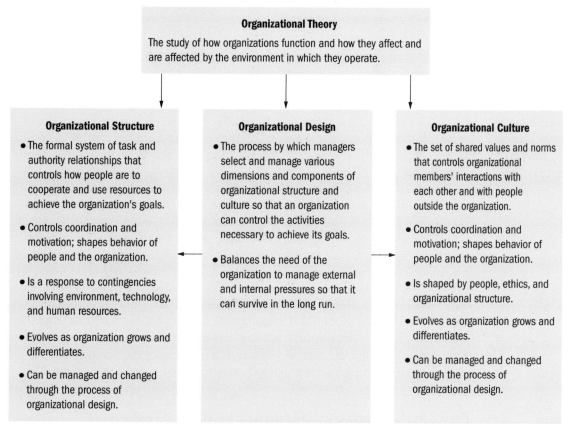

FIGURE 1.4   The Relationship among Organizational Theory and Organizational Structure, Culture, and Design

Organizational culture

The set of shared values and norms that controls organizational members' interactions with each other and with suppliers, customers, and other people outside the organization.

outside the organization. An organization's culture is shaped by the people inside the organization, by the ethics of the organization, by the employment rights given to employees, and by the type of structure used by the organization. Like organizational structure, organizational culture shapes and controls behavior within the organization. It influences how people respond to a situation and how they interpret the environment surrounding the organization. At Microsoft, Bill Gates attempted to create values that encouraged entrepreneurship and risk taking in order to build an organizational culture in which innovation was a valued activity. The small-team structure was helpful because scientists were continually meeting face-to-face to coordinate their activities and to learn from one another, which encouraged them to experiment and to find new ways of solving problems.

The cultures of organizations that provide essentially the same goods and services can be very different. For example, Coca-Cola and PepsiCo are the two largest and most successful companies in the soft-drinks industry. Because they sell similar products and face similar environments, we might expect their cultures to be similar. But they are not. Coca-Cola takes pride in its long-term commitment to employees; its loyal managers, many of whom spend their entire careers with the organization; and its cautious and cooperative approach to planning. By contrast, PepsiCo has a highly political and competitive culture in which conflicts over decision making cause frequent turnover among top managers. Like organizational structure, organizational culture evolves and can be managed and changed through organizational design.

Organizational Design

Organizational design
The process by which managers select and manage aspects of structure and culture so that an organization can control the activities necessary to achieve its goals.

Organizational design is the process by which managers select and manage aspects of structure and culture so that an organization can control the activities necessary to achieve its goals. Organizational structure and culture are the means the organization uses to achieve its goals. Organizational design is about how and why various means are chosen. It is a task that requires managers to strike a balance between external pressures from the organization's environment and internal pressures from, for example, its choice of technology. Achieving the proper balance helps to ensure that the organization will survive in the long run.

Organizations like Microsoft and Intel, which operate in the high-tech computer industry, need to be flexible and capable of quick responses to their rivals' competitive moves, and they need to be innovative in developing and using new technology, such as the Internet.[10] At the same time, such organizations must have stable task relationships that allow their members to work together to create value, solve problems, and accomplish organizational objectives. In contrast, organizations like Nucor and Aluminum Company of America (Alcoa), which produce sheet steel and aluminum, face relatively stable environments in which customer needs are more predictable and technology changes more slowly. Consequently, their organizational design choices are likely to reflect the need for a structure and culture that reduce production costs rather than a structure and culture that promote flexibility. In Chapters 2, 3, 4, and 5 we discuss the organizational structures and cultures that managers can design to help ensure their organizations' survival.

The Importance of Organizational Design

Because of increased global competitive pressures and because of the increasing use of advanced information technologies, organizational design has become one of management's top priorities. Today, as never before, managers are searching for new and better ways to coordinate and motivate their employees to increase the value their organizations can create. There are several specific reasons why designing an organization's structure and culture is such an important task. Organizational design has important implications for a company's ability to deal with contingencies, achieve a competitive advantage, effectively manage diversity, and increase its efficiency and ability to innovate new goods and services.

Contingency *An event that might occur and must be planned for.*

DEALING WITH CONTINGENCIES.   A **contingency** is an event that might occur and must be planned for, such as a changing environment or a competitor like Amazon.com that decides to use new technology in an innovative way. The design of an organization determines how effectively an organization responds to various factors in its environment and obtains scarce resources. For example, an organization's ability to attract skilled employees, loyal customers, or government contracts is a function of the degree to which it can control those three environmental factors.

An organization can design its structure in many ways to increase control over its environment. An organization might change employee task relationships so that employees are more aware of the environment, or it might change the way the organization relates to other organizations by establishing new contracts or joint ventures. For example, when Microsoft wanted to attract new customers for its Windows 98 software both in the United States and globally, it recruited large numbers of customer service representatives and created a new department to allow them to better meet customers' needs. The strategy was very successful, and Windows 98 has become the best-selling operating system in the world.

As pressures from competitors, consumers, and the government increase, the environment facing all organizations is becoming increasingly complex and difficult to respond to, and more effective types of structure and culture are continually being developed and tried. We discuss how organizations influence and control their environments in Chapter 6.

One part of the organizational environment that is becoming more important and more complex is the global environment. Increasingly, U.S. companies like AT&T, IBM, and America Online are being pressured to become global and to produce and sell their products in foreign markets in order to reduce costs, increase efficiency, and survive. Organizational design is important in a global context because to become a global competitor, a company often needs to create a new structure and culture. Chapter 8 looks at the structures and cultures that a company can adopt as it engages in different kinds of global activities.

Changing technology is another contingency to which organizations must respond. Today, the emergence of the Internet as an important new medium through which organizations manage relationships with their employees, customers, and suppliers is fundamentally changing the design of organizational structure. We will examine the changes taking place in almost all the chapters of this book; the issue is that the Internet has become a major contingency to which *all* organizations must respond.

Gaining Competitive Advantage

Competitive advantage *The ability of one company to outperform another because its managers are able to create more value from the resources at their disposal.*

Core Competences *Managers' skills and abilities in value-creating activities.*

Strategy *The specific pattern of decisions and actions that managers take to use core competencies to achieve a competitive advantage and outperform competitors.*

Increasingly, organizations are discovering that organizational design is a source of sustained competitive advantage. **Competitive advantage** is the ability of one company to outperform another because its managers are able to create more value from the resources at their disposal. Competitive advantage springs from **core competences**, managers' skills and abilities in value-creating activities such as manufacturing, research and development, managing new technology, or organizational design. Core competences allow a company to develop a strategy to outperform competitors and produce better products or produce the same products but at a lower cost. **Strategy** is the specific pattern of decisions and actions that managers take to use core competencies to achieve a competitive advantage and outperform competitors.

The *way* the organization designs its structure is an important determinant of how much value the organization creates, because organizational design is the means of implementing an organization's *strategy*. Many sources of competitive advantage, such as skills in research and development that result in novel product features or state-of-the-art technology, quickly disappear because they are relatively easy for competitors to imitate. It is much more difficult to imitate good organizational design that brings into being a successful organizational structure and culture. Such imitation is difficult because structure and culture are embedded in the way people in an organization interact and coordinate their actions to get a job done. Moreover, because successful structures and cultures take a long time to establish and develop, companies that possess them can have a long-term competitive advantage.

Because an organization's strategy is always changing in response to changes in the environment, organizational design must be a continuously evolving managerial activity if managers are to stay one step ahead of the competition. There is never a single optimal or "perfect" organizational design to fit an organization's needs. Managers must constantly evaluate how well their organization's structure and culture work, and they should redesign them on an ongoing basis to improve them. In Chapter 7 we consider how organizations create value by means of their strategy.

Managing Diversity

Differences in the race, gender, and national origin of organizational members have important implications for the values of an organization's culture and for organizational effectiveness. The quality of organizational decision making, for example, is a function of the diversity of the viewpoints that get considered and of the kind of analysis that takes place. Similarly, in many organizations, particularly service organizations, a large part of the workforce is minority employees, whose needs and preferences must be taken into consideration. Also, changes in the characteristics of the workforce, such as an influx of immigrant workers or the aging of the current workforce, require attention and advance planning. An organization needs to design a structure to make optimal use of the talents of a diverse workforce and to develop cultural values that encourage people to work together. An organization's structure and culture determine how effectively managers are able to coordinate and motivate workers.

Efficiency and Innovation

Organizations exist to produce goods and services that people value. The better organizations function, the more value, in the form of more or better goods and services, they create. Historically, the capacity of organizations to create value has increased enormously as organizations have introduced better ways of producing and distributing goods and services. Earlier, we discussed the importance of the division of labor and the use of modern technology in reducing costs and increasing efficiency. The design and use of new and more efficient organizational structures is equally important. In today's global environment, for example, competition from countries with low labor costs is pressuring companies all over the world to become more efficient in order to reduce costs or increase quality.

Similarly, the ability of companies to compete successfully in today's competitive environment is increasingly a function of how well they innovate and how quickly they can introduce new technologies. Organizational design plays an important role in innovation. For example, the way an organization's structure links people in different specializations, such as research and marketing, determines how fast the organization can introduce new products. Similarly, an organization's culture can affect people's desire to be innovative. A culture that is based on entrepreneurial norms and values is more likely to encourage innovation than is a culture that is conservative and bureaucratic because entrepreneurial values encourage people to learn how to respond and adapt to a changing situation.

Organizational design involves a constant search for new or better ways of coordinating and motivating employees. Different structures and cultures cause employees to behave in different ways. We consider structures that encourage efficiency and innovation in Chapters 2, 3, and 4 and cultures that do so in Chapter 5.

The Consequences of Poor Organizational Design

Many management teams fail to understand the effect of organizational design on their company's performance and effectiveness. Although behavior is controlled by organizational structure and culture, managers are often unaware of this relationship and pay scant attention to the way employees behave and their role in the organization—until something happens.

General Motors, IBM, Sears, Eastman Kodak, and AT&T have all experienced enormous problems in the last decade adjusting to the reality of modern global competition and have seen their sales and profits fall dramatically. In response, they have dramatically reduced their workforces, reduced the number of products they make, and even reduced their investment in research and development. Why did the performance of these blue-chip companies deteriorate to such a degree? One reason is that they lost control of their organizational structures and cultures. They became so big and bureaucratic that their managers and employees were unable to change and adapt to changing conditions.

The consequence of poor organizational design or lack of attention to organizational design is the decline of the organization. Talented employees leave to take positions in strong, growing companies. Resources become harder and harder to acquire, and the whole process of value creation slows down. Neglecting organizational design until crisis threatens forces managers to make changes in organizational structure and culture that derail the company's strategy.

Stakeholders People who have an interest, claim, or stake in an organization, in what it does, and in how well it performs.

Inducements Rewards such as money, power, and organizational status.

ORGANIZATIONAL STAKEHOLDERS

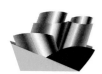

Contributions The skills, knowledge, and expertise that organizations require of their members during task performance.

Organizations exist because of their ability to create value and acceptable outcomes for various groups of **stakeholders**, people who have an interest, claim, or stake in the organization, in what it does, and in how well it performs.[11] In general, stakeholders are motivated to participate in an organization if they receive inducements that exceed the value of the contributions they are required to make.[12] **Inducements** are rewards such as money, power, and organizational status. **Contributions** are the skills, knowledge, and expertise that organizations require of their members during task performance.

There are two main groups of organizational stakeholders: inside stakeholders and outside stakeholders. The inducements and contributions of each group are summarized in Table 1.1.[13]

TABLE 1.1		
Inducements and Contributions of Organizational Stakeholders		
Stakeholder	**Contribution to the Organization**	**Inducement to Contribute**
INSIDE		
Shareholders	Money and capital	Dividends and stock appreciation
Managers	Skills and expertise	Salaries, bonuses, status, and power
Workforce	Skills and expertise	Wages, bonuses, stable employment, and promotion
OUTSIDE		
Customers	Revenue from purchase of goods and services	Quality and price of goods and services
Suppliers	High-quality inputs	Revenue from purchase of inputs
Government	Rules governing good business practice	Fair and free competition
Unions	Free and fair collective bargaining	Equitable share of inducements
Community	Social and economic infrastructure	Revenue, taxes, and employment
General public	Customer loyalty and reputation	National pride

Inside Stakeholders

Inside stakeholders are people who are closest to an organization and have the strongest or most direct claim on organizational resources: shareholders, managers, and the workforce.

SHAREHOLDERS.   Shareholders are the owners of the organization, and, as such, their claim on organizational resources is often considered superior to the claims of other inside stakeholders. The shareholders' contribution to the organization is to invest money in it by buying the organization's stock. The shareholders' inducement to invest is the prospective money they can earn on their investment in the form of dividends and increases in the price of stock. Investment in stock is risky, however, because there is no guarantee of a return. Shareholders who do not believe that the inducement (the possible return on their investment) is enough to warrant their contribution (the money they have invested) sell their shares and withdraw their support from the organization. As the following example illustrates, more and more shareholders are relying on large institutional investment companies to protect their interests and to increase their collective power to influence organizations.

ORGANIZATIONAL INSIGHT

1.1 THE INCREASING POWER OF INSTITUTIONAL INVESTORS

As more and more shareholders rely on mutual fund companies like Fidelity or TIAA/CREF to manage their retirement funds, the power of these companies to intervene in the running of a company has dramatically increased.[14] The California Public Employees Retirement System (Calpers), for example, is the largest public-sector pension fund in the United States, managing $65 billion for over 1 million of its members. Because the fund is so large, it is a major shareholder in many U.S. companies and, therefore, has a vital interest in their performance. During the 1990s Calpers realized that it had a duty to protect the interests of its investors by paying more attention to what the top management and boards of directors of these companies were doing. If mutual fund companies are to protect the interests of their shareholders, they need to monitor and influence the behavior of the companies in which they invest, to make sure that the top managers pursue actions that do not threaten shareholders' interests while enhancing their own.

As a result of this concern for shareholders, Calpers and other mutual funds are taking an active interest in controlling the ability of a corporation's managers to create antitakeover provisions. These provisions protect managers from corporate raiders who might like to take a company over, a process that would earn a lot of money for shareholders but might cost managers their jobs. Mutual funds are also exerting their right as shareholders to intervene in long-run management decisions such as the acquisition of a company that might hurt the value of the acquiring company's stock. Calpers even found errors in one company's accounting procedures.[15] The funds have also been showing an interest in controlling the salaries and bonuses that corporation managers give themselves, many of which have reached record levels in recent years.

As the power of mutual funds and other institutional investors increases, so does the power of shareholders as organizational stakeholders. In a way, large mutual fund companies are the shareholders' equivalent of a union for employees. Just as unions increase the power of individual workers in relation to management, so mutual fund companies increase the power of individual shareholders in dealing with management. Indeed, by the end of the 1990s Calpers and other large funds had formed global alliances to monitor the performance of companies in other countries as they invest more and more abroad.[16]

MANAGERS. Managers are the employees who are responsible for coordinating organizational resources and ensuring that an organization's goals are successfully met. Top managers are responsible for investing shareholder money in resources in order to maximize the future output of goods and services. Managers are, in effect, the agents or employees of shareholders and are appointed indirectly by shareholders through an organization's board of directors to manage the organization's business.

Managers' contributions are the skills they use to direct the organization's response to pressures from within and outside the organization. For example, a manager's skills at opening up global markets, identifying new product markets, or solving transaction-cost and technological problems can greatly facilitate the achievement of the organization's goals.

Various types of rewards induce managers to perform their activities well: monetary compensation (in the form of salaries, bonuses, and stock options) and the psychological satisfaction they get from controlling the corporation, exercising power, or taking risks with other people's money. Managers who do not believe that the inducements meet or exceed their contributions are likely to withdraw their support by leaving the organization.

THE WORKFORCE. An organization's workforce consists of all nonmanagerial employees. Members of the workforce have responsibilities and duties (usually outlined in a job description) to perform. An employee's contribution to the organization is the performance of his or her duties and responsibilities. How well an employee performs is, in some measure, within the employee's control. An employee's motivation to perform well relates to the rewards and punishments that the organization uses to influence job performance. Employees who do not feel that the inducements meet or exceed their contributions are likely to withdraw their support for the organization by reducing the level of their performance or by leaving the organization.

Outside Stakeholders

Outside stakeholders are people who do not own the organization, are not employed by it, but do have some interest in it. Customers, suppliers, the government, trade unions, local communities, and the general public are all outside stakeholders.

CUSTOMERS. Customers are usually an organization's largest outside stakeholder group. Customers are induced to select a product (and, thus, an organization) from alternative products by their estimation of what they are getting relative to what they have to pay. The money they pay for the product is their contribution to the organization and reflects the value they feel they receive from the organization. As long as the organization produces a product whose price is equal to or less than the value customers feel they are getting, they will continue to buy the product and support the organization.[17] If customers refuse to pay the price the organization is asking, they withdraw their support, and the organization loses a vital stakeholder. Southwest Airlines' attention to its customers has resulted in their loyal support.

1.2 SOUTHWEST AIRLINES SERVES ITS CUSTOMERS

Southwest Airlines, based in Dallas, Texas, attributes its success to the way it handles customers. At a time when most airlines are losing money, Southwest posts hefty profits, which CEO Herbert Kelleher attributes to the airline's policy of "dignifying the customer."[18] Southwest sends birthday cards to its frequent fliers, responds personally to the thousands of customer letters it receives each week, and regularly obtains feedback from customers on ways to improve service. Such personal attention makes customers feel valued and inclined to fly Southwest.[19] Moreover, Kelleher believes that if management fails to treat employees right, employees will not treat customers right. So Southwest's employees, most of whom are unionized, own 13 percent of the airline's stock, a stake that was worth over $1 billion by 2000.[20] Ownership of the company increases employees' motivation to contribute to the organization and improve customer service.[21] One stakeholder group (employees) thus helps another (customers).

SUPPLIERS. Suppliers, another important outside stakeholder group, contribute to the organization by providing reliable raw materials and component parts that allow the organization to reduce uncertainty in its technical or production operations and, thus, reduce production costs. Suppliers have a direct effect on the organization's efficiency and an indirect effect on its ability to attract customers. An organization that has high-quality inputs can make high-quality products and attract customers. In turn, as demand for its products increases, the organization demands greater quantities of high-quality inputs from its suppliers.

One of the reasons why Japanese cars remain so popular with U.S. consumers is that they still require fewer repairs than the average U.S.-made vehicle. This reliability is a result of the use of component parts that meet incredibly stringent quality control standards. In addition, Japanese parts suppliers are constantly improving their performance.[22] The close relationship between the large Japanese automakers and their suppliers is a stakeholder relationship that pays long-term dividends for both parties. Realizing this, in the last decade U.S. car manufacturers have also moved to establish strong relationships with their suppliers to increase quality, and the reliability of their vehicles has increased as a result.

THE GOVERNMENT. The government has several claims on an organization. It wants companies to compete in a fair manner and obey the rules of free competition. It also wants companies to obey agreed-upon rules and laws concerning the payment and treatment of employees, workers' health and workplace safety, nondiscriminatory hiring practices, and other social and economic issues about which Congress has enacted legislation. The government makes a contribution to the organization by standardizing regulations so that they apply to all companies and no company can obtain an unfair competitive advantage. The government controls the rules of good business practice and has the power to punish any company that breaks these rules by taking legal action against it.

TRADE UNIONS. The relationship between a trade union and an organization can be one of conflict or cooperation. The nature of the relationship has a direct effect on the productivity and effectiveness of the organization and the union. Cooperation between managers and the union can lead to positive long-term outcomes if both parties agree on an equitable division of the gains from an improvement in a company's fortunes. Managers and the union might agree, for example, to share the gains from cost savings due to productivity improvements that resulted from a flexible work schedule. Traditionally, however, the management-union relationship has been antagonistic because unions' demands for increased benefits conflict directly with shareholders' demands for greater company profits and, thus, greater returns on their investments.

LOCAL COMMUNITIES.   Local communities have a stake in the performance of organizations because employment, housing, and the general economic well-being of a community are strongly affected by the success or failure of local businesses. The fortunes of Seattle, for example, are closely tied to the fortunes of the Boeing Corporation. Similarly, the city of Mexia, Texas (population 6,933), was saved from economic collapse when Ann Richards, the former governor of Texas, overruled a state committee and kept open Mexia's state hospital for mentally handicapped people. By contrast, American Home Products' subsidiary Whitehall Laboratories, which produces Anacin, Advil, and Dristan, closed a plant in Elkhart, Indiana. The layoff of 800 workers had a big impact on Elkhart, a city with a population of 45,000. Merchants suffered declining sales, and the whole community has had to deal with a rise in crime and an increase in the number of clinically depressed unemployed people.[23]

THE GENERAL PUBLIC.   The public is happy when organizations do well against foreign competitors. This is hardly surprising, given that the present and future wealth of a nation is closely related to the success of its businesses and its economic institutions. The French and Italians, for example, prefer domestically produced cars and other products, even when foreign products are clearly superior. To some degree, they are induced by pride in their country to contribute to their country's organizations by buying their products. Typically, U.S. consumers do not support their companies in the same way. They prefer competition to loyalty as the means to ensure the future health of American businesses.

A nation's public also wants its corporations to act in a socially responsible way, which means that corporations refrain from taking any actions that may injure or impose costs on other stakeholders. In 1992, for example, a scandal rocked United Way of America after it was revealed that its president, William Aramony, had misused the agency's funds for lavish personal expenditures. To encourage past contributors, including large donors like Xerox and General Electric, not to withhold contributions, United Way appointed Elaine L. Chao, the former head of the Peace Corps and an experienced investment banker, as the new president of the organization. She quickly introduced strict new financial controls and staved off a serious decline in public contributions, and by 1995 contributions had returned to their former levels.

ORGANIZATIONAL EFFECTIVENESS: SATISFYING STAKEHOLDERS' GOALS AND INTERESTS

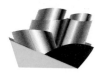

An organization is a value-creating tool that can be used simultaneously by different groups of stakeholders to accomplish a variety of goals. The contributions of all stakeholders are needed for an organization to be viable and to accomplish its mission of producing goods and services. Each stakeholder group is motivated to contribute to the organization by its own set of goals, and each group evaluates the effectiveness of the organization by judging how well it meets the group's specific goals.[24]

Shareholders evaluate an organization by the return they receive on their investment. Customers evaluate an organization by the reliability and value of its products relative to their price. Sometimes goals conflict, and stakeholder groups must bargain among themselves over the appropriate balance between the inducements that they should receive and the contributions that they should make. For this reason, organizations are often regarded as alliances or coalitions of stakeholder groups that directly and indirectly bargain with each other and use their power and influence to alter the balance of inducements and contributions in their favor.[25] An organization is viable as long as a dominant coalition of stakeholders has control over sufficient inducements so that it can obtain the contributions it needs from other stakeholder groups.

There is no reason to assume, however, that all stakeholders will be equally satisfied with the balance between inducements and contributions. Indeed, the implications of the coalition view of organizations is that some stakeholder groups have priority over others. To be effective, however, an organization must at least *minimally* satisfy the interests of *all* the groups that have a stake in the organization.[26] The claims of each group must be addressed; otherwise, a group might withdraw its support and injure the future performance of the organization. When all stakeholder interests are *minimally* satisfied, the relative power of a stakeholder group to control the distribution of inducements determines how the organization will attempt to satisfy different stakeholder goals and what criteria stakeholders will use to judge the organization's performance.

Problems that an organization faces as it tries to win stakeholders' approval include choosing which stakeholder goals to satisfy, deciding how to allocate organizational rewards to different stakeholder groups, and balancing short-term and long-term goals.

Competing Goals

Organizations exist to satisfy stakeholders' goals, but who decides which goals to strive for and which goals are most important? An organization's choice of goals has political and social implications. In a capitalistic country like the United States, it is taken for granted that shareholders, the owners of the organization's accumulated wealth or capital—its machines, buildings, land, and goodwill—have first claim on the value created by the organization. According to this view, the job of managers is to maximize shareholder wealth, and the best way to do so is to maximize the organization's return on investment (a good measure of an organization's relative effectiveness).

Is maximizing shareholder wealth always management's primary goal? According to one argument, it is not. When shareholders delegate to managers the right to coordinate and use organizational skills and resources, a divorce of ownership and control occurs.[27] Although in theory managers are the employees of shareholders, in practice managers' control over organizational resources gives them real control over the corporation even though shareholders own it. The result is that managers may follow goals that promote their own interests but not the interests of shareholders.[28]

An attempt to maximize stockholder wealth, for example, may involve taking risks into uncharted territory and making investments in research and development that may bear fruit only in the long term, as new inventions and discoveries generate new products and, hence, new revenues. Managers, however, may prefer to maximize short-term profits because that is the goal on which they are evaluated by their peers and by market analysts who do not take the long-term view.

Another view is that managers prefer a quiet life in which risks are small, and that they have no incentive to be entrepreneurial because they control their own salaries. Moreover, because managers' salaries are closely correlated to organizational size and growth, managers may prefer to pursue these goals even though they are only loosely associated with profitability.

As those examples suggest, the goals of managers and shareholders may compete, and because managers are in the organizational driver's seat, shareholder goals are not the ones most likely to be followed. But even when there is no competition among different stakeholders over whose goals should be followed, selecting goals that will enhance an organization's chances of survival and future prosperity is no easy task.

Suppose managers decide that the primary goal is to maximize shareholder wealth. What should be done to achieve this goal? Should managers try to increase efficiency and reduce costs to improve profitability? Should they increase the organization's ability to influence its outside stakeholders and perhaps become a global company? Should they invest all organizational resources in research and development or in ways to increase internal skills? An organization could take any of these actions to achieve the goal of maximizing shareholder wealth.

As you can see, there are no easy rules to follow. In many ways, being effective means making more right choices than wrong choices. One thing is certain, however: An organization that does not pay attention to its stakeholders and does not attempt at least *minimally* to satisfy their interests will lose legitimacy in their eyes and be doomed to failure.

Allocating Rewards

Another major problem that an organization has to face is how to allocate the rewards it gains as a result of being effective. How should an organization allocate inducements among various stakeholder groups? An organization needs to minimally satisfy the expectation of each group. But when rewards are more than enough to meet each group's minimum need, how should the "extra" rewards be allocated? How much should the workforce or managers receive relative to shareholders? What determines the appropriate reward for managers? Most people answer that managerial rewards should be determined by the organization's effectiveness. But this answer raises another question: What are the best indicators of effectiveness on which to base managerial rewards? Short-term profit? Long-term wealth maximization? Organizational growth? The choice of different criteria leads to different answers to the question.

The same kinds of consideration are true for other organizational members. What are the appropriate rewards for a middle manager who invents a new process that earns the organization millions of dollars a year or for the workforce as a whole when the company is making record profits? Should they be given short-term bonuses, or should the organization guarantee long-term or lifetime employment as the ultimate inducement for good performance? Similarly, should shareholders receive dividends, or should all profits be invested in the organization to increase its skills and resources? The way in which these goals can come into conflict is illustrated in the following organizational insight.

The allocation of rewards, or inducements, is an important component of organizational effectiveness because the inducements offered to stakeholders now determine their motivation—that is, the form and level of their contributions—in the future. Stakeholders' future investment decisions depend on the return they expect from their investments, whether the returns are in the form of dividends, stock options, bonuses, or wages.

ORGANIZATIONAL INSIGHT

1.3 SHOULD DOCTORS OWN STOCK IN HOSPITALS?

Since the 1990s, there has been an increasing trend for medical doctors to become stockholders in the hospitals and clinics in which they work. Sometimes teams of doctors in a particular area join together to open their own clinic. Other times, large hospital chains give doctors stock in the hospital. Such a trend has the potential to cause a major conflict of interest between doctors and their patients.

Take the case of the Columbia/HCA hospital chain, for example. In 1993, Columbia began offering doctors a financial stake in its chain, a move to encourage doctors to send their patients to a Columbia hospital for treatment.[29] However, when they become owners, doctors then might have the incentive to give their patients minimum-standards care in order to cut costs and increase the hospital's bottom line, or be more likely to overcharge patients for their services and reap extra profits that way. In addition, the financial link between doctors and hospitals means that other hospitals that may have better records in minimizing postoperative infections or in general patient care will not be used by these doctors.

Clearly, the potentially competing goals of doctors and patients when doctors are shareholders have important implications for managing stakeholder interests. Indeed, there has been some support for banning doctors from holding a financial stake in their own clinics and hospitals. However, doctors claim that they are in the same situation as lawyers or accountants, and there is no more reason to suppose that doctors will take advantage of their patients any more than accountants or lawyers take advantage of their clients.

Managing Stakeholder Interests

An organization must carefully balance the claims of all of its stakeholders when choosing criteria for evaluating its performance.[30] However, the interests of managers and shareholders are most commonly used to give direction to the organization's activities because satisfying those stakeholders has the greatest effect on the survival and prosperity of the organization. If the satisfaction of managerial and shareholder interests is the organization's ultimate goal, then satisfying the interests of customers, employees, the government, and other stakeholders can be seen as the *means* for reaching that goal.[31] The way in which managers in the H. B. Fuller Company pay attention to their customers illustrates this well.

Clearly, long-run survival is an organization's ultimate goal—one that overrides the interests of any particular group. In theory the best way to ensure survival is to invest in the skills and resources of the business. Such investment maximizes the organization's ability to create value and to be at the forefront of technical developments that will allow the organization to meet new customer needs. Ensuring the ability of an organization to meet customer and stakeholder needs over time, however, is a difficult managerial task that few organizations seem to do well. Managing the business and relating to its stakeholders pose constant problems. There also are constant problems in managing the resource environment to deal with competition from other organizations, all of which are seeking the same goals: access to scarce and valued resources, including customers, raw materials,

ORGANIZATIONAL INSIGHT

1.4 KEEP YOUR STAKEHOLDERS GLUED TO YOUR COMPANY

H. B. Fuller Company is one of the largest U.S. manufacturers of glue; it supplies glue to many of America's largest companies. For example, it supplies the glue used in Pampers, Procter & Gamble's disposable diapers. Former CEO Tony Anderson, who established Fuller's stance toward its stakeholders, ranked their importance as follows: customers first, employees second, shareholders third, and the community fourth.[32] Anderson believed that shareholders will receive the returns they expect only if customers are offered the goods and services they want. "I don't know how to perform for shareholders over the long term unless I do my best for customers," he has said.[33] Given that this stance has resulted in an annual return to shareholders exceeding 20 percent, H. B. Fuller Company continues to pursue this goal, demonstrating how satisfying the expectations of customers is a way to satisfy other stakeholder groups as well.

and human capital. The ability of an organization to satisfy its stakeholders is virtually synonymous with organization survival.

HOW DO MANAGERS MEASURE ORGANIZATIONAL EFFECTIVENESS?

Because managers are responsible for utilizing organizational resources in a way that maximizes an organization's ability to create value, it is important to understand how they evaluate organizational effectiveness. Researchers analyzing what CEOs and managers do have pointed to control, innovation, and efficiency as the three essential tasks of top management.[34]

In this context, *control* means having control over the external environment and having the ability to attract resources and customers. It also means using the political process to lobby for organizational interests, such as favorable industry conditions, protection from foreign competitors, and industrial and labor relations regulations. *Innovation* means developing an organization's skills and capabilities so that the organization can discover and take advantage of new products and processes, like the Internet. It also means designing and creating new organizational structures and cultures that enhance a company's ability to change, adapt, and improve the way it functions—especially in the era of the Internet.[35] *Efficiency* means developing modern production facilities using new information technologies that can produce and distribute a company's products in a timely and cost-effective manner. It also means introducing techniques like Internet-based information systems, total quality management and just-in-time inventory systems, and e-engineering (discussed in Chapter 10) to improve productivity.[36]

To evaluate the effectiveness with which an organization confronts each of these three tasks, managers can take one of three approaches (see Table 1.2). An organization is effective if it can (1) secure scarce and valued skills and resources from outside the organization (external resource approach); (2) creatively coordinate resources with employee skills to

	TABLE 1.2	
	Approaches to Measuring Organizational Effectiveness	
Approach	**Description**	**Goals to Set to Measure Effectiveness**
External resource approach	Evaluates the organization's ability to secure, manage, and control scarce and valued skills and resources	• Lower costs of inputs • Obtain high-quality inputs of raw materials and employees • Increase market share • Increase stock price • Gain support of stakeholders such as government or environmentalists
Internal systems approach	Evaluates the organization's ability to be innovative and function quickly and responsively	• Cut decision-making time • Increase rate of product innovation • Increase coordination and motivation of employees • Reduce conflict • Reduce time to market
Technical approach	Evaluates the organization's ability to convert skills and resources into goods and services efficiently	• Increase product quality • Reduce number of defects • Reduce production costs • Improve customer service • Reduce delivery time to customer

innovate products and adapt to changing customer needs (internal systems approach); and (3) efficiently convert skills and resources into finished goods and services (technical approach).

The External Resource Approach: Control

External resource approach *A method that allows managers to evaluate how effectively an organization manages and controls its external environment.*

The **external resource approach** allows managers to evaluate how effectively an organization manages and controls its external environment. For example, the organization's ability to influence stakeholders' perceptions in its favor and to receive a positive evaluation by external stakeholders is very important to managers and the organization's survival.[37] Similarly, an organization's ability to utilize its environment and to secure scarce and valuable resources is another indication of its control over the environment.[38]

To measure the effectiveness of their control over the environment, managers use indicators such as stock price, profitability, and return on investment, which compare the performance of their organization with the performance of other organizations.[39] Top managers watch the price of their company's stock very closely because of the impact it has on shareholder expectations. Similarly, in their attempt to attract customers and gauge the performance of their organization, managers gather information on the quality of their company's products as compared to their competitors' products.

Top management's ability to perceive and respond to changes in the environment or to initiate change and be first to take advantage of a new opportunity is another indicator of an organization's ability to influence and control its environment. For instance, the ability and willingness of the Walt Disney Company to manage its environment by seizing any chance to use its reputation and brand name to develop new products that exploit market opportunities are well known. Similarly, Bill Gates has stated that his goal is to be at the forefront of software development in order to maintain Microsoft's competitive advantage in new-product development. By their competitive attitude, these companies signify that they intend to stay in control of their environment so that they can continue to obtain scarce and valued resources such as customers and markets. Managers know that the organization's aggressiveness, entrepreneurial nature, and reputation are all criteria by which stakeholders (especially shareholders) judge how well a company's management is controlling its environment. Indeed, today, being able to make use of the Internet is a major factor differentiating the effectiveness of particular managers.[40]

The Internal Systems Approach: Innovation

Internal Systems Approach *A method that allows managers to evaluate how effectively an organization functions and operates.*

The **internal systems approach** allows managers to evaluate how effectively an organization functions and operates. To be effective, an organization needs a structure and a culture that foster adaptability and quick responses to changing conditions in the environment. The organization also needs to be flexible so that it can speed up decision making and rapidly innovate products and services. Measures of an organization's capacity for innovation include the length of time needed to make a decision, the amount of time needed to get new products to market, and the amount of time spent coordinating the activities of different departments.[41] These factors can often be measured objectively. For example, Hewlett-Packard announced recently that the amount of time it spends in bringing new products to market has been cut in half because of changes in its decision-making systems.

Improvements to internal systems that influence employee coordination or motivation have a direct impact on an organization's ability to respond to its environment. The reduction in product development time allowed Hewlett-Packard to match Japanese companies, which have always enjoyed short development cycles because of their extensive use of product teams in the development process. In turn, Hewlett-Packard's improved ability to get a product to market is likely to make the company attractive to new customers and may bring about an increase in shareholder returns.

The Technical Approach: Efficiency

Technical approach *A method that allows managers to evaluate how efficiently an organization can convert some fixed amount of organizational skills and resources into finished goods and services.*

The **technical approach** allows managers to evaluate how efficiently an organization can convert some fixed amount of organizational skills and resources into finished goods and services. Technical effectiveness is measured in terms of productivity and efficiency (the ratio of outputs to inputs).[42] Thus, for example, an increase in the number of units produced without the use of additional labor indicates a gain in productivity, and so does a reduction in the cost of labor or materials required to produce each unit of output.

Productivity measures are objective measures of the effectiveness of an organization's production operations. Thus, it is common for production line managers to measure productivity at all stages of the production process and for them to be rewarded for reducing costs. In service organizations, where no tangible good is produced, line managers use productivity measures such as amount of sales per employee or the ratio of goods sold to goods returned to judge employee productivity. For most work activities, no matter how complex, there is a way to measure productivity or performance. In many settings the inducements offered to both employees and managers are closely linked to productivity measures, and it is important to select the right measures to evaluate effectiveness.[43] Employees' attitude and motivation and their desire to cooperate are also important factors influencing productivity and efficiency.[44]

Measuring Effectiveness: Organizational Goals

Managers create goals that they use to assess how well the organization is performing. Two types of goals used to evaluate organizational effectiveness are official goals and operative goals. **Official goals** are guiding principles that the organization formally states in its annual report and in other public documents. Usually these goals lay out the **mission** of the organization—that is, they explain why the organization exists and what it should be doing. Official goals include being a leading producer of a product, demonstrating an overriding concern for public safety, and so forth. Official goals are meant to legitimize the organization and its activities and to allow it to obtain resources and the support of its stakeholders.[45]

Operative goals are specific long-term and short-term goals that guide managers and employees as they perform the work of the organization. The goals listed in Table 1.2 are operative goals that managers can use to evaluate organizational effectiveness. Managers can use operative goals to measure how well they are managing the environment. Is market share increasing or decreasing? Is the cost of inputs rising or falling? Similarly, they can measure how well the organization is functioning by measuring how long it takes to make a decision or how great conflict is among organizational members. Finally, they can measure how efficient they are by creating operative goals that allow them to "benchmark" themselves against their competitors—that is, compare their competitors' costs and quality achievements with their own. General Motors used Toyota's cost and quality as benchmarks for what it sought to achieve in its Saturn plant.

Official goals Guiding principles that the organization formally states in its annual report and in other public documents.

Mission Goals that explain why the organization exists and what it should be doing.

Operative goals Specific long-term and short-term goals that guide managers and employees as they perform the work of the organization.

WHAT ARE THE FACTORS AFFECTING ORGANIZATIONS?

We have discussed what an organization is, why organizations exist, how stakeholders and managers measure effectiveness, and how organizations select which goals to pursue. An effective organization is one that designs its organizational structure and culture to meet the needs of its stakeholders so that it can gain a competitive advantage and survive. Chapters 2 through 5 examine the principles on which organizations operate and the choices available for designing their structures and cultures. As these chapters show, the same basic organizational problems occur in all work settings, and the purpose of organizational design is to develop an organizational structure and culture that will respond effectively to these challenges.

Organizational design is complicated by the contingencies that must be considered as an organization makes its design choices. Several types of contingencies—the organization's environment, its technology, and internal processes that develop in an organization over time—cause uncertainty and influence an organization's choice of structure and culture. Throughout the rest of this book we analyze the sources of this uncertainty and how organizations manage it. Figure 1.5 shows how the various chapters fit together and provides a model of the components of organizational theory.

The Organizational Environment

The environment in which an organization operates is a principal source of uncertainty. If customers withdraw their support, if suppliers withhold inputs, or if other stakeholder groups threaten the organization, considerable uncertainty is created. Thus, the orga-

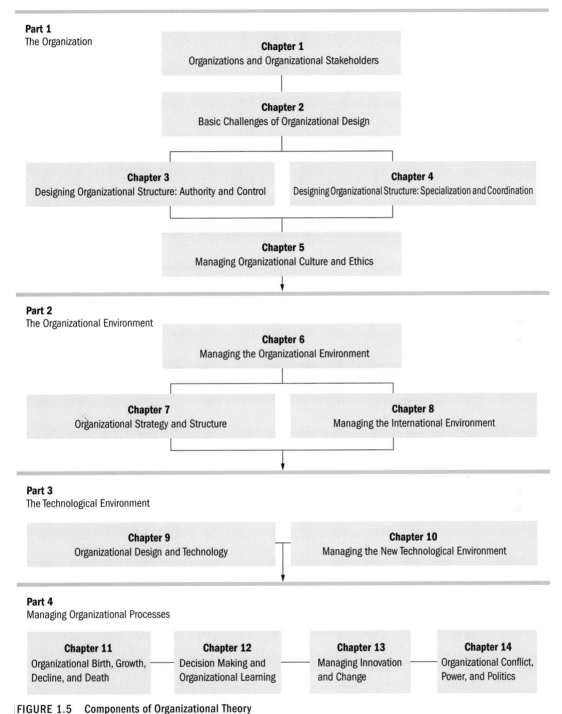

Part 1
The Organization

Chapter 1
Organizations and Organizational Stakeholders

Chapter 2
Basic Challenges of Organizational Design

Chapter 3
Designing Organizational Structure: Authority and Control

Chapter 4
Designing Organizational Structure: Specialization and Coordination

Chapter 5
Managing Organizational Culture and Ethics

Part 2
The Organizational Environment

Chapter 6
Managing the Organizational Environment

Chapter 7
Organizational Strategy and Structure

Chapter 8
Managing the International Environment

Part 3
The Technological Environment

Chapter 9
Organizational Design and Technology

Chapter 10
Managing the New Technological Environment

Part 4
Managing Organizational Processes

Chapter 11
Organizational Birth, Growth, Decline, and Death

Chapter 12
Decision Making and Organizational Learning

Chapter 13
Managing Innovation and Change

Chapter 14
Organizational Conflict, Power, and Politics

FIGURE 1.5   Components of Organizational Theory

nization must design its structure to adequately handle its relationships with stakeholders in the external environment.

In Chapters 6 through 8, we examine how organizations deal with their environment. Chapter 6 presents models that reveal why the environment is a source of uncertainty and theories about how and why organizations design their structure to meet uncertainties in the environment. Resource dependence theory examines how organizations attempt to gain control over scarce resources. Transaction cost theory examines how organizations manage environmental relations to reduce transaction costs. Chapter 7 discusses organizations' attempts to manage their environment by means of the strategies they adopt toward significant stakeholders. We discuss how organizations develop functional, business, and corporate-level strategies to increase their control over and share of scarce resources. Chapter 8 looks at how an organization manages the global environment and at the special challenges an organization faces when it needs to extend its control beyond national boundaries.

The Technological Environment

Organizations produce goods and services. The way they produce goods and services and the uncertainty associated with different production methods are major factors in the design of an organization. In Chapter 9 some theories that describe what technology is and that explain the way in which technology affects organizational structure and culture are discussed. Then in Chapter 10 we look at how new innovations in both manufacturing and information technology, including the Internet, have been affecting organizations and changing organizational structure and culture.

Organizational Processes

When organizations are created and set in motion, various internal processes occur. As organizations grow and mature, many of them experience a predictable series of organizing crises, and as they attempt to change their strategies and structures, they confront similar problems. Chapters 11 through 14 analyze such issues. Chapter 11 presents a life cycle model of organizations and charts the typical problems they confront as they grow, mature, and decline. Here, particular attention is paid to population ecology theory and institutional theory. Chapter 12 discusses organizational learning and decision making. First, the ways in which managers make decisions is examined. Then the increasingly important question of how managers can increase the level of organizational learning to improve the quality of decision making is examined. Chapter 13 then looks at the issue of innovation and change in organizations. It focuses on how managers can find ways to promote the development of new kinds of goods and services. How to foster innovation and manage research and development is a pressing problem, particularly for organizations competing globally. The chapter also looks at the process of organizational change and at the problems managers experience in adjusting their structures and cultures to suit changing contingencies. Finally, Chapter 14 covers problems of politics and conflict that arise as managers and stakeholders pursue their goals. These chapters highlight the complex organizational processes that must be managed if an organization is to be effective.

Organizational theory seeks to understand the principles that govern how organizations operate, evolve, and change their structures and cultures and the factors that affect the way organizations operate, evolve, and change. Its focus is on the organization as a whole. An organization's behavior is the result of its design and the principles behind its operation. Looking inward, an organization's design puts pressure on work groups and individuals to behave in certain ways. Looking outward, the design can cause organizational members to view and respond to the environment in different ways. The theories and concepts covered in this book are intended to provide you with working models that you can use to analyze organizational situations and to propose and implement suitable solutions.

SUMMARY

We have examined what organizations are, why they exist, whose interests they serve, the different ways in which they can be evaluated, and how they set their goals. Organizations play a vital role in increasing the wealth of a society, and organizational theory and design provide important insights into enhancing organizational effectiveness. An organization is a coalition of stakeholders; and to survive and grow, an organization must create value to satisfy the expectations of these stakeholders. Chapter 1 has made the following main points:

1. An organization is a tool used by people to coordinate their actions to obtain something they desire or value—to achieve their goals.

2. Organizations are value-creation systems that take inputs from the environment and use skills and knowledge to transform these inputs into finished goods and services.

3. The use of an organization allows people jointly to increase specialization and the division of labor, use large-scale technology, manage the external environment, economize on transaction costs, and exert power and control—all of which increase the value that the organization can create.

4. Organizational theory is the study of how organizations function and how they affect and are affected by the environment in which they operate.

5. Organizational structure is the formal system of task and authority relationships that controls how people coordinate their actions and use resources to achieve an organization's goals.

6. Organizational culture is the set of shared values and norms that controls organizational members' interactions with each other and with suppliers, customers, and other people outside the organization.

7. Organizational design is the process by which managers select and manage aspects of structure and culture so that an organization can control the activities necessary to achieve its goals. Organizational design has important implications for a company's competitive advantage, its ability to deal with contingencies and manage diversity, its efficiency, its ability to generate new goods and services, its control of the environment, its coordination and motivation of employees, and its development and implementation of strategy.

8. Organizations exist because of their ability to create value and acceptable outcomes for stakeholders. The two main groups of stakeholders are inside stakeholders and outside stakeholders. Effective organizations satisfy, at least minimally, the interests of all stakeholder groups.

9. Problems that an organization faces as it tries to win stakeholders' approval include choosing which stakeholder goals to satisfy, deciding how to allocate organizational rewards to different stakeholder groups, and balancing short-term and long-term goals.

10. Managers can use three approaches to evaluate organizational effectiveness: the external resource approach, the internal systems approach, and the technical approach. Each approach is associated with a set of criteria that can be used to measure effectiveness and a set of organizational goals.

DISCUSSION QUESTIONS

1. How do organizations create value? What is the role of entrepreneurship in this process?

2. What is the relationship among organizational theory, organizational design, and organizational structure and culture?

3. Pick a fast-food restaurant or some other local organization, and outline the inducements and contributions of its stakeholders.
4. Satisfying the claims of shareholders should be the paramount concern of a company. Discuss the arguments for and against this statement.
5. What is organizational effectiveness? Discuss three approaches to evaluating effectiveness and the problems associated with each approach.
6. Draw up a list of effectiveness goals that you would use to measure the performance of (a) a fast-food restaurant and (b) a school of business.

ORGANIZATIONAL THEORY IN ACTION

PRACTICING ORGANIZATIONAL THEORY: OPEN SYSTEMS DYNAMICS

Form groups of three to five people and discuss the following scenario:

Think of an organization you are all familiar with such as a local restaurant, store, or bank, for instance. Once you have chosen an organization, model it from an open systems perspective. For example, identify its input, conversion, and output processes.

1. Identify the specific forces in the environment that have the greatest opportunity to help or hurt this organization's ability to obtain resources and dispose of its goods or services.
2. Using the three views of effectiveness discussed in the chapter, discuss which specific measures are most useful to managers in evaluating this organization's effectiveness.

MAKING THE CONNECTION #1

At the end of every chapter you will find an exercise that requires you to search newspapers or magazines for an example of a real company that is dealing with some of the issues, concepts, challenges, questions, and problems discussed in the chapter.

The purpose of the following exercise for Chapter 1 is to familiarize you with the way organizations impact their stakeholders: Identify a company that has helped or harmed a stakeholder group. Describe the incident, and discuss how it has affected or might affect the relationship among different stakeholder groups.

Analyzing the Organization: Design Module #1

To give you insight into the way real-world organizations work, at the end of every chapter there is an organizational design module for which you must collect and analyze information about an organization that you will select now and study all semester. You will write up the information you collect into a report to be presented to the class at the end of the semester.

Suppose you select General Motors. You will collect the information specified in each organizational design module, present and summarize your findings on GM for your class, and then produce a written report. Your instructor will provide the details of what will be required of you—for example, how long the presentation or report should be and whether you will work in a group or by yourself to complete the assignment. By the end of the semester, by completing each module, you will have a clear picture of how organizations operate and how they deal with problems and contingencies they face.

There are two approaches to selecting an organization. One is to choose a well-known organization about which a lot has been written. Large companies like IBM, Apple Computer, and Procter & Gamble receive extensive coverage in business periodicals such as *Fortune* and *Business Week*. Every year, for example, in one of its April issues, *Fortune* magazine publishes a list of the Fortune 500 manufacturing companies, and in one of its May issues it publishes a list of the Fortune 500 service companies, the biggest companies in the United States. If you choose a company on the Fortune lists, you can be sure that considerable information is published about it.

The best sources of information are business periodicals like *Fortune*, *Business Week*, and *Forbes*; news magazines like *Time* and *Newsweek*; the *Wall Street Journal* and other newspapers; and on-line information services, such as Lotus One Source, that summarize all the articles published about a particular company. *F&S Predicasts, Value Line Investment Survey, Moody's Manuals on Investment*, and many other publications summarize articles written about a particular company. In addition, you should write to "your" company and ask for a copy of its current annual report (you might find previous annual reports in libraries), and you should check industry and trade publications.

Finally, you should take advantage of the Internet and explore the World Wide Web to find information on your company. Most large companies have detailed Web sites that provide a considerable amount of information. You can find these Web sites using a search engine such as Yahoo! (www.yahoo.com) or Altavista (www.altavista.digital.com) and then download the information you need.

If you consult these sources, you will obtain a lot of information that you can use to complete the design modules. You may not get all the specific information you need, but you will have enough to answer many of the design module questions. To obtain information that you lack, do not be afraid to call your organization and ask to speak to its public relations department or even to the CEO. You will be surprised at how much companies will tell you if you ask the right questions.

The second approach to selecting an organization is to choose one located in your city or town—for example, a large department store, manufacturing company, hotel, or nonprofit organization (such as a hospital or school) where you or somebody you know works. You could contact the owners or managers of the organization and ask whether they would be willing to talk to you about the way they operate and how they design and manage their company.

Each approach to selecting a company has advantages and disadvantages. The advantage of selecting a local company and doing your own information gathering is that in face-to-face interviews you can ask for detailed information that may be unavailable from published sources. You will gain an especially rich picture of the way a company operates by doing your research personally. The problem is that the local organization you choose has to be big enough to offer you insight into the way organizations work. In general, it should employ at least 20 people and have at least three levels in its hierarchy.

If you use written sources to study a very large organization, you will get a lot of interesting information that relates to organizational theory because the organization is large and complex and is confronting many of the problems discussed in this book. But you may not be able to obtain all the detailed information you want.

Whichever selection approach you use, be sure that you have access to enough interesting information to complete the majority of the organizational design modules. One module, for example, asks about the international or global dimension of your organization's strategy and structure. If you pick a local company that does not have an international dimension, you will be unable to complete that assignment. However, to compensate for this lack of information, you might have very detailed information about the company's structure or product lines. The issue is to make sure that you can gain access to enough information to write an interesting report.

ASSIGNMENT

Choose a company to study, and answer the following questions about it.

1. What is the name of the organization? Give a short account of the history of the company. Describe the way it has grown and developed.

2. What does the organization do? What goods and services does it produce or provide? What kind of value does it create? If the company has an annual report, what does the report describe as the company's organizational mission?

3. Draw a model of the way the organization creates value. Briefly describe its inputs, throughputs, outputs, and environment.

4. Do an initial analysis of the organization's major problems or issues. What challenges confront the organization today—for example, in its efforts to attract customers, to lower costs, to increase operating efficiency? How does organizational design relate to these problems?

5. Who are the organization's major stakeholders? List the major groups and discuss any problems your company has (or has had) in managing its relations with these stakeholder groups. Is it able to offer an acceptable inducements/contributions package to each group? If not, why not?

6. Are there any conflicts among stakeholder groups? Do the goals of various groups conflict? Which stakeholder groups' goals receive priority in your organization? Does the organization do a good job in managing its stakeholders? How do you know?

7. How do the organization's managers judge its effectiveness? What goals, standards, or targets are they using to evaluate performance? How well is the organization doing when judged by the criteria of control, innovation, and efficiency?

8. What other issues are interesting in this company? For example, are there interesting technology issues? Is there a unique competitive environment? Are there problems with internal workforce issues such as control or motivation?

Case for Analysis:
KINKO'S NEW OPERATING STRUCTURE

Kinko's is the largest chain of 24-hour copying stores in the United States and holds an estimated 25 to 30 percent share of the $6 billion retail copying market. However, by 1996 its founder, Paul Orfalea, realized that his company was facing major problems. First, Kinko's was under intense competitive pressure from other rapidly growing copying chains like Sir Speedy and Quick Copy, which were opening outlets in all of Kinko's major markets, and stores such as Officemax and Office Depot had begun to offer low-priced copying services. Second, the informal, decentralized form of management that Orfalea had been using in the 850 Kinko's stores was not allowing the company to respond quickly enough to the moves of its competitors.[46] Third, Kinko's was having a difficult time managing its own growth and development. In particular, it was experiencing problems in deciding how to effectively service the needs of new kinds of customers like small and large businesses.

Orfalea had begun to feel that Kinko's was in danger of losing its leading industry position because of this and his company's inability to find a new way of operating in the changed industry environment. To help find a solution, Orfalea called on the services of consultants from the New York investment firm of Clayton, Dubilier & Rice. These consultants began to examine and analyze the company's method of operating. They soon realized that the root of the company's troubles was the kind of organizational structure—the task and authority relationships inside the company—Kinko's used to manage its far-flung store operations.[47]

Orfalea had grown his companies by franchising. He had sold to investors the right to open stores using Kinko's name and copying expertise in a particular location, normally a city. Each Kinko's store was an independent operating unit, and the local investor, or franchisee, controlled how it grew in that location.[48] Although this method of operating had let the company grow quickly, it had done little to help the company either control its costs or find better ways of servicing its customers' needs. The consultants decided that what Kinko's needed was a more centralized operating system where, for example, purchasing and financing for the entire company were handled centrally by the head office to reduce costs. Previously, Orfalea had not taken control of any operating activity; indeed, he had even refused to use an official title like "president." The consultants recommended that Kinko's recruit experienced top managers to provide the centralized control that the company needed if it was going to be able to develop a plan of action to respond to the challenges of its competitors and discover new and better ways of meeting its customers' needs. Moreover, they recommended that Kinko's develop a clear set of internal authority relationships so that Kinko's new top managers would be able to orchestrate companywide changes to retain and attract new customers. Given that Kinko's store managers had been in complete control of their operations it was not clear how they would adapt to this new operating structure. However, they all agreed that they had to try to make it work if Kinko's was to survive and prosper in the new, more competitive environment.

1. What were the problems facing Kinko's managers?
2. What steps did managers take to solve these problems?

REFERENCES

1. A. W. Gouldner, "Organizational Analysis," in R. K. Merton, ed., *Sociology Today* (New York: Basic Books, 1959); A. Etzioni, *Comparative Analysis of Complex Organizations* (New York: Free Press, 1961).
2. I. M. Kirzner, *Competition and Entrepreneurship* (Chicago: University of Chicago Press, 1973).
3. www. Amazon.com, "About Amazon.com," 1999.
4. ibid.
5. P. M. Blau, "A Formal Theory of Differentiation in Organizations," *American Sociological Review*, 1970, vol. 35, pp. 201–218; D. S. Pugh and D. J. Hickson, "The Comparative Study of Organizations," in G. Salaman and K. Thompson, eds., *People and Organizations* (London: Penguin, 1977), pp. 43–55.
6. J. Useem, "Internet Defense Strategy: Cannibalize Yourself," *Fortune*, 6 September 1999.
7. P. M. Blau, *Exchange and Power in Social Life* (New York: Wiley, 1964);

P. M. Blau and W. R. Scott, *Formal Organizations* (San Francisco: Chandler, 1962).
8. C. I. Barnard, *The Functions of the Executive* (Cambridge, MA: Harvard University Press, 1948); A. Etzioni, *Modern Organizations* (Englewood Cliffs, NJ: Prentice Hall, 1964).
9. P. R. Lawrence and J. W. Lorsch, *Organization and Environment* (Boston: Graduate School of Business Administration, Harvard University, 1967); W. R. Scott, *Organizations: Rational, Natural, and Open Systems* (Englewood Cliffs, NJ: Prentice Hall, 1981).
10. H. Stucker, "Internet: Useless Without Business Strategy," *National Underwriter*, 1999, vol. 103, p. 16.
11. T. Donaldson and L. E. Preston, "The Stakeholder Theory of the Corporation: Concepts, Evidence, and Implications," *Academy of Management Review*, 1995, vol. 20, pp. 65–91.
12. J. G. March and H. Simon, *Organizations* (New York: Wiley, 1958).

13. Ibid.; J. A. Pearce, "The Company Mission as a Strategic Tool," *Sloan Management Review*, Spring 1982, pp. 15–24.

14. R. Norton, "Who Owns This Company, Anyhow?" *Fortune*, 29 July 1991, pp. 131–142.

15. M. Benson, "Calpers Audit Finds Errors," *Wall Street Journal*, 24 February 1999, p. 16.

16. J. S. Lublin and S. Calian, "Activist Pension Funds in Trans-Atlantic Alliance," *Wall Street Journal*, 23 November 1998, p. 2.

17. C. W. L. Hill and G. R. Jones, *Strategic Management: An Integrated Approach*, 5th ed. (Boston: Houghton Mifflin, 2000).

18. B. O'Reilly, "Where Service Flies Right," *Fortune*, 24 August 1992, pp. 115–116.

19. P. Corbett, "Southwest Airlines Names Vice President of Customer Relations and Rapid Rewards," www.southwest.com, 1 October 1999.

20. www.southwest.com, 2000.

21. K. Cleland, "Southwest Tries Online Ticketing," *Advertising Age*, 1996, vol. 67, p. 39.

22. J. P. Womack, D. T. Jones, D. Roos, and D. Sammons Carpenter, *The Machine That Changed the World* (New York: Macmillan, 1990).

23. K. Kelly, "A Living Hell in Indiana," *Business Week*, 9 March 1992, p. 33.

24. R. F. Zammuto, "A Comparison of Multiple Constituency Models of Organizational Effectiveness," *Academy of Management Review*, 1984, vol. 9, pp. 606–616; K. S. Cameron, "Critical Questions in Assessing Organizational Effectiveness," *Organizational Dynamics*, 1989, vol. 9, pp. 66–80.

25. R. M. Cyert and J. G. March, *A Behavioral Theory of the Firm* (Englewood Cliffs, NJ: Prentice Hall, 1963).

26. R. H. Miles, *Macro Organizational Behavior* (Santa Monica, CA: Goodyear, 1980), p. 375.

27. A. A. Berle and G. C. Means, *The Modern Corporation and Private Property* (New York: Commerce Clearing House, 1932).

28. Hill and Jones, *Strategic Management*, Ch. 2.

29. C. Yang, "Money and Medicine: Physician Disentangle Thyself," *Academic Universe*, 21 April 1997, p. 34.

30. G. T. Savage, T. W. Nix, C. J. Whitehead, and J. D. Blair, "Strategies for Assessing and Managing Organizational Stakeholders," *Academy of Management Executives*, 1992, vol. 5, pp. 61–75.

31. J. P. Campbell, "On the Nature of Organizational Effectiveness," in P. S. Goodman, J. M. Pennings, and Associates, *New Perspectives on Organizational Effectiveness* (San Francisco: Jossey-Bass, 1977).

32. A. Wood, "Adhesives Maker Bonds Business and Ethics," *Chemical Week*, 3 May 1995, p. 366.

33. P. Sellers, "H. B. Fuller: Who Cares About Shareholders?" *Fortune*, 15 June 1992, p. 122.

34. L. Galambos, "What Have CEOs Been Doing?" *Journal of Economic History*, 1988, vol. 18, pp. 243–258.

35. Ibid., p. 253.

36. S. Hamm and M. Stepanek, "From Reengineering to E-Engineering," *Business Week*, 29 March 1999, pp. 62–65.

37. Campbell, "On the Nature of Organizational Effectiveness."

38. F. Friedlander and H. Pickle, "Components of Effectiveness in Small Organizations," *Administrative Science Quarterly*, 1968, vol. 13, pp. 289–304; Miles, *Macro Organizational Behavior*.

39. Campbell, "On the Nature of Organizational Effectiveness."

40. G. Colvin, "How to Be a Great E-CEO," *Fortune*, 1999, vol. 139, pp. 104–114.

41. Ibid., p. 38.

42. J. D. Thompson, *Organizations in Action* (New York: McGraw-Hill, 1967).

43. R. M. Steers, *Organizational Effectiveness: A Behavioral View* (Santa Monica, CA: Goodyear, 1977).

44. D. E. Bowen and G. R. Jones, "Transaction Cost Analysis of Customer-Service Organization Exchange," *Academy of Management Review*, 1986, vol. 11, pp. 428–441.

45. T. M. Jones, "Instrumental Stakeholder Theory: A Synthesis of Ethics and Economics," *Academy of Management Review*, 1995, vol. 20, pp. 404–437.

46. N. Byrnes, "Kinko's Goes Corporate," *Business Week*, 19 August 1996, pp. 58–59.

47. Z. Moutkheiber, "I'm Just a Peddler," *Fortune*, 17 July 1995, pp. 42–43.

48. C. Rubel, "Treating Coworkers Right Is the Key to Kinko's Success," *Advertising Age*, 29 January 1996, p. 5.

C h a p t e r 2

BASIC CHALLENGES of
ORGANIZATIONAL DESIGN

Organizational design involves difficult choices about how to control—that is, coordinate organizational tasks and motivate the people who perform them to maximize an organization's ability to create value. If an organization is to remain effective and successful as it changes and grows and as its environment changes and grows, management must continuously evaluate how the organization divides up the work that needs to be done and how it controls its human, financial, and physical resources.

This chapter examines the challenges of designing an organizational structure so that it achieves stakeholder objectives. First, the factors that lead to differentiation in an organization are discussed. This discussion provides an overview of how an organization develops value-creation skills and abilities in order to survive and grow. Then the organization is analyzed as a system of interlocking roles and some of the basic terms in organizational theory are defined. Next, three more basic design challenges that organizations encounter are examined. Finally, the way in which managers address these challenges and cause the emergence of either a mechanistic or an organic structure is discussed, and the behavior of people who work in mechanistic and organic structures is contrasted.

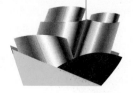

DIFFERENTIATION

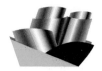

| *Design Challenge 1* | *People in this organization take on new tasks as the need arises and it's very unclear who is responsible for what and who is supposed to report to whom. This makes it difficult to know on whom to call when the need arises and difficult to coordinate people's activities so they work together as a team.*

Differentiation *The process by which an organization allocates people and resources to organizational tasks and establishes the task and authority relationships that allow the organization to achieve its goals.*

As organizations grow, managers must decide how to control and coordinate the activities that are required for the organization to create value. The principal design challenge is how to manage differentiation to achieve organizational goals. **Differentiation** is the process by which an organization allocates people and resources to organizational tasks and establishes the task and authority relationships that allow the organization to achieve its goals.[1] In short, it is the process of establishing and controlling the *division of labor*, or degree of specialization, in the organization.

An easy way to examine why differentiation occurs and why it poses a design challenge is to examine an organization and chart the problems it faces as it attempts to achieve its goals (see Figure 2.1). In a *simple* organization differentiation is low because the division of labor is low. Typically, one person or a few people perform all organizational tasks, so there are few problems with coordinating who does what, for whom, and when. With growth, however, comes complexity. In a *complex* organization both the division of labor and differentiation are high. The story of how the B.A.R. and Grille restaurant grew illustrates the problems and challenges that organizational design must address. As the B.A.R. and Grille changed, its owners had to find new ways to control the activities necessary to meet their goal of providing customers with a satisfying dining experience.

ORGANIZATIONAL INSIGHT

2.1 B.A.R. AND GRILLE RESTAURANT

In 1998, Bob and Amanda Richards (hence, B.A.R.) trained as chefs and obtained the capital they needed to open their own restaurant, the B.A.R. and Grille, a 1950s-style restaurant specializing in hamburgers, hot dogs, french fries, fresh fruit pies, and fountain drinks. At the beginning, with the help of one additional person hired to be a waiter, Bob and Amanda took turns cooking and waiting on tables (see Figure 2.1A). The venture was wildly successful. The combination of good food, served in a "Happy Days" atmosphere, appealed to customers, who swamped the restaurant at lunchtime and every night.

Right away Bob and Amanda were overloaded. They worked from dawn to midnight to cope with all the jobs that needed to be done: buying supplies, preparing the food, maintaining the property, taking in money, and figuring the accounts. It was soon clear that both Bob and Amanda were needed in the kitchen and that they needed additional help. They hired waiters, busboys, and kitchen help to wash mountains of dishes. The staff worked in shifts, and by the end of the third month of operations Bob and Amanda were employing 22 people on a full- or part-time basis (Figure 2.1B).

With 22 staff members to oversee, the Richardses confronted a new problem. Because both of them were working in the kitchen, they had little time to oversee what was happening in the dining room. The waiters, in effect, were running the restaurant. Bob and Amanda had lost contact with the customers and no longer received their comments about the food and service. They realized that to make sure their standards

A. Bob and Amanda, the owners, cook and wait tables as needed. They employ one additional waiter.
(3 individuals in the organization)

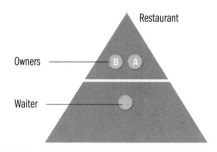

B. Bob and Amanda work in the kitchen full-time. They hire waiters, busboys, and kitchen staff.
(22 individuals in the organization)

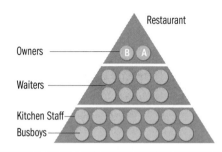

C. Unable to manage both the kitchen and the dining room, they divide tasks into two functions, kitchen and dining room, and specialize. Bob runs the kitchen, and Amanda runs the dining room. They also add more staff.
(29 individuals in the organization)

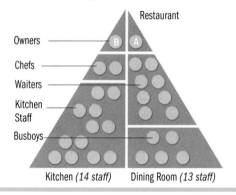

D. The business continues to prosper. Bob and Amanda create new tasks and functions and hire people to manage the functions.
(52 individuals in the organization)

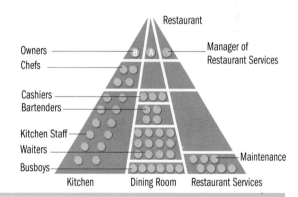

E. The Richardses see new opportunities to apply their core competences in new restaurant ventures. They open new restaurants, put support functions like purchasing and marketing under their direct control, and hire shift managers to manage the kitchen and dining room in each restaurant.
(150 individuals in the organization)

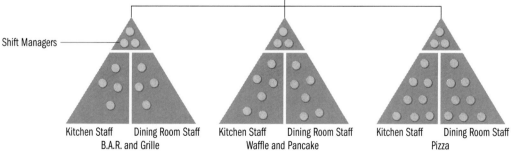

FIGURE 2.1   **Design Challenge.** Differentiation at the B.A.R. and Grille

of customer service were being met, one of them needed to take control of the dining room and supervise the waiters and busboys while the other took control of the kitchen. Amanda took over the dining room, and she and Bob hired two chefs to replace her in the kitchen. Bob oversaw the kitchen and continued to cook. The business continued to do well, so they increased the size of the dining room and hired additional waiters and busboys (Figure 2.1C).

It soon became clear that Bob and Amanda needed to employ additional people to take over specific tasks because they no longer had the time or energy to handle them personally. To control the payment system, they employed full-time cashiers. To cope with customers' demands for alcoholic drinks, they hired a lawyer, got a liquor license, and employed full-time bartenders. To obtain restaurant supplies and manage restaurant services such as cleaning and equipment maintenance, they employed a restaurant manager. The manager was also responsible for overseeing the restaurant on days when the owners took a well-deserved break. By the end of its first year of operation, the B.A.R. and Grille had 50 full- and part-time employees, and the owners were seeking new avenues for expansion (Figure 2.1D).

Eager to use their newly acquired skills to create yet more value, the Richardses began to search for ideas for a new restaurant. Within 18 months they opened a waffle and pancake restaurant, and a year later they opened a pizza restaurant. With this growth, Bob and Amanda left their jobs in the B.A.R. and Grille. They hired shift managers to manage each restaurant, and they spent their time managing central support functions such as purchasing, marketing, and accounting, training new chefs, and developing menu and marketing plans (Figure 2.1E). To ensure that service and quality were uniformly excellent at all three restaurants, they developed written rules and procedures that told chefs, waiters, and other employees what was expected of them—for example, how to prepare and present food and how to behave with customers. After five years of operation, they employed over 150 people full- or part-time in their three restaurants, and their sales volume was over $2 million a year.

The basic design challenge facing the owners of the B.A.R. and Grille was managing the increasing complexity of the organization's activities. At first, Bob and Amanda performed all the major organizational tasks themselves, and the division of labor was low. As the volume of business grew, the owners needed to increase the division of labor and decide which people would do which jobs. In other words, they had to differentiate the organization and allocate people and resources to organizational tasks.

Organizational Roles

Organizational role *The set of task-related behaviors required of a person by his or her position in an organization.*

The basic building blocks of differentiation are organizational roles (see Figure 2.2). An **organizational role** is a set of task-related behaviors required of a person by his or her position in an organization.[2] For example, the organizational role of a B.A.R. and Grille waiter is to provide customers with quick, courteous service to enhance their dining experience. A chef's role is to provide customers with high-quality, appetizing, cooked-to-order meals. A person who is given a role with identifiable tasks and responsibilities can be held accountable for the resources used to accomplish the duties of that position. Bob and Amanda held the waiter responsible for satisfying customers, the restaurant's crucial stakeholder group. The chef was accountable for providing high-quality meals to customers consistently and speedily.

FIGURE 2.2

Building Blocks of Differentiation

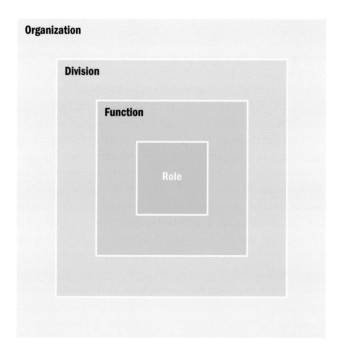

Authority *The power to hold people accountable for their actions and to make decisions concerning the use of organizational resources.*

Control *The ability to coordinate and motivate people to work in the organization's interests.*

Function *A subunit composed of a group of people, working together, who possess similar skills or use the same kind of knowledge, tools, or techniques to perform their jobs.*

As the division of labor increases in an organization, managers specialize in some roles and hire people to specialize in others. Specialization allows people to develop their individual abilities and knowledge, which are the ultimate source of an organization's core competences. At the B.A.R. and Grille, for example, the owners identified various tasks to be done, such as cooking, bookkeeping, and purchasing, and hired people with the appropriate abilities and knowledge to do them.

Organizational structure is based on a system of interlocking roles, and the relationship of one role to another is defined by task-related behaviors. Some roles require people to oversee the behavior of others. Shift managers at the B.A.R. and Grille oversee the waiters and busboys. A person who can hold another person accountable for his or her performance possesses authority over the other person. **Authority** is the power to hold people accountable for their actions and to make decisions concerning the use of organizational resources.[3] The differentiation of an organization into individual organizational roles results in clear authority and responsibility requirements for each role in the system. When an individual clearly understands the responsibilities of his or her role and what a superior can require of a person in that role, the result within the organization is **control**—the ability to coordinate and motivate people to work in the organization's interests.

Subunits: Functions and Divisions

Division *A subunit that consists of a collection of functions or departments that share responsibility for producing a particular good or service.*

In most organizations, people with similar and related roles are grouped into a subunit. The main subunits that develop in organizations are functions (or departments) and divisions. A **function** is a subunit composed of a group of people, working together, who possess similar skills or use the same kind of knowledge, tools, or techniques to perform their jobs. For example, in the B.A.R. and Grille, chefs are grouped together as the kitchen function, and waiters are grouped together as the dining room function. A **division** is a subunit that consists of a collection of functions or departments that share responsibility for producing a particular good or service. Take another look at Figure 2.1E. Each restaurant is a division composed of just two functions—dining room and kitchen—which are responsible for the restaurant's activities. Large companies like General Electric, Textron, and Procter & Gamble, profiled at the end of the chapter in Cases for Analysis, have dozens of separate divisions, each one responsible for producing a particular product. We will see how Procter & Gamble also faced the problem of how to organize these divisions on a global level so the company could create the most value, an issue discussed in detail in Chapter 8.

The number of different functions and divisions that an organization possesses is a measure of the organization's complexity—its degree of differentiation. Differentiation into functions and divisions increases an organization's control over its activities and allows the organization to accomplish its tasks more effectively.

As organizations grow in size, they differentiate into five different kinds of functions.[4] **Support functions** facilitate an organization's control of its relations with its environment and its stakeholders. Support functions include *purchasing*, to handle the acquisition of inputs; *sales and marketing*, to handle the disposal of outputs; and *public relations and legal affairs*, to respond to the needs of outside stakeholders. Bob and Amanda Richards hired a manager to oversee purchasing for all three restaurants and an accountant to manage the books (see Figure 2.1E).

Production functions manage and improve the efficiency of an organization's conversion processes so that more value is created. Production functions include *production operations, production control*, and *quality control*. At the Ford Motor Company, the production operations department controls the manufacturing process; production control decides on the most efficient way to produce cars at the lowest cost; and quality control monitors product quality.

Maintenance functions enable an organization to keep its departments in operation. Maintenance functions include *personnel*, to recruit and train workers and improve skills; *engineering*, to repair broken machinery; and *janitorial services*, to keep the work environment safe and healthy—conditions that are very important to a restaurant like the B.A.R. and Grille.

Adaptive functions allow an organization to adjust to changes in the environment. Adaptive functions include *research and development, market research*, and *long-range planning*, which allow an organization to learn from and attempt to manage its environment and, thus, increase its core competences. At the B.A.R. and Grille, developing new menu choices to keep up with customers' changing tastes is an important adaptive activity.

Managerial functions facilitate the control and coordination of activities within and among departments. Managers at different organizational levels direct the acquisition of, investment in, and control of resources to improve the organization's ability to create value. Top management, for example, is responsible for formulating strategy and establishing the policies the organization uses to control its environment. Middle managers are responsible for managing the organization's resources to meet its goals. Lower-level managers oversee and direct the activities of the workforce.

Differentiation at the B.A.R. and Grille

In the B.A.R. and Grille, differentiation at first was minimal. The owners, with the help of one other person, did all the work. But with unexpected success came the need to differentiate activities into separate organizational roles and functions, with Bob managing the kitchen and Amanda the dining room. As the restaurant continued to grow, Bob and Amanda were confronted with the need to develop skills and capabilities in the five functional areas. For the support role they hired a restaurant services manager to take charge of purchasing supplies and local advertising. To handle the production role, they increased the division of labor in the kitchen and dining room. They hired cleaning staff, cashiers, and an external accountant for maintenance tasks. They themselves handled the adaptive role of ensuring that the organization served customer needs. Finally, Bob and Amanda took on the managerial role of establishing the pattern of task and functional relationships that most effectively accomplished the restaurant's overall task of serving customers good food. Collectively, the five functions constituted the B.A.R. and Grille and gave it the ability to create value.

As soon as the owners decided to open new kinds of restaurants and expand the size of their organization, they faced the challenge of differentiating into divisions to control the operation of three restaurants simultaneously. The organization grew to three divisions, each of which made use of support functions centralized at the top of the organization (see Figure 2.1E). In large organizations each division is likely to have its own set of the five basic functions and is, thus, a *self-contained division.*

As we discussed in Chapter 1, functional skills and abilities are the source of an organization's *core competences*, the set of unique skills and capabilities that gives an organization a competitive advantage.[5] An organization's competitive advantage may lie in any or all of an organization's functions. An organization could have superior low-cost production, exceptional managerial talent, or a leading research and development department.[6] A core competence of the B.A.R. and Grille was the way Bob and Amanda took control of the differentiation of their restaurant and increased its ability to attract customers who appreciated the good food and good service they received. In short, they created a core competence that gave their restaurant a competitive advantage over other restaurants. In turn, this competitive advantage gave them access to resources that allowed them to expand by opening new restaurants.

Vertical and Horizontal Differentiation

Figure 2.3 shows the organizational chart that emerged in the B.A.R. and Grille as differentiation unfolded. An organizational chart is a drawing that shows the end result of organizational differentiation. Each box on the chart represents a role or function in the organization. Each role has a vertical and a horizontal dimension.

The organizational chart *vertically* differentiates organizational roles in terms of the authority that goes with each role. A classification of people according to authority and rank is called a **hierarchy**. Roles at the top of an organization's hierarchy possess more authority and responsibility than do roles farther down in the hierarchy; each lower role is under the control or supervision of a higher one. Managers designing an organization have to make decisions about how much vertical differentiation to have in the organization—that is, how many levels there should be from top to bottom. To maintain control over the various functions in the restaurant, for example, Bob and Amanda realized that they needed to create the role of restaurant manager. Because the restaurant manager would report to them and would supervise lower-level employees, this new role added a level to the hierarchy. **Vertical differentiation** refers to the way an organization designs its hierarchy of authority and creates reporting relationships to link organizational roles and subunits.[7] Vertical differentiation establishes the distribution of authority between levels to give the organization more control over its activities and increase its ability to create value.

The organizational chart *horizontally* differentiates roles according to main task responsibilities. For example, when Bob and Amanda realized that a more complex division of tasks would increase restaurant effectiveness, they created new organizational

Hierarchy A classification of people according to authority and rank.

Vertical differentiation The way an organization designs its hierarchy of authority and creates reporting relationships to link organizational roles and subunits.

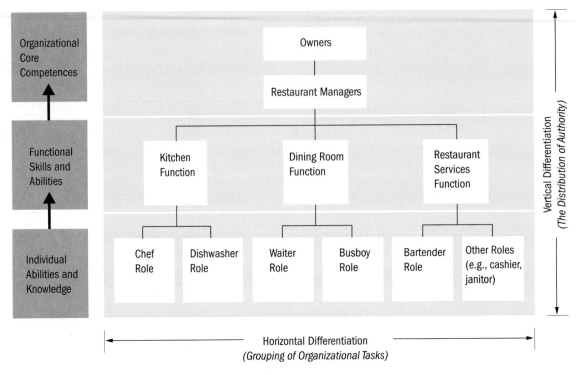

FIGURE 2.3 Organizational Chart of the B.A.R. and Grille

Horizontal differentiation The way an organization groups organizational tasks into roles and roles into subunits (functions and divisions).

roles—such as restaurant manager, cashier, bartender, and busboy—and grouped these roles into functions. **Horizontal differentiation** refers to the way an organization groups organizational tasks into roles and roles into subunits (functions and divisions).[8] Horizontal differentiation establishes the division of labor, which enables people in the organization to become more specialized and productive and increases the organization's ability to create value.

Organizational Design Challenges

We have seen that the principal design challenge facing an organization is to choose the levels of vertical and horizontal differentiation that allow the organization to control its activities in order to achieve its goals. In Chapters 3 and 4 we examine some principles that guide these choices. In the remainder of Chapter 2 we look at two more design challenges that confront managers attempting to create a structure that will maximize their organization's effectiveness. The first of the four is the coordination of organizational activities.

FIGURE 2.4

Organizational Design Challenges

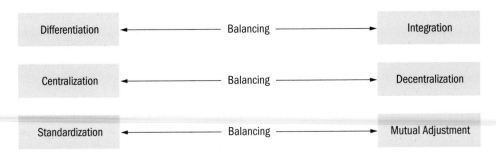

The second is determining who will make decisions. The third is deciding how strictly the organization will control employee activities. The fourth is influencing the informal personal relationships that develop between employees regardless of the formal structure set forth on an organizational chart. The choices managers make as they grapple with all five challenges determine how effectively their organization works.

Managerial Implications: Differentiation

1. No matter what your position in an organization is, draw an organizational chart of the organization so that you can identify the distribution of authority and the division of labor.
2. No matter how few or how many people you work with or supervise, analyze each person's role and the relationships between roles to make sure that the division of labor is best for the task being performed. If it is not, redefine role relationships and responsibilities.
3. If you supervise more than one function or department, analyze relationships between departments to make sure that the division of labor best suits the organization's mission: the creation of value for stakeholders.

BALANCING DIFFERENTIATION AND INTEGRATION

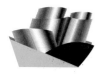

| Design Challenge 2 | *We can't get people to communicate and coordinate in this organization. Specifying tasks and roles is supposed to help coordinate the work process, but here it builds barriers between people and functions.*

Horizontal differentiation is supposed to enable people to specialize and, thus, become more productive. However, companies have often found that specialization limits communication between subunits and prevents them from learning from one another. As a result of horizontal differentiation, the members of different functions or divisions develop a **subunit orientation**—a tendency to view one's role in the organization strictly from the perspective of the time frame, goals, and interpersonal orientations of one's subunit.[9] For example, the production department is most concerned with reducing costs and increasing quality; thus, it tends to have a short-term outlook because cost and quality are production goals that must be met daily. In research and development, on the other hand, innovations to the production process may take years to come to fruition; thus, R&D people usually have a longer-term outlook. When different functions see things differently, communication fails and coordination becomes difficult, if not impossible.

Subunit orientation *A tendency to view one's role in the organization strictly from the perspective of the time frame, goals, and interpersonal orientations of one's subunit.*

To avoid the communication problems that can arise from horizontal differentiation, organizations try to find new or better ways to integrate functions—that is, to promote cooperation, coordination, and communication among separate subunits. Xerox uses its computer systems to find new ways for different functions to share databases, memos, and reports. Increasingly, companies are using electronic means of communication, like e-mail and teleconferencing, to bring different functions together. For example, buyers at Wal-Mart's home office use television linkups to show each store individually the appropriate way to display products for sale.

Integration and Integrating Mechanisms

Integration *The process of coordinating various tasks, functions, and divisions so that they work together and not at cross-purposes.*

How to facilitate communication and coordination among subunits is a major challenge for managers. One reason for problems on this front is that the development of subunit orientations makes communication difficult and complex. Another reason for lack of coordination and communication is that managers often fail to use the appropriate mechanisms to integrate organizational subunits. **Integration** is the process of coordinating various tasks, functions, and divisions so that they work together and are not at cross-purposes. Table 2.1 lists seven integrating mechanisms that managers can use as their organization's level of differentiation increases.[10] The simplest mechanism is a hierarchy of authority; the most complex is a department created specifically to coordinate the activities of diverse functions or divisions. The table includes examples of how a company like

TABLE 2.1		
Types and Examples of Integrating Mechanisms		
Integration Mechanism (in order of increasing complexity)	**Description**	**Example (e.g., in Johnson & Johnson)**
Hierarchy of authority	A ranking of employees integrates by specifying who reports to whom.	Salesperson reports to Diaper Division sales manager.
Direct contact	Managers meet face-to-face to coordinate activities.	Diaper Division sales and manufacturing managers meet to discuss scheduling.
Liaison role	A specific manager is given responsibility for coordinating with managers from other subunits on behalf of his or her subunit.	A person from each of J&J's production, marketing, and research and development departments is given responsibility for coordinating with the other departments.
Task force	Managers meet in temporary committees to coordinate cross-functional activities.	A committee is formed to find new ways to recycle diapers.
Team	Managers meet regularly in permanent committees to coordinate activities.	A permanent J&J committee is established to promote new-product development in the Diaper Division.
Integrating role	A new role is established to coordinate the activities of two or more functions or divisions.	One manager takes responsibility for coordinating Diaper and Baby Soap divisions to enhance their marketing activities.
Integrating department	A new department is created to coordinate the activities of functions or divisions.	A team of managers is created to take responsibility for coordinating J&J's centralization program to allow divisions to share skills and resources.

Johnson & Johnson might use all seven types of integration mechanisms as it goes about managing one major product line—disposable diapers. We will examine each mechanism separately.

HIERARCHY OF AUTHORITY.   The simplest integrating device is an organization's hierarchy of authority, which differentiates people by how much authority they have. Because the hierarchy dictates who reports to whom, it coordinates various organizational roles. Managers must carefully divide and allocate authority within a function and between one function and others to promote coordination. For example, at Becton Dickinson, a high-tech medical instrument maker, the marketing and engineering departments were frequently squabbling over product specifications. Marketing argued that the company's products needed more features to please customers. Engineering wanted to simplify product design to reduce costs.[11] The two departments could not resolve their differences because the head of marketing reported to the head of engineering. To resolve this conflict, Becton Dickinson reorganized its hierarchy so that both marketing and engineering reported to the head of the Instrument Product Division. The head of the division was an impartial third party who had the authority to listen to both managers' cases and make the decision that was best for the organization as a whole.

DIRECT CONTACT.   Direct contact between people in different subunits is an integrating mechanism that is more complex than a hierarchy of authority. The principal problem with integration across functions is that a manager in one function has no authority over a manager in another. Only the CEO or somebody else above the functional level has power to intervene if two functions come into conflict. Consequently, establishing personal relationships between people at all levels in different functions is an important step in overcoming the problems that arise because people (or groups or departments) have different subunit orientations. Managers from different functions who have opportunities for direct contact with each other can work together to solve common problems. If disputes still arise, however, it is important for both parties to be able to appeal to a common superior who is not far removed from the scene of the problem.

LIAISON ROLES.   When the need for communication among subunits increases, one member or a few members from a subunit are likely to have responsibility for coordinating with other subunits. The people who hold these connecting, or liaison, roles are able to develop in-depth relations with people in other subunits. This interaction helps overcome barriers between subunits. Over time, as the people in liaison roles learn to cooperate, they can become increasingly flexible in accommodating other subunits' requests. Figure 2.5A illustrates a liaison role.

TASK FORCES.   As an organization increases in size and complexity, more than two subunits may need to work together to solve common problems. Increasing an organization's ability to serve its customers effectively, for example, may require input from production, marketing, engineering, and research and development. The solution commonly takes the form of a **task force**, a temporary committee set up to handle a specific problem (Figure 2.5B). One person from each function joins a task force, which meets until it finds a solution to the problem. Task force members are responsible for taking the solution back to their functional groups for the groups' input and approval. To increase the effectiveness of task forces, a senior manager from outside all the functions involved usually chairs the meetings.

Task force *A temporary committee set up to handle a specific problem.*

TEAMS.   When the issue a task force is dealing with becomes an ongoing strategic or administrative issue, the task force becomes permanent. A *team* is a permanent task force

A. Liaison Roles

B. Task Force or Team

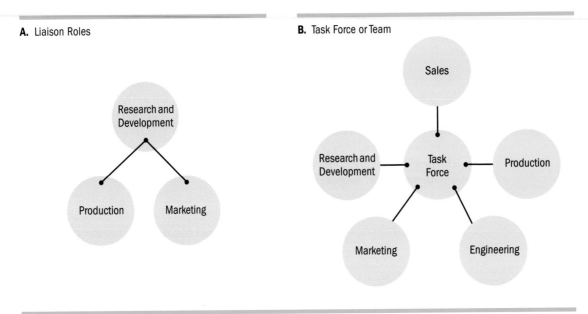

C. Integrating Role or Department

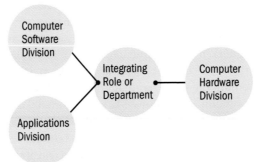

• Indicates managers with responsibility for integration between subunits.

| FIGURE 2.5   Integrating Mechanisms

or committee. Most companies, for example, now have product development and customer contact teams to respond to the threat of increased competition in a global market. Such teams, once a rarity, are now a vital part of most successful U.S. organizations. At Amgen, for example, the team system is proving to be an important factor in the company's success.

Approximately 70 percent of a manager's time is spent in committee meetings.[14] Teams provide the opportunity for the face-to-face contact and continual adjustment that managers need to deal effectively with ongoing complex issues. As they set up teams, managers face the challenge of creating a committee system that gives them effective control over organizational activities. Very often teams are ineffective because the problems facing the organization change but team membership remains unchanged. People often fight to stay on a committee even when their services are no longer needed. Membership on a team gives a person power in the organization, but this power does not necessarily promote organizational goals. At Tenneco, an oil and gas company based in Houston, Texas, however, CEO Michael Walsh established hundreds of minimanagement teams throughout the company to bring about change, improve quality control, and streamline production.

ORGANIZATIONAL INSIGHT

2.2 INTEGRATION AT AMGEN

Amgen is experiencing great success with its recombinant DNA drugs Epogen (an anemia drug) and Neupogen (an immune system stimulant). With Amgen's success has come growth, and the company is seeking new ways to integrate its employees so that it can preserve its small-company atmosphere, which is based on personal contact between employees. Amgen is relying on a team system to coordinate its people. It has devised two types of teams. Product development teams organize the whole process of bringing a new drug to market, and task forces handle other needs of the business down to the level of organizing the firm's annual picnic. The product development teams are composed of people from all areas of the company and report directly to top management. They meet daily or weekly, as needed, and at other times the team members return to their regular jobs in the organization. Any employee can join any team at any time, and in this way the company hopes to keep its levels of innovation and flexibility high.

Amgen prides itself on searching out new ways of organizing itself to minimize the need to standardize work activities. The company's goals are to maximize employees' opportunities to be innovative and to find new ways to integrate employees' skills to speed the development of new products to the market.[12] As Amgen continued to grow, however, it sensed some problems with its use of teams. Employees seemed to be more loyal to their teams than to their regular job assignments, and this situation was starting to cause communication problems between the teams and the regular functions. To control team activities and make sure that the teams coordinated effectively with the functions, Amgen started to fully integrate its teams into its hierarchy of authority to facilitate the flow of information.[13] Amgen had considerable success with its new structure in the 1990s and has become a leading biotechnology company.

Walsh's goal? To use teams to change patterns of authority and decision making to increase interaction and promote creativity among managers.[15]

INTEGRATING ROLES OR DEPARTMENTS.   As organizations become large and complex, communication barriers between functions and divisions are likely to increase. Managers in different product divisions, for example, may never meet one another. In organizations that employ many thousands of people, coordinating subunits becomes especially difficult. One way to overcome these barriers is to create integrating roles that coordinate subunits. An **integrating role** is a full-time position established specifically to improve communication between divisions. (A liaison role, in contrast, is part of a person's full-time job.) Figure 2.5C shows an integrating role that might exist in a large computer company like Compaq or Apple.

The purpose of an integrating role is to promote the sharing of information and knowledge to enhance organizational goals such as innovation and product development, increased flexibility, and heightened customer service. People in integrating roles are often senior managers who have decided to give up authority in a specific function and focus on integration. They often chair task forces and teams and report directly to top management.

When a company has many employees in integrating roles, it creates an integrating department, which coordinates the activities of subunits. Du Pont, the chemical company, has a department that employs over 200 people in integrating roles. In general, the

Integrating role *A full-time position established specifically to improve communication between divisions.*

more complex and highly differentiated an organization is, the more complex are the integration mechanisms needed to overcome communication and coordination barriers between functions and divisions.

Differentiation versus Integration

The design issue facing managers is to establish a level of integration that matches the organization's level of differentiation. Managers must achieve an appropriate balance between differentiation and integration. A highly complex organization that is highly differentiated needs a high level of integration to effectively coordinate it activities. By contrast, an organization that has a relatively simple, clearly defined role structure normally needs to use only simple integrating mechanisms. Its managers may find that the hierarchy of authority provides all the control and coordination they need to achieve organizational goals.

At all costs, managers need to be sure they do not differentiate or integrate their organization too much. Differentiation and integration are both expensive in terms of the number of managers employed and the amount of managerial time spent on coordinating organizational activities. For example, every hour that employees spend on committees that are not really needed costs the organization thousands of dollars because the employees are not being put to their most productive use.

Managers facing the challenge of deciding how and how much to differentiate and integrate must do two things: (1) carefully guide the process of differentiation so that it develops the core competences that give the organization a competitive advantage; and (2) carefully integrate the organization by choosing appropriate integrating mechanisms that allow subunits to cooperate and that build up the organization's core competences.[16]

BALANCING CENTRALIZATION AND DECENTRALIZATION

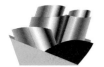

| *Design Challenge 3* | *People in this organization don't take responsibility or risks. They are always looking to the boss for direction and supervision. As a result, decision making is slow and cumbersome, and we miss out on a lot of opportunities to create value.*

In discussing vertical differentiation, we noted that establishing a hierarchy of authority is supposed to improve the way an organization functions because people can be held accountable for their actions and because the hierarchy defines the area of each person's authority within the organization. Many companies, however, complain that when a hierarchy of authority exists, people are constantly looking to their superiors for directions.[17] When something new or unusual occurs, they prefer to let it pass, or they pass it on to their superior rather than assume responsibility and take the risk of dealing with it. As responsibility and risk taking decline, so does organizational performance because the organization does not exploit new opportunities for using its core competences. When nobody is willing to take responsibility, decision making becomes slow and the organization becomes inflexible—that is, unable to change and adapt to new developments.

At Levi Strauss, for example, workers often told former CEO Roger Sant that they felt they couldn't do something because "*They* wouldn't like it." When asked who "they" were, workers had a hard time saying; nevertheless, the workers felt that they did not have the authority or responsibility to initiate changes. Sant started a "Theybusters" campaign to renegotiate authority and responsibility relationships so that workers and managers could take on new responsibilities.[18] The solution involved decentralizing authority so that employees at low levels in the hierarchy had authority to decide on issues within their control. The issues of how much to centralize or decentralize the authority to make decisions offers a basic design challenge for all organizations.

Centralization versus Decentralization of Authority

Authority gives one person the power to hold other people accountable for their actions and the right to make decisions about the use of organizational resources.

As we saw in the B.A.R. and Grille example, vertical differentiation involves choices about how to distribute authority. But even when a hierarchy of authority exists, the problem of how much decision-making authority to delegate to each level must be solved.

It is possible to design an organization in which managers at the top of the hierarchy have all power to make important decisions. Subordinates take orders from the top, are accountable for how well they obey those orders, and have no authority to initiate new actions or use resources for purposes that they believe are important. When the authority to make important decisions is retained by managers at the top of the hierarchy, authority is said to be highly **centralized**.[19] By contrast, when the authority to make important decisions about organizational resources and to initiate new projects is delegated to managers at all levels in the hierarchy, authority is highly **decentralized**.

Each alternative has certain advantages and disadvantages. The advantage of centralization is that it lets top managers coordinate organizational activities and keep the organization focused on its goals. Centralization becomes a problem, however, when top managers become overloaded and so involved in operational decision making about day-to-day resource issues (such as hiring people and obtaining inputs) that they have no time for long-term strategic decision making about future organizational activities (such as deciding on the best strategy to compete globally).

The advantage of decentralization is that it promotes flexibility and responsiveness by allowing lower-level managers to make on-the-spot decisions. Managers remain accountable for their actions but have the opportunity to assume greater responsibilities and take potentially successful risks. Also, when authority is decentralized, managers can make important decisions that allow them to demonstrate their personal skills and competences and may be more motivated to perform well for the organization. The downside of decentralization is that if so much authority is delegated that managers at all levels can make their own decisions, planning and coordination become very difficult and the company may lose control of its decision-making process. The following organizational insight reveals many of the issues surrounding this design choice.

As these examples suggest, the design challenge for managers is to decide on the correct balance between centralization and decentralization of decision making in an organization. If authority is too decentralized, managers have so much freedom that they can pursue their own functional goals and objectives at the expense of the organization's. On the other hand, if authority is too centralized and top management makes all important organizational decisions, managers lower down in the hierarchy become afraid to make new moves and lack the freedom to respond to problems as they arise in their own groups and departments. The ideal situation is a balance between centralization and decentralization of authority so that middle and lower managers who are at the scene of the action are allowed to make important decisions, and top managers' primary responsibility becomes

Centralization *An organizational setup whereby the authority to make important decisions is retained by managers at the top of the hierarchy.*
Decentralization *An organizational setup whereby the authority to make important decisions about organizational resources and to initiate new projects is delegated to managers at all levels in the hierarchy.*

ORGANIZATIONAL INSIGHT

2.3 CENTRALIZE OR DECENTRALIZE?

Is it best to centralize or decentralize authority? It depends on the situation as the following examples illustrate.

In 1998, the United Way was suffering from a public perception that it was spending too much of the donations it received on itself and not enough for the needy people it was set up to serve. The solution? It called in management consultants who recommended that the best way to save money and increase efficiency was to reduce the number of local organizations, and centralize many business functions such as data processing, marketing, and wealthy donor programs. However, many local organizations then became concerned that they would receive a smaller share of donations. To date the United Way is still working out the right balance between centralization and decentralization.[20]

In 1998, Union Pacific, in response to complaints from customers and employees about traffic bottlenecks and poor-quality service made a radical decision. It would abandon its centralized operating system and decentralize authority to regional managers who could make on-the-spot decisions. The result? A significant decrease in the amount of penalties it was forced to pay its customers for late shipments.[21]

To reduce disposal costs and save money, managers at a Chemical Waste plant decided to deliberately turn off the plant's pollution-monitoring equipment. Soon after this decision was made, a container of chemicals exploded, and the company's managers were also accused of mislabeling up to a hundred barrels of hazardous waste to avoid disposal costs. Although Chemical Waste's top managers blamed local management for these problems and denied any knowledge of the situation, the decentralized management style of the company was blamed for the problems. According to former Chemical Waste managers, top managers took no interest in the plant's operations and put local management under intense pressure to reduce costs. The combination of decentralized control and bottom-line pressure led to the problems that occurred. The plant's top managers claimed that Chemical Waste management's attitude was "Don't tell us what's going on; just keep turning out the profit."[22]

managing long-term strategic decision making. The result is a good balance between long-term strategy making and short-term flexibility and innovation as lower-level managers respond quickly to problems and changes in the environment as they occur.

Why were the Levi Strauss managers so reluctant to take on new responsibilities and assume extra authority? A previous management team had centralized authority so that it could retain day-to-day control over important decision making. The company's performance suffered, however, because in spending all their time on day-to-day operations, top managers lost sight of changing customer needs and evolving trends in the clothing industry. The new management team that took over in the early 1990s recognized the need to delegate authority for operational decision making to lower-level managers so that top management could concentrate on long-term strategic decision making. Consequently, top management decentralized authority until they believed they had achieved the correct balance.

As noted earlier, the way managers and workers behave in an organization is a direct result of managers' decisions about how the organization is to operate. Managers who want to discourage risk taking and to maximize control over subordinates' performance centralize authority. Managers who want to encourage risk taking and innovation decentralize authority. In the army, for example, the top brass generally wishes to discourage lower-level officers from acting on their own initiative, for if they did, the power of centralized command would be gone and the army would splinter. Consequently, the army has a highly centralized decision-making system that operates by strict rules and with a well-defined hierarchy of authority. By contrast, at Becton Dickinson, the medical equipment maker, authority is decentralized, and employees are provided with a broad framework within which they are free to make their own decisions and take risks, as long as they are consistent with the company's master plan. High-tech companies generally decentralize authority because decentralization encourages innovation and risk taking.

Decisions about how to distribute decision-making authority in an organization change as the organization changes—that is, as it grows and differentiates. How to balance authority is not a design decision that can be made once and forgotten; it must be made on an ongoing basis and is one part of the managerial task. We examine this issue in more detail in Chapters 3 and 4.

BALANCING STANDARDIZATION AND MUTUAL ADJUSTMENT

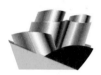

| Design Challenge 4 | *People in this organization pay too much attention to the rules. Whenever I need somebody to satisfy an unusual customer request or need real quick service from another function, I can't get it because no one is willing to bend or break the rules.*

Written rules and standard operating procedures (SOPs) and unwritten values and norms help to control behavior in organizations. They specify how an employee is to perform his or her organizational role, and they set forth the tasks and responsibilities associated with that role. Many companies, however, complain that employees tend to follow written and unwritten guidelines too rigidly instead of adapting them to the needs of a particular situation. Strictly following rules may stifle innovation; rules specifying how decisions are to be made leave no room for creativity and imaginative responses to unusual circumstances. As a result, decision making becomes inflexible, innovation is stifled, and organizational performance suffers.

IBM, for example, was traditionally a company respected for being close to its customers and responsive to their needs. But as IBM grew, it standardized responses to customers' requests, and its sales force was instructed to sell certain kinds of machines to certain kinds of customers, regardless of what the customer needed.[23] Standardizing operations had become more important than giving customers what they wanted. Moreover, internal communication among IBM's divisions and functions was increasingly conducted in accordance with formal rules rather than by relatively informal direct contact. These rigid patterns of communication slowed product development and ultimately resulted in dissatisfied customers.

The challenge facing *all* organizations, large and small, is to design a structure that achieves the right balance between standardization and mutual adjustment. **Standardization** is conformity to specific models or examples—defined by sets of rules and norms—

Standardization Conformity to specific models or examples—defined by sets of rules and norms—that are considered proper in a given situation.

Mutual adjustment *The compromise that emerges when decision making and coordination are evolutionary processes and people use their judgment rather than standardized rules to address a problem.*

that are considered proper in a given situation. Standardized decision-making and coordination procedures make people's actions predictable in certain circumstances.[24] **Mutual adjustment** is the process through which people use their judgment rather than standardized rules to address problems, guide decision making, and promote coordination. The right balance makes some actions predictable so that basic organizational tasks and goals are achieved, yet it gives employees the freedom to behave flexibly so that they can respond to new and changing situations creatively.

Formalization: Written Rules

Formalization is the use of written rules and procedures to standardize operations.[25] In an organization in which formalization and standardization are extensive—for example, the military, Federal Express, or United Parcel Service—everything is done by the book. There is no room for mutual adjustment; rules specify how people are to perform their roles and how decisions are to be made, and employees are accountable for following the rules. Moreover, employees have no authority to break the rules. A high level of formalization typically implies centralization of authority. A low level of formalization implies that coordination is the product of mutual adjustment among people across organizational functions and that decision making is a dynamic process in which employees apply their skills and abilities to respond to change and solve problems. Mutual adjustment typically implies decentralization of authority because employees must have the authority to commit the organization to certain actions when they make decisions.

Since the 1990s, the CEO of IBM, Louis Gerstner, has been trying to increase mutual adjustment so that IBM's decision making can become more flexible.[26] In the last five years, IBM has gone through four major structural reorganizations designed to make the organization less formalized and more decentralized, but changing peoples' behavior has proved difficult because IBM employees have become used to working in a highly formal system. Microsoft manages its organization differently from IBM and, as a result, has been very successful at being innovative and flexible, as the following Organizational Insight illustrates.

ORGANIZATIONAL INSIGHT

2.4 INNOVATIVE CONTROL AT MICROSOFT

Microsoft has grown rapidly throughout the 1990s. As it differentiates into more and more software specialties, such as networking, Internet applications, and multimedia, managers face the challenge of designing an organizational structure hospitable to innovation and flexibility. One approach they have taken is to limit the size of a department to 200 people. In addition, they have divided each department into distinct subgroups, each of which performs a specific task. In this way, people remain accountable for what they do, and each subgroup's task is manageable. With this structure, the organization needs a minimum level of standardization and formalization to coordinate its people. By keeping the operating departments small, Microsoft is able to rely on mutual adjustment and direct methods of communication and integration. E-mail, for example, is a vital medium of communication at Microsoft.[27] Any employee can send an e-mail message directly to CEO Bill Gates or to anybody else in the organization. Similarly, Microsoft's intranet is one of the most advanced and sophisticated in existence, utilizing state-of-the-art streaming video.[28]

Socialization: Understood Norms

Rules *Formal, written statements that specify the appropriate means for reaching desired goals.*

Norms *Standards or styles of behavior that are considered acceptable or typical for a group of people.*

Rules are formal, written statements that specify the appropriate means for reaching desired goals. As people follow rules, they behave in accordance with certain specified principles. **Norms** are standards or styles of behavior that are considered typical for a group of people. People follow a norm because it is a generally agreed-upon standard for behavior. Many norms arise informally as people work together over time. In some organizations it is the norm that people take an hour and a quarter for lunch, despite a formally specified one-hour lunch break. Over time, norms become part of peoples' way of viewing and responding to a particular situation.

Although many organizational norms—such as always behaving courteously to customers and leaving the work area clean—promote organizational effectiveness, many do not. Studies have shown that groups of workers can develop norms that reduce performance. Several studies have found that workers can directly control the pace or speed at which work is performed by imposing informal sanctions on workers who break the informal norms governing behavior in a work group. A worker who works too quickly (above group productivity norms) is called a "ratebuster," and a worker who works too slowly (below group norms) is called a "chiseler."[29] Having established a group norm, workers actively enforce it by physically and emotionally punishing violators.

This process occurs at all levels in the organization. Suppose a group of middle managers has adopted the norm of not rocking the organizational boat. A new manager who enters the picture will soon learn from the others that rocking the boat doesn't pay, or the other managers will find ways to punish the new person for violating the norm and trying to rock the boat—even if a little shaking up is what the organization really needs. Even a new manager who is high in the hierarchy will have difficulty changing the informal norms of the organization.

The taken-for-granted way in which norms affect behavior has another consequence for organizational effectiveness. We noted in the Levi Strauss example that even when an organization changes formal work rules, the behavior of people does not change quickly. Why is behavior rigid when rules change? The reason is that rules may be internalized and become part of a person's psychological makeup so that external rules become internalized norms. When this happens, it is very difficult for people to break a familiar rule and follow a new rule. They slip back into the old way of behaving. Consider, for example, how difficult it is to keep new resolutions and break bad habits.[30]

Paradoxically, an organization often wants members to buy into a particular set of corporate norms and values. IBM and Intel, for example, cultivate technical and professional norms and values as a means of controlling and standardizing the behavior of highly skilled organizational members. However, once norms are established, they are very difficult to change. And when the organization wants to pursue new goals and foster new norms, people find it difficult to alter their behavior. There is no easy solution to this problem. At Levi Strauss, organizational members had to go through a major period of relearning before they understood that they did not need to apply the old set of internalized norms. And IBM is undergoing major upheavals to unlearn its old, conservative norms so that it can develop new ones that encourage innovation and responsiveness to customers.

The name given to the process by which organizational members learn the norms of an organization and internalize these unwritten rules of conduct is **socialization**.[31] In general, organizations can encourage the development of *standardized* responses or *innovative* ones. These issues are examined in more detail in Chapter 5.

Standardization versus Mutual Adjustment

The design challenge facing managers is to find a way of using rules and norms to standardize behavior while at the same time allowing for mutual adjustment to provide employees with the opportunity to discover new and better ways of achieving organizational goals. Managers facing the challenge of balancing the need for standardization against the need for mutual adjustment need to keep in mind that, in general, people at higher levels in the hierarchy and in functions that perform complex, uncertain tasks rely more on mutual adjustment than on standardization to coordinate their actions. For example, an organization wants its accountants to follow standard practices in performing their tasks, but in R&D the organization may want to encourage risk taking that leads to innovation. Many of the integrating mechanisms discussed earlier, such as task forces and teams, can increase mutual adjustment by providing an opportunity for people to meet and work out improved ways of doing things. In addition, an organization can emphasize, as Levi Strauss did, that rules are not set in stone but are just convenient guidelines for getting work done. Managers can also promote norms and values that emphasize change rather than stability. For all organizational roles, however, the appropriate balance between these two variables is one that promotes creative and responsible employee behavior as well as organizational effectiveness.

Focus on New Information Technology:
Amazon.com, Part 2

How did Jeff Bezos address these design challenges given his need to create a structure to manage an e-commerce business that operates through the Internet and never sees its customers but whose mission is to provide customers great selection at low prices? Since the success of his venture depends on providing high-quality customer responsiveness, it is vital that customers find Amazon.com's 1-Click (SM) information system Internet software easy and convenient to use and his service reliable. So his design choices were driven by the need to ensure his software linked customers to the organization most effectively.

First, he quickly realized that customer support was the most vital link between customer and organization, so to ensure good customer service he decentralized control and empowered his employees to find a way of meeting customers' needs quickly. Second, realizing that customers wanted the book quickly, he developed an efficient distribution and shipping system. Essentially, his main problem was handling inputs into the system (customer requests) and outputs (delivered books). So he developed information systems to standardize the work or throughput process to increase efficiency. He also encouraged mutual adjustment at the input or customer end to improve customers' responsiveness by allowing employees to manage exceptions such as lost orders or confused customers as the need arose. (Note that Amazon.com's information system also plays the dominant role in integrating across functions in the organization; it provides the backbone to the company's value creation activities.) Third, because Amazon.com only employs a relatively small number of people (i.e., about 2,100 people worldwide), Bezos was able to make great use of socialization to coordinate and motivate his employees. All Amazon.com employees are carefully selected and socialized by the other members of their functions so that new employees quickly learn their organizational roles and Amazon.com's important norm of providing excellent customer service. Finally, to ensure Amazon.com's employees are motivated to provide the best possible customer service, Bezos gives all employees stock in the company. Employees currently own 10 percent of their company. Amazon.com's rapid growth suggests that Bezos has designed an effective organizational structure.

MECHANISTIC AND ORGANIC ORGANIZATIONAL STRUCTURES

Each design challenge has implications for how an organization as a whole and the people in the organization behave and perform. Useful concepts for addressing the way in which management's responses to the challenges collectively influence how an organizational structure works are the concepts of mechanistic structure and organic structure.[32] The design choices that produce mechanistic and organic structures are contrasted in Figure 2.6 and discussed next.

Mechanistic Structures

Mechanistic structures are designed to induce people to behave in predictable, accountable ways. Decision-making authority is centralized, subordinates are closely supervised, and information flows mainly in a vertical direction down a clearly defined hierarchy. In a mechanistic structure the tasks associated with a role are also clearly defined. There is usually a one-to-one correspondence between a person and a task. Figure 2.7A depicts this situation. Each person is individually specialized and knows exactly what he or she is responsible for, and behavior inappropriate to the role is discouraged or prohibited.

Mechanistic structures result when an organization makes these choices.	Organic structures result when an organization makes these choices.
• Individual Specialization Employees work separately and specialize in one clearly defined task.	• Joint Specialization Employees work together and coordinate their actions to find the best way of performing a task.
• Simple Integrating Mechanisms Hierarchy of authority is clearly defined and is the major integrating mechanism.	• Complex Integrating Mechanisms Task forces and teams are the major integrating mechanisms.
• Centralization Authority to control tasks is kept at the top of the organization. Most communication is vertical.	• Decentralization Authority to control tasks is delegated to people at all levels in the organization. Most communication is lateral.
• Standardization Extensive use is made of rules and SOPs to coordinate tasks, and work process is predictable.	• Mutual Adjustment Extensive use is made of face-to-face contact to coordinate tasks, and work process is relatively unpredictable.
• Status-Conscious Informal Organization Employees protect their area of authority and responsibility from others.	• Expertise-Conscious Informal Organization Employees share their skills with others, and authority and responsibility change over time.

A structure that is simultaneously mechanistic and organic is achieved when the organization balances these choices in a way that matches the contingencies it faces.

FIGURE 2.6 How the Design Challenges Result in Mechanistic or Organic Structures

At the functional level, each function is separate, and communication and cooperation between functions are the responsibility of someone at the top of the hierarchy. Thus, in a mechanistic structure, the hierarchy is the principal integrating mechanism both within and between functions. Because tasks are organized to prevent miscommunication, the organization does not need to use complex integrating mechanisms. Tasks and roles are coordinated primarily through standardization. Formal written rules and procedures specify role responsibilities, and standardization (together with the hierarchy) is the main means of organizational control.

FIGURE 2.7

Task and Role Relationships

A. Individual Specialization in a Mechanistic Structure. A person in a role specializes in a specific task or set of tasks.

B. Joint Specialization in an Organic Structure. A person in a role is assigned to a specific task or set of tasks. However, the person is able to learn new tasks and develop new skills and capabilities.

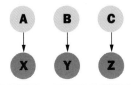

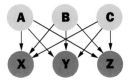

Roles

Tasks

Given this emphasis on the vertical command structure, the organization is very status-conscious, and norms of "protecting one's turf" are common. Promotion is normally slow and steady, tied to performance. One's progress in the organization can be charted for years to come. Because of its rigidity, a mechanistic structure is best suited to organizations that face stable, unchanging environments.

Organic Structures

Organic structures are at the opposite end of the organizational design spectrum from mechanistic structures. Organic structures promote flexibility, so people initiate change and can adapt quickly to changing conditions.

Organic structures are decentralized; that is, decision-making authority is distributed throughout the hierarchy, and people assume the authority to make decisions as organizational needs dictate. Roles are loosely defined—people perform various tasks and continually develop skills in new activities. Figure 2.7B depicts this situation. Each person performs all three tasks, and the result is joint specialization and increased productivity. Employees from different functions work together to solve problems and become involved in each other's activities. As a result, a high level of integration is needed so that employees can share information and overcome problems caused by differences in subunit orientation. The integration of functions is achieved by means of complex mechanisms like task forces and teams (see Figure 2.6). Coordination is achieved through mutual adjustment as people and functions work out role definitions and responsibilities, and as rules and norms emerge from the ongoing interaction of organizational members.

In an organic structure informal norms and values develop that emphasize personal competence, expertise, and the ability to act in innovative ways. Status is conferred by the ability to provide creative leadership, not by any formal position in the hierarchy. The Sony Corporation has become the successful giant it is by maintaining an organic structure.

ORGANIZATIONAL INSIGHT

2.5 SONY'S MAGIC TOUCH

Product engineers at Sony turn out an average of four ideas for new products every day. Despite the fact that Sony is now a huge, diversified organization employing over 115,000 employees worldwide, the company continues to lead the way in innovation in the consumer electronics industry. Why? A large part of the answer lies in the way the company uses its structure to motivate and coordinate employees. First, a policy of "self-promotion" allows Sony engineers, without notifying their supervisors, to seek out projects anywhere in the company where they feel they can make a contribution. If they find a new project to which they can make a contribution, their current boss is expected to let them join the new team. Sony has 23 business groups composed of hundreds of development teams, and this movement of people cross-pollinates ideas throughout the organization.

Sony deliberately emphasizes the lateral movement of people and ideas between design and engineering groups. The "Sony Way" emphasizes communication between groups to foster innovation and change. Sony has a corporate research department full of people in integrating roles who coordinate the efforts of the business groups and product development teams. It is their responsibility to make sure that each team knows what the others are doing, not only to share knowledge but also to avoid overlap or duplication of effort. Once a year, the corporate research department organizes an in-house three-day "special event," open only to Sony employees, where each product development team can display its work to its peers.

That Sony's organic structure works is evident from the company's success in the marketplace and from the number of innovative products Sony turns out. Like many other large Japanese companies, Sony has a policy of lifetime employment, which makes it easy for its engineers to take risks with ideas and encourages the development of norms and values that support innovative efforts. Moreover, Sony rewards its engineers with promotion and more control of resources if they are successful.

Sony is hard-headed, however, when it comes to making the best use of its resources. Top management takes pains to distance itself from decision making inside a team or even a business group, so that the magic of decentralized decision making can work. But it does intervene when it sees different groups duplicating one another's efforts. For example, when Sony made a big push into computers it reorganized the relationship between its audio, video, and computer groups so that they improved the way they coordinate new-product developments.[33] Once again, however, Sony takes a lateral view of the way the organization works, and its vertical chain of command is oriented toward finding ways to decentralize authority and still make the best use of resources. This lateral approach to decision making contrasts dramatically with the old IBM's vertical, centralized product development system, in which getting a decision made was, according to one engineer, like wading through a tub of peanut butter.

Organic and mechanistic structures have very different implications for the way people behave. Is an organic structure better than a mechanistic structure? It seems to encourage the kinds of innovative behaviors that are in vogue at present: teamwork and self-management to improve quality and reduce the time needed to get new products to market. However, would you want to use an organic structure to coordinate the armed forces? Probably not, because of the status problems of getting the army, air force, marines, and navy to cooperate. Would you want an organic structure in a nuclear power plant? Probably not, because a creative, novel response to an emergency might produce a catastrophe. Would you even want an organic structure in a restaurant, in which chefs take the roles of waiters and waiters take the roles of chefs and authority and power relationships are worked out on an ongoing basis? Probably not, because the traditional one-to-one correspondence of person and role allows restaurant employees to perform their roles most effectively. Conversely, would you want to use a mechanistic structure in a high-tech company like Apple Computer or Microsoft, where innovation is a function of the skills and abilities of teams of creative programmers working jointly on a project?

The Contingency Approach to Organizational Design

Obviously, the decision about whether to design an organic or a mechanistic structure depends on the particular situation an organization faces: the environment it confronts, its technology and the nature of the tasks it performs, and the type of people it employs. In general, the contingencies or sources of uncertainty facing an organization shape the or-

Contingency approach
A management approach in which the design of an organization's structure must match the sources of uncertainty facing an organization.

ganization's design. The **contingency approach** to organizational design tailors organizational structure to the sources of uncertainty facing an organization.[34] The structure is designed to respond to various contingencies—things that might happen and, therefore, must be planned for.

Later chapters on the organizational and technological environments examine in detail how to choose the appropriate organizational structure to meet environmental and technological contingencies. For now, it is important to realize that mechanistic and organic structures are ideals: They are useful for examining how organizational structure affects behavior, but they probably do not exist in a pure form in any real-life organization. Most organizations are a mixture of the two types. Indeed, according to one increasingly influential view about organizational design, the most successful organizations are those that have achieved a balance between the two, so that they are simultaneously mechanistic and organic. An organization may tend more in one direction than in the other, but it needs to be able to act in both ways to be effective. The army, for example, is well known for having a mechanistic structure in which hierarchical reporting relationships are clearly specified. However, in wartime, this mechanistic command structure allows the army to become organic and flexible as it responds to the uncertainties of the quickly changing battlefield. Similarly, an organization may design its structure so that some functions (such as manufacturing and accounting) act in a mechanistic way and others (marketing or R&D) develop a more organic approach to their tasks. To achieve the difficult balancing act of being simultaneously mechanistic and organic, organizations need to make appropriate choices (see Figure 2.6). Wal-Mart Corporation offers an interesting insight into how an organization can achieve this balance.

ORGANIZATIONAL INSIGHT

2.6 WAL-MART'S RACE TO THE TOP

Phenomenal growth has made Wal-Mart the largest and most profitable retailer in the United States. While Sears and Kmart have been struggling to raise their profitability, Wal-Mart has been earning record profits and opening new kinds of stores at a rapid rate. Analysts attribute the company's success to the way the organization controls and coordinates activities. The efficiency of its store operations impacts very highly on Wal-Mart's effectiveness as a retailer. To control store operations, Wal-Mart has created a vertical operating structure based on a clear and precise definition of authority and responsibility. Each store is run by a manager, three assistant managers, 15 department heads, and the employees under each department head. Inside each store, decision making is highly centralized at the store-manager level. Moreover, store operations are highly standardized, and each store manager uses the same book of rules and procedures and the same accounting standards to operate each store. Thus, the performances of all stores can be directly compared.

Each store manager reports to a district manager who is in charge of about a dozen stores. District managers, in turn, report to regional vice presidents, who oversee the work of three or four district managers. Regional vice presidents report to the vice president of operations, who is based in Bentonville, Arkansas. District and regional managers frequently visit Wal-Mart stores to learn what is happening at the store level. They take the information back to Bentonville, where top management sits down once a week, on Saturday, to plan a sales campaign for the whole organization. This system allows managers to monitor store operations closely and to intervene and take corrective action if necessary.

Wal-Mart is not just centralized and standardized, however. Mutual adjustment and decentralization of authority are also important parts of its design philosophy. Wal-Mart's approach is based on mutual adjustment as managers scour the country to find innovative products or ideas that they can share with stores to improve their performance. Similarly, although important decisions are made at the top of the organization, Wal-Mart encourages store managers to make quick decisions on their own to improve the success of their stores. Moreover, inside each store, the company encourages its employees, called associates, to make suggestions, and it listens to what the associates have to say, incorporating their suggestions into its operating system. For example, in one year alone the "Yes we can, Sam" suggestion program led to the adoption of over 400 suggestions, which resulted in savings of $38 million.

As Wal-Mart has grown and become more differentiated, it has increased its use of integrating mechanisms. Managers frequently meet in task forces and teams to plan the company's future strategy. Wal-Mart also uses a sophisticated global satellite network to link and coordinate stores and to give the company quick feedback on store needs. Moreover, Wal-Mart has encouraged the development of organizational norms and values that encourage spontaneous behavior. Its employees participate in a stock option plan (some long-term associates have received stock worth over $200,000), sing a company song, and participate in other ways that build the Wal-Mart culture.

The continuing emphasis is on creating an organizational structure that not only allows Wal-Mart to control and monitor its operations so that it can reduce costs but also allows it to change and adapt itself to meet changing conditions in the highly competitive global retailing industry.[35] Wal-Mart's core competences in operating its organization have given the company a competitive advantage over rivals like Sears and Kmart. Although competitors have been copying many aspects of Wal-Mart's organizational design, so far they have not been able to achieve the results that make Wal-Mart stakeholders so happy.[36]

As this example suggests, Wal-Mart has achieved the difficult balancing act of being mechanistic and organic simultaneously. In the next three chapters we look in more detail at the issues involved in designing organizational structure and culture to improve organizational effectiveness.

SUMMARY

This chapter has analyzed how managers' responses to several organizational design challenges affect the way employees behave and interact and how they respond to the organization. We have analyzed how differentiation occurs and examined four other challenges that managers confront as they try to structure their organization to achieve organizational goals. Chapter 2 has made the following main points:

1. Differentiation is the process by which organizations evolve into complex systems as they allocate people and resources to organizational tasks and assign people different levels of authority.

2. Organizations develop five functions to accomplish their goals and objectives: support, production, maintenance, adaptive, and managerial.

3. An organizational role is a set of task-related behaviors required of an employee. An organization is composed of interlocking roles that are differentiated by task responsibilities and task authority.

4. Differentiation has a vertical and a horizontal dimension. Vertical differentiation refers to the way an organization designs its hierarchy of authority. Horizontal differentiation refers to the way an organization groups roles into subunits (functions and divisions).

5. Managers confront five design challenges as they coordinate organizational activities. The choices they make are interrelated and collectively determine how effectively an organization operates.

6. The first challenge is to choose the right extent of vertical and horizontal differentiation.

7. The second challenge is to strike an appropriate balance between differentiation and integration and use appropriate integrating mechanisms.

8. The third challenge is to strike an appropriate balance between the centralization and decentralization of decision-making authority.

9. The fourth challenge is to strike an appropriate balance between standardization and mutual adjustment by using the right amounts of formalization and socialization.

10. Different organizational structures cause individuals to behave in different ways. Mechanistic structures are designed to cause people to behave in predictable ways. Organic structures promote flexibility and quick responses to changing conditions. Successful organizations strike an appropriate balance between mechanistic and organic structures.

11. The particular contingencies that an organization faces determine the appropriate choice of organizational structure.

DISCUSSION QUESTIONS

1. Why does differentiation occur in an organization? Distinguish between vertical and horizontal differentiation.

2. Draw an organizational chart of the business school or college that you attend. Outline its major roles and functions. How differentiated is it? Do you think the distribution of authority and division of labor are appropriate?

3. When does an organization need to use complex integrating mechanisms? Why?

4. What factors determine the balance between centralization and decentralization and between standardization and mutual adjustment?

5. Under what conditions is an organization likely to prefer (a) a mechanistic structure, (b) an organic structure, or (c) elements of both?

ORGANIZATIONAL THEORY IN ACTION

PRACTICING ORGANIZATIONAL THEORY:
GROWING PAINS

Form groups of three to five people and discuss the following scenario:

You are the founding entrepreneurs of Zylon Corporation, a fast-growing Internet software company that specializes in electronic banking. Customer demand to license your software has boomed so much that in just two years you have added over 50 new software programmers to help develop a new range of software products. The growth of your company has been so swift that you still operate informally with a loose and flexible arrangement of roles, and programmers are encouraged to find solutions to problems as they go along. Although this structure has worked well, there are signs that problems are arising.

There have been increasing complaints from employees that good performance is not being recognized in the organization and that they do not feel equitably treated. Moreover, there have been complaints about getting managers to listen to their new ideas and to act on them. A bad atmosphere seems to be developing in the company, and recently several talented employees have left. You are meeting to discuss these problems.

1. Examine your organizational structure to see what might be causing these problems.
2. What kinds of design choices do you need to make to solve them?

MAKING THE CONNECTION #2

Find an example of a company that has been facing one of the design challenges discussed in this chapter. What problem has the company been experiencing? How has it attempted to deal with the problem?

Analyzing the Organization: Design Module #2

This module attempts to get at some of the basic operating principles that your organization uses to perform its tasks. From the information you have been able to obtain, describe the following aspects of your organization's structure.

ASSIGNMENT

1. How differentiated is your organization? Is it simple or complex? List the major roles, functions, or departments in your organization. Does your organization have many divisions? If your organization engages in many businesses, list the major divisions in the company.

2. What core competences make your organization unique or different from other organizations? What are the sources of the core competences? How difficult do you think it would be for other organizations to imitate these distinctive competences?

3. How has your organization responded to the design challenges? (a) Is it centralized or decentralized? How do you know? (b) Is it highly differentiated? Can you identify any integrating mechanisms used by your organization? What is the match between the complexity of differentiation and the complexity of the integrating mechanisms that are used? (c) Is behavior in the organization very standardized, or does mutual adjustment play an important role in coordinating people and activities? What can you tell about the level of formalization by looking at the number and kinds of rules the organization uses? How important is socialization in your organization?

4. Does your analysis in item 3 lead you to think that your organization conforms more to the organic or to the mechanistic model of organizational structure? Briefly explain why you think it is organic or mechanistic.

5. From your analysis so far, what do you think could be done to improve the way your organization operates?

6. Do any factors not covered in the foregoing items seem important in explaining the way your organization operates?

Cases for Analysis:
WHERE SHOULD DECISIONS BE MADE?

In 1995, Procter & Gamble's top managers took a long, hard look at the giant company's global operations and decided that they could make much better use of organizational resources if they changed the level at which decisions were made in their organization. Until 1995, managers in each of Procter & Gamble's divisions, in each country in the world in which it operated, were more or less free to make their own decisions, and decision making was *decentralized*. Thus, managers in charge of the British soap and detergent division operated quite independently from managers in French and German divisions. Moreover, even within Britain, the soap and detergent division operated quite independently from other Procter & Gamble divisions such as its healthcare and beauty products divisions. Top managers believed that this highly decentralized global decision making resulted in the loss of possible gains to be obtained from cooperation both among managers of the same kind of division in the different countries (soap and detergent divisions throughout Europe) and among managers in the different kinds of divisions operating in the same country or world regions.

Therefore, Procter & Gamble's top-management team pioneered a new kind of organizational structure. First, they divided up P&G's global operations into four main areas—North America, Europe, the Middle East and Africa, and Asia—and in each area they created the new role of global executive vice president who is responsible for overseeing the operation of all the different kinds of divisions inside that world region. This approach was something

Procter & Gamble had never attempted before.[37] It is the global vice president's responsibility to get the different kinds of divisions inside each area to cooperate and to share information and knowledge so that authority is *centralized* at the world area level. Each of these new top managers then reports directly to the president of Procter & Gamble, further centralizing authority.

In another change to further centralize authority, P&G's managers grouped together divisions operating in the same area and put them under the control of one manager. For example, the manager of the U.K. soap and detergent division took control over soap and detergent operations in the United Kingdom, Ireland, Spain, and Portugal and became responsible for getting them to cooperate so the company could reduce costs and innovate new products more quickly across Europe.

Procter & Gamble has been delighted with its new balance between centralized and decentralized authority because its top managers feel they are making much better use of organizational resources to meet customers' needs. They believe Procter & Gamble is poised to become the dominant consumer goods company in the world, not merely in the United States, and in 1996 the company earned record operating profits on record global sales.

1. Why did Procter & Gamble move to centralize control?

2. When might managers realize that they have gone too far and "centralized" control too much?

REFERENCES

1. T. Parsons, *Structure and Process in Modern Societies* (Glencoe, IL: Free Press, 1960); J. Child, *Organization: A Guide for Managers and Administrators* (New York: Harper and Row, 1977).

2. R. K. Merton, *Social Theory and Social Structure*, 2nd ed. (Glencoe, IL: Free Press, 1957).

3. D. Katz and R. L. Kahn, *The Social Psychology of Organizing* (New York: Wiley, 1966).

4. Ibid., pp. 39–47.

5. P. Selznick, "An Approach to a Theory of Bureaucracy," *American Sociological Review*, 1943, vol. VIII, pp. 47–54.

6. M. E. Porter, *Competitive Strategy* (New York: Free Press, 1980).

7. R. H. Miles, *Macro Organizational Behavior* (Santa Monica, CA: Goodyear, 1980), pp. 19–20.

8. Child, *Organization*.

9. P. R. Lawrence and J. W. Lorsch, *Organization and Environment* (Boston: Graduate School of Business Administration, Harvard University, 1967).

10. J. R. Galbraith, *Designing Complex Organizations* (Reading, MA: Addison-Wesley, 1973).

11. B. Dumaine, "The Bureaucracy Busters," *Fortune*, 7 June 1991, p. 42.

12. B. P. Sunoo, "Amgen's Latest Secrets," *Personnel Journal*, February 1996, pp. 38–45.

13. A. Erdman, "How to Keep That Family Feeling," *Fortune*, 6 April 1992, pp. 95–96.

14. H. Mintzberg, *The Nature of Managerial Work* (Englewood Cliffs, NJ: Prentice-Hall, 1973).

15. R. Johnson, "Tenneco Restructuring Is Over, But Doubt Remains," *Wall Street Journal*, 8 September 1992, p. 49.

16. P. P. Gupta, M. D. Dirsmith, and T. J. Fogarty, "Coordination and Control in a Government Agency: Contingency and Institutional Theory Perspectives on GAO Audits," *Administrative Science Quarterly*, 1994, vol. 39, pp. 264–284.

17. A detailed critique of the workings of bureaucracy in practice is offered in P. M. Blau, *The Dynamics of Bureaucracy* (Chicago: University of Chicago Press, 1955).

18. Dumaine, "The Bureaucracy Busters," pp. 36–50.

19. D. S. Pugh, D. J. Hickson, C. R. Hinings, and C. Turner, "Dimensions of Organizational Structure," *Administrative Science Quarterly*, 1968, vol. 13, pp. 65–91; D. S. Pugh and D. J. Hickson, "The Comparative Study of Organizations," in G. Salaman and K. Thompson, eds., *People and Organizations* (London: Longman, 1973), pp. 50–66.

20. M. Vevrka, "United Way Weighs Pros and Cons of Centralizing," *Wall Street Journal*, 7 January 1998, p. 2.

21. C. Wian, "Union Pacific to Reorganize," www.cnnfn.com, August 20, 1998.

22. J. Flynn, "The Ugly Mess at Waste Management," *Business Week*, 13 April 1992, pp. 76–77.

23. C. L. Loomis, "Can John Akers Save IBM?" *Fortune*, 22 April 1992, pp. 41–56.

24. See H. Mintzberg, *The Structuring of Organizational Structures* (Engle-

wood Cliffs, NJ: Prentice-Hall, 1979), for an in-depth treatment of standardization and mutual adjustment.

25. Pugh and Hickson, "The Comparative Study of Organizations."

26. Loomis, "Can John Akers Save IBM?" p. 54.

27. K. Rebello and E. I. Schwartz, "Microsoft: Bill Gates's Baby Is on Top of the World. Can It Stay There?" *Business Week*, 24 February 1992, pp. 60–64.

28. Microsoft, Annual Report, 1999.

29. M. Dalton, "The Industrial Ratebuster: A Characterization," *Applied Anthropology*, 1948, vol. 7, pp. 5–18.

30. J. Van Mannen and E. H. Schein, "Towards a Theory of Organizational Socialization," in B. M. Staw, ed., *Research in Organizational Behavior*, vol. 1 (Greenwich, CT: JAI Press 1979), pp. 209–264.

31. G. R. Jones, "Socialization Tactics, Self-Efficacy, and Newcomers' Adjustments to Organizations," *Academy of Management Journal*, 1986, vol. 29, pp. 262–279; Van Maanen and Schein, "Towards a Theory of Organizational Socialization."

32. T. Burns and G. M. Stalker, *The Management of Innovation* (London: Tavistock, 1966).

33. T. Pruzan, "Sony Testing Campaign to Pump Up Minidiscs," *Advertising Age*, 15 July 1996, p. 6.

34. J. Pfeffer, *Organizations and Organizational Theory* (Boston: Pitman, 1982), pp. 147–162; J. Child, "Organizational Structure, Environment, and Performance: The Role of Strategic Choice," *Sociology*, 1972, vol. 6, pp. 1–22.

35. T. Andreoli, "Wal-Mart Sees Potential Fortune in China Debut," *Discount Store News*, 15 July 1996, p. 1.

36. B. Saporito, "A Week Aboard the Wal-Mart Express," *Fortune*, 24 August 1992, pp. 77–84; B. Saporito, "What Sam Walton Taught America," *Fortune*, 4 May 1992, pp. 104–107.

37. "P&G Divides to Rule," *Marketing*, 23 March 1995, p. 15.

Chapter 3

DESIGNING ORGANIZATIONAL STRUCTURE:
AUTHORITY and CONTROL

To protect stakeholders' goals and interests, managers must constantly analyze an organization's structure and continually redesign it so that it most effectively controls people and other resources. In this chapter the vertical dimension of organizational structure—the hierarchy of authority that an organization creates to control its members—is examined.

The way in which a hierarchy of authority emerges in an organization and the process of vertical differentiation are examined. Then the issues involved in designing a hierarchy to coordinate and motivate organizational behavior most effectively are discussed.[1] The way in which the design challenges discussed in Chapter 2 affect the design of the organizational hierarchy are then put under the spotlight. Specifically, the way processes such as centralization and standardization provide methods of control that substitute for the direct, personal control that managers provide is examined. The principles of bureaucratic structure and their implications for the design of effective organizational hierarchies are then outlined. Finally, the chapter focuses on the issues surrounding organizational restructuring. By the end of the chapter you will understand why designing the vertical dimension of an organization's structure—its hierarchy—is a vital part of a manager's role.

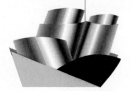

AUTHORITY: HOW AND WHY VERTICAL DIFFERENTIATION OCCURS

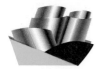

A basic design challenge, identified in Chapter 2, is deciding how much authority to centralize at the top of the organizational hierarchy and how much authority to decentralize to middle and lower levels. (Recall from Chapter 2 that *authority* is the power to hold people accountable for their actions and to directly influence what they do and how they do it.) But what determines the shape of an organization's hierarchy—that is, the number of levels of authority within an organization—and the span of control at each level? This question is important because the shape of an organization (evident in its organizational chart) determines how effectively the organization's decision-making and communication systems work. Decisions concerning the shape of the hierarchy and the balance between centralized and decentralized decision making establish the extent of vertical differentiation in an organization.

The Emergence of the Hierarchy

An organization's hierarchy begins to emerge when the organization experiences problems in coordinating and motivating employees.[2] As an organization grows, employees increase in number and begin to specialize, performing widely different kinds of tasks; the level of differentiation increases; and coordinating employees' activities becomes more difficult.[3] The division of labor and specialization produce motivational problems. When each person performs only a small part of a total task, it is often difficult to determine how well an individual performs and how much he or she actually contributes to the task, and it is often difficult to evaluate individuals' performance. Moreover, if people are cooperating to achieve a goal, it is often impossible to measure individual contributions and to reward individuals for their personal contributions. For example, if two waiters cooperate to serve tables, how does their boss know how much each contributed? If two chefs work together to cook a meal, how is each person's individual impact on food quality to be measured?[4]

An organization does two things to improve its ability to control—that is, coordinate and motivate—its members: (1) It increases the number of managers it uses to monitor, evaluate, and reward employees. (2) It increases the number of levels in its managerial hierarchy, thereby making the hierarchy of authority taller.[5] Increasing both the number of managers and the levels of management increases vertical differentiation and gives the organization direct, face-to-face control over its members—managers *personally* control their subordinates.

Tall organization *An organization in which the hierarchy has many levels relative to the size of the organization.*

Flat organization *An organization that has few levels in its hierarchy relative to its size.*

Figure 3.1 shows two organizations that have the same number of employees, but one has three levels in its hierarchy and the other has seven. An organization in which the hierarchy has many levels relative to the size of the organization is a **tall organization**. An organization that has few levels in its hierarchy is a **flat organization**. The tall organization in Figure 3.1 has four more levels than the flat organization and uses many more managers to personally direct and control members' activities. Research evidence suggests that an organization that employs 3,000 people is likely to have seven levels in its hierarchy. Thus, a 3,000-person organization with only four levels in its hierarchy would be flat, and one with nine levels would be tall.

FIGURE 3.1

Flat and Tall Organizations. A tall organization has more hierarchical levels and more managers to direct and control employees' activities than does a flat organization with the same number of employees.

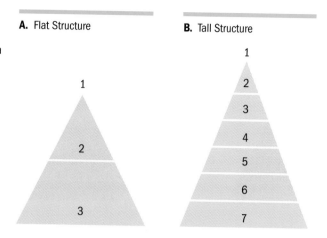

A. Flat Structure

B. Tall Structure

Size and Height Limitations

Figure 3.2 illustrates an interesting research finding concerning the relationship between organizational size and the height of the vertical hierarchy. By the time an organization has 1,000 members, it is likely to have about four levels in its hierarchy: chief executive officer (CEO), function or department heads, department supervisors, and employees. An organization that has grown to 3,000 members is likely to have seven levels. After that size is reached, however, something striking happens: Organizations that employ 10,000 or 100,000 employees typically do not have more than nine or ten levels in their hierarchy. Moreover, large organizations do not increase the numbers of managers at each level to compensate for the limited number of hierarchical levels.[6] Thus, most organizations have a pyramid-like structure and fewer and fewer managers at each level (see Figure 3.3A) rather than a bloated structure (Figure 3.3B) in which proportionally more managers at all levels control the activities of increasing numbers of members.

FIGURE 3.2

The Relationship Between Organizational Size and Number of Hierarchical Levels

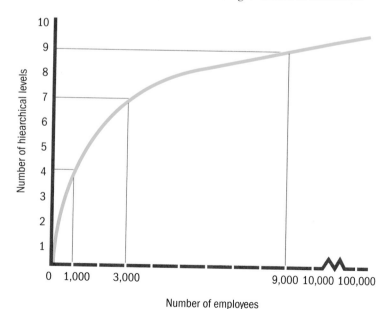

FIGURE 3.3

**Types of Managerial
Hierarchies**

A. Pyramid-like structure with
decreasing numbers of
managers at each level

B. Bloated structure with increasing
numbers of managers at each level

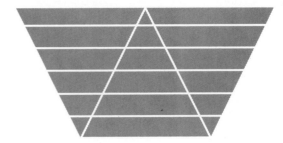

In fact, research suggests that the increase in the size of the managerial component in an organization is *less than proportional* to the increase in size of the organization as it grows.[7] This phenomenon is illustrated in Figure 3.4. An increase from 2,000 to 3,000 employees (a 50 percent increase in organizational size) results in an increase from 300 to 400 managers (a 33 percent increase). However, an increase from 6,000 to 10,000 employees (a 66 percent increase) increases the size of the managerial component by only 100 managers (from 700 to 800, a 14 percent increase).

Why do organizations seem to actively restrict the number of managers and the number of hierarchical levels as they grow and differentiate? The answer is that many significant problems are associated with the use of tall hierarchies.[8]

Problems with Tall Hierarchies

Choosing the right number of managers and hierarchical levels is important because the decision directly influences organizational effectiveness. The choice affects communication, motivation, and bottom-line profitability.[9]

FIGURE 3.4

The Relationship Between Organizational Size and the Size of the Managerial Component

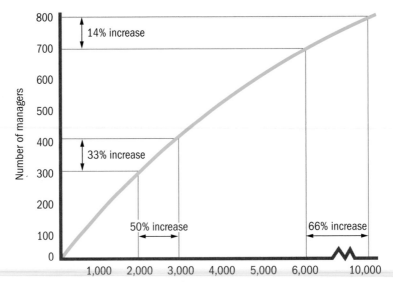

Number of organizational members

COMMUNICATION PROBLEMS.   Having too many hierarchical levels may hinder communication. As the chain of command lengthens, communication between managers at the top and bottom of the hierarchy takes longer. Decision making slows, and the slowdown hurts the performance of organizations that need to respond quickly to customers' needs or the actions of competitors.[10] At Federal Express, fast decision making is a prerequisite for success, so the company has only five hierarchical levels; it believes that with any more levels the speed of communication and decision making would suffer.[11] Similarly, when Liz Claiborne was designing the structure of her organization, she was careful to keep the hierarchy flat—four levels for 4,000 employees—to maximize the organization's ability to respond to quickly changing fashion trends.

Another significant communication problem is distortion. Information becomes distorted as it flows up and down the hierarchy through many levels of management.[12] Experiments have shown that a message that starts at one end of a chain of people can become something quite different by the time it reaches the other end of the chain.

In addition, managers up and down the hierarchy may manipulate information to serve their own interests. It has been demonstrated that managers can lead others to make certain kinds of decisions by restricting the flow of information or by selectively feeding information to them.[13] When this happens, the top of the hierarchy may lose control over the bottom. Managers at low levels may also selectively transmit up the hierarchy only the information that serves their interests. A rational subordinate, for example, may decide to give to a superior only information that makes him or her or the superior look good. Again, when this happens, the top of the hierarchy may have no idea about or control over what is happening below, and the quality of decision making at all levels suffers.

Studies show that communication problems get progressively worse as the number of hierarchical levels increases. Thus, organizations are wise to try to limit the growth of the hierarchy. When the number of levels surpasses seven or eight, communication problems can cause a breakdown in control and slow and unresponsive decision making, as Wang Laboratories' experience demonstrates.

ORGANIZATIONAL INSIGHT

3.1 WANG LABS' NEW STRUCTURE

In the early 1980s Wang Laboratories was the leader in the office word processing and publishing market; the company's stock price soared as investors thought it would become the new IBM. Its founder, An Wang, was a genius, and he had designed a tall centralized structure to run his business, which allowed him to scrutinize every important decision and keep close control over all the company's activities. Yet, only a decade later, the company was bankrupt. Why? Many analysts blame the slow decision making that resulted from the structure Wang created, one that did not allow the company to adapt its technology to the fast-moving conditions in the computer industry.

The future of Wang looked dim indeed until a new CEO, Joseph Tucci, took control of the company and reinvented the firm's business. Tucci decided to enter the software services market, helping companies install and operate their computer systems rather than providing the software or hardware itself. To compete with market leaders like IBM and EDS Tucci realized he needed a structure that would allow the company to be flexible and responsive to customers. He knew that the structure Wang had created would not be suitable, so he set out to redesign it.

Tucci acted quickly. In the old structure there had been seven levels of management between him and the lowest-level employee. Tucci wiped out the entire top two layers of management and reorganized the rest of the hierarchy so that now only three layers existed.[14] In addition, he decentralized control to individuals giving them greater responsibility and held them accountable through quarterly reviews. The new structure performed just as he hoped. Employees were energized to provide good customer service, the number of accounts grew, and by 1999 Wang became the fourth largest provider in the United States.

MOTIVATION PROBLEMS.   As the number of levels in the hierarchy *increases*, the relative difference in the authority possessed by managers at each level *decreases*, as does their area of responsibility. A flat organization (see Figure 3.1) has fewer managers and hierarchical levels than a tall organization, so a flat organization's managers possess relatively more authority and responsibility than a tall organization's managers. Many studies have shown that the more authority and responsibility a person has, the more motivating is the person's organizational role, other things being equal. Thus, motivation in an organization with a flat structure may be stronger than motivation in a tall organization. Also, when a hierarchy has many levels, it is easy for managers to pass the buck and evade responsibility—actions that worsen the problem of slow decision making and poor communication.

BUREAUCRATIC COSTS.   Managers cost money. The greater the number of managers and hierarchical levels, the greater the bureaucratic costs—that is, the costs associated with running and operating an organization. It has been estimated that the average middle manager costs over $300,000 per year in salary, bonuses, benefits, and an office. Employing a thousand excess managers, therefore, costs an organization $300 million a year—an enormous sum that companies often belatedly recognize they do not need to pay. Because of the cost of a tall and bloated hierarchy, it is common, especially during a recession, for a company to announce that it will reduce the number of levels in its hierarchy and lay off excess employees to reduce bureaucratic costs. In 1996, for example, Miller Brewing Company announced that it would eliminate two levels in its hierarchy and lay off 500 managers for a savings of $500 million. Du Pont expects to save $1 billion from streamlining its managerial hierarchy.

Why do companies suddenly perceive the need to reduce their workforce drastically, thus subjecting employees to the uncertainty and misery of the unemployment line with a minimum of notice? Why do companies not have more foresight and restrict the growth of managers and hierarchical levels to avoid large layoffs? Sometimes, layoffs are unavoidable as when a totally unexpected situation arises in the organization's environment: For example, technical innovation may render technology obsolete or uncompetitive, or a general economic crisis may abruptly reduce demand for an organization's product. Much of the time, however, dramatic changes in employment and structure are simply the result of bad management.

Managers of an organization that is doing well often do not recognize the need to control, prune, and manage the organization's hierarchy as the organization confronts new or changing situations. Or they may see the need but prefer to do nothing, as occurred at Sunbeam. As organizations grow, managers usually pay little attention to the hierarchy; their most pressing concern is to satisfy customer needs by bringing products or services to the market as quickly as possible. As a result, hierarchical levels multiply as new people are added without much thought about long-term consequences. When an organization matures, its structure is likely to be streamlined as two or more managerial positions are combined into one and levels in the hierarchy are eliminated to improve decision making and reduce costs. The terms *restructuring* and *downsizing* are used to describe the process by which managers streamline hierarchies and lay off managers and workers to reduce bureaucratic costs. This issue is discussed in more detail at the end of the chapter.

The Parkinson's Law Problem

While studying administrative processes in the British Navy, C. Northcote Parkinson, a former British civil servant, came upon some interesting statistics.[15] He discovered that from 1914 to 1928 the number of ships in operation had decreased by 68 percent but the number of dockyard officials responsible for maintaining the fleet had increased by 40 percent and the number of top brass in London responsible for managing the fleet had increased by 79 percent. Why had this situation come about? Parkinson argued that growth in the number of managers and hierarchical levels is controlled by two principles: (1) "An official wants to multiply subordinates not rivals," and (2) "Officials make work for one another."[16]

Managers in hierarchies value their status in the hierarchy. The fewer managers at their hierarchical level and the greater the number of managers below them, the bigger is their "empire" and the higher is their status in the hierarchy. Not surprisingly, therefore, managers seek to increase the number of their subordinates. In turn, these subordinates realize the status advantages of having subordinates, so they try to increase the number of their subordinates, causing the hierarchy to become taller and taller. As the number of levels increases, managers spend more of their time monitoring and controlling the actions and behaviors of their subordinates and, thus, create work for themselves. More managers lead to more work—hence, the British Navy results. Parkinson further contended that his principles apply to all hierarchies if they are not controlled. Because managers in hierarchies make work for each other, "Work expands so as to fill the time available." That is Parkinson's Law.

The Ideal Number of Hierarchical Levels: The Minimum Chain of Command

Managers should base the decision to employ an extra manager on the difference between the *value added* by the last manager employed and the cost of the last manager employed. However, as Parkinson noted, a person may have no second thoughts about spending the organization's money to improve his or her own position, status, and power. Well-managed organizations control this problem by simple rules—for example, "Any new recruitment has to be approved by the CEO"—that prompt upper-level managers to evaluate whether another lower-level manager or another hierarchical level is necessary. An even more general principle for designing a hierarchy is the principle of minimum chain of command.

According to the **principle of minimum chain of command**, an organization should choose the minimum number of hierarchical levels consistent with its goals and the environment in which it exists.[17] In other words, the organization should be kept as flat as possible, and managers should be evaluated for their ability to control organizational activities with the smallest number of managers possible.

An organization with a flat structure will experience fewer communication, motivation, and cost problems than will a tall organization. The only reason why an organization should choose a tall structure over a flat structure is that it needs a high level of direct

Principle of minimum chain of command An organization should choose the minimum number of hierarchical levels consistent with its goals and the environment in which it operates.

control or personal supervision over subordinates. Nuclear power plants, for example, typically have very tall managerial hierarchies so that managers can maintain effective supervision of operations. Because any error could produce a disaster, upper-level managers constantly oversee and cross-check the work of lower-level managers to ensure that rules and standard operating procedures are followed accurately and consistently.

In Chapters 9 and 10 we examine how factors such as technology and task characteristics make tall structures the preferred choice. Here, the issue is that organizations should strive to keep hierarchical levels to the minimum necessary to accomplish their mission. Organizational problems produced by factors such as Parkinson's Law do not satisfy any stakeholder interest, for sooner or later they will be discovered by a new management team, which will purge the hierarchy to reduce excess managers, as happened at Sunbeam.

Span of Control

Span of control *The number of subordinates a manager directly manages.*

Organizations that become too tall inevitably experience problems. Nevertheless, an organization that is growing must control the activities of newly hired personnel. How can an organization avoid becoming too tall? One way is by increasing managers' **span of control**—the number of subordinates a manager directly manages.[18] If the span of control of each manager increases as the number of employees increases, then the number of managers or hierarchical levels does *not* increase in proportion to increases in the number of employees. Instead, each manager coordinates the work of more subordinates, and the organization substitutes an increase in the span of control for an increase in hierarchical levels.

Figure 3.5 depicts two different spans of control. Figure 3.5A shows an organization with a CEO, five managers, and ten employees, and each manager supervises two people. Figure 3.5B shows an organization with a CEO, two managers, and ten employees, but Manager A supervises two people, and Manager B supervises eight people. Why does Manager A's span of control extend over only two people and Manager B's extend over eight? Or, more generally, what determines the size of a manager's span of control?

Perhaps the single most important factor limiting a manager's span of control is the manager's inability to supervise increasing numbers of subordinates adequately. It has been demonstrated that an arithmetic increase in the number of subordinates is accompanied

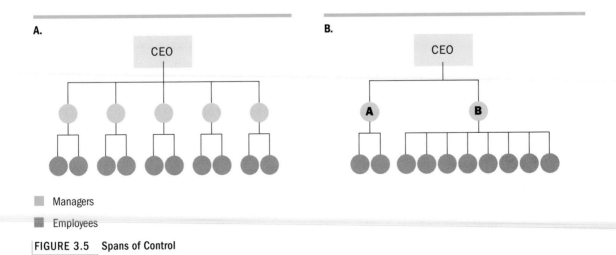

A.

B.

Managers

Employees

FIGURE 3.5   Spans of Control

FIGURE 3.6

The Increasing Complexity of a Manager's Job as the Span of Control Increases

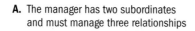

A. The manager has two subordinates and must manage three relationships

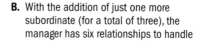

B. With the addition of just one more subordinate (for a total of three), the manager has six relationships to handle

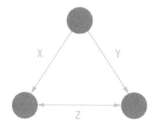

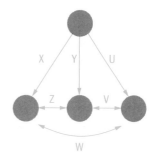

by an exponential increase in the number of subordinate relationships that a manager has to manage.[19] Figure 3.6 illustrates this point.

The manager in Figure 3.6A has two subordinates and must manage three relationships: X, Y, and Z. The manager in Figure 3.6B has only one more subordinate than the manager in Figure 3.6A but must manage six relationships: X, Y, and Z, as well as U, V, and W. [The number of relationships is determined by the formula $n(n - 1)/2$.] Thus, a manager with eight subordinates, as in Figure 3.6B, has 28 relationships to manage. If managers lose control of their subordinates and the relationships among them, subordinates will have the opportunity to follow their own goals, to coast along on the performance of other group members, or to shirk their responsibilities.

Given these problems, there seems to be a limit to how wide a manager's span of control should be.[20] If the span is too wide, the manager loses control over subordinates and cannot hold them accountable for their actions. In general, a manager's ability to directly supervise and control subordinates' behavior is limited by two factors: the complexity and the interrelatedness of subordinates' tasks.

When subordinates' tasks are complex and dissimilar, a manager's span of control needs to be small. If tasks are routine and similar so that all subordinates perform the same task, the span of control can be widened. In mass-production settings, for example, it is common for a supervisor's span of control to extend over 30 or 40 people. But in the research laboratory of a biotechnology company, supervising employees is more difficult, and the span of control is much narrower. It is sometimes argued that the span of control of a CEO should not exceed six people because of the complexity of the tasks performed by the CEO's subordinates.

When subordinates' tasks are closely interrelated, so that what one person does has a direct effect on what another person does, coordination and control are greater challenges for a manager. In Figure 3.6B, the interrelatedness of tasks means that the manager has to manage relationships V, W, and Z. When subordinates' tasks are not closely interrelated, the horizontal relationships between subordinates become relatively unimportant (in Figure 3.6B, relationships V, W, and Z would be eliminated) and the manager's span of control can be dramatically increased.

Managers supervising subordinates who perform highly complex, interrelated tasks have a much narrower span of control than managers supervising workers who perform separate, relatively routine tasks. Indeed, one of the reasons why organizations are often pictured as a pyramid is that at the upper levels the tasks are complex and interrelated and the span of control narrows.

Summary

Together, design choices concerning the number of hierarchical levels and the span of control determine the shape of the organizational hierarchy. There are limits to how much an organization can increase the number of levels in the hierarchy, the number of managers, or the span of control. Even though a hierarchy of authority emerges to provide an organization with control over its activities, if the structure becomes too tall or too top-heavy with managers, or if managers become overloaded because they are supervising too many employees, the organization can lose control of its activities. How can an organization maintain adequate control over its activities as it grows but avoid problems associated with a hierarchy that is too tall or a span of control that is too wide?

CONTROL: FACTORS AFFECTING THE SHAPE OF THE HIERARCHY

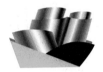

When there are limits on the usefulness of direct personal supervision by managers, organizations have to find other ways to control their activities. Typically, organizations first increase the level of horizontal differentiation and then decide on their responses to the other design challenges discussed in Chapter 2. Keep in mind that successful organizational design requires managers to meet all of those challenges (see Figure 3.7).

Horizontal Differentiation

Horizontal differentiation leads to the emergence of specialized subunits—functions or divisions. Figure 3.8 shows the horizontal differentiation of an organization into five functions. Each triangle represents a specific function in which people perform the same kind of task.

An organization that is divided into subunits has many different hierarchies, not just one. Each distinct function, department, or division has its own hierarchy. Horizontal dif-

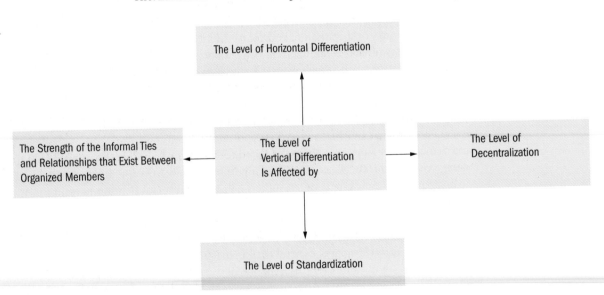

FIGURE 3.7   Factors Affecting the Shape of the Hierarchy

FIGURE 3.8

Horizontal Differentiation into Functional Hierarchies. The sales and R&D departments have three levels in their hierarchies; manufacturing has seven.

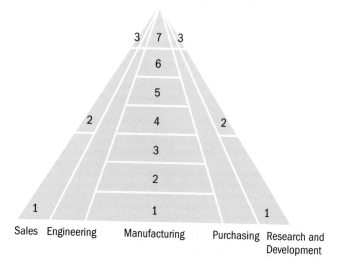

Sales   Engineering   Manufacturing   Purchasing   Research and Development

ferentiation is the principal way in which an organization retains control over employees when it cannot increase the number of levels in the organizational hierarchy without encountering the sorts of problems discussed earlier in the chapter.

In Figure 3.8, the hierarchy of the manufacturing department has seven levels. The production manager, at level 7, reports to the CEO. In contrast, both the research and development and the sales functions have only three levels in their hierarchies. Why? Like the organization as a whole, each function follows the principle of minimum chain of command when designing its hierarchy. Each function chooses the lowest number of hierarchical levels it can live with, given its tasks and goals.[21] The manufacturing function traditionally has many levels because management needs to exert tight and close control over subordinates and closely monitor and control costs. The sales department has fewer levels because both standardization by means of formalization and output controls are used to monitor and control salespeople; extensive supervision is not needed. The research and development function also usually has few levels but for a different reason. Personal supervision on a continuing basis is superfluous. R&D tasks are complex, and even if managers monitor researchers, they really cannot evaluate how well the researchers are performing because years may pass before significant research projects come to fruition. In an R&D context, control is generally achieved by scientists working in small teams, where they can monitor and learn from each other. As a result, there can be yet another level of horizontal differentiation within an organization: that within a function or department.

Figure 3.9 shows the horizontal differentiation of the R&D function into project teams. Each team focuses on a specific task, but the teams' tasks are likely to be related. The use of teams is a way to keep the span of control small, which is necessary when tasks are complex and interrelated. Moreover, in an R&D setting, informal norms and values are used to standardize behavior, and the "informal" organization is an important means of linking R&D to other functions.

Increasing horizontal differentiation increases vertical differentiation within an organization. But horizontal differentiation avoids many of the problems of tall hierarchies because it leads to the development of many subunit hierarchies, which allow the organization to remain flat. Nevertheless, the problems associated with horizontal differentiation such as the development of subunit orientations (see Chapter 2), cause additional coordination and motivation problems. Managers can control these problems by making wise choices concerning centralization, standardization, and the influence of the informal organization. (In Chapter 4 we discuss the coordination of activities between subunits.[22])

FIGURE 3.9

Horizontal Differentia-
tion Within the R&D
Function

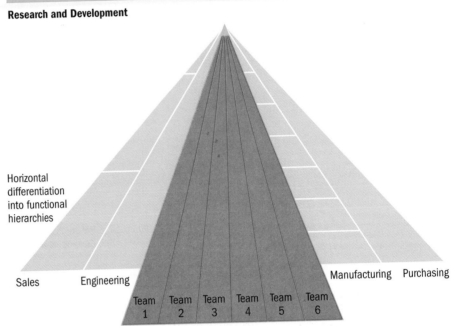

Research and Development

Horizontal
differentiation
into functional
hierarchies

Sales   Engineering   Manufacturing   Purchasing

Team 1   Team 2   Team 3   Team 4   Team 5   Team 6

Horizontal differentiation into research and development teams

Centralization

As the organizational hierarchy becomes taller and the number of managers increases, communication and coordination problems grow, and soon a manager's principal task is monitoring and supervising other managers' activities. When this happens, the organization loses sight of its goals. A solution to the problem of too many managers and levels is to decentralize authority. With decentralization, less direct managerial supervision is needed. When authority is decentralized, the authority to make significant decisions is delegated to people throughout the hierarchy, not concentrated at the top. The delegation of authority to lower-level managers reduces the monitoring burden on upper-level managers and reduces the need for managers to monitor managers. The following organizational insight illustrates how two organizations took steps to decentralize authority so that they could flatten their structures.

Decentralization alone may not eliminate the need for many hierarchical levels in a large and complex organization that has to control work activities between many subunits. However, it can reduce the amount of direct supervision needed *within* a subunit and can allow even a relatively tall structure to be flexible in its responses to changes in the external environment and other challenges.

Standardization

Managers can gain control over organizational activities by standardizing work activities to make them predictable. Standardization reduces the need for managers and extra levels in the hierarchy because rules and standard operating procedures *substitute* for direct supervision—that is, rules replace face-to-face contact. Organizations standardize activities by creating detailed work rules and by socializing employees to organizational norms and values. As subordinates' tasks are increasingly standardized and controlled by means of rules and

ORGANIZATIONAL INSIGHT

3.2 HOW MUCH TO DECENTRALIZE?

Quaker Oats experienced many problems in the 1990s as its management made many poor acquisitions and competitors like Kraft and Heinz forged ahead with many new innovative product ideas. In 1998, Quaker Oats's new CEO, Robert S. Morrison, decided that the problem was that the organization's structure put authority in the wrong place—with top executives above the level of the heads of the different food divisions, rather than with the heads of the food divisions themselves. So he took action. First, he decided to eliminate the entire upper level of management—even though it contained many competent executives. Then he promoted the next level of managers, the division heads, who now reported directly to him, and made them totally responsible for the food products under their control. In this way he flattened and decentralized control at the same time. By 1999, this new organizational structure was having some success as product sales increased in several areas.

Coca-Cola Enterprises, Inc., is the bottling arm of the soft-drink giant. When CEO Summerfield Johnston, Jr., took control of Coca-Cola Enterprises in the early 1990s, he noted the that the company's inability to respond quickly to the needs of the different regions in which Coke is bottled was costing the company sales and profits. Johnston decided that centralized control (regional operations were controlled from the Atlanta head office) was hurting the bottling operations. Because of the long chain of command, many problems that the regions were experiencing were being dealt with slowly, and managers at the head office were often unaware of the problems faced by people on the front line. Moreover, the hierarchy was very expensive to operate, and Johnston believed that bureaucratic costs could be reduced at the regional level if there were more local control over marketing and production.

Johnston took steps to redesign the management hierarchy. He fired 100 middle and top managers at company headquarters, eliminating several levels in the hierarchy. He then decentralized operations to 10 regional units, one for each region, and put a strong vice president in charge of each unit. Each regional vice president was given the responsibility to streamline regional operations and cut costs.[23] By 1999, these moves helped Coca-Cola Enterprises to innovate many new kinds of regional marketing campaigns, which increased its market share and profitability.

norms, and the amount of supervision that is required lessens, a manager's span of control can be increased. Salespeople, for instance, are typically controlled by a combination of sales quotas that they are expected to achieve and written reports that they are required to submit after calling on their clients. Managers do not need to monitor salespeople directly because they can evaluate their performance through those two standardized output controls. Standardization also allows upper-level managers to delegate responsibility more confidently when subordinates have clearly specified procedures to follow.

Summary

We have seen that an organization can control its members and their activities in different ways, ranging from personal control by managers in the hierarchy, to control through formalization and standardization, to informal control by means of norms and values. Structuring an organization to solve control problems requires decisions about all the different methods of control. The structure of every organization reflects the particular contingencies the organization faces, so all organizations' structures are different. Nevertheless, some generalizations can be made about how organizations fashion a structure to control people and resources.

First, managers increase the level of vertical differentiation, paying particular attention to keeping the organization as flat as possible and to maintaining an appropriate balance between centralization and decentralization. Second, they increase horizontal differentiation and thereby also increase vertical differentiation. Third, they decide how much they can use rules, SOPs, and norms to control activities. The more they can use them, the less they will need to rely on direct supervision from the managerial hierarchy, and the need for managers and for additional levels in the hierarchy will be reduced.

Organizational design is difficult because all these decisions affect one another and must be made simultaneously. For example, managers very often start out by designing an organic structure (see Chapter 2) with a flat hierarchy and rely on norms and values rather than on rules to control organizational activities. Very quickly, however, as the organization grows, they are forced to add levels to the hierarchy and to develop rules and SOPs to maintain control. Before managers realize it, their organization has a mechanistic structure, and they face a new set of control problems. Organizational structure evolves and has to be managed constantly if an organization is to maintain its competitive advantage.

Managerial Implications: Authority and Control

1. Managers must control the organizational hierarchy and make sure that it matches the current needs of the organization. Periodically, managers should draw a new organizational chart of their organization or department and measure (a) the number of current employees, (b) the number of levels in the hierarchy, and (c) the size of the span of control of managers at different levels.
2. Using that information, managers should consider whether the hierarchy has grown too tall or too centralized. If they find the hierarchy has grown too tall, they should combine managerial positions and eliminate levels in the hierarchy by reassigning the responsibilities of the eliminated positions to managers in the level above or, preferably, by decentralizing the responsibilities to managers or employees in the levels below.
3. If managers find the hierarchy does not provide the control they need to maintain adequate supervision over people and resources, they should consider how to increase organizational control. They may need to add a level to the organizational hierarchy or, preferably, use an alternative means of control, such as increasing standardization or decentralization or making better use of the norms and values of the informal organization.
4. Managers should periodically meet in teams to consider how best to design and redesign the hierarchy so that it allows the organization to create the most value at the lowest operating cost.

THE PRINCIPLES OF BUREAUCRACY

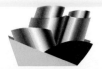

Around the turn of the century, Max Weber (1864–1920), a German sociologist, developed principles for designing a hierarchy so that it effectively allocates decision-making authority and control over resources.[24] Weber's interest was in identifying a system of orga-

---

TABLE 3.1

The Principles of Bureaucratic Structure

Principle One: A bureaucracy is founded on the concept of rational-legal authority.

Principle Two: Organizational roles are held on the basis of technical competence.

Principle Three: A role's task responsibility and decision-making authority and its relationship to other roles should be clearly specified.

Principle Four: The organization of roles in a bureaucracy is such that each lower office in the hierarchy is under the control and supervision of a higher office.

Principle Five: Rules, standard operating procedures, and norms should be used to control the behavior and the relationship between roles in an organization.

Principle Six: Administrative acts, decisions, and rules should be formulated and put in writing.

---

nization or an organizational structure that could improve the way organizations operated—that is, increase the value they produced and make them more effective.

Bureaucracy *A form of organizational structure in which people can be held accountable for their actions because they are required to act in accordance with rules and standard operating procedures.*

A **bureaucracy** is a form of organizational structure in which people can be held accountable for their actions because they are required to act in accordance with well-specified and agreed-upon rules and standard operating procedures. Weber's bureaucratic organizing principles offer clear prescriptions for how to create and differentiate organizational structure so that task responsibility and decision-making authority are distributed in a way that maximizes organizational effectiveness. Because his work has been so influential in organizational design, it is useful to examine the six bureaucratic principles that, Weber argued, underlie effective organizational structure (see Table 3.1). Together these principles define what a bureaucracy or bureaucratic structure is.

| *Principle One* | *A bureaucracy is founded on the concept of rational-legal authority.*

Rational-legal authority *The authority a person possesses because of his or her position in an organization.*

Rational-legal authority is the authority a person possesses because of his or her position in an organization. In a bureaucracy, obedience is owed to a person not because of any personal qualities that he or she might possess (such as charisma, wealth, or social status) but because of the level of authority and responsibility that is associated with the organizational position the person occupies. Thus, we obey a policeman not because he wears an impressive uniform and carries a gun but because he holds the position of policeman, which brings with it certain powers, rights, and responsibilities that compel obedience. In theory, a bureaucracy is impersonal. People's attitudes and beliefs play no part in determining the way a bureaucracy operates. If people base decisions and orders on their personal preferences instead of on organizational goals, effectiveness suffers.

Weber's first principle indicates that choices that affect the design of an organization's hierarchy should be based on the needs of the task, not on the needs of the person performing the task.[25] Thus, subordinates obey the CEO because of the authority and power vested in the position, not because of the individual currently filling it. For a bureaucracy to be effective, however, the distinction between positions and the people who hold them must be clear: People are appointed to positions; they do not own them.

| Principle Two | *Organizational roles are held on the basis of technical competence, not because of social status, kinship, or heredity.*

In a well-designed hierarchy, roles are occupied by people because they can do the job, not because of whom they are or whom they know. Although this principle seems to indicate the only logical way to run an organization, it has often been ignored. Until 1850, for example, an officer's commission in the British Army could be bought by anybody who could afford the price. The higher the rank, the more the commission cost. As a result, most officers were rich aristocrats who had little or no formal army training. Today, in many organizations and industries, old-boy networks—personal contacts and relations—and not job-related skills influence the decision about who gets a job. The use of such criteria to fill organizational roles can be harmful to an organization because talented people get overlooked, particularly women and minorities, who are rarely included in such networks.

Picking the best person for the job seems an obvious principle to follow. In practice, however, following this principle is a difficult process that requires managers to view all potential candidates objectively. It is important for people to always remember that holding a role in an organization in a legal sense means that their job is to use the organization's resources wisely for the benefit of all stakeholders, not just for personal gain.

Weber's first two principles establish the organizational role (and not the person in that role) as the basic component of bureaucratic structure. The next three principles specify how the process of differentiation should be controlled.

| Principle Three | *A role's task responsibility and decision-making authority and its relationship to other roles in the organization should be clearly specified.*

According to Weber's third principle, a clear and consistent pattern of vertical differentiation (decision-making authority) and horizontal differentiation (task responsibility) is the foundation for organizational effectiveness. When the limits of authority and control are specified for the various roles in an organization, the people in those roles know how much power they have to influence the behavior of others. Similarly, when the tasks of various roles are clearly specified, people in those roles clearly know what is expected of them. Thus, with those two aspects of a person's role in an organization clearly defined, a stable system emerges in which each person has a clear expectation and understanding of the rights and responsibilities attached to other organizational roles. In such a stable system all individuals know how much their supervisor can require of them and how much they can require of their subordinates. People also know how to deal with their peers—people who are at the same level in the organization as they are and over whom they have no authority and vice versa.

Clear specification of roles avoids many problems that can arise when people interact. If, for example, some task responsibilities are assigned to more than one role, the people in those roles may have to fight over the same set of resources or claim responsibility for the same tasks. Is sales or marketing responsible for handling customer requests for information? Is the head of the army or the head of the air force responsible for invasive operations into enemy territory? The military is a vast bureaucracy in which the division of labor among the armed services is continually being negotiated to prevent such problems from emerging.

A clear pattern of vertical (authority) and horizontal (task) differentiation also cuts down on role conflict and role ambiguity.[26] **Role conflict** occurs when two or more people have different views of what another person should do and, as a result, make conflict-

Role conflict *The state of opposition that occurs when two or more people have different views of what another person should do and, as a result, make conflicting demands on the person.*

Role ambiguity *The un-certainty that occurs for a person whose tasks or authority are not clearly defined.*

ing demands on the person. The person may be caught in the crossfire between two supervisors or the needs of two functional groups. **Role ambiguity** occurs when a person's tasks or authority are not clearly defined and the person becomes afraid to act on or take responsibility for anything. Clear descriptions of task and authority relationships solve conflict and ambiguity problems; when people know the dimensions of their position in the organization, they find it easier to take responsibility for their actions and to interact with one another.

| Principle Four | *The organization of roles in a bureaucracy is such that each lower office in the hierarchy is under the control and supervision of a higher office.*

To control vertical authority relationships, the organization should be arranged hierarchically so that people can recognize the chain of command.[27] The organization should delegate to each person holding a role the authority needed to make certain decisions and to use certain organizational resources. The organization can then hold the person in the role accountable for the use of those resources. The hierarchical pattern of vertical differentiation also makes clear that a person at a low level in the hierarchy can go to someone at a higher level to solve conflicts at the low level. In the U.S. court system, for example, participants in a court case can ask a higher court to review the decision of a lower court if they feel a bad decision was made. The right to appeal to a higher organizational level also needs to be specified in case a subordinate feels that his or her immediate superior has made a bad or unfair decision.

| Principle Five | *Rules, standard operating procedures, and norms should be used to control the behavior and the relationship between roles in an organization.*

Rules, including standard operating procedures (SOPs), are formal, written instructions that specify a series of actions to be taken to achieve a given end; for example, if A happens, then do B. Norms are unwritten standards or styles of behavior that govern how people act and lead people to behave in predictable ways. Rules, SOPs, and norms provide behavioral guidelines that can increase efficiency because they specify the best way to accomplish a task. Over time, all guidelines should change as improved ways of doing things are discovered.

Rules, SOPs, and norms clarify people's expectations about one another and prevent misunderstandings over responsibility or the use of power. Such guidelines can prevent a supervisor from arbitrarily increasing a subordinate's task and can prevent a subordinate from ignoring tasks that are a legitimate part of his or her job. A simple set of rules established by the supervisor of some custodial workers (Crew G) at a university building clearly established task responsibilities and clarified expectations.

Rules and norms enhance the integration and coordination of organizational roles at different levels and of different functions. Vertical differentiation and horizontal differentiation break the organization up into distinct roles that must be coordinated and integrated to accomplish organizational goals.[28] Rules and norms are important aspects of integration. They specify how roles interact, and they provide procedures that people should follow to jointly perform a task.[29] For example, a rule could stipulate that "Sales must give production five days' notice of any changes in customer requirements." Or an informal norm could require underutilized waiters to help waiters who have fallen behind in serving their customers.

ORGANIZATIONAL INSIGHT

3.3 CREW G'S RULES OF CONDUCT

1. All employees must call their supervisor or leader before 5:55 A.M. to notify of absence or tardiness.
2. Disciplinary action will be issued to any employee who abuses sick leave policy.
3. Disciplinary action will be issued to any employee whose assigned area is not up to custodial standards.
4. If a door is locked when you go in to clean an office, it's your responsibility to lock it back up.
5. Name tags and uniforms must be worn daily.
6. Each employee is responsible for buffing hallways and offices. Hallways must be buffed weekly, offices periodically.
7. All equipment must be put in closets during 9:00 A.M. and 11 A.M. breaks.
8. Do not use the elevator to move trash or equipment from 8:50 to 9:05, 9:50 to 10:05, 11:50 to 12:05, or 1:50 to 2:05, to avoid breaks between classes.
9. Try to mop hallways when students are in classrooms, or mop floors as you go down to each office.
10. Closets must be kept clean, and all equipment must be clean and operative.
11. Each employee is expected to greet building occupants with "Good morning."
12. Always knock before entering offices and conference rooms.
13. Loud talking, profanity, and horseplay will not be tolerated inside buildings.
14. All custodial carts must be kept uniform and cleaned daily.
15. You must have excellent "public relations" with occupants at all times.

Your supervisor stands behind workers at all times when the employee is in the right and you are doing what you are supposed to. But when you are wrong, you are wrong. Let's try to work together to better Crew G, because there are many outstanding employees in this crew.

| Principle Six | *Administrative acts, decisions, and rules should be formulated and put in writing.*

When rules and decisions are written down, they become official guides to the way the organization works. Thus, even when someone leaves an organization, an indication of what that person did is part of the organization's written records. A bureaucratic structure provides an organization with memory, and it is the responsibility of members to train successors and ensure that there is continuity in the organizational hierarchy. Written records also ensure that organizational history cannot be altered and that people can be held accountable for their decisions.

The Advantages of Bureaucracy

Almost every organization possesses some features of bureaucracy.[30] The primary advantage of a bureaucracy is that it lays out the ground rules for designing an organizational hierarchy that controls interactions between organizational members and increases the efficiency of those interactions.[31] Bureaucracy's clear specification of vertical authority and horizontal task relationships means that there is no question about each person's role in the organization. Individuals can be held accountable for what they do, and such accountability reduces the transaction costs that arise when people must continually negotiate and define their organizational tasks. Similarly, the specification of roles and the use of rules, SOPs, and norms to regulate how tasks are performed reduce the costs associated with monitoring the work of subordinates and increase integration within the organization. Finally, written rules regarding the reward and punishment of employees, such as rules for promotion and termination, reduce the costs of enforcement and evaluating employees' performance.

Another advantage of bureaucracy is that it separates the position from the person. The fairness and equity of bureaucratic selection, evaluation, and reward systems encourage organizational members to advance the interests of all organizational stakeholders and meet organizational expectations.[32] Bureaucracy provides people with the opportunity to develop their skills and pass them on to their successors. In this way, a bureaucracy fosters differentiation, increases the organization's core competences, and improves its ability to compete in the marketplace against other organizations for scarce resources.[33] Bureaucracies provide the stability necessary for organizational members to take a long-run view of the organization and its relationship to its environment.

If a bureaucracy is based on such clear guidelines for allocating authority and control in an organization, why is bureaucracy considered a dirty word by some people, and why are terms like *bureaucrats* and *bureaucratic red tape* meant as insults? Why do bureaucratic structures cause such disgust?

One of the problems that emerges with a bureaucracy is that over time managers fail to properly control the development of the organizational hierarchy. As a result, an organization can become very tall and centralized. Decision making begins to slow down, the organization begins to stagnate, and bureaucratic costs increase because managers start to make work for each other.

Another problem with bureaucracy is that organizational members come to rely too much on rules and SOPs to make decisions, and this overreliance makes them unresponsive to the needs of customers and other stakeholders. Organizational members lose sight of the fact that their job is to create value for stakeholders. Instead, their chief goal is to follow rules and procedures and obey authority.

Organizations that suffer from those problems are accused of being bureaucratic or of being run by bureaucrats. However, whenever we hear this claim, we must be careful to distinguish between the principles of bureaucracy and the people who manage bureaucratic organizations. Remember: There is nothing intrinsically bad or inefficient about a bureaucracy. When organizations become overly bureaucratic, the fault lies with the people who run them—with managers who prefer the pursuit of power and status to the pursuit of operating efficiency, who prefer to protect their careers rather than their organizations, and who prefer to use resources to benefit themselves rather than stakeholders.

Managerial Implications: Using Bureaucracy to Benefit the Organization

1. If organizational hierarchies are to function effectively and the problems of overly bureaucratized organizations are to be avoided, both managers and employees must follow bureaucratic principles.
2. Both employees and managers should realize that they do not own their positions in an organization and that it is their responsibility to use their authority and control over resources to benefit stakeholders and not themselves.

3. Managers should strive to make human resource decisions such as hiring, promoting, or rewarding employees as fair and equitable as possible. Managers should not let personal ties or relationships influence their decisions, and employees should complain to managers when they feel that their decisions are inappropriate.
4. Periodically, the members of a work group or function should meet to ensure that reporting relationships are clear and unambiguous and that the rules members are using to make decisions meet current needs.
5. Both managers and employees should adopt a "questioning attitude" toward the way the organization works in order to uncover the taken-for-granted assumptions and beliefs on which it operates. For example, to make sure that they are not wasting organizational resources by performing unnecessary actions, they should always ask questions such as "Is that rule or SOP really necessary?" and "Who will read the report that I am writing?"

THE INFLUENCE OF THE INFORMAL ORGANIZATION

The hierarchy of authority designed by management that allocates people and resources to organizational tasks and roles is a blueprint for how things are supposed to happen. However, at all levels in the organization decision making and coordination frequently take place outside the formally designed channels as people interact informally on the job. Moreover, many of the rules and norms that employees use to perform their tasks emerge out of informal interactions between people and not from the formal blueprint and rules established by managers. Thus, while establishing a formal structure of interrelated roles, managers are also creating an informal social structure that affects behavior in ways that may differ from the ways the managers intended. The importance of understanding the way in which the network of personal relationships that develops over time in an organization, which is known as the *informal organization*, affects the way the "formal" hierarchy works is illustrated in the following Organizational Insight.[34]

By reintroducing the plant's formal hierarchy of authority, the new management team at General Gypsum Company totally changed the informal organization that had been governing the way workers thought they should act. The changes destroyed the norms that had made the plant work smoothly (though not very effectively from top management's perspective). The result of changing the informal organization was lower productivity because of the strikes.

This case shows that managers need to consider the effects of the informal organization on individual and group behavior when they make any organizational changes, because altering the formal structure may disrupt the informal norms that make the organization work. Because an organization is a network of informal social relations, as well as a hierarchy of formal task and authority relations, managers must harness the power of the informal organization in order to achieve organizational goals. People in organizations go to enormous lengths to increase their status and prestige and always want others to know about and recognize their status. Every organization has an established informal organization that does not appear on any formal chart but is familiar to all employees. Much of what gets done in an organization gets done through the informal organization, in ways not revealed by the formal hierarchy. Managers need to consider carefully the implications of the interactions between the formal and informal hierarchies when changing the ways they motivate and coordinate employees.

The informal organization can actually enhance organizational performance. New approaches to organization design argue that managers need to tap into the power of the informal organization to increase motivation and provide informal avenues for employ-

---

ORGANIZATIONAL INSIGHT

3.4 WILDCAT STRIKES IN THE GYPSUM PLANT

Gypsum is a mineral that is extracted from the ground, crushed, refined, and compacted into wallboard. A gypsum mine and processing plant owned by the General Gypsum Company[35] was located in a rural community, and farmers and laborers frequently supplemented their farm income by working in the plant. The situation in the mine was stable, the management team had been in place for many years, and workers knew exactly what they had to do. Coordination in the plant took place through long-established informal routines that were taken for granted by management and workers alike. Workers did a fair day's work for a fair day's pay. For its part, management was very liberal. It allowed workers to take wallboard for their own personal use and overlooked absences from work, which were especially common during the harvest season.

The situation changed when the corporate office sent a new plant manager to take over the plant's operations and improve its productivity. When the new man arrived, he was amazed by the situation. He could not understand how the previous manager had allowed workers to take wallboard, break work rules (such as those concerning absenteeism), and otherwise take advantage of the company. He decided that these practices had to stop, and he took steps to change the way the company was operated.

He began by reactivating the formal rules and procedures, which, though they had always existed, had never been enforced by the previous management team. He reinstituted rules concerning absenteeism and punished workers who were excessively absent. He stopped the informal practice of allowing employees to take wallboard, and he took formal steps to reestablish management's authority in the plant. In short, he reestablished the formal organizational structure—one based on a strict hierarchy of authority and strictly enforced rules that no longer indulged the employees.

The results were immediate. The workforce walked out and, in a series of wildcat strikes, refused to return until the old system was restored. It made no difference to the workers that the formal rules and procedures had always been on the books. They were used to the old, informal routines, and they wanted them back. Eventually, after prolonged negotiation about new work practices, the union and company reached an agreement that defined the relative spheres of authority of management and the union and established a bureaucratic system for managing future disputes. When the new work routines were in place, the wildcat strikes ended.

---

ees to use to improve organizational performance. The formal hierarchical structure is the main mechanism of control, but there is no reason not to use the informal structure along with the formal one to allow people to work out solutions to their problems.

RESTRUCTURING THE ORGANIZATION

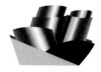

As noted earlier, **restructuring** refers to the process by which managers change task and authority relationships to improve organizational effectiveness. One type of organizational restructuring that has become very common in recent years is **downsizing**, the process

Restructuring *The process by which managers change task and authority relationships to improve organizational effectiveness.*

by which managers streamline the organizational hierarchy and lay off managers and workers to reduce bureaucratic costs. The size and scope of recent restructuring and downsizing efforts have been enormous. It is estimated that in the last 10 years Fortune 500 companies have downsized so much that they now employ about 10 percent fewer managers than they used to. Moreover, in 1998, despite the fact that the economy was booming, companies laid off record numbers of employees as they restructured to reduce costs and improve efficiency.

The drive to reduce bureaucratic costs is often a response to increasing competitive pressures in the environment as companies fight to increase their performance and introduce new information technology.[36] For example, the wave of mergers and acquisitions that occurred in the 1990s in many industries such as telecommunications, banking, and defense has also resulted in downsizing because merged companies typically require fewer managers. For example, the merger of Time Warner with Turner Broadcasting System in 1996 resulted in the layoff of over 8,000 managers as the merged company combined many of its operating functions such as finance and accounting. Often, after one industry company downsizes, other industry companies are forced to examine their own structures to search out inefficiencies; thus, downsizing waves take place across companies in an industry. For example, in 1996 Molson Breweries, the largest Canadian brewing company, announced that it was reducing the size of its headquarters staff to reduce costs. Apparently, Molson's top managers had watched its main competitor, Labatt Breweries, reduce its headquarters staff to 110 and decided that Molson did not need the 200 headquarters staff it employed.[37]

Downsizing *The process by which managers streamline the organizational hierarchy and lay off managers and workers to reduce bureaucratic costs.*

While there is no doubt that companies have realized considerable cost savings by downsizing and streamlining their hierarchies, some analysts are now wondering whether this process has gone far enough or even too far.[38] There are increasing reports that the remaining managers in downsized organizations are working under severe stress, both because they fear they might be the next employees to be let go and because they are forced to do the work that was previously performed by the lost employees—work, which often they cannot cope with.

Moreover, there are concerns that in pushing their downsizing efforts too far organizations may be trading off short-term gains from cost savings for long-term losses because of lost opportunities. The argument is that organizations always need some level of "surplus" managers who have the time and energy to improve current operating methods and search the environment to find new opportunities for growth and expansion.[39] Downsized organizations lack the middle managers who perform this vital task, and this may hurt them in the future. Hence, the terms *anorexic* or *hollow* been coined to refer to organizations that have downsized too much and have too few managers.

While clearly there are disadvantages associated with excessive downsizing, it remains true that many organizations became too tall and bloated because their past top-management teams failed to control the growth of their hierarchies and design their organizational structures appropriately, as in the Sunbeam case given at the end of the chapter. In such cases, managers are forced to restructure their organizations to remain competitive and even to survive. The huge savings in bureaucratic costs that can be obtained from restructuring by downsizing are illustrated in the following Organizational Insight, which describes the efforts of the U.S. Postal Service to restructure itself at a time when it was under intense public pressure to keep mail prices down.

Empowerment *The process of giving employees throughout an organization the authority to make important decisions and to be responsible for their outcomes.*

Other important trends that go hand in hand with restructuring and downsizing are the increasing use of empowered workers, self-managed teams, and contingent or temporary workers. **Empowerment** is the process of giving employees throughout an orga-

---

ORGANIZATIONAL INSIGHT

3.5 BIG CHANGES AT THE POST OFFICE

The U.S. Postal Service is huge. It employs 740,000 workers, including 130,000 managers, to handle what amounts to 40 percent of the world's volume of mail. In recent years, it has been battling to reduce its massive staff and cut other costs in order to stem losses that have been rising steadily in spite of 50,000 jobs already cut. To help cut losses, Marvin Runyon, the former head of the Tennessee Valley Authority (TVA), was recruited to become the nation's seventieth Postmaster General. While at the TVA, he had slashed the managerial hierarchy, eliminated 14,000 jobs, and reduced total overhead costs by 30 percent, to achieve a savings of $1.8 billion. Analysts hoped that he could perform the same feat at the Postal Service. He did. Runyon announced that he would cut the postal workforce by 30,000 employees from all levels in the organization. Then he announced that he would cut top-management personnel from 42 to 24 and eliminate two layers of management. Then he decided to close five regional offices and more than 50 district offices, eliminating another management layer. He argued that the Postal Service had become too tall: It had local, regional, divisional, and headquarters managers, most of whom duplicated one another's work and slowed the pace of change in the organization. Eliminating jobs directly saved an estimated $2 billion in costs. Moreover, he began a drive to install the latest information technology in the post office to keep costs down.

Runyon's reorganization shook up the Postal Service; it increased productivity and facilitated faster decision making. His efforts have been so successful that the post office made record profits in the 1990s while keeping prices low. In 1997, Postmaster General Bill Henderson took over with a new mission, to remake the post office so it could respond to the challenges of operating in a growing Internet environment where on-line shopping generates hundreds of millions more parcels each year.[40]

Self-managed teams

Work groups consisting of people who are jointly responsible for ensuring that the team accomplishes its goals and who lead themselves.

nization the authority to make important decisions and to be responsible for their outcomes. **Self-managed teams** are formal work groups consisting of people who are jointly responsible for ensuring that the team accomplishes its goals and who lead themselves. As discussed earlier, decentralizing authority to lower-level employees and placing them in teams reduce the need for direct, personal supervision by managers, and organizations become flatter.

The movement to flatten organizations by empowering workers in this way has been increasing steadily since the 1990s and has met with great success according to many stories in the popular press. However, while some commentators have forecasted the "end of hierarchy" and the emergence of new organizational forms based purely on lateral relations both inside and between functions, other commentators are not so sure. They argue that even a flat, team-based organization composed of empowered workers must have a hierarchy and some minimum set of rules and standard operating procedures if the organization is to have enough control over its activities. Organizations sacrifice the gains from bureaucratic structure only at their peril.[41] The problem for managers is to combine the best aspects of both systems—of bureaucratic structure and empowered work groups. Essentially, what this comes down to is that managers must be sure they have the right blend of mechanistic and organic structure to meet the contingencies they face. Managers should use bureaucratic principles to build a mechanistic structure, and they should enhance the organization's ability to act in an organic way by empowering employees and making teams a principle way of increasing the level of integration in an organization.

Finally, as organizations have downsized and flattened their structures, there has been an increasing trend for companies to employ contingent workers to keep costs down. **Contingent workers** are workers who are employed for temporary periods by an organization and who receive no indirect benefits such as health insurance or pensions. Contingent workers may work by the day, week, or month performing some functional task, or may contract with the organization for some fee to perform a specific service to the organization. Thus, for example, an organization may employ 10 temporary accountants to "do the books" when it is time or it may contract with a software programmer to write some specialized software for a fixed fee.

The advantages an organization obtains from contingent workers are that they cost less to employ since they receive no indirect benefits and they can be let go easily when their services are no longer needed. However, there are also some disadvantages associated with contingent workers. First, coordination and motivation problems may arise because temporary workers may have less incentive to perform at a high level given that there is no prospect for promotion or job security. Second, organizations must develop core competences in their functions to gain a competitive advantage, and it is unlikely that contingent workers will help them develop such competences since they do not remain with the organization very long and are not committed to it.

Nevertheless, it has been estimated that 20 percent of the U.S workforce today consists of contingent workers, and this figure is expected to increase as managers spend more time studying their organizational structures to find new ways of reducing bureaucratic costs. Indeed, one method that managers are already employing to keep their structures flat is the use of outsourcing and network structures, which are discussed in detail in the next chapter.

Contingent workers

Workers who are employed for temporary periods by an organization and who receive no indirect benefits such as health insurance or pensions.

SUMMARY

Stakeholder goals and objectives can be achieved only when organizational skills and capabilities are controlled through organizational structure. The activities of organizational members would be chaotic without a structure that assigns people to roles and directs the activities of people and functions.[42] This chapter has examined how organizations should design their hierarchy of authority and choose control systems that create an effective organizational structure. The shape of the hierarchy determines how decision making takes place. It also determines how motivated people will be to pursue organizational goals. Designing the hierarchy should be one of management's major tasks, but, as we have seen, it is a task that many organizations do not do well or fail to consider at all. Chapter 3 has made the following main points:

1. The height of an organization's structure is a function of the number of levels in the hierarchy, the span of control at each level, and the balance between centralization and decentralization of authority.

2. As an organization grows, the increase in the size of the managerial component is less than proportional to the increase in the size of the organization.

3. Problems with tall hierarchies include communication, motivation, and bureaucratic costs.

4. According to the principle of minimum chain of command, an organization should choose the minimum number of hierarchical levels consistent with the contingencies it faces.

5. The span of control is the number of subordinates a manager directly manages. The two main factors that affect the span of control are task complexity and task interrelatedness.

6. The shape of the hierarchy and the way it works are also affected by choices concerning horizontal differentiation, centralization versus decentralization, differentiation versus integration, standardization versus mutual adjustment, and the influence of the informal organization.

7. The six principles of bureaucratic theory specify the most effective way to design the hierarchy of authority in an organization.

8. Bureaucracy has several advantages. It is fair and equitable, and it can promote organizational effectiveness by improving organizational design. However, problems can arise if bureaucratic principles are not followed and if managers allow the organization to become too tall and centralized.

9. Managers need to recognize how the informal organization affects the way the formal hierarchy of authority works and make sure they fit to enhance organizational performance.

10. Managers are increasingly restructuring and downsizing their organizations to reduce bureaucratic costs. Also, to keep their organizations as flat as possible they are creating self-managed work teams of empowered workers and turning to contingent workers to keep costs low.

DISCUSSION QUESTIONS

1. How do corporate, divisional, and functional managers differ? What different roles do they play in the organization?

2. In what ways can a CEO influence organizational effectiveness?

3. Choose a small organization in your city, such as a restaurant or school, and draw a chart showing its structure. Do you think the number of levels in its hierarchy and the span of control at each level are appropriate? Why or why not?

4. In what ways can the informal organization and the norms and values of its culture affect the shape of an organization?

5. What factors determine the appropriate authority and control structure in (a) a research and development laboratory, (b) a large department store, and (c) a small manufacturing company?

6. How can the principles of bureaucracy help managers to design the organizational hierarchy?

7. When does bureaucracy become a problem in an organization? What can managers do to prevent bureaucratic problems from arising?

ORGANIZATIONAL THEORY IN ACTION

ORGANIZATIONAL THEORY:
HOW TO RESTRUCTURE AN ORGANIZATION

Form groups of three to five people and discuss the following scenario:

You are the managers charged with restructuring your division to reduce high operating costs. You have been instructed by the CEO to eliminate 25 percent of the company's managerial positions and then to reorganize the remaining positions so that the organization still exercises adequate supervision over its employees.

1. How would you go about analyzing the organizational hierarchy to decide which managerial positions should be cut first?
2. How will you be able to ensure adequate supervision with fewer managers?
3. What can you do to help make the downsizing process less painful for those who leave and for those who remain?

MAKING THE CONNECTION #3

Find an example of a company that recently changed its hierarchy of authority or its top-management team. What changes did it make? Why did it make them? What does it hope to accomplish as a result of them? What happened as a result of the changes?

Analyzing the Organization: Design Module #3

This module focuses on vertical differentiation and understanding the managerial hierarchy in your organization and the way the organization allocates decision-making authority.

ASSIGNMENT

1. Draw an organizational chart of the top management in your organization. Write down the names of the top managers and the positions they occupy. As far as you can discover, who is a member of the top-management team? If you are using published sources, write to the company and ask for a copy of its organizational chart.

2. What do you know about the CEO's management approach? Does the CEO or the top-management team behave in any characteristic way? From your contacts or published sources, can you discover any management principles on which the CEO relies? What is the company's philosophy of doing business?

3. Describe the top-management team. How old are its members? What are their backgrounds? Has the CEO chosen a successor?

4. What is your general impression of the company's top management? Are you favorably impressed by what you have learned? Why or why not?

5. To what degree has your organization followed bureaucratic principles in designing its hierarchy? How bureaucratized is it? How do you know?

6. How many people does the organization employ?

7. How many levels are there in the organization's hierarchy?

8. Is the organization tall or flat?

9. Does the organization experience any of the problems associated with tall hierarchies? Which ones?

10. What is the span of control of the CEO? Is this span appropriate, or is it too wide or too narrow?

11. How do centralization, standardization, and horizontal differentiation affect the shape of the organization?

12. Do you think your organization does a good or a poor job in managing its hierarchy of authority? Give reasons for your answer.

Cases for Analysis:
ALL CHANGE AT SUNBEAM

On July 1996, Sunbeam Corporation, the well-known small-appliance maker, reported a 37 percent drop in net income even though its sales had increased by 12 percent. Soon after this announcement Sunbeam's board of directors, believing that the company's poor performance was the result of poor management, forced the resignation of Sunbeam's CEO, Roger Schipke. They then replaced him with Albert J. Dunlap, a manager well known for his ability to restructure and turn around a failing company, and a manager fond of saying, "If it can't be done in a year it can't be done at all."

Dunlap's last restructuring job had been at Scott Paper where, to reduce costs, he had streamlined operations through sweeping job cuts at all levels. At Scott he had fired most of top management on the first day, and before he was finished he had cut the number of levels of management from eight to five and laid off thousands of managers and workers while centralizing control of many of Scott's operating functions at the head office.

At Sunbeam, he began the same way. Dunlap fired the chief operating officer on the same day he was appointed, and within weeks not one member of Sunbeam's previous top-management team was left. To replace them he brought into the company managers with whom he had previously worked and he promoted several Sunbeam managers who bravely came to him with their plans for how Sunbeam should be restructured to turn the company around.

Arguing that the company had too many people, too many products, too many plants, and too many divisional headquarters, Dunlap then began to look at where he could streamline the company's operations. He decided to centralize decision-making authority at the top, arguing that "autonomy is nonsense, the last thing we need is for people to be setting up empires."[43] He then began to sell off marginal products and businesses to restructure the company to make it easier and less expensive to manage. As was the case at Scott Paper, the layoff of thousands of managers and workers will result in a "downsized" or "rightsized" organization and Dunlap expects a much flatter organizational structure, one with fewer levels in the hierarchy, to emerge from his efforts.

Dunlap has no qualms about laying off these thousands of employees, attributing the need to do so to the poor management by the previous management team whom he believed deserved to be "hung." Indeed, Dunlap argues that the remaining employees will keep their jobs only if he can find a new strategy and structure to turn the company around and restore its profitability—something that will be possible to do only after he has restructured and streamlined the company.

1. What happened to Sunbeam's hierarchy when downsizing took place?

2. How do managers know when downsizing has gone too far?

Cases for Analysis:

THE SHAKE-UP IN GM'S HIERARCHY

On April 6, 1992, the normally quiescent board of directors of General Motors, under the leadership of outside director John G. Smale, instituted a revolt against the company's top-management team. Horrified by GM's $4.5 billion loss in 1991 and angry at the slow pace of change instituted by GM chairman and chief executive officer Robert Stempel, the board decided to teach GM's top management a lesson.

Stempel lost his leadership of the board's executive committee (GM's top policy-making committee) to Smale, who effectively became his overseer. The board then dismantled Stempel's handpicked team of top managers and replaced them with managers in whom the board had more confidence: John F. ("Jack") Smith, who became president and chief operating officer (COO); and William E. Hoagland, who became the new chief financial officer (CFO). In making these changes, the board effectively told Stempel that if he could not quickly turn around the company's disappointing performance, the board would replace him with Smith and Hoagland. Both men had extensive experience in reducing costs and instituting a turnaround. Jack Smith, for example, had dramatically increased the performance of GM's European operations.

In October 1992, Stempel fell ill, and the board decided to act immediately to finish the changes it had begun in GM's top management. Stempel was forced to retire. Jack Smith became the new CEO. Smale became the new chairman of the board. Hoagland became Smith's right-hand man as GM's new president. With these changes complete, the new top-management team moved quickly to change the rest of GM's chain of command.

The problem, in the opinion of car industry analysts, was that GM had become too tall—that is, it had developed too many levels of management. Because the corporate staff was huge, decision making was slow and cumbersome and change difficult to introduce. The task facing GM's new top-management team was to flatten the hierarchy, eliminating hierarchical levels and reducing the size of the managerial staff. The team hoped that this move would reduce operating costs, improve communication, and encourage innovation. The task was enormous, however. Some analysts believed that Jack Smith needed to cut GM's bloated management staff by 50 percent, which would mean terminating 20,000 managers.

The board clearly believed that shareholders' interests would be best served by a new management team that would make tough organizational design decisions. As the new team began a reassessment of operations, the pace of change quickened at GM. In 1993 GM announced its intention to cut 50,000 hourly and 24,000 salaried jobs and to close or consolidate 21 parts and assembly plants by 1995. It was estimated that this would eventually save the automaker many billions of dollars.[44] The hope was that the changes would result in an organization in which managers would be close to the scene of the action and decision making would be fast and responsive to the needs of customers.

1. What problems were associated with GM's managerial hierarchy before Jack Smith became CEO?
2. What was Jack Smith's approach to managing the hierarchy?

REFERENCES

1. R. H. Miles, *Macro Organizational Behavior* (Santa Monica, CA: Goodyear, 1980), pp. 19–20.

2. J. R. Galbraith, *Designing Complex Organizations* (Reading, MA: Addison-Wesley, 1973).

3. P. R. Lawrence and J. W. Lorsch, *Organization and Environment* (Boston: Graduate School of Business Administration, Harvard University, 1967).

4. G. R. Jones, "Task Visibility, Free Riding, and Shirking: Explaining the Effect of Organization Structure on Employee Behavior," *Academy of Management Review*, 1984, vol. 4, pp. 684–695.

5. P. M. Blau, "A Formal Theory of Differentiation in Organizations," *American Sociological Review*, 1970, vol. 35, pp. 201–218.

6. J. Child, *Organization: A Guide for Managers and Administrators* (New York: Harper and Row, 1977), pp. 10–15; P. Blau, "A Formal Theory of Differentiation."

7. P. Blau, "A Formal Theory of Differentiation"; W. R. Scott, *Organizations: Rational, Natural, and Open Systems* (Englewood Cliffs, NJ: Prentice Hall, 1981), pp. 235–240.

8. D. D. Baker and J. C. Cullen, "Administrative Reorganization and the Configurational Context: The Contingent Effects of Age, Size, and Changes in Size," *Academy of Management Journal*, 1993, vol. 36, pp. 1251–1277.

9. P. M. Blau and R. A. Schoenherr, *The Structure of Organizations* (New York: Basic Books, 1971).

10. R. Carzo and J. N. Zanousas, "Effects of Flat and Tall Structure," *Administrative Science Quarterly*, 1969, vol. 14, pp. 178–191; A. Gupta and V. Govindarajan, "Business Unit Strategy, Managerial Characteristics, and Business Unit Effectiveness at Strategy Implementation," *Academy of Management Journal*, 1984, vol. 27, pp. 25–41.

11. W. H. Wagel, "Keeping the Organization Lean at Federal Express," *Personnel*, 1984, vol. 4, p. 4.

12. D. Katz and R. L. Kahn, *The Social Psychology of Organizing* (New York: Wiley, 1966), p. 255.

13. A. M. Pettigrew, *The Politics of Organizational Decision Making* (London: Tavistock, 1973).

14. E. Nee, "Reboot," *Forbes*, 4 May 1990, p. 37.

15. C. N. Parkinson, *Parkinson's Law* (New York: Ballantine Books, 1964).

16. Ibid., p. 17.

17. See, for example, "Preparing the Company Organization Manual," *Studies in Personnel Policy*, no. 157 (New York: National Industrial Conference Board, 1957), p. 28.

18. V. A. Graicunas, "Relationships in Organizations," in L. Gulick and L. Urwick, eds., *Papers in the Science of Administration* (New York: Institute of Public Administration, 1937), pp. 181–185.

19. Ibid.

20. D. D. Van Fleet, "Span of Management Research and Issues," *Academy of Management Journal*, 1983, vol. 4, pp. 546–552.

21. J. W. Lorsch and J. J. Morse, *Organizations and Their Members: A Contingency Approach* (New York: Harper and Row, 1974).

22. Lawrence and Lorsch, *Organization and Environment*.

23. W. Konrad, "The Bottleneck at Coca-Cola Enterprises," *Business Week*, 14 September 1992, pp. 28–30.

24. M. Weber, *From Max Weber: Essays in Sociology*, in H. H. Gerth and C. W. Mills, eds. (New York: Oxford University Press, 1946); M. Weber, *Economy and Society*, in G. Roth and C. Wittich, eds. (Berkeley: University of California Press, 1978).

25. C. Perrow, *Complex Organizations*, 2nd ed. (Glenview, IL: Scott, Foresman, 1979).

26. R. L. Kahn, D. M. Wolfe, R. P. Quinn, J. D. Snoek, and R. A. Rosenthal, *Organizational Stress: Studies in Role Conflict and Ambiguity* (New York: Wiley, 1964).

27. Weber, *From Max Weber*, p. 331.

28. Lawrence and Lorsch, *Organization and Environment*; J. R. Galbraith, *Organization Design* (Reading, MA: Addison-Wesley, 1977).

29. Lawrence and Lorsch, *Organization and Environment*.

30. Perrow, *Complex Organizations*.

31. G. R. Jones and C. W. L. Hill, "Transaction Cost Analysis of Strategy-Structure Choice," *Strategic Management Journal*, 1989, vol. 9, pp. 159–172.

32. See Perrow, *Complex Organizations*, Ch. 1, for a detailed discussion of these issues.

33. P. S. Adler and B. Borys, "Two Types of Bureaucracy," *Administrative Science Quarterly*, 1996, vol. 41, pp. 61–89.

34. A. W. Gouldner, *Wildcat Strike: A Study of Worker-Management Relationships* (New York: Harper and Row, 1954).

35. This is a pseudonym used by Gouldner, ibid.

36. S. J. Freeman and K. S. Cameron, "Organizational Downsizing: A Convergence and Reorientation Framework," *Organizational Science*, 1993, vol. 4, pp. 10–29.

37. P. Brent, "3 Molson Executives Ousted in Decentralization Move," *Financial Post-Toronto*, 20 December 1995, p. 3.

38. R-L. DeWitt, "The Structural Consequences of Downsizing," *Organizational Science*, 1993, vol. 4, pp. 30–40.

39. "The Salaryman Rides Again," *The Economist*, 4 December 1995, p. 64.

40. "Industry Leaders Discuss Postal Service Role in Internet Commerce," *PR Newswire*, 29 September 1999.

41. L. Donaldson, *Redeeming the Organization* (New York: The Free Press, 1996).

42. Child, *Organization: A Guide for Managers and Administrators*, pp. 50–72.

43. R. Frank, "New Sunbeam CEO Presses Restructuring," *Wall Street Journal*, 6 August 1996, p. A1.

44. J. Treece, "The Board Revolt—Business as Usual Won't Cut It Anymore at a Humbled GM," *Business Week*, 20 April 1992, pp. 31–36; "Shakeup at General Motors," *Motor Trend*, July 1992, p. 26.

Chapter 4

DESIGNING ORGANIZATIONAL STRUCTURE: SPECIALIZATION and COORDINATION

In this chapter the second principal issue in organizational design is addressed: how to group and coordinate tasks to create a division of labor that gives an organization a competitive advantage. The design challenge is to create the optimal pattern of vertical and horizontal relationships among roles, functions, teams, and divisions that will enable an organization to best coordinate and motivate people and other resources to achieve its goals.

Later chapters discuss in detail the way in which a changing environment, strategy, and technology affect the process of organizational design and choice of structure over time. This chapter discusses the various kinds of organizational structures that managers can choose from and outlines their advantages and disadvantages.

First, the advantages of a functional structure are examined. Then the various control problems that can emerge with a functional structure as organizations grow and differentiate are considered. Then the issue of how to reengineer an organization to increase performance is examined.

Next, the more complex kinds of structures from which managers can choose to coordinate organizational activities to gain a competitive advantage are outlined. Specifically, three types of divisional structure (product, geographic, and market structure), matrix structure, and network structure are examined. By the end of the chapter you will understand why designing a structure to coordinate people and resources is a vital part of a manager's role.

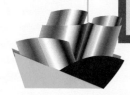

FUNCTIONAL STRUCTURE

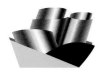

Functional structure A design that groups people together on the basis of their common expertise and experience or because they use the same resources.

In Chapter 2 we noted that the tasks involved in running the B.A.R. and Grille became more numerous and more complex as the number of customers increased and the organization needed to serve more meals. At first, the owners, Bob and Amanda Richards, performed multiple roles, but as the business grew, they became overloaded and were forced to develop specialized roles and institute a division of labor. As we saw in Chapter 2, the assignment of one person to a role is the start of specialization and horizontal differentiation. As this process continues, the result is a **functional structure**, a design that groups people together on the basis of their common skills and expertise or because they use the same resources. At the B.A.R. and Grille, waiters and busboys were grouped into the dining-room function, and chefs and kitchen staff were grouped into the kitchen function (see Figure 2.1). Similarly, research and development scientists at companies like Amazon.com and Johnson & Johnson are grouped together in specialized laboratories because they use the same skills and resources, and accountants are grouped together in an accounting function.

Functional structure is the bedrock of horizontal differentiation. An organization groups tasks into functions to increase the effectiveness with which it achieves its principal goal: providing customers with high-quality products at reasonable prices.[1] As functions specialize, skills and abilities improve, and the core competences that give an organization a competitive advantage emerge. Different functions emerge as an organization responds to increasingly complex task requirements. The owner of a very small business, for example, might hire outside specialists to handle accounting and marketing. As an organization grows in size and complexity, however, it normally develops those functions internally because handling accounting and marketing itself becomes more efficient than hiring outside contractors. This is how organizations become more complex as they grow: They develop not only more functions but also more specialization within each

Focus on New Information Technology: Amazon.com, Part 3

As we saw in Chapter 1, Jeff Bezos, the founder of Amazon.com, achieved phenomenal success with his concept for an on-line bookstore. In large part, his success has been due to the functional structure that he created for his company that has allowed Amazon.com's proprietary Internet software to be used so effectively to link employees to customers. (See Figure 4.1.)

First, Bezos created the research and development department to continue to develop and improve the in-house software that he had initially developed for Internet-based retailing. Then he also established the information systems department to handle the day-to-day implementation of these systems and to manage the interface between the customer and the organization. Third, he created the materials management/logistics department to devise the most cost-efficient ways to obtain books from book publishers and book distributors and then to ship them quickly to customers. Currently, the department is trying to develop new information systems to ensure one-day shipping to customers. Fi-

nally, as Amazon.com grew, he created a separate financial department and a strategic planning department to help chart the company's future. As we will see in later chapters, these departments have helped Amazon.com to expand into providing many other kinds of products for its customers such as music CDs, electronics, and gifts.

By focusing on the best way to divide into functions the total task facing the organization (the creation of value for customers), and recruiting experienced functional managers from other organizations like Wal-Mart to run them, Bezos created core competences that allowed his on-line bookstore to compete effectively with bricks-and-mortar bookstores. Stores that can't provide customers with the range of books and convenient service that Amazon.com is able to because of the way it has developed a structure to effectively manage its new information technology are going out of business.

FIGURE 4.1

Functional Structure

A. This format shows that each function has its own hierarchy.

CEO

Research and Development   Sales and Marketing   Manufacturing   Materials Management   Finance

B. This format shows the position of each function within the organization's hierarchy.

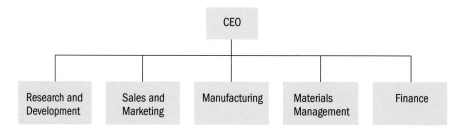

function. (They also become vertically differentiated and develop a hierarchy of authority, as we saw in Chapter 3.) A good example of the way in which horizontal differentiation leads to the development of a functional structure is provided by Amazon.com.

Advantages of a Functional Structure

Functional structure develops first and foremost because it provides people with the opportunity to learn from one another and become more specialized and productive. When people with skills in common are assembled into a functional group, they can learn the best way to solve problems and the most efficient techniques for performing a task from one another. The most skilled employees can train new recruits, and the most skilled people can be promoted to supervisors and managers so that they can hire, train, and develop new employees. In this way an organization can increase its store of skills and abilities. For example, Microsoft has revenues of over $4 billion per year but only 30,000 employees. Microsoft's value is in the skills and abilities of its employees and in the way the organization groups and organizes them to promote and develop their skills.

Another advantage of the functional structure is that people who are grouped together by common skills can supervise one another and control each other's behavior. We discussed in Chapter 3 how a hierarchy develops within each function to help the organization control its activities (see Figure 3.5). In addition to functional managers, peers in the same function can monitor and supervise one another and keep work activities on track. Peer supervision is especially important when work is complex and relies on cooperation; in such situations, supervision from above is very difficult.

Finally, people in a function who work closely with each other over extended time periods develop norms and values that allow them to become more effective at what they do. They become team members who are committed to organizational activities. This commitment may develop into a core competence of the organization.

Control Problems in a Functional Structure

All organizations are initially organized by function because the development of separate functions allows organizations to manage an increase in specialization and the division of labor most efficiently. As in Amazon.com, functional structure breeds core competences and increases an organization's ability to control its people and resources. However, as an organization continues to grow and differentiate, functional structure creates problems. Often the problems arise from the organization's success: As the organization's skills and abilities increase and the organization is able to produce better or more varied goods or services, the organization's ability to service the needs of its growing product line is strained. For example, it becomes increasingly difficult for sales and marketing to provide the in-depth attention that the launch of new products requires, so new products tend not to do well. Similarly, as more customers perceive value in what an organization creates, customer demand goes up. Increasing demand may strain the ability of manufacturing to produce products fast enough or in sufficient quantity. Moreover, costs start to rise as manufacturing is forced to increase production. In turn, the pressure of staying on top and beating the competition puts more pressure on R&D or engineering to further improve the quality or increase the sophistication of products.

The problem facing a successful organization is how to keep control of increasingly complex activities as it grows and differentiates. As it produces more and more products, becomes geographically diverse, or faces increasing competition for customers, control problems impede the organization's ability to coordinate activities.[2]

COMMUNICATION PROBLEMS. As more organizational functions develop, each with its own hierarchy, they become increasingly distant from one another. They develop different subunit orientations, which cause communication problems.[3] For example, sales thinks the organization's main problem is the need to satisfy customer demands quickly to increase revenues; manufacturing thinks the main problem is to simplify products to reduce costs; and R&D thinks the biggest problem is to increase a product's technical sophistication. As a result of such differences in perception, communication problems develop that reduce the level of coordination and mutual adjustment among functions and make it more difficult for the organization to respond to customer and market demands. Thus, as we discussed in Chapter 2, differentiation produces communication problems that companies try to solve by means of integrating mechanisms.

MEASUREMENT PROBLEMS. To exercise control over something, there has to be a way to measure it. Otherwise, there is no basis for evaluation. However, as organizations grow and the number and complexity of their functions, products, and services increase, the information needed to measure the contribution of any one functional group to overall profitability is often difficult to obtain. The reason for the difficulty is that the cost of each group's contribution to product development cannot be isolated. Because of the inability to measure each function's contribution, the organization may not be making the best use of its resources.

LOCATION PROBLEMS.   As a company grows, it may need to set up shop in different geographical regions in order to serve customer needs. Geographical spread can pose a control problem within a functional structure if centralized control at one geographical location does not allow the organization to handle manufacturing and sales and other support activities on a regional basis. An organization with more than one location has to develop an information system that can balance the need to centralize decision-making authority with the need to decentralize authority to regional operations. In fact, as Amazon.com has grown, it has established five main U.S. distribution centers in Delaware, Nevada, Georgia, Kansas, and Kentucky.

CUSTOMER PROBLEMS.   As the range and quality of an organization's goods and services increase, the kinds of customers who are attracted to the organization change. Servicing the needs of new kinds of customers and tailoring products to suit them are relatively difficult in a functional structure. Functions like production, marketing, and sales have little opportunity to specialize in the needs of a particular customer group; instead, they are responsible for servicing the complete product range. Thus, in an organization with a functional structure, the ability to identify and satisfy customer needs may fall short.

STRATEGIC PROBLEMS.   Top managers may spend so much time trying to find solutions to everyday coordination problems that they have no time to address the longer-term strategic problems facing the company. For example, they are likely to be so involved in solving communication and integration problems that they have no time to plan for future product development. As a result, the organization loses direction.

Reengineering Functional Structure to Solve Control Problems

Sometimes managers can solve the control problems associated with a functional structure, such as poor communication between functions, by redesigning the functional structure to increase integration between functions (see Figure 4.2). For example, one ongoing organizational challenge is how to manage the relationship between sales and marketing. Figure 4.2A shows the traditional relationship between them: Each is a separate function with its own hierarchy. Many organizations have recognized the need to alter this design and have combined those activities into one function. Figure 4.2B shows that modification. Such changes to the functional structure increase control by increasing integration between functions.

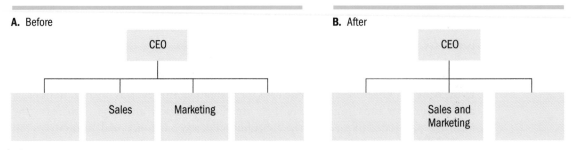

FIGURE 4.2   **Improving Integration in a Functional Structure by Combining Sales and Marketing**

Reengineering *The fundamental rethinking and radical redesign of business processes to achieve dramatic improvements in critical, contemporary measures of performance such as cost, quality, service, and speed.*

Recently, the term *reengineering* has been coined to refer to the process by which managers redesign how tasks are bundled into roles *and* functions to improve organizational effectiveness. In the words of Michael Hammer and J. Champy, who popularized the term, **reengineering** involves the fundamental rethinking and radical redesign of business processes to achieve dramatic improvements in critical, contemporary measures of performance such as cost, quality, service, and speed.[4] "Processes, not organizations, are the object of reengineering. Companies don't reengineer their sales or manufacturing departments; they reengineer the work the people in those departments do."[5]

As this definition suggests, an organization that undertakes reengineering must completely rethink how it goes about its business. Instead of focusing on an organization's *functions* in isolation from one another, managers make *business processes* the focus of attention. A business process is any activity, such as order processing, inventory control, or product design, that cuts across functional boundaries. It is the ability of people and groups to act in a *cross-functional way* that is the vital factor in determining how quickly goods and services are delivered to customers and in promoting high quality or low costs. Business processes involve activities *across functions*. Because reengineering focuses on business processes and not functions, an organization must rethink the way it approaches organizing its activities.

Organizations that take up reengineering deliberately ignore the existing arrangement of tasks, roles, and work activities. They start the reengineering process with the customer (not the product or service) and ask the question: "How can I reorganize the way we do our work, our business processes, to provide the best-quality, lowest-cost goods and services to the customer?" Frequently, when companies ask this question they realize that there are more effective ways of organizing their activities. For example, a business process that currently involves members of 10 different functions working sequentially to provide goods and services might be performed by one or a few people at a fraction of the cost after reengineering.

A good example of how to use reengineering to increase functional integration and increase control of activities comes from attempts to redesign the materials management function to improve its effectiveness (see Figure 4.3).[6] In the past, the three main components of materials management—purchasing (responsible for obtaining inputs), production control (responsible for using inputs most efficiently), and distribution (responsible for disposing of the finished product)—were typically in separate functions and had little to do with one another. Figure 4.3A shows the traditional functional design. The problem with the traditional design is that when all aspects of materials management are separate functions, coordinating their activities is difficult. Each function has its own hierarchy, and there are problems in both vertical and horizontal communication. The structure shown in Figure 4.3A makes it difficult to process information quickly in order to secure cost savings. Computerized production and warehousing, for example, require the careful coordination of activities, but the traditional design of materials management activities does not provide enough control for this to be achieved.

Realizing that this separation of activities has often slowed down production and raised costs, many organizations have moved to reengineer the materials management process. Today, most organizations put all three of the *functional* activities involved in the materials management *process* inside one function, as shown in Figure 4.3B. In the structure shown in Figure 4.3B, in contrast, one hierarchy of managers is responsible for all three aspects of materials management, and communication among those managers is easy because they are within the same function. Three guidelines for performing reengineering successfully are:[7]

FIGURE 4.3

Improving Integration in Functional Structure in Creating a Materials Management Function

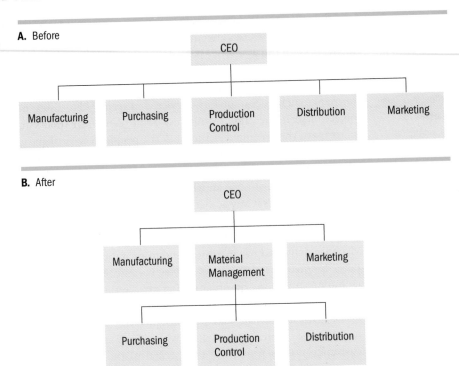

A. Before

B. After

- *Organize around outcomes, not tasks.* Where possible, organize work so that one person or one function can perform all the activities necessary to complete the process, thus avoiding the need for transfers (and integration) between functions.
- *Have those who use the output of the process perform the process.* Since the people who use the output of the process know best what they want, establish a system of rules and SOPs that will allow them to take control over it.
- *Decentralize decision making to the point at which the decision is made.* Allow the people on the spot to decide how best to respond to specific problems that arise.

The increasing popularity of reengineering suggests that improving integration between functions can solve control problems and increase organizational effectiveness. Later in the chapter we discuss some more examples of reengineering when we discuss product team structures, which are based on the use of cross-functional teams. However, many types of loss-of-control problems cannot be handled just by reengineering a functional structure. In many cases, an organization also needs to move to a more complex structure if it is to perform effectively as it grows and differentiates.

FROM FUNCTIONAL STRUCTURE TO DIVISIONAL STRUCTURE

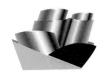

If an organization (1) limits itself to producing a small number of similar products, (2) produces those products in one or a few locations, and (3) sells them to only one general type of client or customer, a functional structure will be able to manage most of its control problems. As organizations grow, however, they are likely to produce more and more products, which may be very different from one another. For example, General Electric pro-

> ### Managerial Implications:
> ### Functional Structure
>
> 1. For an entrepreneur starting a small business, or for a manager of a work group or department, creating the correct division of labor within a function and between functions is a vital design task.
> 2. To ensure that the division of labor is correct, list the various functions that currently exist in your organization, and itemize the tasks they perform.
> 3. Draw a diagram of task relationships both within and between functions, and evaluate to what degree your organization is obtaining the advantages of the functional structure (such as the development of new or improved skills) or experiencing the disadvantages of the functional structure (such as lack of integration between functions).
> 4. Experiment with different ways of reengineering the design of the functional structure to increase effectiveness—for example, by transferring task responsibilities from one function to another or by eliminating unnecessary roles.

duces hundreds of different models of refrigerators, ranges, and washing machines; its NBC television studio produces hundreds of different kinds of television shows; and its financial services unit is involved in many different kinds of activities, from providing loans to providing insurance. Moreover, when an organization increases its production of goods and services, it usually does so at an increasing number of locations and for many different types of customers.

When organizations grow in these ways, what is needed is a structure that will increase the organization's control of its different subunits so that they can better meet product and customer needs. The move to a more complex structure is based on three design choices:

1. *Increasing vertical differentiation.* To regain control in a vertical direction, the organization needs to increase vertical differentiation. This typically involves (a) increasing the number of levels in the hierarchy; (b) deciding how much decision-making authority to centralize at the top of the organization; and (c) deciding how much to use rules, SOPs, and norms to standardize behavior and, hence, exert control over low-level employees.

2. *Increasing horizontal differentiation.* To regain control in a horizontal direction, the organization needs to increase horizontal differentiation. This involves overlaying a functional grouping with some other kind of subunit grouping—most often, self-contained product teams or product divisions that possess all the functional resources they need to meet their goals.

3. *Increasing integration.* To regain control both vertically and horizontally, the organization needs to increase integration between subunits. The higher the level of differentiation, the more complex are the integrating mechanisms that an organization needs in order to control its activities. Recall from Chapter 2 that complex integrating mechanisms include task forces, teams, and integrating roles. Organizations need to increase integration between subunits to increase their ability to coordinate activities and motivate employees.

The way those three design choices increase differentiation and integration is shown in Figure 4.4. The organization illustrated in Figure 4.4A has two levels in its hierarchy and

FIGURE 4.4

Differentiation and Integration: How Organizations Increase Control over Their Activities

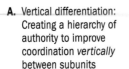

A. Vertical differentiation: Creating a hierarchy of authority to improve coordination *vertically* between subunits

Horizontal differentiation: Creating separate subunits to increase control *within* a subunit

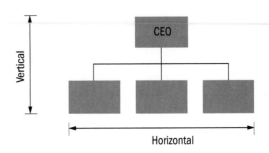

B. Integration: Creating integrating mechanisms, such as a task force, *laterally* to improve coordination between subunits

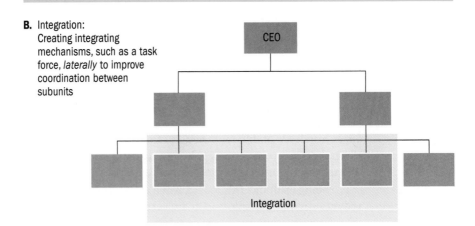

three subunits, and the only integrating mechanism that it uses is the hierarchy of authority. Figure 4.4B shows the effects of growth and differentiation. To manage its more complex activities, the organization has developed three levels in its hierarchy and has eight subunits. Because of the increase in differentiation, it needed a greater degree of integration and, thus, created a series of task forces to control activities between subunits.

All of the complex organizational structures discussed in the remainder of this chapter come into being as a result of managers' design decisions about vertical differentiation, horizontal differentiation, and integration. The move to a complex structure normally involves changes in all three characteristics.

Moving to a Divisional Structure

Divisional structure A structure in which functions are grouped together according to the specific demands of products, markets, or customers.

The structure that organizations most commonly adopt to solve the control problems that result from producing many different kinds of products in many different locations for many different types of clients is the divisional structure. A **divisional structure** groups functions according to the specific demands of products, markets, or customers. The goal behind the change to a divisional structure is to create smaller, more manageable subunits within an organization. The type of divisional structure managers select depends on the specific control problems to be solved. If the control problem is due to the number and complexity of products, the organization will divide its activities by product and use a *product structure*. If the control problem is due to the number of locations in which the organization produces and sells its products, the organization will divide its activities by region and use a *geographic structure*. If the control problem is due to the need to service a large number of different customer groups, the organization will divide its activities by customer group and use a *market structure*.

Next we discuss these types of divisional structure, which are designed to solve specific control problems. Each type of divisional structure has greater vertical and horizontal differentiation than a functional structure and employs more complex integrating mechanisms.

DIVISIONAL STRUCTURE I: THREE KINDS OF PRODUCT STRUCTURE

Product structure A divisional structure in which products (goods or services) are grouped into separate divisions, according to their similarities or differences.

As an organization increases the kinds of goods it manufactures or the services it provides, a functional structure becomes less effective at coordinating task activities. Imagine the coordination problems a furniture maker like Drexel Heritage would experience if it were to produce 100 styles of sofas, 100 styles of tables, and 50 styles of chairs in the same manufacturing unit. Adequately controlling value-creation activities would be impossible. To maintain effectiveness and simplify control problems as the range of its products increases, an organization is likely to group activities not only by function but also by type of product. To simplify control problems, a furniture maker might create three product groups: one for sofas, one for tables, and one for chairs. A **product structure** is a divisional structure in which products (goods or services) are grouped into separate divisions, according to their similarities or differences, to increase control.

An organization that decides to group activities by product must also decide how to coordinate its product divisions with support functions like research and development, marketing and sales, and accounting. In general, there are two choices that the organization can make: (1) centralize the support functions at the top of the organization so that one set of support functions services all the different product divisions, or (2) create multiple sets of support functions, one for each product division. In general, the decision that an organization makes reflects the degree of complexity of and difference between its products. An organization whose products are broadly similar and aimed at the same market will choose to centralize support services and use a *product division* structure. An organization whose products are very different and that operates in several different markets or industries will choose a *multidivisional structure*. An organization whose products are very complex technologically or whose characteristics change rapidly to suit changes in customer preferences will choose a *product team structure*.

Product Division Structure

Product division structure A divisional structure in which a centralized set of support functions services the needs of a number of different product lines.

A **product division structure** is a structure in which a centralized set of support functions services the needs of a number of different product lines. A product division structure is commonly used by food processors, furniture makers, and companies that make personal care products, paper products, or other products that are broadly similar and use the same set of support functions. Figure 4.5 shows a product division structure for a large food processor such as H. J. Heinz Company.

Because controlling the production of different foods within the same manufacturing unit proved to be very difficult and very expensive, Heinz created separate product divisions that produce frozen vegetables, frozen entrees, canned soups, and baked goods. This design decision increased horizontal differentiation within the organization, for each

FIGURE 4.5

Product Division Structure. Each product division manager (PDM) has responsibility for coordinating with each support function.

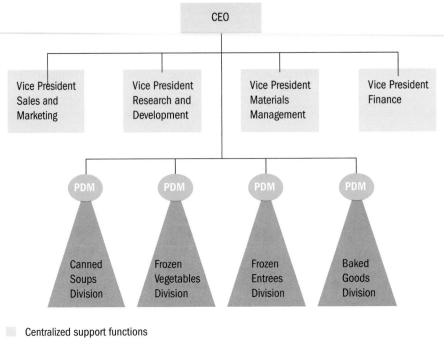

Centralized support functions

Divisions

division is a separate manufacturing unit that has its own hierarchy headed by a product division manager. Each product division manager (PDM on Figure 4.5) is responsible for his or her division's manufacturing and service activities. The product division manager is also responsible for coordinating manufacturing and service activities with the activities of central support functions like marketing and materials management. The role of product division manager adds a level to the organizational hierarchy and, thus, increases vertical differentiation.

Figure 4.5 shows that in a product division structure, support functions such as sales and marketing, research and development, materials management, and finance are centralized at the top of the organization. Each product division uses the services of the central support functions and does not have its own support functions. Creating separate support functions for each product division would be expensive and could be justified only if the needs of the different divisions were so great or so different that different functional specialists were required for each type of product.

Each support function is divided into product-oriented teams of functional specialists who focus on the needs of one particular product division. Figure 4.6 shows the grouping of the research and development function into four teams, each of which focuses on a separate product division. This arrangement allows each team to specialize and become expert in managing the needs of "its" product group. However, because all of the R&D teams belong to the same centralized function, they can share knowledge and information with each other. The R&D team that focuses on frozen vegetables can share discoveries about new methods for quick-freezing vegetables with the R&D team for frozen entrees. Such sharing of skills and resources increases a function's ability to create value across product divisions.

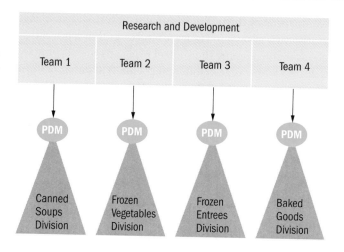

Multidivisional Structure

Multidivisional structure A structure in which support functions are placed in self-contained divisions.

As an organization begins to produce a wide range of complex products, such as many car or truck models, or to enter new industries and produce completely different products, such as cars and fast food, the product division structure cannot provide the control the organization needs. Managing complex and diverse value-creation activities requires a **multidivisional structure**, a structure in which support functions are placed in self-contained divisions. Figure 4.7 depicts the multidivisional structure used by a large consumer products company. Four divisions are illustrated, although a company such as GE, IBM, Johnson & Johnson, or Matsushita might have 150 different operating divisions.

FIGURE 4.7

Multidivisional Structure. Each division is independent and has its own set of support functions. The corporate headquarters staff oversees the activities of the divisional managers, and there are three levels of management: corporate, divisional, and functional.

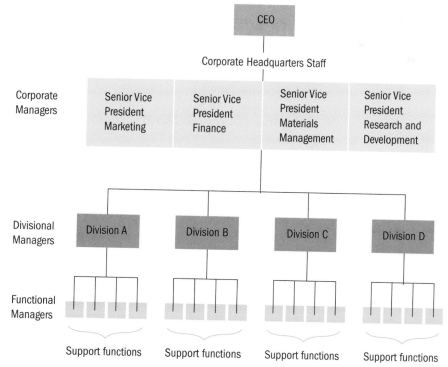

Self-contained division
A division that has its own set of support functions and controls its own value creation activities.

Corporate headquarters staff Corporate managers who are responsible for overseeing the activities of the divisional managers heading up the different divisions.

A comparison of the multidivisional structure shown in Figure 4.7 with the product division structure shown in Figure 4.5 indicates that a multidivisional structure has two innovations that overcome the control problems that a company experiences as it grows and produces a wide range of different products in different industries.[8] The first innovation is the independence of each division. In a multidivisional structure, each division is independent and self-contained (in a product division structure, the divisions share the services of a set of centralized functions). When divisions are **self-contained**, each division has its own set of support functions and controls its own value-creation activities. Each division needs its own set of support functions because it is impossible for one centralized set of support functions to service the needs of totally different products—such as automobiles, computers, and consumer electronics. As a result, horizontal differentiation increases.

The second innovation in a multidivisional structure is a new level of management, a **corporate headquarters staff**, composed of corporate managers who are responsible for overseeing the activities of the divisional managers heading up the different divisions.[9] The corporate headquarters staff is functionally organized, and one of the tasks of corporate managers is to coordinate the activities of the divisions. For example, managers at corporate headquarters can help the divisions share information and learn from one another so that divisional innovations can be quickly communicated throughout the organization. Recall from Chapter 2 that managers acting in that way are performing an *integrating role*.

Because corporate managers constitute another level in the hierarchy, there is an increase in vertical differentiation, which provides more control. The heads of the divisions (divisional managers) link corporate headquarters and the divisions. Compared to a functional or a product division structure, a multidivisional structure provides additional differentiation and integration, which facilitate the control of complex activities.

A corporate staff and self-contained divisions are two factors that distinguish a multidivisional structure from a product division structure. But there are other important differences between them. A product division structure can only be used to control the activities of a company that is operating in one business or industry. In contrast, a multidivisional structure is designed to allow a company to operate in many different businesses. Each division in a multidivisional structure is essentially a different business. Moreover, it is the responsibility of each divisional manager to design the divisional structure that best meets the needs of the products and customers of his or her division. Thus, one or more of the independent divisions within a multidivisional structure could use a product division structure or any other structure to coordinate its activities. This diversity is illustrated in Figure 4.8.

The multidivisional organization depicted in Figure 4.8 has three divisions, each with a different structure. The Automobile Products Division has a functional structure because it produces a small range of simple components. The Personal Computers Division has a product division structure. Each of its divisions develops a different kind of computer. The Consumer Electronics Division has a matrix structure (which we discuss later in the chapter) because it has to respond quickly to customer needs. At its peak, Beatrice International Foods, a food and consumer products company, had over a hundred different divisions. Both its Samsonite Division, which produced luggage, and its Hunt and Wesson Division, best known for tomato-based products, operated with product division structures; but the whole Beatrice empire was operated through a multidivisional structure.

Most Fortune 500 companies use a multidivisional structure because it allows them to grow and expand their operations while maintaining control over their activities. Only when an organization has a multidivisional structure does the management hierarchy expand to include three of the levels of management: corporate managers who oversee the

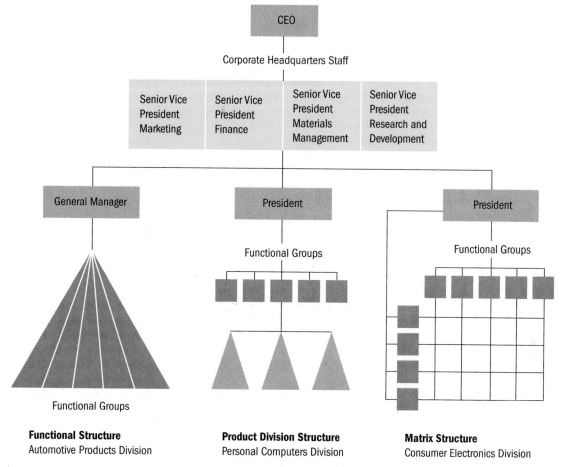

FIGURE 4.8   A Multidivisional Structure in Which Each Division Has a Different Structure

operations of *all* the divisions; divisional managers who run the individual divisions; and functional managers who are responsible for developing the organization's core competences. The story of General Motors' decision to move to a multidivisional structure illustrates many of the issues involved in operating a multidivisional structure and the difference between it and a product division structure.

As the GM story suggests, operating a multidivisional structure is no easy task. It is perhaps the biggest challenge that top management faces. Because the multidivisional structure is so widely used, we need to look closely at its advantages and disadvantages.

ADVANTAGES OF A MULTIDIVISIONAL STRUCTURE.   When the multidivisional structure is managed effectively, it provides a large organization with several advantages.[13]

Increased Organizational Effectiveness.   A division of labor generally increases organizational effectiveness. In a multidivisional structure there is a clear division of labor between corporate and divisional managers. Divisional managers are responsible for the day-to-day operations of their respective divisions and for tailoring divisional activities to the needs of customers. Corporate managers are responsible for long-term planning for the corporation as a whole and for tailoring the mission of the divisions to suit the goals of the whole organization.

ORGANIZATIONAL INSIGHT

4.1 CREATING GM'S MULTIDIVISIONAL STRUCTURE

William C. Durant formed the General Motors Company on September 16, 1908. Into it he brought about 25 different companies. Only four of them—Buick, Olds (now Oldsmobile), Oakland (now Pontiac), and Cadillac—survive as operating divisions today. Originally, each company retained its own operating identity, and the General Motors organization was simply a holding company, a central office surrounded by 25 satellites. When Alfred P. Sloan took over as president of GM in 1923, he inherited this collection of independently managed car companies, which made their own decisions, did their own research and development, and produced their own range of cars.

GM's principal competitor, the Ford Motor Car Company, was organized very differently. From the beginning, Henry Ford had emphasized the advantages of economies of scale and mass production and had designed a mechanistic structure to achieve them. He built a highly centralized hierarchy in which he had complete personal control over decision making. To reduce costs, Ford at first produced only one vehicle, the Model T, and gave enormous attention to finding improved ways of producing the car. Because of its organizational design, Ford's company was initially much more profitable than General Motors. The problem facing Sloan was to compete with Ford, not only in terms of product but in financial performance, too.

Confronted with Ford's success, Sloan must have been tempted to close several of GM's small operations and concentrate production in a few locations where the company could enjoy the benefits of fewer models and cost savings from economies of scale. For example, he could have adopted a product division structure, created three product divisions to manufacture three kinds of car, and centralized support functions such as marketing, research and development, and engineering to reduce costs. Sloan, however, recognized the importance of the diverse sets of research, design, and marketing skills and competencies present in the small car companies. He realized that there was a great risk of losing this diversity of talent if he combined all these skills into one centrally located research and design department. Moreover, if the same set of support functions, such as engineering and design, worked for all of GM's divisions, there was a danger that all GM cars would begin to look alike. Nevertheless, Sloan also recognized the advantages of centralized control in achieving economies of scale, controlling costs, and providing for the development of a strategic plan for the company as a whole, rather than for each company separately. So he searched for an organizational structure that would allow him to achieve all these objectives simultaneously, and he found his answer in the multidivisional structure. In 1920, he instituted this change, noting that General Motors, "needs to find a principle for coordination without losing the advantages of decentralization."[10]

Each of GM's different businesses was placed in a self-contained operating division with support services like sales, production, engineering, and finance. Each division became a profit center and was evaluated on its return on investment. Sloan was quite clear about the main advantage of linking decentralization to return on investment: It raised the visibility of each division's performance. And, Sloan observed, it (1) "increases the morale of the organization by placing each operation on its own foundation,…, assuming its own responsibility and contributing its share to the final result"; (2) "develops statistics correctly reflecting…. the true measure of efficiency"; and (3) "enables the corporation to direct the placing of additional capital where it will result in the greatest benefit to the corporation as a whole."[11]

Sloan recommended that transactions between divisions be set by a transfer pricing scheme based on cost plus some predetermined rate of return. However, to avoid protecting a high-cost internal supplier, he also recommended a number of steps involving analysis of the operations of outside competitors to determine the fair price. Sloan established a strong, professional, centralized headquarters management staff to perform such calculations. Corporate management's primary role was to audit divisional performance and to plan strategy for the total organization. Divisional managers were to be responsible for all product-related decisions.

In the 1980s, after fierce competition from the Japanese, General Motors took a hard look at its multidivisional structure. The duplication of research and development and engineering and the purchasing of inputs by each division independently were costing the company billions of extra dollars. In 1984, GM's five autonomous car divisions were combined into two groups: Chevrolet and Pontiac would concentrate on small cars; Buick, Oldsmobile, and Cadillac would focus on large cars.[12]

GM hoped that the reorganization would reduce costs and speed product development, but it was a disaster. With control of design and engineering more centralized at the group level, the cars of the different divisions started to look the same. Nobody could tell a Buick from a Cadillac or an Oldsmobile. Sales plummeted. Moreover, the reorganization did not speed decision making. It increased the number of levels in the hierarchy by introducing the group level into the organization. As a result, GM had 13 levels in its hierarchy as compared with Toyota, for example, which had just five. Once again the company was in trouble: Before the reorganization, it had been too decentralized; now it was too centralized. What to do?

Realizing its mistake, GM moved to return control over product design to the divisions while continuing to centralize high-cost functions like engineering and purchasing. This restructuring has had some success. Cadillac's management moved quickly to establish a new product identity and design new models. However, there is still a long way to go. Currently, GM is reducing the number of different models it produces and is contemplating the elimination of a division. What GM seems to need is fewer divisions and a flatter structure to reflect the realities of the new competitive marketplace.

Increased Control.   Corporate managers monitor the performance of divisional managers. The extra control provided by the corporate office can encourage the stronger pursuit of internal organizational efficiency by divisional managers. Knowing that they have to answer to corporate managers, divisional managers may curb their inclination to increase the size of their personal staffs and thus increase their status. They may also think twice before investing in products that increase their status but do little to promote corporate performance.

More generally, as the GM example suggests, the creation of self-contained divisions means that corporate managers can develop control systems to compare the performance of one division with the performance of another by measuring profitability or product development time. Consequently, corporate managers are in a good position to intervene and take selective action to correct inefficiencies when they arise.

Profitable Growth.   When each division is its own profit center—that is, when its individual profitability can be clearly evaluated—corporate headquarters can identify the divisions in which an investment of funds is likely to yield the greatest returns.[14] Thus, corporate executives can make better capital resource allocation decisions to promote corporate growth. At the same time, their role as monitor rather than as administrator means that they can manage a greater number of different businesses and activities. The multidivisional structure allows a company to grow without suffering from the problems of communication or information overload that can occur when the two roles are mixed, as they are in the functional structure.

Internal Labor Market. The most able divisional managers are promoted to become corporate managers. Thus, divisional managers have an incentive to perform well because superior performance could result in promotion to high office. A large divisional company possesses an internal labor market, which increases motivation for people at all levels to increase organizational effectiveness.

DISADVANTAGES OF A MULTIDIVISIONAL STRUCTURE. Like other structures, multidivisional structures are associated with certain problems. Although good management can control most of the problems, it cannot eliminate them.

Managing the Corporate-Divisional Relationship. The central management problem posed by a multidivisional structure is how much authority to centralize at the corporate level and how much authority to decentralize to the operating divisions. On the one hand, each division is closest to its particular operating environment and is in the best position to develop plans and objectives to increase its own effectiveness, so decentralization is a logical choice. On the other hand, headquarters' role is to adopt the long-term view and to tailor divisional activities to the needs of the whole organization, so centralization has advantages, too. The balance between the two has to be managed all the time. Too much centralization of authority can straitjacket the divisions and let headquarters take responsibility for decision making, and the result can be poor performance. General Motors' attempt to centralize decision making to reduce costs was a disaster because all GM cars started to look the same! Too much decentralization, however, can result in giving the divisions so much freedom that they slack off and fail to control their costs. The corporate-divisional relationship needs to be managed continually. Over time, as the operating environment changes, the decision about which activities to centralize and which to decentralize will change.

Coordination Problems Between Divisions. When a multidivisional structure is created, measures of effectiveness such as return on investment can be used to compare divisions' performance, and corporate headquarters can allocate capital to the divisions on the basis of their performance. One problem with this approach, however, is that divisions may begin to compete for resources, and the rivalry may prevent them from cooperating with each other. Such a rivalry can harm organizational performance when a company's effectiveness depends on the divisions' sharing of knowledge and information about innovations to enhance the performance of all divisions. It would be counterproductive, for example, if one of General Motors' divisions invented a new superefficient engine and refused to share the information with other divisions.

Transfer price The price at which one division sells a product or information about innovations to another division.

Transfer Pricing. Problems between divisions often revolve around the **transfer price**—the price at which one division sells a product or information about innovations to another division. To maximize its own return on investment, a division will want a high transfer price, but that will penalize the other division, which is, after all, part of the same organization. Thus, as each division pursues its own goals, coordination problems inside the organization can emerge. The role of the corporate center is to manage such problems, as Sloan of GM noted. It is very important that a multidivisional organization establish integrating mechanisms that enable managers from different divisions to cooperate. Mechanisms like integrating roles and integrating departments are very important in promoting cooperation. The corporate office itself is a type of *integrating department.*

Bureaucratic Costs.   Multidivisional structures are very expensive to operate. Each division has a full complement of support functions, including research and development. Thus, there is extensive duplication of activities within the organization. The cost of operating a multidivisional structure must constantly be evaluated, and if the benefits relative to the costs seem to be falling, the company should either move to reduce the number of divisions or find a way to reduce the costs of its support functions. It might be possible, for example, for an organization to change to a product division structure or to a product team structure (discussed later) and service the needs of its different products through one set of centralized support functions. When a company is operating in different businesses and producing very different products such as cars and fast food, however, such a restructuring is rarely possible.

Communication Problems.   Tall hierarchies tend to have communication problems, particularly the distortion of information. These problems are common in multidivisional structures because they tend to be the tallest of all the structures that organizations use. In them, the gap between the corporate center and the divisions is especially wide. A divisional manager may deliberately disguise falling performance in his or her division in order to receive larger capital allocations; and when a company has 200 divisions, such deception can be hard to detect. In addition, it may take so long for decisions to be made and transmitted down to the divisions that responses to competitors are too slow. The more centralized an organization is, the more of a problem communication will be.

Product Team Structure

In a product division structure, members of support functions such as marketing and R&D coordinate with the different divisions as their services are needed, but their main loyalty is to their function, *not* to the division. Increasingly, organizations are finding that the functional orientation of specialists is not in the organization's best interests because industry competition has become focused on the product and especially on the need to customize the product to suit customer needs. Moreover, increased competition has made it important to reduce the time needed to bring a product to market by speeding product development while reducing product development costs. One solution to this problem might be a multidivisional structure in which each division has its own set of support functions. But, as we just discussed, this structure is very expensive to operate, and communication problems between divisions can slow innovation and product development. Many companies, in their search for a new structure to solve these problems, have reengineered their divisional structures into a product team structure.

Product team structure
A divisional structure in which specialists from the support functions are combined into product development teams that specialize in the needs of a particular kind of product.

A product team structure is a cross between the product division structure, in which the support functions are centralized, and the multidivisional structure, in which each division has its own support functions. In a **product team structure**, specialists from the support functions are combined into product development teams that specialize in the needs of a particular kind of product. (See Figure 4.9.) Each team is, in effect, a self-contained division headed by a product team manager (PTM in Figure 4.9), who supervises all the operational activities associated with developing and manufacturing the product. The product teams focus on the needs of one product (or client) or a few related products, and they owe their allegiance not to their functions but to the product team they join. The

FIGURE 4.9

Product Team Structure. Each product team manager (PTM) supervises the activities associated with developing and manufacturing a product.

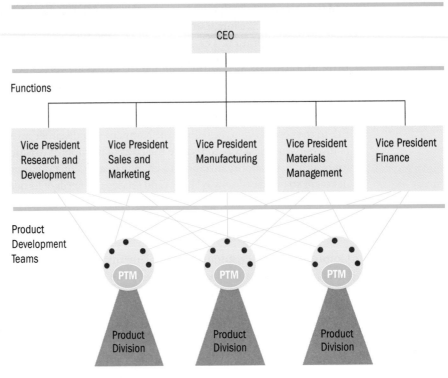

- Functional specialist
PTM   Product Team Manager

vice presidents of the functions, at the top of the organization, retain overall functional control, but decision-making authority for each product is decentralized to the team, and each team becomes responsible for the success of a project. Both Xerox and Hallmark Cards have found this approach to coordinating functions and products to be an effective way to develop new products quickly.

Throughout the 1980s, both Xerox and Hallmark experienced severe problems with their structures. Xerox simply could not match the speed at which Japanese competitors like Canon and Fuji were able to introduce new and better copying machines. So Xerox reengineered from a product division structure to a product team structure and created nine product teams around its major products—office document systems, copiers, and so on. Each team had most of the support functions it needed and was nearly a self-contained division. Xerox even went so far as to create and implement the idea of a "focused factory," in which each team is responsible for manufacturing its particular products.[15] This change in structure brought Xerox's product development time and product quality in line with its Japanese competitors.

Hallmark Cards had been using a functional structure to coordinate activities. A large number of artists, writers, lithographers, and designers working in different functional departments produced a huge array of greeting cards. The problems of coordinating the activities of 700 writers and artists across functional boundaries became so complex and difficult that it was taking Hallmark two years to develop a new card. To solve its product development problems, Hallmark reengineered to a product team structure. Artists and writers were formed into product teams around particular categories of greeting cards, such as Mother's Day cards, Christmas cards, and so on. With no differences in subunit orientation to impede the flow of information, mutual adjustment became much easier, and work was performed much more quickly. Product development time shrank from years to weeks.

A product team structure is more decentralized than a functional structure or a product division structure, and specialists in the various product teams are permitted to make on-the-spot decisions—something particularly important in service organizations. The grouping into self-contained divisions increases integration because each product team becomes responsible for all aspects of its operations. Through close collaboration, team members become intensely involved in all aspects of product development and in tailoring the product to its market. Moreover, the high level of integration produced by teams makes it possible to make decisions quickly to respond to changes in customer requirements. Chrysler was very successful in reengineering to a product team structure after experiencing problems with the more traditional product division structure.

ORGANIZATIONAL INSIGHT

4.2 IACOCCA PIONEERS CHRYSLER'S TEAM STRUCTURE

After Lee Iacocca took over the Chrysler Corporation, the company changed its approach to product development. Formerly, the company had come up with an idea for a new model of car, formed a product division to take control of the idea, and made the division managers responsible for obtaining the inputs of the various functions located at the top of the organization. The divisions had made their contributions sequentially; so, for example, design had the idea, engineering designed the prototype, purchasing and supply ordered the inputs, manufacturing made the vehicle, and marketing and sales sold it. Iacocca saw that this approach was very ineffective. Typically, Chrysler took seven or eight years to bring a new car to market, more than twice as long as the three years needed by Toyota or Nissan. Moreover, this system resulted in products with higher costs and lower quality than Japanese products. Why?

According to Iacocca, when a company like Chrysler produces a range of complex and technically sophisticated products, getting the different functional support groups to cooperate and coordinating their activities to arrive at the final product design is a nightmare. One function's activities may conflict with another function's activities, and no function learns anything from another because of the strength of their respective subunit orientations. The engineering department says, "Our aim is to develop an aerodynamic, lightweight car that gets good mileage, and we are not really interested in how difficult it is to assemble or how costly it is to build." The marketing department says, "You engineers and production folks had better control your costs so that we can price this car competitively."

Iacocca was determined to change this situation. As an experiment, he used what he called a "platform team" to develop the Dodge Viper, a luxury sports car. In a platform team, which is the same as a product development team, the functions are organized around the product. A team consists of product and manufacturing engineers, planners and buyers, designers, financial analysts, and marketing and sales people, and each team has sole responsibility for getting its car to the market. The team concept encourages different specialists to interact and, thus, speeds communication and allows problems to be solved quickly, creatively, and efficiently. Moreover, as the specialists begin to learn from one another, the quality of the product improves, and the pace of innovation quickens. The concept was wildly successful at Chrysler. "Team Viper" got the product to market in three years—a record time for the organization. Moreover, the car was a hit, and customers lined up to buy it.

With the success of the platform team concept established, Iacocca reengineered the rest of Chrysler's functionally organized product development operations into product-oriented platform teams. Chrysler now has four such teams: large car, small car, minivan, and Jeep/truck.[16] Three of these teams operate out of Chrysler's billion-dollar technology center in Auburn Hills, Michigan, where all the research and engineering resources that the teams need are readily available. Chrysler's new team-based structure resulted in a continuing trend toward lower costs, higher quality, and faster development time. Indeed, both Ford and GM imitated Chrysler's team approach to achieve these gains and the sales and profits of all these companies have soared throughout the 1990s.

Summary

The division of activities by product is the second most common method organizations use to group activities—after grouping them by function. Product structure increases horizontal differentiation and vertical differentiation and leads to the differentiation of managers into corporate-level, divisional-level, and functional-level managers. In recent years, many large companies have reengineered from one type of product structure to another in an attempt to save money or make better use of their functional resources. It is important for managers to continually evaluate how well their product structure is working because it has a direct impact on the effectiveness of their organization.

DIVISIONAL STRUCTURE II: GEOGRAPHIC STRUCTURE

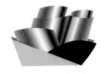

Geographic divisional structure *A divisional structure in which divisions are organized according to the requirements of the different locations in which an organization operates.*

Of the three types of product structure discussed earlier, the multidivisional structure is the one most often used by large organizations. It provides the extra control that is important when a company produces a wide array of complex products or services or enters new industries and needs to deal with different sets of stakeholders and competitive forces. However, when the control problems that companies experience are a function of geography, a **geographic divisional structure**, in which divisions are organized according to the requirements of the different locations in which an organization operates, is available.

As an organization grows, it may develop a national customer base. As it spreads into different regions of a country, it needs to adjust its structure to align its core competencies with the needs of customers in different geographic regions. A geographic structure allows some functions to be centralized at one headquarters location and others to be decentralized to a regional level. For example, the can manufacturer Crown Cork and Seal produces many of the cans used in canning soft drinks, personal hygiene products, vegetables, and fruits. Because cans are bulky objects that are expensive to transport, it makes sense to establish manufacturing plants in the different parts of the country where cans are most used. Also, there is a limit to how many cans the company can efficiently produce at one plant location; when economies of scale become exhausted at one location, it makes sense to establish another plant in a new location. Recognizing these limiting factors, Crown Cork and Seal operates several manufacturing plants throughout the United States and Canada. Each plant has its own purchasing, quality control, and sales departments. Research and development and engineering, however, are centralized at its headquarters location.

FIGURE 4.10

Geographic Structure

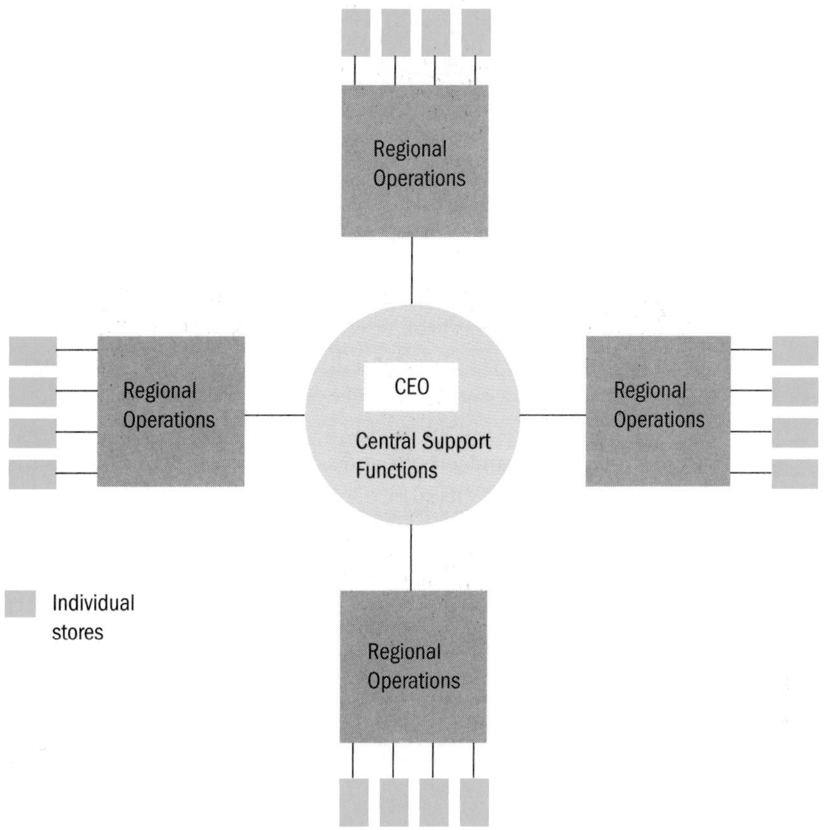

Neiman-Marcus, the specialty department store, also has a geographic structure, but for a different reason. When Neiman-Marcus operated only in Texas, it used a functional structure to coordinate activities. But as it opened stores at selected sites across the United States, it confronted a dilemma: how to respond to the customer needs of different regions while achieving the cost advantages of central purchasing. Neiman-Marcus's solution was to establish a geographic structure that groups stores by region (see Figure 4.10). Individual stores are under the direction of a regional office, which is responsible for coordinating the market needs of the stores in its region and for responding to specific product needs—for example, surfboards in Los Angeles and down parkas in Chicago. The regional office feeds information back to headquarters in Dallas, where centralized purchasing functions make decisions for the company as a whole.

Both Crown Cork and Seal and Neiman-Marcus superimposed a geographic grouping over their basic functional grouping, thereby increasing horizontal differentiation. The creation of a new level in the hierarchy—regional managers—and the decentralization of control to regional hierarchies also increased vertical differentiation. The regional hierarchies provide more control than is possible with one centralized hierarchy and, in the cases of Crown Cork and Seal and Neiman-Marcus, have increased effectiveness. The following Organizational Insight profiles Wal-Mart's geographic structure.

4.3 WAL-MART GOES NATIONAL, THEN GLOBAL

As we discussed in Organizational Insight 2.6, Wal-Mart has found the right balance between a mechanistic and an organic style of operating and has prospered. Its explosive growth continued through the 1990s, and in 1999 alone the company opened 125 supercenters, 50 discount stores, 50 to 60 international stores, and 10 Sam's clubs. Analysts estimate these new openings will add another $17 billion in sales.[17] The problem facing Wal-Mart has been to choose a structure complex enough to operate its growing empire and yet one that will allow it to maintain its mechanistic/organic balance. The structure it chose was a geographic structure (See Figure 4.11.)

Under the control of CEO David Glass and COO Lee Scott, Wal-Mart centralizes its materials management and sales and marketing activities at corporate headquarters. Then it divides its store operations into regions, including international operations, and gives its regional managers input in what mix of products should be sold in their regions to maximize sales. At the moment, Wal-Mart is working on replicating its materials management and marketing activities in Europe where it intends to become one, if not the biggest, retailer in the decade ahead. As it expands the global scope of its operations no doubt it will further subdivide its international division to meet its customers' needs.

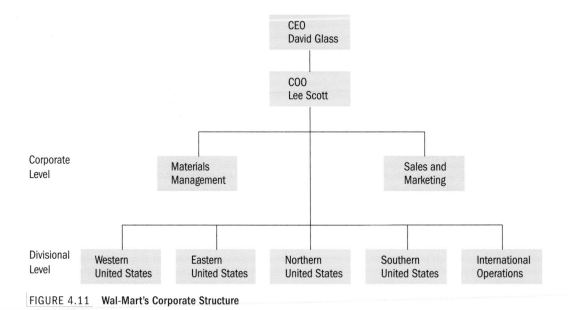

FIGURE 4.11   Wal-Mart's Corporate Structure

DIVISIONAL STRUCTURE III: MARKET STRUCTURE

The grouping of activities by product or geography makes the product or region the center of attention. In contrast, a market structure aligns functional skills and activities with the needs of different customer groups. Marketing, not manufacturing, becomes the basis on which the organization establishes divisions. Figure 4.12 shows a market structure designed to meet the needs of commercial, consumer, corporate, and government customers.

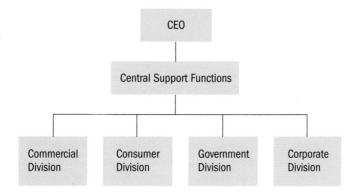

Each customer group has a different marketing focus, and the job of each group is to develop products to suit the needs of its specific customers. Each group makes use of centralized support functions. Engineering tailors products to suit the various needs of each group, and manufacturing follows each group's specifications. Because the market structure focuses the activities of the whole organization on the needs of the customer, the organization can quickly sense changes in its market and transfer skills and resources to satisfy the needs of this important stakeholder group. Mellon Bank had great success when it moved from a product structure to a market structure.

ORGANIZATIONAL INSIGHT

4.4 TAILORING STRUCTURE TO CUSTOMERS

Mellon Bank used to group activities around its principal products: certificates of deposit (CDs), insurance, mortgages, credit cards, and customer deposits. Each product division had its own manager and set of support services, and this arrangement created a lot of problems. Each product manager ignored the effect of his or her actions on the products of the other managers, and potential customer-attracting linkages among product divisions were ignored because the product, not the customer, was the focus of each product division. Although the product divisions may have been maximizing the sale of their own products, sales across product divisions were not as large as they could have been if there had been cooperation among divisions. The company was missing out on an important opportunity to increase sales by offering each customer an array of banking services.[18]

To provide customers with a full line of banking services, Mellon decided to reorganize to a market-based structure in which a range of financial products would be offered to targeted customer groups—for example, affluent customers (those with a portfolio of over $1 million) and corporate clients. The new structure enhanced communication among product divisions and made it easier for them to share information because they were not competing for each other's customers.

To provide a centralized support service for the customer groups, Mellon decided to centralize the support functions of advertising, market research, and computers. This change produced major benefits, saving $2 million from economies of scale. With the product focus, these support functions had often been in conflict with the product managers over the best use of the bank's resources. With the market focus, those conflicts disappeared, and the customer groups were able to coordinate their activities much more effectively.

1. As an organization grows, be sensitive to the need to change a functional structure to improve the control of organizational activities.
2. When the control problem is to manage the production of a wide range of products, consider using a form of divisional structure.
3. Use a product division structure if the organization's products are generally similar.
4. Move to a multidivisional structure if the organization produces a wide range of different or complex goods and services or operates in more than one business or industry.
5. When the control problem is to reduce product development time by increasing the integration among support functions, consider using a product team structure.
6. When the control problem is to customize products to the needs of customers in different geographic areas, consider using a geographic structure.
7. When the control problem is to coordinate the marketing of all of a company's products to several distinct groups of customers, use a market structure.
8. Always weigh the benefits that will arise from moving to a new structure (i.e., the control problems that will be solved) against the costs that will arise from moving to the new structure (i.e., the higher operating costs associated with managing a more complex structure) to see whether changing organizational structure will increase organizational effectiveness.

MATRIX STRUCTURE

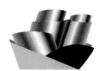

The search for better and faster ways to develop products and to respond to customer needs has led companies to adopt a matrix structure, a design that groups people and resources in two ways simultaneously: by function and by product.[19] A matrix structure is both similar to and different from a product team structure.

Before examining those differences, it is necessary to examine how a matrix structure works (see Figure 4.13). In the context of organizational design, a matrix is a rectangular grid that shows a *vertical* flow of *functional* responsibility and a *horizontal* flow of *product* responsibility. In Figure 4.13 the boxes at the top represent the grouping of tasks by function, and the boxes at the side represent the grouping of tasks by product. An organization with a matrix structure is differentiated into whatever functions the organization needs to achieve its goals. The organization itself is very flat, having minimal hierarchical levels within each function and decentralized authority. Functional employees report to the heads of their respective functions (usually, functional vice presidents) but do not work under their direct supervision. Instead, the work of functional personnel is determined primarily by membership in one of several cross-functional product teams under the leadership of a product manager. The members of the team are called **two-boss employees** because they report to two superiors: the product team manager and the functional manager. The defining feature of a matrix structure is the fact that team members have two superiors.

The team is both the basic building block of the matrix and the principal mechanism for coordination and integration. Role and authority relationships are deliberately vague because the underlying assumption of the matrix structure is that when team members are given responsibility without being given more authority, they are forced to cooperate to get the job done. The matrix, thus, relies on minimal vertical control from the formal hierarchy and maximal horizontal control from the use of integrating mechanisms—

Two-boss employees

Employees who report to two superiors: the product team manager and the functional manager.

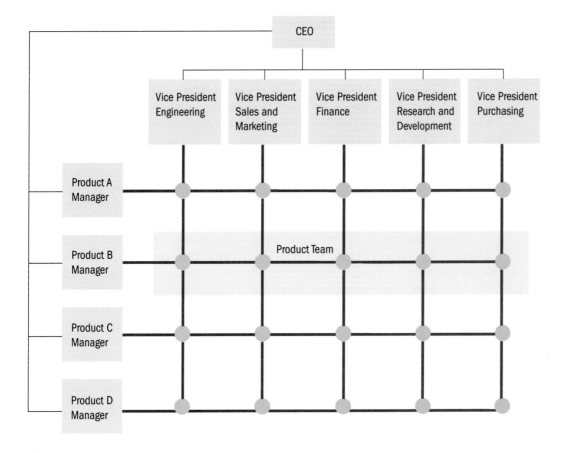

Two-boss employees

FIGURE 4.13   **Market Structure.** Team members are two-boss employees because they report to both the product team manager and the functional manager

teams—which promote mutual adjustment. Matrix structures are a type of organic structure (see Chapter 2).

Both matrix structure and product team structure make use of teams to coordinate activities, but they differ in two major respects. First, team members in a product team structure have only one boss: the product team manager. Team members in a matrix structure have two bosses—the product manager and the functional manager—and, thus, divided loyalty. They must juggle the conflicting demands of the function and the product. Second, in the matrix structure, team membership is not fixed. Team members move from team to team—to where their skills are most needed.

In theory, because of those two differences, the matrix structure should be more flexible than the product team structure, in which lines of authority and coordination are more stable. The matrix is deliberately designed to overcome differences in functional orientation and to force integration on its members. Does it work?

Advantages of a Matrix Structure

A matrix structure has four significant advantages over more traditional structures.[20] First, the use of cross-functional teams is designed to reduce functional barriers and overcome the problem of subunit orientation. With differentiation between functions kept to a minimum, integration becomes easier to achieve. In turn, the team structure facilitates adaptation and learning for the whole organization. The matrix's team system is designed to make the organization flexible and able to respond quickly to changing product and customer needs. Not surprisingly, matrix structures were first used in high-tech companies for which the ability to develop technologically advanced products quickly was the key to success. TRW Systems, one of the largest U.S. defense contractors, used the matrix system to develop the Atlas and Titan rockets, which were the heart of the U.S. space program in the 1960s.

A second advantage of the matrix structure is that it opens up communication between functional specialists and provides an opportunity for team members from different functions to learn from one another and develop their skills. Thus, matrix structure facilitates technological progress because the interactions of different specialists produce the innovations that give a company its core competences.

Third, the matrix enables an organization to maximize its use of skilled professionals, who move from product to product as needed. At the beginning of a project, for example, basic skills in R&D are needed, but after early innovation, the skills of engineers are needed to design and make the product. People move around the matrix to wherever they are most needed; team membership is constantly changing to suit the needs of the product.

Fourth, the dual functional and product focus promotes concern for both cost and quality. The primary goal of functional specialists is likely to be technical: producing the highest-quality, most innovative product possible (regardless of cost). In contrast, the primary goals of product managers are likely to concern cost and speed of development—doing whatever can be done given the amounts of time and money that are available. This built-in focus on both quality and cost keeps the team on track and keeps technical possibilities in line with commercial realities.

Disadvantages of a Matrix Structure

In theory, the principles underlying matrix structures seem logical. In practice, however, many problems arise.[21] To identify the sources of these problems, consider what is missing in a matrix.

A matrix lacks the advantages of bureaucratic structure (discussed in Chapter 3). With a flat hierarchy and minimal rules and SOPs, the matrix lacks a control structure that leads employees to develop stable expectations of one another. In theory, team members continually negotiate with one another about role responsibilities, and the resulting give-and-take makes the organization flexible. In practice, many people do not like the role ambiguity and role conflict that matrix structures can produce. For example, the functional boss, focused on quality, and the product boss, focused on cost, often have different expectations of the team members. The result is role conflict. Team members become unsure of what to do, and a structure designed to *promote* flexibility may actually *reduce* it if team members become afraid to assume responsibility.

The lack of a clearly defined hierarchy of authority can also lead to conflict between functions and product teams over the use of resources. In theory, product managers are supposed to buy the services of the functional specialists on the team (say, for example, the services of 10 engineers at $500 per day). In practice, however, cost and resource allocation become fuzzy as products exceed their budgets and specialists are unable to overcome technical obstacles. Power struggles emerge between product and functional managers, and politicking takes place to gain the support of top management.

As those examples show, matrix structures have to be carefully managed to retain their flexibility. They do not automatically produce the high level of coordination that is claimed of them, and people who work in a matrix often complain about high levels of stress and uncertainty.

Over time, people in a matrix structure are likely to experience a vacuum of authority and responsibility and move to create their own bureaucracy to provide themselves with some sense of structure and stability. Informal leaders emerge within teams. These people become increasingly recognized as experts or as great "team leaders." A status hierarchy emerges within teams. Team members often resist transfer to other teams in order to remain with their colleagues.

When top managers do not get the results they expect, they sometimes try to increase their control over the matrix and to increase their power over decision making. Slowly but surely, as people jockey for power and authority, a system that started out very flat and decentralized turns into a centralized, less flexible structure. The matrix becomes bureaucratized, and all the bureaucratic problems noted in Chapter 3 arise because every principle of bureaucracy is being improperly implemented. Digital Equipment Corporation offers an interesting insight into the way a matrix can hamper decision making and company performance.

ORGANIZATIONAL INSIGHT

4.5 DEC'S PROBLEMS WITH ITS MATRIX

Digital Equipment Corporation experienced increasing problems in the 1990s as its sales and profits plunged. In 1998, it was finally taken over by Compaq and has been integrated into Compaq's operations. Why did a company that was once one of the most powerful companies in the computer industry suffer such trauma? Analysts attribute a major part of its problem to the way DEC's founder and CEO, Kenneth Olsen, designed and managed the company's structure.

In the early days of the computer industry, companies had the time and opportunity to perfect a product's technical capabilities because product cycles were slow, and Olsen had created a matrix structure to manage DEC's new-product development. In that matrix, rival product teams worked side by side on different designs. When one superior design emerged, it was chosen for further development. The winning team's members became organizational heroes and rose quickly in the corporation, winning the right to direct future product teams and claim a large share of company resources. The other teams were disbanded so that their members could work on other products.

At first this system worked well and led to early successes. But then the speed of product development within the computer industry quickened as new competitors entered the market, and DEC lost ground. As DEC faltered, resources tightened, and the product teams began to compete with each other for scarce company resources, such as marketing and engineering support. Intense rivalries broke out between product teams. Members felt that their careers were in jeopardy because DEC rewarded only the winners.[22]

As a result of the competition for company resources and the competition between teams, the product teams did not pool their knowledge and expertise, and integration between functions declined. Thus, at DEC the matrix structure, whose claim to fame is its flexibility and its ability to utilize resources effectively, had an unintended effect: It resulted in inertia, infighting, slow product development, and victory for DEC's competitors in the new-product war. Clearly, DEC had not chosen a structure that made the best use of people's talents.[23]

Matrix structures need to be managed carefully if their advantages are to outweigh their disadvantages. However, matrix structures are not designed for use in normal, everyday, organizational situations. They are appropriate in situations in which a high level of coordination among functional experts is needed because the organization needs to respond quickly to changing conditions. Given the problems associated with managing a deliberately ambiguous matrix structure, many growing companies have chosen to overlay a functional structure or a product division structure with product teams rather than attempt to manage a full-fledged matrix.

The Multidivisional Matrix Structure

Multidivisional structures allow an organization to coordinate activities effectively but are difficult to manage. Communication and coordination problems arise simply because of the high degree of differentiation within a multidivisional structure. Consequently, a company with several divisions needs to be sure that it has sufficient integration mechanisms in place to handle its control needs. Sometimes the corporate center becomes very remote from divisional activities and is unable to play this important integrating role. When that happens, organizations sometimes introduce the matrix structure at the top of the organization and create a **multidivisional matrix structure**, a structure that provides for more integration between corporate and divisional managers and among divisional managers. Figure 4.14 depicts this structure.

Multidivisional matrix structure A structure that provides for more integration between corporate and divisional managers and between divisional managers.

As the figure shows, this structure allows senior vice presidents at the corporate center to send corporate-level specialists to each division to perform an in-depth analysis of the division's performance and to devise a functional action plan for all divisions. Divisional executives meet with corporate executives to trade knowledge and information and to coordinate divisional activities. The multidivisional matrix structure makes it much

FIGURE 4.14

Multidivisional Matrix Structure

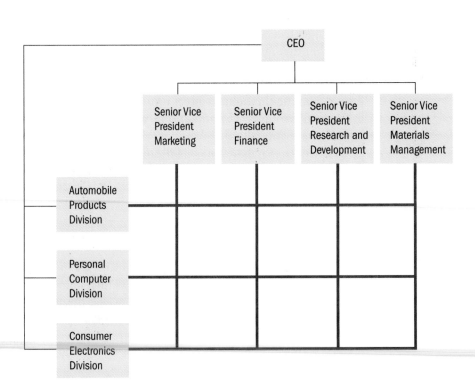

easier for top executives from the divisions and from the corporate center to cooperate and jointly coordinate organizational activities. Many large international companies that operate globally use this structure. However, a discussion of how to design an international organizational structure is left until Chapter 8.

Network Structure and the Boundaryless Organization

Network structure A cluster of different organizations whose actions are coordinated by contracts and agreements rather than through a formal hierarchy of authority.

Outsourcing The moving of a value-creation activity that was done inside an organization to the outside, where it is done by another company.

Recently, another innovation in organizational architecture has been sweeping through the United States: the use of network structures. A **network structure** is a cluster of different organizations whose actions are coordinated by contracts and agreements rather than through a formal hierarchy of authority.[24] Very often one organization takes the lead in creating the network as it searches for a way to increase effectiveness. For example, a clothing manufacturer may search for ways to produce and market clothes more cheaply. Rather than manufacturing the clothes in its own factories, the company decides to outsource its manufacturing to a low-cost Asian company; it also forms an agreement with a large Madison Avenue advertising agency to design and implement its sales campaign. **Outsourcing** is moving a value-creation activity that was done *inside* an organization to the *outside*, where it is done by another company.

Often network structures become very complex as a company forms agreements with a whole range of suppliers, manufacturers, and distributors to outsource many of the value creation activities involved in producing and marketing goods and services.[25] For example, Nike, the largest and most profitable sports shoe manufacturer in the world, has developed a very complex network structure to produce its shoes. At the center of the network is Nike's product design and research function located in Beaverton, Oregon, where Nike's designers pioneer new innovations in sports shoe design, such as the air pump and "Air Jordans." Almost all the other functional specialisms that Nike needs to produce and market its shoes have been outsourced to companies around the world! How does Nike manage the relationships among all the companies in its network? Principally through the use of modern information technology (discussed in depth in Chapter 10). Nike's designers use computer-aided design (CAD) to design shoes, and all new-product information, including manufacturing instructions, is stored electronically. When the designers have done their work, they relay all the blueprints for the new products electronically to Nike's network of suppliers and manufacturers in Southeast Asia.[26] For example, instructions for the design of a new sole may be sent to a supplier in Taiwan, and instructions for the leather uppers to a supplier in Malaysia. These suppliers produce the shoe parts, which are then sent for final assembly to a manufacturer in China with whom Nike has established an alliance. From China these shoes are shipped to distributors throughout the world and are marketed in each country by an organization with which Nike has formed a contract.

Advantages of Network Structures

Why does Nike use a network structure to control the value-creation process rather than perform all the functional activities itself? There are several advantages that Nike, and other organizations, can realize by using a network structure.

First, to the degree that an organization can find a network partner that can perform a specific functional activity reliably, and at a lower cost, production costs are reduced.[27] Almost all of Nike's manufacturing is done in Asia, for example, because wages in Southeast Asia are a fraction of what they are in the United States. Second, to the degree that an organization contracts with other organizations to perform specific value-creation activities, it avoids the high bureaucratic costs of operating a complex organizational structure. For example, the hierarchy can be kept as flat as possible and fewer managers are needed. Because Nike outsources many functional activities, for example, it is able to stay small and flexible. Control of the design process is decentralized to teams that are assigned to develop each of the new kinds of sports shoes for which Nike is known.

Third, a network structure allows an organization to act in an organic way. If the environment changes, for example, and new opportunities become apparent, an organization can quickly alter its network in response. For example, it can sever the links to companies whose services it no longer needs and develop new ones with companies that have the skills it needs. An organization that performed all of its own functional activities would take a longer time to respond to the changes taking place. Fourth, if any of its network partners fail to perform up to Nike's standards, they can be replaced with new partners. Finally, a very important reason for the development of networks has been that organizations gain access to low-cost foreign sources of inputs and functional expertise, something crucial in today's changing global environment.

Disadvantages of Network Structures

Although network structure has several advantages, it also has some drawbacks in certain situations. To see what these are, imagine a high-tech company racing to bring to market proprietary hardware and software faster than its competitors. How easy would it be to outsource the functional activities necessary to ensure that the hardware and software are compatible and bug-free? Not easy at all. Close interaction is needed between the hardware and software divisions, and among the various groups of hardware and software programmers responsible for designing the different parts of the system. A considerable level of mutual adjustment is needed to allow the groups to interact so that they can learn from one another and constantly improve the final product. Also, managers must be there to integrate the activities of the groups to make sure their activities mesh well. The coordination problems arising from having different companies perform different parts of the work process would be enormous. Moreover, there has to be considerable trust among the different groups so that they can share their ideas, something necessary for successful new-product development.

It is unlikely that a network structure would provide an organization with the ability to control such a complex value-creation process because managers would lack the means at their disposal to effectively coordinate and motivate the various network partners. First, it would be difficult to obtain the ongoing learning that builds core competences over time *inside* a company because separate companies have less incentive to make such an investment.[28] As a result, many opportunities to cut costs and increase quality would be lost. Second, if one of Nike's suppliers failed to perform well, Nike could easily replace it by forming a contract with another. But how easy is it to find reliable software companies who can both do the job and be trusted not to take proprietary information and give it to a company's competitors?

In general, the more complex the value-creation activities necessary to produce and market goods and services the more problems there are associated with using a network structure.[29] Like the other structures discussed in this chapter, network structures are appropriate in some situations and not in others. We look at more issues concerning network structures in Chapter 6.

The Boundaryless Organization

The ability of managers to develop a network structure to produce or provide the goods and services their customers want, rather than create a complex organizational structure to do so, has led many researchers and consultants to popularize the idea of the boundaryless organization. The boundaryless organization is composed of people who are linked by computers, faxes, computer-aided design systems, and video teleconferencing, and who may rarely or ever see one another face-to-face.[30] People come and go as their services are needed, much as in a matrix structure, but they are not formal members of an organization, just functional experts who form an alliance with an organization, fulfill their contractual obligations, and then move on to the next project.

The use of outsourcing and the development of network organization are increasing rapidly as organizations recognize the many opportunities they offer to reduce costs and increase flexibility. U.S. companies spent $100 billion on outsourcing in 1996, and companies like EDS, which manages the information systems of large organizations like Xerox and Kodak, are major beneficiaries of this new organizing approach. Clearly, managers have to carefully assess the relative benefits of having their own organization perform a functional activity or make a particular input versus forming an alliance with another organization to do so to increase organizational effectiveness. Designing organizational structure is becoming an increasingly complex management activity in today's complex world.

 SUMMARY

Designing organizational structure is a difficult and challenging task. Managers have to manage the vertical and horizontal dimensions of the structure continually and choose an appropriate allocation of authority and task responsibilities. As an organization grows and becomes more complex, changing its structure to respond to changing needs or contingencies becomes important.

Designing a structure that fits a company's needs is a large challenge. Each structure has advantages and disadvantages, and managers have to be ready and willing to redesign their organizations in order to obtain the advantages and anticipate and minimize the problems of whichever structure they choose. An organization that is in control of its structure has an important competitive advantage over one that is not.

Many organizations ignore the coordination problems inherent in the organizing process. Too often, an organization waits until it is already in trouble (in decline) before attempting to deal with coordination and motivation problems. The characteristics of the top-management team are very important in this regard because they determine how decisions get made and how top managers perceive the problems the organization is experiencing. Chapter 4 has made the following main points:

1. A functional structure is a design that groups people together because they have similar skills or use the same resources. Functional groups include finance, R&D, marketing, and engineering. All organizations begin as functional structures.

2. An organization needs to adopt a more complex structure when it starts to produce many products or when it confronts special needs, such as the need to produce new products quickly, to deal with different customer groups, or to handle growth into new regions.

3. The move to a more complex structure is based on three design choices: increasing vertical differentiation, increasing horizontal differentiation, and increasing integration.

4. Most organizations move from a functional structure to some kind of divisional structure: a product structure, a geographic structure, or a market structure.

5. There are three kinds of product structure: product division structure, multidivisional structure, and product team structure.

6. Product division structure is used when an organization produces broadly similar products that use the same set of support functions.

7. Multidivisional structures are available to organizations that are growing rapidly and producing a wide variety of products or are entering totally different kinds of industries. In a multidivisional structure, each product division is a self-contained division with the operating structure that best suits its needs. A central headquarters staff is responsible for coordinating the activities of the divisions in the organization. When a lot of coordination between divisions is required, a company can use a multidivisional matrix structure.

8. Product team structures put the focus on the product being produced. Teams of functional specialists are organized around the product to speed product development.

9. Geographic structures are used when organizations expand into new areas or begin to manufacture in many different locations.

10. Market structures are used when organizations wish to group activities to focus on the needs of distinct customer groups.

11. Matrix structures group activities by function and product. They are a special kind of structure that is available when an organization needs to deal with new or technically sophisticated products in rapidly changing markets.

12. Network structures are formed when an organization forms agreements or contracts with other organizations to perform specific functional value-creation activities.

DISCUSSION QUESTIONS

1. Grouping by function is the foundation of all types of organizational structure. Why?

2. As organizations grow and differentiate, what problems can arise with a functional structure?

3. How do the product division structure and the multidivisional structure differ?

4. Why might an organization prefer to use a product team structure rather than a matrix structure?

5. Under what conditions are the advantages of the matrix structure most likely to be realized?

6. What are the principal differences between a functional structure and a multidivisional structure? Why does a company change from a functional to a multidivisional structure?

7. What are the advantages and disadvantages associated with network structures?

ORGANIZATIONAL THEORY IN ACTION

PRACTICING ORGANIZATIONAL THEORY:
HOW TO REENGINEER AN ORGANIZATION

Form groups of three to five people and discuss the following scenario:

The IBM Credit Corporation is responsible for providing credit to customers who purchase IBM computers.[31] In the early 1990s, IBM's salespeople were complaining about how long it took—often seven days—for credit personnel to give them a decision about whether or not a potential customer was creditworthy. Customers didn't like the delay and often shopped around at other computer manufacturers while they were waiting, which often resulted in lost sales. IBM credit managers decided to look at the work system to see if they could speed up the credit-issuing process. What they found was that employees were organized as shown in the following figure. When a request came in, the applicant's credit was first checked by the credit department; then an interest rate for the deal was chosen by the pricing department; next the formal contracts were drawn up by the contracts department; and then the final documents were put together and sent to the salesperson responsible for the deal. IBM's managers decided that there must be a better way of doing the job and set out to find it.

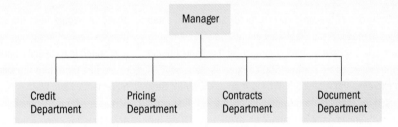

1. What structure is IBM using to manage the work process?
2. How would you reengineer the work process to reduce the time it takes to process a credit application?

MAKING THE CONNECTION #4

Find an example of a company that has changed its horizontal differentiation in some way. What did the company do? Why did it make the change? What does it hope to accomplish as a result of the change? To what structure has it changed?

Analyzing the Organization: Design Module #4

This module focuses on horizontal differentiation in your organization and on the structure the organization uses to coordinate its tasks and roles.

ASSIGNMENT

1. What kind of structure (e.g., functional, product division, multidivisional) does your organization have? Draw a diagram showing its structure, and identify the major subunits or divisions in the organization.

2. Why does the company use this kind of structure? Provide a brief account of the advantages and disadvantages associated with this structure for your organization.

3. Is your organization experiencing any particular problems in managing its activities? Can you suggest a more appropriate structure that your company might adopt to solve these problems?

4. How do the characteristics of the top managers in your organization affect organizational decision making?

5. What other issues pertaining to your organization's structure strike you as important?

Cases for Analysis:
STEIN & CO. MAKES A MAJOR CHANGE

Stein & Co. is one of the most successful full-service real estate companies in the Midwest. Employing about 250 real estate professionals, it is a relatively small company, yet its clients number among the largest of the Fortune 500 companies, such as AT&T, Federal Express, and Ameritech. Why is it so successful? Stein has focused its energies on providing its clients with first-class, personalized service as they embark on major real estate projects, such as acquiring land and building large-scale factory and office complexes.

In the early 1990s Richard Stein, the CEO, and Julia Stasch, president and COO, confronted a major problem, which paradoxically had been brought about by the company's very success: Its level of customer service was slipping because the organization had outgrown its current operating structure. Stein used a functional structure to organize its activities. Four main functions, including brokering and program management services, cooperated to provide the high level of service its customers had come to expect. However, in the early 1990s the number of its employees had increased rapidly, and it had attracted a growing range of clients. The increased complexity of its activities had led to major problems in coordinating the activities of its four functions across the widely different needs of its clients—the result of which was a fall in the level of customer service.

Stein and Stasch searched for a way to reorganize the company to make it easier for the employees in its various functions to service client needs. Their solution was to eliminate the four functional groups and replace them with 10 product teams composed of people from the various functional groups, who could provide each client group with the full-line specialized service best suited to its specific needs. Clients were assigned to whichever product team had the skills to best satisfy their particular requirements. Each team is headed by two team managers: a sales manager, who is responsible for looking outside the organization and attracting new clients, and an organization manager, whose task it is to control the ongoing operations of the team.

Stein and Stasch, who chair the top-level management committee composed of the team leaders, believe that their new structure has several advantages over the old functional structure. First, each team is now closer to its clients and is, thus, in a better position to provide high-quality service. Second, the team managers are in a better position to coordinate and monitor the activities of team members and reward them appropriately. Third, each team now operates as a separate profit center, which allows top managers to decide where to best place the company's resources to encourage continued growth and profitability. Stein and Stasch are convinced that they have in place a structure that will facilitate the development of long- term personal relationships with clients, something vital in today's highly competitive real estate market.

1. What steps did Stein and Stasch take to reengineer their company?

2. What factors might make reengineering difficult in practice?

Cases for Analysis:
A NEW CATERPILLAR EMERGES

A reputation for low-cost manufacturing combined with excellent distribution and after-sales service made Caterpillar one of the largest and most prosperous of all construction equipment companies. In 1982, however, it found itself under intense competition from Komatsu, Kubota, and Hitachi, Japan's biggest construction equipment manufacturers. By adopting the latest techniques in robotics, just-in-time inventory systems, and flexible manufacturing technology, these Japanese companies had obtained a large cost advantage over Caterpillar and could easily undercut its prices. As a result, Caterpillar's low-cost reputation was slipping, its market share was eroding, and the company was in trouble.

Recognizing the crisis, Caterpillar quickly moved to change its organizational structure. The prime mover of this restructuring was Donald V. Fites, who became chairman of Caterpillar in 1990. During his rise through Caterpillar's managerial hierarchy, Fites had spent much time in Japan. While there, he had noticed two characteristics of Japanese companies' organizational structures that did not exist in his company. First, Japanese companies relied heavily on teams of people from different functions for product development. Each team focused on only one product and paid exclusive attention to improving the quality and reducing the costs of that product. Second, Japanese companies were very decentralized in their approach to decision making; decisions about a product were made by the people most familiar with the product and its market, not by executives far removed in corporate headquarters. Fites saw that the combination of up-to-the-minute technology, cross-functional teams of workers empowered to make decisions about their product, and decentralized control was the ultimate source of the Japanese companies' competitive advantage. Once in control at Caterpillar, he quickly moved to institute Japanese-style organizational practices.

Fites introduced cross-functional teams into Caterpillar's product development process. Each product development team was given its own marketing staff, product designers, and manufacturing engineers, all of whom worked together to integrate their functional specialties. This structural change cut product development time in half. Next, he decentralized control over marketing from corporate headquarters to the regional level—in North America and globally—in order to speed Caterpillar's response to its customers. Manufacturing, too, experienced far-reaching changes. The company embarked on a billion-dollar plant-modernization program based on the use of computer-integrated flexible manufacturing systems by groups of employees in product teams. This new system helped boost productivity by 30 percent.[32]

The full extent of Fites's push to simultaneously exploit the advantages of product teams, decentralized decision making, and plant modernization was seen in 1990. Fites orchestrated a major structural reorganization of Caterpillar, changing it from a company organized on a functional basis to one organized by product divisions. Although Caterpillar continued to centralize research and development, purchasing, and some support services in four "service divisions," Fites created 14 product divisions, each of which is a profit center and each of which is required to satisfy a 15 percent return-on-assets target. Each product division has a Japanese-like product team structure in which cross-functional teams are responsible for all aspects of product performance.

Caterpillar's new decentralized structure contrasts sharply with the old structure, in which decisions were made at the top of the various functions and then fed down throughout the organization.[33] With its new structure in place, Caterpillar is poised to reap the fruits of its long and difficult reorganization and compete effectively in the global marketplace.

1. What were the problems with Caterpillar's old organizational structure?
2. How did Fites change Caterpillar's structure to improve its effectiveness?

REFERENCES

1. J. Child, *Organization: A Guide for Managers and Administrators* (New York: Harper and Row, 1977); R. Duncan, *"What Is the Right Organization Structure?"* *Organization Dynamics*, Winter 1979, pp. 59–80; J. R. Galbraith and R. K. Kazanjian, *Strategy Implementation: Structure, System, and Process*, 2nd ed. (St. Paul, MN: West, 1986).

2. O. E. Williamson, *Markets and Hierarchies: Analysis and Antitrust Implications* (New York: Free Press, 1975).
3. P. R. Lawrence and J. W. Lorsch, *Organization and Environment* (Boston: Graduate School of Business Administration, Harvard University, 1967).

4. M. Hammer and J. Champy, *Reengineering the Corporation* (New York: Harper Collins, 1993).

5. Ibid., p. 117.

6. J. G. Miller and P. Gilmour, "Materials Managers: Who Needs Them?" *Harvard Business Review*, July–August 1979, p. 57.

7. M. Hammer, "Reengineering Work: Don't Automate, Obliterate," *Harvard Business Review*, July–August 1990, pp. 104–112.

8. A. D. Chandler, *Strategy and Structure* (Cambridge, MA: MIT Press, 1962); Williamson, *Markets and Hierarchies*.

9. Chandler, *Strategy and Structure*; B. R. Scott, *Stages of Development* (Cambridge, MA: Harvard Business School, 1971).

10. A. P. Sloan, *My Years at General Motors* (Garden City, NY: Doubleday, 1946), p. 46.

11. Ibid., p. 50.

12. A. Taylor, III, "Can GM Remodel Itself?" *Fortune*, 13 January 1992, pp. 26–34; W. Hampton and J. Norman, "General Motors: What Went Wrong?" *Business Week*, 16 March 1987, pp. 102–110.

13. C. W. L. Hill and G. R. Jones, *Strategic Management*, 4th ed. (Boston: Houghton Mifflin, 1998); G. R. Jones and C. W. L. Hill, "Transaction Cost Analysis of Strategy-Structure Choice," *Strategic Management Journal*, 1988, vol. 9, pp. 159–172.

14. Sloan, *My Years at General Motors*.

15. T. Stewart, "The Search for the Organization of Tomorrow," *Fortune*, 18 May 1992, pp. 92–98.

16. J. Halliday, "Plymouth Drives Comeback Trail,' *Advertising Age*, 15 July 1996, p. 28.

17. M. Troy, "The Culture Remains the Constant," *Discount Store News*, 8 June 1999, pp. 59–98.

18. "Mellon: A Sweeter Mix," *Financial World*, 1 August 1995, p. 24.

19. S. M. Davis and P. R. Lawrence, *Matrix* (Reading, MA: Addison-Wesley, 1977); J. R. Galbraith, "Matrix Organization Designs: How to Combine Functional and Project Forms," *Business Horizons*, 1971, vol. 14, pp. 29–40.

20. L. R. Burns, "Matrix Management in Hospitals: Testing Theories of Matrix Structure and Development," *Administrative Science Quarterly*, 1989, vol. 34, pp. 349–368; Duncan, "What Is the Right Organization Structure?"

21. S. M. Davis and P. R. Lawrence, "Problems of Matrix Organization," *Harvard Business Review*, May–June 1978, pp. 131–142; E. W. Larson and D. H. Gobelli, "Matrix Management: Contradictions and Insight," *California Management Review*, Summer 1987, pp. 126–138.

22. "Through the Mill," *The Economist*, 10 October 1994, p. 76.

23. G. McWilliams, "Crunch Time at DEC," *Business Week*, 4 May 1992, pp. 30–33.

24. R. E. Miles and C. C. Snow, "Causes of Failure in Network Organizations," *California Management Review*, July 1992, pp. 53–72.

25. W. Baker, "The Network Organization in Theory and Practice." In N. Nohria and R. Eccles, eds., *Networks and Organizations* (Boston: Harvard Business School, 1992), pp. 397–429.

26. G. S. Capowski, "Designing a Corporate Identity," *Management Review*, June 1993, pp. 37–38.

27. J. Marcia, "Just Doing It," *Distribution*, January 1995, pp. 36–40.

28. R. A. Bettis, S. P. Bradley, and G. Hamel, "Outsourcing and Industrial Decline," *Academy of Management Executive*, February 1992, pp. 7–22.

29. C. C. Snow, R. E. Miles, and H. J. Coleman, Jr., "Managing 21st Century Network Organizations," *Organizational Dynamics*, Winter 1992, pp. 5–20.

30. J. Fulk and G. Desanctis, "Electronic Communication and Changing Organizational Forms," *Organizational Science*, 1995, vol. 6, pp. 337–349.

31. Case is adapted from information in M. Hammer and J. Champy, *Reengineering the Organization*.

32. T. E. Benson, "Caterpillar Wakes Up," *Industry Week*, 20 May 1991, pp. 33–37; K. Kelly, A. Bernstein, and R. Neff, "Caterpillar's Don Fites: Why He Didn't Blink," *Business Week*, 10 August 1992, pp. 56–57.

33. "Upgrade for Caterpillar," *Fleet Equipment*, 1996, vol. 22, p. 71.

C h a p t e r   5

MANAGING ORGANIZATIONAL
CULTURE and ETHICS

In this chapter, the hard-to-define concept of organizational culture is examined. First, culture is discussed in terms of the values and norms that give an organization its competitive advantage, influence its members' behavior, determine how its members interpret the environment, and bond its members to the organization. Then the way in which individuals learn culture both formally (i.e., the way an organization intends them to learn it) and informally (i.e., by seeing what goes on in the organization) is discussed. To understand how an organization's culture, like its structure, can be designed or managed, four factors that account for cultural differences among organizations are examined: (1) the characteristics of people within the organization, (2) organizational ethics, (3) the property rights system used by the organization, and (4) organizational structure. Finally, an important aspect of organizational culture—organizational ethics and corporate social responsibility—is focused on in detail.

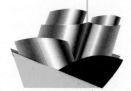

WHAT IS ORGANIZATIONAL CULTURE?

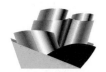

Organizational culture
The set of shared values and norms that controls organizational members' interactions with each other and with people outside the organization.
Values *General criteria, standards, or guiding principles that people use to determine which types of behaviors, events, situations, and outcomes are desirable or undesirable.*
Terminal value *A desired end state or outcome that people seek to achieve.*
Instrumental value *A desired mode or pattern behavior.*

Previous chapters have discussed how the most important function of organizational structure is to control—that is, coordinate and motivate—people within an organization. In Chapter 1, we defined **organizational culture** as the set of shared values and norms that controls organizational members' interactions with each other and with suppliers, customers, and other people outside the organization. Just as an organization's structure can be used to achieve competitive advantage and promote stakeholder interests, an organization's culture can be used to increase organizational effectiveness.[1] This is because organizational culture controls the way members make decisions, the way they interpret and manage the organization's environment, what they do with information, and how they behave.[2] Culture, thus, affects an organization's competitive position.

What are organizational values, and how do they affect behavior? **Values** are general criteria, standards, or guiding principles that people use to determine which types of behaviors, events, situations, and outcomes are desirable or undesirable. There are two kinds of values: terminal and instrumental values (see Figure 5.1).[3] A **terminal value** is a desired end state or outcome that people seek to achieve. Organizations might adopt any of the following as terminal values, that is, as guiding principles: excellence, responsibility, reliability, profitability, innovativeness, economy, morality, quality. Large insurance companies, for example, may value excellence, but their terminal values are often stability and predictability because the company must be there to pay off policyholders' claims. An **instrumental value** is a desired mode of behavior. Modes of behavior that organizations advocate include working hard, respecting traditions and authority, being conservative and cautious, being frugal, being creative and courageous, being honest, taking risks, and maintaining high standards.

An organization's culture, thus, consists of the end states that the organization seeks to achieve (its *terminal values*) and the modes of behavior the organization encourages (its *instrumental values*). Ideally, instrumental values help the organization to achieve its terminal goals. For example, a computer company whose culture emphasizes the terminal value of innovativeness may attain this outcome through the instrumental values of work-

FIGURE 5.1

Terminal and Instrumental Values in an Organization's Culture

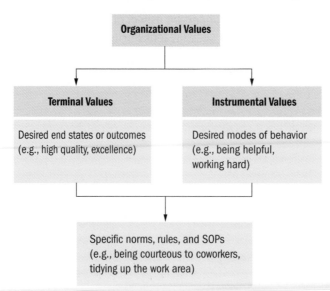

ing hard, being creative, and taking risks. That combination of terminal and instrumental values leads to an entrepreneurial culture. Similarly, a computer company that desires stability and predictability may emphasize caution and obedience to authority. The result will be a conservative culture.

Terminal values are reflected in an organization's mission statement and official goals, which tell organization members and other stakeholders that the company values excellence and has high ethical standards. So that members understand instrumental values—that is, the modes of behavior that they are expected to follow as they pursue desired end states—an organization develops specific norms, rules, and standard operating procedures (SOPs) that embody its instrumental values. In Chapter 2, we defined **norms** as standards or styles of behavior that are considered acceptable or typical for a group of people. The specific norms of being courteous and keeping the work area clean, for example, will develop in an organization whose instrumental values include being helpful and working hard.

Many of the most powerful and crucial values of an organization are not written down. They exist only in the shared norms, beliefs, assumptions, and ways of thinking and acting that people within an organization use to relate to each other and to outsiders and to analyze and deal with problems facing the organization. Members learn from each other how to interpret and respond to various situations in ways that are consistent with the organization's accepted values. Eventually, members choose and follow appropriate values without even realizing that they are making a choice. Over time, they internalize the organization's values and the specific rules, norms, and SOPs that govern behavior; that is, organizational values become part of members' mind-set—peoples' own values systems—and affect their interpretation of a situation.[4]

Values and norms work in a subtle fashion yet have a powerful effect on behavior.[5] To get a feel for the effect of organizational values, consider how differences in behavior at Southwest Airlines and Value Line reflect differences in values.

The terminal and instrumental values that Kelleher and Buttner developed to manage their organizations produced very different responses in their employees. The cultural values at Southwest led employees to perceive that they were appreciated by the organization and that the organization wanted to reward behavior that supported its goals. The cultural values at Value Line alienated employees, reduced commitment and loyalty, and increased employee turnover.

Organizational culture is based on relatively enduring values embodied in organizational norms, rules, SOPs, and goals. People in the organization draw on these cultural values in their actions and decisions and when dealing with ambiguity and uncertainty inside and outside the organization.[7] The values in an organization's culture are important shapers of members' behavior and responses to situations, and they increase the reliability of members' behavior.[8] In this context, *reliability* does not necessarily mean consistently obedient or passive behavior; it may also mean consistently innovative or creative behavior.[9]

Cultural values are also important facilitators of mutual adjustment in an organization. When shared cultural values provide a common reference point, employees do not need to spend much time establishing rapport and overcoming differences in their perceptions of events. Cultural values can smooth interactions among organizational members. People who share an organization's values may come to identify strongly with the organization, and feelings of self-worth may flow from their membership in it.[10] Employees of Southwest Airlines, for example, seem to value greatly their membership in the organization and are committed to it.

Norms *Standards or styles of behavior that are considered acceptable or typical for a group of people.*

ORGANIZATIONAL INSIGHT

5.1 A TALE OF TWO CULTURES

In an attempt to give Southwest Airlines a competitive advantage based on low-cost, high-quality service, CEO Herbert Kelleher has developed terminal and instrumental values that make Southwest's culture the envy of its competitors. Southwest managers and employees alike are committed to the success of the organization and do all they can to help one another and to provide customers with excellent service (a terminal value). Four times a year, Southwest managers work as baggage handlers, ticket agents, and flight attendants so that they get a feel for the problems facing other employees. An informal norm makes it possible for employees to gather with Kelleher every Friday at noon in the company's Dallas parking lot for a company cookout.

Kelleher keeps the organization as flat and informal as possible, and managers encourage employees to be creative and to develop rules and norms to solve their own problems. To please customers, for example, employees dress up on special days like Halloween and Valentine's Day and wear "fun uniforms" every Friday. In addition, they try to develop innovative ways to improve customer service and satisfaction. All employees participate in a bonus system that bases rewards on company performance, and employees own over 18 percent of the airline's stock. The entrance hall at company headquarters at Love Field in Dallas is full of plaques earned by employees for their outstanding performance. Everybody in the organization cooperates to achieve Southwest's goal of providing low-cost, high-quality service. And the culture of excellence that Southwest created seems to be working to its advantage. Southwest increased its operating routes and profits every year in the 1990s and is one of the most profitable airlines flying today.

Contrast Southwest's CEO and culture with that of Value Line, Inc. Jean Buttner, publisher of the Value Line Investment Survey, has fashioned a culture that the company's employees apparently hate and that no one envies. In her attempt to reduce costs and improve efficiency, she has created instrumental values of frugality and economy that are poisoning employees' attitudes toward the organization. Employees must sign in by 9:00 A.M. every day and sign out when leaving. If they fake their arrival or departure time, they face dismissal. Because at Value Line messy desks are considered signs of unproductivity, Buttner requires department managers to file a "clean surfaces report" every day, certifying that employees have tidied their desks.[6] She keeps salary increases as small as possible and has kept the company's bonus plan and health plan under tight rein.

How have these values paid off? Many highly trained, professional workers have left Value Line because of the hostile atmosphere produced by these "economical" values and by work rules that devalue employees. This turnover has generated discontent among the company's customers. So bad have feelings between employees and Buttner become that employees reportedly put up a notice on their bulletin board criticizing Buttner's management style and suggesting that the company could use some new leadership. Buttner's response to this message from a significant stakeholder group was to remove the bulletin board. Clearly, at Value Line there is no culture of cooperation between managers and employees.

HOW IS AN ORGANIZATION'S CULTURE TRANSMITTED TO ITS MEMBERS?

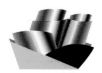

The ability of an organization's culture to motivate employees and increase organizational effectiveness is directly related to the way in which members learn the organization's values. Organizational members learn pivotal values from an organization's formal socialization practices and from the stories, ceremonies, and organizational language that develop informally as an organization's culture matures.

Socialization and Socialization Tactics

Newcomers to an organization must learn the values and norms that guide existing members' behavior and decision making.[11] Can they work from 10:00 A.M.. TO 7:00 P.M. instead of from 8:00 A.M. TO 5:00 P.M.? Can they challenge their peers' and superiors' views of a situation, or should they simply stand and listen? Newcomers are outsiders, and only when they have learned and internalized the organization's values and act in accordance with its rules and norms will longtime members accept them as insiders.

To learn an organization's culture, newcomers must obtain information about cultural values. They can learn values indirectly by observing how existing members behave and inferring what behaviors are appropriate and inappropriate. From the organization's perspective, however, the indirect method is risky because newcomers might observe and learn habits that are *not* acceptable to the organization. From the organization's perspective, the most effective way for newcomers to learn appropriate values is through **socialization**, which, as we saw in Chapter 2, is the process by which members learn and internalize the norms of an organization's culture.

Socialization The process by which members learn and internalize the values and norms of an organization's culture.

Role orientation The characteristic way in which newcomers respond to a situation.

Van Mannen and Schein developed a model of socialization that suggests how organizations can structure the socialization experience so that newcomers learn the values that the organization wants them to learn. In turn, these values influence the role orientation that the newcomers adopt.[12] **Role orientation** is the characteristic way in which newcomers respond to a situation: Do they react passively and obediently to commands and orders? Are they creative and innovative in searching for solutions to problems?

Van Mannen and Schein identified 12 socialization tactics that influence a newcomer's role orientation (see Table 5.1). The use of different sets of these tactics leads to two different role orientations: institutionalized and individualized. An *institutionalized role orientation* results when individuals are taught to respond to a new context in the same way that existing organizational members respond to it. An institutionalized orientation encourages obedience and conformity to rules and norms. An *individualized role orientation* results when individuals are allowed and encouraged to be creative and to experiment with changing norms and values so that an organization can better achieve its values.[13] The following list contrasts the tactics used to socialize newcomers to an institutionalized orientation with those tactics used to develop an individualized orientation.

1. *Collective vs. Individual.* Collective tactics provide newcomers with common learning experiences designed to produce a standardized response to a situation. With individual tactics, each newcomer's learning experiences are unique, and newcomers can learn new, appropriate responses for each situation.
2. *Formal vs. Informal.* Formal tactics segregate newcomers from existing organizational members during the learning process. With informal tactics, newcomers learn on the job as members of a team.

TABLE 5.1	
How Socialization Tactics Shape Employees' Role Orientation	
Tactics That Lead to an Institutionalized Orientation	Tactics That Lead to an Individualized Orientation
Collective	Individual
Formal	Informal
Sequential	Random
Fixed	Variable
Serial	Disjunctive
Divestiture	Investiture

3. *Sequential vs. Random.* Sequential tactics provide newcomers with explicit information about the sequence in which they will perform new activities or occupy new roles as they advance in an organization. With random tactics, training is based on the interests and needs of individual newcomers because there is no set sequence to the newcomers' progress in the organization.

4. *Fixed vs. Variable.* Fixed tactics give newcomers precise knowledge of the timetable associated with completing each stage in the learning process. Variable tactics provide no information about when newcomers will reach a certain stage in the learning process; once again, training depends on the needs and interests of the individual.

5. *Serial vs. Disjunctive.* When serial tactics are employed, existing organizational members act as role models and mentors for newcomers. Disjunctive processes require newcomers to figure out and develop their own way of behaving; they are not told what to do.

6. *Divestiture vs. Investiture.* With divestiture, newcomers receive negative social support—that is, they are ignored or taunted—and existing organizational members withhold support until newcomers learn the ropes and conform to established norms. With investiture, newcomers immediately receive positive social support from other organizational members and are encouraged to be themselves.

When organizations combine these tactics as suggested in Table 5.1, there is some evidence that they can influence an individual's role orientation.[14] Military-style socialization, for example, leads to an extremely institutionalized orientation. New soldiers are placed in platoons with other new recruits (*collective*); are segregated from existing organizational members (*formal*); go through preestablished drills and learning experiences (*sequential*); know exactly how long this will take them and what they have to do (*fixed*); have superior officers who are their role models (*serial*); and are treated with zero respect and tolerance until they have learned their duties and "gotten with the program" (*divestiture*). As a result, new recruits develop an institutionalized role orientation in which obedience and conformity to organizational norms and values are the signs of success. New members who cannot or will not perform according to these norms and values leave (or are asked to leave), so that by the end of the socialization process the people who stay are clones of existing organizational members.

No organization controls its members to the extent that the military does, but other organizations do use similar practices to socialize their members. Arthur Andersen, a large accounting and consulting firm, has a very institutionalized program. Recruits are carefully selected for employment because they already possess the values that Arthur Andersen wants—for example, they appear to be hardworking, cautious, or creative. After they are hired, all new recruits attend a six-week course at a training center outside Chicago, where they are indoctrinated as a group into Arthur Andersen's way of doing business. In formal eight-hour-a-day classes, existing organizational members serve as role models and tell newcomers what will be expected of them. Newcomers also learn informally over meals and during recreation what it means to be working for Arthur Andersen. By the end of this socialization process, they have learned the values of the organization and the rules and norms that govern the way they are expected to behave when they represent Andersen's clients.

Should an organization encourage an institutionalized role orientation in which newcomers accept the status quo and passively accept and perform their jobs? Or should an organization encourage an individualized role orientation in which newcomers are allowed to develop creative and innovative responses to the jobs that the organization requires of them? The answer to this question depends on the organization's mission. Arthur Andersen wants to standardize the way its employees perform auditing activities. The firm's credibility and reputation with clients depend on its integrity, so it wants to have control over what its employees do. Thus, it needs to adopt a strong socialization program that will reinforce its cultural values.

The danger of institutionalized socialization lies in the sameness it may produce among members of an organization. If all employees have been socialized to share the same way of looking at the world, how will the organization be able to change and adapt when that world changes? When confronted with changes in the organizational environment (e.g., a new product, a new competitor, or a change in customer demands), employees indoctrinated into old values will be unable to develop new values that might allow them to innovate. As a result, they—and, thus, the organization—cannot adapt and respond to the new conditions.

An organization whose mission is to provide innovative products for customers should encourage informal, random experiences from which individuals working on the job gain information as they need it. By all accounts, many of the new Internet companies such as Yahoo!, Amazon.com, and eBay rely on individualized socialization tactics and allow members to develop skills in areas that capitalize on their skills and interests.[15] These companies take this approach because their effectiveness (unlike Arthur Andersen's) depends not on standardizing individual behavior but on innovation and the ability of members to come up with new and improved solutions to Internet software problems. Thus, an organization's socialization practices not only help members learn the organization's cultural values and the rules and norms that govern behavior but also support the organization's mission.

Stories, Ceremonies, and Organizational Language

The cultural values of an organization are often evident in the stories, ceremonies, and language found in the organization.[16] At Southwest Airlines, for example, employees wearing costumes on Halloween, the Friday cookouts with CEO Kelleher, and managers periodically working with employees to perform the basic organizational jobs all reinforce and communicate the company's culture to its members.

Organizations use several types of ceremonial rites to communicate cultural norms and values (see Table 5.2).[17] *Rites of passage* mark an individual's entry to, promotion in, and

TABLE 5.2		
Organizational Rites		
Type of Rite	**Example of Rite**	**Purpose of Rite**
Rite of passage	Induction and basic training	Learn and internalize norms and values
Rite of integration	Office Christmas party	Build common norms and values
Rite of enhancement	Presentation of annual award	Motivate commitment to norms and values

departure from the organization. The socialization programs used by the army and by Arthur Andersen are rites of passage; so too are the ways in which an organization grooms people for promotion or retirement. *Rites of integration*, such as shared announcements of organizational success, office parties, and company cookouts, build and reinforce common bonds between organizational members. *Rites of enhancement*, such as awards dinners, newspaper releases, and employee promotions, publicly recognize and reward employees' contributions. Triad Systems uses its annual trade show to integrate and enhance its organizational culture.

ORGANIZATIONAL INSIGHT

5.2 TRIAD SYSTEMS BUILDS A CULTURE BASED ON SUCCESS

Triad Systems Corporation, a computer company based in Livermore, California, has annual sales of over $250 million. Each year it holds a trade show in which all its major divisions and many of its suppliers are represented. At the annual show managers give out awards to recognize employees for excellent service. With much hoopla the Grindstone Award is given to "individuals who most consistently demonstrate initiative, focus, dedication, and persistence"; the Innovator Award to those who "conceive and carry out innovative ideas"; and the Busting the Boundaries Award to "those who work most effectively across departmental and divisional boundaries to accomplish their work."[18] Each year, over 700 of Triad's 1,500 employees win awards.

The goal of Triad's trade show and awards ceremony is to develop organizational folklore to support its work teams and build a productive culture. Triad believes that giving praise and recognition builds a community of employees who share similar values and will jointly strive for organizational success. Also, providing members with organizational experiences in common promotes the development, across functional groups, of a common corporate language that bonds people together and allows them to better coordinate their activities. So far, Triad has been very successful with its approach. It has received a national award for quality, and its sales have exceeded its forecasts in every quarter to date.

Organizational stories and the language of an organization are important media for communicating culture. Stories (whether fact or fiction) about organizational heroes and villains, such as Herb Kelleher and Jean Buttner, provide important clues about cultural values and norms. Such stories can reveal the kinds of behaviors that the organization values and the kinds of practices on which the organization frowns. Studying stories and language can reveal the values that guide behavior.[19] because language is the principal medium of communication in organizations, the characteristic phrases that frame and describe events provide important clues about norms and values. For example, if any manager in IBM's old laptop-computer division used the phrase "I nonconcur" to disagree with a proposed plan of action, the plan was abandoned because achieving consensus used to be an important instrumental value at IBM. After divisions were given the authority to control their own activities, however, the language changed. A manager who tried to "nonconcur" was told by other managers, "We no longer recognize that phrase," indicating that the division had adopted new terminal values that made old instrumental values obsolete.

The concept of organizational language encompasses not only spoken language but how people dress, the offices they occupy, the company cars they drive, and how they formally address one another. In Microsoft and some other organizations casual dress is the norm, but in IBM and Arthur Andersen—to name just two—only conservative suits are acceptable and even on "dress-down" days it is clear just what kind of informal attire is suitable.

Many organizations have technical languages that facilitate mutual adjustment among organizational members.[20] At 3M, inside entrepreneurs have to emphasize the relationship between their product and 3M's terminal values in order to push ideas through the product development committee. Because many 3M products are flat, ignoring compact discs, Post-it notepads, floppy disks, paper, and transparencies, the quality of flatness embodies 3M's terminal values, and "flatness" is often a winning theme in 3M's corporate language. At Microsoft, employees have developed a shorthand language of technical software phrases to describe communication problems. Technical languages are used by the military, by sports teams, in hospitals, and in many other specialized work contexts. Like socialization practices, organizational language, ceremonies, and stories help people learn the ropes and the organization's cultural values.

Finally, organizational symbols often convey an organization's cultural values to its members and to others outside the organization. In some organizations, for example, the size of peoples' offices, their location on the third floor or the thirty-third floor, and the luxury with which they are equipped are symbols that convey images about the values in an organization's culture. Is the organization hierarchical and status-conscious, for example, or are informal, participative work relationships encouraged? In General Motors, the executive suite on the top floor of its Detroit headquarters is isolated from the rest of the building and open only to top GM executives. A private corridor and stairway link top managers' offices, and a private elevator connects to their heated parking garage. Sometimes the very design of the building itself is a symbol of an organization's values. For example, the Walt Disney Company hired famed Japanese architect Arata Isozaki to design the Team Disney Building, which houses Disney's "imagineering unit" in Orlando, Florida. This building's contemporary and unusual design featuring unusual shapes and bright colors conveys the importance of imagination and creativity to the Walt Disney Company and to the people who work in it.

Managerial Implications: Analyzing Organizational Culture

1. Study the culture of your organization, and identify the terminal and instrumental values on which it is based in order to assess how they affect organizational behavior.
2. Assess whether the goals, norms, and rules of your organization are effectively transmitting the values of the organizational culture to members. Identify areas for improvement.
3. Examine the methods your organization uses to socialize new members. Assess whether these socialization practices are effective in helping newcomers learn the organization's culture. Recommend ways to improve the process.
4. Try to develop organizational ceremonies to help employees learn cultural values, to enhance employee commitment, and to bond employees to the organization.

WHERE DOES ORGANIZATIONAL CULTURE COME FROM?

Now that you have seen what organizational culture is and how members learn and become part of an organization's culture, some difficult questions can be addressed: Where does organizational culture come from? Why do different companies have different cultures? Why might a culture that for many years helped an organization pursue its corporate mission suddenly harm the organization? Can culture be managed?

Organizational culture develops from the interaction of four factors: the personal and professional characteristics of people within the organization, organizational ethics, the property rights that the organization gives to employees, and the structure of the organization (see Figure 5.2). The interaction of these factors produces different cultures in different organizations and causes changes in culture over time. The way in which people's personal characteristics shapes culture is discussed first.

FIGURE 5.2

Where an Organization's Culture Comes From

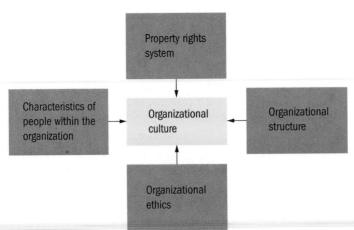

Characteristics of People Within the Organization

The ultimate source of organizational culture is the people who make up the organization. If you want to know why cultures differ, look at their members. Organizations A, B, and C develop distinctly different cultures because they attract, select, and retain people who have different values, personalities, and ethics.[21] People may be attracted to an organization whose values match theirs; similarly, an organization selects people who share its values. Over time, people who do not fit in leave. The result is that people inside the organization become more and more similar, the values of the organization become more and more parochial, and the culture becomes more and more distinct from that of similar organizations.

The founder of an organization has a substantial influence on the organization's initial culture because of his or her personal values and beliefs.[22] Founders set the scene for the later development of a culture because they not only establish the new organization's values but also hire its first members. Presumably, the people selected by the founder have values and interests similar to the founder's.[23] Over time, members buy into the founder's vision and perpetuate the founder's values in the organization.[24]

American Online and Prudential Insurance Company provide good illustrations of the important role the founder plays in establishing organizational culture. At American Online, CEO Steve Chase has pioneered an entrepreneurial culture based on instrumental values of creativity and hard work. At Prudential, John Dryden pioneered the notion that an insurance company should be operated in the interests of its policyholders, and the terminal value of customer satisfaction gave rise to a philanthropic, caring culture at Prudential. The type of culture that pervades an organization, however, is not always good for the organization, as the story of the way Procter & Gamble's culture has developed over time illustrates.

ORGANIZATIONAL INSIGHT

5.3 A NEW CEO TRIES TO CHANGE PROCTER & GAMBLE'S CULTURE

Procter & Gamble (P&G), the well-known soap and detergent company, is widely recognized as having one of the most distinct and insular corporate cultures in the United States. Although it does try to recruit people from diverse backgrounds, once they join the company, they encounter such a strong and homogeneous set of organizational values and norms that they begin to sound alike, think alike, and even look alike, at least so say the company's critics. Is this a good or a bad thing?

According to P&G's new CEO, Durk I. Jager, who took control of the company in 1999, it is a bad thing. As a part of his attempt to learn about P&G, Jager took a world tour of the company's facilities. He came to the conclusion that P&G's values and norms that emphasize consensus, obedience to the hierarchy, respect for authority, and participative decision making were causing a bureaucratic nightmare. He believed that P&G's managers were spending over 50 percent of their time working on "non–value-added" work such as memo writing and group meetings rather than in innovating new products and marketing strategies. In Japan, one worker complained to him that all he did was to write and rewrite management charts.[25]

Jager's goal? To break up the stodgy culture that has caused slow decision making and disappointing sales growth and to install a new entrepreneurial spirit in the company. He wants P&G's manager to take risks. In 1999, he started to change the company's culture. He fired 15,000 employees or 13 percent of P&G's workforce; he transferred thousands more to new jobs and linked managers' pay directly to their and to P&G's performance. After shaking up P&G's workforce, he then announced that in future, "stretch, innovation, and speed" would be the company's new terminal and instrumental values and that rewards and promotion would come not from conformity but from demonstrating the ability to break out of the mold and increase value.[26] Analysts are waiting to see if the changes he has made will increase bottom-line performance or whether P&G's old culture will be too strong to overcome.

As this story illustrates, an important implication of the view that people create the organizational culture is that as organizational members become similar over time, their ability to respond to changes in the environment may lessen.[27] This situation explains in part why organizations experience inertia in their decision making and why they may be slow to respond to change, as we saw at P&G. Some people argue that an organization can guard against inertia and stagnation by deliberately selecting as members people who share different beliefs and values. An organization that does this guards against groupthink and can better adapt to changes in the environment. In Chapter 12, we will discuss in depth how factors such as the background or skills of top-management teams, for example, may improve decision making and organizational learning. The "people make the place" view of organizational culture explains how an organization develops the shared cultural values that become such a powerful tool, and it implies that the culture of an organization can be changed by changing the people who control and lead it.[28]

Organizational Ethics

Many cultural values derive from the personality and beliefs of the founder and the top-management team and are in a sense out of the control of the organization. These values are what they are because of who the founder and top managers are. Microsoft founder Bill Gates is a workaholic who often works 18 hours a day. His terminal values for Microsoft are excellence, innovation, and high quality, and the instrumental values he advocates are hard work, creativity, and high standards. Gates expects his employees to put in long workdays because he requires this level of commitment from himself, and he expects them to do everything they can to promote innovation and quality because this is what he does. Employees who do not buy into these values leave Microsoft, and those who remain are pressured by organizational norms to stay on the job after the normal workday is over and to go out of their way to help others and take on new tasks that will help the organization. Cultural values at Microsoft are out of the organization's control because they are based on who Gates is.

An organization can, however, consciously and purposefully develop some cultural values to control members' behavior. Ethical values fall into this category. **Organizational ethics** are the moral values, beliefs, and rules that establish the appropriate way for organizational stakeholders to deal with one another and with the organization's environment. (See Figure 5.3.)

In developing cultural values, top management must constantly make choices about the right or appropriate thing to do. IBM or Sears, for example, might wonder whether it

Organizational ethics
The moral values, beliefs, and rules that establish the appropriate way for organizational stakeholders to deal with one another and with the organization's environment.

FIGURE 5.3

Factors Influencing the Development of Organizational Ethics

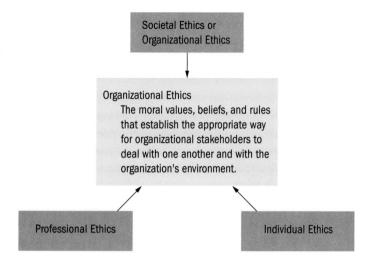

should develop procedural guidelines for giving advance notice to employees and middle managers about impending layoffs or store closings. Traditionally, companies have been reluctant to do so because they fear employee hostility and apathy. In 1993 General Motors had to decide whether to recall some trucks because of an unprotected gas tank that could cause harm or injury to passengers. Similarly, a company has to decide whether to allow its managers to pay bribes to government officials in foreign countries where such payoffs are an illegal yet accepted way of doing business. In such situations managers deciding on a course of action have to balance the interests of the organization against the interests of other stakeholder groups.[29]

To make these decisions, managers rely on ethical instrumental values embodied in the organization's culture.[30] Such values outline the right and wrong ways to behave in a situation in which an action may help one person or stakeholder group but hurt another.[31] Ethical values, and the rules and norms that they embody, are an inseparable part of an organization's culture because they help shape the values that members use to manage situations and make decisions.

Organizational ethics evolve through negotiation, compromise, and bargaining between stakeholders. Ethical rules can also evolve from conflict and competition, in which the ability of one stakeholder group to impose its solution on another decides which ethical rules will be followed. For example, employees might pressure management to improve working conditions or to warn them of impending layoffs, and shareholders might demand that top management not invest capital in countries that practice racism, violate human rights, or employ children in factories under conditions close to slavery.[32] Levi Strauss, for example, terminated 30 contracts with overseas suppliers that flouted basic human rights and failed to meet acceptable health and safety standards for their employees.

In some instances, organizational ethics become so commonplace that they become law, and behavior that once was just questionable on ethical grounds becomes illegal. The employment of children in U.S. factories, for example, was made illegal only after human rights pioneers lobbied Congress to outlaw the practice.

Organizational ethics are a product of societal, professional, and individual ethics.[33]

SOCIETAL ETHICS.   The ethics of the society in which an organization exists are important determinants of organizational ethics. Societal ethics are the moral values formalized in a society's legal system, in its customs and practices, and in the unwritten norms and values that people follow in their daily lives. Most people automatically follow the ethical norms and values of the society in which they live because they have internalized them and made them their own.[34] When societal ethics are codified into law (rules), an organization is legally required to follow all the laws and to deal with stakeholders in a legal way.

One of top management's main responsibilities is to ensure that organizational members obey the law. Indeed, in certain situations top managers can be held accountable for the conduct of their subordinates. One of the main ways in which top managers can ensure the legality of organizational behavior is to create an organizational culture that instills ethical instrumental values so that members reflexively deal with stakeholders in an ethical manner. While some companies, such as Johnson & Johnson and Merck, are well known for their ethical cultures, many organizations do act illegally, immorally, and unethically and take few steps to develop ethical values for their employees to follow. The management team that used to be in control at Beech-Nut put personal interests before customers' health and above the law.

ORGANIZATIONAL INSIGHT

5.4 APPLE JUICE OR SUGAR WATER?

In the early 1980s Beech-Nut, a maker of baby foods, was in financial trouble as it strived to compete with Gerber Products, the market leader. Threatened with the failure of the company if costs could not be lowered, Beech-Nut entered into an agreement with a low-cost supplier of apple juice concentrate. The agreement was supposed to save the company over $250,000 annually at a time when every dollar counted. Soon one of Beech-Nut's research and development specialists became concerned about the quality of the concentrate. He believed that it was not made from apples alone but contained large quantities of corn syrup, cane sugar, and malic acid. He brought this information to the attention of top managers at Beech-Nut, but they were obsessed with the need to keep costs down and chose to ignore it. The company continued to produce and sell its product as pure apple juice.

Eventually, investigators from the U.S. Food and Drug Administration (FDA), acting on other information, confronted Beech-Nut with evidence that the concentrate was adulterated. The top managers issued denials and quickly shipped the remaining stock of apple juice to the market before their inventory could be seized.

The research and development specialist who had questioned the purity of the apple juice had resigned from Beech-Nut, but he decided to blow the whistle on the company. He told the FDA that Beech-Nut's top management had known of the problem with the concentrate and had acted to maximize company profits rather than to inform customers about the additives in the apple juice. In 1987, the company pleaded guilty to charges that it had deliberately sold adulterated juice and was fined over $2 million. Its top managers were also found guilty and were sentenced to prison terms (which were eventually overturned on a technicality). Consumer trust in Beech-Nut products plummeted, as did the value of Beech-Nut stock. The company was eventually sold to Ralston Purina, which completely revamped it and its management and promoted strict new ethical values to establish a new culture in the organization.[35]

PROFESSIONAL ETHICS.   Professional ethics are the moral values that a group of similarly trained people develop to control their performance of a task or their use of resources.[36] People internalize the rules and values of their professional culture just as they do those of their society, and they reflexively adhere to professional rules and values when deciding how to behave.[37] Some organizations have many groups of professional employees—nurses, lawyers, researchers, doctors, and accountants—whose behavior is governed by professional ethics. These ethics help shape the organization's culture and determine the values members use in their dealings with other stakeholders. Medical ethics, for example, control doctors' and nurses' performance of their tasks and, thus, help establish the culture of a hospital. Professional ethics prevent doctors from performing unnecessary medical procedures and encourage them to act in the patient's best interest, not their own. Similarly, at companies like Merck and Johnson & Johnson, professional ethics induce scientists and technicians to behave ethically when preparing and presenting the results of their research.

Most professional groups can enforce the ethical standards of their profession. Doctors and lawyers, for example, can be banned from practicing their profession if they violate professional rules.

INDIVIDUAL ETHICS.   Individual ethics are the personal moral values that individuals use to structure their interactions with other people. In many instances, personal ethics mirror societal ethics and originate in law. But personal ethics are also the result of an individual's upbringing and may stem from family, friends, or membership in a church or some other social organization. Behaviors that one person finds unethical may be considered ethical by someone else. As long as the behaviors in question are not illegal, individuals may agree to disagree about their ethical beliefs. They may also try to impose their beliefs on others or try to make their ethical beliefs into law. When personal ethics conflict with law, a person may be subject to legal sanction.

Because personal ethics influence how a person will act in an organization, an organization's culture is strongly affected by the people who are in a position to establish its ethical values. As we saw earlier, the founder of an organization plays a particularly important role in establishing ethical norms and values.

Property Rights

Property rights *The rights that an organization gives to its members to receive and use organizational resources.*

The values in an organization's culture reflect the ethics of individuals in the organization, of professional groups, and of the society in which the organization exists. The values in an organization's culture also stem from how the organization distributes **property rights**—the rights that an organization gives to its members to receive and use organizational resources.[38] Property rights define the rights and responsibilities of each inside stakeholder group and cause the development of different norms, values, and attitudes toward the organization. Table 5.3 identifies some of the property rights commonly given to managers and the workforce.

Shareholders have the strongest property rights of all stakeholder groups because they own the resources of the company and share in its profits. Top managers often have strong property rights because they are given large amounts of organizational resources, such as high salaries, the rights to large stock options, or golden parachutes, which guarantee them large sums of money if they are fired when their company is taken over. Top managers' rights to use organizational resources are reflected in their authority to make decisions and control organizational resources. Managers are usually given strong rights

TABLE 5.3

Common Property Rights Given to Managers and the Workforce

Managers' Rights	Workforce Rights
Golden parachutes	Notification of layoffs
Stock options	Severance payments
Large salaries	Lifetime employment
Control over organizational resouces	Long-term employment
Decision making	Pension and benefits
	Employee stock ownership plans
	Participation in decision making

because if they do not share in the value that the organization creates, they are unlikely to be motivated to work hard on behalf of the organization and its other stakeholders.

An organization's workforce may be given strong property rights, such as a guarantee of lifetime employment and involvement in an employee stock ownership plan (ESOP) or in a profit-sharing plan. Most workers, however, are not given very strong property rights. Few are given lifetime employment or involved in ESOPs, though they may be guaranteed long-term employment or be eligible for bonuses. Often workers' property rights are simply the wages they earn and the health and pension benefits they receive. Workers' rights to use organizational resources are reflected in their responsibilities in the level of control they have over their tasks.

The distribution of property rights has a direct effect on the instrumental values that shape employee behavior and motivate organizational members.[39] We saw how Jean Buttner's attempt to limit Value Line employees' benefits and reduce their rights to receive and use resources resulted in hostility and high turnover. We also saw how Herbert Kelleher, by establishing a companywide stock option system and by encouraging employees to use organizational resources to find better ways of serving customers, fostered commitment and loyalty at Southwest Airlines.

The distribution of property rights to different stakeholders determines (1) how effective an organization is and (2) the culture that emerges in the organization. How different property rights systems promote the development of different cultures is evident in the story of what occurred after General Motors' acquisition of Electronic Data Systems.

As that account illustrates, the distribution of property rights influences not only expectations about how people should behave but also the values people use in their dealings with other stakeholders. Managers accustomed to one property rights system will find it hard to function in another. GM managers were used to a conservative, cautious culture that did not reward innovation (in this case, potentially cost-saving behavior). They found it hard to relate to managers in EDS's more entrepreneurial culture, who were rewarded for performance. In fact, GM and many other companies have since moved to rewarding their managers with stock options to encourage division managers to become more entrepreneurial.

The power of property rights over people's expectations is also apparent in a situation that occurred at Apple Computer. For its first 10 years in operation, Apple had never

ORGANIZATIONAL INSIGHT

5.5   A CLASH OF TWO CULTURES

When Roger Smith, General Motors CEO at the time, bought Electronic Data Systems (EDS), he bought a company recognized as one of the best computer systems specialists in the world. The deal worked out between Smith and EDS founder Ross Perot was that EDS would take control of GM's computer systems and computer staffs and would manage all of GM's software needs. EDS would make contracts with each GM car division and would price its services as if it were operating in the open market—that is, the price would include a markup for EDS's services even though EDS was part of General Motors. This practice gave rise to a problem.

The managers of GM's car divisions typically earned a straight salary; they received neither bonuses nor stock options as rewards for performance. Moreover, when they bought inputs from GM's parts divisions, they paid whatever price the parts division asked. There was no incentive for the car division managers to bargain over prices because reducing costs had no effect on their salaries.

At EDS, in contrast, Perot had rewarded his executives with generous stock options on the basis of contract profits. Thus, EDS managers were more entrepreneurial than the GM car division managers and had an incentive to strike the best deal they could get (cost plus a markup for profit) with the car divisions. The difference in the way property rights were awarded to employees in EDS and GM led to a culture clash. GM's car division managers did not want to sign contracts with managers from GM's new EDS division because the EDS managers would personally gain from the markup charged to the car divisions. GM's 57 car division managers refused to sign contracts with EDS because they did not want to enrich other GM employees.[40] Thus, the potential gains to the corporation as a whole from EDS management of GM's hundred different computer networks were only slowly realized. GM, realizing that EDS would be better off on its own, allowed EDS once again to become an independent company free to pursue its own interests.

had a layoff, and employees had come to take job security for granted. Although no written document promised job security, employees believed they were appreciated and possessed an implicit property right to their jobs. Imagine, then, what happened in 1991 when Apple announced the layoff of several thousand middle- and lower-level personnel to reduce costs. Employees were dumbfounded: This was not how Apple treated its employees. They demonstrated outside Apple headquarters for several weeks. What effect did the layoff have on Apple's culture? It destroyed the belief that Apple valued its employees, and it destroyed an organizational culture in which employees had been motivated to put forth effort above and beyond their formal job descriptions. It was as if Southwest Airlines' culture had turned into Value Line's culture overnight. At Apple, employee loyalty turned into hostility.

Apple, Sears, General Motors, Westinghouse, and other large companies that have recently laid off large numbers of employees are in the peculiar position of needing increased commitment from those who remain in order to turn their businesses around. Can they reasonably expect this? How can they encourage it? Perhaps they can give remaining employees property rights that will engender commitment to the organization. That task is the responsibility of top managers.

TOP MANAGEMENT AND PROPERTY RIGHTS.   Top managers are in a strong position to establish the terms of their own employment, their salary and benefits packages, and their termination and pension benefits. Top managers also determine the property rights received by others and, thus, determine what kind of culture will develop in an organization. The core competences of Apple Computer and Microsoft, for example, depend on the skills and capabilities of their personnel. To gain employee commitment, these organizations reward their top programmers and functional experts highly and give them very strong property rights. Apple has a position called "Apple Fellow," which gives top programmers the right to work on any project in the corporation or start any new project that they find promising. Both corporations reward important employees with large stock options. Over 1,500 people who joined Microsoft in the 1970s and 1980s, for example, are now multimillionaires as a result of stock options that they received in the past and continue to receive. It is not difficult to imagine how committed they are to the organization. Microsoft founder Bill Gates does not hand out stock options because he is generous, however; he does so because he wants to encourage terminal values of excellence and innovation and instrumental values of creativity and hard work. He also wants to prevent his best people from leaving to found their own firms (which would most likely compete with Microsoft) or going to work for Microsoft's competitors!

Does giving stronger property rights to production line or staff workers produce a culture in which they are committed to the organization and motivated to perform highly? The introduction of an employee stock option plan at Bimba Manufacturing had dramatic effects on employee behavior and the culture of the organization.

As the Bimba story illustrates, changing the property rights system changes the corporate culture by changing the instrumental values that motivate and coordinate employees. At Bimba, gone is the need for close supervision and the use of rigid rules and procedures to control behavior. Instead, coordination is achieved by teams of employees who value cooperation and are motivated by the prospect of sharing in the value created by the new work system.

CAN PROPERTY RIGHTS BE TOO STRONG?   As the Bimba story suggests, the *worth* of a person's behavior and the level of his or her performance are, in part, consequences of the rights the person is given. Sometimes, however, employees can be given property rights that are so strong that the organization and its employees are actually harmed over time.

For example, over the years IBM had developed a very conservative culture in which employees had strong rights, such as the implicit promise of lifetime employment. As a result, according to CEO Lou Gerstner, IBM employees had become cautious and noninnovative. Gerstner claimed that the organization protected IBM employees so well that they had no motivation to perform, to take risks, or to rock the boat. He suggested that the property rights of IBM employees were too strong.

It is easy to understand how property rights can become too strong. Chapter 3 discussed how people in bureaucracies can come to believe that they own their positions and the rights that go with them. When this happens, people take steps to protect their rights and resist attempts by others to wrest their rights away. The result is conflict, internal power struggles, and a loss of flexibility and innovation as the organization loses sight of its mission because its members are preoccupied with their own and not the organization's interests. Property rights, therefore, must be assigned on the basis of performance and in a discriminating way. Managers must continually evaluate and address this difficult challenge.

ORGANIZATIONAL INSIGHT

5.6 BIMBA CHANGES ITS PROPERTY RIGHTS SYSTEM

The Bimba Manufacturing Company, based in Monee, Illinois, manufactures aluminum cylinders. Its owner, Charles Bimba, decided to sell the company to its employees by establishing an employee stock ownership plan. He kept 10 percent of the shares; the other 90 percent was sold to employees. Some of the employees' money came from an already existing profit-sharing plan; the rest was borrowed from a bank.

Changes in the company since the ESOP was introduced have been dramatic, and the orientation of the workforce to the organization has totally changed. Previously, the company had two groups of employees: managers who made the rules and workers who carried them out. Workers rarely made suggestions and generally just obeyed orders. Now, cross-functional teams composed of managers and workers meet regularly to discuss problems and find new ways to improve quality. These teams also meet regularly with customers to better meet their needs.

Because of the incentives provided by the new ESOP, management and workers have developed new working relationships based on teamwork to achieve excellence and high quality. Each team hires its own members and spends considerable time socializing new employees in the new culture of the organization. The new cooperative spirit in the plant has forced managers to relearn their roles. They now listen to workers and act as advisers rather than superiors.

So far, changing the company's property rights system has paid off. Sales have increased by 70 percent and the workforce has grown by 59 percent. Bimba has expanded to a new, large facility and has opened a facility in England. Furthermore, workers have repaid over 60 percent of the loan they took out to finance the employee stock purchase. The ESOP has totally changed Bimba's corporate culture and altered the commitment of its workforce. In the words of one worker, it has led to "an intense change in the way we look at our jobs."[41]

Gerstner took steps to change IBM's property rights system and create an entrepreneurial culture by distributing more rewards based on performance and by eliminating employees' expectations of lifetime employment. To create a certain kind of culture, an organization needs to create a certain kind of property rights system. In part, organizational culture reflects the values that emerge as a result of an organization's property rights system.

Organizational Structure

We have seen how the values that coordinate and motivate employees result from the organization's people, its ethics, and the distribution of property rights among various stakeholders. The fourth source of cultural values is organizational structure. Recall from Chapter 1 that *organizational structure* is the formal system of task and authority relationships that an organization establishes to control its activities. Because different structures give rise to different cultures, managers need to design a certain kind of organizational structure to create a certain kind of organizational culture. Mechanistic structures and organic structures, for example, give rise to totally different sets of cultural values. The values, rules, and norms in a mechanistic structure are different from those in an organic structure.

Recall from Chapter 2 that *mechanistic structures* are tall, highly centralized, and standardized, and *organic structures* are flat and decentralized and rely on mutual adjustment. In a tall, centralized organization, people have relatively little personal autonomy, and desirable behaviors include being cautious, obeying superior authority, and respecting traditions. Thus, mechanistic structure is likely to give rise to a culture in which predictability and stability are desired end states. In a flat, decentralized structure, people have more freedom to choose and control their own activities, and desirable behaviors include being creative or courageous and taking risks. Thus, an organic structure is likely to give rise to a culture in which innovation and flexibility are desired end states.

An organization's structure can promote cultural values that foster integration and coordination. Out of stable task and role relationships, for example, emerge shared norms and rules that help reduce communications problems, prevent the distortion of information, and speed the flow of information. Moreover, norms, values, and a common organizational language can improve the performance of teams and task forces. It is relatively easy for different functions to share information and trust one another when they share similar cultural values. One reason why product development time is short and the organization is flexible in product team structures and matrix structures is that the reliance on face-to-face contact among functional specialists in teams forces those teams to quickly develop shared values and common responses to problems.

Whether a company is centralized or decentralized also leads to the development of different kinds of cultural values. By decentralizing authority, an organization can establish values that encourage and reward creativity or innovation. The founders of Hewlett-Packard established the "Hewlett-Packard Way," an organizational philosophy that gives employees access to equipment and resources so that they can be creative and conduct their own research informally, outside of their normal job responsibilities. At 3M, employees are informally encouraged to spend 15 percent of their time working on personal projects. In both these companies, the organizational structure produces cultural values that tell members that it is all right to be innovative and to do things in their own way, as long as their actions are consistent with the good of the organization.

Conversely, in some organizations, it is important that employees do not make decisions on their own and that their actions be open to the scrutiny of superiors. In such cases, centralization can be used to create cultural values that reinforce obedience and accountability. For example, in nuclear power plants, values that promote stability, predictability, and obedience to superior authority are deliberately fostered to prevent disasters.[42] Through norms and rules, employees are taught the importance of behaving consistently and honestly, and they learn that sharing information with supervisors, especially information about mistakes or errors, is the only acceptable form of behavior.[43]

In sum, organizational structure affects the cultural values that guide organizational members as they perform their activities. In turn, culture improves the way structure coordinates and motivates organizational resources to help an organization achieve its goals. One source of a company's competitive advantage is its ability to design its structure and manage its culture so that there is a good fit between the two. This gives rise to a core competence that is hard for other organizations to imitate. However, when companies fail to achieve a good fit, or when structural changes produce changes in cultural values, problems start to occur. Over time, IBM's structure grew tall and centralized, and the entrepreneurial values that originally energized the organization were smothered by new conservative values. As companies grow and differentiate, they need to pay attention to maintaining the values on which they were founded; otherwise, like IBM, they risk losing their competitive advantage.

CAN ORGANIZATIONAL CULTURE BE MANAGED?

Managers interested in understanding the interplay between an organization's culture and the organization's effectiveness at creating value for stakeholders must take a hard look at all four of the factors that produce culture: the characteristics of organizational members (particularly the founder), organizational ethics, the property rights system, and organizational structure. To change a culture can be very difficult because those factors interact and because major alterations are often needed to change an organization's values.[44] To change its culture, an organization might need to redesign its structure and revise the property rights it uses to motivate and reward employees. The organization might also need to change its people, especially its top-management team. Keeping in mind the difficulty of managing organizational culture, let's look at how Microsoft's culture evolved as a result of the interaction of the four factors.

As we discussed earlier, Bill Gates's personal values and beliefs and his vision of what Microsoft could achieve form the core of Microsoft's culture with its terminal values of excellence and innovation. With its initial success established by its MS-DOS and Microsoft Word systems, Microsoft began to attract the best software engineers in the world. Gates was therefore, in a position to select those people who bought into his values and who could perform at the level that he and his managers required. Over time, norms based on the need for individual initiative (to enhance the instrumental values of creativity and risk taking) and for teamwork (to enhance cooperation) emerged, and Microsoft built a campus-like headquarters complex to promote the development of an informal atmosphere in which people could develop strong working bonds.

Gates designed an organic structure for Microsoft and kept it as flat and decentralized as possible by using small teams to coordinate work activities. This design encourages risk taking and creativity. He also used a product team structure to reinforce the team atmosphere and norms of "team spirit." Gates also established a culture for innovation by rewarding successful risk taking and creativity with strong property rights. Many key employees receive stock options based on company performance, and all employees are eligible to receive bonuses. Furthermore, Microsoft offers high-quality pensions and benefits and has never had to lay off any employees. Finally, the company has a history of behaving ethically toward its employees and customers. Microsoft's people, its structure, its property rights, and its ethics interact and fit together to make up Microsoft's culture.

Compare Microsoft's culture to the one Louis Gerstner, IBM's CEO, has been trying to change: IBM had a conservative, stable culture produced by (1) property rights tied not to performance but to employee longevity in the organization and (2) a tall, centralized structure that promoted obedience and conformity. The people attracted to and retained by this IBM culture were those who liked working in a stable environment where they knew their place, who accepted the status quo, and who did not mind that the culture limited their opportunities to innovate or be creative. Although there was a match among the factors producing IBM's culture, the culture did not serve the company well. Because its cultural values emphasized stability, IBM was unable to adapt to changes in the environment, such as changes in technology and customer needs.

Can a company maintain a creative, entrepreneurial culture as it grows? Analysts have asked whether Gates will be able to maintain Microsoft's dynamic and freewheeling culture as the company grows. He has said that his policy of using small product development teams and spinning off into a separate product team any unit that reaches 200 people will help Microsoft preserve its entrepreneurial values and prevent the development of inertia and complacency.

To prevent an organization's culture from changing in ways that reduce effectiveness as the organization grows, top managers must design its structure to offset the control problems that occur with large size and complexity.[45] IBM, for example, was reorganized into 13 autonomous business units in an attempt to break IBM's old conservative culture and give each unit the opportunity to develop a new culture supportive of values such as customer responsiveness and excellence. IBM also made changes in its property rights system to try to change the cultural values guiding employee behavior; now performance, not seniority, determines the distribution of property rights. Furthermore, Gerstner decided to build IBM a new campus-style headquarters building to encourage its members to adopt a more flexible, team-based, cross-divisional perspective.

Will changing the structure, property rights, and top people be enough to change cultural values? Many studies have demonstrated that norms and values are stable and resistant to change.[46] Under Gerstner's leadership IBM's culture has changed. Although, Gerstner has on several occasions complained about how difficult it has been and still is to get people to change, he has changed the foundations on which the old culture was built and a new, more entrepreneurial culture is emerging as values and norms change. IBM's performance soared by the end of the 1990s.

Managerial Implications: Designing Organizational Culture

1. Try to identify the source of the values and norms of your organization's culture and analyze the relative effects of people, ethics, property rights, and structure on influencing organizational culture.
2. Use this analysis to produce an action plan for redesigning the culture of the organization to improve effectiveness.
3. Be sure that the action plan takes all four factors into consideration, for each one affects the others. Changing one factor alone may not be sufficient to change organizational culture.
4. Make the development of ethical organizational values one of your major priorities.

THE ADVANTAGES OF ETHICAL BEHAVIOR

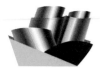

Ethics—the moral values, beliefs, and rules that govern the way organizational stakeholders should act toward one another—form an important part of an organization's cultural values. In an age when many different stakeholders scrutinize an organization's actions, and competition is fierce, organizations cannot afford to engage in actions that will hurt their reputation. Neither can they allow employees to take advantage of their position to commit unethical acts. Thus, creating an ethical organizational culture is one of top management's major priorities. Managers create an ethical culture by making a personal commitment to uphold ethical values and transmit them to subordinates. All organizations are expected to develop and follow ethical values because of the advantages that ethical behavior confers on an organization and on society.

One of the most important effects of ethical rules is the regulation of the pursuit of self-interest. To understand why self-interest needs to be regulated, consider the "tragedy of the commons." When common land—that is, land owned by everyone in a town or city—exists, it is rational for every person to maximize his or her use of it because it is a free resource. Thus, all owners will graze their cattle on the land to promote their individual interests. As a result, the land will be overgrazed and defenseless against the eroding effects of wind and rain, and the rational pursuit of individual self-interest results in a collective disaster. The same thing can happen in organizations: Left to their own devices, people will pursue their own goals at the expense of collective goals. Top managers, for example, may run the organization in their own interests and harm shareholders, employees, and the general public. Similarly, powerful unions may raise wages so high that in the long run a company becomes uncompetitive.

Ethical values and rules control self-interested behavior that might threaten society's collective interests. Ethical values establish desired end states—for example, equitable or "good" business practices—and the modes of behavior needed to achieve those end states, such as being honest or being fair. Free and fair competition between organizations is possible only when values and norms constrain people's actions in certain situations. It is ethical for a businessperson to compete with a rival and drive that rival out of business if the basis for competition is legal. Competition based on price and quality is legal and ethical. It is not ethical to compete by shooting a rival, blowing up a rival's factory, spreading false rumors about a competitor's products, or stealing information from a rival's organization. Quality and price competition creates value for an organization's stakeholders and the general public; competition by underhanded means hurts stakeholders and goes against the public interest. Note that ethical practices do not ensure that nobody gets hurt—the rival forced out of business does get hurt—but the harm done to the rival has to be weighed against the gain to consumers.

Ethical values in an organization's culture reduce the costs people incur in deciding what is right or appropriate. By reflexively following an ethical rule, people spend less time and effort trying to weigh, measure, or balance, and decide what is the right thing to do.[47]

When an organization's behavior follows accepted ethical rules, the organization gains a positive *reputation effect*.[48] Over time, people will most likely view with suspicion and hostility an organization that is known for engaging in illegal acts. However, an organization that always follows the rules and is known for its ethical business practices over and above strict legal requirements will have a good reputation—a valuable asset that makes people want to deal with it. Although unethical organizations might reap short-term benefits, they are penalized in the long run because eventually people will refuse to deal with them. The following example shows how United Way's reputation was harmed by new operating policies that established values that caused employees to behave unethically.

Reputation effects help explain why managers and employees follow ethical rules. If an organization behaves unethically, what will be the position of its employees? Outsiders are likely to tar employees and the unethical organization with the same brush because they assume that employees were following the organization's code of ethics. Even if an organization's unethical behavior was the product of only a few self-seeking individuals, it will affect and harm all employees.

In 1992, United Way of America was rocked by scandal after it was revealed that its president and top management had spent United Way funds on high salaries and large expense accounts for themselves. One top manager had charged to the United Way a $4,700-a-month apartment in Manhattan and a $1,200 membership in an exclusive lunch club. To prevent the scandal from causing a big drop in contributions, the United Way board tried to regain the public trust by appointing an outsider, Elaine L. Chao, as its new president. Chao, an experienced investment banker and a former head of the Peace Corps, moved quickly to institute strict new accounting standards and to introduce new rules governing salaries and perks at United Way.

In sum, acting ethically as individuals and as organizations promotes the good of a society and the well-being of its members. More value is created in societies where people follow ethical rules, and where criminal and unethical behavior are prevented by law, social custom, and practice. Personal reputation is the outcome of behaving ethically, and the esteem or respect of one's peers has always been a reward that most people desire and value.

WHY DOES UNETHICAL BEHAVIOR OCCUR?

If there are good reasons for individuals and organizations to behave ethically, why do we see so many instances of unethical behavior?

Lapses in Individual Ethics

In theory, individuals learn ethical principles and codes of morality as they mature. Ethics are learned from family, friends, religious institutions, schools, professional associations, and other organizations. From their experiences, people learn to differentiate right from wrong. However, imagine that your father is a mobster, your mother is a political terrorist, or your family belongs to a warring ethnic or religious group. Brought up in such a context, you may believe that it is ethical to do anything and to perform any act—including murder—to benefit your family, friends, or group. In a similar way, individuals within an organization may come to believe that any action that promotes or protects the organization is acceptable, even if it does harm to others. That sort of thinking prompted the Beech-Nut management team to approve the sale of sugar water labeled as apple juice.

Ruthless Pursuit of Self-Interest

We normally confront ethical issues when we weigh our personal interests against the effects that our actions will have on others. Suppose you will be promoted to vice president of your company if you can secure a $100 million contract, but that to get the contract, you must bribe the contractor with $1 million. Your career and future will probably be assured if you perform this act. "What harm will it do?" you ask yourself. Bribery is common, and if you don't pay the million dollars, you are certain that somebody else will. So what do you do? Research suggests that people who believe they have the most at stake are the ones most likely to act unethically. Similarly, it has been shown that organizations that are doing badly economically and are struggling to survive are the ones most likely to commit unethical and illegal acts such as price fixing or bribery, although many other organizations will do so if they are given the opportunity.[49]

Outside Pressure

Many studies have found that the likelihood of unethical or criminal behavior increases when people feel outside pressure to perform. If company performance is deteriorating, for example, top managers may feel pressures from shareholders to boost performance, and, fearful of losing their jobs, they may engage in unethical behavior to increase the value of corporate stock. That is what happened at Beech-Nut. If all outside pressures work in the same direction, it is easy to understand why unethical organizational cultures develop. Managers at all levels buy into unethical acts, and the view that the end justifies the means comes to permeate the organization. As organizational members pull together to disguise their unethical actions and to protect one another from prosecution, the organization becomes increasingly defensive.

The temptation for organizations to collectively engage in unethical and illegal behavior is very great. Industry competitors can clearly see the advantages of acting together to raise prices because of the extra profits they will earn. The harm they inflict as a result of their collusion is difficult to see because their customers may number in the millions. Unethical companies may rationalize by saying that individual customers are affected so slightly that they are hardly hurt at all. However, if every company in every industry behaved unethically, and if all companies tried to extract money from their customers, customers would have much less to spend, and the nation's economy as a whole would suffer. Moreover, price fixing results in a misallocation of society's resources. Companies spend less and less on improving their products because they have no incentive to improve them. Simply by increasing prices, they can make all the money they want with the products they already have.

The social costs of unethical behavior are hard to measure but can be easily seen in the long run. They take the form of mismanaged organizations that become less innovative and spend less and less on research and development and more and more on advertising or managerial salaries. When new competitors arrive that refuse to play the game, the mismanaged organization starts to crumble.

CORPORATE SOCIAL RESPONSIBILITY

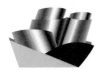

Social responsibility is an organization's moral responsibility to stakeholder groups that are affected directly or indirectly by the organization's actions. An organization can adopt a narrow or a broad stance on social responsibility.

The Narrow Stance

An organization with a *narrow stance* believes that it is behaving socially responsibly as long as it acts within the law and plays by the (often unwritten) rules of the game in its particular environment. One proponent of the narrow stance is the economist Milton Friedman, who states that as long as an organization conforms to the basic rules of a society, as embodied in its laws and ethical customs and practices, an organization is free to act as it wishes.[50]

Supporters of the narrow stance say that it is up to society to create an ethical framework for organizations to work within. According to their view, society must decide on the rules for the treatment of organizational members, employees, suppliers, customers, and other stakeholders. Organizations are responsible only for following the rules that exist. They have no responsibility to go beyond these rules and may "creatively interpret" these rules to their own advantage when the rules are not specific enough in outlining what is or is not legal or appropriate behavior.

Because so many organizations *do* act illegally and "creatively," the law is a vital safeguard against self-interested behaviors, such as those of the Beech-Nut managers.

The Broad Stance

An organization with a *broad stance* on social responsibility accepts the premise that organizations are moral agents and, like individuals, have a duty to examine every situation from a moral perspective. According to this view, even when no laws or societal ethics are applicable to a given situation, the organization should act to produce the most good or the least harm for its stakeholders.

In general, an organization can decide which action or behavior is the most ethical in a particular situation by applying certain moral principles. One important principle is the golden rule. One way to decide whether a behavior or action is ethical is to ask, "Would I like to be treated in this way?" This principle makes a clear case against acts like theft or cheating. But it does not offer much help to a manager who must lay off employees. In that situation, a different moral principle may be more helpful: "The right action produces the greatest benefit for the most people." Using this rule, the manager can weigh the costs of layoff to the employees against the direct benefits (lower costs) to the organization and the indirect benefit to society that results from reallocating resources (i.e., employees' salaries) to their most productive use. As a result of this cost/benefit analysis, the manager may still decide it is morally right to give employees a generous severance payment to compensate for the disruption caused by the layoff.

After applying moral values and principles to analyze actions and behavior, the manager can develop moral rules that specify behaviors appropriate for organizational members. Some rules are truisms and are accepted by almost everybody—for example, "It is unethical to kill, harm, or steal from stakeholders." Other rules are more controversial because there is no way to determine whether an action is right. For example, is it ethical to use animals in laboratory experiments that may result in the saving of thousands of human lives? Is it ethical to use animals to test cosmetics? Is it ethical for a company to bribe officials in countries where bribery is an accepted practice even though it is illegal in the United States? Is it ethical to transfer jobs from the United States to countries with lower wages in order to provide American consumers with low-cost products?

The broad stance on social responsibility requires much more thought and judgment by an organization and its members than does the narrow stance. Often, moral choices such as donating money to worthy causes, not closing a factory, not laying off thousands of employees, or not polluting the atmosphere reduce company profits. Some stakeholders, such as the workforce and the public at large, gain; others, such as shareholders, may lose.

Who decides which is the ethical course and which stakeholders should gain or lose? Very often, the founder of an organization makes these decisions. For example, Sheri Poe, founder of Ryka Inc., a company that makes running shoes exclusively for women, contributes 7 percent of the company's profits to a foundation she created to help female victims of violent crime. A rape victim herself, Poe decided that her company would use its resources to help this stakeholder group. The founders of Ben & Jerry's Homemade also have a very clear idea about their company's moral priorities.

In sum, if an organization's ethics violate society's ethics as embodied in law, the organization is acting illegally and will be subject to sanction. If organizational ethics violate generally accepted business and social customs and practices, organizations may lose their reputations. Beyond these two limits on ethical behavior, an organization's ethics are a function of the moral values of its stakeholders and of the power of the different stakeholder groups to impose these values on the organization.

ORGANIZATIONAL INSIGHT

5.7 BEN AND JERRY'S ETHICAL CULTURE

Ben Cohen and Jerry Greenfield, two former hippies, founded Ben & Jerry's Home-made, Inc., in 1978. Their ground-breaking ice-cream flavors—such as New York Super Fudge Chunk, Cherry Garcia (named after Jerry Garcia of the Grateful Dead), and Wavy Gravy—were wildly successful. In 1999, the company had record profits and sales.[51] Cohen and Greenfield's corporate objectives go beyond making a good dessert and a good profit, however. Ben and Jerry believe that the job of business is not just to make goods and services but to be a powerful tool for social change.

Inside the organization, Ben and Jerry want to create an organizational culture in which socially responsible corporate values, norms, and rules control employee behavior and daily supervision is superfluous. They want to encourage in their employees a sense of "social mission" toward other organizational stakeholders—that is, an awareness of the responsibility that each employee, as a person, has toward others in the organization and in society.

Ben and Jerry are specific about how they want workers to be socially responsible and active, and workers' participation in the company's social mission is evaluated in their performance reviews. Employees might help run a haunted house for a local charity or participate in an environmental cleanup, for example. Workers who ignore the social mission lose points toward raises.

Ben and Jerry have hired managers to take over the running of the business so that they can focus on its social mission. They formalized the policy that 7.5 percent of pretax profits would be distributed as grants to support socially responsible activities. The amount they contribute to charitable purposes is many times greater than the charitable gifts of much larger companies. Overseeing the use of these grants has become Ben and Jerry's major responsibility. They have sponsored local concerts and film festivals in their Vermont community, given away free ice cream at charitable events, and renovated a New York subway station. Every year the scope of their activities increases as their profits increase.

The social mission was brought inside the organization when they established a rule that the top salary paid to an employee could be no more than five times as large as the lowest salary (changed to seven times to attract a new CEO in 1995). This rule, however, does not directly affect Ben and Jerry. They get dividends from the shares they own.[52]

Ben & Jerry's Homemade exemplifies a culture based on a broad view of social responsibility that keeps employees focused on the company's social mission whether they like it or not. Although most employees like Ben and Jerry personally, not all employees like to be told what to do and how to spend their free time. Many, however, are reluctant to disagree publicly with the duo. The founders push their social values upon employees and are likely to hire only employees who have similar values.[53]

CREATING AN ETHICAL ORGANIZATION

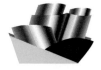

In what ways can ethical behavior be promoted so that, at the very least, organizational members resist the temptation to engage in illegal acts that promote personal or organizational interests at the expense of society's interests? Ultimately, an organization is ethical if the people inside the organization are ethical. How can people judge if they are making ethical decisions and, thus, acting ethically? One way is as follows: If a person (a) makes a decision (or takes an action) that falls within the accepted values or standards that typically apply in the organization's environment; (b) is willing to see the decision communicated to all parties affected by it, for example, having it reported in newspapers or on television; and (c) believes that other people with whom the person has a significant personal relationship, such as family members, friends, or even managers in other organizations, would approve the decision, then the decision is probably acceptable on ethical grounds. By contrast, an unethical decision would be one that a manager would wish to disguise or hide from other people because the decision harms other stakeholders in ways that are not acceptable based on the standards or values in the environment, or benefits him or her personally.

Beyond personal considerations, an organization can encourage people to act ethically by putting in place incentives for ethical behavior and disincentives to punish those who behave unethically. Because top managers have the ultimate responsibility for setting policy, they establish the ethical culture of the organization. There are many ways in which they can influence organizational ethics. A manager outlining a company's position on business ethics acts as a figurehead and personifies the organization's ethical position. As a leader, a manager can promote moral values that result in the specific ethical rules and norms that people use to make decisions. Outside the organization, as a liaison or spokesperson, a manager can inform prospective customers and other stakeholders about the organization's ethical values and demonstrate those values through his or her behavior toward stakeholders—such as by being honest and acknowledging errors. A manager also sets employees' incentives to behave ethically and can develop rules and norms that state the organization's ethical position. Finally, a manager can make decisions to allocate organizational resources and pursue policies based on the organization's ethical position, as Ben and Jerry did.

Designing an Ethical Structure and Control System

Ethics influence the choice of the structure and culture that coordinate resources and motivate employees.[54] Managers can design an organizational structure that reduces the incentives for people to behave unethically. The creation of authority relationships and rules that promote ethical behavior and punish unethical acts, for example, will encourage members to behave in a socially responsible way. In 1992, the federal government announced a new set of uniform standards of conduct for employees of the executive branch. Before the introduction of this new code, there were general guidelines that each department interpreted for itself. Not surprisingly, different government agencies interpreted the guidelines differently. Since 1992, the rules have been clearly stated, apply to all executive branch employees, and are evaluated by one central agency. The new standards cover ethical issues such as giving and receiving gifts, impartiality in government work and the assignment of contracts, conflicting financial interests, and outside work activities. These regulations affect approximately 5 million federal workers.[55]

Often an organization uses its mission statement to guide employees in making ethical decisions.[56] Johnson & Johnson uses its mission statement to define the ethical values that J&J employees are expected to follow. By acting ethically, Johnson & Johnson emerged from the Tylenol crisis with its reputation intact and even enhanced.

Whistle-blowing occurs when an employee informs an outside person or agency, such as a government agency or a newspaper or television reporter, about an organization's (its managers') illegal or immoral behavior. Employees typically become whistle-blowers

Whistle-blowing *Informing (by an employee) an outside person or agency, such as a government agency or a newspaper or television reporter, about an organization's (its managers') illegal or immoral behavior.*

when they feel powerless to prevent an organization from committing an unethical act or when they fear retribution from the company if they voice their concerns. However, an organization can take steps to make whistle-blowing an acceptable and rewarded activity.[57] Procedures that allow subordinates access to upper-level managers to voice concerns about unethical organizational behavior can be set up. The position of ethics officer can be established to investigate claims of unethical behavior, and ethics committees can make formal ethical judgments. Ten percent of Fortune 500 companies have ethics officers who are responsible for keeping employees informed about organizational ethics, for training employees, and for investigating breaches of ethical conduct. Ethical values flow down from the top of the organization but are strengthened or weakened by the design of the organizational structure.

Creating an Ethical Culture

The values, rules, and norms that define an organization's ethical position are part of the organization's culture. The behavior of top managers strongly influences organizational culture. An ethical culture is most likely to emerge if top managers are ethical, and an unethical culture can become an ethical one if the top-management team is changed. This transformation occurred at General Dynamics and other defense contracting firms in which corruption was common at all levels and overbilling and cheating the government had become a popular managerial sport. But neither culture nor structure can make an organization ethical if its top managers are not ethical. The creation of an ethical corporate culture requires commitment at all levels of an organization, from the top down.[58]

Supporting the Interests of Stakeholder Groups

Shareholders are the owners of an organization. Through the board of directors they have the power to hire and fire top management and, thus, in theory can discipline managers who engage in unethical behavior. Shareholders want higher profits, but do they want them to be gained by unethical behavior? In general, the answer is no because unethical behavior will make a company a riskier investment. If an organization loses its reputation, the value of its shares will be lower than the value of shares offered by firms that behave ethically. In addition, many shareholders do not want to hold stock in companies that engage in socially questionable activities.

Pressure from outside stakeholders can also promote ethical organizational behavior.[59] The government and its agencies, industry councils and regulatory bodies, and consumer watchdog groups all play a role in establishing the ethical rules that organizations should follow when doing business. Outside regulation sets the rules of the competitive game and, as noted earlier, plays an important part in creating and sustaining ethics in society.

Large organizations possess enormous power to benefit and harm society. But if corporations act to harm society and their own stakeholders, society will move to regulate and control business to minimize its ability to inflict harm. Societies, however, differ in the extent to which they are willing to impose regulations on organizations. In general, poor countries have the least restrictive regulations. In many countries, people pay large bribes to government officials to get permission to start a company; and once in business, they operate unfettered by any regulations pertaining to child labor, minimum wages, or employee health and safety. Americans, in contrast, take ethical behavior on these fronts for granted because laws as well as custom and practice discourage child labor, slave wages, and unsafe working conditions.

SUMMARY

Organizational culture exercises a potent form of control over the interactions of organizational members with each other and with outsiders. By supplying people with a toolbox of values, norms, and rules that tell them how to behave, organizational culture is instrumental in determining how they interpret and react to a situation. Thus, an organization's culture can be a source of competitive advantage. Chapter 5 has made the following main points:

1. Organizational culture is a set of shared values that provides organizational members with a common understanding of how they should act in a situation.

2. There are two kinds of organizational values: terminal (a desired end state or outcome) and instrumental (a desired mode of behavior). Ideally, instrumental values help the organization to achieve its terminal goals.

3. Organizational culture affects organizational effectiveness because it can (a) provide an organization with a competitive advantage, (b) improve the way an organizational structure works, and (c) increase the motivation of employees to pursue organizational interests.

4. Culture is transmitted to an organization's members by means of (a) socialization and training programs and (b) stories, ceremonies, and language used by members of the organization.

5. Organizational culture develops from the interaction of (a) the characteristics of organization members, (b) organizational ethics, (c) the property rights distributed among the people in the organization (especially managers and the workforce), and (d) organizational structure.

6. Different organizations have different kinds of cultures because they attract, select, and retain different kinds of people. Because an organization's founder is instrumental in initially determining what kind of people get selected, a founder can have a long-lasting effect on an organization's culture.

7. Ethics are the moral values, beliefs, and rules that establish the right or appropriate ways in which one person or stakeholder group should interact and deal with another individual or stakeholder group. Organizational ethics are a product of societal, professional, and individual ethics.

8. Property rights are the rights that an organization gives to its members to receive and use organizational resources. Property rights cause the development of different norms, values, and attitudes toward the organization.

9. Different organizational structures give rise to different patterns of interaction among people. These different patterns lead to the formation of different organizational cultures.

10. The ethical values of an organization's culture develop to increase the wealth that can be produced by people and organizations. Ethical values protect people and their interests.

11. Social responsibility is an organization's moral responsibility to stakeholder groups affected by the organization's actions.

12. There are two stances on social responsibility: a narrow stance and a broad stance. They have very different implications for organizational behavior.

13. Top managers can create an ethical organization by (a) designing an ethical structure and control system, (b) creating an ethical culture, and (c) supporting the interests of stakeholder groups.

DISCUSSION QUESTIONS

1. What is the origin of organizational culture? Why do different organizations have different cultures?
2. How do newcomers learn the culture of an organization? How can an organization encourage newcomers to develop (a) an institutionalized role orientation and (b) a individualized role orientation?
3. In what ways can organizational culture increase organizational effectiveness? Why is it important to obtain the right fit between organizational structure and culture?
4. "An organization should always adopt a broad stance on social responsibility." Explain why you agree or disagree with this statement.

ORGANIZATIONAL THEORY IN ACTION

PRACTICING ORGANIZATIONAL THEORY: DEVELOPING A SERVICE CULTURE

Form groups of three to five people and discuss the following scenario:

You are the owner/manager of a new five-star resort hotel opening up on the white sand beaches of the western coast of Florida. For your venture to succeed you need to make sure that hotel employees focus on providing customers with the highest-quality customer service possible. You are meeting to discuss how to create a culture that will promote such high-quality service, that will encourage employees to be committed to the hotel, and that will reduce the level of employee turnover and absenteeism, which are typically high in the hotel business.

1. What kinds of organizational values and norms encourage employees to behave in ways that lead to high-quality customer service?
2. Using the concepts discussed in this chapter (e.g., people, property rights, socialization) discuss how you will create a culture that promotes the learning of these customer service values and norms.
3. Which factor is the most important determinant of the kind of culture you expect to find in a five-star hotel?

MAKING THE CONNECTION #5

Identify an organization that has been trying to change its culture. Describe the culture that it is trying to alter. Why is this culture no longer effective? How has the organization tried to bring about change? How successful has it been?

Analyzing the Organization: Design Module #5

In this module you will analyze the culture of your organization, discuss the characteristic ways in which members act, and identify the organization's ethical stance.

Cases for Analysis:
CHANGING THE CULTURE OF UTC

United Technologies Corporation (UTC) is a $21 billion conglomerate composed of six different businesses: Pratt & Whitney (aircraft engines), Otis (elevators), Carrier (air conditioners), Hamilton Standard (aviation systems), Sikorsky (helicopters), and UT (automotive systems). When George David took over as CEO, he found himself in charge of a collection of companies, some of which, like Otis, were performing well, some of which, like Pratt & Whitney, were performing poorly. Indeed, in the early 1990s, Pratt & Whitney was losing over $500 million a year. As David started to analyze why some units were performing well and some poorly, he began to realize that at least part of the answer lay in the way the different divisions operated.

Pratt & Whitney was the company's oldest business and had the most prestige in the organization. In the jet aircraft business, it takes many years to develop a new engine, and research and development costs are enormous, often running into the billions. Possessing this long-term research orientation, Pratt & Whitney had gradually developed a very tall, inflexible organizational structure that was coordinated from the top. The master plan for new engine development was decided by the top-management team, which then allocated to various teams of design engineers the responsibility for developing specific parts for the new engine. Top managers coordinated the whole project, and over the years this top-down, centralized approach had slowed project development. Moreover, middle managers had become internally focused on their part of the project and not externally on the needs of the company's customers—the airlines that provided passenger service. The result was that the company had missed opportunities to develop aircraft engines that suited the needs of airlines in the new deregulated airline industry, which valued fuel efficiency and engines that were easy and cheap to maintain.

David compared this stodgy, conservative operating culture with the way Otis, the division of which he had previously been in charge, operated. At Otis, managers' mind-set was very different

and they had entrepreneurial, quick-moving, and customer-driven values.[60] At Otis, managers had to work closely with their customers to understand their specific needs. Every elevator project is different, and each elevator must be custom-built for the building in which it is to be placed. Consequently, top managers had decentralized decision making to lower-level managers, empowering the people on the spot to find the best way to respond to each customer's unique needs. This decentralized approach also speeded up decision making and project completion. The division's entrepreneurial values also encouraged managers to experiment with new elevator designs and to search for new kinds of customers, particularly international customers, with the result that Otis had become the largest and most profitable elevator company in the world.

David decided that to increase the profitability of the whole UTC empire he needed to transfer Otis's culture to the other divisions—in particular, to Pratt & Whitney, the loss-making division. In a series of radical moves, David replaced many of Pratt & Whitney's top managers with Otis executives, including Karl J. Krapek, who became president. He then slashed Pratt & Whitney's workforce by 40 percent, laying off many middle managers. David then began to empower middle managers and created product development teams, which were given the authority and responsibility to coordinate the new engine development process. These teams were also given the responsibility to liaise with important customers to ensure that the new engines that Pratt & Whitney developed suited the needs of airlines in the 1990s and beyond. David and Krapek's goal is to replace the long-term engineering mind-set of Pratt & Whitney's managers with a new customer-driven focus.

1. Why were the cultures of Pratt & Whitney and the Otis divisions different?
2. How has David tried to change Pratt & Whitney's culture, and what more can he and Krapek do?

ASSIGNMENT

1. Do managers and employees use certain words and phrases to describe the behavior of people in the organization? Are any stories about events or people typically used to describe the way the organization works?

2. How does the organization socialize employees? Does it put them through formal training programs? What kind of programs are used, and what is their goal?

3. What beliefs and values seem to characterize the way people behave in the organization? How do they affect people's behavior?

4. Given the answers to the first three questions, how would you characterize the organization's culture?

5. What advantages and disadvantages are associated with the organization's culture? How could the culture be improved?

6. What is the relationship between the organization's structure, which you analyzed in Module 4, and the organization's culture? Is there a fit or a misfit?

7. What do you think has the strongest impact on the organization's culture: the people, organizational structure, or property rights? Explain.

8. Do you have any other impressions of the organization's culture, norms, and values that seem to explain the way the organization operates?

9. Can you find a written statement of the organization's ethical stance? Is there one in its mission statement or annual report? If you are interviewing the organization's managers personally, ask about the organization's ethical position. In what situations have they been confronted with ethical problems? Are there stories in the press about the company? If there are, what do they say?

10. What is the company's stance on social responsibility? Does the company seem to have a narrow or a broad stance?

11. As far as you can discover, how does the organization attempt to create an ethical climate?

12. Present any other related information or impressions that you have gained about your organization from your research.

REFERENCES

1. L. Smircich, "Concepts of Culture and Organizational Analysis," *Administrative Science Quarterly*, 1983, vol. 28, pp. 339–358.
2. S. D. N. Cook and D. Yanow, "Culture and Organizational Learning," *Journal of Management Inquiry*, 1993, vol. 2, pp. 373–390.
3. M. Rokeach, *The Nature of Human Values* (New York: The Free Press, 1973).
4. P. L. Berger and T. Luckman, *The Social Construction of Reality* (Garden City, NY: Anchor Books, 1967).
5. E. H. Schein, "Culture: The Missing Concept in Organization Studies," *Administrative Science Quarterly*, 1996, vol. 41, pp. 229–240.
6. A. Bianco, "Value Line: Too Lean, Too Mean," *Business Week*, 16 March, 1992, pp. 104–106.
7. J. P. Walsh and G. R. Ungson, "Organizational Memory," *Academy of Management Review*, 1991, vol. 1, pp. 57–91.
8. K. E. Weick, "Organizational Culture as a Source of High Reliability," *California Management Review*, 1984, vol. 9, pp. 653–669.
9. J. A. Chatman and S. G. Barsade, "Personality, Organizational Culture, and Cooperation: Evidence from a Business Simulation," *Administrative Science Theory*, 1995, vol. 40, pp. 423–443.
10. A. Etzioni, *A Comparative Analysis of Organizations* (New York: The Free Press, 1975).
11. G. R. Jones, "Psychological Orientation and the Process of Organizational Socialization: An Interactionist Perspective," *Academy of Management Review*, 1983, vol. 8, pp. 464–474.
12. J. Van Mannen and E. H. Schein, "Towards a Theory of Organizational Socialization," in B. M. Staw, ed., *Research in Organizational Behavior*, vol. 1 (Greenwich, CT: JAI Press, 1979), pp. 209–264.
13. G. R. Jones, "Socialization Tactics, Self-Efficacy, and Newcomers' Adjustments to Organizations," *Academy of Management Review*, 1986, vol. 29, pp. 262–279.
14. Ibid.
15. M. A. Cusumano and R. W. Selby, *Microsoft's Secrets* (New York: The Free Press, 1995).
16. H. M. Trice and J. M. Beyer, "Studying Organizational Culture Through Rites and Ceremonials," *Academy of Management Review*, 1984, vol. 9, pp. 653–669.
17. H. M. Trice and J. M. Beyer, *The Cultures of Work Organizations* (Englewood Cliffs, NJ: Prentice Hall, 1993).
18. M. Ramundo, "Service Awards Build Culture of Success," *Human Resources Magazine*, August 1992, pp. 61–63.
19. Trice and Beyer, "Studying Organizational Culture Through Rites and Ceremonials."
20. A. M. Pettigrew, "On Studying Organizational Cultures," *Administrative Science Quarterly*, 1979, vol. 24, pp. 570–582.
21. B. Schneider, "The People Make the Place," *Personnel Psychology*, 1987, vol. 40, pp. 437–453.
22. E. H. Schein, "The Role of the Founder in Creating Organizational Culture," *Organizational Dynamics*, 1983, vol. 12, pp. 13–28.

23. J. M. George, "Personality, Affect, and Behavior in Groups," *Journal of Applied Psychology*, 1990, vol. 75, pp. 107–116.

24. E. Schein, *Organizational Culture and Leadership*, 2nd ed. (San Francisco: Jossey-Bass, 1992).

25. T. Parker-Pope, "New CEO Preaches Rebellion for P&G's 'Cult'," *Wall Street Journal*, 11 December 1998, p. B1.

26. G. Fairclough, "P&G to Slash 15,000 Jobs, Shut 10 Plants," *Wall Street Journal*, 10 June 1999, p. A3.

27. M. Hannan and J. Freeman, "Structural Inertia and Organizational Change," *American Sociological Review*, 1984, vol. 49, pp. 149–164.

28. George, "Personality, Affect, and Behavior in Groups"; D. Miller and J. M. Toulouse, "Chief Executive Personality and Corporate Strategy and Structure in Small Firms," *Management Science*, 1986, vol. 32, pp. 1389–1409.

29. R. E. Goodin, "How to Determine Who Should Get What," *Ethics*, July 1975, pp. 310–321.

30. T. M. Jones, "Ethical Decision Making by Individuals in Organizations: An Issue Contingent Model," *Academy of Management Review*, 1991, vol. 2, pp. 366–395.

31. T. L. Beauchamp and N. E. Bowie, eds., *Ethical Theory and Business* (Englewood Cliffs, NJ: Prentice Hall, 1979); A. MacIntyre, *After Virtue* (South Bend, IN: University of Notre Dame Press, 1981).

32. *The Economist*, 31 March 1993, p. 25.

33. B. Victor and J. B. Cullen, "The Organizational Bases of Ethical Work Climates," *Administrative Science Quarterly*, 1988, vol. 33, pp. 101–125.

34. L. Kohlberg, "Stage and Sequence: The Cognitive-Development Approach to Socialization," in D. A. Goslin, ed., *Handbook of Socialization Theory and Research* (Chicago: Rand McNally, 1969), pp. 347–380.

35. "What Led Beech-Nut Down the Road to Disgrace," *Business Week*, 22 February 1988, pp. 124–128; "Bad Apples in the Executive Suite," *Consumer Reports*, May 1989, p. 296; R. Johnson, "Ralston to Buy Beech-Nut, Gambling It Can Overcome Apple Juice Scandal," *Wall Street Journal*, 18 September 1989, p. B11.

36. M. S. Frankel, "Professional Codes: Why, How, and with What Impact?" *Journal of Business Ethics*, 1989, vol. 8, pp. 109–115.

37. J. Van Mannen and S. R. Barley, "Occupational Communities: Culture and Control in Organizations," in B. Staw and L. Cummings, eds., *Research in Organizational Behavior*, vol. 6 (Greenwich, CT: JAI Press, 1984), pp. 287–365.

38. H. Demsetz, "Towards a Theory of Property Rights," *American Economic Review*, 1967, vol. 57, pp. 347–359.

39. G. R. Jones, "Transaction Costs, Property Rights, and Organizational Culture: An Exchange Perspective," *Administrative Science Quarterly*, 1983, vol. 28, pp. 454–467.

40. T. Moore, "Make or Break Time for General Motors," *Fortune*, 15 February 1988, pp. 32–42.

41. "ESOP Binges Change in Corporate Culture," *Employee Benefit Plan Review*, July 1992, pp. 25–26

42. C. Perrow, *Normal Accidents* (New York: Basic Books, 1984).

43. H. Mintzberg, *The Structuring of Organizational Structures* (Englewood Cliffs, NJ: Prentice Hall, 1979).

44. G. Kunda, *Engineering Culture* (Philadelphia: Temple University Press, 1992).

45. J. P. Kotter and J. L. Heskett, *Corporate Culture and Performance* (New York: The Free Press, 1992).

46. K. L. Bettenhausen and J. K. Murnighan, "The Emergence of Norms in Competitive Decision Making Groups," *Administrative Science Quarterly*, 1985, vol. 30, pp. 350–372.

47. T. M. Jones, "Instrumental Stakeholder Theory: A Synthesis of Ethics and Economics," *Academy of Management Review*, 1995, vol. 20, pp. 404–437.

48. J. Dobson, "Corporate Reputation: A Free Market Solution to Unethical Behavior," *Business and Society*, 1989, vol. 28, pp. 1–5.

49. M. S. Baucus and J. P. Near, "Can Illegal Corporate Behavior Be Predicted? An Event History Analysis," *Academy of Management Journal*, 1991, vol. 34, pp. 9–36.

50. M. Friedman, "A Friedman Doctrine: The Social Responsibility of Business Is to Increase Its Profits," *New York Times Magazine*, 13 September 1970, p. 33.

51. A. Urbanski, "Pro-File; Keeper of the Counterculture," *Promo*, April 1999, p. 6.

52. R. E. Sullivan, Jr., "Just Desserts," *Rolling Stone*, 9–23 July 1992, pp. 75–79.

53. J. Pereira, "Ben & Jerry's Chief Executive Resigns After Disagreement with Founders," *Wall Street Journal*, 1996, 30 September 1996, p. B5.

54. P. E. Murphy, "Implementing Business Ethics," *Journal of Business Ethics*, 1988, vol. 7, pp. 907–915.

55. "Ethics Office Approves Executive-Branch Rules," *Wall Street Journal*, 7 August 1992, p. A14.

56. P. E. Murphy, "Creating Ethical Corporate Structure," *Sloan Management Review*, Winter 1989, pp. 81–87.

57. J. B. Dozier and M. P. Miceli, "Potential Predictors of Whistle-Blowing: A Prosocial Behavior Perspective," *Academy of Management Review*, 1985, vol. 10, pp. 823–836; J. P. Near and M. P. Miceli, "Retaliation Against Whistle-Blowers: Predictors and Effects," *Journal of Applied Psychology*, 1986, vol. 71, pp. 137–145.

58. J. A. Byrne, "The Best-Laid Ethics Programs...," *Business Week*, 9 March 1992, pp. 67–69.

59. D. Collins, "Organizational Harm, Legal Consequences and Stakeholder Retaliation," *Journal of Business Ethics*, 1988, vol. 8, pp. 1–13.

60. T. Smart, "Global Mission," *Business Week*, 1 May 1995, pp. 132–134.

Chapter 6

MANAGING the ORGANIZATIONAL ENVIRONMENT

An organization's environment is the complex network of changing forces that affects the way the organization operates. The environment is a major contingency for which an organization must plan and to which it must adapt. Furthermore, it is a source of uncertainty that an organization must try to control. There are several theories about how and why organizations attempt to manage their environments to gain the resources they need to achieve their goals and create value for their stakeholders.

This chapter examines the forces that make an organization's environment uncertain and how an organization seeks to adapt to and control these forces. Three theories that explain how and why an organization chooses ways to structure its activities to respond to this uncertainty are discussed: contingency theory, resource dependence theory, and transaction cost theory.

This discussion of the organizational environment continues in the next two chapters. In Chapter 7 the specific strategies or ways of creating value that an organization can adopt to compete effectively with other organizations for resources in particular industry environments are examined. Chapter 8 examines the specific issues involved in managing the international environment. Chapters 6, 7, and 8 focus on the ways in which organizations manage their environments to increase their ability to satisfy stakeholders.

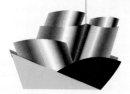

WHAT IS THE ORGANIZATIONAL ENVIRONMENT?

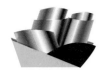

Organizational environment *The set of forces surrounding an organization that has the potential to affect the way it operates and its access to scarce resources.*

Organizational domain *The particular range of goods and services that the organization produces and the customers and other stakeholders whom it serves.*

The **organizational environment** is the set of forces surrounding an organization that has the potential to affect the way it operates and its access to scarce resources. Scarce resources include the raw materials and skilled workers the organization needs to produce goods and services; the information it needs to improve its technology or decide on its competitive strategy; and the support of outside stakeholders, such as the customers who buy its goods and services, and the banks and financial institutions that supply the capital that sustains it. Forces in the environment that affect an organization's ability to secure these scarce resources include competition from rivals for customers; rapid changes in technology, which might erode an organization's competitive advantage; and an increase in the price of important inputs, which raises the organization's costs.

An organization attempts to manage the forces in its environment to obtain the resources necessary to produce goods and services for customers and clients (see Figure 6.1). The term **organizational domain** refers to the particular range of goods and services that the organization produces and the customers and other stakeholders whom it serves.[1] An organization establishes its domain by deciding *which* customers it is going to serve and then deciding *how* to manage the forces in its environment to maximize its ability to secure needed resources. To obtain inputs, for example, an organization has to decide which suppliers to deal with from the range of possible suppliers and how to manage its relationships with its chosen suppliers. To obtain money, an organization has to decide which bank to deal with and how to manage its relationship with the bank so that the bank will be inclined to authorize a loan.

An organization attempts to structure its transactions with the environment to protect and enlarge its domain so that it can increase its ability to create value for customers, shareholders, employees, and other stakeholders. For example, Gerber Products' domain

FIGURE 6.1

The Organizational Environment. In the specific environment are forces that directly affect an organization's ability to obtain resources. In the general environment are forces that shape the specific environments of all organizations.

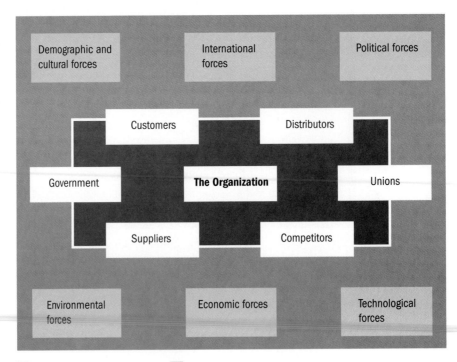

is a wide range of baby foods and other baby-related products (clothing, diapers, pacifiers) that the company makes to satisfy the needs of babies and their families. Gerber structures transactions with its environment—that is, with suppliers, bankers, customers, and other stakeholders—to obtain the resources it needs to protect and enlarge its domain.

Recall that Bob and Amanda Richards, owners of the B.A.R. and Grille, initially selected the hamburger segment of the restaurant market as their organizational domain. When their organization prospered, they decided to extend their domain to include the pizza and the waffle and pancake segments. That decision meant that they had to manage a more complex set of transactions with the environment to obtain resources. They had to deal with different sets of customers, different sets of suppliers, and so on.

Before discussing the ways in which organizations manage their environment to protect and enlarge their domain, we must understand in detail which forces in the environment affect organizations. The concepts of specific environment and general environment provide a useful basis of analysis.[2]

The Specific Environment

Specific environment
The forces from outside stakeholder groups that directly affect an organization's ability to secure resources.

The **specific environment** consists of forces from outside stakeholder groups that directly affect an organization's ability to secure resources.[3] Customers, distributors, unions, competitors, suppliers, and the government are all important outside stakeholders who can influence and pressure organizations to act in certain ways (see Figure 6.1).

For baby-food maker Gerber, competitors, such as Beech-Nut and H. J. Heinz, are an important force that affects the organization's ability to attract resources: customer revenue. Competition makes resources scarce and valuable because the greater the competition for resources, the more difficult they are to obtain. Competitors can be domestic or foreign. Each type has different implications for a company's ability to obtain resources. Foreign competitors have not been as important a force in the baby-food industry as they have been in the U.S. automobile industry, where they have reduced the U.S. car companies' ability to attract resources.

Changes in the number of and types of customers and changes in customer tastes are another force that impacts on an organization. An organization must have a strategy to manage its relationships with customers and attract their support, and the strategy must change over time as customer needs change. Gerber has a national reputation based on its high standards of purity, quality, and caring, and it has gained the support of so many U.S. consumers that it holds 65 percent of the baby-food market. However, in the 1990s, increasing demands from customers for additive-free, organic baby food led Gerber to change the formulation of some of its food products.

Besides responding to the needs of customers, organizations must decide how to manage relationships with suppliers and distributors to obtain access to the resources they provide. An organization has to make many choices concerning how to manage these exchanges in order to most effectively secure a stable supply of inputs or dispose of its products in a timely manner. For example, should Gerber buy or make its inputs? Should it raise cattle and chickens and vegetables and fruits? Should it make glass jars? Or should it buy all of these inputs from suppliers? The purity of baby foods is a vital issue; can input suppliers be trusted to ensure product quality? What is the best way for Gerber to distribute its products to ensure their quality? Should Gerber own its own fleet of vehicles and sell directly to retail stores, or should it use wholesalers to distribute its products? (We examine how an organization chooses to manage its input and output transactions later in the chapter.)

Other outside stakeholders include the government, unions, and consumer interest groups. Various government agencies are interested in Gerber's policies concerning equal employment opportunity, food preparation and content, and health and safety standards, and these agencies pressure the organization to make sure it follows legal rules. Unions pressure Gerber to secure favorable wages and benefits, and to protect the jobs of their members who work for Gerber. Consumer interest groups seek to prevent Gerber from reducing the quality of its foods, as Beech-Nut once did (see Organizational Insight 5.4).

An organization must engage in transactions with each of the forces in its specific environment if it is to obtain the resources it requires to survive and to protect and enhance its domain. Over time, the size and scope of its domain will change as those transactions change. For example, an organization that decides to expand its domain to satisfy the needs of new customers by producing new kinds of products will encounter new sets of forces and may need to engage in a different set of transactions with the environment to gain resources. A good example of an organization that changed its domain is the March of Dimes. Having funded research that led to a cure for polio, the March of Dimes changed its domain and announced that henceforth it would support research on birth defects.

The General Environment

General environment

The forces that shape the specific environment and affect the ability of all organizations in a particular environment to obtain resources.

The **general environment** consists of forces that shape the specific environment and affect the ability of all organizations in a particular environment to obtain resources (see Figure 6.1). *Economic forces*, such as interest rates, the state of the economy, and the unemployment rate, determine the level of demand for products and the price of inputs. *International forces*, such as the foreign exchange rate, foreign interest rates, and the cost of production abroad, determine where companies buy inputs, manufacture products, and try to sell products. Levi Strauss, for example, moved jean production from the United States to Mexico and the Dominican Republic to reduce production costs. (Chapter 8 looks specifically at how and why an organization manages international exchanges.)

Technological forces, such as the development of new production techniques and new information-processing equipment, influence many aspects of organizations' operations. The use of computerized manufacturing technology can increase productivity. Similarly, investment in advanced research and development activities influences how organizations interact with each other and how they design their structures. (The role of technology is examined further in Chapters 9 and 10.) *Demographic and cultural forces*, such as the age, education, and norms and values of a nation's people, shape organizations' customers, managers, and employees. The demand for baby products, for example, is linked to national birthrates and age distributions.

Political forces influence government policy toward organizations and their stakeholders. For example, laws that favor particular business interests, such as a tariff on imported cars, influence organizations' customers and competitors.

Environmental forces, such as pressure to reduce air pollution or a desire to decrease the nation's level of solid waste, affect organizations' production costs. Environmentally friendly product design and packaging may alter organizations' relationships with competitors, customers, and suppliers.

If an organization manages the forces in its general and specific environments effectively, so that it obtains the resources it needs, its domain will grow as it attracts new customers and produces more goods and services. If an organization manages the forces in its general and specific environments poorly, stakeholders will withhold their support, the organization will not obtain scarce resources, and the organization's domain may shrink. Eventually, unless it can find a better way to manage its environment, the organization may cease to exist.

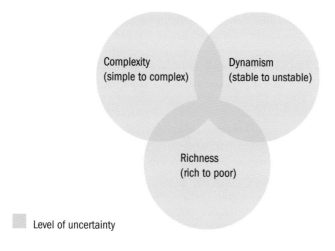

FIGURE 6.2

Three Factors Causing Uncertainty. As the environment becomes more complex, less stable, and poorer, the level of uncertainty increases.

Level of uncertainty

Sources of Uncertainty in the Organizational Environment

An organization likes to have a steady and abundant supply of resources so that it can easily manage its domain and satisfy its stakeholders. All organizations, however, face uncertainty, which makes it impossible for managers to control and predict the flow of resources. Three factors give rise to environmental uncertainty: the complexity, dynamism, and richness of the environment. As the environment becomes more complex, less stable, and poorer, the level of uncertainty increases (see Figure 6.2).

Environmental complexity The strength, number, and interconnectedness of the specific and general forces that an organization has to manage.

ENVIRONMENTAL COMPLEXITY.   **Environmental complexity** is a function of the strength, number, and interconnectedness of the specific and general forces that an organization has to manage.[4] The greater the number, and the greater the differences among them, the more complex and uncertain is the environment and the more difficult to predict and control. Xerox, for example, used to obtain inputs from over 3,000 different suppliers. To reduce the uncertainty associated with dealing with so many suppliers, Xerox embarked on a program to reduce their number and, thus, reduce the complexity of its environment. Now Xerox deals with fewer than 300 suppliers, and acquiring the information needed to manage its relationships with them is much easier than acquiring information to facilitate dealings with ten times that number. Complexity also increases when a company produces different products for different groups of customers. For example, if a company like McDonald's suddenly decided to enter the insurance and banking businesses, it would need a massive infusion of information to reduce the uncertainty surrounding the new transactions.

Complexity can increase greatly when specific and general forces in the environment become interconnected—that is, when they begin to interact and their effect on the organization becomes unpredictable.[5] The more interconnected the forces in an organization's specific and general environments are, the more uncertainty the organization faces. Suppose a major breakthrough in car-making technology makes existing factories obsolete. This general force will cause the price of car manufacturers' stock to fluctuate wildly and will send financial markets into a turmoil. Car manufacturers will be unsure how the breakthrough will affect their business, competition between rivals will increase (a specific force), and both management and the unions will be uncertain of the effect it will have on jobs and the future of the organization. If customers then stop buying cars (another specific force) until new models made with the new technology come out, the result may be layoffs and further decreases in the price of car company stocks.

The more complex an organization's environment, the greater the uncertainty about that environment. Predicting and controlling the flow of resources becomes extremely difficult, and problems associated with managing transactions with the environment increase.

Environmental dynamism The degree to which forces in the specific and general environments change quickly over time and, thus, contribute to the uncertainty an organization faces.

ENVIRONMENTAL DYNAMISM. **Environmental dynamism** is a function of how much and how quickly forces in the specific and general environments change over time and, thus, contribute to the uncertainty an organization faces.[6] An environment is *stable* if forces affect the supply of resources in a predictable way. An environment is *unstable and dynamic* if an organization cannot predict the way in which the forces will change over time. If technology, for example, is changing as rapidly as it does in the computer industry, the environment is very dynamic. An organization in a dynamic, unstable environment will seek ways to make the environment more predictable and thereby lessen the organization's uncertainty about its environment. Later in the chapter, we discuss strategies for managing potentially dynamic parts of the environment, including long-term contracts and vertical integration.

Environmental richness The amount of resources available to support an organization's domain.

ENVIRONMENTAL RICHNESS. **Environmental richness** is a function of the amount of resources available to support an organization's domain.[7] In rich environments, resources are plentiful and uncertainty is low because organizations need not compete for resources. Biotechnology companies in Boston, for example, have a large pool of high-quality scientists to choose from because of the presence of so many universities in the area (MIT, Harvard, Boston University, Boston College, Tufts, Brandeis, among others). In poor environments, resources are scarce and uncertainty is high because organizations have to compete for the scarce resources. The supply of high-quality scientists in Alaska, for example, is very limited, and meeting the demand for them is very expensive.

Environments may be poor for two reasons: (1) The organization is located in a poor country or in a poor region of a country. (2) There is a high level of competition, and organizations are fighting over available resources.[8] In poor environments, organizations have to battle to attract customers or to obtain the best inputs or the latest technology. The end result of these battles is greater uncertainty for the organization. The poorer the environment, the more difficult the problems organizations face in managing resource transactions. In an environment that is poor, unstable, and complex, resources are especially hard to obtain and organizations face the greatest uncertainty. By contrast, in a rich, stable, and simple environment, resources are easy to come by and uncertainty is low.

Airline companies, such as American, Continental, and Delta, are currently experiencing a highly uncertain environment. New, low-cost airlines are entering the industry, which has increased the level of industry competition. As a result, the environment has become poorer as airlines fight for customers (a resource) and are forced to offer lower prices to attract them. The airlines' environment is complex because competing airlines (part of each airline's specific environment) are very interconnected: If one airline reduces prices, they all reduce prices to protect their domains, and these actions further increase uncertainty. Finally, the price of oil, the threat of foreign competition, and the state of the economy are all interconnected in the airlines' environment and change over time, making it difficult to predict or plan for contingencies.

In contrast, the environment of the pharmaceutical industry is relatively certain. Merck, Bristol-Myers-Squibb, Upjohn, and other large companies that invent drugs receive patents and are the sole providers of their respective new drugs for 17 years. The patent-owning company can charge a high price for its drug because it faces no competition and customers have no option but to buy the drug from the original manufacturer.

Organizations in the pharmaceutical industry exist in a stable, rich environment: Competition is low, and no change occurs until patents expire. Because of a huge increase in the price of drugs during the 1990s, however, the government moved to control drug prices. That move increased the complexity of the environment and, thus, made pharmaceutical organizations less certain about it. To manage complexity and slow the pace of change, the industry successfully lobbied Congress to safeguard its interests. Throughout the rest of this chapter, we discuss in more detail the strategies that organizations pursue to manage their environments. First, however, it is useful to examine the nature of the environment that confronted Jeff Bezos after he founded Amazon.com.

Focus on New Information Technology: Amazon.com, Part 4

The book distribution and book-selling industry was changed forever in July 1995 when Jeff Bezos brought virtual bookseller Amazon.com on-line. His new company changed the whole nature of the environment. Previously, book publishers had sold their books either indirectly to book wholesalers who supplied small bookstores or directly to large book chains like Barnes & Noble or Borders or to book-of-the-month clubs. There were so many book publishers and so many book sellers that the industry was relatively stable with both large and small bookstores enjoying a comfortable niche in the market. In this relatively stable, simple, rich environment uncertainty was low and all companies enjoyed good revenues and profits.

Amazon.com's electronic approach both to buying and selling books changed all this. First, since it was able to offer customers quick access to all books in print (over 1.5 million) and it discounted the prices of its books, this led to a higher level of industry competition and made the industry environment poorer. Second, since it also negotiated directly with the large book publishers over price and supply because it wanted to get books quickly to its customers, this led to an increase in the complexity of the environment because all players (book publishers, wholesalers, stores, and customers) became more closely linked. Third, as a result of these factors and continuing changes in information technology, the environment became more unstable and resources harder to secure.

What have been the results of the increase in uncertainty in the environment brought about by these changes? First, these changes directly threatened the prosperity of small bookstores, many of which have closed their doors and left the business because they can't compete with on-line bookstores. Second, the large book sellers like Barnes & Noble and Borders have started their own on-line bookstores to compete with Amazon.com. Third, Amazon.com and the other on-line bookstores have been engaged in a price war and the prices of books have been further discounted, resulting in an even more competitive and uncertain environment. What will be the outcome in the future? Nobody knows, but Amazon.com has yet to make a profit, and profits are falling in the industry as uncertainty has increased.

Managerial Implications: Analyzing the Environment

1. Managers at all levels and in all functions should periodically analyze the organizational environment and identify sources of uncertainty.
2. To manage transactions with the organizational environment effectively, managers should chart the forces in the organization's specific and general environments, noting (a) the number of forces that will affect the organization, (b) the pattern of interconnectedness or linkages among these forces, (c) how rapidly these forces change, and (d) the extent and nature of competition, which affect how rich or poor the environment is.
3. Taking that analysis, managers should plan how to deal with contingencies. Designing the structure of their organization to match the environment in which they operate is the first stage in this process.

CONTINGENCY THEORY

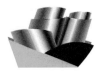

A common assumption in the study of how organizations manage their environments is that the environment is a contingency—a source of uncertainty that has to be planned for. According to **contingency theory**, in order to manage its environment effectively, an organization should design its structure to fit with the environment in which the organization operates.[9] In other words, an organization must design its *internal* structure to control the *external* environment (see Figure 6.3). A poor fit between structure and environment leads to failure; a close fit leads to success. Support for contingency theory comes from two studies of the relationship between structure and the environment. These studies, conducted by Paul Lawrence and Jay Lorsch and by Tom Burns and G. M. Stalker, are examined next.

Lawrence and Lorsch on Differentiation, Integration, and the Environment

Contingency theory *A management theory that states that in order to manage its environment effectively, an organization should design its structure to fit with the environment in which the organization operates.*

The strength and complexity of the forces in the general and specific environments have a direct effect on the extent of differentiation *inside* an organization.[10] The number and size of an organization's functions mirror the organization's needs to manage exchanges with forces in its environment (see Figure 6.4). Which function handles exchanges with suppliers? Purchasing does. Which function handles exchanges with customers? Sales and marketing. With the government and consumer organizations? Legal and public relations. A *functional structure* emerges, in part, to deal with the complexity of environmental demands.

Paul Lawrence and Jay Lorsch investigated how companies in different industries differentiate and integrate their structures to fit the characteristics of the industry in which they compete.[11] They selected three industries that they argued experienced different levels of uncertainty as measured by variables such as rate of change (dynamism) in the environment. The three industries were the plastics industry, which they said experienced the greatest level of uncertainty, the food-processing industry, and the container or can-manufacturing industry, which they said experienced the least uncertainty. Uncertainty was highest in plastics because of the rapid pace of technological and product change. It was lowest in containers because organizations produce a standard array of products that changes little from year to year. Food-processing companies were in-between because, although they introduce new products frequently, the technology of production is quite stable.

Lawrence and Lorsch measured the degree of differentiation in the production, research and development, and sales departments of a set of companies in each industry.

FIGURE 6.3

The Fit Between the Organization and Its Environment. A poor fit leads to failure; a close fit leads to success.

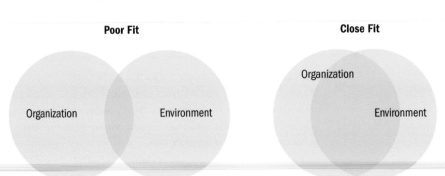

Degree of fit

FIGURE 6.4

Functional Differentia-tion and Environmental Demands. A functional structure emerges in part to deal with the complexity of demands from the environment.

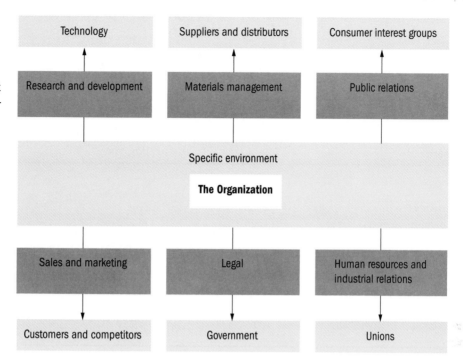

They were interested in the degree to which each department adopted a different internal structure of rules and procedures to coordinate its activities. They also measured differences in subunit or functional orientations (differences in time, goal, and interpersonal orientations). They were interested in the differences between each department's attitude toward the importance of different organizational goals, such as sales or production goals or short-term and long-term goals. They also measured how companies in different industries integrated their functional activities.

They found that when the environment was perceived by each of the three departments as very complex and unstable, the attitudes and orientation of each department diverged significantly. Each department developed a different set of values, perspectives, and way of doing things that suited the part of the specific environment with which it was dealing. Thus, the extent of differentiation among departments was greater in companies that faced an uncertain environment than in companies that were in stable environments.

Lawrence and Lorsch also found that when the environment is perceived as unstable and uncertain, organizations are more effective if they are less formalized, more decentralized, and more reliant on mutual adjustment. When the environment is perceived as relatively stable and certain, organizations are more effective if they have a more centralized, formalized, and standardized structure. Moreover, they found that effective companies in different industries had levels of integration that matched their levels of differentiation. In the uncertain plastics industry, very effective organizations were highly differentiated but were also highly integrated. In the relatively stable container industry, very effective companies had a low level of differentiation, which was matched with a low level of integration. Companies in the moderately uncertain food-processing industry had levels of differentiation and integration in between the other two. Table 6.1 summarizes these relationships.

As Table 6.1 shows, a complex, uncertain environment (such as the plastics industry) requires that different departments develop different orientations toward their tasks (a high level of differentiation) so that they can deal with the complexity of their specific environment. As a result of this high degree of differentiation, such organizations require

TABLE 6.1
The Effect of Uncertainty on Differentiation and Integration in Three Industries

	Degree of Uncertainty		
VARIABLE	PLASTICS INDUSTRY	FOOD-PROCESSING INDUSTRY	CONTAINER INDUSTRY
Environmental Variable			
Uncertainty (complexity dynamism, richness)	High	Moderate	Low
Structural Variables			
Departmental differentiation	High	Moderate	Low
Cross-functional integration	High	Moderate	Low

more coordination (a high level of integration). They make greater use of integrating roles among departments to transfer information so that the organization as a whole can develop a coordinated response to the environment. By contrast, no complex integrating mechanisms such as integrating roles are found in companies in stable environments because the hierarchy, rules, and SOPs provide sufficient coordination.

The message of Lawrence and Lorsch's study was that organizations must adapt their structures to match the environment in which they operate if they are to be effective. This conclusion reinforced that of a study by Burns and Stalker.

Burns and Stalker on Organic versus Mechanistic Structures and the Environment

Tom Burns and G. M. Stalker also found that organizations need different kinds of structure to control activities when they need to adapt and respond to change in the environment.[12] Specifically, they found that companies with an organic structure were more effective in unstable, changing environments than were companies with a mechanistic structure. The reverse was true in a stable environment. There the centralized, formalized, and standardized way of coordinating and motivating people that is characteristic of a mechanistic structure worked better than the decentralized team approach that is characteristic of an organic structure.

What is the reason for those results? When the environment is rapidly changing and on-the-spot decisions need to be made, lower-level employees need to have the authority to make important decisions—in other words, they need to be empowered. Moreover, in complex environments, rapid communication and information sharing are often necessary to respond to customer needs and develop new products.[13] When the environment is stable, in contrast, there is no need for complex decision-making systems. Managing resource transactions is easy, and better performance can be obtained by keeping authority centralized in the top-management team and using top-down decision making. Burns and Stalker's conclusion was that organizations should design their structure to match the dynamism and uncertainty of their environment. Figure 6.5 summarizes the conclusions from Burns and Stalker's and Lawrence and Lorsch's contingency studies.

McDonald's offers an interesting insight into the way a change in an organization's environment can bring about a change in its structure.

ORGANIZATIONAL INSIGHT

6.1 MCDONALD'S CHANGING ENVIRONMENT

McDonald's environment is changing rapidly and becoming increasingly difficult to manage, and the company has been experiencing increasing problems since the late 1990s. Consumer tastes are shifting as a health-conscious public is eating less beef and less fat. Environmentalists are attacking the packaging that McDonald's uses. Competitors are becoming more numerous and are seizing McDonald's customers. Chili's and the Olive Garden are luring away upscale customers, and Rally's, Taco Bell, and Wendy's are challenging McDonald's for patrons who want a quick, cheap meal. McDonald's has been searching for ways to increase its control of an environment that is becoming poorer, more complex, and less predictable.

At the center of its new approach is a dramatic change in McDonald's view of its domain. In the past, at the heart of McDonald's were its standardized production operation and its mechanistic structure based on formalization, which together ensured that burgers and fries served in London and Moscow tasted and looked the same as burgers and fries served in New York. The operations manual for the kitchen alone was 600 pages long!

New customers, however, demanded new kinds of food, so McDonald's new approach to production is based on flexibility. It has experimented with over 200 kinds of food—from barbecue to pizza to lobster—and is allowing franchisees to design a menu that appeals to local customers. For example, McDonald's restaurants on the eastern shore of Maryland serve crab-cake sandwiches; in Mexico, it has introduced a guacamole burger.[14] McDonald's is also allowing franchisees to design a decor to suit their location. For instance, the McDonald's on Wall Street has a grand piano.[15] Also, McDonald's has opened many different types of restaurants, for example, Wal-Mart store and air-conditioned playhouse restaurants. In addition, McDonald's is experimenting with owning different kinds of restaurants—it bought a small pizza chain in 1999 and invested in a Mexican restaurant in 1997, for example.[16]

All this flexibility placed a severe strain on McDonald's mechanistic structure. The organization was forced to develop a more organic structure to allow its 8,800 restaurants to fashion their own approaches to decor and bill of fare. Moreover, it decentralized authority to managers in the regions to make the important decisions that most affected them. In the new environment, the name of the game is flexibility and quick response to changes in customers' needs and competitors' moves. Nevertheless, McDonald's also needs to maintain the standards of quality and cleanliness that are among its claims to fame; thus, it needs the centralized control that has always been the key to the operation of its structure.

Forces in McDonald's specific and general environments have combined to produce a high level of uncertainty that has compelled the organization to change the way it operates. The impact of a force of nature on Burger King, a major competitor of McDonald's, also illustrates the importance of flexibility in the face of the unexpected. When

FIGURE 6.5

The Relationship Between Environmental Uncertainty and Organizational Structure.
Studies by Lawrence and Lorsch and by Burns and Stalker indicate that organizations should adapt their structure to reflect the degree of uncertainty in their environment. Companies with a mechanistic structure tend to fare best in a stable environment. Those with an organic structure tend to fare best in an unstable, changing environment.

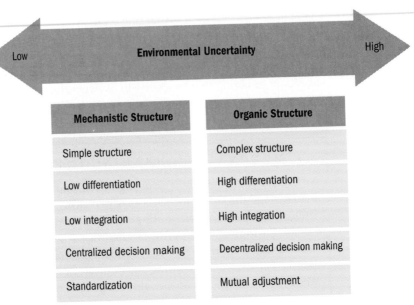

Mechanistic Structure	Organic Structure
Simple structure	Complex structure
Low differentiation	High differentiation
Low integration	High integration
Centralized decision making	Decentralized decision making
Standardization	Mutual adjustment

Hurricane Andrew struck Miami in 1992, it destroyed Burger King's corporate headquarters. Over 300 of the company's 700 corporate executives lost their homes and belongings. Overnight, CEO Barry Gibbons initiated sweeping management changes. He empowered employees to set their own work hours, allowed them to bring their children to work, abolished the company dress code because many had few clothes to wear, and widened job descriptions and job duties to encourage employees to perform a wide range of tasks.[17] Its new temporary headquarters had no private offices, so managers and employees were forced to develop new ways of communicating and coordinating.

The results of this turmoil astonished Burger King management. The pace of work remained the same, but the culture of the organization completely changed. People enjoyed the new open atmosphere created by the new headquarters and the new work rules. So beneficial were the changes to the organization's culture that top management rebuilt its headquarters building in a way that allowed it to retain its new corporate values. Burger King's sales have soared in the 1990s as it competes head to head with McDonald's.

RESOURCE DEPENDENCE THEORY

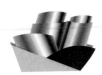

Organizations are dependent on their environment for the resources they need to survive and grow. The supply of resources, however, is dependent on the complexity, dynamism, and richness of the environment. If an environment becomes poorer because important customers are lost or new competitors enter the market, resources are likely to become scarce and more valuable, and uncertainty is likely to increase. Organizations attempt to manage their transactions with the environment to ensure access to the resources on which they depend. They want their access to resources to be as predictable as possible because predictability simplifies the managing of their domain and promotes survival.

According to **resource dependence theory**, the goal of an organization is to minimize its dependence on other organizations for the supply of scarce resources in its environment and to find ways of influencing them to make resources available.[18] Thus, an organization must simultaneously manage two aspects of its resource dependence: (1) It

Resource dependence theory *A management theory that states that the goal of an organization is to minimize its dependence on other organizations for the supply of scarce resources in its environment and to find ways of influencing them to make resources available.*

has to exert influence over other organizations so that it can obtain resources, and (2) it must respond to the needs and demands of the other organizations in its environment.[19]

The strength of one organization's dependence on another for a particular resource is a function of two factors. One factor is how vital the resource is to the organization's survival. Scarce and valuable inputs (such as component parts and raw materials) and resources (such as customers and distribution outlets) are very important to an organization's survival.[20] The other factor is the extent to which the resource is controlled by other organizations. Crown Cork and Seal and other can manufacturers, for example, need aluminum to produce cans, but for many years the supply of aluminum was controlled by Alcoa, which had a virtual monopoly.

The personal computer industry illustrates the operation of both factors. Personal computer manufacturers—such as Compaq, Gateway, and Dell—depend on organizations such as Intel that supply memory chips and integrated circuits. Some like Apple and IBM that do not sell on-line (Dell and Gateway are the on-line leaders) also depend on chains of computer stores and other retail stores that stock their products, and on school systems and corporate customers that buy large quantities of their products. When there are few suppliers of a resource such as integrated circuits, or few organizations that distribute and sell a product, companies become very dependent on the organizations that do exist. Intel, for example, makes many of the most advanced microchips and, thus, has a lot of power over computer makers who need its fastest chips to compete successfully. The greater the dependence of one organization on another, the more power the latter has over the former, and the more it can threaten or exploit the dependent organization if it wishes to do so.

To manage their resource dependence and control their access to scarce resources, organizations develop various strategies.[21] Just as nations attempt to craft an international policy to increase their ability to influence world affairs, so organizations try to find ways of increasing their influence over their environment. Microsoft offers a good example of the management of the environment to control resource dependence.

ORGANIZATIONAL INSIGHT

6.2 MIGHTY MICROSOFT

Microsoft dominates the operating systems market and is attempting to build its market share in the Internet, spreadsheet, word-processing, graphics, and local area networking markets as well. In 1998, competitors accused Microsoft of using its dominant industry position to harm rivals and gain power over suppliers and other companies that rely on it, and in 1999 the federal government sued Microsoft in court arguing it, is a monopolist. Competitors believe Microsoft has an unfair advantage because it controls the development of basic computer operating systems, such as Windows 98, which in turn determines how well software applications work. In effect, Microsoft controls the input that other companies require—its widely used operating system. Rival software developers believe that Microsoft's expertise in operating systems gives Microsoft software designers an unfair opportunity to make Microsoft products run better than theirs. Adobe Systems, which makes software typefaces, thinks that Microsoft's Windows operating system was designed to print Microsoft's typefaces at twice the speed of Adobe's, and Adobe's sales suffered. Logitech Inc. complained that Microsoft's refusal to allow it to package Windows with its mouse made it difficult for Logitech to offer customers a competitive product. Netscape complained that Microsoft forced users of Windows 98 to use Microsoft's Web browser rather than Netscape's.

> Other companies are dependent on Microsoft, but Microsoft is not dependent on them. Microsoft produces not only all kinds of software products but also the hardware—mouse and CD-ROM products, for example—that backs up its software. Moreover, if it wants to quickly enter a lucrative new market niche, it often takes over the dominant software company in that niche. Microsoft's power to control resources has been so strong that some analysts suggest that Microsoft should be broken up into a number of smaller companies, or it should be prevented from taking over any more. However, Microsoft claims it has done nothing wrong.[22]

INTERORGANIZATIONAL STRATEGIES FOR MANAGING RESOURCE DEPENDENCIES

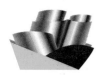

As the Microsoft example shows, the flow of resources among organizations is uncertain and problematic. To reduce uncertainty, an organization needs to devise interorganizational strategies to manage the resource interdependencies in its specific and general environments. Managing these interdependencies allows an organization to protect and enlarge its domain. In the specific environment, an organization needs to manage its relationships with forces such as suppliers, unions, and consumer interest groups. If they restrict access to resources, they can increase uncertainty.

In the specific environment, two basic interdependencies cause uncertainty: symbiotic and competitive.[23] Interdependencies are symbiotic when the outputs of one organization are inputs for another; thus, **symbiotic interdependencies** generally exist between an organization and its suppliers and distributors. Intel and computer makers like Compaq and Dell have a symbiotic interdependency. **Competitive interdependencies** exist among organizations that compete for scarce inputs and outputs.[24] Compaq and Dell are in competition for customers for their computers and for inputs such as Intel's latest microchips.

Symbiotic interdependencies *Interdependencies that exist between an organization and its suppliers and distributors.*

Competitive interdependencies *Interdependencies that exist among organizations that compete for scarce inputs and outputs.*

Organizations can use various linkage mechanisms to control symbiotic and competitive interdependencies.[25] The use of these mechanisms, however, requires the actions and decisions of the linked organizations to be coordinated. This need for coordination reduces each organization's freedom to act independently and perhaps in its own best interests. Suppose that Compaq, to protect its future supply of chips, signs a contract with Intel agreeing to use only Intel chips. But then a new chip manufacturer comes along with a less expensive chip. The contract with Intel obliges Compaq to pay Intel's higher prices even though doing so is not in Compaq's best interests.

Whenever an organization involves itself in an interorganizational linkage, it must balance its need to reduce resource dependence against the loss in autonomy or freedom of choice that will result from the linkage.[26] In general, an organization aims to choose the interorganizational strategy that offers the most reduction in uncertainty for the least loss of control.[27]

In the next two sections we examine the interorganizational strategies that organizations can use to manage symbiotic interdependencies and competitive interdependencies. A linkage is formal when two or more organizations agree to coordinate their interdependencies directly in order to reduce uncertainty. The more formal a linkage is, the greater are both the direct coordination and the likelihood that coordination is based on an explicit, written agreement or involves some common ownership between organizations. The more informal a linkage is, the more indirect or loose is the method of coordination and the more likely is the coordination to be based on an implicit or unspoken agreement.

STRATEGIES FOR MANAGING SYMBIOTIC RESOURCE INTERDEPENDENCIES

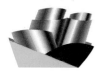

To manage symbiotic interdependencies, organizations have a range of strategies from which to choose. Figure 6.6 indicates the relative degree of formality of four strategies. The more formal a strategy is, the greater is the prescribed area of cooperation between organizations.

Developing a Good Reputation

Reputation *A state in which an organization is held in high regard and trusted by other parties because of its fair and honest business practices.*

The least formal, least direct way to manage symbiotic interdependencies with suppliers and customers is to develop a **reputation**, a state in which an organization is held in high regard and trusted by other parties because of its fair and honest business practices. For example, paying bills on time and providing high-quality goods and services lead to a good reputation and trust on the part of suppliers and customers. If a car repair shop has a reputation for excellent repair work and fair prices for parts and labor, customers will return to the shop whenever their cars need servicing, and the organization will be managing its linkages with customers successfully.

The De Beers diamond cartel uses trust and reputation to manage its linkages with suppliers and customers. De Beers customers are a select group of the world's biggest diamond merchants. When these merchants buy from De Beers, they ask for a certain quantity of diamonds—say, $10 million worth. De Beers then selects an assortment of diamonds that it values at $10 million. Customers have no opportunity to bargain with De Beers over the price or quality of the diamonds. They can buy or not buy, but they always buy because they know that De Beers will not cheat them. The organization's reputation and survival depend on maintaining customers' goodwill.

Reputation and trust are probably the most common linkage mechanisms for managing symbiotic interdependencies. Over the long run, companies that behave dishonestly are likely to be unsuccessful; thus, organizations as a group tend to become more honest over time.[28] Acting honestly, however, does not rule out active bargaining and negotiating over the price and quality of inputs and outputs. Every organization wants to strike the deal that best suits it and, therefore, attempts to negotiate terms in its favor.

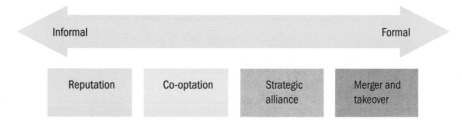

FIGURE 6.6   **Interorganizational Strategies for Managing Symbiotic Interdependencies.** Symbiotic interdependencies generally exist between an organization and its suppliers and distributors. The more formal a strategy is, the greater is the cooperation between organizations.

Co-optation

Co-optation A strategy that manages symbiotic interdependencies by neutralizing problematic forces in the specific environment.

Co-optation is a strategy that manages symbiotic interdependencies by neutralizing problematic forces in the specific environment.[29] An organization that wants to bring opponents over to its side gives them a stake in or claim on what it does and tries to satisfy their interests. Pharmaceutical companies co-opt physicians by sponsoring medical conferences, giving away free samples of drugs, and advertising extensively in medical journals. Physicians become sympathetic to the interests of the pharmaceutical companies, which bring them onto the "team" and tell them that they and the companies have interests in common. Co-optation is an important political tool.

A common way to co-opt problematic forces such as customers, suppliers, or other important outside stakeholders is to bring them within the organization and, in effect, make them inside stakeholders. If some stakeholder group does not like the way things are being done, an organization co-opts the group by giving it a role in changing the way things are. All kinds of organizations use this strategy. Local schools, for example, attempt to co-opt parents by inviting them to become members of school boards or by establishing teacher-parent committees. In such an exchange, the organization gives up some control but usually gains more than it loses.

Interlocking directorate A linkage that results when a director from one company sits on the board of another company.

Outsiders can be brought inside an organization through bribery, a practice widespread in many countries but illegal in the United States. They can also be brought inside through the use of an **interlocking directorate**—a linkage that results when a director from one company sits on the board of another company. An organization that uses an interlocking directorate as a linkage mechanism invites members of powerful and significant stakeholder groups in its specific environment to sit on its board of directors.[30] An organization might invite the financial institution from which it borrows most of its money to send someone to sit on the organization's board of directors. Outside directors interact with an organization's top-management team, ensuring supplies of scarce capital, exchanging information, and strengthening ties between organizations.

Strategic Alliances

Strategic alliance An agreement that commits two or more companies to share their resources to develop joint new business opportunities.

Strategic alliances are becoming an increasingly common mechanism for managing symbiotic (and competitive) interdependencies. A **strategic alliance** is an agreement that commits two or more companies to share their resources to develop joint new business opportunities. For example, Digital Equipment Corporation (DEC) agreed to buy a 10 percent stake in Olivetti, the Italian consumer products firm, so that it could use Olivetti's vast European sales network (Olivetti's resource) to sell its new computer workstation technology (DEC's resource).[31] This arrangement lets DEC compete with IBM, Hewlett-Packard, and Sun Microsystems for the huge European office computer market. IBM and Sears established a joint venture called Prodigy to create an on-line information service for customers. The venture combined IBM's computer skills (its resource) with Sears's huge customer base (its resource).[32]

There are several types of strategic alliance. Figure 6.7 indicates the relative degree of formality of long-term contracts, networks, minority ownership, and joint ventures. The more formal an arrangement is, the stronger and more prescribed is the linkage and the tighter is control of the joint activities. In general, as uncertainty increases, organizations choose a more formal alliance to protect their access to resources.

LONG-TERM CONTRACTS.   At the informal end of the continuum shown in Figure 6.7 are alliances spelled out in long-term contracts among two or more organizations.

FIGURE 6.7

Types of Strategic Alliance. Companies linked by a strategic alliance share resources to develop joint new business joint new business opportunities. The more formal an alliance is, the stronger is the link between allied organizations.

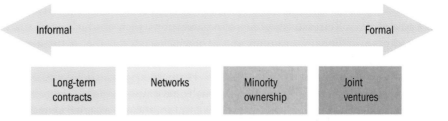

The purpose of these contracts is usually to reduce costs by sharing resources or by sharing the risk of research and development, marketing, construction, and other activities. Contracts are the least formal type of alliance because no ties link the organizations apart from the agreement set forth in the contract. For example, to reduce financial risk, Bechtel Corporation and Willbros Group, Inc., two leading multinational construction companies, agreed to pool their resources to construct an $850 million oil pipeline in the Caspian Sea.[33] J. B. Hunt Transport, a trucking company, formed an alliance with Sante Fe Pacific Corporation, a railroad company. Sante Fe agreed to carry Hunt's trailers across the country on railroad cars. At the end of the trip, the trains were met by Hunt's trucks, which transported the trailers to their final destination. This arrangement lowered Hunt's costs while increasing Sante Fe's revenues.

Contracts can be oral or written, casual, shared or implicit. The CEOs or top managers of two companies might agree over lunch to meet regularly to share information and ideas on some business activity, such as standardizing computer systems or changing customer needs. Some organizations, in contrast, develop written contracts to specify procedures for sharing resources or information and for using the benefits that result from such agreements. Kellogg Company, the breakfast cereal manufacturer, enters into written contracts with the farmers who supply the corn and rice it needs. Kellogg agrees to pay a certain price for their produce regardless of the market rate prevailing when the produce is harvested. Both parties gain because a major source of unpredictability (fluctuations in corn and rice prices) is eliminated from their environments.

NETWORKS.   As discussed in Chapter 4, a network or network structure is a cluster of different organizations whose actions are coordinated by contracts and agreements rather than through a formal hierarchy of authority. Members of a network work closely to support and complement one another's activities. The alliance resulting from a network is more formal than the alliance resulting from a contract because more ties link member organizations and there is greater formal coordination of activities.[34] Chapter 4 discussed how Nike and other organizations establish networks to build long-term relationships with suppliers, distributors, and customers while keeping the core organization from becoming too large or too bureaucratic.

The goal of the organization that created the network is to share its R&D skills with its partners and have them use those skills to become more efficient and help it to reduce its costs or increase quality. For example, AT&T created a network organization and linked its partners together so that it could produce answering machines at low cost. AT&T electronically sends designs for new component parts and assembly instructions for new products to its network partners who coordinate their activities to produce the components in the desired quantities and then ship them to the final assembly point.[35]

MINORITY OWNERSHIP.   A more formal alliance emerges when organizations buy a minority ownership stake in each other. Ownership is a more formal linkage than contracts and network relationships. Minority ownership makes organizations extremely interdependent, and that interdependence forges strong cooperative bonds.

Keiretsu *A group of organizations, each of which owns shares in the other organizations in the group, that work together to further the group's interests.*

The Japanese system of keiretsu shows how minority ownership networks operate. **Keiretsu** is a group of organizations, each of which owns shares in the other organizations in the group, and all of which work together to further the group's interests. Japanese companies employ two basic forms of keiretsu. Capital keiretsu are used to manage input and output linkages. Financial keiretsu are used to manage linkages among many diverse companies and usually have at their center a large bank.[36]

A particularly good example of the way a capital keiretsu network can benefit all the companies in it, but particularly the dominant ones, comes from the Japanese auto industry.[37] Toyota is one of the most profitable car companies in the world. Its vehicles are consistently ranked among the most reliable, and the company enjoys strong customer support. Interdependencies with its customers are not problematic because Toyota has a good reputation among them. One of the reasons for this good reputation is the way Toyota controls its input interdependencies.

Because a car's reliability depends on the quality of its inputs, managing this crucial linkage is important. To control its inputs, Toyota owns a minority stake, often as much as 49 percent, in most of the companies that supply its components. Because of these formal ownership ties, Toyota can exercise strong control over the prices that suppliers charge and over the quality of their products. An even more important result of this formal alliance, however, is that it allows Toyota and its suppliers to work together to improve product quality and reliability.

Toyota is not afraid to share proprietary information with its suppliers because of its ownership stake. As a result, suppliers participate in the car design process, and their participation can lead to the discovery of new ways to improve the quality and reduce the cost of components. Both Toyota and the suppliers share in the benefits that accrue from this close cooperation, and over time, this alliance has given Toyota a competitive advantage. In turn, this competitive advantage translates into control over important environmental interdependencies. Note also that Toyota's position as a shareholder in its suppliers' businesses means that there is no reason for Toyota to exploit them ruthlessly and depress their profits. All partners benefit from the sharing of activities. These close linkages paid off once again when Toyota introduced the latest model of the Camry sedan. By taking advantage of the skills in its network, Toyota was able to engineer $1,700 in cost savings in the new model and to introduce it at a price below that of the old model.

A financial keiretsu, dominated by a large bank, functions like a giant interlocking directorate. The dominant members of the financial keiretsu, which is composed of diverse companies, sit on the board of directors of the bank and often on the boards of each other's companies. The companies are linked by substantial long-term stock holdings, most of which are managed by the bank at the center of the keiretsu. Member companies are able to trade proprietary information and knowledge that benefit them collectively. Indeed, one of the benefits that comes from a financial keiretsu is the way businesses can transfer and exchange managers to strengthen the network.

Figure 6.8 shows the Fuyo keiretsu, which centers on Fuji Bank. Its members include Nissan, NKK, Hitachi, and Canon. The directors of Fuji Bank link all the largest and most significant keiretsu members. Each large member company has its own set of satellite companies. For example, Nissan has a minority ownership stake in many of the suppliers that provide inputs for its auto operations.

Joint venture *A strategic alliance among two or more organizations that agree to jointly establish and share the ownership of a new business.*

JOINT VENTURE. A **joint venture** is a strategic alliance among two or more organizations that agree to jointly establish and share the ownership of a new business.[38] Joint ventures are the most formal of the strategic alliances because the participants are bound by a formal legal agreement that spells out their rights and responsibilities. For example,

FIGURE 6.8

The Fuyo Keiretsu. A financial keiretsu centered around Fuji Bank in which organizations in the kereitsu are linked by minority share ownership in each other.

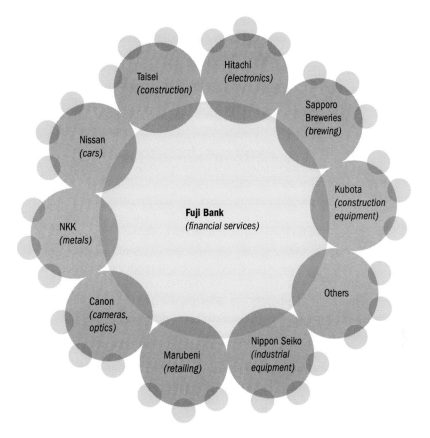

Satellite companies affiliated with one of the dominant members of the keiretsu.

Company A and Company B agree to set up a new organization, Company C, and then jointly design its organizational structure and select its top-management team (see Figure 6.9). Both Company A and Company B send executives to manage Company C, and they also provide the resources Company C needs to grow and prosper. Participants in a joint venture often pool their distinctive competences. One, for example, might supply expert knowledge on efficient production techniques, and the other might supply some R&D skills. The pooling of skills in a new venture increases the value that can be produced.

The shared ownership of a joint venture reduces the problems of managing complex interorganizational relationships that might arise if the basis of the strategic alliance was simply a long-term contract. Moreover, the newly created organization (Company C in Figure 6.9) is free to develop the structure that best suits its needs, and the problems of managing interdependencies with the parent companies are reduced. A joint venture may allow the founding companies (Company A and Company B) to stay small and entrepreneurial.

FIGURE 6.9

Joint Venture Formation. Two separate organizations pool resources to create a third organization. A formal legal document specifies the terms of this type of strategic alliance.

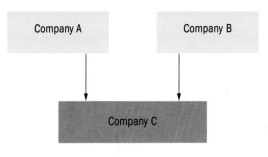

In sum, organizations use informal and formal strategic alliances to manage symbiotic resource interdependencies. The degree of formality increases as environmental uncertainty increases. (The issue of which type of alliance an organization should select is discussed in more detail later in the section on transaction cost theory.)

Merger and Takeover

The most formal strategy (see Figure 6.6) for managing symbiotic (and competitive) resource interdependencies is to merge with or take over a supplier or distributor. As a result of a merger or a takeover, resource exchanges occur *within* one organization rather than *between* organizations, and an organization can no longer be held hostage by a powerful supplier (that might demand a high price for its products) or by a powerful customer (who might try to drive down the price it pays for a company's products).[39] For example, Conoco, a major producer of chemicals, owns several oil fields and, thus, controls the prices of its oil and petroleum products, which are vital inputs for chemical manufacturing. Similarly, McDonald's owns vast ranches in Brazil, where it rears, at a low cost, cattle for hamburger. Alcoa owns or manages most of the world's supply of aluminum ore and has effectively controlled the world aluminum industry for decades. Ford Motor Company, owner of Hertz Rent-a-Car, has a ready-made customer for its products.

An organization that takes over another company normally incurs great expense and faces the problems of managing the new business. Thus, an organization is likely to take over a supplier or distributor only when it has a very great need to control a crucial resource or manage an important interdependency.

STRATEGIES FOR MANAGING COMPETITIVE RESOURCE INTERDEPENDENCIES

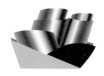

Organizations do not like competition. Competition threatens the supply of scarce resources and increases the uncertainty of the specific environment. Intense competition can threaten the very survival of an organization as product prices fall to attract fickle customers and the environment becomes poorer and poorer. For example, in 1999, AT&T was forced to reduce the price of its long-distance services to just 7 cents a minute to compete with MCI Worldcom, SBC Communications, and Qwest, which had been making large inroads into its market share.[40] The stronger competition is, the greater the number of companies that go bankrupt.[41] Ultimately, an organizational environment consists of a handful of the strongest survivors competing head-to-head for resources.

Organizations use a variety of techniques to directly manipulate the environment to reduce the uncertainty of their competitive interdependent activities.[42] Figure 6.10 indicates

FIGURE 6.10

Interorganizational Strategies for Managing Competitive Interdependencies. Competitive interdependencies exist between an organization and its rivals. The more formal a strategy is, the more explicit is the attempt to coordinate competitors' activities.

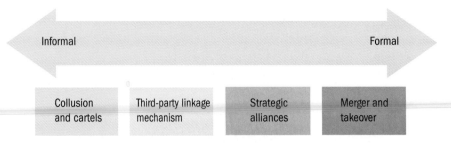

Informal			Formal
Collusion and cartels	Third-party linkage mechanism	Strategic alliances	Merger and takeover

the relative formality of four strategies. The more formal a strategy is, the more explicit is the attempt to coordinate competitors' activities. Some of these strategies are illegal, but unethical organizations use them to gain an edge.

Collusion and Cartels

Collusion *A secret agreement among competitors to share information for a deceitful or illegal purpose.*

Cartel *An association of firms that explicitly agree to coordinate their activities.*

Collusion is a secret agreement among competitors to share information for a deceitful or illegal purpose. Organizations collude in order to reduce the competitive uncertainty they experience. A **cartel** is an association of firms that explicitly agree to coordinate their activities.[43] Cartels and collusion increase the stability and richness of an organization's environment and reduce the complexity of relations among competitors. Both of them are illegal in the United States.

Competitors in an industry can collude by establishing industry standards.[44] Industry standards function like rules of conduct and may tell competitors, for example, what prices they should charge, what their product specifications should be, or what a product's profit markup should be. Industry standards may result from price leadership. The dominant organization is likely to be the price leader. It sets the prices for its products, and then the weaker organizations charge prices that conform to the price leader's price. In this way, industry prices are fixed. Organizations can always make more profit if they collectively coordinate their activities than if they compete. Price fixing enables competitors to maintain artificially high prices and prevent destructive price competition. Customers lose because the prices that are established may be artificially high.

In the United States today, price leadership is occurring in the market for large trucks. A 25 percent import duty on large trucks keeps out foreign trucks that otherwise would be less expensive than American-made trucks. Behind this protective wall, General Motors and Ford indirectly coordinate their prices to keep the prices of large trucks artificially high. It has been estimated that 35 percent of the cost of a large American truck is profit, compared with 10 to 15 percent for a sedan.[45] So high is the markup that Toyota introduced a large truck in 1993, paid the 25 percent import duty, and still made a 10 to 15 percent profit.

Organizations can also collude and form a cartel without formal written agreement by signaling their intentions to each other by public announcements about their future strategy. For example, they can announce price increases that they are contemplating and see whether their rivals will match those increases.

Organizations in an industry can try to discipline organizations that break informal competitive industry rules. Some large companies have a reputation for ruthlessly going after competitors that break their industry's informal pricing rules. American Airlines has been accused of reducing prices below the level of its price-cutting rivals and keeping them there to deliberately punish weaker price-cutting firms. In the 1970s, the large airlines jointly conspired to drive a price-cutting small firm—Britain's Laker Airlines—out of business so that they could keep prices high.

Third-Party Linkage Mechanisms

Third-party linkage mechanism *A regulatory body that allows organizations to share information and regulate the way they compete.*

A more formal but still indirect way for competing organizations to coordinate their activities is through a **third-party linkage mechanism**—a regulatory body that allows organizations to share information and regulate the way they compete.[46] An example is a trade association, an organization that represents companies in the same industry and enables competitors to meet, share information, and informally make agreements that allow them to monitor one another's activities.[47] This interaction reduces the fear that one organization may deceive or outwit another. A trade association has the collective resources (obtained from member organizations) to lobby strongly for government policies that protect the interests of its industry. We saw earlier how the pharmaceutical industry uses its powerful lobby to fend off attempts to reduce the price of drugs. The cable TV industry, defense, farming, and virtually every other industry seek to protect their own interests and increase their access to scarce resources.

Other examples of third-party linkage mechanisms include agencies such as the Chicago Board of Trade, stock markets, the National Collegiate Athletic Association (NCAA), and any other organization that is set up to regulate competitive interdependencies. Third-party linkage mechanisms provide rules and standards that stabilize industry competition and, thus, increase the richness of the environment. They reduce the complexity of the environment because they regulate the interactions of organizations. And, by increasing the flow of information, they enable organizations to react more easily to change or to the dynamism of the environment. In short, third-party linkage mechanisms provide a way for competing organizations to manage resource interdependencies and reduce uncertainty.

Organizations that use a third-party linkage mechanism co-opt themselves and jointly receive the benefits of the coordination that they obtain from the third-party linkage mechanism. For example, Microelectronics and Computer Corporation, an applied R&D cooperative funded by industry members such as Intel and Motorola, was set up to improve research in semiconductors. This organization channels the results of its research to its funding members. After three years, the funding members can license the results to other companies in the industry.[48] The number of U.S. research and development cooperatives formed by competitors to fund joint research interests is rapidly increasing as global competition increases. Japan is the model for such third-party linkage mechanisms. Its Ministry of International Trade and Industry (MITI) has a long history of promoting industry cooperation among domestic rivals to foster joint technical developments that allow Japanese companies to dominate the global marketplace.

Strategic Alliances

Strategic alliances can be used to manage not only symbiotic interdependencies but also competitive interdependencies.[49] Competitors can cooperate and form a joint venture to develop common technology that will save them all a lot of money, even though they may be in competition for customers when their final products hit the market. Apple Computer and IBM, for example, formed a long-term joint venture to share the costs of developing a common microchip that will make their machines compatible, even though they will be competitors in the personal computer market. Both Ford and Mazda have benefited from a strategic alliance (Ford owns a 25 percent stake in Mazda). Ford gained detailed knowledge of Japanese production techniques, and Mazda and Ford jointly cooperated to produce vehicles in the same U.S. plant.

Although the kinds of joint ventures just described are not anticompetitive, organizations sometimes use joint ventures to deter new entrants or harm existing competitors. Philips and Grounding, two of the largest German consumer electronics companies, signed an agreement to share their VCR and camcorder businesses in order to compete with the Japanese giants Sony and Panasonic.[50] Organizations can also form a joint venture to develop a new technology that they can then protect from other rivals by obtaining and defending patents. The use of strategic alliances to manage competitive interdependencies is limited only by the imagination of rival companies. The situation in the telecommunications industry provides an interesting example of how joint ventures can reduce the uncertainty surrounding competitive industry relations.

ORGANIZATIONAL INSIGHT

6.3 COMPETITIVE ALLIANCES IN TELECOMMUNICATIONS

The telecommunications industry is experiencing a wave of strategic alliances and joint ventures. The introduction of new technologies and the linking of these technologies with computer networks and with satellite networks have made the industry one of the most dynamic and uncertain. For example, the development of the next generation of digital switching technology is very expensive, and several different companies are trying to develop the technology that will become the industry standard. Consequently, companies are becoming strategic allies and are forming joint ventures to link their operations. This strategy allows them to reduce risks and costs. Figure 6.11 shows how complex such an alliance system can be.

As the figure shows, Mitsui has direct alliances with Hughes Aircraft, Unisys, Toshiba, Nippon Telephone and Telegraph, Nippon Electric Company, Hitachi, and Olivetti. These companies, all of which are competitors, are jointly attempting to develop the next generation of digital telephone technology to seize the growing European market, which is presently being deregulated. In another competitive alliance, AT&T is cooperating with Sun Microsystems, Ricoh, Plessey, and Philips, among other companies, to develop the technology to seize this market. Thus, on a global level, competitors are forming strategic alliances to compete with the alliances formed by other organizations. Industry competition is becoming a complex game.

Merger and Takeover

The ultimate weapon in an organization's armory for managing problematic competitive (and symbiotic) interdependencies is merger with, or takeover of, a competing organization.[51] Mergers and takeovers can improve a company's competitive position by allowing the company to strengthen and enlarge its domain and increase its ability to produce a wider range of products to better serve more customers. For example, NationsBank bought up smaller banks at a very fast rate, and in 1998 merged with Bank of America to become the biggest bank in the United States. Liz Claiborne purchased bankrupt Russ Togs (whose clothes are in a significantly lower price range than Liz Claiborne brand clothes) to expand its product line and serve the needs of shoppers at discount stores such as Kmart and Wal-Mart.[52]

Many organizations might like to use merger to become a monopoly, the sole player in the marketplace. Fortunately for consumers, and for organizations themselves, monopolies are illegal in the United States and in most other developed countries, and if organizations become too strong and dominant, they are prevented by antitrust law from taking over other companies. An organization that is too dominant is itself the whole competitive environment and has virtually no need to manage organization-environment

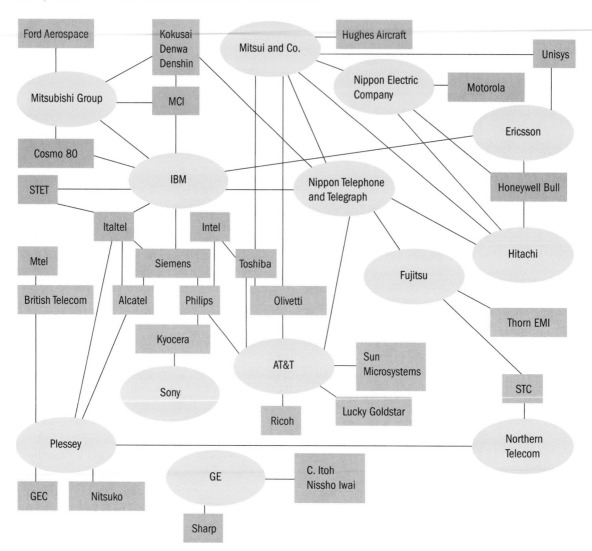

FIGURE 6.11   Competitive Alliances in Telecommunications.

Source: "How to Form and Manage Successful Strategic Alliances," *Prospectus* March 1990, p. 18. Reprinted with permission.

relations.[53] Nevertheless, cartels, collusion, and other anticompetitive practices can ultimately be bad for the organizations themselves. In the long run, as a result of changes in technology, cheap sources of labor, changes in government policy, and so forth, new entrants will eventually be able to enter the industry, and existing companies that have reduced competition among themselves will then find themselves ineffective competitors. Protected from competition in an environment where uncertainty has been low, these monopoly-like organizations will have developed tall, centralized, mechanistic structures weighed down by overly complex bureaucratic rules and procedures. Their decision making will be slow and cumbersome, and in the short run they will be unable to meet the challenges of the new, rapidly changing environment. GM, IBM, and Xerox are organizations that controlled their competitive environments for a very long time and suffered greatly when the environment changed and allowed more agile foreign and domestic competitors to enter and beat the established companies at their own game.

Managerial Implications: Resource Dependence Theory

1. To maintain an adequate supply of scarce resources, study each resource transaction individually in order to decide how to manage it.
2. Study the benefits and costs associated with an interorganizational strategy before using it.
3. To maximize the organization's freedom of action, always prefer an informal to a formal linkage mechanism. Use a more formal mechanism only when the uncertainty of the situation warrants it.
4. When entering into strategic alliances with other organizations, be careful to identify the purpose of the alliance and future problems that might arise between organizations, in order to decide whether an informal or a formal linkage mechanism is most appropriate. Once again, choose an informal rather than a formal alliance whenever possible.
5. Use transaction cost theory (discussed next) to identify the benefits and costs associated with the use of different linkage mechanisms to manage particular interdependencies.

TRANSACTION COST THEORY

Transaction costs The costs of negotiating, monitoring, and governing exchanges between people.

As we have seen, organizations have at their disposal many interorganizational strategies to manage uncertain resource dependencies. The effect of all these strategies is to make the environment friendlier and to increase an organization's control over forces in its specific and general environments. Most large organizations probably use every one of the strategies and change strategies to suit a changing environment. Transaction cost theory sheds light on why and under what conditions they select and change strategies.

In Chapter 1, we defined **transaction costs** as the costs of negotiating, monitoring, and governing exchanges between people. Whenever people work together, there are costs—transaction costs—associated with controlling their activities.[54] Transaction costs also arise when organizations exchange resources or information. Organizations interact with other organizations to get the resources they require, and they have to control those symbiotic and competitive interdependencies. According to resource dependence theory, organizations attempt to gain control of resources and minimize their dependence on other organizations. According to **transaction cost theory**, the goal of the organization is to minimize the costs of exchanging resources in the environment and the costs of managing exchanges inside the organization.[55] Every dollar or hour of a manager's time spent in negotiating or monitoring exchanges with other organizations, or with managers inside one organization, is a dollar or hour that is not being used to create value. Thus, organizations try to minimize transaction costs and bureaucratic costs because they siphon off productive capacity. Organizations try to find mechanisms that make interorganizational transactions relatively more efficient.

Transaction cost theory A theory that states that the goal of an organization is to minimize the costs of exchanging resources in the environment and the costs of managing exchanges inside the organization.

Health care provides a dramatic example of just how large transaction costs can be and why reducing them is so important. It is estimated that 42 percent of the health care budget in the United States is spent handling exchanges (such as bills and insurance claims) between doctors, hospitals, the government, insurance companies, and other parties.[56] Clearly, any improvements that reduce transaction costs would result in a major saving of resources. The desire to reduce transaction costs was the impetus for the formation of health maintenance organizations (HMOs) and other networks of health care providers. HMO providers agree to reduce their costs in return for a more certain flow of patients, among other things. This trade-off reduces the uncertainty they experience.

Sources of Transaction Costs

Transaction costs result from a combination of human and environmental factors.[57] (See Figure 6.12.)

ENVIRONMENTAL UNCERTAINTY AND BOUNDED RATIONALITY.   The environment is characterized by considerable uncertainty and complexity. People, however, have only a limited ability to process information and to understand the environment surrounding them.[58] Because of this limited ability, or bounded rationality, the higher the level of uncertainty is in an environment, the greater is the difficulty of managing transactions between organizations.

Suppose Organization A wants to license a technology developed by Organization B. The two organizations could sign a contract. Considerable uncertainty, however, would surround this contract. For example, Organization B might want to find new ways of using the technology to make new products for itself. Given bounded rationality, it would be difficult and prohibitively expensive to try to write a contract that not only protected Organization B, which developed the technology, but also spelled out how the two organizations might jointly share in the future benefits from the technology. In this situation, the developing company (Organization B) might prefer to proceed alone and not exchange resources with Organization A, even though it knows it could create more value by engaging in the exchange. Thus, because of bounded rationality and the high transaction costs of drawing up a contract, potential value that could have been created is lost. Environmental uncertainty may make the cost of negotiating, monitoring, and governing agreements so high that organizations resort to more formal linkage mechanisms—such as strategic alliances, minority ownership, or even mergers—to lower transaction costs.

OPPORTUNISM AND SMALL NUMBERS.   Most people and organizations behave honestly and reputably most of the time, but some always behave opportunistically—that is, they cheat or otherwise attempt to exploit other forces or stakeholders in the environment.[59] For example, an organization contracts for component parts of a particular quality. To reduce costs and save money, the supplier deliberately substitutes inferior materials but bills for the more expensive, higher-quality parts. Individuals, too, act opportunistically: Managers pad their expense reports or exploit customers by manufacturing inferior products.

FIGURE 6.12

Sources of Transaction Costs

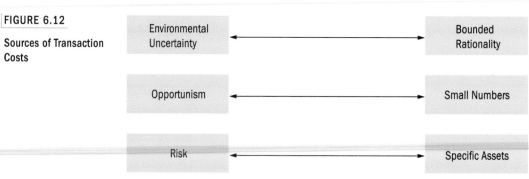

When an organization is dependent on one supplier or on a small number of trading partners, the potential for opportunism is great. The organization has no choice but to transact business with the supplier, and the supplier, knowing this, might choose to supply inferior inputs to reduce costs and increase profit.

When the prospect for opportunism is high because of the small number of suppliers to which an organization can go for resources, the organization has to expend resources to negotiate, monitor, and enforce agreements with its suppliers to protect itself. For example, the U.S. government spends billions of dollars a year to protect itself from being exploited by defense contractors such as Hughes Aircraft and General Dynamics, which have been known to take advantage of their ability to exploit the government because they have so few competitors for defense-related work.

Specific assets *Investments—in skills, machinery, knowledge, and information—that create value in one particular exchange relationship but have no value in any other exchange relationship.*

RISK AND SPECIFIC ASSETS.   **Specific assets** are investments—in skills, machinery, knowledge, and information—that create value in one particular exchange relationship but have no value in any other exchange relationship. A company that invests $100 million in a machine that makes microchips for IBM machines only has made a very specific investment in a very specific asset. An organization's decision to invest money to develop specific assets for a specific relationship with another organization in its environment involves a high level of risk. Once the investment is made, the organization is locked into it. If the other party tries to exploit the relationship by saying, for example, "We will not buy your product unless you sell it to us for $10 less per unit than you're charging now," the organization is in a very difficult situation. This tactic is akin to blackmail.

An organization that sees any prospect of being trapped or blackmailed will judge the investment in specific assets to be too risky. The transaction costs associated with the investment become too high, and value that could have been created is lost.[60]

Transaction Costs and Linkage Mechanisms

Organizations base their choice of interorganizational linkage mechanisms on the level of transaction costs involved in an exchange relationship. Transaction costs are low when these conditions exist:

1. Organizations are exchanging nonspecific goods and services.
2. Uncertainty is low.
3. There are many possible exchange partners.

In these environmental conditions, it is easy for organizations to negotiate and monitor interorganizational behavior. Thus, in a low-transaction-cost environment, organizations can use relatively informal linkage mechanisms, such as reputation and unwritten, word-of-mouth contracts.

Transaction costs increase when these conditions exist:

1. Organizations begin to exchange more specific goods and services.
2. Uncertainty increases.
3. The number of possible exchange partners falls.

In this kind of environment, an organization will begin to feel that it cannot afford to trust other organizations, and it will start to monitor and use more formal linkages, such as long-term contracts, to govern its exchanges. Contracts, however, cannot cover every situation that might arise. If something unexpected happens, what will the other party to the exchange do? It has a perfect right to act in the way that most benefits itself, even though its actions are harmful to the other organization.

How does an organization act in a high-transaction-cost situation? According to transaction cost theory, an organization should choose a more formal linkage mechanism to manage exchanges as transaction costs increase. The more formal the mechanism used, the more control organizations have over each other's behavior. Formal mechanisms include strategic alliances (joint ventures), merger, and takeover, all of which internalize the transaction and its cost. In a joint venture, two organizations establish a third organization to handle their joint transactions. Establishing a new entity that both organizations own equally reduces each organization's incentives to cheat the other and provides incentives for them to do things (e.g., invest in specific assets) that will create value for them both. With mergers, the same arguments hold because one organization now owns the other.

From a transaction cost perspective, the movement from less formal to more formal linkage mechanisms (see Figures 6.6, 6.7, and 6.10) occurs because of an organization's need to reduce the transaction costs of its exchanges with other organizations. Formal mechanisms minimize the transaction costs associated with reducing uncertainty, opportunism, and risk.

Bureaucratic Costs

If formal linkage mechanisms are such an efficient way to minimize the transaction costs of exchanges with the environment, why do organizations not use these mechanisms all the time? Why do they ever use an informal linkage mechanism such as a contract if a joint venture or a merger gives them better control of their environment? The answer is that bringing the transactions inside the organization minimizes but does not eliminate the costs of managing transactions.[61] Managers must still negotiate, monitor, and govern exchanges between people inside the organization. Internal transaction costs are called bureaucratic costs to distinguish them from the transaction costs of exchanges between organizations in the environment.[62] We saw in Chapter 2 how difficult communication and integration between functions and divisions are. Now we see that integration and communication are not only difficult to achieve but cost money because managers have to spend their time in meetings rather than creating value.[63] Thus, managing an organization's structure is a complex and expensive problem that becomes much more expensive and complex as the organization grows—as GM and IBM have discovered.

Using Transaction Cost Theory to Choose an Interorganizational Strategy

Transaction cost theory can help managers choose an interorganizational strategy by enabling them to weigh the savings in transaction costs achieved from using a particular linkage mechanism against the bureaucratic costs of operating the linkage mechanism.[64] Because transaction cost theory brings into focus the costs associated with different linkage mechanisms to reduce uncertainty, it is able to make better predictions than is resource dependence theory about why and when a company will choose a certain interorganizational strategy. Managers deciding which strategy to pursue must take the following steps:

1. Locate the sources of transaction costs that may affect an exchange relationship and decide how high the transaction costs are likely to be.
2. Estimate the transaction cost savings from using different linkage mechanisms.
3. Estimate the bureaucratic costs of operating the linkage mechanism.

4. Choose the linkage mechanism that gives the most transaction cost savings at the lowest bureaucratic cost.

The experience of the Ekco Group offers an interesting example of how a supplier can use a linkage mechanism to reduce transaction costs for customers in order to gain their support. Ekco and its customers jointly benefit from close, personal ties, and there is no need for formal and expensive mechanisms to coordinate their interorganizational exchanges.

ORGANIZATIONAL INSIGHT

6.4 EKCO AND ITS SUPPLIERS

The Ekco Group of Nashua, New Hampshire, makes a wide range of bakeware products, kitchen tools and equipment, household plastic products (such as laundry baskets), and pest-control devices.[65] It produces thousands of nonelectric consumer and office products that require no assembly and are replaced rather than repaired when they wear out.

Ekco's wide product range reflects the needs of retail customers like Wal-Mart and Kmart, which are continually trying to reduce the transaction costs associated with obtaining products. Obtaining a wide range of products from one supplier reduces the transaction costs associated with building many supplier relationships. By offering a broad range of products that Kmart, Wal-Mart, and others are interested in carrying, Ekco helps the retailers minimize the number of companies they must go to for the products they want to carry. In this way, Ekco is implicitly inviting customers to increase their links with Ekco.

To foster long-term commitment and trust with its customers, Ekco recently installed a state-of-the-art $4 million data-processing system (a specific asset) that allows Ekco to provide a just-in-time inventory service to retailers that supply the company with data. This system simplifies retailers' ordering and tracking of their inventory. By managing customers' transactions at no cost to them, the Ekco system further reduces the retailers' transaction costs with Ekco and strengthens their perception that Ekco is a good company to do business with. Ekco's attempt to develop informal linkage mechanisms with its customers has paid off. Sales to its major customers increase every year, and in 1999 Ecko was acquired by Corning Consumer Products for over $300 million, a premium price for its shareholders.[66]

The implication of a transaction cost view is that a formal linkage mechanism should be used only when transaction costs are high enough to demand it. An organization should take over and merge with its suppliers or distributors, for example, only if the saving in transaction costs outweighs the costs of managing the new acquisition.[67] Otherwise, like Ekco and its customers, the organization should rely on less formal mechanisms, such as strategic alliances and long-term contracts, to handle exchange relationships. The relatively informal linkage mechanisms avoid the need for an organization to incur bureaucratic costs. Three linkage mechanisms that enable organizations to avoid bureaucratic costs while still minimizing transaction costs are keiretsu, franchising, and outsourcing.

KEIRETSU. The Japanese system of keiretsu can be seen as a mechanism for achieving the benefits of a formal linkage mechanism without incurring its costs.[68] The policy of owning a minority stake in its suppliers' companies gives Toyota substantial control over the exchange relationship and allows it to avoid problems of opportunism and uncertainty with its suppliers. Toyota also avoids the bureaucratic costs of actually owning and managing its suppliers. Indeed, keiretsu was developed to provide the benefits of full ownership without the costs.

In contrast, General Motors has full ownership of more suppliers than does any other car manufacturer and pays more for its inputs than the other car companies pay for theirs. Critics charge that these high costs arise because GM's internal suppliers are in a protected situation. GM is a captive buyer, so its supplying divisions have no incentive to be efficient and, thus, behave opportunistically.[69]

What should GM do? One course of action would be to divest its inefficient suppliers and then establish strategic alliances or long-term contracts with them to encourage them to lower their costs and increase their efficiency. If they cannot improve their cost or quality, GM would form new alliances with new suppliers. GM has been trying to do exactly that. In 1999 it spun off its Delco electronic parts subsidiary into an independent operating company.[70] GM is trying to obtain the benefits that Toyota has achieved from its strategy of minority ownership. Conversely, if General Motors were experiencing problems with obtaining the benefits from a strategic alliance (e.g., its partner was acting opportunistically), it should move to a more formal linkage mechanism and buy and merge with its suppliers. GM is not in this situation, however. Its problem is finding the combination of ownership, strategic alliances, and long-term contracts that will minimize its input costs, which are still about $1,000 higher per car than the input costs of Japanese car manufacturers.

FRANCHISING.   A franchise is a business that is authorized to sell a company's products in a certain area. The franchiser sells the right to use its resources (e.g., its name or operating system) to a person or group (the franchisee) in return for a flat fee or a share of the profits. Normally, the franchiser provides the inputs used by the franchisee, who deals directly with the customer. The relationship between franchiser and franchisee is symbiotic. The transaction cost approach offers an interesting insight into why interorganizational strategies such as franchising emerge.[71]

Consider the operational differences between McDonald's and Burger King. A very large proportion of McDonald's restaurants are owned by franchisees, but most Burger King restaurants are owned by the company. Why does McDonald's not own its restaurants? Why is McDonald's willing to make its franchisees millionaires instead of enriching its stockholders? From a transaction cost point of view, the answer lies in the bureaucratic costs that McDonald's would incur if it managed its own restaurants.

The single biggest challenge for a restaurant is to maintain the quality of its food. If McDonald's employed managers in company-owned restaurants, would those managers have the same incentive to maintain as high a quality of customer service as franchisees, who directly benefit from high performance? McDonald's believes that if it owned and operated all its restaurants—that is, if it used a formal linkage mechanism—the bureaucratic costs incurred to maintain the quality and consistency of the restaurants would exceed any extra value the organization and its shareholders would obtain from ownership. Thus, McDonald's generally owns only those restaurants that are located in big cities or near highways. In big cities, it can spread the costs of employing a management team over many restaurants and reduce bureaucratic costs. On interstate highways, McDonald's believes, franchisees realize that they are unlikely to see the same travelers ever again and have no incentive to maintain standards.

The same issue arises on the output side when an organization is choosing how to distribute its products. Should an organization own its distribution outlets? Should it sell directly to customers? Should it sell only to franchised dealers? Again the answer depends on the transaction cost problems the organization can expect in dealing with the needs of its customers. Generally, the more complex products are and the more information customers need about how they work or how to repair them, the greater is the likelihood that organizations have formal hierarchical control over their distributors and franchisees or own their own distribution outlets.[72]

Cars are typically sold through franchised dealers because of the need to provide customers with reliable car repair. Also, because cars are complicated products and customers need a lot of information before they buy one, it is effective for manufacturers to have some control over their distributors. Thus, car manufacturers have considerable control over their dealerships and monitor and enforce the service that dealerships give to customers. Toyota, for example, closely monitors the number of customer complaints against a dealership. If the number of complaints gets too high, it punishes the dealership by restricting its supply of new cars. As a result, dealers have strong incentives to give customers good service. In contrast, the transaction costs involved in handling simple products like clothes or food are low. Thus, few clothing or food companies choose to use formal linkages to control the distribution of their products. Less formal mechanisms such as contracts with wholesalers or with retail stores become the preferred distribution strategy.

OUTSOURCING.   Another strategy for managing interdependencies is outsourcing. As discussed in Chapter 4, **outsourcing** is moving a value creation activity that was performed inside an organization to outside where it is done by another company, for example, hiring a company to manage a company's computer network or to distribute its products instead of performing the activity itself. Increasingly, organizations are turning to specialized companies to manage their information-processing needs. Eastman Kodak and IBM, for example, have set up divisions that supply this specialized service to companies in their environments.

What prompts an organization to outsource a function is the same calculation that determines whether an organization makes or buys inputs. Does the extra value that the organization obtains from performing its own marketing or information processing exceed the extra bureaucratic costs of managing such functions? If the answer is yes, the organization develops its own function. If it is no, the organization outsources the activity.[73] This decision is likely to change over time. Perhaps in 1998 it was best to have an information-processing department inside the organization. By 2002, however, specialized organizations may be able to process information more cheaply, and then it will pay to outsource that function. Outsourcing within networks, such as the one established by Nike, is another example of how outsourcing helps hold down the bureaucratic costs of managing exchanges inside an organization.

In summary, a transaction cost approach sheds light on why and how organizations choose different linkage mechanisms to manage their interdependencies. It improves our ability to understand the process that organizations use to manage their environments to enhance their chances for growth and survival. Solutions exist for managing uncertain resource exchanges and organizational interdependencies. These solutions range from less formal mechanisms like contracts to more formal mechanisms like ownership. The best mechanism for an organization is one that minimizes transaction and bureaucratic costs.

 # SUMMARY

Managing the organizational environment is a crucial task for an organization. The first step is identifying sources of uncertainty. Contingency theory suggests that the design of an organization's structure should reflect the level of uncertainty in the organization's environment. The more rapidly an organization's environment changes, the more complex its structure needs to be.

An organization needs to choose appropriate interorganizational linkage mechanisms for managing transactions between the organization and its environment. To do this, organizations need to continually evaluate the benefits and costs of different interorganizational strategies. Managers have to constantly monitor the linkage mechanisms they are using because environmental conditions may change and alter the benefits and costs associated with specific mechanisms. Different theories provide different but related approaches to understanding what these benefits and costs are.

Resource dependence theory weighs the benefit of securing scarce resources against the cost of a loss of autonomy. Transaction cost theory weighs the benefit of reducing transaction costs against the cost of increasing bureaucratic costs. An organization must examine the whole array of its exchanges with its environment in order to devise the combination of linkage mechanisms that will maximize its ability to create value. Chapter 6 has made the following main points:

1. The organizational environment is the set of forces that affects the way an organization operates and its ability to gain access to scarce resources.

2. The organizational domain is the range of goods and services that the organization produces and the clients that it serves. An organization devises interorganizational strategies to protect and enlarge its domain.

3. The specific environment consists of forces that most directly affect an organization's ability to secure resources. The general environment consists of forces that shape the specific environments of all organizations.

4. Uncertainty in the environment is a function of the complexity, dynamism, and richness of the environment.

5. Contingency theory argues that in order to manage its environment effectively, an organization should design its structure and control systems to fit with the environment in which the organization operates.

6. Resource dependence theory argues that the goal of an organization is to minimize its dependence on other organizations for the supply of scarce resources and to find ways of influencing them to make resources available.

7. Organizations have to manage two kinds of resource interdependencies: symbiotic interdependencies with suppliers and customers and competitive interdependencies with rivals.

8. The main interorganizational strategies for managing symbiotic relationships are the development of a good reputation, co-optation, strategic alliances, and merger and takeover. The main interorganizational strategies for managing competitive relationships are collusion and cartels, third-party linkage mechanisms, strategic alliances, and merger and takeover.

9. Transaction costs are the costs of negotiating, monitoring, and governing exchanges between people and organizations. There are three sources of transaction costs: the combination of uncertainty and bounded rationality, opportunism and small numbers, and specific assets and risk.

10. Transaction cost theory argues that the goal of organizations is to minimize the costs of exchanging resources in the environment and the costs of managing exchanges inside the organization. Organizations try to choose interorganizational strategies that minimize transaction costs and bureaucratic costs.

11. Interorganizational linkage mechanisms range from informal types such as contracts and reputation to formal types such as strategic alliances and ownership strategies such as merger and takeover.

DISCUSSION QUESTIONS

1. Pick an organization, such as a local travel agency or supermarket. Describe its organizational domain; then draw a map of the forces in its general and specific environments that affect the way it operates.

2. What are the major sources of uncertainty in an environment? Discuss how these sources of uncertainty affect a small biotechnology company and a large automaker.

3. What are the main findings of contingency theory? What current industry conditions might affect the way organizations design their structures?

4. According to resource dependence theory, what motivates organizations to form interorganizational linkages? What is the advantage of strategic alliances as a way of exchanging resources?

5. According to transaction cost theory, what motivates organizations to form interorganizational linkages? Under what conditions would a company prefer a more formal linkage mechanism to a less formal one?

ORGANIZATIONAL THEORY IN ACTION

PRACTICING ORGANIZATIONAL THEORY:
PROTECTING YOUR DOMAIN

Break up into groups of three to five people and discuss the following scenario:

You are a group of entrepreneurs who have recently launched a new kind of root beer, made from exotic herbs and spices, that has quickly obtained a loyal following in a large southwestern city. Inspired by your success, you have decided that you would like to increase production of your root beer to serve a wider geographical area with the eventual goal of serving the whole of the United States and Canada.

The problem you have is deciding what is the best way to secure your domain and manage the environment as you grow. On the one hand, both the ingredients in your root beer and your method of making it are secret, so that you have to protect it from potential imitators at all costs—large soda companies that will quickly copy it if they have a chance. On the other hand, you lack the funds for quick expansion, and finding a partner who can help you grow quickly and establish a brand-name reputation would be an enormous advantage.

1. Analyze the pros and cons of each of the types of strategic alliances (long-term contracts, networks, minority ownership, and joint ventures) as your means of managing the environment.

2. Based on this analysis, which one would you choose to maximize your chance of securing a stable niche in the soda market?

MAKING THE CONNECTION #6

Find an example of a company that is using a specific interorganizational strategy, such as a joint venture or a long-term contract. What linkage mechanism is it using? Use resource dependence theory or transaction cost theory to explain why the organization might have chosen that type of mechanism.

Analyzing the Organization: Design Modul #6

This module and the modules in the next two chapters allow you to analyze the environment of your organization and to understand how the organization tries to manage its environment to control and obtain the resources it needs to protect its domain.

Cases for Analysis:
AT&T'S CHANGING ENVIRONMENT

AT&T's environment began to change rapidly in 1982, after the company's parent, the Bell Corporation, was forced to divest the 22 "Baby Bells," the providers of local telephone service. The divestiture occurred because the U.S. government decided not to allow AT&T to compete in the emerging computer and telecommunications industry as long as it controlled both local and long-distance telephone service. Since AT&T wanted to enter the computer industry and become a major player in it, it agreed to the spin-off, and in 1984 the seven regional Bell telephone companies, such as Nynex and Ameritech, emerged. The government also deregulated long-distance telephone service at this time and new competitors, such as Sprint and MCI, entered the long-distance telephone market. As a result, AT&T faced competition for the first time in its long-distance markets.

AT&T's environment continued to change in the 1980s when technological advances such as the advent of wireless communications and cellular telephones and paging ushered in a whole new kind of competition. AT&T watched as wireless telephone companies like McCaw Cable became industry leaders. Realizing that it needed a strong foothold in the wireless market, AT&T decided to acquire McCaw Cable in 1993 to give it a strong foothold in this important new segment of the market.

During the early 1990s, AT&T's environment began to change rapidly as the government moved to deregulate the telecommunications industry further. In 1996, the "Baby Bells" finally received permission to provide long-distance service to their local customers and became a direct threat to AT&T's major business. In response, AT&T announced that it would enter the local telephone market to fight back. In addition, the increasing popularity of the Internet and the possibility of new technological developments that would make telephone conversations over the Internet quick and easy became a major threat to AT&T. AT&T re-

sponded by forming strategic alliances with Internet software companies like Netscape and decided to become a provider of on-line service to its long-distance customers. Seeing the threat from new communications media like satellite-to-home linkups (which would bypass AT&T's wired system), AT&T also formed a joint venture with Hughes Aircraft and made a major investment in its planned new global satellite system.

In the meantime, AT&T's venture into computers, which had started the whole move toward deregulation in the 1980s, had proved a disaster. AT&T had never been able to compete successfully with computer companies like Compaq and Dell, or with software providers like Microsoft and Novell. It had acquired NCR, a major computer maker, but this merger had proved to be a disaster because NCR was even then having its own problems surviving in the rapidly evolving computer industry.[74]

In the 1980s, AT&T also experienced stiff competition from Panasonic, Sony, and other Japanese companies that had seized control of the market for telecommunications equipment such as telephones, answering machines, and fax machines. Formerly, AT&T had a monopoly in this area, too. To fight back, AT&T developed a global network of strategic alliances to allow it to reduce production costs, and by 1995 it had won back a significant share of the market. Finally, by 1985, AT&T had begun to realize the importance of the international environment as a source of increased sales, and it entered into a series of alliances with foreign telephone companies to provide them with products and support services. The company also participated in industry consortia, such as Sematech, a partnership between the Department of Defense and industry focused on developing world-leading semiconductor technology, to keep on top of the rapidly changing environment.

In 1996, recognizing the significance of the profound changes taking place in all its different industry environments (long-distance and local phone service, Internet service, telecommunications products, and computers), AT&T announced that it was breaking up into three separate companies—AT&T, which would continue to do battle in the telephone service and Internet market; Lucent, which was AT&T's research and development arm, including Bell Laboratories, which produced all of AT&T's telecommunications products; and NCR, which would now be spun off.[75] In essence, AT&T had decided that it could not successfully manage all these different businesses through one corporate hierarchy.[76] Its response to the increasing turbulence in its environment was to split apart and allow three different management teams to find solutions to the problems they were experiencing in managing their respective environments.

1. How did AT&T's environment change over time?
2. What strategies did AT&T adopt to manage these changes?

ASSIGNMENT

1. Draw a chart of your organization's domain. List the organization's products and customers and the forces in the specific and general environments that have an effect on it. Which are the most important forces with which the organization has to deal?

2. Analyze the effect of the forces on the complexity, dynamism, and richness of the environment. From this analysis, how would you characterize the level of uncertainty in your organization's environment?

3. Review your analyses of organizational structure in Chapters 2, 3, and 4. How has your organization designed its structure to match the environment in which it operates? For example, how do its degree of differentiation and its use of integrating mechanisms reflect the uncertainty of its environment?

4. Draw a chart of the main interorganizational linkage mechanisms (e.g., long-term contracts, strategic alliances, mergers) that your organization uses to manage its symbiotic resource interdependencies. Using resource dependence theory and transaction cost theory, discuss why the organization chose to manage its interdependencies in this way. Do you think the organization has selected the most appropriate linkage mechanisms? Why or why not?

5. Draw a chart of the main interorganizational linkage mechanisms (e.g., collusion, third-party linkage mechanisms, strategic alliances) that your organization uses to manage its competitive resource interdependencies. Using resource dependence theory or transaction cost theory, discuss why the organization chose to manage its interdependencies in this way. Do you think the organization has selected the most appropriate linkage mechanisms? Why or why not?

6. In view of the analysis you have just made, do you think your organization is doing a good or a not-so-good job of managing its environment? What recommendations would you make to improve its ability to obtain resources?

REFERENCES

1. J. D. Thompson, *Organizations in Action* (New York: McGraw-Hill, 1967).

2. R. H. Hall, *Organizations: Structure and Process* (Englewood Cliffs, NJ: Prentice Hall, 1972).

3. R. H. Miles, *Macro Organizational Behavior* (Santa Monica, CA: Goodyear, 1980).

4. J. Child, "Organizational Structure, Environment, and Performance: The Role of Strategic Choice," *Sociology*, 1972, vol. 6, pp. 1–22; G. G. Dess and D. W. Beard, "Dimensions of Organizational Task Environments," *Administrative Science Quarterly*, 1984, vol. 29, pp. 52–73.

5. F. E. Emery and E. L. Trist, "The Causal Texture of Organizational Environments," *Human Relations*, 1965, vol. 18, pp. 21–32.

6. H. Aldrich, *Organizations and Environments* (Englewood Cliffs, NJ: Prentice Hall, 1979).

7. W. H. Starbuck, "Organizations and Their Environments," in M. D. Dunnette, ed., *Handbook of Industrial Psychology* (Chicago: Rand McNally, 1976), pp. 1069–1123; Dess and Beard, "Dimensions of Organizational Task Environments."

8. Aldrich, *Organizations and Environments.*

9. J. Pfeffer, *Organizations and Organizational Theory* (Boston: Pitman, 1982).

10. P. R. Lawrence and J. W. Lorsch, *Organization and Environment* (Boston: Graduate School of Business Administration, Harvard University, 1967).

11. Ibid.

12. T. Burns and G. M. Stalker, *The Management of Innovation* (London: Tavistock, 1961).

13. J. A. Courtright, G. T. Fairhurst, and L. E. Rogers, "Interaction Patterns in Organic and Mechanistic Systems," *Academy of Management Journal*, 1989, vol. 32, pp. 773–802.

14. "McDonald's Goes Local With a Guacamole Burger," *Daily World Wire*, 16 March 1999, p. 1.

15. L. Therrien, "McRisky," *Business Week*, 21 October 1991, pp. 114–122.

16. A. Edgecliffe-Johnson, "McDonald's Buys Pizza Restaurant Chain in Midwest," *Financial Times*, 7 May 1999, p. 19.

17. M. Billiard, "Change Blows in with Hurricane at Burger King," *Houston Chronicle*, 4 October 1992, p. 5E.

18. J. Pfeffer and G. R. Salancik, *The External Control of Organizations* (New York: Harper and Row, 1978).

19. Pfeffer, *Organizations and Organizational Theory*, p. 193.

20. Pfeffer and Salancik, *The External Control of Organizations*, pp. 45–46.

21. D. Miller and J. Shamsie, "The Resource-Based View of the Firm in Two Environments: The Hollywood Film Studios from 1936–1965." *Academy of Management Journal*, 1996, vol. 39, pp. 519–543.

22. K. Rebello and M. Lewyn, "Did Microsoft Shut the Windows on Competitors?" *Business Week*, 28 September 1992, pp. 32–33.

23. Pfeffer and Salancik, *The External Control of Organizations*, p. 114.

24. H. R. Greve, "Patterns of Competition: The Diffusion of Market Position in Radio Broadcasting," *Administrative Science Quarterly*, 1996, vol. 41, pp. 29–60.

25. J. M. Pennings, "Strategically Interdependent Organizations," in J. Nystrom and W. Starbuck, eds., *Handbook of Organizational Design* (New York: Oxford University Press, 1981), pp. 433–455.

26. J. Galaskeiwicz, "Interorganizational Relations," *Annual Review of Sociology*, 1985, vol. 11, pp. 281–304.

27. G. R. Jones and M. W. Pustay, "Interorganizational Coordination in the Airline Industry, 1925–1938: A Transaction Cost Approach," *Journal of Management*, 1988, vol. 14, pp. 529–546.

28. C. W. L. Hill, "Cooperation, Opportunism, and the Invisible Hand," *Academy of Management Review*, 1990, vol. 15, pp. 500–513.

29. P. Selznick, *TVA and the Grassroots* (New York: Harper and Row, 1949).

30. J. Pfeffer, "Size and Composition of Corporate Boards of Directors," *Administrative Science Quarterly*, 1972, vol. 17, pp. 218–228; R. D. Burt, "Co-optive Corporate Actor Networks: A Reconsideration of Interlocking Directorates Involving American Manufacturing," *Administrative Science Quarterly*, 1980, vol. 25, pp. 557–581.

31. J. B. Levine, "A Helping Hand for Europe's High-Tech Heavies," *Business Week*, 13 July 1992, pp. 43–44.

32. E. I. Schwartz, "Prodigy Installs a New Program," *Business Week*, 14 September 1992, pp. 96–97.

33. "Bechtel, Willbros to Build Pipeline at Caspian Sea," *Wall Street Journal*, 26 October 1992, p. A3.

34. W. W. Powell, K. W. Kogut, and L. Smith-Deorr, "Interorganizational Collaboration and the Locus of Innovation: Networks of Learning in Biotechnology," *Administrative Science Quarterly*, 1996, vol. 41, pp. 116–145.

35. R. Miles and C. Snow, "Causes of Failure in Network Organizations," *California Management Review*, 1992, vol. 4, pp. 13–32.

36. M. Aoki, *Information, Incentives, and Bargaining in the Japanese Economy* (New York: Cambridge University Press, 1988).

37. D. Roos, D. T. Jones, and J. P. Womack, *The Machine That Changed the World* (New York: Macmillan, 1990).

38. B. Kogut, "Joint Ventures: Theoretical and Empirical Perspectives," *Strategic Management Journal*, 1988, vol. 9, pp. 319–333.

39. J. Pfeffer, "Merger as a Response to Organizational Interdependence," *Administrative Science Quarterly*, 1972, vol. 17, pp. 382–394.

40. I. Simpson, "AT&T Slashes Calls to 7 Cents a Minute," Reuters, 30 August 1999.

41. F. M. Scherer, *Industrial Market Structure and Economic Performance*, 2nd ed. (Boston: Houghton Mifflin, 1980).

42. A. Phillips, "A Theory of Interfirm Competition," *Quarterly Journal of Economics*, 1960, vol. 74, pp. 602–613; J. K. Benson, "The Interorganizational Network as a Political Economy," *Administrative Science Quarterly*, 1975, vol. 20, pp. 229–250.

43. D. W. Carlton and J. M. Perloff, *Modern Industrial Organization* (Glenview, ILL: Scott, Foresman, 1990).

44. K. G. Provan, J. M. Beyer, and C. Kruytbosch, "Environmental Linkages and Power in Resource Dependence Relations Between Organizations," *Administrative Science Quarterly*, 1980, vol. 25, pp. 200–225.

45. "Why Networks May Fail,' *The Economist.*

46. H. Leblebichi and G. R. Salancik, "Stability in Interorganizational Exchanges: Rule-Making Processes in the Chicago Board of Trade," *Administrative Science Quarterly*, 1982, vol. 27, pp. 227–242; A. Phillips, "A Theory of Interfirm Competition."

47. M. Olson, *The Logic of Collective Action* (Cambridge, MA: Harvard University Press, 1965).

48. A. Allison, "Computer Vendors Consolidate Resources," *Mini-Micro Systems*, 19 June 1992, pp. 54–57.

49. B. Kogut, "Joint Ventures: Theoretical and Empirical Perspectives," *Strategic Management Journal*, 1988, vol. 9, pp. 319–332.

50. J. B. Levine, "A Helping Hand for Europe's High-Tech Heavies," *Business Week*, 13 July 1992, pp. 43–44.

51. Scherer, *Industrial Market Structure and Economic Performance.*

52. *Fortune*, 5 October 1992, pp. 49–54.

53. J. Cook, "When 2 + 2 = 5," *Forbes*, 8 June 1992, pp. 128–129.

54. A. Alchian and H. Demsetz, "Production, Information Costs, and Economic Organization," *American Economic Review*, 1972, vol. 62, pp. 777–795.

55. O. E. Williamson, *Markets and Hierarchies* (New York: The Free Press, 1975); O. E. Williamson, "The Governance of Contractual Relationships," *Journal of Law and Economics*, 1979, vol. 22, pp. 232–261.

56. www.msnbc.com, September 1999.

57. Williamson, *Markets and Hierarchies*.

58. H. A. Simon, *Models of Man* (New York: Wiley, 1957).

59. Williamson, *Markets and Hierarchies*.

60. B. Klein, R. Crawford, and A. Alchian, "Vertical Integration Appropriable Rents and the Competitive Contracting Process," *Journal of Law and Economics*, 1978, vol. 21, pp. 297–326.

61. R. H. Coase, "The Nature of the Firm," *Economica* N.S., 1937, 4, pp. 386–405.

62. G. R. Jones, "Transaction Costs, Property Rights, and Organizational Culture: An Exchange Perspective," *Administrative Science Quarterly*, 1983, vol. 28, pp. 454–467.

63. R. A. D'Aveni and D. J. Ravenscraft, "Economies of Integration Versus Bureaucracy Costs: Does Vertical Integration Improve Performance?" *Academy of Management Journal*, 1994, vol. 37, pp. 1167–1206.

64. G. R. Jones and C. W. L. Hill, "Transaction Cost Analysis of Strategy-Structure Choice," *Strategic Management Journal*, 1988, vol. 9, pp. 159–172.

65. "Ekco Group," *Fortune*, 21 September 1992, p. 87.

66. "CCPC Acquisition Corp. Completes Acquisition of EKCP Group Inc.," Company Press Release, 1999.

67. G. Walker and D. Weber, "A Transaction Cost Approach to Make or Buy Decisions," *Administrative Science Quarterly*, 1984, vol. 29, pp. 373–391.

68. J. F. Hennart, "A Transaction Cost Theory of Equity Joint Ventures," *Strategic Management Journal*, 1988, vol. 9, pp. 361–374.

69. K. G. Provan and S. J. Skinner, "Interorganizational Dependence and Control as Predictors of Opportunism in Dealer-Supplier Relations," *Academy of Management Journal*, 1989, vol. 32, pp. 202–212.

70. www.gm.com, Press release, 1998.

71. S. A. Shane, "Hybrid Organizational Arrangements and Their Implications for Firm Growth and Survival: A Study of New Franchisors," *Academy of Management Journal*, 1996, vol. 39, pp. 216–234.

72. D. E. Bowen and G. R. Jones, "Transaction Cost Analysis of Service Organization-Customer Exchange," *Academy of Management Review*, 1986, vol. 11, pp. 428–441.

73. E. Anderson and D. C. Schmittlein, "Integration of the Sales Force: An Empirical Examination," *Rand Journal of Economics*, 1984, vol. 26, pp. 65–79.

74. "Fatal Attraction," *The Economist*, 23 March 1996, p. 73.

75. A. Sloan, "The Howling Wolves," *Newsweek*, 7 October 1996, p. 59.

76. J. J. Keller, "The New AT&T Faces Daunting Challenges," *Wall Street Journal*, 24 September 1996, p. B1.

77. K. Kelly, O. Port, G. George, and Z. Schiller, "Learning from Japan," *Business Week*, 27 January 1992, pp. 52–60.

Chapter 7

ORGANIZATIONAL STRATEGY
and STRUCTURE

Finding the right strategy to respond to changes taking place in the environment, such as changes in the needs of customers or actions of competitors, is a complex issue facing managers. In an uncertain environment it is easy to make mistakes, and managers must constantly monitor their strategies and structures to make sure that they are working effectively. This chapter focuses on how managers of an organization can develop a strategy to compete successfully for scarce and valuable resources like customers.

First, the way managers use functional-level strategy to develop core competences that allow an organization to create value and give it a competitive advantage is examined. Second, the way managers then combine their organization's distinctive functional competences to create a business-level strategy that allows them to compete for scarce resources is analyzed. Third, the ways successful organizations—those that have been able to secure scarce resources—develop a corporate-level strategy to enter new domains where they can continue to grow and create value are scrutinized. The way managers must match strategy to structure and culture at each level—functional, business, and corporate—to increase their ability to create value is addressed throughout the chapter. By the end of this chapter you will understand why organizational strategy is a vital component of managing the organizational environment.

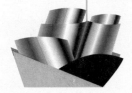

WHAT IS ORGANIZATIONAL STRATEGY?

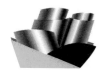

Strategy *The specific pattern of decisions and actions that managers take to use core compe- tences to achieve a com- petitive advantage and outperform competitors.*
Core competences *The skills and abilities in value creation activities that allow a company to achieve superior efficien- cy, quality, innovation, or customer responsiveness.*

As discussed in Chapter 1, an organization's **strategy** is a specific pattern of decisions and actions that managers take to use core competences to achieve a competitive advantage and outperform competitors.[1] An organization develops a strategy to increase the value it can create for its stakeholders. In this context, *value* is anything that satisfies the needs and desires of organizational stakeholders. Stockholders want a company to set goals and de- velop an action plan that maximizes the long-run profitability of the company and the value of their stock. Customers are likely to respond to a strategy that is based on the goal of offering high-quality products and services at appropriate prices.

Through its strategy, an organization seeks to use and develop core competences to gain a competitive advantage so that it can increase its share of scarce resources in its en- vironment. Recall that **core competences** are skills and abilities in value creation activi- ties, such as manufacturing, marketing, or R&D, that allow a company to achieve superior efficiency, quality, innovation, or customer responsiveness. An organization that possess- es superior core competences can outperform its rivals. Organizational strategy allows an organization to shape and manage its domain to exploit its existing core competences and develop new competences that make it a better competitor for resources.

McDonald's, for example, used its existing core competences in the production of fast food such as burgers and fries to provide fast food for the breakfast segment of the fast-food domain. By investing in food-testing facilities, McDonald's developed R&D competences that led to the development of breakfast items (such as the Egg McMuffin) that could be produced quickly. By using its existing core competences in new ways, and by developing new competences, McDonald's created a new line of breakfast food, which contributes 35 percent to McDonald's revenues. Similarly, Gillette applied its skills in marketing razor blades to selling men's toiletries and expanded its domain into toiletries.

The more resources an organization can obtain from the environment, the better able it is to set ambitious long-term goals and then develop a strategy and invest resources to create core competences to allow it to achieve those goals. In turn, improved competences give an organization a competitive advantage, which allows the organization to attract new resources—for example, new customers, highly qualified employees, or new sources of financial support. Figure 7.1 shows this cyclical value-creation process.

FIGURE 7.1

The Value Creation Cycle. Ample resources, a well-thought-out strate- gy, and distinctive com- petences give an organization a competi- tive advantage, which fa- cilitates the acquisition of still more resources.

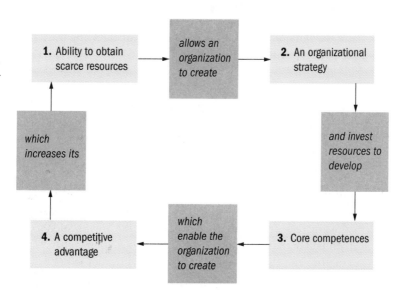

Sources of Core Competences

The ability to develop a strategy that allows an organization to create value and outperform competitors is a function of the organization's core competences. The strength of its core competences is a product of the specialized resources and coordination abilities that it possesses and other organizations lack.[2]

Functional resources
The skills possessed by an organization's functional personnel.

SPECIALIZED RESOURCES.   Two kinds of resources give an organization a competitive advantage: functional resources and organizational resources. **Functional resources** are the skills possessed by an organization's functional personnel. The skills of Microsoft's software design groups constitute Microsoft's single biggest functional resource. The quality of 3M's R&D department is the source of 3M's continued growth. Procter & Gamble's skill in new-product development is P&G's greatest functional resource. High-quality functional resources, however, are not enough to give an organization a competitive advantage. To be a source of competitive advantage, a function's core competence must be unique or special and difficult to imitate.[3] Microsoft's claim to uniqueness rests in the breadth and depth of the software talent that it possesses. In theory, a rich competitor like IBM could come along and buy up Microsoft's best people, or Du Pont could lure away 3M's scientists. If that were to happen, those companies' claims to uniqueness would disappear. To maintain its long-term competitive advantage, an organization needs to protect the source of its functional competences. That is why Microsoft gives its best people strong property rights, including making them owners in the company, and why 3M is well known for its long-term employment policies.

Organizational resources *The attributes that give an organization a competitive advantage such as the skills of the top-management team or possession of valuable and scarce resources.*

Organizational resources are the attributes that give an organization a competitive advantage. They include the skills of a company's top-management team, the vision of its founder or CEO, and the possession of valuable and scarce resources such as land, capital reserves, and plant equipment. They also include intangibles such as a company's brand name and its corporate reputation.[4] Like functional resources, to provide a competitive advantage, organizational resources must be unique or difficult to imitate. When organizations can hire away one another's managers, or when any organization can buy the most advanced computer-controlled manufacturing technology from Hitachi or Caterpillar, organizational resources are not unique and do not give an organization a competitive advantage. However, brand names like Coca-Cola and Levi Strauss and reputations such as Toyota's and Microsoft's are organizational resources that are unique and difficult to imitate. Obtaining those resources would entail buying the whole company, not just hiring away individual managers.

Coordination ability *An organization's ability to coordinate its functional and organizational resources to create maximal value.*

COORDINATION ABILITIES.   Another source of core competences is **coordination ability**, an organization's ability to coordinate its functional and organizational resources to create maximal value. Effective coordination of resources (achieved through the control provided by organizational structure and culture) leads to a competitive advantage.[5] The control systems that an organization uses to coordinate and motivate people at the functional and organizational levels can be a core competence that contributes to the organization's overall competitive advantage. Similarly, the way an organization decides to centralize or decentralize authority or the way it develops and promotes shared cultural values increases its effectiveness and allows the organization to manage and protect its domain better than its competitors can protect theirs. For example, Microsoft designs its structure and culture around small teams in order to coordinate activities in a way that facilitates the rapid development and launch of new products.

An organization's ability to use its structure and culture to coordinate its activities is also important at the functional and organizational levels.[6] The way an organization coordinates people and resources within functions determines the strength of its core competences. For example, several organizations have access to fast-food production technology (a functional resource) similar to the technology that McDonald's uses, but none has been able to imitate the rules, standard operating procedures, and norms that make McDonald's production operations so efficient. Competitors have been unable to duplicate the coordination of people and resources that enables McDonald's to produce hamburgers so efficiently and reliably.

Similarly, at the organizational level, the ability to use structure and culture to coordinate and integrate activities between departments or divisions gives some organizations a core competence and thus a competitive advantage. For example, the success of 3M and Procter & Gamble can be explained in part by their ability to develop integrating mechanisms that allow their marketing, product development, and manufacturing departments to combine their skills to develop innovative products. Similarly, PepsiCo's success stems in part from its sharing of resources among its different divisions (Pepsi-Cola, Frito-Lay, and so on).

Although many functional and organizational resources are not unique and can be imitated, an organization's ability to coordinate and motivate its functions and departments is difficult to imitate. It might be possible to buy the functional experts or technical knowledge of 3M or Microsoft, but the purchase would not include access to the practices and methods that either organization uses to coordinate its resources. These intangible practices are embedded in the way people interact in an organization—in the way organizational structure controls behavior—and they make these companies successful competitors.

Three Levels of Strategy

An organization should match its strategy and structure so that it can create value from its functional and organizational resources. But where is an organization's strategy created and by whom? Strategy is formulated at three organizational levels: the functional, business, and corporate levels. An organization's ability to create value at one level is an indication of its ability to manage the value creation process at the other levels (see Figure 7.2).

FIGURE 7.2

Three Levels of Organizational Strategy

Functional-level strategy *A plan of action to strengthen an organization's functional and organizational resources, as well as its coordination abilities, in order to create core competences.*

Functional-level strategy is a plan of action to strengthen an organization's functional and organizational resources, as well as its coordination abilities, in order to create core competences.[7] Daimler-Chrysler, for example, invests heavily to improve its skills in R&D and product design, and Coca-Cola invests heavily to devise innovative approaches to marketing. To strengthen their technical and human resources, functional managers train and develop subordinates to ensure that the organization has skills that match or exceed the skills of its competitors. Another part of the functional manager's job is to scan and manage the functional environment to ensure that the organization knows what is going on both inside and outside its domain.

R&D functional managers, for example, need to understand the techniques and products of their rivals. R&D functional managers at car companies routinely buy competitors' cars and strip them down to their component parts to study the technology and design that went into their manufacture. Taking this information, they can imitate the best aspects of competitors' products. It is also the job of R&D experts to scan other industries to find innovations that may help their company. Innovations in the computer software and microchip industries, for example, are important in product development in the car industry. If all of the functional managers in an organization monitor their respective functional environments and develop their functional resources and abilities, the organization will be better able to manage the uncertainty of its environment.[8]

Business-level strategy *A plan to combine functional core competences in order to position the organization so that it has a competitive advantage in its domain.*

Business-level strategy is a plan to combine functional core competences in order to position the organization so that it has a competitive advantage in its domain.[9] Mercedes-Benz takes its skills in R&D and positions itself in the luxury segment of the car market. Coca-Cola uses its marketing skills to defend its niche against PepsiCo.

Business-level strategy is the responsibility of the top-management team (the CEO and vice presidents in charge of various functions). Their job is to decide how to position the organization to compete for resources in its environment. CBS, NBC, and ABC, for example, compete with each other and with Fox, CNN, and Turner Broadcasting to attract the viewers (customers). Programming is the key variable that these companies can manipulate. They rely on functional experts in their news, documentary, comedy, and soap opera departments (among others) to scan the environment and identify future viewing trends so that they can commission programs that will give them a competitive advantage. Because all of the networks are doing this and are trying to outguess their rivals, programming is a complex and uncertain process.

Corporate-level strategy *A plan to use and develop core competences so that the organization can not only protect and enlarge its existing domain but can also expand into new domains.*

Corporate-level strategy is a plan to use and develop core competences so that the organization not only can protect and enlarge its existing domain but can also expand into new domains.[10] Mercedes-Benz used its competences in R&D and product development to enter the household products and aerospace industries. Coca-Cola took its marketing skills and applied them globally in the soft-drinks industry.

Corporate-level strategy is the responsibility of corporate-level managers and the heads of an organization's operating divisions—the top-management team of a multi-business organization. Their responsibility is to take the value creation skills present in the divisions and in corporate headquarters and combine them to improve the competitive position of each division and of the organization as a whole. Corporate strategists use the combined resources of the organization to create more value than could be obtained if each division operated alone and independently. For example, Honda takes its strengths in engine production and uses them to produce many different kinds of products such as cars, motor bikes, jet skis, and lawnmowers, creating value in many different markets. How does strategy at each level advance the goal of creating value?

FUNCTIONAL-LEVEL STRATEGY

The strategic goal of each function is to create a core competence that gives the organization a competitive advantage. As we have seen, McDonald's production and marketing functions have given the organization important core competences. No competitor can match the efficiency of McDonald's production process, and no competitor has developed the brand-name reputation that McDonald's enjoys.

An organization creates value by applying its functional skills and knowledge to inputs and transforming them into outputs of finished goods and services. To gain a competitive advantage, an organization must be able to do at least one of the following: (1) perform functional activities at a cost lower than that of its rivals or (2) perform functional activities in a way that clearly differentiates its goods and services from those of its rivals—by giving its products unique qualities that customers greatly desire.[11]

Strategies to Lower Costs or Differentiate Products

Any function that can lower the cost at which a product is produced or that can differentiate a product adds value to the product and to the organization. Table 7.1 summarizes the ways in which different organizational functions can advance the goal of value creation.

The manufacturing function can lower the costs of production by pioneering the adoption of the most efficient production methods, such as computer-controlled flexible manufacturing systems. Because manufacturing skills and competence can improve product quality and reliability, manufacturing can also contribute to product differentiation.[12] Sony and Toyota, for example, lead the world in "lean" manufacturing techniques, which both reduce production costs and increase quality by lowering the number of defects. Manufacturing, thus, gives Sony and Toyota products a low-cost advantage and a differentiation advantage.

On the input side, the human resource management (HRM) function can lower costs by designing appropriate control and reward systems to increase employee motivation and reduce absenteeism and turnover.[13] HRM can contribute to differentiation by selecting and hiring high-quality employees and managers and by running innovative training programs. The use of employee stock ownership plans, the linking of pay to performance for different job categories, and the development of flexible work hours to allow employees to dovetail work activities with nonwork obligations are all ways in which the HRM function can advance the cause of value creation. Arthur Andersen, Xerox, and other companies have developed sophisticated HRM systems for selecting and training their employees.

The role of materials management on both the input and the output sides is also crucial. Just-in-time inventory systems and computerized warehousing reduce the costs of carrying and shipping inventory. Purchasing managers' skills in developing long-term links with suppliers and distributors and in fostering an organization's reputation can lead to a low-cost or differentiation advantage.[14] Suppliers that trust an organization may offer more favorable payment terms or be more responsive to the organization when it needs more or different types of inputs in a hurry. The quality of a company-supplier relationship can also affect the quality of inputs. A supplier has more incentive to invest in specialized equipment to produce higher-quality inputs if it trusts the organization.[15] Highly skilled purchasing negotiators may be able to strike good contract terms with suppliers, too.

TABLE 7.1		
Low-Cost and Differentiation Advantages Resulting from Functional-Level Strategy		
Value-Creating Function	Source of Low-Cost Advantage	Source of Differentiation Advantage
Manufacturing	• Development of skills in flexible manufacturing technology	• Increase in product quality and reliability
Human resource management	• Reduction of turnover and absenteeism	• Hiring of highly skilled personnel • Development of innovative training programs
Materials management	• Use of just-in-time inventory system/computerized warehousing • Development of long-term relationships with suppliers and customers	• Use of company reputation and long-term relationships with suppliers and customers to provide high-quality inputs and efficient distribution and disposal of outputs
Sales and marketing	• Increased demand and lower production costs	• Targeting of customer groups • Tailoring products to customers • Promoting brand names
Research and development	• Improved efficiency of manufacturing technology	• Creation of new products • Improvement of existing products

VF Company, the clothes manufacturer that makes Lee and Wrangler jeans, has developed a low-cost core competence on the output side of the value creation process. VF Company has a state-of-the-art inventory control system. A computer network links its manufacturing and distribution plants directly to its retail customers. When a Kmart customer buys a pair of VF jeans, for example, a record of the sale is transmitted electronically from Kmart to a VF warehouse, which restocks the retailer within five days. When a specified number of garments has been shipped from the VF warehouse, a reorder is automatically placed with the manufacturing plant. This system allows the VF organization to maintain a 97 percent in-stock rate (the industry average is 70 percent) and reduce lost sales for both the retailer and the manufacturer.

At the output end of the value creation process, the skills and expertise of sales and marketing can contribute directly to a low-cost or differentiation advantage. A core competence in marketing can lower the cost of value creation activities. Suppose a marketing department devises a campaign that significantly increases the sales of a product and, as a result, the organization's market share steadily rises. As the organization expands its output to satisfy the increased demand, it is likely to obtain manufacturing economies of scale, and its costs are likely to fall. Sony and Panasonic have a low-cost advantage because their marketing and sales efforts have developed global markets whose enormous size enables the companies to produce huge volumes of a product at lower and lower unit costs.

Marketing and sales help differentiate products because they tell customers about why one company's products are better than another's. They target customer groups and discover, analyze, and transmit to the product development and R&D departments the needs of customers so that those functions can design new products to attract more customers.[16] A core competence in marketing can allow an organization to quickly discover and respond to customer needs. This speed gives the organization's products a differentiated appeal. Coca-Cola, Philip Morris, and Campbell Soup are all known for innovative marketing that constantly promotes their brand names and protects their domains from competitors.

Research and development can also contribute significantly to an organization's value creation activities.[17] R&D can reduce costs by developing cheaper ways of making a product. Skills in R&D have allowed Japanese companies to develop low-cost, flexible manufacturing techniques that are being copied by Xerox, Hewlett-Packard, Daimler-Chrysler, and other U.S. manufacturers. A core competence in R&D that results in the improvement of existing products or the creation of new products gives an organization a strong competitive advantage through differentiation. Intel's creation of faster and improved microchips is an example of incremental product improvement. CD-ROM technology developed by Microsoft and other companies has led to the birth of a new generation of computer products. All makers of personal computers rush to modify their products to use a new chip; otherwise, they fear, their products are likely to lose their differentiated appeal.

Using Interorganizational Strategies

Interorganizational strategies to develop functional resources and coordination abilities are becoming increasingly important for many organizations. As competition in an industry increases, so does the pressure to develop core competences. As we saw in Chapter 6, materials management has responded to the competitive challenge by developing linkages with suppliers that lower the costs of inputs. The use of minority ownership in suppliers and the development of long-term contracts to develop just-in-time inventory systems are other ways in which an organization can lower the costs of value creation. Similarly, it is increasingly common for companies to lower the cost of research and development by establishing strategic alliances and joint ventures to pool their knowledge and engage in joint R&D activities. All parties share the knowledge produced from such agreements. Finally, many organizations enter into long-term contracts with other organizations for help in developing functional resources. Many consulting companies exist to provide specialized knowledge and expertise in marketing, accounting, finance, human resource development, and other functions.

Functional-Level Strategy and Structure

Every function in an organization can develop a core competence that allows the organization to perform value creation activities at a cost lower than its rivals' costs or that allows the organization to create clearly differentiated products. One goal of the organization is to provide its functions with the resources and the setting they need to develop superior skills and expertise. Thus, organizational structure and culture are very important to the development of functional-level strategy. We first consider structure.

The strength of a function's core competence depends not only on the function's resources but also on its ability to coordinate the use of its resources. An organization's coordination abilities are, in turn, a product of its structure.[18] In Chapter 6 we discussed Lawrence and Lorsch's findings about how the degree of functional differentiation in the production, sales, and research and development departments within an organization and the extent of integration among those functions directly affect organizational performance. In the most effective organizations, each of the three departments develops an orientation specific to its functional tasks and develops its own ways of responding to its particular functional environment.

According to contingency theory, an organization's design should permit each function to develop a structure that suits its human and technical resources. We will continue to follow the contingency theory approach as we examine how to design a structure that allows the R&D, manufacturing, and sales functions to develop core competences.[19] Figure 7.3 summarizes the characteristics of structures that support the development of core competences by those three functions.

Successful research and development reflects the ability of R&D experts to apply their skills and knowledge in innovative ways and to combine their activities with technical resources to produce new products. The structure most conducive to the development of functional abilities in R&D is a flat, decentralized structure in which mutual adjustment among teams is the main means of coordinating human and technical resources. In such an organic structure, functional norms and values based on self-control and team control are likely to emerge, and a core competence in R&D is likely to be developed.

FIGURE 7.3

Structural Characteristics Associated with the Development of Core Competences in Production, Sales, and Research and Development

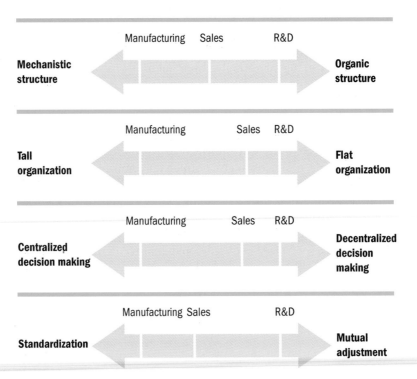

What sort of structure supports the development of a core competence in production? Traditionally, the manufacturing function has used a tall hierarchy in which decision making is centralized and the speed of the production line controls the pace of work.[20] Standardization is achieved through the use of extensive rules and procedures, and the result of these design choices is a mechanistic structure. Has such a structure led to a core competence in manufacturing for American companies? If we compare American manufacturing companies with Japanese manufacturing companies, we see that American companies today do not have a core competence in manufacturing. What do the Japanese do differently? Chapter 10 takes an in-depth look at new manufacturing systems, but one common theme in the development of a new structure for manufacturing is the empowerment of workers—that is, allowing workers to participate directly in decision making and giving them responsibility for making incremental improvements in the production process. The manufacturing function in Japanese companies has a more organic structure than the manufacturing function in American companies has: It is flatter, more decentralized, and relies more on mutual adjustment.

A core competence based on coordination abilities in sales is another important source of competitive advantage that should be planned for in an organization's strategy. Typically, the sales function uses a flat, decentralized structure to coordinate its activities because incentive pay systems, rather than direct supervision by managers, are the primary control mechanism in sales settings.[21] Salespeople are generally paid on the basis of how much they sell, and information about customer needs and changing customer requirements is relayed to the salespeople's superiors through a standardized reporting system. Because salespeople often work alone, mutual adjustment is relatively unimportant. Thus, the structure of the sales function is likely to be relatively mechanistic, compared to that used by the R&D function, but not as mechanistic as that used by manufacturing.

In some sales settings, however, a differentiated appeal to customers is necessary. Luxury department stores such as Nordstrom and Neiman-Marcus do not use incentive compensation. In such settings, the last thing the organization wants to do is encourage a standardized hard sell to customers. Instead, it wants salespeople to develop competence in a sales technique based on a courteous, personalized, customer-oriented approach. The same strategic considerations shape the structure of other organizational functions—accounting, human resources, materials management, and so on. The coordination abilities of each function reflect the skill with which managers design the functional structure to suit the resources the function uses in its value creation activities. The greater the organization's skills at coordinating functional resources, the stronger are the core competences the organization develops and the greater is its competitive advantage.

Functional-Level Strategy and Culture

The development of functional abilities that lead to core competences is also a result of the culture that emerges in a function or department. Recall from Chapter 5 that organizational culture is a set of shared values that organizational members use when they interact with one another and with other stakeholders. What is the importance of culture for functional-level strategy? A competitor can easily imitate another organization's structure, but it is very difficult for a competitor to imitate another organization's culture, for culture is embedded in the day-to-day interactions of functional personnel. Culture is very difficult to control and manage, let alone imitate or copy, so a company that has an effective culture has an important source of competitive advantage.[22]

Many organizations imitated General Motors and Du Pont and moved to a multidivisional structure to improve their ability to control their operations. Organizations can also imitate one another's incentive pay systems. GM has moved to give its managers stock options like those offered by its competitors, and retail stores have copied Wal-Mart's policy of establishing an employee stock ownership plan. Kmart, however, despite changes to its structure, has found it very difficult to imitate Wal-Mart's cultural values of thrift and economy, and GM (except for its Saturn plant) does not operate like Toyota even though it has imitated many of Toyota's operating systems. The reason for such differences (despite structural similarities) is that the coordination abilities that stem from an organization's culture emerge gradually and are a product of many factors: an organization's property rights system, its structure, its ethics, and the characteristics of its top-management team. Because these factors can be combined in many different ways, reproducing another organization's culture is difficult.

To develop functional abilities and produce a core competence, it is necessary to choose the property rights, functional structure, and functional managers that seem most likely to enhance a function's coordination ability. We just saw that R&D uses a flat, decentralized structure and small teams to create norms and values that emphasize teamwork and cooperation. There are other ways in which an organization can build a culture to reinforce those norms and values. Employees can be given strong property rights, including job tenure and a share in the organizational profits; and an organization can recruit people who share its terminal values and socialize them to its functional instrumental values.[23] Microsoft deliberately creates an entrepreneurial culture by using small teams to socialize its programmers to its instrumental values of hard work and cooperation. The same is true in biotech companies like Amgen and Genentech and consumer products companies like Sony.

The coordination abilities of the manufacturing function are also affected by its culture. In some manufacturing cultures (as in the United States traditionally), the focus is on reducing the level of skill required to perform a task, transferring control to managers, and creating a mechanistic hierarchy in which workers have minimal control over tasks. In such settings, management develops a culture based on values of economy to reduce production costs. As we saw earlier, however, empowering workers and developing cultural values and norms that encourage participation, cooperation, and commitment may be the source of the increased product quality traditionally enjoyed by Japanese automakers. Honda claims that its American manufacturing plant can produce cars more cheaply than its Japanese plants. Honda empowers its workers, involves them in decision making, and uses a pay system based on performance. In 1993, when demand for the Accord dropped because Honda was introducing a new model, Honda showed its commitment to its American workforce by using the downtime in production to train the workers to repair broken machinery rather than laying them off until demand for the new model increased. Similarly, at GM's Saturn plant, values and norms based on employee involvement have dramatically increased product quality. The kind of abilities that a function develops are a product of organizational design decisions and organizational culture.

In sum, to create value at the functional level, the organizational strategy must allow and encourage each function to develop a core competence in lowering costs or differentiating its products from those of competitors. Ultimately, the sources of core competences lie in the resources that the organization assigns to each function and in the abilities of functional experts to coordinate those resources. To gain a competitive advantage, an organization needs to design its functional structure and culture to provide a setting in which core competences develop. The more a function's core competence is based on coordination abilities embedded in the way people in the organization interact, the more

---

Managerial Implications: Functional-Level Strategy

1. As a member or manager of a function, identify the functional resources or coordination abilities that give your function a core competence. Having identified the sources of your function's core competence, establish a plan to improve or strengthen them, and create a set of goals to measure your progress.
2. Study your competitors and the methods and practices they use to control their functional activities. Pick your most effective competitor, study its methods, and use them as a benchmark for what you wish to achieve in your function.
3. Analyze the way your functional structure and culture affect functional resources and abilities. Experiment to see whether changing a component of structure or culture can enhance your function's core competence.

---

difficult it is for competing organizations to duplicate the core competence and the greater is the organization's competitive advantage.

BUSINESS-LEVEL STRATEGY

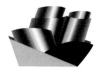

At the business level the task facing the organization is to take the core competences created by the functions and combine them to exploit opportunities in the organizational environment. Strategists at the business level select and manage the domain in which the organization uses its value creation resources and coordination abilities to obtain a competitive advantage.[24] For example, core competences in three functions—manufacturing, marketing, and materials management—jointly give McDonald's a competitive advantage over rivals such as Burger King and Wendy's. Obtaining a competitive advantage is important because, as we noted in Chapter 6, organizations in the same environment (e.g., fast food) are in competition for scarce resources. Any organization that fails to devise a business-level strategy to attract resources is at a disadvantage vis-à-vis its rivals and in the long run is likely to fail. Thus, the organization needs a business-level strategy that does both of the following: (1) selects the domain the organization will compete in and (2) positions the organization so that it can use its resources and abilities to manage its specific and general environments in order to protect and enlarge that domain. (See Figure 7.4.)

FIGURE 7.4

Types of Business-Level Strategy

Strategy	Number of Market Segments Served	
	Many	**Few**
Low cost	●	
Focused low cost		●
Differentiation	●	
Focused differentiation		●

Strategies to Lower Costs or Differentiate Products

We have seen that the two basic ways in which an organization can create value are by reducing the cost of its value creation activities and by performing those activities in a way that gives its products a differentiated appeal. Business-level strategy focuses on selecting the domain in which an organization can exploit its functional-level core competences.

Recall from Chapter 6 that the *organizational domain* is the range of goods and services that the organization produces to attract customers and other stakeholders. Once an organization has chosen its domain, it has two bases on which it can position itself to compete with its rivals. It can use its skills in low-cost value creation to produce for a customer group that wants low-priced goods and services. This plan is called a **low-cost business-level strategy**. Or it can use its skills at differentiation to produce for a customer group that wants and can afford differentiated products that command a high or premium price. This plan is called a **differentiation business-level strategy**.[25] Wal-Mart and Kmart, for example, specialize in selling low-price clothing to customers who want or can afford to pay only a modest amount for their attire. Neiman-Marcus and Saks Fifth Avenue specialize in selling high-priced clothing made by exclusive designers to wealthy customers.

Both Wal-Mart and Neiman-Marcus are in the retail clothing industry but have chosen different domains in which to compete. They have decided to sell different products to different groups of customers. In essence, Neiman-Marcus and Saks have chosen a business-level strategy based on core competences in differentiation in order to charge a premium price, and Wal-Mart and Kmart have chosen a business-level strategy based on core competences in low-cost value creation activities in order to charge a low price.

The choice of strategy determines which companies will be an organization's direct competitors. Clearly, Neiman-Marcus and Wal-Mart do not compete directly. Wal-Mart's main competitors are Kmart and Sears, organizations that have staked out the same domain as Wal-Mart. Currently, Wal-Mart is outperforming both competitors because it possesses a stronger set of core competences. Wal-Mart has a strong competence in low-cost materials management because of its very efficient purchasing and distribution systems. In marketing, too, it takes a low-cost approach, deliberately spending less on advertising than Sears and other rivals spend. Wal-Mart seeks to develop a low-cost competence in every function because it knows that strategy will enable it to charge low prices to its customers. This low-cost business-level strategy gives Wal-Mart a competitive advantage and enhances its ability to attract customers and the resources they bring with them.

At the other extreme is Neiman-Marcus, whose competitors include Saks Fifth Avenue, Macy's, and Nordstrom. Competition among these organizations is as intense as competition among organizations in the low-cost domain. In the high-price domain, however, an organization's competitive strength depends on its ability to provide customers with both products and a retail setting that have a differentiated appeal. As a result of this emphasis, functional competences in differentiation become important. Neiman-Marcus enjoys a competitive advantage because of the quality of its sales function; the luxuriousness of each store and its managers' skills in creating an upscale, classy atmosphere for shopping; the quality and uniqueness of the merchandise obtained by its purchasing executives; and the brand-name reputation of the organization, achieved through memorable advertising and canny marketing. Nordstrom has developed a core competence in the high end of the retail market: extraordinary customer service. Core competences such as the provision of differentiated high-quality merchandise and willingness to satisfy customers allow Neiman-Marcus and Nordstrom to follow a differentiation business-level strategy and to charge premium prices.

Low-cost business-level strategy A plan whereby an organization produces low-priced goods and services for all customer groups.

Differentiation business-level strategy A plan whereby an organization produces high-priced, quality products aimed at particular market segments.

To compete successfully, an organization must develop a low-cost or differentiation strategy to protect and enlarge its domain. An organization can also attempt to pursue both strategies simultaneously and produce differentiated products at low cost.[26] Doing so is extremely difficult and requires an exceptionally strong set of core competences. Mc-Donald's is an organization that has successfully pursued both strategies simultaneously. McDonald's has developed a unique brand-name reputation by means of sophisticated advertising and marketing and has developed low-cost skills in its manufacturing and distribution functions. Moreover, McDonald's has used many of the interorganizational strategies discussed in Chapter 6 to pursue both strategies simultaneously. It has formed strategic alliances with suppliers and obtains bread, rolls, and restaurant fittings (tables, chairs, lights, and so on) from companies with which it has long-term contracts or in which it has a minority ownership interest. McDonald's uses franchising to maintain the reliability and efficiency of its retail outlets and owns many of the sources of its inputs, such as herds of cattle in Brazil.

Over time, an organization has to change its business-level strategy to match changes in its environment. New technological developments, foreign competitors, and changes in customer needs and tastes may all affect the way an organization tries to compete for resources. Amazon.com offers an interesting example of the way changes in information technology affect a company's choice of business-level strategy.

Focus on New Information Technology: Amazon.com, Part 5

Before the advent of on-line bookstores, competition among bookstores was limited at best. The market was essentially divided between two kinds of competitors: (1) large bookstore chains, such as Barnes & Noble and Borders, whose stores were often located in malls and that offered customers the latest lines of best-selling books, and (2) independent bookstores that could be very large and offer a huge selection of books, or could be small, specialized bookstores found in most cities in the United States. The large bookstore chains used their huge purchasing power to negotiate low prices with book publishers and they pursued a low-cost strategy, often offering price discounts. Independent bookstores that offered a large selection of books or that specialized in some way pursued a differentiation strategy. Thus, the different kinds of bookstores were not in competition and all were able to make comfortable profits.

Jeff Bezos's idea of using new Internet information technology to sell books on-line made it possible to develop a simultaneous low-cost and differentiation strategy and, thus, outperform existing bookstore competitors. First, on the differentiation side, the ability of a computerized on-line catalog to both describe and make available to customers every book in the English language offered customers a selection that could not be rivaled even by the largest bookstores in cities like New York and San Francisco. Second, on the low-cost side, his use of information technology to interface inexpensively with book publishers, distributors, and customers allowed him to offer these customers books at discounted prices, and to get them quickly to customers as well.

Small wonder then that this new low-cost/differentiation strategy has given Amazon.com a competitive advantage over its rivals. Many small and large stand-alone bookstores have exited the market; the large chains have responded by opening up book superstores and by going on-line themselves. However, they have yet to repeat Amazon.com's success story; Amazon.com has over 18 million customers in its database and claims that over 45 percent of its business is from repeat customers. Its share price has soared as investors believe it possesses the business-level strategy that will dominate in the years ahead.

As Amazon.com's strategy suggests, organizations have to defend, protect, and sometimes alter the sources of their competitive advantage if they are to successfully control their environment in the long run. Industry leaders, such as Amazon.com, Toyota, and McDonald's, are able to sustain their competitive advantage by maintaining and developing their functional-level resources and abilities. Amazon.com, for example, is constantly updating its information systems to take advantage of any new developments, such as streaming audio and video.

Focus Strategy

Another business-level strategy is the focus strategy—specializing in one segment of a market, and focusing all of the organization's resources on that segment.[27] KFC specializes in the chicken segment of the fast-food market; Tiffany specializes in the high-price, luxury segment of the jewelry market; Rolls-Royce focuses on the highest-price segment of the car market—a Rolls-Royce Silver Sprite costs $265,000.

A focus strategy allows an organization to get close to its customers and tailor its goods or services to their needs. Typically, focus companies are relatively small companies that, by specializing in one market segment, avoid head-to-head competition with low-cost or differentiated companies. As a result, they can be very profitable because they have few competitors inside the specialized domain they have staked out for themselves. Before the advent of Amazon.com, for example, huge specialty bookstores had no competitors. Now many are struggling and some have closed their doors.

Business-Level Strategy and Structure

The value that an organization creates at the business level depends on the organization's ability to use its core competences to gain a competitive advantage. This ability is a product of the way the organization designs its structure.[28] An organization pursuing a differentiation business-level strategy generally confronts design choices different from those faced by organizations pursuing a low-cost strategy. Figure 7.5 summarizes the differences.

The competitive strengths of an organization with a differentiation strategy come from functional skills that give the organization's products unique or state-of-the-art features that distinguish them from the products of competitors. An organization pursuing a differentiation strategy has to be able to develop products quickly because only if it gets its products to customers ahead of its competitors can it exploit its differentiation advantage. Close cooperation between functions is likely to be required to bring new products

FIGURE 7.5

Business-Level Strategies for Enlarging the Organizational Domain.
Source: Adapted from H. I. Ansoff, *Corporate Strategy.* London, Penguin, 1984, p. 99. (McGraw-Hill, 1968). Reprinted with permission of the author.

	Product	
	Existing	New
Domain — Existing	Market penetration strategy	Product development strategy
Domain — New	Market development strategy	Diversification strategy

to market quickly. For example, R&D, marketing, manufacturing, and product development must be able to communicate easily and adjust their activities to one another smoothly to speed the development process. All these factors make it likely that an organization pursuing a differentiation strategy has an organic structure. An organic structure permits the development of a decentralized, cross-functional team approach to decision making, which is the key to speedy new-product development.

A low-cost strategy is associated with the need for close control of functional activities to monitor and lower the costs of product development.[29] Manufacturing and materials management become the central functions for an organization pursuing a low-cost strategy. The other functions (R&D, marketing, and so on) tailor their skills to achieve the goal of producing a low-cost product. A speedy response to market changes is not vital to the competitive success of a low-cost organization. Often, because product development is so expensive, such an organization waits to develop a new or improved product until customers clearly demand it. The low-cost organization generally imitates the differentiator's product and always remains one step behind to keep costs low. Consequently, a mechanistic structure is often the most appropriate choice for an organization pursuing a low-cost strategy (see Figure 7.6). Centralized decision making allows the organization to maintain close control over functional activities and, thus, over costs. Also, because there is no pressing need to respond quickly or innovatively, a mechanistic structure provides sufficient coordination to meet the demands of the competitive domain.

Further evidence for the match between differentiation strategy and organic structure and the match between low-cost strategy and mechanistic structure comes from contingency theory. Recall from Chapter 6 that contingency theory suggests that organizations in uncertain, rapidly changing environments require a greater degree of differentiation and integration than do organizations in more stable environments.[30] Because differentiators generally compete in a complex, uncertain environment where they need to react quickly to rivals' actions, and because low-cost companies usually compete in slow-moving environments, contingency theory suggests that effective differentiators will have greater differentiation and integration than low-cost companies have. Given that organizational structures with extensive differentiation and integration are costly to operate, contingency theory implies that low-cost companies should use the simplest structure possible because it will help to keep down the cost of value creation.[31]

FIGURE 7.6

Characteristics of Organizational Structure Associated with Business-Level Differentiation and Low-Cost Strategies

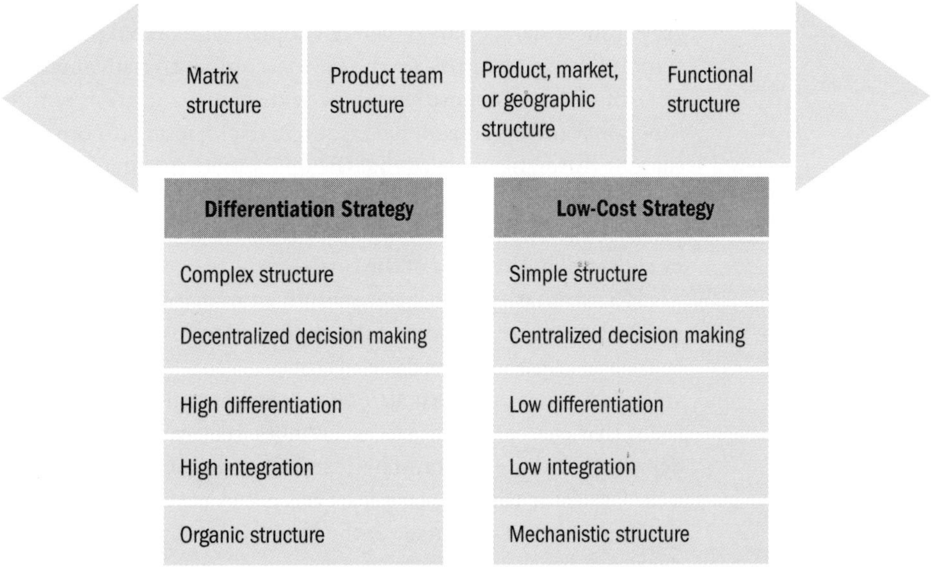

Matrix structure	Product team structure	Product, market, or geographic structure	Functional structure

Differentiation Strategy	Low-Cost Strategy
Complex structure	Simple structure
Decentralized decision making	Centralized decision making
High differentiation	Low differentiation
High integration	Low integration
Organic structure	Mechanistic structure

In addition to examining the relationship between business-level strategy and organic and mechanistic structures, we can look at the relationship between strategy and the types of organizational structure discussed in Chapter 4: functional, divisional, and matrix structures. From a strategy perspective, three factors affect an organization's choice of a structure to create a competitive advantage for itself:

1. As an organization produces a wider range of products, it will need greater control over the development, marketing, and production of these products.
2. As an organization seeks to find new customer groups for its products, it will need a structure that allows it to serve the needs of its customers.
3. As the pace of new product development in an industry increases, an organization will need a structure that increases coordination among its functions.

Organizations following a low-cost strategy typically focus on producing one product or a few products in order to reduce costs. BIC Corporation, for example, produces one disposable razor for both men and women. A low-cost company does not face the problems of dealing with a wide range of products or with many customer groups. Moreover, low-cost companies are not leaders in product development. Because they are imitators, they do not have the problems of coordinating the activities of different functional groups. For all these reasons, low-cost companies generally adopt the simplest structure that is consistent with their strategy. Normally, a *functional structure* (one in which people are grouped by common skills or use of similar resources) is sufficient to coordinate the core competences of a low-cost organization.

In contrast, differentiators typically produce a wide range of products to suit the needs of different groups of customers. Also, to the degree that competition between differentiators is based on the development of new and innovative products (a situation found in the car and personal computer industries), differentiators need a structure that allows functional experts to cooperate so that they can quickly develop and introduce new products. For these reasons, differentiators are likely to adopt a more complex structure. If the pressing need is to handle a wide range of products, a *product structure* (in which products are grouped into separate divisions that are served by the same set of support functions) is the appropriate choice. If handling different groups of customers is the key to success, a *market structure* or a *geographic structure* (in which functional activities are grouped to best meet the needs of different types of customers) will best fit the differentiator's needs. A *product team structure* or a *matrix structure* (in which product development is coordinated by teams of cross-functional specialists) can be adopted when rapid product development and speedy response to competitors are the keys to competitive advantage.

All of those structures can provide an organization with the ability to coordinate functional and organizational resources to create a core competence. Intel, the microchip manufacturer, has decided that the only way to maintain its lead in the industry is to produce several generations of microchips at the same time. Therefore, it has established a product team structure in which teams of research and development specialists work side by side to plan the chips of the future.[32]

To summarize, an organization must match its business-level strategy to the organizational structure that allows the organization to use its functional and organizational resources to create a competitive advantage. A top-quality R&D department is useless unless an organization has a structure that coordinates R&D activities with a marketing department that can correctly forecast changes in customer needs and a product development department that can translate research and marketing findings into commercial products. Choosing the right structure has major payoffs by giving an organization a low-cost or differentiation advantage at the business level, as the following Organizational Insight demonstrates.

ORGANIZATIONAL INSIGHT

7.1 PEPSICO CHOOSES A NEW STRUCTURE

PepsiCo, the soft-drink company, had a difficult time battling against Coca-Cola, its principal competitor, in the 1990s. Coke, with its innovative marketing and new-product expertise, had been gaining in market share; it also had increased its lead globally. PepsiCo realized the need to change both its strategy and structure to fight back, and it began this process in 1998 when it announced that it was spinning off its restaurant business (it used to own Taco Bell and KFC) in order to focus its attention on its core soft-drink business. After this spinoff, its CEO, Philip Martineau, announced that he was going to reengineer the company from top to bottom to improve the company's relationships with its customers and to improve the marketing of its products.

At the heart of the change in structure was a new pattern of horizontal differentiation. PepsiCo used to operate with a geographic structure, and customers in each of the regions in which it operated would be approached by representatives from its bottling operations, not from its marketing function. The result was that its marketing efforts were often badly coordinated, and there was no central thrust from the top of the organization.

Henceforth, PepsiCo announced that it was creating a new marketing research and development function, and this function would be responsible for coordinating all the company's marketing activities throughout all regions. In the new structure, all bottling and production activities would follow the lead of marketing; marketing would decide on new-product introductions, for example, and then feed this information to the other functions so that they could then move to implement the new-product strategies most effectively.[33]

Essentially, Martineau moved to centralize decision making and move to a new kind of functional structure to build PepsiCo's differentiation advantage. At the same time, he hopes that the new structure, which is both flatter and more streamlined than before, will also speed product development and reduce costs since the regional bureaucracy has been eliminated. As of 1999, the new structure has seemed to work effectively, PepsiCo's sales and profits have increased, and according to Martineau, PepsiCo has improved relations with customers.

Business-Level Strategy and Culture

Organizational culture is another major determinant of an organization's ability to use functional and organizational resources effectively. The challenge at the business level is to develop organizationwide values and specific norms and rules, all of which allow the organization to combine and use its functional resources to the best advantage. Over time, different functions may develop different subunit orientations, which impede communication and coordination. But if the various functions share values and norms, communication and coordination problems can be overcome. If managers in different functions can develop common ways of dealing with problems, an organization's competitive advantage will be enhanced.

How does the culture of a low-cost organization differ from that of a differentiator? Organizations pursuing a low-cost strategy must develop values of economy and frugality.[34] Frequently, specific norms and rules develop that reflect the organization's terminal and instrumental values. For example, Ken Iverson, CEO of Nucor, a leading low-cost steel manufacturer, is proud of the frugal way he operates the company. Top managers at Nucor work in a small, unpretentious corporate office with few of the trappings of luxury. They drive their own cars to work, fly economy class, and on business trips share rooms in hotels to reduce costs.

The functions within a low-cost organization are likely to develop goals that reflect the organization's values of economy. Marketing views its job as finding the most efficient ways of attracting customers. R&D sees its role as developing new products that offer the greatest potential return for the smallest investment of organizational resources.

In low-cost organizations, a common "language" and a code of behavior based on low-cost values develop. In a differentiator, in contrast, the need to be different from competitors and to develop innovative products puts product development or marketing at center stage. Values that promote innovation and responsiveness to customers, stories of products that became winners or of winning products that were not developed, and boosting the status of employees who create new products all make organizational members aware of the need to be the first or the best.[35] Cultural values of innovation, quality, excellence, and uniqueness help a differentiator implement its chosen strategy, and they become a source of competitive strength. The following insight offers a glimpse at the way culture can influence a company's business-level strategy.

ORGANIZATIONAL INSIGHT

7.2 HOW CULTURE DERAILED THE MERGER BETWEEN AHP AND MONSANTO

In June 1998, American Home Products(AHP), the giant pharmaceutical maker, announced that it would buy Monsanto, another large pharmaceutical and chemical company, for $33 billion. Analysts applauded the merger, believing that it would provide important differentiation and low-cost advantages for the combined firm. Specifically, the merged companies would have a much broader product range, and the merger would eliminate expensive duplication of production facilities leading to major cost savings.

Analysts were, therefore, shocked when in October 1998, the two companies announced that the merger was off because it was not in the best interests of shareholders. Why were the companies forced to give up these potential sources of competitive advantage? AHP has a culture characterized by a short-term focus on bottom-line profits. Its managers are cost conscious and only want to invest in products that have a short-term payoff. Monsanto, on the other hand, has a long-term orientation. It is driven by a desire to produce innovative new products, many of which may not pay off except in the long run. Thus, it has strong values of innovation and excellence.

Managers at these companies came to realize that it was impossible to harmonize these different cultures and driving values. They foresaw that the potential low-cost and differentiation gains might be wiped out by politics and infighting between managers of these two companies, and it was just not worth the risk to go ahead with the merger.

An organizational culture that promotes norms and rules that increase effectiveness can be a major source of competitive advantage. In Chapter 5, we saw how organizations deliberately shape their culture to achieve their goals. Sony and Microsoft, for example, promote innovation by establishing norms and rules that enable employees to move to positions where their talents are most valuable to the organization. Arthur Andersen socializes new recruits to the values that it considers most important.

Recall, too, that organizational structures are chosen because of their effect on culture. Organic structures foster the development of cultural values of innovation and quality. In contrast, mechanistic structures foster economical values that focus attention on improving existing rules and SOPs, not finding new ones. Low-cost companies that seek to develop Japanese-style, lean production systems will find a mechanistic structure useful because it focuses all efforts on improving existing work procedures.

In sum, organizational culture is another important factor shaping an organization's business-level strategy for improving its value creation skills. As technology changes, as new products and markets come into being, and as the environment changes, an organization's culture likewise will change. Like organizational structure, the way in which organizational culture supports an organization's strategy for value creation can also be a source of competitive advantage. That is one reason why there has been continuing interest in culture as an explanation for differences in organizational effectiveness.

Managerial Implications: Business-Level Strategy

1. Managers in each function should understand their function's contribution to the organization's low-cost advantage or differentiated appeal. Members of a function should examine their interactions with members of other functions to see if they can devise new ways of reducing costs or develop a differentiated appeal.
2. Managers should act like entrepreneurs and always be on the lookout for new opportunities to protect and enlarge the domain of their organization. They must continually experiment to see whether they can enlarge the existing organizational domain, find new uses for existing products, or develop new products to satisfy customer needs.
3. Managers must always evaluate whether the current organizational structure and culture are congruent with the organization's business-level strategy. If they are not, managers should move quickly to make changes that can improve their competitive position.

CORPORATE-LEVEL STRATEGY

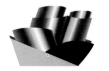

Corporate-level strategy
A plan whereby an organization searches for new domains in which to exploit and defend an organization's ability to create value from the use of its low-cost or differentiation core competences.

Often, an organization that cannot create more value in its current domain tries to find a new domain in which to compete for resources. **Corporate-level strategy** involves a search for new domains in which to exploit and defend an organization's ability to create value from the use of its low-cost or differentiation core competences.[36] Corporate-level strategy is a continuation of business-level strategy because the organization takes its existing core competences and applies them in new domains. If an organization takes marketing skills developed in one domain and applies them in a new domain, for example, it can create value in that new domain. When Philip Morris took marketing skills developed in the tobacco industry, applied them to Miller Brewing, and made Miller Light the market leader, it created value for Miller's customers and for Philip Morris's shareholders. Next we look in detail at how vertical integration and diversification, two important corporate-level strategies, can help an organization create value. In the next chapter we examine global expansion, the other main kind of corporate strategy.

Vertical Integration

Vertical integration A strategy in which an organization takes over and owns its suppliers (backward vertical integration) or its distributors (forward vertical integration).

An organization pursuing a strategy of **vertical integration** establishes or takes over and buys its suppliers (*backward* vertical integration) or its distributors (*forward* vertical integration).[37] In this way it controls the production of its inputs or the disposal of its outputs (see Figure 7.7). As an illustration, Figure 7.8 shows a soft-drink company that enters new domains that overlap its core domain so that it can use, enhance, or protect its low-cost or differentiation value creation skills.

How does vertical integration allow an organization to use or enhance its core competence in value creation? An organization that supplies its own inputs or disposes of its own outputs may be able to keep for itself the profits previously earned by its suppliers. Moreover, production cost savings can sometimes be obtained when an organization owns its input suppliers. Inputs can be designed so that they can be assembled at a lower cost, and control of the reliability and quality of inputs can save an organization a great deal of money if products eventually have to be repaired under guarantee.

An organization can call attention to its uniqueness by making its products different from its rivals' products. One way to do this is by controlling the inputs that make a prod-

FIGURE 7.7

Corporate-Level Strategies for Entering New Domains

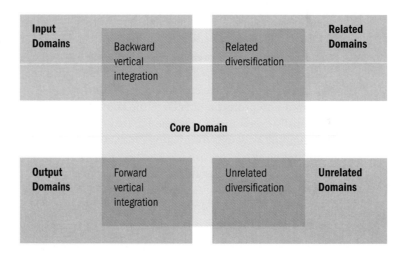

FIGURE 7.8

Soft-Drink Company's Corporate-Level Strategies for Entering New Domains

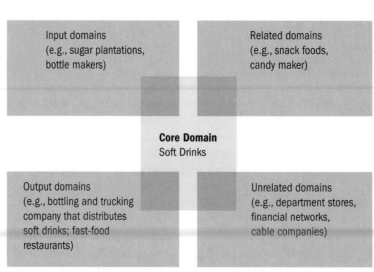

uct unique. Coca-Cola, for example, has sole control over the Coke formula, so Coca-Cola tastes like no other cola drink. Controlling inputs also helps the organization control quality, which confers uniqueness on a product. Rolls-Royce carefully tends the flocks of sheep from which it obtains the leather for its car upholstery. The sheep are kept in enclosures without barbed wire and are protected so that the leather has no flaws and blemishes. Finally, taking over a supplier by vertical integration avoids the problem that results when there are only a few suppliers in an industry and they act opportunistically and try to cheat an organization by, for example, inflating the costs or reducing the quality of its inputs.

Controlling the way a product is distributed can also result in a low-cost or differentiation advantage. Tandy Corporation, for example, owns Radio Shack, so Tandy obtains all the profit from sales of Radio Shack consumer electronic products and accessories, profit that otherwise would have been made by other retail stores. Tandy can also control the quality of the sales and repair service that Radio Shack customers receive and, thus, build customer loyalty—a differentiation advantage.

Control of overlapping input and output domains enhances an organization's competitive advantage in its core domain and creates new opportunities for value creation. But an organization also needs to look at the bureaucratic costs associated with full ownership of suppliers and distributors.[38] The organization needs to evaluate whether minority ownership, strategic alliances, and other interorganizational strategies are viable alternatives to vertical integration.[39] The value creation advantages of vertical integration can sometimes be obtained at much lower bureaucratic costs by means of strategic alliances with already existing businesses because an organization avoids the costs associated with having to operate the business. The more an organization pursues vertical integration, the larger the organization becomes, and the bureaucratic costs associated with managing the strategy are likely to rise sharply because of communication and coordination problems and the simple fact that managers are expensive to employ. Too much vertical integration can be a strategic mistake. Thus, managers must be careful to make design choices about organizational structure and culture that will enhance and support such a strategy.

Related Diversification

Related diversification
The entry into a new domain that is related in some way to an organization's domain.

Related diversification occurs when an organization enters a new domain in which it can exploit one or more of its existing core competences to create a low-cost or differentiated competitive advantage in that new domain. When Honda entered the small-car market, for example, it entered a domain in which it could exploit functional skills in engine design and manufacture that it had developed in its core domain, motorbikes, to achieve a low-cost advantage. When the owners of the B.A.R. and Grille opened a pizza restaurant and a waffle restaurant, they were exploiting the coordination abilities they had developed in food operations, purchasing, and restaurant management to create a differentiation advantage for their new restaurants. Whenever an organization enters a new domain to exploit an opportunity to use any of its core competences in a way that can lower costs or create uniqueness, it creates value through related diversification.

Unrelated diversification   The entry into a new domain that is not related in any way to an organization's core domain.

Unrelated Diversification

The value created by *related* diversification comes from exploiting *any* of an organization's core competences in a new domain. When a company pursues **unrelated diversification**, it enters new domains that have nothing in common with its core domain. The value created by unrelated diversification comes from exploiting one particular core competence: a top-management team's ability to control a set of organizations better than the organizations' existing top-management teams.[40]

Suppose a retail organization's top-management team has developed unique skills in economizing on bureaucratic costs by designing and managing organizational structure. If the team sees an organization in some new domain—for example, fast food—that is being managed inefficiently and is not making the best use of its resources, team members may see an opportunity for their organization to expand into this new domain and create value there. If the top-management team takes over the inefficient organization, restructures its operations, reduces bureaucratic costs, and increases its profitability, it has created value that did not previously exist in the fast-food organization.

An organization that takes over inefficient companies and restructures them to create value is pursuing a strategy of unrelated diversification. If it continues to manage these organizations from a pure profitability standpoint and buys and sells them on the basis of their return on investment, it is also pursuing a strategy of unrelated diversification. For example, Hanson Trust, an organization that is a collection of unrelated British and American divisions, seeks out underperforming organizations, sells off the divisions it does not want, and keeps the divisions it feels it can restructure and operate profitably. Designing an efficient organizational structure is an important part of the strategy of unrelated diversification because companies that perform poorly often do so because they have high bureaucratic costs.

As noted earlier, an organization is likely to pursue all three corporate-level strategies (vertical integration, related diversification, and unrelated diversification) as it searches for new ways to exploit its core competences. As an organization pursues more and more opportunities, its activities expand and may diverge increasingly from those it pursued in its original domain. Greyhound Corporation offers a good example of a diversification strategy. In its original domain, Greyhound provided transportation throughout the United States through its well-known bus operations. Greyhound also integrated vertically, manufacturing its own buses. During the 1980s, it diversified into unrelated domains, buying companies such as Armor-Dial Corporation, which manufactured products ranging from processed meat to soap. When the bus operations became unprofitable because of falling customer demand and rising labor costs, Greyhound Corporation eventually sold them and withdrew from its original domain. It changed its name to Dial Corporation in 1990 and now principally manufacturers consumer goods such as Liquid Dial soap and Breck shampoo.

Corporate-Level Strategy and Structure

The appropriate organizational structure must be chosen at the corporate level in order to realize the value associated with vertical integration and related and unrelated diversification. In general, as we discussed in Chapter 4, for organizations that are operating in more than one domain a multidivisional structure is the appropriate choice (see Figure 4.7). The use of self-contained operating divisions supported by a corporate headquarters staff provides the control the organization needs to coordinate resource transfers between divisions so that core competences can be shared across the organization. There are a few variants of the multidivisional structure. Each is suited to realizing the benefits associated with either unrelated or related diversification.

CONGLOMERATE STRUCTURE AND UNRELATED DIVERSIFICATION. Organizations pursuing a strategy of unrelated diversification attempt to create value by purchasing underperforming businesses, restructuring them, and then managing them more efficiently. This strategy frees the managers of the parent organization from involvement in the day-to-day running of the various companies that the organization owns. After the restructuring, corporate management's only role is to monitor each company's performance and intervene to take selective action when necessary. Organizations with a strategy of unrelated diversification are likely to use a conglomerate structure.

Conglomerate structure

A structure in which each business is placed in a self-contained division and there is no contact between divisions.

As Figure 7.9 shows, in a **conglomerate structure**, each unrelated business is a self-contained division. Because there is no need to coordinate activities between divisions, only a small corporate headquarters staff is needed. Communication is from the top down and occurs most often on issues that concern bureaucratic costs, such as decisions about the level of financial expenditure necessary to pursue new value creation opportunities. Hanson Trust, for example, has a corporate staff of only 120 people to oversee more than 50 companies, and it operates primarily through rules that control bureaucratic costs. Hanson Trust has a rule that requires a corporate executive to approve any expenditure over $3,000.[41] Beyond this, it makes little attempt to intervene in the affairs of the operating divisions unless some restructuring is necessary.

STRUCTURES FOR RELATED DIVERSIFICATION. An organization pursuing a strategy of related diversification tries to obtain value by sharing resources or by transferring functional skills from one division to another—processes that require a great amount of coordination and integration. Related diversification requires lateral communication between divisions as well as vertical communication between divisions and corporate headquarters. As a result, integrating roles and teams of functional experts are needed to coordinate skill and resource transfers. Coordination is complicated because divisions may fight for resources and may not wish to share information and knowledge unless they are equitably rewarded for doing so. To obtain from related diversification a set of gains comparable to those obtained from unrelated diversification, a much larger corporate headquarters staff is required to coordinate interdivisional activities, and much more managerial time and effort are needed. Hitachi's corporate structure offers an interesting insight into the management of a strategy of related diversification.

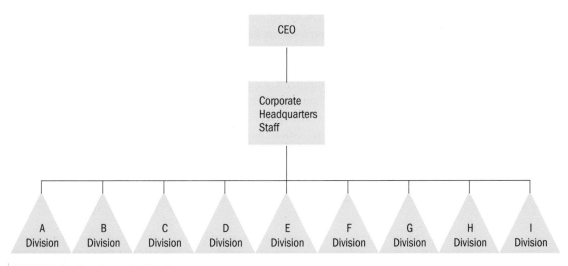

FIGURE 7.9 **Conglomerate Structure**

ORGANIZATIONAL INSIGHT

7.3 HITACHI LTD.

Hitachi Ltd. is one of Japan's biggest and most innovative companies. Every year the $62 billion giant accounts for 6 percent of Japan's expenditures on R&D and over 2 percent of Japan's gross domestic product. Like its biggest competitors, IBM and Fujitsu, Hitachi is a major computer organization. Unlike them, however, it is also engaged in noncomputer businesses that rely heavily on computer technology: consumer electronics, power plants, transportation, medical equipment, and telecommunications.[42] It is pursuing a strategy of related diversification on a grand scale, and research and development forms the bedrock of the organization and its value creation activities.

Hitachi has 28 divisions. Each has its own R&D laboratory and is responsible for product development from the initial conception to design and final marketing. Control is decentralized to each division, and each division has the ultimate responsibility for choosing its domain. This decentralized approach puts a heavy burden on Hitachi to find ways to integrate and coordinate its divisions so that they can share skills and resources and increase their level of innovation.

Hitachi has responded to the need for interdivisional coordination by adopting various integrating mechanisms:

1. Hitachi employs a large number of corporate executives in integrating roles to oversee each division's activities and control information flows from one division to another.
2. Hitachi has a corporate R&D laboratory that has the responsibility for coordinating the flow of new knowledge among the divisions' R&D laboratories and for disseminating the knowledge it creates to the divisions.
3. Hitachi uses a sophisticated telecommunications and teleconferencing network to link its laboratories, so that scientists and engineers in different labs can effectively work face-to-face to trade knowledge and cooperate on joint research.
4. Hitachi has developed a strong corporate culture based on values of cooperation and teamwork between scientists, and norms that support innovation flourish.

Through all those means, Hitachi has enhanced its ability to transfer its R&D skills around the organization and secure the gains from its strategy of related diversification.

In Hitachi, there are enormous opportunities for finding new ways to create value because the divisions are related to one another through their reliance on computer and electronic technology. The bureaucratic costs of pursuing this strategy, however, are very high because so much time and money are spent on integrating the 28 R&D laboratories in order to keep them aware of each other's activities. The enormous costs of operating so many R&D units also eat into profits. Hitachi has chosen to bear these costs in order to obtain the benefits of its strategy of related diversification. Because it has a time horizon for product development that extends well into the future, it is not concerned with the bottom-line results of any single division in the short run. What matters to Hitachi is maintaining its long-term ability to create value.

Hitachi has 28 operating divisions, and its coordination problem is intense. Imagine the coordination problem that arises when an organization has over 150 divisions, as do General Electric and Textron. Often the coordination problem becomes so severe that a multidivisional matrix structure is used to increase integration (see Figure 4.14). As we saw in

Chapter 4, this structure provides the coordination between the divisions and corporate headquarters that allows for the transfer of skills and the sharing of resources around the organization. It gives top-level functional, divisional, and corporate managers the opportunity to meet in teams to plan the organization's future strategy.

The bureaucratic costs associated with managing related diversification (whether in a multidivisional structure or a matrix multidivisional structure) are much greater than those associated with vertical integration or unrelated diversification.[43] Considerably more communication and coordination are needed to create value from related diversification than from the other corporate-level strategies. Bureaucratic costs increase as the size of the corporate staff and the amount of time that both divisional and corporate managers spend in coordinating with other divisions increase. In contrast, the bureaucratic costs associated with unrelated diversification are likely to be low because there is no need to coordinate resource transfers between divisions—the divisions do not exchange anything.

Corporate-Level Strategy and Culture

Just as a move to a more appropriate organizational structure can reduce bureaucratic costs, so can a move to a more appropriate organizational culture. Cultural values and the common norms, rules, and goals that reflect those values can greatly facilitate the management of a corporate strategy. For example, Hanson Trust, which pursues a strategy of unrelated diversification, values economy, cost cutting, and the efficient use of organizational resources. Divisional managers at Hanson Trust cannot spend large amounts of money without the approval of corporate executives. They know that their performance is scrutinized closely, and their actions are shaped by corporate values tied to bottom-line results. Both managers and workers are socialized to cost-cutting norms and rules.

By contrast, suppose an organization is pursuing a strategy of related diversification. What kinds of values, norms, and rules are most useful in managing the strategy? Because the creation of value from related diversification requires a large amount of coordination and integration, norms and values that emphasize cooperation between divisions are important. This type of culture lowers the costs of exchanging resources and is likely to feature a common corporate language that the various divisions can use in their dealings with one another. Each division will have its own culture, but the corporate culture can overcome differences in divisional orientation, just as at the business level an organization's culture can overcome differences in functional orientation.

At Sony, for example, corporate values of innovation and entrepreneurship are passed on in the stories that organizational members use to frame significant corporate events. New employees are socialized to the innovative culture and learn the corporate language from their interactions with other people. In its promotions to the corporate headquarters staff, Sony also sends a message about the kinds of values and behaviors that are associated with success in the organization—actions that lead to innovative new products. Similarly, an organization that rewards managers who successfully manage interdivisional attempts to share skills and trade resources has a culture that supports a strategy of related diversification.

Thus, different cultures help organizations pursue different corporate-level strategies. An organization needs to create a culture that reinforces and builds on the strategy it pursues and the structure it adopts. In an organization that has a conglomerate structure, in which there is no connection between divisions, it would be pointless to develop a common corporate culture across divisions because the managers in the different divisions will not know one another. A multidivisional matrix structure, in contrast, does support the development of a cohesive corporate culture because it permits the rapid interchange of ideas and the transfer of norms and values around the organization. In sum, as we saw in Chapter 5, corporate culture is an important tool that organizations can use to coordinate and motivate employees.

Using Interorganizational Strategies

As at the business level, the interorganizational strategies discussed in Chapter 6 are an important means of increasing the value an organization can create through its corporate strategy. Interorganizational strategies increase value by allowing the organization to avoid the bureaucratic costs often associated with managing a new organization in a new domain. As the number of an organization's divisions increases, for example, the bureaucratic costs associated with managing interdivisional activities increase. Interorganizational strategies such as strategic alliances may allow an organization to obtain the gains from cooperation between divisions without experiencing the costs. Suppose two organizations establish a joint venture to produce a range of products in a domain that is new to both of them. Each organization contributes a different skill or resource to the venture. One provides low-cost manufacturing skills; the other, differentiated R&D and marketing skills. By establishing the joint venture, they have avoided the bureaucratic costs that would be incurred if one organization took over the other or if either organization had to internally coordinate the new resource transfers necessary to make the new venture work. Similarly, the gains from vertical integration can often be realized through minority ownership or long-term contracts, which avoid the need to own the supplier or distributor. An organization that can use an interorganizational strategy to enter and compete in a new domain can often secure the benefits of the diversification and integration strategies without incurring bureaucratic costs.

Managerial Implications: Corporate-Level Strategy

1. To protect the organization's existing domains and to exploit the organization's core competences to create value for stakeholders, managers should carefully analyze the environment.
2. To distinguish between a value creation opportunity and a value losing opportunity, managers should carefully evaluate the benefits and costs associated with entering a new domain.
3. As part of this analysis, managers should weigh the benefits and costs of various strategies for entering the domain—for example, takeover of an existing company versus establishing a new organization versus using a strategic alliance such as a joint venture.
4. No matter which corporate strategy managers pursue, as the organization grows, managers must be careful to match their organization's structure and culture to the strategy they are pursuing.

 SUMMARY

Organizational strategy is a plan of action that an organization undertakes to create value. Organizations that do not constantly set ambitious new goals and try to find effective means of reaching those goals are likely to be threatened by younger, more agile competitors in search of ways to seize resources for themselves. Consequently, organizational members at all levels in the organization—functional, business, and corporate—must develop their value creation skills and abilities. Managers must manage the interrelationship of strategy (at all levels), structure, and culture to maximize the organization's ability to manage, enhance, and protect its domain so that it can create value to satisfy stakeholders. Chapter 7 has made the following main points:

1. The value that an organization creates by means of its strategy is a function of how the organization positions itself in its environment so that it can use its core competences to compete for resources.

2. An organization's core competences are products of its functional and organizational resources and its coordination ability.

3. An organization must formulate strategy at three levels: the functional level, the business level, and the corporate level.

4. The goal of functional-level strategy is to create in each function a low-cost or differentiation competence that gives the organization a competitive advantage.

5. Functional structure and culture produce functional abilities that support the development of functional resources.

6. The goal of business-level strategy is to combine functional low-cost and differentiation competences in order to exploit opportunities in the organizational environment. Business-level strategy selects and manages the domain in which an organization uses its value creation resources and coordination abilities.

7. The two main business-level strategies are low-cost business-level strategy and differentiation business-level strategy.

8. An organization chooses a structure and culture to develop coordination abilities that support its business-level strategy.

9. The goal of corporate-level strategy is to use and develop low-cost and differentiation competences so that the organization can protect and enlarge its existing domain and expand into new domains.

10. Four main types of corporate-level strategy are vertical integration, related diversification, unrelated diversification, and global expansion.

11. An appropriate corporate-level structure and culture can help reduce the bureaucratic costs of managing a strategy.

12. At the functional, business, and corporate levels, an organization should use interorganizational strategies to help reduce the bureaucratic costs associated with its value creation activities.

DISCUSSION QUESTIONS

1. How should an organization design its structure and culture to obtain a core competence in manufacturing and in research and development?

2. Select an organization such as a restaurant or a department store, and analyze how it might pursue a low-cost or a differentiation strategy.

3. What is the difference between a low-cost strategy and a differentiation strategy? How should a differentiated biotechnology organization and a low-cost, fast-food organization design their structures and cultures to promote their respective competitive advantages?

4. Compare the competitive advantages enjoyed by a large restaurant chain, such as Steak and Ale or Red Lobster, and the sources of competitive advantages enjoyed by a small, local restaurant.

5. Why would an organization choose a corporate-level strategy to expand its value creation activities beyond its core domain? Discuss how an organization's structure and culture might change as the organization begins to enter new domains.

ORGANIZATIONAL THEORY IN ACTION

PRACTICING ORGANIZATIONAL THEORY: WHAT KIND OF SUPERMARKET?

Form groups of three to five people and discuss the following scenario:

You are a group of investors who are contemplating opening a new supermarket in your city. You are trying to decide what business-level strategy would provide your supermarket with a competitive advantage that would allow you to attract customers and outperform your prospective rivals.

1. List the supermarket chains in your city and identify their business-level strategies (e.g., low cost, differentiation, or focus). Also list any particular kinds of functional strengths or weaknesses that they might have (such as a great bakery or a lousy fish counter).
2. On the basis of this analysis, what type of business-level strategy do you think will best succeed in the local market? What will the specific elements of this strategy be? (For example, what kind of supermarket will it be? What kind of functional strengths will you try to develop? What kinds of customers will you aim for? What will you do to attract them?)

MAKING THE CONNECTION #7

Find an example of an organization pursuing a business- or a corporate-level strategy. What kind of strategy is it pursuing? Why did it choose this strategy? How does the strategy create value? How does the strategy affect the organization's structure or culture?

Analyzing the Organization: Design Module #7

This module focuses on the kinds of goods and services that your organization produces, the markets in which it competes, and the kinds of strategies that it uses to create value for its stakeholders.

ASSIGNMENT

1. Briefly describe your organization's domain—that is, the goods and services that it produces and the customer groups that it serves.
2. What core competences give the organization a competitive advantage? What are the organization's functional-level strategies?
3. What is your organization's principal business-level strategy: low cost or differentiation? How successfully is the organization pursuing this strategy? In what ways does it need to improve its core competences to improve its competitive position? Is it pur-

suing one of the other business-level strategies, such as product development or market development?

4. In what ways do your organization's structure and culture match its strategy? Is there a good match? In what ways could the match be improved? Is the organization experiencing any problems with its structure?

5. Is your organization operating in more than one domain? If it is, what corporate-level strategies is it pursuing? How is it creating value from these strategies? Is it successful?

6. What is your overall impression of your organization's value creation activities? Is there a good or a not-so-good fit between its functional-, business-, and corporate-level strategies?

Cases for Analysis:
CAN LONG JOHN'S GET BACK ON BOTH FEET?

Long John Silver's Inc., the 1,488-store seafood chain, has been experiencing hard times recently, and its sales and profits have fallen dramatically. Its new CEO, John Cranor III, who was brought in to turn around the company's performance, believes that a large part of the seafood chain's problem was the previous management team's inability to find the right strategy for the company to compete effectively and attract customers.

Long John's started out as a cheap fast-food restaurant that sold only fish products. However, in the early 1990s, riding the wave of the increasing popularity of fish as a health food, the seafood chain decided to go for more upscale customers. It improved its food quality and service and increased its prices, becoming a midscale restaurant—neither fast-food nor expensive. To implement the new midscale strategy, the company moved to a geographic-based structure to encourage restaurants in each region of the United States to take advantage of local seafood specialties (e.g., redfish in the Gulf region or lobster in the Northeast) and to develop special meals for its customers. This new upscale differentiation strategy was a disaster.

Long John's customers were not the kind of people who wanted higher prices and better service; they wanted meals that were served fast and were value for money. Moreover, Long John's had started its strategy at a time when there was intense competition between fast-food chains. Both Taco Bell and McDonald's were *reducing* prices to keep their customers and build market share. They were pursuing a low-cost strategy in contrast to Long John's differentiation approach.

At first Long John's managers attributed their falling sales not to their new midscale strategy but to the fact that they were focusing on too narrow a niche—Long John's served only seafood. Managers decided that Long John's must expand its range of prod-

uct offerings, so in early 1996 the company announced that it was seeking alliances with other chains like Arby's (which specializes in roast beef and meat sandwiches) and with regional taco chains like Taco Time. The idea behind the strategy was that each store should sell the food offerings of the other stores so that they would all offer customers a much broader product range—one that could compete with the likes of McDonald's. For example, Long John's would offer seafood, roast beef sandwiches, and tacos.

By the summer of 1996, it was clear that this new strategy was not working and that customers were not attracted by the idea of eating tacos in a Long John's restaurant. With sales plunging, the new CEO decided that Long John's only hope was to return to its initial strategy and focus on providing cheap, fast seafood. Cranor instructed Long John's franchisees to cut prices and the range of food offerings. To further reduce costs, he also demolished the company's new regional structure, cutting 150 middle managers and wiping out two levels in the corporate hierarchy.[44] Cranor then centralized support services. He hopes that operating with a simpler functional structure will allow the company as a whole to respond more quickly to the needs of its customers and the changing patterns of competition in the fast-food industry. He also hopes the company can more effectively compete with a new competitor, Captain D's (a division of Shoney's), which has also staked out the seafood segment of the fast-food market and is rapidly expanding the number of its restaurants.

1. What problems was Long John's experiencing in its environment?

2. How did it change its strategy to manage them?

REFERENCES

1. A. D. Chandler, *Strategy and Structure: Chapters in the History of the Industrial Enterprise* (Cambridge, MA: MIT Press, 1962).

2. C. W. L. Hill and G. R. Jones, *Strategic Management: An Integrated Approach*, 4th ed. (Boston: Houghton Mifflin, 1998).

3. M. E. Porter, *Competitive Strategy* (New York: The Free Press, 1980).

4. K. Weigelt and C. Camerer, "Reputation and Corporate Strategy," *Strategic Management Journal*, 1988, vol. 9, pp. 443–454.

5. Hill and Jones, *Strategic Management*, Ch. 10.

6. R. R. Nelson and S. Winter, *An Evolutionary Theory of Economic Change* (Cambridge, MA: Harvard University Press, 1982).

7. M. E. Porter, *Competitive Advantage: Creating and Sustaining Superior Performance* (New York: The Free Press, 1985).

8. R. W. Ruekert and O. C. Walker, "Interactions Between Marketing and R&D Departments in Implementing Different Business Strategies," *Strategic Management Journal*, 1987, vol. 8, pp. 233–248.

9. Porter, *Competitive Strategy*.

10. K. N. M. Dundas and P. R. Richardson, "Corporate Strategy and the Concept of Market Failure," *Strategic Management Journal*, 1980, vol. 1, pp. 177–188.

11. Porter, *Competitive Advantage*.

12. S. C. Wheelright, "Manufacturing Strategy: Defining the Missing Link," *Strategic Management Journal*, 1984, vol. 5, pp. 77–91.

13. D. Ulrich, "Linking Strategic Planning and Human Resource Planning," in L. Fahey, ed., *The Strategic Planning Management Reader* (Englewood Cliffs, NJ: Prentice Hall, 1989), pp. 421–426.

14. E. S. Buffa, "Positioning the Production System—A Key Element in Manufacturing Strategy," in Fahey, *The Strategic Planning Management Reader*, pp. 387–395.

15. O. E. Williamson, *Markets and Hierarchies* (New York: The Free Press, 1975).

16. R. M. Johnson, "Market Segmentation: A Strategic Management Tool," *Journal of Marketing Research*, 1971, vol. 8, pp. 15–23.

17. V. Scarpello, W. R. Boulton, and C. W. Hofer, "Reintegrating R&D into Business Strategy," *Journal of Business Strategy*, 1986, vol. 6, pp. 49–56.

18. D. Miller, "Strategy Making and Structure: Analysis and Implications for Performance," *Academy of Management Journal*, 1987, vol. 30, pp. 7–32.

19. P. R. Lawrence and J. W. Lorsch, *Organization and Environment* (Boston: Graduate School of Business Administration, Harvard University, 1967).

20. J. Woodward, *Industrial Organization: Theory and Practice* (London: Oxford University Press, 1965).

21. K. M. Eisenhardt, "Control: Organizational and Economic Approaches," *Management Science*, 1985, vol. 16, pp. 134–138.

22. J. B. Barney, "Organization Culture: Can It Be a Source of Sustained Competitive Advantage?" *Academy of Management Review*, 1986, vol. 11, pp. 791–800.

23. S. M. Oster, *Modern Competitive Analysis* (New York: Oxford University Press, 1990).

24. Porter, *Competitive Strategy*, Ch. 2.

25. Ibid.

26. R. E. White, "Generic Business Strategies, Organizational Context and Performance: An Empirical Investigation," *Strategic Management Journal*, 1986, vol. 7, pp. 217–231; G. R. Jones and J. E. Butler, "Costs, Revenue, and Business Level Strategy," *Academy of Management Review*, 1988, vol. 13, pp. 202–213.

27. Porter, *Competitive Strategy*.

28. White, "Generic Business Strategies, Organizational Context and Performance"; D. Miller, "Configurations of Strategy and Structure," *Strategic Management Journal*, 1986, vol. 7, pp. 223–249.

29. S. Kotha and D. Orne, "Generic Manufacturing Strategies: A Conceptual Synthesis," *Strategic Management Journal*, 1989, vol. 10, pp. 211–231.

30. P. R. Lawrence and J. W. Lorsch, *Organization and Environment* (Cambridge, MA: Harvard University Press, 1967).

31. D. Miller, "Strategy Making and Structure: Analysis and Implications for Performance," *Academy of Management Journal*, 1987, vol. 30, pp. 7–32.

32. A. Deutschman, "If They're Gaining on You, Innovate," *Fortune*, 2 November 1992, p. 86.

33. N. Deogun, "Pepsi Alters Structure of U.S. marketing," www.msnbc.com, 4 November 1988.

34. T. J. Peters and R. H. Waterman, Jr., *In Search of Excellence* (New York: Harper and Row, 1982).

35. E. Deal and A. A. Kennedy, *Corporate Cultures* (Reading, MA: Addison-Wesley, 1985).

36. M. E. Porter, "From Competitive Advantage to Competitive Strategy," *Harvard Business Review*, May–June 1987, pp. 43–59.

37. Based on Chandler, *Strategy and Structure*.

38. Chandler, *Strategy and Structure*; J. Pfeffer and G. R. Salancik, *The External Control of Organizations* (New York: Harper and Row, 1978).

39. Williamson, *Markets and Hierarchies*; K. R. Harrigan, *Strategic Flexibility* (Lexington, MA: Lexington Books, 1985).

40. Porter, "From Competitive Advantage to Competitive Strategy."

41. C. W. L. Hill, "Hanson PLC," in C. W. L. Hill and G. R. Jones, *Strategic Management: An Integrated Approach*, 4th ed. (Boston: Houghton Mifflin, 1998), pp. 764–783.

42. "New In-Flight Adapter Adds to Hitachi's Mobilized Computing Vision and Extends Flexibility and Mobility," *Business Wire*, 20 October 1997.

43. G. R. Jones and C. W. L. Hill, "Transaction Cost Analysis of Strategy-Structure Choice," *Strategic Management Journal*, 1988, vol. 9, pp. 159–172.

44. "Cranor Streamlines LJS' Structure," *Nation's Restaurant News*, 22 July 1996, p. 1.

Chapter 8

MANAGING the
INTERNATIONAL ENVIRONMENT

Chapter 6 noted that forces in the international environment can affect an organization's domain, and Chapter 7 noted that one major corporate-level strategy that an organization can pursue to enlarge and protect its domain is global expansion. Global expansion allows an organization to seek new opportunities to exploit its core competences to create value for stakeholders. This chapter discusses how organizations expand globally and manage the international environment. It focuses on how an organization creates value by global expansion and examines some strategies managers can use to extend its international domain. Each strategy creates value in a different way, and each is associated with a different set of management problems. If the benefits of each strategy are to be realized, it must be matched to a particular type of organizational structure and culture. Complex strategies require complex forms of structure, and this chapter examines the range of choices open to companies competing internationally, including strategic alliances. By the end of this chapter, you will understand why managing the international environment is a crucial challenge facing the managers of all organizations.

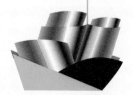

WHAT IS THE INTERNATIONAL ENVIRONMENT?

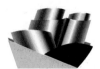

American companies have been heavily involved in international trade since colonial days, when they shipped their stocks of tobacco and sugar to Europe in return for manufactured products. Throughout the twentieth century, General Motors, H. J. Heinz, Campbell Soup, Procter & Gamble, and thousands of other U.S. companies have established foreign divisions and have transferred their domestic core competences abroad to produce goods and services valued by foreign consumers. Indeed, U.S. companies have been established in foreign countries for so long that they are often treated as domestic companies by people in those countries. People in Britain, for example, regard H. J. Heinz, Hoover, Ford, and Eastman Kodak as British companies, often forgetting their U.S. origins. Similarly, the fact that Britain is the biggest foreign investor in the United States and that British companies own or have owned such "American" institutions as Burger King, Howard Johnson, and Jacuzzi is not generally known by Americans.

Today, the international environment is of increasing concern to U.S. companies and other companies around the world because it is both a major opportunity and a major threat. On one hand, the existence of huge new markets and the possibility of gaining access to new resources and new core competences provide opportunities for an organization to enlarge its domain and create more value for its stakeholders. On the other hand, international forces make the organizational environment more uncertain and difficult to predict and control. As companies are increasingly drawn into competition both at home and abroad, the environment becomes increasingly complex (there are greater numbers of forces to be managed, and the forces are interconnected) and increasingly dynamic (the forces change rapidly).

In the United States, Sony, Toyota, Philips, BMW, and other foreign companies compete with American companies for consumers. Abroad, American companies face competition from organizations both inside and outside the countries in which they operate. The European divisions of General Motors and Ford, for example, compete not only with European car companies such as Fiat, Peugeot, and BMW but also with Japanese companies such as Toyota and Honda. Indeed, during the 1990s, Japanese car companies operating in Europe have established plants with the capacity to produce 450,000 new cars a year and, thus, threaten the prosperity of Volkswagen, Renault, Fiat, and Volvo.

Whenever an organization confronts the international environment, it has to manage forces that are similar to the ones that operate in the domestic environment. These forces, however, differ from country to country and from region to region and, thus, increase the complexity of transactions in the organization's specific and general international environments. Figure 8.1 identifies these forces.

The Specific International Environment

Several forces in the specific international environment increase the problems an organization experiences in managing its domain and gaining access to scarce resources.

CUSTOMERS.   In the international environment, satisfying customer needs presents new challenges because customers differ from country to country. For example, customers in Europe—unlike Americans—typically do not like their cereal sweetened, so Kellogg and General Mills modify their products to suit local European tastes. An organization must be willing and able to tailor or customize its products to suit the tastes and preferences of different consumers if it expects to attract their business.

FIGURE 8.1

The International Environment. In the specific international environment are outside stakeholders that directly affect an organization's ability to obtain resources. In the general international environment are forces that shape the specific international environments of all organizations.

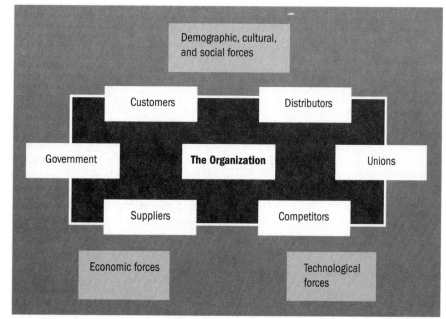

■ General international environment
■ Specific international environment

FOREIGN COMPETITORS.   More often than not, foreign competitors have some kind of competitive advantage over U.S. companies in foreign markets or in the U.S. market because of their possession of a low-cost or differentiation competence. Small European breakfast food companies and beer and wine producers have been attracting American consumers who like the unique taste of their products. Americans at first favored Japanese cars because of their low prices and high quality but have continued to purchase them even though they now cost more than American cars. The large number of competitors in the international environment makes it especially difficult to attract consumers because each competitor offers consumers an extra product choice.

SUPPLIERS.   In the international environment, supplies of inputs can be obtained not just from domestic sources but from any country in the world. We saw in Chapter 6 how network organizations, which contract with other organizations to perform value creation activities like manufacturing or marketing, take advantage of the existence of low-cost sources of supplies in foreign countries to increase their ability to pursue a low-cost strategy. If U.S. companies do not explore opportunities to lower the cost of their inputs by locating abroad or by buying from foreign suppliers, they know that their foreign competitors will do so and will hurt their competitive advantage. AT&T, for example, found it impossible to compete with Panasonic and Hitachi for the lucrative telephone-answering-machine market until it started to buy and assemble its inputs abroad. AT&T components are made in Taiwan, China, and Hong Kong, and access to low-cost inputs has allowed AT&T to reduce its prices and recapture the market from its Japanese competitors.

DISTRIBUTORS AND MARKETERS.   The challenges associated with distributing and marketing products increase in the international environment. Because the tastes of customers vary from country to country, many advertising and marketing campaigns are country specific, and many products are customized to foreign customers' preferences. Moreover, in Japan and some other countries, domestic producers tightly control distribution systems, and that arrangement makes it very hard for foreign companies to sell their products. Global distribution also becomes difficult when an organization's products are complex and customers need a lot of information to operate or use them successfully. All of these factors mean that an organization has to carefully consider how to handle the global distribution of its products to attract and retain customer support. Should the organization handle foreign sales and distribution itself? Should it sell to a wholesaler in the foreign market? Should it enter into a strategic alliance with an organization in the foreign country and allow that company to market and distribute its products? Organizations operating in many countries must weigh all these options.

THE WORKFORCE.   An organization that establishes foreign operations has to forge a working relationship with its new workforce and develop relationships with any unions that represent its new employees. If a Japanese manufacturer opens a new plant in the United States, the Japanese management team has to understand the expectations of its American workers—that is, their attitudes toward pay, seniority, and other conditions of employment. A foreign organization has to adapt its management style to fit with the workforce's style, and workers have to modify their expectations.

GOVERNMENT.   Each country has its own system of government and its own laws and regulations that govern the conduct of business. A U.S. company that enters a foreign country must conform to the host country's institutional and legal system. Sometimes, as in the European Community (EC), the rules governing business conduct are standardized across several countries. Increasingly, U.S. companies are complaining about the protection that host governments offer their own companies. Boeing, for example, complains that subsidies from European taxpayers allow Airbus Industries to undercut the price of Boeing's airplanes. Similarly, U.S. farmers complain that European tariffs protect inefficient European farmers and close the market to the products of more efficient U.S. producers. Often, domestic competitors lobby their home governments to combat "unfair" foreign competition.

The General International Environment

Similar general forces operate in the international environment and in the domestic organizational environment. But country-to-country differences make it especially difficult for an organization to manage its domain.

ECONOMIC FORCES.   National differences in interest rates, exchange rates, wage levels, gross domestic product, and per capita income have a dramatic effect on the way organizations operate internationally. Generally, organizations attempt to obtain their inputs or to manufacture their products in the country with the lowest labor or raw-materials costs. Both Smith Corona and Zenith recently closed their last U.S. manufacturing plants and moved their operations to Mexico because doing so enabled them to match the low costs of their foreign competitors. Obviously, a foreign competitor based in a country with low wages has a competitive advantage that may be crucial in the battle for the price-conscious U.S. consumer. Many U.S. companies are forced to move their operations abroad to compete with the low-cost operations of foreign manufacturers.

TECHNOLOGICAL FORCES.   The international transfer of technology has important implications for an organization's competitive advantage. Organizations must be able to learn about and have access to technological developments abroad that might provide a low-cost or differentiation advantage. Traditionally, the United States has exported its technology and foreign companies have been eager to use it, but American companies have been slow to take advantage of foreign technological developments. Critics charge that global learning has been one-way—from the United States to the rest of the world—to the detriment of U.S. competitiveness. It has been estimated that after World War II Japanese companies paid U.S. companies $100 million for the rights to license certain technologies and in return gained over $100 billion in sales revenue from U.S. consumers. The willingness and ability of U.S. companies to learn from their foreign competitors are becoming increasingly important. Such technological learning allows an organization to develop its core competences and apply them around the world to create value, as Amazon.com has done.

Focus on New Information Technology: Amazon.com, Part 6

New information technology is not specialized to any one country or world region. Access to the Internet and the World Wide Web means that an on-line company can sell to customers around the world, providing, of course, that its products are suitable or can be customized to the needs of foreign competitors. Jeff Bezos was quick to realize that his U.S.-based Amazon.com information systems could be profitably customized and transferred to other countries to sell books. However, his ability to enter new foreign markets was limited by one major factor: Amazon.com offers its customers the biggest selection of books written in the English language. Therefore, he has to find foreign customers who can read English. Where to locate then?

An obvious first choice would be the United Kingdom since its population speaks English, followed other English-speaking nations such as Australia, New Zealand, India, and Germany. Germany? Probably of any nation in the world Germany has the highest proportion of English as a second language speakers because English is taught in all its high schools.

So far, Bezos has replicated his company's value creation functions and customized its information systems for two nations. In the United Kingdom it bought the company Bookpages, installed its proprietary technology, and renamed it Amazon.co.uk in 1996. In Germany, it acquired a new on-line venture ABC Bücherdienst/Telebuch.de, and created Amazon.de in 1998.[1] Analysts wonder which nations will be next, especially if Bezos decides to customize Amazon.com's technology for other languages such as Spanish or Chinese. Already Amazon.com ships its English language books to anywhere in the world.

DEMOGRAPHIC, CULTURAL, AND SOCIAL FORCES.   The value of a product to a customer is a function of a nation's lifestyle, norms, values, and customs. Similarly, cultural and social values affect a country's attitudes toward foreign products and foreign companies. Thus, demographic, cultural, and social forces are an important source of uncertainty in the international environment because they directly affect the tastes and needs of foreign customers. Customers in France and Italy, for example, generally prefer domestically produced cars even though foreign products are superior in quality and value.

A U.S. company establishing operations in a foreign country must be attuned to the host country's business methods and practices. Countries differ in how they do business and in the nature of their business institutions. They also differ in their attitudes toward union-management relationships, in their ethical standards, and in their accounting and financial practices. In some countries bribery and corruption are acceptable business practices. In Japan, the law supports organizations in their attempt to protect their market and distribution systems against the entry of foreign competitors. Antitrust sentiment is far weaker in Japan and South Korea than in the United States. That attitude enables domestic Japanese and Korean companies to collude to keep foreign rivals out of their respective markets.

CREATING VALUE FROM GLOBAL EXPANSION

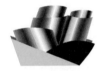

Global expansion strategy *A plan whereby an organization extends its value creation activities into foreign countries.*

To compete effectively on a global basis, an organization has to manage the forces in its specific and general international environments. Before we examine the strategies that organizations use to manage activities in the international environment, we need to examine how organizations create value from their international activities and the factors that influence the choice of strategy.

Global expansion strategy is an organization's plan to extend its value creation activities into foreign countries. Figure 8.2 summarizes four ways in which global expansion allows an organization to create value for its stakeholders and enhances the organization's core competences.

Transferring Core Competences Abroad

Global network *Sets of task and reporting relationships among managers, functions, and divisions that link an organization's value creation activities around the world.*

Value creation at the global level begins when an organization transfers a core competence in one or more of its value creation functions to a foreign market in order to produce cheaper or improved products that will give the organization a low-cost or differentiation advantage over its competitors in the foreign market. For example, Microsoft, with its competence in the production of technologically advanced software, takes this differentiation advantage and produces software tailored to the needs of foreign consumers. As a result of the transfer of its core competences to foreign markets, over 50 percent of Microsoft's revenue comes from foreign sales. McDonald's, using the competence in fast-food production that has made it a low-cost leader, applies its skills abroad to establish restaurants around the globe. Similarly, in the 1950s, companies such as Ford and H. J. Heinz took their core skills and established divisions in several countries.

Establishing a Global Network

Factor costs *The costs of raw materials, unskilled or skilled labor, land, and taxes.*

Generally, when an organization decides to transfer its competences abroad, it locates its value creation activities in countries where economic, political, and cultural conditions are likely to enhance its low-cost or differentiation advantage. It then establishes a **global network**—sets of task and reporting relationships among managers, functions, and divisions that link an organization's value creation activities around the world. To lower costs, an organization may locate its value creation functions in the countries in which **factor costs**—the costs of raw materials, unskilled or skilled labor, land, and taxes—are lowest. To lower costs, a video game company like Nintendo may perform its assembly opera-

FIGURE 8.2

The Creation of Value Through Global Expansion

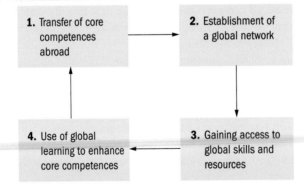

tions in one country and its design operations in another, have its headquarters in a third country, and buy its inputs and raw materials from still other countries. To link these far-flung activities, the organization creates a global network.

An organization can also establish a global network of distributors to sell and service its products. The access to foreign consumers that a global sales network brings can result in a huge sales volume, which, in turn, allows the organization to manufacture very large quantities of goods, realize global economies of scale in production, and strengthen its low-cost advantage. Matsushita, Sony, and Panasonic, for example, sell billions of electronic components to their global customers. Because of their huge volumes, they can produce in such large quantities that their economies of scale in production give them a low-cost advantage over American competitors such as General Electric and Zenith.

Gaining Access to Global Resources and Skills

An organization with a global network has access to resources and skills throughout the world. Because each country has unique economic, political, and cultural conditions, different countries have different resources and skills that give them a competitive advantage. So, for example, an American organization is likely to benefit from establishing itself in foreign countries with low-cost or differentiation core competences so that it can gain access to and learn how to develop these competences. If organizations in one country have an R&D competence, it would pay a U.S. company to establish operations in that country to gain access to the competence. Japan, for example, has skills in lean production and total quality manufacturing, and Xerox, Eastman Kodak, IBM, Ford, and other companies have established foreign divisions in Japan to learn these skills. Many U.S. companies developed skills in managing just-in-time inventory systems from their Japanese divisions and transferred this knowledge to their other domestic and global operations. Moreover, as we saw in Chapter 6, Japanese companies pioneered the development of strategic alliances through their use of keiretsu. In the United States, strategic alliances have become a way for an organization to enhance its core competences and improve its competitive advantage.

Toys "R" Us, the world's largest toy retailer, is an American company that has benefited from a global network. The company established a network of stores throughout Europe to take advantage of its core competence in the distribution and retailing of toys. While establishing a network of suppliers in Europe, Toys "R" Us found many new, high-quality toys, produced by German and Swiss companies, that it believed would appeal to American consumers; arranged to sell these toys in its American stores; and, thus, enhanced its differentiation advantage, creating more value. Similarly, Microsoft and McDonald's have entered foreign countries and enlarged their domains to exploit their competences and have established global networks to give them access to global resources and skills. In foreign markets, they have learned new skills that they have transferred to their business divisions in the other countries in which they operate.

Using Global Learning to Enhance Core Competences

Organizations set up their global activities to gain access to knowledge that will allow them to improve their core competences. The access to global resources and skills that a global network provides exposes an organization to new ways of improving itself. After an organization masters these new skills, it can transfer them to its domestic base to enhance its core competences and then transfer its enhanced competences back to its foreign operations to increase its competitive advantage abroad. For example, after World War II, the founders of Toyota, Panasonic, and other Japanese companies came to the United States to learn American production and marketing methods, which they then took back to Japan. They were not content just to learn the new techniques, however; they spent considerable time and effort trying to improve them. The engineers who founded Toyota studied GM's and Ford's production techniques and took what they had learned back to Japan, where they improved upon it and adapted it to the Japanese environment. As a result, Japanese companies obtained a competitive advantage over U.S. companies, which

ORGANIZATIONAL INSIGHT

8.1 XEROX LEARNS FROM THE JAPANESE

As we noted in Chapter 4, Xerox went from being a high-cost, low-quality organization to an effective global competitor that has adjusted well to the new realities of low-cost competition and the rapid pace of product innovation in the photocopier industry. In large part, the turnaround happened because Xerox was willing to learn from its Japanese division.

In the early 1960s, while Xerox still controlled a patent on its copying process, it established Fuji Xerox, a joint venture in Japan with Fuji (a manufacturer of photographic equipment and materials). Xerox entered into this joint venture so that it could distribute and market Xerox products in Japan. (Japanese law requires a foreign company to enter into an agreement with a Japanese company before it can begin operations in Japan. The law was enacted to give Japanese companies access to foreign technologies.)

Xerox did nothing to tailor its products to the Japanese market. By 1970, Fuji Xerox had convinced its American parent to allow it to produce copiers tailored to the needs of Japanese customers, and five years later Fuji Xerox had redesigned and was producing and marketing copiers in Japan with considerable success. By 1980, Fuji Xerox, over the objections of Xerox's engineers in the United States, was also designing its own new machines. By applying Japanese expertise in lean production and quality control, Fuji Xerox was able to produce a new generation of low-cost, high-quality copiers for sale only in the Japanese market.[2]

Meanwhile, in the United States, where patents protected Xerox from competitors, Xerox had done little to improve its machines and develop new technology for the day when its patents would expire. When they did expire, Xerox found itself under such intense price and quality pressure from Japanese companies like Canon and Murata, and American companies like IBM, that it had to fight for survival. Xerox's market share dropped by half, to less than 40 percent, as customers chose the products of its competitors.

Fuji Xerox saved its parent from collapse. The American company finally woke up and began to adopt its Japanese division's technology in the design and manufacture of copying machines in the United States. Xerox transferred its Japanese core competences to the United States. It redesigned its structure, adopting a product team structure, which enabled it to exploit the advantages offered by the new methods and technology. Recognition of the importance of a global approach and the two-way transfer of skills and resources transformed Xerox into an effective value-creating global organization.

made no attempt to improve the techniques they were using. Xerox recently reversed the flow of information by learning Japanese methods and adapting them to its worldwide operations.

FACTORS INFLUENCING THE CHOICE OF GLOBAL EXPANSION STRATEGY

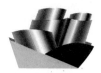

The three factors that influence the choice of strategy for global expansion are pressures for global integration, pressures for local responsiveness, and bureaucratic costs.

Pressures for Global Integration

As global learning takes place, and as an organization's global network expands, opportunities open for the transfer of skills from one country to another to enhance an organization's ability to create value. Indeed, the additional value that global expansion can create puts pressure on an organization to integrate its global value creation activities and use its skills and resources more efficiently to lower costs and increase quality—that is, to create a *low-cost competitive advantage*. An organization knows that whether or not it moves to exploit global learning, its foreign competitors will, and doing nothing will cost the organization its competitive advantage. This pressure is the first major consideration in an organization's choice of strategy for managing the international environment.

Pressures for Local Responsiveness

Our discussion so far may seem to rest on the assumption that an organization pursuing a global expansion strategy simply takes its core competences and transfers them directly to a foreign country to create value. But that is generally not what happens. Because countries around the world differ greatly, the relationships that an organization has to develop with its foreign suppliers and workforce are likely to differ from country to country. Also, because consumers in different countries may demand different qualities from any given product, an organization may have to customize its products and tailor its distinctive competences to suit the needs of its foreign customers.[3] McDonald's, for example, responds to the different tastes and preferences of foreign customers and customizes its menu to suit them. Similarly, Microsoft modifies its software to suit the language and customers of each country for which it produces software.

The greater the differences among countries, the greater are the pressures for local responsiveness. In response to these pressures, an organization customizes products, processes, and operating methods to suit conditions in the country in which it is operating, in order to create a differentiation competitive advantage.

Bureaucratic Costs

The greater the pressures for global integration and for local responsiveness, the greater are the bureaucratic costs associated with managing an organization's foreign operations. Coordinating resource transfers from one country to another takes managerial time and effort and, thus, is very expensive. Customizing products to foreign markets requires the coordination of value creation activities, which is also expensive. The specific global expansion strategy that an organization pursues also affects the level of bureaucratic costs.

We now examine four strategies for managing the international environment. We then turn to the issue of matching strategy to the appropriate organizational structure and culture in order to economize on the bureaucratic costs of global expansion.

STRATEGIES FOR MANAGING THE INTERNATIONAL ENVIRONMENT

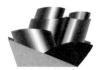

The four basic strategies that companies can use to enter and compete in the international environment are a multidomestic strategy, an international strategy, a global strategy, and a transnational strategy.[4] Each has different advantages and disadvantages and is associated with a different approach to creating value through global expansion. Figure 8.3 classifies these four strategies on two dimensions: (1) pressures for local responsiveness and (2) pressures for global integration.[5]

Multidomestic Strategy

A **multidomestic strategy** is a plan that responds to pressures for local responsiveness. An organization pursuing a multidomestic strategy customizes its products to suit the needs of customers in each country in which it competes. The organization transfers to foreign countries the core competences it has developed at home and establishes a wholly owned foreign division. Strategic control is decentralized to each foreign division, which

FIGURE 8.3

Four Strategies for
Global Expansion

	Pressures for Global Integration	
	(Value creation activities are coordinated on a country-by-country basis) Low	*(Value creation activities are coordinated simultaneously on a global and a country basis)* High
High *(Products and approaches are highly customized for each local market)*	(Goal of strategy is local differentiation advantage) **Multidomestic Strategy** (Bureaucratic costs are lowest)	(Goal of strategy is both differentiation and low-cost advantage) **Transnational Strategy** (Bureaucratic costs are highest)
Pressures for local Responsiveness		
Low *(The same standardized products are offered to customers in all countries)*	(Goal of strategy is global differentiation advantage) **International Strategy** (Bureaucratic costs are low)	(Goal of strategy is low-cost advantage) **Global Strategy** (Bureaucratic costs are high)

Multidomestic strategy
A plan that responds to pressures for local responsiveness and customizes the organization's products to suit the needs of customers in each country in which the organization competes.

operates autonomously and develops its own set of value creation activities. Manufacturing, R&D, product design, and marketing are all located in the foreign country. H. J. Heinz, Ford, and General Motors pursued a multidomestic strategy when they entered European markets. They transferred their core competences abroad and allowed managers in their foreign divisions to gradually develop products to suit the local market. Often the only connection between the parent company and its foreign divisions occurs when profits and dividends are transferred to the parent.

By locating abroad, organizations pursuing a multidomestic strategy gain access to the resources and skills present in the countries in which they operate. Foreign divisions are often able to obtain a differentiation advantage over local rivals by combining local core competences with the competences they received from the parent organization. This advantage allows them to become the dominant competitor in the local or host country.

In pursuing a multidomestic strategy, however, the parent organization often gains nothing but money from its foreign divisions. Because domestic and foreign divisions are autonomous and deal with very different markets, they grow apart, and little global learning occurs to enhance the parent company's core competences. Ford Motor Company established Ford of Europe as an autonomous entity. Ford of Europe used its parent's skills and resources to become the dominant European carmaker, producing a range of small cars tailored to the European market. Ford in the United States, however, believed that Americans wanted large cars and, thus, made little or no attempt to use its European division's design skills and expertise in small-car production to produce cars for the American market. When the Japanese entered the U.S. market and showed how wrong this assumption was, it was too late for Ford to catch up quickly and customize European cars for the U.S. market. The Japanese seized the small-car end of the market, and Ford spent the next 10 years playing catch-up. Ford could not exploit the advantages of global learning that entry into foreign markets makes possible because it was pursuing a multidomestic strategy and its autonomous divisions did not exchange skills or resources.

Another example of how a multidomestic strategy can cause problems for an organization over the long run comes from the experiences of Philips, the Dutch electronics manufacturer. Philips's European headquarters pioneered a new VCR format, the V2000, and attempted to establish it as the world industry standard against Sony's Betamax and Matsushita's VHS. When Philips tried to convince its U.S. division to adopt the new standard for the U.S. market, however, the division refused, arguing that VHS was the way of the future. Philips's U.S. division bought VCRs from Matsushita and sold them under the Magnavox brand name, and Philips lost the chance to profit from its own technology.

In short, the goal of a multidomestic strategy is to respond to the needs of customers in foreign markets and obtain a differentiation advantage. This strategy can result in the establishment of a series of successful foreign divisions, each of which may dominate its own domestic market. This approach also economizes on the bureaucratic costs of managing international businesses. The main disadvantage of this strategy is that an organization loses the potential gains that come from the sharing of core competences—resources and skills—by its various divisions and, thus, eliminates the opportunity for global learning that might generate long-term gains in value creation.

International Strategy

An organization pursuing an international strategy attempts to replicate certain aspects of its operations in each country or world region in which it operates. As with a multidomestic strategy, the organization transfers its core competences in manufacturing and distribution to the foreign country so that it can create a differentiation advantage. With an international strategy, however, an organization's core competences in R&D, product development, and marketing are centralized at home. The organization's foreign divisions merely manufacture and market their products, using approaches developed by the parent organization.

International strategy
A plan that offers customers in all countries a standardized product and allows foreign divisions to adapt products to local preferences only slightly.

An **international strategy** is a plan that offers customers in all countries a standardized product; foreign divisions are allowed to adapt products to local preferences only slightly. Because product customization is limited, consumers abroad buy an organization's products because they find in them the same value that attracts consumers at home. Coca-Cola, Pepsi-Cola, McDonald's, and Toys "R" Us all pursue an international strategy. Coca-Cola's marketing message is the same around the world, and the global appeal of Coke often forms the basis of its marketing campaign. Similarly, although the McDonald's menu is customized to suit the tastes of foreign diners, the Big Mac and Quarter Pounder are always at center stage, and manufacturing and marketing methods abroad, though adapted to foreign conditions, are basically the same as those in the United States.

The disadvantage of limited local responsiveness is balanced in part by the continual transfer of core competences to foreign markets. The latest R&D competences flow abroad in the form of product improvements, which attract consumers. This ability to draw on the distinctive competences of domestic operations may provide foreign divisions with a differentiation advantage over local rivals.

The international strategy has other disadvantages besides limited local responsiveness. Production costs may be higher. Because the parent organization produces in many countries, there is a loss of economies of scale that might be realized from producing at one low-cost location. An organization pursuing an international strategy does not capitalize on global learning and does not benefit from access to foreign resources and skills because it always exports its core competences. The bureaucratic costs of pursuing this strategy are higher than those of a multidomestic strategy because of the need to coordinate resource flows between headquarters and the foreign divisions.

Despite the drawbacks, the international strategy has been the strategy that most large U.S. companies have traditionally used. It made perfect sense for U.S. companies, the early leaders in mass production and marketing techniques that brought low-cost and differentiation advantages, to adopt this approach. In the past two decades, however, many aspects of the international environment have changed, and two new strategies that increase the value that organizations can create in their international domains have arisen: global strategy and transnational strategy.

Global Strategy

Global strategy *A plan whereby an organization reduces production costs so that it can offer foreign consumers products priced lower than the products that their domestic companies offer.*

The principal challenge to U.S. organizations pursuing a multidomestic or an international strategy has been the increasing use of global strategy by large Japanese companies such as Toyota, Sony, and Matsushita. A **global strategy** is a plan to reduce production costs so that an organization can offer foreign consumers products priced lower than the products that their domestic companies offer. With a global strategy, a standardized product is manufactured at a few low-cost locations and then offered to the global market. As with the international strategy, only limited customizing to suit the tastes of individual markets is allowed.[6] Cars, stereos, cameras, and televisions are well suited to this strategy: Good gas mileage and high-quality sound and pictures are preferred the world over. Product standardization allows an organization to achieve huge global economies of scale, which translate into lower costs and lower prices. When low price is accompanied by high quality, the organization has a very strong competitive advantage.

In contrast to an international strategy, however, a global strategy does not transfer manufacturing, distribution, and other value creation activities to every foreign country in which a company operates. With a global strategy, a company develops a global network to reduce the costs of value creation. It locates its value creation functions in the country that can provide it with a cost advantage, and it establishes long-term contracts for its inputs with the suppliers—domestic or foreign—that have the lowest prices. Over time, if factor costs change and a country becomes high priced, a company pursuing a global strategy will change its suppliers or relocate its value creation functions (particularly its manufacturing) to countries with lower costs to keep its prices low. For example, Mattel, the toy manufacturer, has established plants in China, Indonesia, Italy, Malaysia, Spain, and Mexico to produce Barbie dolls (50 percent of which are sold outside the United States) at low cost.

Companies with a global strategy tend to be highly centralized. Resource transfers between value creation functions in the global network are controlled by managers at a company's corporate headquarters. This degree of centralization means that the bureaucratic costs of coordinating this strategy tend to be relatively high. Significant costs are associated with managing resource transfers in the global network to realize a low-cost advantage. For example, to compete with the Japanese and obtain a low-cost advantage in the manufacturing of a new line of telephone-answering machines, AT&T's U.S. telephone division managers coordinated the flow of inputs from factories in Thailand, Malaysia, Hong Kong, and Japan with design and marketing information from the United States and France to an assembly plant in China from which telephones were distributed to Europe, the United States, New Zealand, and Australia.

The principal disadvantage associated with a global strategy is the organization's inability to respond to the needs of different customers in different countries (e.g., all of AT&T's telephones are the same color, beige; no black or white ones, which are very popular in Europe, are offered). This lack of responsiveness to local preferences reduces the potential demand for products. The products of a company with a global strategy do not have the differentiated appeal of products customized to local tastes, which is a main advantage that a company pursuing a multidomestic strategy achieves. Moreover, reluctance to establish value creation operations in many of the countries in which it operates limits the company's opportunity to learn from foreign competitors how to differentiate its products. In essence, in pursuing a global strategy, a company is trading off the advantages of differentiation for a low-cost advantage. Arvin Industries is an interesting example of an organization that has recently adopted a global strategy to compete in the world auto-parts industry.

ORGANIZATIONAL INSIGHT

8.2 ARVIN INDUSTRIES GOES GLOBAL

In 1981, Arvin Industries was a little-known auto-parts maker in Columbus, Indiana, producing auto parts for the Big Three automakers. Almost none of its revenues came from abroad. James K. Baker, Arvin CEO, decided that Arvin had to grow in order to survive and had to attract Japanese carmakers as customers, given their expanding presence in the United States.

Baker set out to improve Arvin's core competences. He decided to focus company resources on exhaust and suspension systems. He acquired the Gabriel shock absorber company and the MacPherson strut company to enhance Arvin's skills in suspension systems. With improved, differentiated products to offer, Baker then set out to find new customers. Arvin now sells to 17 automakers, including Toyota, Honda, and Hyundai.[7]

Rising sales led to economies of scale and allowed Arvin to develop a low-cost skill in muffler manufacturing to supplement the differentiation advantage that had come from its acquisition of MacPherson struts and Gabriel shock absorbers. To capitalize on its competences, Baker decided to take the company global. First, he began to acquire European auto-parts manufacturers: Amortex of France, AP Amortiguadores of Spain, and Bainbridge Silencers and Cheswick of Britain. To each acquisition, he transferred the U.S. division's manufacturing and materials management expertise. He also established new factories in Europe to manufacture catalytic converters, antipollution devices now required on all cars manufactured in Europe. Arvin now manufactures parts in 16 countries and ships its products to over 130. Over 35 percent of its sales come from abroad.

As part of its global strategy, Arvin has tried to enter the Japanese market, both to sell its products and to acquire Japanese skills in manufacturing. Although entry has been difficult, Arvin has been able to establish two joint ventures with Japanese companies to facilitate global learning. It allowed Kayaba, Japan's biggest shock-absorber manufacturer, to take a 25 percent minority stake in its Spanish shock-absorber company; and in the United States it joined with Sango, Japan's largest muffler maker, in a venture to supply mufflers to Toyota in Kentucky. In 1997, Arvin expanded its foreign operations with Kayaba opening new plants in Spain.[8] And in 1998 the two companies announced a U.S. joint venture to make ride control products for all North American car and truck manufacturers.[9] Clearly, Arvin has become a major player in the global auto-parts industry.

Transnational Strategy

Transnational strategy
A plan that simultaneously achieves the advantages of both a global strategy and a multidomestic strategy.

Competitive pressures are so intense in the international environment that Christopher A. Bartlett and Sumantra Ghoshal have suggested that in many industries companies must pursue a **transnational strategy**, a plan that simultaneously achieves the advantages of both a global strategy and a multidomestic strategy.[10] To obtain the advantages of a global strategy, organizations locate value creation activities in foreign countries where factor costs give them a low-cost advantage. To obtain the differentiation advantage of a multidomestic strategy, companies locate value creation activities in most of the countries in which they operate, so they can customize products to suit customer needs. The goal of a transnational strategy is, thus, to obtain both low-cost and differentiation advantages simultaneously. How is this achieved?

First, the transnational organization must transfer core competences to the countries where they can be used most successfully to create value from both low costs and a differentiated appeal. Next, the organization creates a global network to provide the coordination that will allow domestic and foreign divisions to share skills and resources to improve their core competences. Each foreign division is expected to build on and develop the skills and resources it receives from the other divisions and to transfer enhanced products and processes to the other divisions. The goal of a transnational strategy is to develop a core competence in the global coordination of organizational resources between divisions throughout the world. In this way, the organization's products have a differentiated appeal, a low cost, and high quality.

Unlike a company with a purely global strategy that delivers a standardized product to customers in all countries, a company pursuing a transnational strategy has to act like a multidomestic company and customize its products to meet the needs of global customers and, thus, increase demand for its products. Customizing requires a transnational company to locate value creation activities such as manufacturing and marketing in almost every country or world region in which it operates and raises the bureaucratic costs associated with coordinating the flow of resources through the global network. In fact, a transnational strategy generates the highest bureaucratic costs of all four global expansion strategies because of the need to coordinate the resources and skills necessary for customizing products and at the same time obtain the gains from global learning. The problem of designing a structure and control system to coordinate activities is much more complex for a company with a transnational strategy than it is for companies pursuing the other three strategies. One company that has adopted a transnational strategy to make better use of its resources and gain a competitive advantage is Procter & Gamble.

ORGANIZATIONAL INSIGHT

8.3 PROCTER & GAMBLE'S TRANSNATIONAL STRATEGY

Procter & Gamble (P&G) became one of the largest soap and detergent companies by pursuing a multidomestic strategy. To expand globally, it created a foreign division to produce and customize soaps and detergents for each local market in which it operated. By 1980, P&G had over 20 autonomous operating divisions in Europe alone, and each of them had total responsibility for its local market. In the early 1980s, however, P&G saw its costs rising as a result of the duplication of manufacturing facilities in every country in which it operated. Moreover, product development costs were rocketing because divisions in each country were conducting their own research programs. To reduce costs, Procter & Gamble switched to more of a global strategy.

To pursue a global strategy, P&G reorganized its value creation activities to lower costs. The organization centered its main product development activities in the United States, and this focusing of resources in one location dramatically lowered the cost of product development. To further cut costs, P&G reduced the number of countries in which it manufactured soap and detergent. In Europe, for example, it concentrated the production of soap powders in only three locations. As a result of these changes, bottom-line profitability increased, and the potential of P&G's global strategy was revealed.

Nevertheless, Procter & Gamble recognized the product-customization benefits that its foreign divisions provided and the degree to which its brand name in each foreign country was a crucial determinant of its local success. The organization, thus, searched for a way to combine the low-cost advantages of a global strategy and the differentiation advantages of a multidomestic strategy. By 1990, it had reorganized its activities to pursue a transnational strategy. Now, P&G coordinates its skills and resources to reduce costs across countries and to increase its differentiation advantage inside each country as well. The new strategy gives Procter & Gamble a competitive advantage over Unilever, the Anglo-Dutch company that is its main rival. The ability to coordinate resources on a global level allows P&G to develop new products quickly and to share these product innovations among its foreign divisions, which are responsible for customizing them for each foreign market. As a result, P&G has consistently surpassed Unilever in the bringing of new or improved products to market.

Moreover, Tide, P&G's leading laundry detergent, is now sold under the Tide brand name throughout Europe and has both a differentiated appeal and a low-cost advantage. Clearly, Procter & Gamble's new strategy has allowed the organization to become the dominant global player. Trying to recoup, Unilever has been imitating Procter & Gamble's transnational strategy. However, it has been unable to catch up, and throughout the 1990s Procter & Gamble reported record global sales and continued to pull ahead of Unilever.

To summarize, increased competition is forcing many companies to develop a transnational strategy to achieve the advantages of low cost and differentiation simultaneously. In some industries, the costs of a multidomestic strategy are so high that organizations pursuing this strategy cannot compete against organizations with global strategies. In turn, in some industries, organizations pursuing global and international strategies cannot compete against companies that are obtaining both the differentiation and the low-cost advantages of a transnational strategy. As a result, many companies are being forced to act like transnationals. Decisions about organizational structure and culture and interorganizational strategies have a major impact on an organization's success in its effort to exploit opportunities in the international environment. How an organization should match its global expansion strategy, its organizational structure, and its organizational culture is the subject of the next section.

Managerial Implications: Global Expansion Strategy

1. All organizations, large and small, are affected by the international environment, and managers must devise a strategy to manage it in order to protect or enlarge their organization's domain. Managers need to consider carefully the benefits and costs of whatever strategy they choose.
2. Small companies should exploit the opportunities for exporting that a global market offers and should enter into contracts with distributors in foreign countries to market and sell their products locally.
3. Large organizations that are in a position to benefit from global learning and from the transfer of skills and resources from one country to another should choose one of the four global expansion strategies to manage their international domains.
4. Increasingly, organizations that are pursuing a transnational strategy are gaining a competitive advantage over companies that are pursuing one of the other strategies. For this reason, many companies are merging and forming global networks to give them access to the skills and resources that allow them to compete on a truly global level—a transnational level.

GLOBAL EXPANSION STRATEGY, ORGANIZATIONAL STRUCTURE, AND ORGANIZATIONAL CULTURE

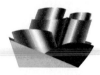

The key factor influencing a company's choice of structure is the degree of control and coordination that its chosen strategy requires. For example, managing a transnational strategy is far more difficult than managing a multidomestic strategy because the problems involved in coordinating and managing resource transfers required by a transnational strategy are much greater. Moreover, as we have just seen, bureaucratic costs increase as an organization moves from a multidomestic to an international, a global, or a transnational strategy. These costs rise because of the increase in managerial time and effort spent coordinating organizational resources. As bureaucratic costs go up, organizations need a more complex structure that allows them to coordinate their activities. Consequently, we need to look at the design choices that organizations make as they expand internationally. Specifically, we need to examine how an organization achieves the degree of differentiation and integration most appropriate to coordinating its global activities. Table 8.1 indicates the appropriate structure for organizations pursuing each of the four global expansion strategies.

TABLE 8.1			
Strategy-Structure Relationships in the International Environment			
	Multidomestic Strategy	**International Strategy**	**Global Strategy**	**Transnational Strategy**
	Low ⟵————— Need for Coordination —————⟶ High			
Vertical Differentiation Choices				
Levels in the hierarchy	Relatively flat	Relatively tall	Relatively tall	Relatively flat
Centralization of authority	Decentralized	Core competences centralized, others decentralized	Centralized	Simultaneously centralized and decentralized
Horizontal Differentiation	Global geographic structure	Global product group structure	Global product group structure	Global matrix or "matrix in the mind"
Integration				
Need for integrating mechanisms such as task forces and integrating roles	Low	Medium	Medium	High
Need for electronic integration and management networks	Medium	High	High	Very high
Need for integration by international organizational culture	Low	Medium	High	Very high
	Low ⟵————— Bureaucratic Costs —————⟶ High			

Vertical Differentiation in the International Environment

Recall from Chapter 2 that *vertical differentiation* deals with choices about how many levels an organization should have in its hierarchy and whether the organization should centralize or decentralize decision-making authority to effectively coordinate activities.

TALL VERSUS FLAT HIERARCHY.   As we saw in Chapter 3, according to the *principle of minimum chain of command*, an organization should keep its structure as flat as possible to reduce communication and motivation problems. International expansion, however, tends to increase the number of hierarchical levels that an organization needs to control its activities. Major coordination and motivation problems arise because of differences in economic, political, and social conditions and the distances between different countries. The size of the increase in hierarchical levels that occurs as a company expands internationally depends on the degree of coordination the company's strategy requires between corporate headquarters and foreign divisions or between foreign divisions.

In general, a company pursuing a *multidomestic strategy* requires relatively little coordination between corporate headquarters and foreign divisions and has a relatively flat structure. By contrast, companies pursuing an *international strategy* or a *global strategy* tend to have taller hierarchies because of their greater need to coordinate value creation activities at home and abroad. With both of those strategies, many core competences are located at home, and coordinating the transfer of skills and resources to divisions in foreign countries poses a problem. A company with a *transnational strategy* has the greatest need for coordination: between divisions and between divisions and corporate headquarters. Thus, we might expect the transnational strategy to result in the tallest hierarchy. But, in practice, a tall structure cannot solve the complex control problems associated with managing a transnational strategy.

Tall hierarchies are not suited to managing complex exchanges of resources between divisions and world areas. As an organization develops a long chain of command to deal with these matters, it encounters the communication and motivation problems associated with tall hierarchies (see Chapter 3). For example, it may take managers at corporate headquarters a long time to respond to the problems facing foreign divisions, and they may fail to understand those problems because they are so far away from the scene of the action. An organization pursuing a transnational strategy has to look to the other characteristics of organizational structure for solutions to its control problem. Its preferred structure is normally a relatively flat (matrix) structure. The way an organization chooses to centralize and decentralize authority is another important design choice.[11]

CENTRALIZATION VERSUS DECENTRALIZATION.   As noted in Chapter 2, an important design challenge affecting vertical differentiation is deciding how much authority to decentralize to departments and divisions and how much authority to centralize at corporate headquarters. The choice is different for each of the four global expansion strategies.

An organization that pursues a *multidomestic strategy* generally decentralizes authority to its foreign divisions. Each division directs its own operations and produces and customizes products to suit each country. Because multidomestic strategy requires little global learning, there is little need for coordination between corporate headquarters and foreign divisions or between foreign divisions. Financial information (return on investment, sales increases, etc.) provides corporate headquarters with information about the performance of foreign divisions. Companies that pursue a multidomestic strategy tend to have a flat, decentralized structure (see Table 8.1).

With an *international strategy*, authority shifts from the foreign division to the parent organization. Because the goal of the parent organization is to transfer core competences to its foreign divisions, strategic decisions about transfers of skills and resources are made centrally, by corporate headquarters personnel. The responsibility for local manufacturing and marketing decisions, however, is decentralized to managers in the foreign divisions. This strategy achieves a balance between centralized and decentralized control that allows the organization to protect core competences yet customize products for the local market.

With a *global strategy*, decision making is centralized at corporate headquarters. Foreign divisions provide important information about local conditions (such as local customer needs or factor prices), and they control local distribution and marketing activities. But all important decision making about the coordination of resource transfers between countries in order to lower costs is centralized in the corporate parent. Generally, corporate headquarters personnel use rules and standard operating procedures to manage foreign operations from afar. Toyota, for example, has a geographical distribution system in the United States with four regional distribution centers. Each regional center uses the same standard operating procedures to monitor and evaluate the performance of each of its dealerships (by measuring the number of customer complaints, sales volume, etc.) and can move quickly to intervene and discipline dealerships for substandard performance. Companies that pursue a global strategy tend to be relatively tall and centralized.

With a *transnational strategy*, the great need for coordination makes the centralization versus decentralization decision especially complex. On the one hand, an organization needs centralized control to facilitate global learning and the transfer of core competences around the world. On the other hand, an organization needs to decentralize authority to its foreign divisions so that each one can develop its own approach to the local market and can develop its own core competences. The challenge facing a transnational organization is to foster a simultaneous "loose-tight" organizational decision-making ability.[12] This ability is apparently one of the key reasons for the success of Nestlé and Procter & Gamble, two companies that are leaders in building a transnational strategy to capitalize on their global competences.

Horizontal Differentiation in the International Environment

The way in which an organization designs its hierarchy and distributes decision-making authority (vertical differentiation) is related to the way the organization creates separate tasks and roles and groups them to coordinate activities: *horizontal differentiation*.[13] Recall from Chapter 4 that an organization can use any of a number of structures to coordinate its activities as the range of products it manufactures increases or as it expands geographically. Here, we look at three global structures that complement the strategy that organizations pursue as they expand globally (see Table 8.1).

GLOBAL GEOGRAPHIC STRUCTURE.   Many organizations first begin to expand internationally by exporting their products to foreign countries. They establish foreign divisions simply to distribute and market their products in these foreign countries. Small, specialized European food companies like Carr's of Carlisle and liquor companies like Moët and Chandon and Hennessey have foreign divisions that coordinate the sale of their products to local retailers.

As the volume of sales in foreign markets increases, the pressure to be responsive to local needs intensifies. In response, the organization is likely to transfer its value creation

FIGURE 8.4

Global Geographic
Structure

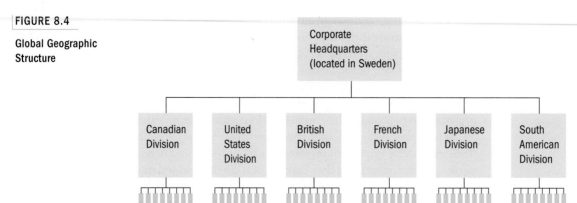

Functional activities

functions abroad and set up manufacturing operations in the foreign countries in which it operates.[14] If the organization chooses to pursue a *multidomestic strategy*, then the appropriate structure is a global geographic structure (see Figure 8.4).

Global geographic struc-
ture *A structure in*
which foreign divisions
are created in every
country or world region
in which an organization
operates to replicate all
its domestic value cre-
ation activities.

An organization with a **global geographic structure** establishes foreign divisions to replicate all its domestic value creation activities in every country or world region in which it operates. To start operations in the foreign country, the parent organization permanently or temporarily transfers executives from headquarters. When a foreign division has been established, the "foreign" managers are responsible for creating core competences in their locations, and authority is decentralized so that each division can customize products to suit local tastes. Corporate headquarters monitors the divisions, and corporate managers can intervene selectively in foreign operations and take corrective action if needed. Because, as we have seen, foreign divisions eventually act autonomously, global geographic structure does not facilitate global learning.

GLOBAL PRODUCT GROUP STRUCTURE.   Once global learning becomes important, as it does for an international or a global strategy, an organization needs a structure that can coordinate resource transfers between corporate headquarters and foreign divisions or between foreign divisions. To coordinate resource transfers between divisions and countries, an organization generally adopts a global product group structure (see Figure 8.5).

Global product group
structure *A structure in*
which product group
headquarters coordinate
the activities of the
domestic and foreign
divisions within each
product group.

An organization with a **global product group structure** creates product group headquarters to coordinate the activities of the domestic and foreign divisions within each product group. Product group managers are responsible for organizing all aspects of value creation on a global basis. The product group structure allows product group managers to decide how best to pursue an international strategy or a global strategy—for example, by deciding which activities should be performed in which country. We saw earlier how Xerox transferred the product development skills of its Japanese division to other Xerox divisions throughout the world to enhance their skills. An organization pursuing an *international strategy* might find many ways to improve its domestic core competences through international technology transfers between divisions. Similarly, an organization pursuing a *global strategy* can transfer manufacturing or input activities to the country where costs are lowest. Honda, for example, as part of its global strategy, recently had to choose a European country in which to locate its manufacturing facilities to overcome EC tariffs on foreign-made cars. It chose Britain, which has some of the lowest labor costs in western Europe and has been least hostile to Japanese imports.

FIGURE 8.5

Global Product Group
Structure

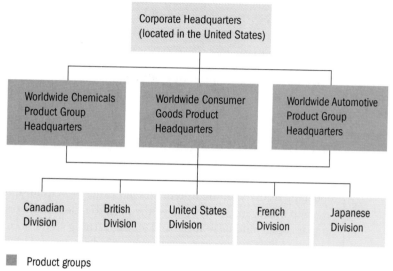

Unilever, a giant consumer products company and maker of soaps and detergents, originally operated with a global geographic structure. Whenever it entered a new country, it set up a foreign division to handle all value creation activities. In the 1980s, however, it saw its business increasingly threatened by Procter & Gamble, which had developed a global product group structure to coordinate its global strategy. P&G took advantage of its product group structure to quickly transfer product developments from one country to the next; it also concentrated the production of detergents in a few locations to obtain economies of scale.

Unilever decided that it would have to copy this structure in order to compete with Procter & Gamble. It created a European product group to control the activities of its 17 separate European divisions. Soon, product group managers began consolidating their activities to reduce costs and speed product development. They introduced new procedures for sharing information and reduced the time needed to introduce a new product in another country from five years to one year. To reduce costs, Unilever now makes soap in two locations, not ten.[15]

Perkin-Elmer, a specialty instruments maker, is another organization that switched from a global geographic to a global product group structure.

The principal disadvantage of a global product group structure is that the organization trades off local responsiveness for global learning and integration. Because resource decisions in a product group structure are made with a global focus, less product customization occurs than in a decentralized global geographic structure, in which foreign division managers control decision making. Because product group managers make the decisions, the needs of the individual countries or regions are often not taken into consideration.

For the global learning and local responsiveness characteristic of a transnational strategy to take place, an organization has to establish a global network of role relationships to coordinate the activities of product groups across countries and world regions. Designing a structure that effectively allows an organization to manage global learning is the most difficult task facing global organizations. There is no accepted "best" design to accomplish this process. Different organizations have been experimenting with different structures and using different integrating mechanisms, including organizational culture, to make the structures work.

ORGANIZATIONAL INSIGHT

8.4 PERKIN-ELMER CHANGES TRACK

Perkin-Elmer Corporation is a manufacturer of specialty laboratory instruments. When its profits dropped in the early 1990s as it faced intense pressure from foreign competitors, Perkin-Elmer realized it could no longer bear the costs of operating its instruments businesses in different countries around the world. Research and development costs were exorbitant, and there was considerable R&D overlap, for R&D teams in different countries worked on the same projects but were not aware of one another's activities. No global learning was going on, and the only advantage Perkin-Elmer was obtaining from its multidomestic strategy came from its local responsiveness.

Top management recognized the need to redesign the organizational structure so that costs could be reduced and global learning could occur. Perkin-Elmer divided its instruments businesses into three product groups—life sciences, organic sciences, and inorganic sciences—and created a global product group structure to coordinate the groups' activities.[16] With this structure, Perkin-Elmer believed it would be able to focus its research activities to gain a competitive advantage in the rapidly developing instruments business. Perkin-Elmer also hoped that this global learning advantage would compensate for the loss of local responsiveness. Perkin-Elmer's managers were right: The company's new structure performed as expected and the company made record profits throughout the 1990s.

GLOBAL MATRIX STRUCTURE.   Nestlé, ABB, Dow Chemical, and other companies use a global matrix structure to manage their international business activities. A **global matrix structure** coordinates organizational activities and resources along two dimensions: product groups and world areas (see Figure 8.6). This structure is a global variant of the matrix structure discussed in Chapter 4 (see Figure. 4.13). On the vertical axis are product groups, which are responsible for coordinating the flow of skills and resources to foreign business divisions. On the horizontal axis are world areas subdivided into countries. The foreign divisions in each area are responsible for customizing products to suit local conditions and for developing their own core competences, which they can transfer back to the product groups. Thus, the Chemicals Product Group of the organization portrayed in Figure 8.6 and the divisions in the European Area are jointly responsible for deciding how to manufacture and market products in Europe. At the intersection of the axes are individual business divisions headed by two-boss managers who answer to a product group boss and to an area boss and are responsible for matching the needs of their respective areas to the resource flows originating from their respective product groups. Motorola Corporation, considered one of the best-run, most successful organizations in the world, successfully pursues a *transnational strategy* by means of a global matrix structure.

In Chapter 4 we discussed how matrix structures can speed decision making and enhance the development of an organization's core competences. We also noted, however, that matrix structures are difficult and expensive to manage because of ambiguous authority and task relationships. These problems also arise in a global matrix structure. Transferring information and knowledge across the world is a time-consuming and difficult process that is further complicated by the distortion of meaning that occurs because of language differences. Moreover, managers in different countries and different regions may have different subunit orientations and develop conflicting attitudes toward the problems

Global matrix structure

A structure that coordinates organizational activities and resources along two dimensions: product groups and world areas.

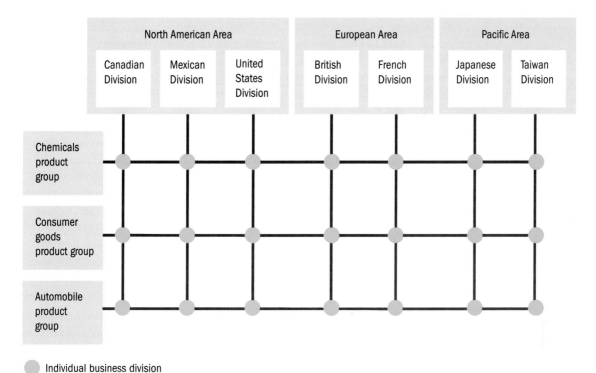

FIGURE 8.6   **Global Matrix Structure**

8.5 MOTOROLA GOES TO A GLOBAL MATRIX

In 1980, Motorola, the cellular communications and semiconductor manufacturer, was content to pursue a multidomestic strategy using a global geographic structure to organize its international operations. It defined a set of world regions, and it decentralized authority for production, marketing, and most operational decisions to those regions. Motorola soon found, however, that this decentralized approach caused a major problem: It prevented Motorola from coordinating its value creation activities on a global basis to reduce costs. Motorola found that it was impossible to develop a global approach to manufacturing, product development, or research and development because its geographic structure gave most control to the foreign divisions. As Japanese companies successfully pursued their low-cost global strategies, Motorola's markets were threatened by its high costs and disjointed efforts at product development.

Motorola's answer to the Japanese challenge was to restructure, to change to a global matrix structure that organizes the company's businesses by product group and by region. Now, three regions in cooperation with three product groups make investment and product development decisions, and Motorola's skills and resources are coordinated globally. Each region has the primary responsibility for the research and development of particular product technologies. Motorola's U.S. product group, for example, has overall control of cellular phone technology. All operational decisions, however, are handled locally at the country and plant level.

Twice a year, six representatives—one from each region and one from each product group—meet to plan Motorola's product development strategy for the next six months. To facilitate their efforts, Motorola exploits its organizational skills in cellular communications to quicken and increase the transfer of information around the matrix, thus improving coordination between product group managers and regional managers.

The global matrix structure has produced some significant benefits. It has allowed Motorola to reduce costs by locating its manufacturing and input activities in low-cost countries. It has enabled Motorola to make better use of its resources and create a differentiation advantage. Motorola now can match any Japanese challenge in cellular phone technology and semiconductors. Moreover, the global network produced by the global matrix structure has allowed Motorola to exploit the advantages of global learning. The company has imitated and improved upon Japanese lean manufacturing techniques and has become a global low-cost producer in its own right. Its efforts have been rewarded: Its stock price skyrocketed in the 1990s and it has become a major global player in the telecommunications industry.

that they encounter. Foreign managers are likely to be most concerned with the needs of their country or region, and product group managers generally have a more global focus. A power struggle between product managers and regional managers may develop over the control of resources. Such a struggle would lead to conflict and a slowdown in decision making and communication that would make it difficult for the organization to adjust quickly to changing market conditions.

Because of these problems, organizations have looked for ways to coordinate and control resource exchanges that either make the matrix structure work more effectively or allow the organization to obtain the global learning and local response benefits from a transnational strategy without resorting to a formal matrix structure. These approaches are attempts to achieve a "matrix in the mind," an organization in which coordination between domestic and foreign managers is accomplished not with a formal matrix structure but with a simpler structure, such as a product group structure, that incorporates new integrating mechanisms and organizational culture to improve organizational effectiveness.

Increasing Integration in the International Environment

Chapters 2 and 4 explained why an organization needs to adopt increasingly complex integrating mechanisms as its structure becomes more complex. Integrating roles and integrating departments, such as the headquarters staff of a multidivisional company, are often used to coordinate interdivisional activities. In a global organization the pressures to coordinate activities are especially acute. In addition to the relatively common integrating mechanisms, such as task forces and integrating roles, new integrating mechanisms—various electronic means and management networks—have been developed to raise the level of global integration. These new mechanisms are useful for any international structure but are especially relevant for operating complex global product group and global matrix structures (see Table 8.1).

ELECTRONIC INTEGRATION.   Integration through electronic means such as teleconferencing and e-mail is becoming increasingly important in global organizations. Teleconferencing allows managers in different countries to meet face-to-face through television hookups to coordinate decision making. It facilitates global learning when managers in foreign and domestic divisions meet to confront important issues and to solve mutual problems. Recall from Organizational Insight 7.3 that Hitachi uses an on-line teleconferencing system to coordinate its 28 R&D laboratories. American companies, such as Hewlett-Packard and IBM, make extensive use of teleconferencing so that foreign and domestic divisions share information and knowledge.

Because the success of a transnational strategy depends on communication between world areas and product groups that are likely to be in separate countries, the value of teleconferencing in a global matrix structure is obvious. It reduces communication problems and allows decisions to be made quickly. E-mail and high-speed data-transfer systems are also becoming extremely important ways of quickly sharing information across the globe. Microsoft is using its expertise to spearhead the use of these electronic media in its international exchanges.

MANAGEMENT NETWORKS.   To help product and country managers to develop a global orientation, more and more organizations are rotating their managers to foreign divisions so that they begin to understand the problems and opportunities present in foreign countries.[17] These "foreign" managers constitute a **management network**—a set of managers who have developed an array of personal contacts with other managers throughout the world—that helps individual managers to learn from one another and helps to overcome a major obstacle to effective integration: subunit orientations that stymie communication and coordination.

Management network
Set of managers who have developed an array of personal contacts with other managers throughout the world.

Donald Fites, CEO of Caterpillar, rose to his present position because of the knowledge of lean manufacturing techniques that he gained from his experiences as a Caterpillar manager in Japan. Jack Smith, CEO of General Motors, rose to his position because of his successful introduction of lean manufacturing to GM's European division. Motorola recently established a new Asian presence by building a factory in Tianjin, a port city near Beijing. Tam Chung Ding, who directs Motorola's Asian operations, commented that personal connections between managers in the same organization and between organizations are more important in Asia than anywhere else in the world. In Asia, integration inside an organization and the formation of strategic alliances between organizations often depend on the personal connections established through a management network.[18]

International experience is a prerequisite for developing a management network that will enhance the integration of geographic areas and product groups. Such a network enables managers from all over the world to discuss problems and solutions and to transfer information and knowledge—and, thus, facilitates global learning. A management network fosters the development of informal linkages among managers throughout the global organization so that when they have a problem they will feel comfortable contacting a manager in another division who might be able to help them solve the problem.

Suppose that a product development manager (PDM) in Europe is attempting to customize for the European market a new dishwashing detergent originally developed in the United States. The product does not dissolve in the low wash-water temperatures usual in European countries, and the PDM needs additional information about the product in order to customize it. The PDM's manager does not personally know anybody on the original U.S. product development team but does know several U.S. marketing managers because of their involvement in marketing the new product in Europe. The PDM's manager calls one of the U.S. marketing managers, who calls someone else, who quickly finds out who headed the original product development team and puts the European product development manager in contact with that person through e-mail.

A management network is able to bypass formal communication channels.[19] Management networks work around the formal structure and constitute a type of informal organization. Recall from Chapter 2 that the informal organization can enhance the effectiveness of the formal organizational structure. Management networks improve the performance of global product group or global matrix structures because they promote communication between managers even when distances are great and interests diverge.

Developing an International Organizational Culture

For an organization interested in gaining the advantages of global learning, the development of an international organizational culture becomes very important.[20] Cultural values are the oil that makes the global network operate smoothly and effectively. As noted in Chapter 5, *organizational culture* is the set of shared values that controls how organizational members interact with one another. Shared values and the specific organizational norms and rules in an organization's culture help people to communicate with each other and to understand each other's positions. Thus, organizational culture is an important means through which an organization can control transfers of resources and skills and gain all available advantages from its global network.[21] A cohesive set of cultural values can help to overcome cultural and language differences that are inevitable when an organization expands internationally. Arthur Andersen, the accounting firm, takes great pains to socialize its American employees so that they learn the company's values. Arthur Andersen also sends English-speaking recruits from throughout the world to its training center in Chicago. In this way the organization develops a global corporate language, and both domestic and international employees learn the organization's values.

Organizational culture has always been an important control mechanism for international organizations. In the past, most organizations pursued a *multidomestic strategy* when they expanded into the international domain, and they were able to delegate authority without fear of abuse because the heads of their foreign divisions were trusted executives from the parent organization. Those top-management executives shared the same corporate values and norms because they had been socialized into the same corporate culture. With a multidomestic strategy, however, the development of an international organizational culture below the top-management level of a division is not important, because the different foreign divisions are not in contact with one another. Each division operates independently, so there is no reason to cultivate a truly global corporate culture that encourages resource sharing (see Table 8.1).

As soon as resource sharing becomes significant, the development of an international organizational culture becomes important at all management levels. For example, it is common for Japanese companies that pursue a *global strategy* or an *international strategy* to send trusted Japanese managers to head and work in their foreign divisions. Normally, a Japanese manager heads U.S. or European operations. In addition, a Japanese manager is likely to be inside each value creation function. This arrangement ensures that the corporate values and interests of the parent organization are followed and the organization can obtain the benefits of global learning.

If a common culture is not developed in an organization pursuing a global strategy, domestic and foreign divisions may compete as they seek to outperform each other, as we saw in the Philips example. When each division is out to improve its own core competences, a global orientation does not develop. Shared cultural values make it much easier for divisions to transfer and exchange core competences and to learn from one another so that products and processes can be improved and adapted to the needs of each country. Shared values also make it easier for an organization to react quickly to changing markets, factor costs, and local conditions in its world areas so that it can, for example, quickly change manufacturing operations and relocate value creation activities to take advantage of lower costs.

For an organization pursuing a *transnational strategy*, an organizationwide international culture is a necessity.[22] An international organizational culture helps provide the extra integration and trust necessary for creating value from resource transfers and global learning between countries. Culture plays an especially important role in a global matrix structure because it allows managers in the different world areas and product groups to develop the shared perspective on which organizational effectiveness depends. Management networks also develop more quickly and can be used more effectively when managers share the same understanding of a situation—an understanding that comes from their common organizational culture.

In summary, numerous complicated problems are associated with the operation of global organizational structures. The simplest way to reduce these problems is to use a multidomestic strategy in which each country operates as a self-contained unit so that bureaucratic costs are low (see Table 8.1). This simple strategy, however, does not allow an organization to obtain the many benefits of global learning. In today's increasingly interdependent international environments, an organization is under constant pressure from competitors that follow strategies and develop structures and cultures that facilitate the building and sharing of core competences, the basis of global learning. Thus most organizations that want to grow internationally must design for themselves a more complex structure, and when they do so, they must use more complex integrating mechanisms and develop an international corporate culture. Integration and culture allow for the development of a "matrix in the mind," regardless of whether a formal global matrix structure is used to reap the benefits of local responsiveness and global learning.

Are there other ways in which an organization can obtain the advantages of global learning and local responsiveness and simultaneously economize on the bureaucratic costs of operating a complex global organizational structure? One way is for the organization to create strategic alliances with other organizations in the international environment.

Managerial Implications:
Matching Global Strategy and Structure

1. To gain the benefits of global expansion, managers must achieve a match between their global strategies and structures.
2. To decide what structure to use, and in particular how to choose the appropriate degrees of differentiation and integration, managers must identify the bureaucratic costs associated with each strategy.
3. The bureaucratic costs of coordinating a strategy increase as the complexity of an organization's global exchanges of skills and resources increases. The more complex a strategy is, the more complex is the structure that the organization will require.
4. Creating an international organizational culture is one way in which managers can coordinate the flow of skills and resources. To facilitate the transfer of corporate values on a global basis, managers must develop global socialization programs and rotate employees to develop a global management network that enhances global learning.
5. By using international strategic alliances to coordinate resource exchanges, managers can gain the benefits of global expansion without incurring the bureaucratic costs of using a complex organizational structure.

INTERNATIONAL STRATEGIC ALLIANCES

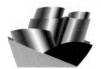

The principal problem associated with managing global product group and global matrix structures is the high number of linkages that have to be coordinated through the organizational structure.[23] Bureaucratic costs increase as the number and complexity of the linkages between value creation functions and countries that an organization has to manage increases. As we saw in Chapter 7, one way to reduce bureaucratic costs is to form strategic alliances. To secure the gains from global expansion and maintain a competitive advantage, organizations are increasingly being forced to form strategic alliances by means of long-term contracts, network organizations, minority ownership, and joint ventures.[24]

Long-Term Contracts

An organization has to decide whether it is likely to benefit financially from setting up a division in a foreign country to manufacture and market its goods or services. Many organizations might be better off establishing a long-term contract with a foreign company and giving that company the license or franchise to use the organization's core competences in return for a share in the profits. For example, because the bureaucratic costs of operating hotel chains to maintain consistently high-quality service are enormous, Hilton, Sheraton, and other hotel companies transfer to foreign companies the rights to use their brand names and functional competences in return for a fixed fee or a share in the profits. Similarly, when the Walt Disney Company established Tokyo Disney, it gave Japanese investors the rights to use the Disney organization's resources and skills in Japan in return for a share in the profits. In this way, the benefits of global expansion, such as an increase in the number of customers, are obtained without the costs.

Network Organizations

An increasingly popular way to organize resource linkages without bearing the bureaucratic costs of managing them is to create a network of interlinked global companies to perform value creation activities. A network promotes a "matrix in the mind" and avoids the need for formal coordination. Nike, for example, protects its core competence in shoe design by locating its research and development in the United States. However, rather than pursue an international strategy and establish its own marketing and production operations in different countries, Nike created a network organization by establishing a network of companies to perform its functional activities in locations where factor costs are most favorable. Manufacturing takes place in China, but inputs come from the lowest-cost source of supply, which may be Hong Kong, Taiwan, or Malaysia. By using a network organization, a global organization can avoid the need to establish foreign divisions to perform value creation activities. If Nike had created a global matrix organization and established a whole set of functional divisions in several world regions instead of using a network structure, Nike would be managing many more complex linkages to bring its product to market, and its bureaucratic costs would be much higher.

Minority Ownership

When the development of loyalty within a network organization is important, a parent organization is likely to use minority ownership to improve the effectiveness of its strategic alliances. Global learning is often facilitated by the formalization of ties between organizations. Recall from Chapter 6, for example, that Toyota owns a minority stake in many of its important suppliers, and both parties share in the gains from lowering costs and improving quality. Toyota extended this strategy to its relationships with foreign suppliers when it established manufacturing operations in the United States and Europe. Minority ownership also encourages the development of common cultural norms and values among network partners, so the network can function like a matrix even though formal reporting relationships are not present.

Joint Ventures

Many organizations use joint ventures to obtain the benefits of global expansion while avoiding the problems associated with managing complex resource linkages.[25] A joint venture is a strategic alliance between two or more organizations for the examples of pooling resources and establishing a new organization. A joint venture allows partners to share the benefits from the transfer of their core competences and reduces bureaucratic costs by decentralizing decision making to the new organization.

Joint ventures are becoming increasingly important in the international arena as new technologies link previously independent industries. For example, General Mills—unlike Kellogg Company, its major U.S. competitor—had never established a presence in Europe. In 1992, however, General Mills announced that it was forming joint ventures with Nestlé to produce and market its cereals to European consumers. This strategic alliance instantly gave General Mills strength to combat Kellogg.[26] Similarly, General Mills and PepsiCo's Frito-Lay Division formed a 60 percent–40 percent joint venture to exploit the European snack foods market. Michael Dolan, the head of this joint venture, set a goal of $2 billion in sales by the year 2000 and wants to redefine the whole European market by exploiting the joint skills of the two organizations.[27]

In general, the use of strategic alliances to manage global relationships reduces the problems associated with operating complex global matrix and product group structures. An organization that manages its less crucial resource interdependencies through strategic alliances can focus on managing its core competences. To enter the Japanese market, for example, Toys "R" Us allied itself with the Japanese entrepreneurs who had engineered McDonald's entry into the Japanese market. Toys "R" Us used its expertise and knowledge of local retail conditions to expand quickly in Japan before Japanese competitors could imitate its purchasing and marketing systems. Its Japanese partners demanded a 20 percent stake in the venture, but Toys "R" Us gained far more by using a joint venture than it would have gained from acting alone and establishing a wholly owned division. An organization has to decide whether long-term contracts, joint ventures, or full ownership by merger is the best way to defend and protect its competitive international position.

Managing the international environment also involves creating a strategy to reduce the environmental uncertainty that comes from foreign competition.[28] Sometimes a domestic company joins forces with its foreign competitors in a strategic alliance to share their joint skills. GM, for example, joined with Toyota to establish a state-of-the-art factory in California to produce the Chevrolet GEO. Toyota supplied its skills in lean manufacturing, GM its marketing and distribution skills. By cooperating in this venture, both organizations created value, although they continued to compete in other segments of the car market. Sometimes domestic competitors form alliances to protect themselves against foreign manufacturers. To reduce development costs, GM, Ford, and Chrysler created an alliance to conduct joint research in advanced plastics used to create car-body parts. Their alliance was a response to Japanese car manufacturers, who have formed many alliances to share resources to lower input costs.

SUMMARY

Managing the international environment is a complex task that adds a new dimension to organizational design. An organization has to choose not only an appropriate strategy for managing global expansion but also the right organizational structure and international strategic alliances for managing the resource exchanges on which its competitive advantage rests. Chapter 8 has made the following main points:

1. Forces in the specific and general international environments differ from country to country and create a new set of resource problems for an organization.
2. Value creation at the global level depends on the transfer of core competences abroad, the establishment of a global network, gaining access to global resources and skills, and the use of global learning to enhance core competences.
3. Three factors that influence the choice of strategy for global expansion are pressures for global integration, pressures for local responsiveness, and bureaucratic costs.
4. The four strategies that companies use to manage the international environment are a multidomestic strategy, an international strategy, a global strategy, and a transnational strategy. Each is associated with a different approach to value creation and a different set of organizational design problems.
5. An organization's decisions about vertical differentiation pertain to the number of hierarchical levels needed to coordinate the organization's international activities and how much authority to centralize at its domestic headquarters and how much to decentralize to its foreign operations.
6. An organization's decisions about horizontal differentiation influence the match between organizational structure and strategy for global expansion.
7. Complementary strategy-structure combinations include (a) multidomestic strategy and global geographic structure, (b) international strategy and global product group structure, (c) global strategy and global product group structure, and (d) transnational strategy and global matrix structure.
8. The more complex an organization's structure is, the greater is the need for complex integrating mechanisms, new integrating mechanisms such as management networks and electronic integration, and a cohesive international organizational culture.
9. Strategic alliances are an important interorganizational strategy in the international environment. Long-term contracts, network organizations, minority ownership, and joint ventures allow an organization to quickly develop a global network. They also facilitate global learning and reduce bureaucratic costs.

DISCUSSION QUESTIONS

1. What problems might an organization encounter if it moves from a global strategy to a transnational strategy?
2. Why is global learning so important to an organization?

3. How does a global product group structure differ from a global matrix structure? What new problems is an organization likely to encounter in moving from a global product group structure to a global matrix structure?

4. How and why do bureaucratic costs increase as a company goes from a multidomestic to an international to a global to a transnational strategy?

5. What steps should a transnational company take to develop a cohesive global corporate culture?

6. Why are strategic alliances becoming an increasingly popular way of managing the international environment? What problems are associated with managing international strategic alliances?

ORGANIZATIONAL THEORY IN ACTION

PRACTICING ORGANIZATIONAL THEORY: GOING GLOBAL

Form groups of three to five people and discuss the following scenario:

You are the managers of a root beer company that two years ago innovated a new kind of root beer, made from an exotic blend of herbs and spices, which has taken North America by storm. Customers cannot get enough of the drink, and both Coke and Pepsi are facing bankruptcy because consumers have turned en masse to your product. With your domain in North America secure, you now desire to take your product and your company global and you are trying to decide how best to achieve this (e.g., what kind of organizational structure or interorganizational linkage mechanism to use). Your goal is to move into Europe first, then Asia, and then into South America and Africa. Your success in the United States has given you all the capital you need for expansion, so your major goal is to protect the quality and integrity of your product as you expand abroad as quickly as you can.

1. Which of the four strategies for managing the international environment is the most suitable choice for your company at this time?
2. Which type of organizational structure will allow you to expand globally most effectively?
3. To what extent will the use of strategic alliances be an important part of your strategy?

MAKING THE CONNECTION #8

Find an example of an organization that has recently been altering or changing the organizational structure it uses to manage the international environment. Why is it changing its structure? What problems led to the change?

Analyzing the Organization: Design Module #8

The purpose of this module is to explore your organization's international activities. You may find a good account of these activities in the organization's annual reports. If your organization has no international activities, go to the library and research how AT&T has developed its global strategy and structure.

ASSIGNMENT

1. Using whatever information is available, describe the kinds of international activities in which your company is engaged. How have they changed over time? How do the organization's international activities relate to its domestic activities? For example, do they allow the organization to exploit a low-cost or differentiation advantage?

2. What kind of strategy is your organization pursuing in the international environment? Why is your organization pursuing this strategy? How does it provide a differential or low-cost advantage? What problems are associated with this strategy?

3. What kind of structure does your organization use to manage its strategy? Draw a diagram showing the organization's structure. How does this structure allow the organization to control its international activities? Do the strategy and structure complement one another? Should any changes be made to the structure? Why or why not?

4. How important are international integration and culture in your organization? Is the organization currently expanding its global presence? What form is this global expansion taking? How important is global learning in the organization? How does the organization's strategy, structure, or culture facilitate global learning?

5. What international strategic alliances is your organization engaged in? Draw a diagram showing these relationships. What advantages does your organization obtain from these interorganizational arrangements? How important are these arrangements to its global expansion strategy? What management problems are associated with maintaining these strategic alliances?

6. What problems do you think your organization will encounter in managing the international environment in the future? Do you think it will need to make any changes to its global expansion strategy and structure? Why or why not?

Cases for Analysis:
ABB'S MATRIX STRUCTURE

Asea Brown Boveri (ABB) is a maker of electrical systems and equipment headquartered in Zurich, Switzerland. Formed by the merger of two separate companies in 1987, ABB generates over $25 billion in sales revenue and employs over 240,000 people in 1,100 individual business divisions throughout the world.[29]

Under new CEO, Goran Lindahl, ABB pursues a transnational strategy designed to allow ABB as a whole to gain both a differentiation advantage by exploiting its core competences across world markets and a low-cost advantage by exploiting global economies of scale. Each business division in the corporation is also expected to respond to the needs of the local markets in which it competes.

An organization that pursues a transnational strategy wants its individual businesses to think globally but act locally. To implement such an ambitious strategy, an organization must be able to organize and coordinate its skills and resources on a global basis. Its managers must have a dual focus: (1) a local (country-specific) focus on how to use the corporation's global resources to develop products tailored to the needs of local consumers and

(2) a global focus that prompts them to search out opportunities to use local skills and resources to produce goods and services for the global marketplace. To achieve those goals, ABB developed a global matrix structure to organize the transfer of its core competences among its worldwide individual business divisions (see Figure 8.7).

In charge of the whole company are CEO Barnevik and his top-management team of 12 executives—the executive committee. They meet every three weeks in various countries to guide the corporate-level strategy. Reporting to the executive committee are 50 business area leaders (shown on the vertical axis in Figure 8.7). They are responsible for managing the global focus of ABB's 1,100 individual business divisions. The job of a business area leader is to coordinate the transfer of core competences among divisions within a business area or in related business areas. Business area leaders also globally organize manufacturing to reduce costs, and they arrange for the global purchase of inputs from the lowest-cost sources. In addition, they oversee the global rotation of managers to create an international corporate culture that fosters the transfer of new skills and technology to individual business divisions. Also reporting to the executive committee are country leaders (shown on the horizontal axis of Figure 8.7). Each country leader is the managing director of a national holding company and is responsible for monitoring and controlling the activities of the individual business divisions in a specific country. The managing director of ABB Germany, for example, oversees the operations of all ABB-owned business divisions in Germany, prepares their financial statements, and makes sure that each division conforms to the regulations of Germany's institutional and legal system.

At the intersections of the global matrix are the 1,100 individual business divisions, which operate throughout the world. The heads of the individual business divisions are two-boss managers who report both to the country leader of the country in which

they operate and to the business area leader who controls the global focus of their division. ABB's two-boss managers are responsible for tailoring products to the local market and for transferring skills and resources to other divisions in their business area to enhance ABB's core competences as a whole. Because managers at all levels are required to think globally but act locally, they need a centralized orientation toward the corporation and a decentralized orientation toward their own division. The ability to perform this delicate balancing act makes a global manager effective in today's international environment.

Although this global matrix structure works fine on paper, corporate and divisional politics can quickly lead to problems. In theory, the activities of the country leaders and the business area leaders are complementary; but in practice, they often compete, for business division managers may have no incentive to act

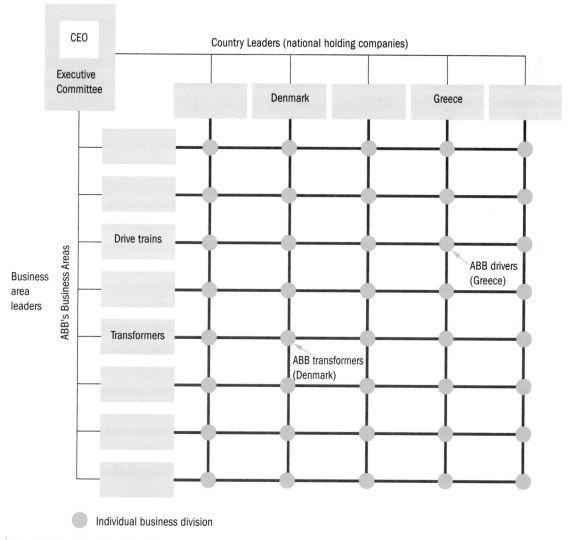

Individual business division

FIGURE 8.7   **The Global Matrix Structure of ABB.**

The managers of ABB's 1,100 individual business division report to both a country leader and a business area leader.

globally (e.g., to share resources with related divisions) if such action causes them problems at the country level. Moreover, the country leaders control the resources of the business divisions. If the country leaders prefer to act locally rather than globally and do not want to cooperate with the business area leaders, who can make them?

Making a global matrix work requires finesse. At ABB, only if all three kinds of managers—business area leaders, country leaders, and business division managers—act cooperatively can the organization achieve the benefits of a transnational strategy. Without balance and cooperation, the matrix will degenerate into an un-

wieldy bureaucracy that pits countries against business areas and managers against managers. ABB's structure helped it to become a dominant player in the European and global marketplaces in the 1990s, and its stock price doubled in 1999.[30]

1. What are the different responsibilities of the business area leaders, country leaders, and business division managers?
2. In what ways does ABB hope that the global matrix structure will increase its ability to create value?

REFERENCES

1. Amazon.com Web site.
2. G. Jacobson and J. Hillkirk, *Xerox: American Samurai* (New York: Macmillan, Collier Books, 1986).
3. K. Ohmae, "Managing in a Borderless World," *Harvard Business Review*, May–June 1989, pp. 152–161.
4. This section draws heavily on C. A. Bartlett and S. Ghoshal, *Managing Across Borders: The Transnational Solution* (Boston: Harvard Business School Press, 1991).
5. Y. Doz, C. A. Bartlett, and C. K. Prahalad, "Global Competitive Pressures v. Host Country Demands: Managing Tensions in Multinational Corporations," *California Management Review*, 1981, vol. 23, pp. 63–74.
6. T. Leavitt, "The Globalization of Markets," *Harvard Business Review*, May–June 1983, pp. 92–102.
7. P. Nulty, "A Quick Course in Going Global," *Fortune*, 13 January 1992, p. 64.
8. K. Buchholz, "Arvin Industries Opens Plant in Spain," *Automotive Engineering*, December 1997, p. 39.
9. "Arvin Industries, Inc. & Kayaba Industry Co., Ltd. Announce North American Joint Venture, Company press release, 1998.
10. Bartlett and Ghoshal, *Managing Across Borders*.
11. B. R. Baliga and A. M. Jaeger, "Multinational Corporations: Control Systems and Delegation Issues," *Journal of International Business Studies*, Fall 1984, pp. 25–40.
12. T. J. Peters and R. H. Waterman, *In Search of Excellence* (New York: Harper and Row, 1982).
13. S. M. Davis, "Managing and Organizing Multinational Corporations," in C. A. Bartlett and S. Ghoshal, eds., *Transnational Management* (Homewood, IL: Irwin, 1992).
14. J. M. Stopford and L. T. Wells, *Strategy and Structure of Multinational Enterprise* (New York: Basic Books, 1972).
15. G. de Jonquieres, "Unilever Adopts a Clean Sheet Approach," *Financial Times*, 21 October 1991, p. 13.
16. R. Abelson, "Getting Its Act Together," *Forbes*, 31 August 1992, pp. 44–45.
17. A. Edstrom and J. R. Galbraith, "Transfer of Managers as a Coordination and Control Strategy in Multinational Organizations," *Administrative Science Quarterly*, 1977, vol. 22, pp. 248–263.
18. "Asia Beckons," *The Economist*, 30 May 1992, pp. 63–64.
19. D. Cray, "Control and Coordination in Multinational Corporations," *Journal of International Business Studies*, Fall 1984, pp. 58–98.
20. J. C. Abegglen, *The Japanese Organization: Aspects of Its Social Organization* (New York: The Free Press, 1958).
21. A. M. Jaeger, "The Transfer of Organizational Culture Overseas: An Approach to Control in the Multinational Corporation," *Journal of International Business Studies*, Fall 1983, pp. 91–114.
22. Bartlett and Ghoshal, *Managing Across Borders*, Ch. 10.
23. C. A. Bartlett, Y. Doz, and G. Hedlund, eds., *Managing the Global Firm* (New York: Routledge, 1990).
24. D. Lei and J. W. Slocum, Jr., "Global Strategic Alliances: Payoffs and Pitfalls," *Organizational Dynamics*, Winter 1991, pp. 17–29.
25. B. Kogut, "Joint Ventures: Theoretical and Empirical Perspectives," *Strategic Management Journal*, 1988, vol. 9, pp. 319–332.
26. L. Therrien and C. Hoots, "Cafe au Lait, a Croissant—and Trix," *Business Week*, 24 August 1992, pp. 50–51.
27. W. Echikson, "Hey Europe, Let's Do Munch!" *Fortune*, 2 November 1992, p. 14.
28. S. Ghoshal and C. A. Bartlett, "The Multinational Corporation as an Interorganizational Network," *Academy of Management Review*, 1990, vol. 15, pp. 603–625.
29. W. Taylor, "The Logic of Global Business: An Interview with ABB's Percy Barnevik," *Harvard Business Review*, March–April 1991, pp. 90–105.
30. R. C. Morais, "ABB Reenergized," Forbes, 23 August 1999, p.58.

Chapter 9

ORGANIZATIONAL DESIGN and TECHNOLOGY

This chapter focuses on technology and examines how organizations use it to create value. First, this chapter analyzes the attributes of different types of technology that make effective management of technology difficult. Then it discusses why certain kinds of organizational structures are likely to be used with certain kinds of technology (just as earlier chapters used a similar **contingency approach** to examine why certain environments or strategies typically require the use of certain kinds of structure). Chapter 10 then extends this analysis and examines recent developments in both production and information technology that affect how organizations design their activities and their structure to be effective in today's competitive environment.

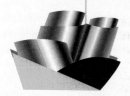

WHAT IS TECHNOLOGY?

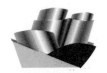

Technology *The combination of skills, knowledge, abilities, techniques, materials, machines, computers, tools, and other equipment that people use to convert or change raw materials into valuable goods and services.*

Mass production *The organizational technology that uses conveyor belts and a standardized, progressive assembly process to manufacture goods.*

Craftswork *The technology that involves groups of skilled workers who interact closely to produce custom-designed products.*

When we think of an organization, we are likely to think of it in terms of what it does. We think of a manufacturing organization like General Electric as a place where people use their skills in combination with machinery and equipment to assemble inputs into light bulbs and other finished products. We view a service organization like a hospital as a place where people apply their skills in combination with machinery or equipment to make sick people well. In all manufacturing and service organizations, actions are taken to create value—that is, inputs are converted into goods and services that satisfy people's needs. **Technology** is the combination of skills, knowledge, abilities, techniques, materials, machines, computers, tools, and other equipment that people use to convert or change raw materials into valuable goods and services. When people at Ford, the Mayo Clinic, and H&R Block use their skills, knowledge, materials, machines, and so forth to produce a finished car, a cured patient, or a completed tax return, they are using technology to *bring about change* to something to *add value* to it.

Inside an organization, technology exists at three levels: individual, functional or departmental, and organizational. At the *individual* level, technology is the personal skills and knowledge that individual women and men possess. At the *functional* or *departmental* level, the procedures and techniques that groups use to perform their work and create value constitute technology. The interactions of the members of a surgical operating team, the cooperative efforts of scientists in a research and development laboratory, and techniques developed by assembly-line workers are all examples of technology at the functional or departmental level.

The way an organization converts inputs into outputs is often used to characterize technology at the *organizational* level. **Mass production** is the organizational technology that uses conveyor belts and a standardized, progressive assembly process to manufacture goods. **Craftswork** is the technology that involves groups of skilled workers who interact closely to produce custom-designed products. The difference between these two forms of technology is clearly illustrated by the way Henry Ford revolutionized car production.

ORGANIZATIONAL INSIGHT

9.1 PROGRESSIVE MANUFACTURE AT FORD

In 1913, Henry Ford opened the Highland Park plant to produce the Model T car. In doing so, he changed forever the way complex products like cars are made, and the new technology of *progressive manufacture* (Ford's term), or mass production, was born. Before Ford introduced mass production, most cars were manufactured by craftswork. A team of workers—a skilled mechanic and a few helpers—performed all the operations necessary to make the product. Individual craftsworkers in the automobile and other industries have the skills to deal with unexpected situations as they arise during the manufacturing process. They can modify misaligned parts so that they fit together snugly, and they can follow specifications and create small batches of a range of products. Because craftswork relies on workers' skills and expertise, it is a costly and slow method of manufacturing. In searching for new ways to improve the efficiency of manufacturing, Ford developed the process of progressive manufacture.

Ford outlined three principles of progressive manufacture:

1. Work should be delivered to the worker; the worker should not have to find the work.[1] At the Highland Park plant, a mechanized, moving conveyer belt brought cars to the workers. Workers did not move past a stationary line of cars under assembly.
2. Work should proceed in an orderly and specific sequence so that each task builds on the task that precedes it. At Highland Park, the implementation of this idea fell to managers, who worked out the most efficient sequence of tasks and coordinated them with the speed of the conveyer belt.
3. Individual tasks should be broken down into their simplest components in order to increase specialization and create an efficient division of labor. The assembly of a taillight, for example, might be broken into two separate tasks to be performed all day long by two different workers. One person puts light bulbs into a reflective panel; the other person screws a red lens onto the reflective panel.

By following those three principles, Ford made the conversion of inputs (component parts) into outputs (finished cars) much more controllable and predictable than it had been with craftswork. The speed of the conveyor belt relieved supervisors of the need to monitor and direct each employee. In the new work system, a supervisor's job was to evaluate performance and discipline workers for poor performance. Ford's three principles reduced the level of skill needed by production workers: A new worker needed only two days to learn the skills necessary to perform a typical assembly-line job.

As a result of this new work system, by 1914 Ford plants employed 15,000 workers but only 255 supervisors (not including top management) to oversee them. The ratio of workers to supervisors was 58 to 1. This very wide span of control was possible because the sequence and pacing of the work were not directed by the supervisors but were controlled by work programming and the speed of the production line.[2] The mass-production system helped Ford control many workers with a relatively small number of supervisors, but it also created a tall hierarchy. The hierarchy at a typical Ford plant had six levels, reflecting the fact that management's major preoccupation was the vertical communication of information to top management, which controlled decision making for the whole plant.

The introduction of mass-production technology to auto making was only one of Henry Ford's technological manufacturing innovations. Another was the use of interchangeable parts. When parts are interchangeable, the components from various suppliers fit together; they do not need to be altered to fit during the assembly process. With the old craftswork method of production, supposedly identical components provided by different manufacturers often differed in size or quality. Ford insisted that component manufacturers follow detailed specifications so that parts needed no remachining and his relatively unskilled workforce would be able to assemble them easily. Eventually, the desire to control the quality of inputs led the Ford Motor Company to embark on a massive program of vertical integration. Ford mined iron ore in its mines in Upper Michigan and transported the ore in a fleet of Ford-owned barges to Ford's steel plants in Detroit, where it was smelted, rolled, and stamped into standard body parts.

As a result of these technological innovations in manufacturing, by the early 1920s Henry Ford's organization was making over 2 million cars a year. Because of his efficient manufacturing methods, Ford reduced the price of a car by two-thirds. This low-price advantage, in turn, created a mass market for his product.[3] Clearly, as measured by standards of technical efficiency and the ability to satisfy external stakeholders such as customers, Ford Motor Company was a very effective organization. Inside the factories, however, the picture was not so rosy.

Workers hated their work. Ford managers responded to their discontent with repressive supervision. Workers were watched constantly. They were not allowed to talk on the production line, and their behavior both in the plant and outside was closely monitored (e.g., they were not allowed to drink alcohol, even when they were not working). Supervisors could instantly fire workers who disobeyed any rules. So repressive were conditions that by 1914 so many workers had been fired or had quit that 500 new workers had to be hired each day to keep the workforce at 15,000 employees.[4] Clearly, the new technology of mass production was imposing severe demands on individual workers.

TECHNOLOGY AND ORGANIZATIONAL EFFECTIVENESS

Recall from Chapter 1 that organizations take inputs from the environment and create value from the inputs by transforming them into outputs through conversion processes (see Figure 9.1). Although we usually think of technology only at the conversion stage, technology is present in all organizational activities: input, conversion, and output.[5]

At the *input* stage, technology—skills, procedures, and techniques—allows each organizational function to handle relationships with outside stakeholders so that the organization can effectively manage its specific environment. The human resource function, for example, has techniques such as interviewing procedures and psychological testing that it uses to recruit and select qualified employees. The materials management function has techniques for dealing with input suppliers, for negotiating favorable contract terms, and for obtaining low-cost, high-quality component parts. The finance department has techniques for obtaining capital at a cost favorable to the company.

At the *conversion* stage, technology—a combination of machines, techniques, and work procedures—transforms inputs into outputs. The best technology allows an organization

FIGURE 9.1

Input, Conversion, and
Output Processes

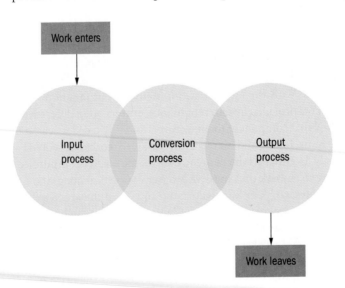

to add the most value to its inputs at the least cost of organizational resources. Organizations often try to improve the efficiency of their conversion processes, and they can improve it by training employees in new time-management techniques and by allowing employees to devise better ways of performing their jobs.

At the *output* stage, technology allows an organization to effectively dispose of finished goods and services to external stakeholders. To be effective, an organization must possess techniques for testing the quality of the finished product, for selling and marketing the product, and for managing after-sales service to customers.

The technology of an organization's input, conversion, and output processes is an important source of a company's competitive advantage. Why is Microsoft the most successful software company? Why is Toyota the most efficient car manufacturer? Why is McDonald's the most efficient fast-food company? Why does Wal-Mart consistently outperform Kmart and Sears? Each of these organizations excels in the development, management, and use of technology to manage the organizational environment and create value for stakeholders.

Recall from Chapter 1 the three principal approaches to measuring and increasing organizational effectiveness (see Table 1.2). An organization taking the *external resource approach* uses technology to increase its ability to manage and control external stakeholders. Any new technological developments that allow an organization to improve its service to customers, such as the ability to customize products or to increase products' quality and reliability, increases the organization's effectiveness.

An organization taking the *internal systems approach* uses technology to increase the success of its attempts to innovate, to develop new products, services, and processes, and to reduce the time needed to bring new products to market. As we saw earlier, the introduction of mass production at the Highland Park plant allowed Henry Ford to make a new kind of product—a car for the mass market.

An organization taking the *technical approach* uses technology to improve efficiency and reduce costs while simultaneously enhancing the quality and reliability of its products. Ford increased his organization's effectiveness by organizing its functional resources to create better-quality cars at lower costs to both manufacturer and consumer.

Organizations use technology to become more efficient, more innovative, and better able to meet the needs and desires of stakeholders. Each department or function in an organization is responsible for developing and maintaining technology that allows it to make a positive contribution to organizational performance. When an organization has technology that enables it to create value, it needs a structure that maximizes the effectiveness of the technology. Just as environmental characteristics require organizations to make certain organizational design choices, so do the characteristics of different technologies affect an organization's choice of structure.

In the next three sections we examine three theories of technology that are attempts to capture the way different departmental and organizational technologies work and affect organizational design. Note that these three theories are *complementary* in that each illuminates some aspects of technology that the others don't. All three theories are needed to understand the characteristics of different kinds of technologies. Managers, at all levels and in all functions, can use these theories to (1) choose the technology that will most effectively transform inputs into outputs and (2) design a structure that allows the organization to operate the technology effectively. Thus, it is important for these managers to understand the concept of technical complexity, the underlying differences between routine and complex tasks, and the concept of task interdependence. We will examine each of these topics in the remainder of this chapter.

TECHNICAL COMPLEXITY:
THE THEORY OF JOAN WOODWARD

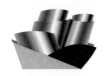

Programmed technology
*A technology in which
the procedures for con-
verting inputs into out-
puts can be specified in
advance so that tasks
can be standardized and
the work process can be
made predictable.*

Technical complexity *A
measure of the extent to
which a production
process can be pro-
grammed so that it can
be controlled and made
predictable.*

Some kinds of technology are more complex and difficult to control than others because some are more difficult to program than others. Technology is said to be **programmed** when procedures for converting inputs into outputs can be specified in advance so that tasks can be standardized and the work process is made predictable. McDonald's uses a highly programmed technology to produce hamburgers, and Ford uses a highly programmed technology to produce cars. They do so to control the quality of their outputs—hamburgers or cars. The more difficult it is to specify the process for converting inputs into outputs, the more difficult it is to control the production process and make it predictable.

According to one researcher, Joan Woodward, the **technical complexity** of a production process—that is, the extent to which it can be programmed so that it can be controlled and made predictable—is the important dimension that differentiates technologies.[6] *High technical complexity* exists when conversion processes can be programmed in advance and fully automated. With full automation, work activities and the outputs that result from them are standardized and can be predicted accurately. *Low technical complexity* exists when conversion processes depend primarily on people and their skills and knowledge and not on machines. With increased human involvement and less reliance on machines, work activities cannot be programmed in advance, and results depend on the skills of the people involved.

The production of services, for example, typically relies much more on the knowledge and experience of employees who interact directly with customers to produce the final output than it relies on machines and other equipment. The labor-intensive nature of the production of services makes standardizing and programming work activities and controlling the work process especially difficult. When conversion processes depend primarily on the performance of people, rather than on machines, technical complexity is low, and the difficulty of maintaining high quality and consistency of production is great.

Joan Woodward identified 10 levels of technical complexity, which she associated with three types of production technology: (1) small-batch and unit technology, (2) large-batch and mass-production technology, and (3) continuous-process technology (see Figure 9.2).[7]

Small-Batch and Unit Technology

Organizations that employ small-batch and unit technology make one-of-a-kind, customized products or small quantities of products. Examples of such organizations include a furniture maker that constructs furniture designed to suit the tastes of a few individuals; a printer that supplies engraved wedding invitations for specific couples; and teams of surgeons and hospitals, which provide a great variety of services customized to the needs of individual patients. Small-batch and unit technology scores lowest on the dimension of technical complexity (see Figure 9.2) because any machines used during the conversion process are less important than people's skills and knowledge. People decide how and when machines will be used, and the production process reflects their decisions about how to apply their knowledge. A custom furniture maker, for example, uses an array of tools—including lathes, hammers, planes, and saws—to transform boards into a cabinet. However, which tools are used and the order in which they are used depends on how the furniture maker chooses to build the cabinet. With small-batch and unit technology, the

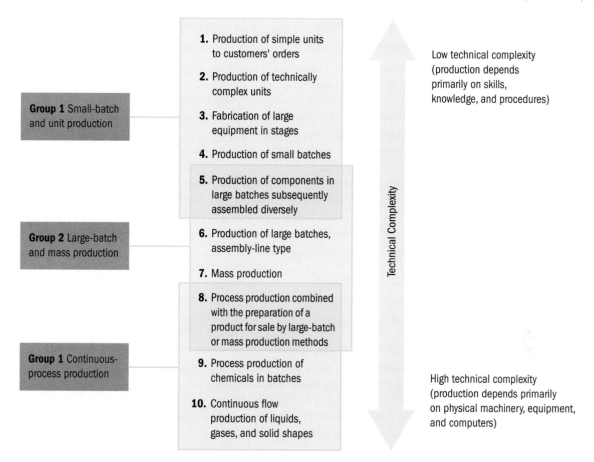

FIGURE 9.2   Technical Complexity and Three Types of Technology.

Joan Woodward identified 10 levels of technical complexity, which she associated with three types of production. *Source:* Adapted from Joan Woodward, "*Management and Technology.*" London: Her Majesty's Stationery Office, 1958, p. 11. Reproduced with permission of the Controller of Her Britannic Majesty's Stationery Office.

conversion process is flexible because the worker adapts techniques to suit the orders of individual customers.

The flexibility of small-batch technology gives an organization the capacity to produce a wide range of products that can be customized for individual customers. For example, high-fashion designers and makers of products such as fine perfume, custom-built cars, and specialized furniture use small-batch technology. Small-batch technology allows a custom furniture maker, for example, to satisfy the customer's request for a certain style of table made from a certain kind of wood.

Small-batch technology is relatively expensive to operate because the work process is unpredictable and the production of customized, made-to-order products makes advance programming of work activities difficult. However, flexibility and the ability to respond to a wide range of customer requests make this technology ideally suited to producing new or complex products. Microsoft uses small-batch technology when it assigns a team of programmers to work together to develop new software applications (see Organizational Insight 3.4).

Large-Batch and Mass-Production Technology

To increase control over the work process and make it predictable, organizations try to increase their use of machines and equipment—that is, they try to increase the level of technical complexity and to increase their efficiency. Organizations that employ large-batch or mass-production technology produce large volumes of standardized products such as cars, razor blades, aluminum cans, and soft drinks. Examples of such organizations include Ford, Gillette, Crown Cork and Seal, and Coca-Cola. With large-batch and mass-production technology, machines control the work process. Their use allows tasks to be specified and programmed in advance. As a result, work activities are standardized, and the production process is highly controllable.[8] Instead of a team of craftsworkers making custom furniture piece by piece, for example, high-speed saws and lathes cut and shape boards into standardized components that are assembled into thousands of identical tables or chairs by unskilled workers on a production line.

The control provided by large-batch and mass-production technology allows an organization to save money on production and charge a lower price for its products. Henry Ford changed manufacturing history when he replaced small-batch production (the assembly of cars one by one by skilled craftsworkers) with mass production to manufacture the Model T. The use of a conveyor belt, standardized and interchangeable parts, and specialized, progressive tasks made conversion processes at the Highland Park plant more efficient and productive. Production costs plummeted, and Ford was able to lower the cost of a Model T and create a mass market for his product.

Mass-production technology is usually associated with the heavy use of automated equipment to produce and assemble inputs into outputs. But if labor costs are low enough, people are used to perform assembly operations. In factories owned by Samsung, Sony, and Panasonic in third-world countries, for example, individual employees assemble component parts to produce a complete television set, radio, or videocassette recorder. U.S. companies' decisions to move their mass-production operations abroad to places where costs are low has stirred considerable controversy on ethical grounds.

ORGANIZATIONAL INSIGHT

9.2 THE ETHICS OF MASS PRODUCTION

To reduce the cost of manufacturing and make their prices more competitive, many U.S. companies have moved their assembly operations from the United States to countries where labor costs are very low. Several of these companies, however, have found that their foreign producers are children or adults forced to work for very low wages and in conditions that would not be tolerated or legal in the United States. Wal-Mart, which buys a large quantity of goods assembled abroad, was embarrassed to learn that many of the clothes it was selling had been made by children working in sweatshops in Bangladesh. Sears discovered that some of its products had been produced by forced labor in China. And female employees in Indonesia netted between $34 and $46 per month for making Nike sneakers that sell for twice that per pair.

Under pressure from customers, many companies are starting to police the way their products are made in foreign countries. Levi Strauss, for example, laid down stringent guidelines and standards for its 600 foreign suppliers. The company inspected each supplier's business and, as a result of this inspection, dropped 30 suppliers and demanded that another 120 reform their hiring practices to prevent the hiring of children.[9] Levi Strauss withdrew its business from Myanmar (formerly Burma), citing that country's frequent human rights violations. Home Depot, the home improvement retailer, recently asked its foreign suppliers to see whether any of the products it sells have been assembled by children or convicts.

Recently, Nike has come under many attacks for producing its shoes in foreign factories where workers are paid a pittance and often work under harsh conditions.[10] It has responded by announcing strict new standards by which these factories must abide, but critics say it is not enforcing these standards actively enough. Recently, concern about sweatshop conditions has spread to Europe and more and more companies are having to defend their buying practises.[11]

Continuous-Process Technology

With continuous-process technology, technical complexity reaches its height (see Figure 9.2). Organizations that employ continuous-process technology include companies that make oil-based products and chemicals, such as Exxon, Du Pont, and Conoco, and brewing companies such as Anheuser-Busch and Miller Brewing. In continuous-process production, the conversion process is almost entirely automated and mechanized; employees generally are not directly involved. Their role in production is to monitor the plant and its machinery and ensure its efficient operation.[12] The task of employees engaged in continuous-process production is primarily to manage exceptions in the work process, such as a machine breakdown or malfunctioning equipment.

The hallmark of continuous-process technology is the smoothness of its operation. Production continues with little variation in output and rarely stops. In an oil refinery, for example, crude oil brought continuously to the refinery by tankers flows through pipes to cracking towers where its individual component chemicals are extracted and sent to other parts of the refinery for further refinement. Final products such as gasoline, fuel oil, benzene, and tar leave the plant in tankers to be shipped to customers. Workers in a refinery or in a chemical plant rarely see what they are producing. Production takes place through pipes and machines. Employees in a centralized control room monitor gauges and dials to ensure that the process functions smoothly, safely, and efficiently.

Continuous-process production tends to be more technically efficient than mass production because it is more mechanized and automated and, thus, is more predictable and easier to control. It is more cost-efficient than both unit and mass production because labor costs are such a small proportion of its overall cost. When operated at full capacity, continuous-process technology has the lowest production costs.

Woodward noted that an organization usually seeks to increase its use of machines (if it is practical to do so) and move from small-batch to mass production to continuous-process production in order to reduce costs. (In Chapter 10 we discuss several recent technological developments that have facilitated the move to continuous-process production.) There are, however, exceptions to this progression. For many organizational activities, the move to automate production is not possible or practical. Prototype development, basic research into new drugs or computers, and the operation of hospitals and schools, for example, are intrinsically unpredictable and, thus, would be difficult to program in advance with an automated machine. A pharmaceutical company cannot say, "Our research department will invent three new drugs—one for diabetes and two for high blood pressure—every six months." Such inventions are the result of trial and error and depend on the skills and knowledge of the researchers. Moreover, many customers are willing to pay high prices for custom-designed products that suit their individual tastes, such as custom-made suits, jewelry, or even cars. Thus, there is a market for the products of small-batch companies even though production costs are high.

Technical Complexity and Organizational Structure

One of Woodward's goals in classifying technologies according to their technical complexity was to discover whether an organization's technology affected the design of its structure. Specifically, Woodward wanted to see whether effective organizations had structures that matched the needs of their technologies. When she compared the structural characteristics of organizations pursuing each of the three types of technology, she found systematic differences in the technology-structure relationship. Figure 9.3 shows some of her findings together with a simplified model of the organizational structure associated with each type of technology.

	Low Technical Complexity High		
Structural Characteristics	**Small-Batch Technology**	**Mass Production Technology**	**Continuous-Process Technology**
Level in the hierarchy	3	4	6
Span of control of CEO	4	7	10
Span of control of first-line supervisor	23	48	15
Ratio of managers to nonmanagers	1 to 23	1 to 16	1 to 8
Approximate shape of organization	*Relatively flat, with narrow span of control*	*Relatively tall, with wide span of control*	*Very tall, with very narrow span of control*
Type of structure	Organic	Mechanistic	Organic
Cost of operation	High	Medium	Low

FIGURE 9.3   Technical Complexity and Organizational Structure.

Woodward's research indicated that each technology presents different control and coordination problems and is, thus, associated with a different organizational structure. *Source:* Adapted from J. Woodward, "*Industrial Organization: Theory and Practice.*" London: Oxford University Press, 1965. Reprinted by permission of Oxford University Press.

On the basis of her findings, Woodward argued that each technology is associated with a different structure because each technology presents different control and coordination problems. Organizations with small-batch technology typically have three levels in their hierarchy; organizations with mass-production technology, four levels; and organizations with continuous-process technology, six levels. As technical complexity increases, organizations become taller, and the span of control of the CEO widens. The span of control of first-line supervisors first expands and then narrows. It is relatively small with small-batch technology, widens greatly with mass-production technology, and contracts dramatically with continuous-process technology. These findings result in the very differently shaped structures shown at the bottom of Figure 9.3. Why does the nature of an organization's technology produce these results?

The main coordination problem associated with *small-batch technology* is the impossibility of programming conversion activities because production depends on the skills and experience of people working together. An organization that uses small-batch technology has to give people the freedom to make their own decisions so that they can respond quickly and flexibly to the customer's requests and produce the exact product the customer wants. For this reason, such an organization has a relatively flat structure (three levels in the hierarchy), and decision making is decentralized to small teams where first-line supervisors have a relatively small span of control (23 employees). With small-batch technology, each supervisor and work group decides how to manage each decision as it occurs at each step of the input-conversion-output process. This type of decision making requires mutual adjustment—face-to-face communication with coworkers and often with customers. The most appropriate structure for unit and small-batch technology is an organic structure in which managers and employees work closely to coordinate their activities to meet changing work demands—hence, the relatively flat structure shown in Figure 9.3.[13]

In an organization that uses *mass-production technology*, the ability to program tasks in advance allows the organization to standardize the manufacturing process and make it predictable. The first-line supervisor's span of control increases to 48 because formalization through rules and procedures becomes the principal method of coordination. Decision making becomes centralized, and the hierarchy of authority becomes taller (four levels) as managers rely on vertical communication to control the work process. A *mechanistic structure* becomes the appropriate structure to control work activities in a mass-production setting, and the organizational structure becomes taller and wider, as shown in Figure 9.3.

In an organization that uses *continuous-process technology*, tasks can be programmed in advance, and the work process is predictable and controllable in a technical sense, but there is still the potential for a major systems breakdown. The principal control problem facing the organization is monitoring the production process to control and correct unforeseen events before they lead to disaster. The consequences of a faulty pipeline in an oil refinery or chemical plant, for example, are potentially disastrous. Accidents at a nuclear power plant, another user of continuous-process technology, can also have catastrophic effects, as accidents at Chernobyl and Three Mile Island showed.

The need to constantly monitor the operating system, and to make sure that each employee conforms to accepted operating procedures, is the reason why continuous-process technology is associated with the tallest hierarchy of authority (six levels). Managers at all levels closely monitor their subordinates' actions. The diamond-shaped hierarchy shown in Figure 9.3 reflects the fact that first-line supervisors have a narrow span of control. Many supervisors are needed to supervise lower-level employees and to monitor and control sophisticated equipment. Because employees also work together as a team and jointly work out procedures for managing and reacting to unexpected situations, mutual adjustment becomes the primary means of coordination. Thus, an *organic structure* is the appropriate structure for managing continuous-process technology because the potential for unpredictable events requires the capability to provide quick, flexible responses.

One researcher, Charles Perrow, argues that complex continuous-process technology such as the technology used in nuclear power plants is so complicated that it is uncontrollable.[14] Perrow acknowledges that control systems are designed with backup systems to handle problems as they arise and that backup systems exist to compensate for failed backup systems. He believes nevertheless that the number of unexpected events that can occur when technical complexity is very high (as it is in nuclear power plants) is so great that managers cannot react quickly enough to solve all the problems that might arise. Perrow argues that some continuous-process technology is so complex that no organizational structure can allow managers to safely operate it, no standard operating procedures can be devised to manage problems in advance, and no use of mutual adjustments will be able to solve problems as they arise. One implication of Perrow's view is that nuclear power stations should be closed because they are too complex to operate safely. Other researchers, however, disagree, arguing that when the right balance of centralized and decentralized control is achieved, the technology can be operated safely.

The Technological Imperative

Technological imperative *The argument that technology determines structure.*

Woodward's results, which have been replicated by several researchers, strongly suggest that technology is a main factor determining the design of organizational structure.[15] Her results imply that if a company operates with a certain technology, then it needs to adopt a certain kind of structure to be effective. If a company uses mass-production technology, for example, then it should have a mechanistic structure with six levels in the hierarchy, a span of control of 1 to 48, and so forth, to be effective. The argument that technology determines structure is known as the **technological imperative**.

Other researchers also interested in the technology-structure relationship became concerned that Woodward's results may have been a consequence of the sample of companies she studied and may have overstated the importance of technology.[16] They pointed out that most of the companies that Woodward studied were relatively small (82 percent had fewer than 500 employees) and suggested that her sample may have biased her results. They acknowledged that technology may have a major impact on structure in a small manufacturing company because improving the efficiency of manufacturing may be management's major priority. But they suggested that the structure of an organization (such as Exxon, General Motors, or IBM) that has 5,000 or 500,000 employees is less likely to be determined primarily by the technology used to manufacture its various products.

In a series of studies known as the Aston Studies, researchers agreed that technology has some effect on organizational structure: The more an organization's technology is mechanized and automated, the more likely is the organization to have a highly centralized and standardized mechanistic structure. But, the Aston Studies concluded, organizational size is more important than technology in determining an organization's choice of structure.[17] We have seen in earlier chapters that as an organization grows and differentiates, control and coordination problems emerge that must be addressed by changes in the organization's structure. The Aston researchers argued that although technology may strongly affect the structure of small organizations, the structure adopted by large organizations may be a product of other factors that cause an organization to grow and differentiate.

We saw in Chapter 7, for example, that organizational strategy and the decision to produce a wider range of products and enter new markets can cause an organization to grow and adopt a more complex structure. Thus, the strategic choices that an organization—especially a large organization—makes about what outputs to produce for which markets are at least as important to the design of the organization's structure as the technology the organization uses to produce the outputs. For small organizations or for functions or departments within large organizations, the importance of technology as a predictor of structure may be more important than it is for large organizations.[18]

ROUTINE TASKS AND COMPLEX TASKS: THE THEORY OF CHARLES PERROW

To understand why some technologies are more complex (more unpredictable and difficult to control) than others, it is necessary to understand why the tasks associated with some technologies are more complex than the tasks associated with other technologies. What causes one task to be more difficult than another? Why, for example, do we normally think that the task of serving hamburgers in a fast-food restaurant is more routine—that is, more predictable and controllable—than the task of programming a computer or performing brain surgery? If we think of the range of tasks that people perform, what characteristics of these tasks cause us to believe that some are more complex than others? According to Charles Perrow, two dimensions underlie the difference between routine and nonroutine or complex tasks and technologies: task variability and task analyzability.[19]

Task Variability and Task Analyzability

Task variability *The number of exceptions—new or unexpected situations—that a person encounters while performing a task.*

Task variability is the number of exceptions—new or unexpected situations—that a person encounters while performing a task. Exceptions may occur at the input, conversion, or output stage. Task variability is high when a person can expect to encounter many new situations or problems when performing his or her task. In a hospital operating room during the course of surgery, for example, there is much opportunity for unexpected problems to develop. The patient's condition may be more serious than the doctors thought it was, or the surgeon may make a mistake. No matter what happens, the surgeon and the operating team must have the capacity to adjust quickly to new situations as they occur. Similarly, great variability in the quality of the raw materials makes it especially difficult to manage and maintain consistent quality during the conversion stage.

Task variability is low when a task is highly standardized or repetitive so that a worker encounters the same situation time and time again.[20] In a fast-food restaurant, for example, the number of exceptions to a given task is limited. Each customer places a different order, but all customers must choose from the same limited menu, so employees rarely confront unexpected situations. In fact, the menu in a fast-food restaurant is designed for low task variability, which keeps costs down and efficiency up.

Task analyzability *The degree to which search activity is needed to solve a problem.*

Task analyzability is the degree to which search activity is needed to solve a problem. The more analyzable a task is, the more routine it is because the procedures for completing it have been worked out or programmed in advance. For example, although a customer may select thousands of combinations of food from a menu at a fast-food restaurant, the order taker's task of fulfilling each customer's order is relatively easy. The problem of combining foods in a bag is easily analyzable: The order taker picks up the drink and puts it in the bag, then adds the fries, burger, and so on, folds down the top of the bag, and hands the bag to the customer. Little thought or judgment is needed to complete an order.

Tasks are hard to analyze when they cannot be programmed—that is, when procedures for carrying them out and dealing with exceptions cannot be worked out in advance. If a person encounters an exception, procedures for dealing with it must be sought. For example, a scientist trying to develop a new cancer-preventing drug that has no side effects, or a software programmer working on a program to enable computers to understand the spoken word, has to spend considerable time and effort working out the procedures for solving problems and may fail because he or she cannot find a solution. People working on tasks with low analyzability have to draw on their knowledge and judgment to search for new procedures to solve problems. When a great deal of search activity is needed to find a solution to a problem and procedures cannot be programmed in advance, tasks are complex and nonroutine.

Together, task analyzability and task variability explain why some tasks are more routine than others. The greater the number of exceptions that workers encounter in the work process, and the greater the amount of search behavior that is required to find a solution to each exception, the more complex and less routine are tasks. For tasks that are routine, there are, in Perrow's words, "well-established techniques which are sure to work and these are applied to essentially similar raw materials. That is, there is little uncertainty about methods and little variety or change in the task that must be performed."[21] For tasks that are complex, "there are few established techniques; there is little certainty about methods, or whether or not they will work. But it also means that there may be a great variety of different tasks to perform."[22]

Four Types of Technology

Perrow used task variability and task analyzability to differentiate among four types of technology: routine manufacturing, craftswork, engineering production, and nonroutine research (see Figure 9.4).[23] Perrow's model can be used to categorize the technology of an organization and the technology of departments and functions inside an organization.

FIGURE 9.4

Task Variability, Task Analyzability, and Four Types of Technology.
Charles Perrow defined two factors—task variability and task analyzability—that account for differences between tasks and technologies. *Source:* Adapted from Charles Perrow, *Organizational Analysis: A Sociological View* (Belmont, CA: Wadsworth, 1970), p. 78.

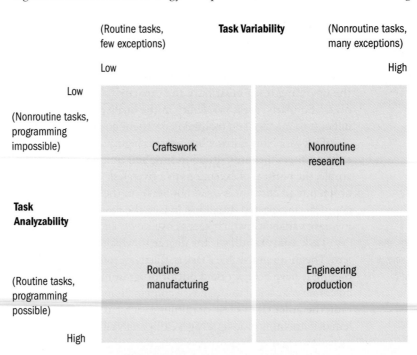

ROUTINE MANUFACTURING.   Routine manufacturing is characterized by low task variability and high task analyzability. Few exceptions are encountered in the work process, and when an exception does occur, little search behavior is required to deal with it. Mass production is representative of routine technology.

In mass-production settings, tasks are broken down into simple steps to minimize the possibility that exceptions will occur, and inputs are standardized to minimize disruptions to the production process. There are standard procedures to follow if an exception or a problem presents itself. The low-cost advantages of mass production are obtained by making tasks low in variability and high in analyzability. One reason why McDonald's costs are lower than its competitors' costs is that McDonald's constantly streamlines its menu choices and standardizes its work activities to reduce task variability and increase task analyzability.

CRAFTSWORK.   With craft technology, task variability is low (only a narrow range of exceptions is encountered), and task analyzability is also low (a high level of search activity is needed to find a solution to problems). Employees in an organization using this kind of technology need to adapt existing procedures to new situations and find new techniques to handle existing problems more effectively. This technology was used, for example, to build early automobiles by Ford Motor Company. Other examples of craftswork are the manufacture of specialized or customized products such as furniture, clothing, and machinery, and trades such as carpentry and plumbing. The tasks that a plumber, for example, is called on to perform center on installing or repairing bathroom or kitchen plumbing. But because every house is different, a plumber needs to adapt the techniques of the craft to each situation and find a unique solution for each house.

ENGINEERING PRODUCTION.   With engineering production technology, task variability is high and task analyzability is high. The number or variety of exceptions that workers may encounter in the task is high, but finding a solution is relatively easy because well-understood standard procedures have been established to handle the exceptions. Because these procedures are often codified in technical formulas, tables, or manuals, solving a problem is often a matter of identifying and applying the right technique. Thus, in organizations that use engineering production technology, existing procedures are used to make many kinds of products. A manufacturing company may specialize in custom building machines such as drill presses or electric motors. A firm of architects may specialize in customizing apartment buildings to the needs of different builders. A civil engineering group may use its skills in constructing airports, dams, and hydroelectric projects to service the needs of clients throughout the world. Like craftswork, engineering production is a form of small-batch technology because people are primarily responsible for developing techniques to solve particular problems.

NONROUTINE RESEARCH.   Nonroutine research technology is characterized by high task variability and low task analyzability and is the most complex and least routine of the four technologies in Perrow's classification. Tasks are complex because not only is the number of unexpected situations large but search activity is high. Each new situation creates a need to expend resources to deal with it.

High-tech research and development activities are examples of nonroutine research. For people working at the forefront of technical knowledge, there are no prepackaged solutions to problems. There may be a thousand well-defined steps to follow when building the perfect bridge (engineering production technology), but there are few well-defined steps to take to discover a cure for AIDS.

An organization's top-management team is another example of a group that uses research technology. The team's job is to chart the future path of the organization and make resource decisions that are likely to ensure its success. They make these decisions in an uncertain context, however, not knowing how successful they will be. Planning and forecasting by top management, and other nonroutine research activities, are inherently risky and uncertain because the technology is difficult to manage.

Routine Technology and Organizational Structure

Just as the types of technology identified by Woodward have implications for an organization's structure, so do the types of technology in Perrow's model. Perrow and others have suggested that an organization should move from a mechanistic to an organic structure as tasks become more complex and less routine.[24] Table 9.1 summarizes this finding.

When technology is routine, employees perform clearly defined tasks according to well-established rules and procedures. The work process is programmed in advance and standardized. Because the work process is standardized in routine technology, employees need only learn the procedures for performing the task effectively. For example, McDonald's uses written rules and procedures to train new personnel so that the behavior of all McDonald's employees is consistent and predictable. Each new employee learns the right way to greet customers, the appropriate way to fulfill customer orders, and the correct way to make Big Macs.

Because employee tasks can be standardized with routine technology, the organizational hierarchy is relatively tall and decision making is centralized. Management's responsibility is to supervise employees and to manage the few exceptions that may occur, such as a breakdown of the production line. Because tasks are routine, all important production decisions are made at the top of the production hierarchy and are transmitted down the chain of command as orders to lower-level managers and workers. It has been suggested that organizations with routine technology, such as that found in mass-production settings, deliberately "deskill" tasks, meaning that they simplify jobs by using ma-

TABLE 9.1		
Routine and Nonroutine Tasks and Organizational Design		
Structural Characteristic	**Nature of Technology**	
	ROUTINE TASKS	NONROUTINE TASKS
Standardization	High	Low
Mutual adjustment	Low	High
Specialization	Individual	Joint
Formalization	High	Low
Hierarchy of authority	Tall	Flat
Decision-making authority	Centralized	Decentralized
Overall structure	Mechanistic	Organic

chines to perform complex tasks and by designing the work process to minimize the degree to which workers' initiative or judgment is required.[25]

The result of all these design choices is a mechanistic structure for organizations operating a routine technology. However, as we will see in the next chapter, this choice may no longer be appropriate for an organization seeking to maintain a competitive advantage in the global environment.

Nonroutine Technology and Organizational Structure

Organizations operating a nonroutine technology face a different set of factors that affects the design of the organization.[26] As tasks become less routine and more complex, an organization has to develop a structure that allows employees to quickly respond to and manage an increase in the number and variety of exceptions and to develop new procedures to handle new problems.[27] As we saw in Chapter 2, an organic structure allows an organization to adapt rapidly to changing conditions. Organic structures are based on mutual adjustment between employees who work together, face-to-face, to develop procedures to find solutions to problems. Mutual adjustment through task forces and teams becomes especially important in facilitating communication and increasing integration among team members. Employees often perform closely related activities in which it is difficult to separate out each individual's contribution.[28]

The more complex an organization's work processes are, the more likely the organization is to have a relatively flat and decentralized structure that allows employees the authority and autonomy to cooperate to make decisions quickly and effectively.[29] The use of work groups and product teams to facilitate rapid adjustment and feedback among employees performing complex tasks is a key feature in such an organization. The San Diego Zoo recently adopted a product team structure to manage its new, more complex approach to organizing its activities.

ORGANIZATIONAL INSIGHT

9.3 THE SAN DIEGO ZOO CHANGES ITS STRIPES

Every year the San Diego Zoo competes with nearby Sea World and Disneyland for its share of tourists. A few years ago, public concern about the way the animals were housed and displayed prompted the zoo, a renowned scientific and conservation organization, to change its way of operating.

Before the change, animals were displayed by type (all big cats were shown together, as were all monkeys, reptiles, and so on), and tasks were organized on strictly functional lines and were very routine. The zoo's 1,200 employees were grouped into over 50 departments, such as animal keeping, maintenance, fund raising, and food service. Each department controlled its own tasks and worked separately to meet goals that the organization had set for it. After working with consultants, the zoo changed the way the animals were displayed and adopted a new approach to organizing its tasks—an approach that fundamentally changed functional relationships.

The zoo now groups animals by bioclimatic zone. Animals that live in African rain forests or in the Australian desert, for example, are displayed together. This new arrangement made functional tasks less routine and more complex because close cooperation was required to design, operate, and maintain the new bioclimatic displays. Thus, the zoo needed a new way to manage its technology to deal with the new, more complex tasks.

The zoo adopted a radical solution. It dissolved its functional structure and created teams focused on individual bioclimatic displays. Each display is run by a team that consists of animal specialists, maintenance workers, construction workers, and others. Team members together work out ways to design, operate, and improve the displays. The zoo also decentralized decision making to each team. Team members have the responsibility for monitoring and controlling the quality and cost of their activities. Team members have been forced to learn one another's jobs and, as a result, team members who leave are not always replaced because others can do their jobs. The new self-directed teams have freed managers from day-to-day monitoring activities, so they can devote their time to marketing the zoo to external stakeholders to obtain a bigger share of San Diego's tourist dollars.

The results of making tasks more complex and technology less routine and of altering the organization's structure to fit with the new technology have been impressive. Employees are happier and more motivated because they have a bigger sense of ownership in the zoo and what it does, and the zoo has enjoyed yearly increases in attendance, which gave it the resources to pursue and enlarge upon its new mode of operation. Indeed, in 1999 the zoo announced its intention of expanding its operations in Balboa Park and increasing the number of animal exhibits to better satisfy the needs of its visitors.[30]

The same design considerations are applicable at the departmental or functional level: To be effective, departments employing different technologies need different structures.[31] In general, departments performing nonroutine tasks are likely to have organic structures, and those performing routine tasks are likely to have mechanistic structures. An R&D department, for example, is typically organic, and decision making in it is usually decentralized; but the manufacturing and sales functions are usually mechanistic, and decision making within them tends to be centralized. The kind of technology employed at the departmental level determines the choice of structure.[32]

TASK INTERDEPENDENCE: THE THEORY OF JAMES D. THOMPSON

Task interdependence
The manner in which different organizational tasks are related to one another.

Woodward focused on how an organization's technology affects its choice of structure. Perrow's model of technology focuses on the way in which the complexity of tasks affects organizational structure. Another view of technology, developed by James D. Thompson, focuses on the way in which **task interdependence**, the manner in which different organizational tasks are related to one another, affects an organization's technology and structure.[33] When task interdependence is low, people and departments are individually specialized—that is, they work separately and independently to achieve organizational goals. When task interdependence is high, people and departments are jointly specialized—that is, they depend on one another for supplying the inputs and resources they need to get the work done. Thompson identified three types of technology: mediating, long-

FIGURE 9.5

Task Interdependence and Three Types of Technology. James D. Thompson's model of technology focuses on how the relationship among different organizational tasks affects an organization's technology and structure.

Type of technology	Form of task interdependence	Main type of coordination	Strategy for reducing uncertainty	Cost of coordination
Mediating	Pooled Ⓧ Ⓨ Ⓩ (e.g., piecework or franchise)	Standardization	Increase in the number of customers served	Low
Long-linked	Sequential Ⓧ→Ⓨ→Ⓩ (e.g., assembly-line or continuous-process plant)	Planning and scheduling	Slack resources Vertical integration	Medium
Intensive	Reciprocal Ⓧ⇄Ⓨ⇄Ⓩ (e.g., general hospital or research and development laboratory)	Mutual adjustment	Specialism of task activities	High

linked, and intensive (see Figure 9.5). Each of them is associated with a different form of task interdependence.

Mediating Technology and Pooled Interdependence

Mediating technology A technology characterized by a work process in which input, conversion, and output activities can be performed independently of one another.

Mediating technology is characterized by a work process in which input, conversion, and output activities can be performed independently of one another. Mediating technology is based on *pooled task interdependence*, which means that each part of the organization—whether a person, team, or department—contributes separately to the performance of the whole organization. With mediating technology, task interdependence is low because people do not directly rely on others to help them perform their tasks. As illustrated in Figure 9.5, each person or department—X, Y, and Z—performs a separate task. In a management consulting firm or hair salon, each consultant or hairdresser works independently to solve a client's problems. The success of the organization as a whole, however, depends on the collective efforts of everyone employed. The activities of a gymnastic team also illustrate pooled task interdependence. Each team member performs independently and can win or lose a particular event, but the collective score of the team members determines which team wins. The implications of mediating technology for organizational structure can be examined at both the departmental and the organizational level.

At the departmental level, piecework systems best characterize the way this technology operates. In a piecework system, each employee performs a task independently from other employees. In a machine shop, each employee might operate a lathe to produce bolts, and each is evaluated and rewarded on the basis of how many bolts he or she produces. The performance of the manufacturing department as a whole depends on how well each employee individually performs, but employees themselves are not interdependent because one employee's actions have no effect on the actions of others. Similarly, the performance of the sales department depends on the performance of each salesperson, but the performance of one salesperson is not affected by the performance of others in the department.

The use of a mediating technology to accomplish departmental or organizational activities makes it easy to monitor, control, and evaluate the performance of each individual because the output of each person is observable and the same standards can be used to evaluate each employee.[34]

At the organizational level, mediating technology is found in organizations where the activities of different departments are performed separately and there is little need for integration between departments to accomplish organizational goals. In a bank, for example, the activities of the loan department and the checking account department are essentially independent. The routines involved in lending money have no relation to the routines involved in receiving money, but the performance of the bank as a whole depends on how well each department does its job.[35]

Mediating technology at the organizational level is also found in organizations that use franchise arrangements to organize their businesses or that operate a chain of stores. For example, each McDonald's franchise or Wal-Mart store operates essentially independently. The performance of one store does not affect another store, but together all stores determine the performance of the whole organization. Indeed, one strategy for improving organizational performance for an organization operating a mediating technology is to try to attract new sets of customers by increasing the number of operating units or the number of products it offers. A fast-food chain can open a new restaurant. A retail organization can open a new store. A bank can increase the number of financial services it offers customers to attract new business. Indeed, one major goal of banks is to be given the right to sell stocks or mutual funds to increase their population of potential customers.

Over the past decades the use of mediating technology has been increasing because it is relatively inexpensive to operate and manage. Costs are low because organizational activities can be controlled by standardization. Bureaucratic rules and procedures can be used to specify how the activities of different departments are to be coordinated and to outline the procedures that a department needs to follow to ensure that its activities are compatible with those of other departments. Standard operating procedures and electronic media such as e-mail provide the coordination necessary to manage the business. Wal-Mart, for example, coordinates its stores through a nationwide satellite system that informs managers about new-product introductions or changes in rules and procedures.

As computers become more important in coordinating the activities of independent employees or departments, it becomes possible to use a mediating technology to coordinate more types of production activities. Network organizations, discussed in Chapter 6, are developing as computer technologies allow the different departments of an organization to operate separately and at different locations. Similarly, the growth of outsourcing—companies' contracting with other companies to perform their value creation activities (like production or marketing) for them—shows the increasing use of mediating technology as a way of doing business.

Recall from Chapter 6 how Nike contracts with manufacturers throughout the world to produce and distribute products to its customers on a global basis. Nike designs a shoe but then contracts manufacturing, marketing, and other functional activities out to other organizations. Coordination is achieved by standardization of the product range. Nike has rules and procedures specifying the required quality of input materials, the nature of the manufacturing process, and the required quality of the finished product. Nike constantly monitors production and sales information from its network by means of a sophisticated global computer system.

Long-Linked Technology and Sequential Interdependence

Long-linked technology
A technology characterized by a work process in which input, conversion, and output activities must be performed in series.

Long-linked technology, the second type of technology that Thompson identified, is based on a work process in which input, conversion, and output activities must be performed in series. Long-linked technology is based on *sequential task interdependence*, which means that the actions of one person or department directly affect the actions of another, so work cannot be successfully completed by allowing each person or department to operate independently. Figure 9.5 illustrates the dynamics of sequential interdependence. X's activities directly affect Y's ability to perform her task, and in turn the activities of Y directly affect Z's ability to perform.

Mass-production technology is based on sequential task interdependence. The actions of the employee at the beginning of the production line determine how successfully the next employee can perform his task and so forth on down the line. Because sequential interactions have to be carefully coordinated, long-linked technology requires more coordination than mediating technology. One result of sequential interdependence is that any error that occurs at the beginning of the production process becomes magnified at later stages. Sports activities such as relay races or football, in which the performance of one person or group determines how well the next can perform, are based on sequential interdependence. In football, for example, the performance of the defensive line determines how well the offense can perform. If the defense is unable to secure the ball, the offense cannot perform its task: scoring touchdowns.

An organization with long-linked technology can respond in a variety of ways to the need to coordinate sequentially interdependent activities. The organization can program the conversion process to standardize the procedures used to transform inputs into outputs. The organization can also use planning and scheduling to manage linkages between input, conversion, and output processes. To reduce the need to coordinate the input, con-

Slack resources *Extra or surplus resources that enhance an organization's ability to deal with unexpected situations.*

version, and output stages of production, an organization often creates **slack resources**— that is, extra or surplus resources that enhance an organization's ability to deal with unexpected situations. For example, a mass-production organization stockpiles inputs and holds inventories of component parts so that the conversion process is not disrupted if there is a problem with suppliers. Similarly, an organization may stockpile finished products so that it can respond quickly to an increase in customer demand without changing its established conversion processes. Another strategy to control the supply of inputs or distribution of outputs is *vertical integration*, which, as we saw in Chapter 7, involves a company taking over its suppliers or distributors.

The need to manage the increased level of interdependence increases the coordination costs associated with long-linked technology. However, this type of technology provides the organization with enormous benefits, stemming primarily from specialization and the division of labor associated with sequential interdependence. Changing the method of production in a pin factory from a system in which each worker produces a whole pin to a system in which each worker is responsible for only *one* aspect of pin production, such as sharpening the pin, for example, can result in a major gain in productivity. Essentially, the factory moves from using a *mediating* technology, in which each worker performs all production tasks, to a *long-linked* technology, in which tasks become sequentially interdependent.

Tasks are routine in long-linked technology because sequential interdependence allows managers to simplify tasks so that the variability of each worker's task is reduced and the analyzability of each task is increased. On mass-production assembly lines, for example, the coordination of tasks is achieved principally by the speed of the line and the way tasks are ordered. Programming and the constant repetition of simple tasks increase production efficiency. As we saw earlier, Henry Ford was the innovator of long-linked technology. Capitalizing on the gains from specialization and the division of labor, he recognized the cost savings that could result from organizing tasks sequentially and controlling the pace of work by the speed of the production line. This system, however, has two major disadvantages. Employees do not become highly skilled (they learn only a narrow range of simple tasks), and they do not develop the ability to improve their skills because they must follow specified procedures. These drawbacks have had serious consequences, as we will see in the next chapter.

At the organizational level, sequential interdependence means that the outputs of one department become the inputs for another and one department's performance determines how well another department performs. The performance of the manufacturing department depends on the ability of the materials management department to obtain adequate amounts of high-quality inputs in a timely manner. The ability of the sales function to sell finished products depends on the quality of the products coming out of the manufacturing department. Failure or poor performance at one stage has serious consequences for performance at the next stage and for the organization as a whole. In the 1970s, for example, U.S. car manufacturers' ability to sell their products was seriously hampered by the poor quality of the cars they were making in their outdated factories, and their inefficient manufacturing was in part the result of outdated materials management practices.

The pressures of competition in today's global markets are increasing the need for interdependence between departments and, thus, are increasing organizations' need to coordinate departmental activities. As we saw in Chapter 4, many organizations in all industries (Xerox and Hallmark Cards are two we looked at) are moving toward the product team structure to increase interdepartmental coordination. This type of coordination encourages different departments to develop procedures that lead to greater production innovation and efficiency. The United States Automobile Association, a major insurance company, changed its structure when it increased task interdependence between departments to improve its response to customer needs.

ORGANIZATIONAL INSIGHT

9.4 USAA IMPROVING THE DELIVERY OF INTANGIBLE SERVICES

United States Automobile Association (USAA) is the fifth-largest insurer of privately owned cars and homes in the United States. It services the needs of over 2 million customers, manages over $21 billion in assets, and has an enviable record for delivering high-quality customer service. The company was not always so effective, however. Its success is the result of radical changes in the organizing of its tasks and its structure.

Insurance is an intangible service product: It cannot be held, worn, or eaten. Thus, customers base their evaluation of an insurance company on its responsiveness to their needs—on the efficiency with which it processes their claims and services their requests as their insurance needs change. Now, imagine a company where on any given day a customer file had a fifty-fifty chance of being lost because employees were swamped in a sea of paperwork and 300 people were employed simply to go from desk to desk searching for lost files! Imagine also a workplace in which there was a total lack of cooperation between departments, where department managers fought turf battles, and where employees in the actuarial department (which establishes risk and premiums and writes policies) and in the claims service department (which processes clients' claims) did not speak to one another and performed their activities in isolation. This was the situation at USAA, which was using a mediating technology to service clients' needs.

One cause of these problems, according to CEO Robert F. McDermott, was that USAA controlled its activities through a highly centralized structure in which employees had little customer focus because they were overwhelmed by paperwork that they could not process. Vertical communication channels were emphasized, and there was little lateral coordination between departments to solve customers' problems and respond to their needs. The organizational structure was preventing employees from providing the quick, flexible response to customers that is vital in a company where the quality of service is the only criterion that customers use to judge organizational effectiveness.

USAA set out to find a better way to organize its task relationships. CEO McDermott decided that the company should move to a long-linked technology in which the tasks of the different departments were more interdependent and customers could be given quicker feedback and service. To achieve this change, the policy-writing and service departments were linked together and then divided into five separate groups. Each group was assigned to service the needs of one-fifth of the company's clients. This move to sequential interdependence brought employees who were writing policies into closer contact with the service employees, and all employees were brought closer to the customer. In each of the five groups, decisions were made closer to the source of the problem, and employees developed new ways of responding to the customer. Moreover, the five groups were placed in competition with each other because the same criteria would be used to evaluate each group. The criteria included the number of customer complaints and growth in insurance sales.[36] Competition among groups motivated employees to find better ways of coordinating their activities and servicing customers.

As a result of the change in technology, the organizational hierarchy became flatter, for supervisors were required only to handle exceptions that employees themselves were unable to solve. Decision-making authority was decentralized to the five groups, which were given responsibility for developing new procedures for increasing their effectiveness. In the new flatter, decentralized structure, supervisors were freed from the need to monitor the flow of paperwork and mediate cross-functional disputes. They too could develop improved work procedures and develop better ways to deliver customer service. The new structure was backed by an incentive system that rewarded customer service, and new opportunities for promotion opened up as the company attracted new clients with its improved service. As a result of all these changes, USAA's client base grew from 650,000 in 1970 to over 2.5 million in 1999.[37] For USAA, the development of a new structure that matched its new technology paid off.

Intensive Technology
and Reciprocal Interdependence

Intensive technology

A technology character-ized by a work process in which input, conversion, and output activities are inseparable.

Intensive technology, the third type of technology identified by Thompson, is charac-terized by a work process in which input, conversion, and output activities are insepara-ble. Intensive technology is based on *reciprocal task interdependence*, which means that the activities of all people and all departments are fully dependent on one another. Not only do X's actions affect what Y and Z can do, but the actions of Z also affect Y's and X's per-formance. The task relationships of X, Y, and Z are reciprocally interdependent (see Fig-ure 9.5). Reciprocal interdependence makes it impossible to program in advance a sequence of tasks or procedures to solve a problem because, in Thompson's words, "the selection, combination, and order of [the tasks'] application are determined by *feedback from the object [problem] itself.*"[38] Thus, the move to reciprocal interdependence and intensive technology has two effects: Technical complexity declines as the ability of managers to control and predict the work process lessens, and tasks become more complex and nonroutine.

Hospitals are organizations that operate an intensive technology. A hospital's great-est source of uncertainty is the impossibility of predicting the types of problems for which patients (clients) will seek treatment. At any time, a general hospital has to have on hand the knowledge, machines, and services of specialist departments capable of solving a huge number and great variety of medical problems. The hospital requires, for example, an emergency room, X-ray facilities, a testing laboratory, an operating room and staff, skilled nursing staff, doctors, and hospital wards. What is wrong with each patient determines the selection and combination of activities and technology to convert a hospital's inputs (sick people) into outputs (well people). The uncertainty of the input (patient) means that tasks cannot be programmed in advance, as they can be when interdependence is sequential.

Basketball, soccer, and rugby are other activities that depend on reciprocal interde-pendence. The current state of play determines the sequence of moves from one player to the next. The fast-moving action of these sports requires players to make judgments quick-ly and obtain feedback from the state of play before deciding what moves to make.

On a departmental level, research and development departments operate with an in-tensive technology. The sequence and content of an R&D department's activities are de-termined by the problems the department is trying to solve—for example, a cure for cancer. R&D is so expensive because the unpredictability of the input-conversion-output process makes it impossible to specify in advance the skills and resources that will be need-ed to solve the problem at hand. A pharmaceutical company such as Merck, for example, creates many different research and development teams. Every team is equipped with whatever functional resources it needs in the hope that at least one team will stumble onto a wonder drug that will justify the immense resource expenditures (each new drug costs about $400 million to develop).

The difficulty of specifying the sequencing of tasks that is characteristic of intensive technology makes necessary a high degree of coordination and makes intensive technol-ogy more expensive to manage than either mediating or long-linked technology. Mutu-al adjustment replaces programming and standardization as the principal method of coordination. Product team and matrix structures are suited to operating intensive tech-nologies because they provide the coordination and the decentralized control that allow departments to cooperate to solve problems. At Microsoft, for example, the whole com-pany is organized into product teams so that it can quickly shift resources to the projects that seem most promising. Also, mutual adjustment and a flat structure allow an orga-nization to quickly exploit new developments and areas for research that arise during the research process itself. Hewlett-Packard designed a new organizational structure to operate its new intensive approach to product development.

ORGANIZATIONAL INSIGHT

9.5 A NEW APPROACH AT HEWLETT-PACKARD

In 1989, Hewlett-Packard (H-P), based in the high-tech Silicon Valley of California, was under siege by competitors that were bringing out competing products such as computer workstations and minicomputers at a rate that H-P could not match. Then CEO John A. Young traced the source of the problem to H-P's product development process. Product development at H-P was a sequential process. New projects went from one department to another, and 23 committees oversaw every decision in every department before moving a project to the next stage—for example, from product R&D to engineering to manufacturing to marketing. The result was slow decision making and late-to-market products.

Young decided to reorganize the technology of the conversion process and the form of task interdependence between departments. His goal was to cut the time needed to bring out H-P's next generation of workstations or laser printers. He reorganized several functions into small product development teams in which people from each function worked together from the beginning to the end of a project.

To manage the complexity of this reciprocal task interdependence, Young redesigned the company's structure. He flattened the organizational hierarchy by cutting two layers of management, he decentralized control of the product development process to the team, and he assigned each team its own sales staff to speed the introduction of the product to the market. He also dissolved much of the committee structure that had slowed decision making.[39] With this new, streamlined, organic structure, H-P has dramatically cut the time it takes to bring new products to market. What used to take months or years now takes only weeks, and the company once again became a dominant force in the computer industry.

However, by the late 1990s, H-P was once again in trouble because of the speed at which developments in the Internet software industry had changed the nature of the competitive game. In 1999 H-P appointed a new CEO, Carly Fiorino, to try to speed up the company's product development program, and she has already instituted changes to help H-P employees act more entrepreneurially and to loosen up the company's famous culture, which has been unable to respond fast enough to the changes currently taking place.[40]

Organizations do not voluntarily use an intensive technology to achieve their goals because it is so expensive to operate. They are forced to use it by the nature of the output they choose to produce. Whenever possible, organizations attempt to reduce the task interdependence necessary to coordinate their activities and revert to a long-linked technology, which is more controllable and predictable. In recent years, for example, hospitals have attempted to control escalating management costs by using forecasting techniques to determine how many resources they need to have on hand to meet customer (patient) demands. If, over a specified period, a hospital knows on average how many broken bones or cardiac arrests it can expect, it knows how many operating theaters it will need to have in readiness and how many doctors, nurses, and technicians to have on call to meet patient demand. This knowledge allows the hospital to control costs. Similarly, in R&D, an organization needs to develop decision-making rules that allow it to decide when to stop investing in a line of research that is showing little promise of success and how to allocate resources among projects to try to maximize potential returns from the investment.

Specialism *Producing only a narrow range of outputs.*

Another strategy that organizations can pursue to reduce the costs associated with intensive technology is **specialism**—producing only a narrow range of outputs. A hospital that specializes in the treatment of cancer or heart disease narrows the range of problems to which it is exposed and can target all its resources to solving those problems. It is the general hospital that faces the most uncertainty. Similarly, a pharmaceutical company typically restricts the areas in which it does research. A company may decide to focus on drugs that combat high blood pressure or diabetes or depression. This specialist strategy allows the organization to use its resources efficiently and reduces problems of coordination.[41]

Managerial Implications: Analyzing Technology

1. Analyze an organization's or a department's input-conversion-output processes to identify the skills, knowledge, tools, and machinery that are central to the production of goods and services.
2. Analyze the level of technical complexity associated with the production of goods and services. Evaluate whether technical complexity can be increased to improve efficiency and reduce costs. For example, is an advanced computer system available; are employees using up-to-date techniques and procedures?
3. Analyze the level of task variety and task analyzability associated with organizational and departmental tasks. Are there ways to reduce task variability or increase task analyzability to increase effectiveness? For example, can procedures be developed to make the work process more predictable and controllable?
4. Analyze the form of task interdependence inside a department and between departments. Evaluate whether the task interdependence being used results in the most effective way of producing goods or servicing the needs of customers. For example, would raising the level of coordination between departments improve efficiency?
5. After analyzing an organization's or a department's technology, analyze its structure, and evaluate the fit between technology and structure. Can the fit be improved? What costs and benefits are associated with changing the technology-structure relationship?
6. Study the principles of advanced manufacturing technology discussed in the next chapter, and evaluate whether they can be used to increase the value created by an organization or department.

TECHNOLOGY AND CULTURE

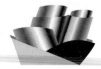

This chapter has discussed in detail the relationship between technology and structure, but so far it has not spent much time examining the relationship between technology and culture. The technology-culture relationship is important, however, for there is a stream of research that suggests that the nature of an organization's technology has important effects on the kinds of values and norms that emerge in an organization, which affect the way people and subunits behave.[42]

One of the first pieces of research that revealed the nature of the relationship between technology and culture emerged from a study of changing work practices in the British coal-mining industry.[43] After World War II, new technology that changed work relationships between miners was introduced into the British mining industry. Previously, coal mining had, for the most part, been a small-batch or craft process, which meant that teams of skilled miners dug the coal from the coal face underground and performed all the other activities necessary to transport the cut coal to the surface. Work took place in a confined space under difficult and dangerous conditions where productivity depended on close cooperation among team members. In other words, there was a high level of reciprocal interdependence present in the work process. To manage this high level of task interdependence, and to combat the stress of their dangerous and confining working conditions, workers developed strong values and norms to get the job done. Workers knew one another intimately; they had their own informal status hierarchy, with those who had the most skill in cutting coal at the top; and the informal team leader managed the work process and prescribed acceptable instrumental values.

This method of coal mining, called the "hand got method," approximated small-batch technology. However, after the war, to increase efficiency, managers on the surface decided to replace small-batch technology with a new technology called the "longwall method" of coal mining. This method involved a mechanized, mass-production technology. Coal was now cut using powered drills and transported to the surface on conveyer belts. Tasks became more routine as the work process was programmed and standardized. On paper, this new technology was expected to dramatically increase mining efficiency. After its introduction, however, efficiency rose only slowly, and absenteeism among miners, which had always been high because of the nature of the work, increased dramatically.

Consultants were called into the mine to study why the expected gains in efficiency were not obtained. The explanation they offered for the poor results was that to operate the new technology efficiently, management had changed the structure of task and role relationships among the miners to reflect the more mechanized production system. However, the new task and role relationships had destroyed the strong system of values and norms that provided miners with social support, disrupted long-established informal working relationships among the miners, and disrupted group cohesiveness. In other words, by changing technology and moving to a more mass-production method, managers had wrecked the old organizational culture, and nothing had emerged to replace it.

The solution to the problem advocated by the researchers was to link the new technology with the old social system by recreating the old system of tasks and roles and decentralizing authority to the work group. In this way, they hoped to recreate a modified form of the old culture based on values and norms similar to those that had existed previously. When management redesigned the work process to achieve this, productivity did improve and absenteeism declined.

Sociotechnical systems theory The idea that managers need to "jointly optimize" the workings of an organization's technical and social systems to promote effectiveness.

This study led to the development of **sociotechnical systems theory,** which argues that managers need to fit or "jointly optimize" the workings of an organization's technical and social systems—or, in terms of the present discussion, culture—to promote effectiveness.[44] A poor fit between an organization's technology and social system leads to failure, but a close fit leads to success. The lesson to take from this theory is that, when changing task and role relationships, managers must recognize the need to gradually adjust the technical and social systems so that the culture and cohesiveness of a subunit are not disrupted.

This pioneering study has been followed by many other studies that show the importance of the link between type of technology and cultural values and norms.[45] Managers need to be sensitive to the fact that the way they structure the work process affects the way people and groups behave. Compare the following two mass-production settings, for example. In the first, managers routinize the technology, standardize the work process, and require workers to perform repetitive tasks as quickly as possible; workers are assigned to a place on the production line and are not allowed to move or switch jobs; and managers monitor workers closely and make all the decisions involving control of the work process. In the second, managers standardize the work process but encourage workers to find better ways to perform tasks; workers are allowed to switch jobs; and workers are formed into teams that are empowered to monitor and control important aspects of their own performance. What differences in values and norms will emerge between these two types of sociotechnical systems? And what will be their effect on performance? Many researchers have argued that the more team-based system will promote the development of values and norms that will boost efficiency and product quality. Indeed, the goal of total quality management, the continuous improvement in product quality, draws heavily on the principles embedded in sociotechnical systems theory. Total quality management is discussed in detail in the following chapter.

SUMMARY

Technical complexity, the differences between routine and nonroutine tasks, and task interdependence jointly explain why some technologies are more complex and difficult to control than others and why organizations adopt different structures to operate their technology. In general, input, conversion, and output processes that depend primarily on people and departments cooperating and trading knowledge that is difficult to program into standard operating routines require the most coordination. An organization that needs extensive coordination and control to operate its technology also needs an organic structure to organize its tasks.

Managers can use the concepts of technical complexity, nonroutine tasks, and task interdependence to analyze the technology in use and design an appropriate structure to manage the technology. Chapter 9 has made the following main points:

1. Technology is the combination of skills, knowledge, abilities, techniques, materials, machines, computers, tools, and other equipment that people use to convert raw materials into valuable goods and services.

2. Technology is involved in an organization's input, conversion, and output processes. An effective organization manages its technology to meet the needs of stakeholders, foster innovation, and increase operating efficiency.

3. Technical complexity is the extent to which a production process is controllable and predictable. According to Joan Woodward, technical complexity differentiates small-batch and unit production, large-batch and mass production, and continuous-process production.

4. Woodward argued that each technology is associated with a different organizational structure because each technology presents different control and coordination problems. In general, small-batch and continuous-process technologies are associated with an organic structure, and mass production is associated with a mechanistic structure.

5. The argument that technology determines structure is known as the technological imperative. According to the Aston Studies, however, organizational size is more important than technology in determining an organization's choice of structure.

6. According to Charles Perrow, two dimensions underlie the difference between routine and nonroutine tasks and technologies: task variability and task analyzability. The higher the level of task variability and the lower the level of task analyzability, the more complex and nonroutine are organizational tasks.

7. Using task variability and analyzability, Perrow described four types of technology: craftswork, nonroutine research, engineering production, and routine manufacturing.

8. The more routine tasks are, the more likely an organization is to use a mechanistic structure. The more complex tasks are, the more likely an organization is to use an organic structure.

9. James D. Thompson focused on the way in which task interdependence affects an organization's technology and structure. Task interdependence is the manner in which different organizational tasks are related to one another and the degree to which the performance of one person or department depends on and affects the performance of another.

10. Thompson identified three types of technology, which he associated with three forms of task interdependence: mediating technology and pooled interdependence; long-linked technology and sequential interdependence; and intensive technology and reciprocal interdependence.

11. The higher the level of task interdependence, the more likely an organization is to use mutual adjustment rather than standardization to coordinate work activities.

12. Sociotechnical systems theory argues that to promote effectiveness, managers must jointly optimize an organization's technical and social systems. Values, norms, and organizational culture are all affected by the way managers perform this task.

DISCUSSION QUESTIONS

1. How can technology increase organizational effectiveness?

2. How does small-batch technology differ from mass-production technology?

3. Why is technical complexity greatest with continuous-process technology? How does technical complexity affect organizational structure?

4. What makes some tasks more complex than others? Give an example of an organization that uses each of the four types of technology identified by Perrow.

5. What level of task interdependence is associated with the activities of (a) a large accounting firm, (b) a fast-food restaurant, and (c) a biotechnology company? What different kinds of structure are you likely to find in these organizations? Why?

6. Find an organization in your city and analyze how its technology works. Use the concepts discussed in this chapter: technical complexity, nonroutine tasks, and task interdependence.

ORGANIZATIONAL THEORY IN ACTION

PRACTICING ORGANIZATIONAL THEORY:
CHOOSING A TECHNOLOGY

Form groups of three to five people and discuss the following scenario:

You are investors who are planning to open a large computer store in a big city on the western seaboard. You plan to offer a complete range of computer hardware ranging from UNIX-based workstations, to powerful PCs and laptop computers, to a full range of printers and scanners. In addition, you propose to offer a full range of software products, from office management systems to personal financial software and children's computer games. Your strategy is to be the "one stop" shopping place where all kind of customers—from large companies to private individuals—can get everything they want from salespeople who can design a complete system to meet each customer's unique needs.

You are meeting to decide which kind of technology—that is, which combination of skills, knowledge, techniques, and task relationships—will best allow you to achieve your goal.

1. Analyze the level of (a) technical complexity and (b) task variability and task analyzability associated with the kinds of tasks needed to achieve your strategy.
2. Given your answer to question 1, what kind of task interdependence between employees and departments will best allow you to pursue your strategy?
3. Based on this analysis, what kind of technology will you choose in your store, and what kind of structure and culture will you create to manage your technology most effectively?

MAKING THE CONNECTION #9

Find an example of a company operating with one of the technologies identified in this chapter. Which technology is the company using? Why is the company using it? How does this technology affect the organization's structure?

Analyzing the Organization: Design Module #9

This module focuses on the technology your company uses to produce goods and services and the problems and issues associated with the use of this technology.

ASSIGNMENT

Using the information at your disposal, and drawing inferences about your company's technology from the activities in which your organization engages, answer the following questions.

1. What kinds of goods or services does your organization produce? Are input, conversion, or output activities the source of greatest uncertainty for your organization?
2. What role does technology in the form of knowledge play in the production of the organization's goods or services?
3. What role does materials technology play in the production of the organization's goods and services?
4. What is the organization's level of technical complexity? Does the organization use a small-batch, mass-production, or continuous-process technology?

5. Use the concepts of task variability and task analyzability to describe the complexity of your organization's activities. Which of the four types of technology identified by Perrow does your organization use?

6. What forms of task interdependence between people and between departments characterize your organization's work process? Which of the three types of technology identified by Thompson does your organization use?

7. The analysis you have done so far might lead you to expect your company to operate with a particular kind of structure. What kind? To what extent does your organization's structure seem to fit with the characteristics of the organization's technology? For example, is the structure organic or mechanistic?

8. Do you think that your organization is operating its technology effectively? Do you see any ways in which it could improve its technical efficiency, innovativeness, or ability to respond to customers?

Case for Analysis:
THE SHAPE OF THINGS TO COME

Intense global competition in the 1990s caused many companies to take another look at the way they manufacture products. In Japan, in particular, the soaring price of the yen in the 1990s put particular pressure on large car and electronics manufacturers to look at ways to cut production costs. To find ways to cut costs, Japanese companies scrutinized the technology they were using, and the mass-production system was the subject of most of this attention.

Traditionally, Japanese companies have used the conveyer belt system pioneered by Ford to mass-produce large volumes of identical products. In this system, workers are positioned along a straight or linear production line that can be hundreds of feet long. In examining how this system works, Japanese production managers have come to realize that a considerable amount of handling time is wasted as the product being assembled is passed from worker to worker, and that a line can only move as fast as the least capable worker. Moreover, this system is only efficient when large quantities of the same product are being produced. If customized products are needed, the production line is typically down while it is being retooled for the next product.

Recognizing these problems, production engineers began to search for assembly-line layouts that could alleviate these problems and experimented with layouts of various shapes, such as spirals, Ys, 6s, or even insects. At a Sony camcorder plant in Kohda, Japan, for example, Sony dismantled its previous mass-production system in which 50 workers worked sequentially to build a camcorder and replaced it with a spiral arrangement only 40 feet long in which four workers perform all the operations necessary to assemble the camcorder. Sony says this new arrangement is 10 percent more efficient than the old system. Why? Because it allows the most efficient assemblers to perform at a higher level by re-ducing handling time and not passing work from one worker to another.[46]

In the United States, too, these new production layouts, which are normally referred to as cell layouts, are becoming increasingly common. It has been estimated that 40 percent of small companies and 70 percent of large companies have experimented with the new designs. Bayside Controls Inc., for example, a small gearhead manufacturer in Queens, New York, converted its 35-person assembly line into a four-cell design in which seven to nine workers form a cell. The members of each cell perform all the operations involved in making the gearheads, such as measuring, cutting, and assembling the new gearheads. Bayside's managers say that the average production time it takes to make a gear has dropped to two days, from six weeks, and it now makes 75 gearheads a day (up from 50 before the change) so costs have also gone down.[47] Once again, there has been a large savings in handling costs, inventory costs are lower because production is faster, and employees are more motivated to produce high-quality products with the new system. An additional advantage is that cell designs allow companies to be very responsive to the needs of individual customers because this system permits the quick manufacture of small quantities of customized products.

1. How do the new "cell" designs change the level of technical complexity, task variability and task analyzability, and task interdependence?

2. Based on this analysis, of what type of technology discussed in the chapter does the new system remind you?

3. What are the advantages associated with the use of the new technology?

REFERENCES

1. H. Ford, "Progressive Manufacture," *Encyclopedia Britannica*, 13th ed. (New York: The Encyclopedia Co., 1926).
2. R. Edwards, *Contested Terrain: The Transformation of the Workplace in the Twentieth Century* (New York: Basic Books, 1979).
3. "Survey: The Endless Road," *The Economist*, 17 October 1992, p. 4.
4. Edwards, *Contested Terrain*, p. 119.
5. D. M. Rousseau, "Assessment of Technology in Organizations: Closed Versus Open Systems Approaches," *Academy of Management Review*, 1979, vol. 4, pp. 531–542; W. R. Scott, *Organizations: Rational, Natural, and Open Systems* (Englewood Cliffs, NJ: Prentice Hall, 1981).
6. J. Woodward, *Management and Technology* (London: Her Majesty's Stationery Office, 1958), p. 12.
7. Woodward, *Management and Technology*, p. 11.
8. J. Woodward, *Industrial Organization: Theory and Practice* (London: Oxford University Press, 1965).
9. "The Supply Police," *Newsweek*, 15 February 1993, pp. 48–49.
10. H. V. Dion, "Nike Hit With Suit on Labor Practises," *Chicago Tribune*, 21 April 1998, p. 3.
11. W. Echison, "It's Europe's Turn to Sweat About Sweatshops," *Business Week*, 19 July 1999, p. 96.
12. Woodward, *Industrial Organization*.
13. Woodward, *Management and Technology*.
14. C. Perrow, *Normal Accidents: Living with High-Risk Technologies* (New York: Basic Books, 1984).
15. E. Harvey, "Technology and the Structure of Organizations," *American Sociological Review*, 1968, vol. 33, pp. 241–259; W. L. Zwerman, *New Perspectives on Organizational Effectiveness* (Westport, CT: Greenwood, 1970).
16. D. J. Hickson, D. S. Pugh, and D. C. Pheysey, "Operations Technology and Organizational Structure: An Empirical Reappraisal," *Administrative Science Quarterly*, 1969, vol. 14, pp. 378–397; D. S. Pugh, "The Aston Program of Research: Retrospect and Prospect," in A. H. Van de Ven and W. F. Joyce, eds., *Perspectives on Organizational Design and Behavior* (New York: Wiley, 1981), pp. 135–166; H. E. Aldrich, "Technology and Organizational Structure: A Reexamination of the Findings of the Aston Group," *Administrative Science Quarterly*, 1972, vol. 17, pp. 26–43.
17. J. Child and R. Mansfield, "Technology, Size, and Organization Structure," *Sociology*, 1972, vol. 6, pp. 369–393.
18. Hickson, Pugh, and Pheysey, "Operations Technology and Organizational Structure."
19. C. Perrow, *Organizational Analysis: A Sociological View* (Belmont, CA: Wadsworth, 1970).
20. Ibid.
21. Ibid., p. 21.
22. Ibid.
23. This section draws heavily on C. Perrow, "A Framework for the Comparative Analysis of Organizations," *American Sociological Review*, 1967, vol. 32, pp. 194–208.
24. Perrow, *Organizational Analysis*; C. Gresov, "Exploring Fit and Misfit with Multiple Contingencies," *Administrative Science Quarterly*, 1989, vol. 34, pp. 431–453.
25. Edwards, *Contested Terrain*.
26. J. Beyer and H. Trice, "A Re-Examination of the Relations Between Size and Various Components of Organizational Complexity," *Administrative Science Quarterly*, 1985, vol. 30, pp. 462–481.
27. L. Argote, "Input Uncertainty and Organizational Coordination of Subunits," *Administrative Science Quarterly*, 1982, vol. 27, pp. 420–434.
28. G. R. Jones, "Task Visibility, Free Riding, and Shirking: Explaining the Effect of Structure and Technology on Employee Behavior," *Academy of Management Review*, 1984, vol. 9, pp. 684–696.
29. R. T. Keller, "Technology-Information Processing Fit and the Performance of R&D Project Groups: A Test of Contingency Theory," *Academy of Management Review*, 1994, vol. 37, pp. 167–179.
30. J. Steinberg, "Zoo Hires Expansion Opponent as Advisor; Officials Take a New Look at Balboa Plan," *San Diego Tribune*, 8 October 1999, p. 7.
31. C. Perrow, "Hospitals: Technology, Structure, and Goals," in J. March, ed., *The Handbook of Organizations* (Chicago: Rand McNally, 1965), pp. 910–971.
32. D. E. Comstock and W. R. Scott, "Technology and the Structure of Subunits," *Administrative Science Quarterly*, 1977, vol. 22, pp. 177–202; A. H. Van de Ven and A. L. Delbecq, "A Task Contingent Model of Work Unit Structure," *Administrative Science Quarterly*, 1974, vol. 19, pp. 183–197.
33. J. D. Thompson, *Organizations in Action* (New York: McGraw-Hill, 1967).
34. W. G. Ouchi, "The Relationship Between Organizational Structure and Organizational Control," *Administrative Science Quarterly*, 1977, vol. 22, pp. 95–113.
35. Thompson, *Organizations in Action*.
36. T. Thomas, "Service Comes First: An Interview with USAA's Robert F. McDermott," *Harvard Business Review*, September–October 1991, pp. 116–127.
37. www.usaa.com, Annual Report, 1999.
38. Thompson, *Organizations in Action*, p. 17.
39. R. D. Hof, "From Dinosaur to Gazelle," *Business Week*, 12 August 1992.
40. "Hewlett-Packard Sees Pressure On Sales," *Investor's Business Daily*, 4 October 1999, p. A7.
41. Thompson, *Organizations in Action*; G. R. Jones, "Organization-Client Transactions and Organizational Governance Structures," *Academy of Management Journal*, 1987, vol. 30, pp. 197–218.
42. See, for example, E. Jaques, *The Changing Culture of a Factory* (New York: Dryden Press, 1951); S. Barley, "Technology as an Occasion for Structuring: Observations on CT Scanners and the Social Order of Radiology Departments," *Administrative Science Quarterly*, 1986, vol. 31, pp. 78–108; G. Kunda, *Engineering Culture* (Philadelphia: Temple University Press, 1992).
43. E. L. Trist and K. W. Bamforth, "Some Social and Psychological Consequences of the Long Wall Method of Coal Mining," *Human Relations*, 1951, vol. 4, pp. 3–38; F. E. Emery and E. L. Trist, *Socio-Technical Systems*, Proceedings of the 6th Annual International Meeting of the Institute of Management Sciences, pp. 92–93. London, 1965.
44. E. L. Trist, G. Higgins, H. Murray, and A. G. Pollock, *Organizational Choice* (London: Tavistock, 1965); J. C. Taylor, "The Human Side of Work: The Socio-Technical Approach to Work Design," *Personnel Review*, 1975, vol. 4, pp. 17–22.
45. For a review, see, D. R. Denison, "What Is the Difference Between Organizational Culture and Organizational Climate? A Native's Point of View on a Decade of Paradigm Wars," *Academy of Management Review*, 1996, vol. 21, pp. 619–654.
46. M. Williams, "Back to the Past," *Wall Street Journal*, 24 October 1994, p. A1.
47. S. N. Mehta, "Cell Manufacturing Gains Acceptance at Smaller Plants," *Wall Street Journal*, 15 September 1994, p. B2.

Chapter 10

MANAGING
the NEW TECHNOLOGICAL
ENVIRONMENT

Effective organizations are always searching for ways to create more value and increase effectiveness. This chapter examines how organizations have adopted both advanced manufacturing and advanced information technologies to increase their effectiveness. First, the chapter examines how new technological developments have dramatically changed the way production activities are carried out in organizations. The three dimensions of technology discussed in Chapter 9—technical complexity, nonroutine tasks, and task interdependence—are used to frame this discussion of the impact of new technology on organizations. Second, the chapter discusses how changes in information technology, particularly the use of the Internet and computers and computer-related hardware and software, have changed the way work is done and impacted organizational structure and culture. By the end of this chapter, you will understand how recent advances in technology have changed the way organizations and their members operate.

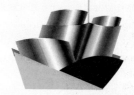

FROM MASS PRODUCTION TO ADVANCED MANUFACTURING TECHNOLOGY

One of the most influential advances in technology in this century was the introduction of mass-production technology by Henry Ford. It allowed his company to produce large volumes of a standardized product (the Model T car) at a low cost and to pursue a low-cost business-level strategy.[1] (Recall from Chapter 7 that a low-cost strategy attracts customers by providing them with low-priced products.) To reduce costs, a mass-production company must maximize the gains from economies of scale and from the division of labor associated with large-scale production. There are two ways to do this. One is by using dedicated machines and standardized work procedures. The other is by protecting the conversion process against production slowdowns or stoppages.

Dedicated machines
Machines that can perform only one operation at a time.

Traditional mass production is based on the use of **dedicated machines**—machines that can perform only one operation at a time, such as repeatedly cutting or drilling or stamping out a car body part.[2] To maximize volume and efficiency, a dedicated machine produces a narrow range of products but does so cheaply. Thus, this method of production traditionally resulted in low production costs.

When the component being manufactured needs to be changed, a dedicated machine must be retooled—that is, fitted with new dies or jigs—before it can handle the change. When Ford retooled one of his plants to switch from the Model T to the Model A, he had to close the plant for over six months. Because retooling a dedicated machine can take days, during which no production is possible, long production runs are required for maximum efficiency and lowest costs. Thus, for example, Ford might make 50,000 right-side door panels in a single production run and stockpile them until they are needed because the money saved by using dedicated machines outweighs the combined costs of lost production and carrying the doors in inventory. In a similar way, both the use of a production line to assemble the final product and the employment of **fixed workers**—workers who perform standardized work procedures—increase an organization's control over the conversion process.

Fixed workers *Workers who perform standardized, repetitive work procedures.*

A mass-production organization also attempts to reduce costs by protecting its conversion processes from the uncertainty that results from disruptions in the external environment.[3] Threats to the conversion process come from both the input and the output stages, but an organization can stockpile inputs and outputs to reduce these threats (see Figure 10.1a).

At the input stage, an organization tries to control its access to inputs by keeping raw materials and semifinished components on hand to prevent shortages that would lead to a slowdown or break in production. The role of purchasing, for example, is to negotiate with suppliers contracts that guarantee the organization an adequate supply of inputs. At the output stage, an organization tries to control its ability to dispose of its outputs. It does so by stockpiling finished products so that it can respond quickly to customer demands. An organization can also advertise heavily to maintain customer demand. In that case, the role of the sales department is to maintain demand for an organization's products so that production does not need to slow down or stop because no one wants the organization's outputs. An organization can further increase certainty at both stages by vertically integrating and taking over its suppliers and distributors to protect its access to raw materials and to its customers (see Chapter 7).

The high technical complexity, the routine nature of production tasks, and the sequential task interdependence characteristic of mass production all make an organization very inflexible. The term *fixed automation* is sometimes used to describe the traditional way of organizing production. The combination of dedicated machines (which perform only

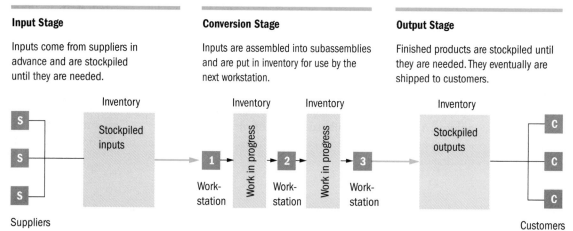

Input Stage

Inputs come from suppliers in advance and are stockpiled until they are needed.

Conversion Stage

Inputs are assembled into subassemblies and are put in inventory for use by the next workstation.

Output Stage

Finished products are stockpiled until they are needed. They eventually are shipped to customers.

A. The Work Flow in Mass Production. Inventory is used to protect the conversion process and to prevent slowdowns or stoppages in production.

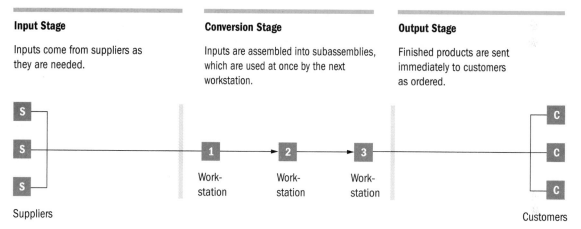

Input Stage

Inputs come from suppliers as they are needed.

Conversion Stage

Inputs are assembled into subassemblies, which are used at once by the next workstation.

Output Stage

Finished products are sent immediately to customers as ordered.

B. The Work Flow with Advanced Manufacturing Technology. No inventory buffers are used between workstations.

FIGURE 10.1

A. The Work Flow in Mass Production.
Inventory is used to protect the conversion process and to prevent slowdowns or stoppages in production.
B. The Work Flow with Advanced Manufacturing Technology.
No inventory buffers are used between workstations.

a narrow range of operations), fixed workers (who perform a narrow range of fixed tasks), and large stocks of inventory (which can be used to produce only one product or a few related products) makes it very expensive and difficult for an organization to begin to manufacture different kinds of products when customer preferences change.

Suppose an organization had a new technology that allowed it to make a wide range of products—products that could be customized to the needs of individual customers. This ability would increase demand for its products. If the new technology also allowed the organization to rapidly introduce new products that incorporated new features or the latest design trends, demand would increase even more. Finally, suppose the cost of producing this wide range of new, customized products with the new technology was the same as, or only slightly more than, the cost of producing a narrow, standardized product line. Clearly, the new technology would greatly increase organizational effectiveness

Advanced manufacturing technology (AMT)
Innovations in materials and knowledge technology that change the work process of traditional mass-production organizations.

and allow the organization to pursue both a low-cost and a differentiation strategy, to attract customers by giving them advanced, high-quality, reliable products at low prices.[4]

What changes would an organization need to make to its technology to make it flexible enough to respond to customers while controlling costs? In the last 20 years, many new technological developments have allowed organizations to achieve these two goals. The new developments are sometimes called *flexible production, lean production*, or *computer-aided production*. Here we will consider them to be components of advanced manufacturing technology.[5] **Advanced manufacturing technology** (AMT) consists of innovations in *materials technology* and in *knowledge technology* that change the work process of traditional mass-production organizations.

ADVANCED MANUFACTURING TECHNOLOGY: INNOVATIONS IN MATERIALS TECHNOLOGY

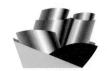

Materials technology
Machinery, computers, and other equipment.

Materials technology comprises machinery, other equipment, and computers. Innovations in materials technology are based on a new view of the linkages among input, conversion, and output activities.[6] Traditional mass production tries to protect the conversion process from disruptions at the input and output stages by using stockpiles of inventory as buffers to increase control and reduce uncertainty. With AMT, however, the organization actively seeks ways to increase its ability to integrate or coordinate the flow of resources among input, conversion, and output activities. AMT allows an organization to reduce uncertainty not by using inventory stockpiles but by developing the capacity to quickly adjust and control its procedures to eliminate the need for inventory at both the input and the output stages (see Figure 10.1b).[7] Several innovations in materials technology allow organizations to reduce the costs and speed the process of producing goods and services. Computer-aided design, computer-aided materials management, just-in-time inventory systems, and computer-integrated manufacturing affect one another and jointly improve organizational effectiveness. The first three are techniques for coordinating the input and conversion stages of production. The last one increases the technical complexity of the conversion stage.

Computer-Aided Design

Mass-production systems are set up to produce a large quantity of a few products. To some degree, this arrangement reflects the fact that a large part of the cost associated with mass production is incurred at the design stage.[8] In general, the more complex a product is, the higher are the design costs. The costs of designing a new car, for example, are enormous. Ford's new world car, the Mondeo, cost over $6 billion to develop. At Rolls-Royce, 80 percent of the cost of production is consumed by the design of the 2,000 components that constitute a Rolls-Royce car.

Computer-aided design (CAD) *An AMT that greatly simplifies and enhances the design process.*

Traditionally, the design of new parts involved the laborious construction of prototypes and scale models, a process akin to unit or small-batch production. **Computer-aided design (CAD)** is an advanced manufacturing technique that greatly simplifies the design process. CAD makes it possible to design a new component or microcircuit on a computer screen and then press a button, not to print out the plans for the part but to physically produce the part itself. Several research groups at Massachusetts Institute of Technology are working on "printers" that squirt a stream of liquid metal droplets to create three-dimensional objects. Detailed prototypes can be sculpted according to the computer program and can be redesigned quickly if necessary. Thus, for example, an engineer at Ford who wants to see how a new gear will work in a transmission assembly, or an engineer at Intel who wonders how a new chip will function, can experiment quickly and cheaply to fine-tune the design of these inputs.[9]

Cutting the costs of product design by using CAD can contribute to both a low-cost and a differentiation advantage. Design advances that CAD makes possible can improve the efficiency of manufacturing. Well-designed components are easily fitted together into a subassembly, and well-designed subassemblies are easily fitted to other subassemblies. Improvements at the input design stage also make selling and servicing products easier at the output stage. The risk of later failure or of breakdown is reduced if potential problems have been eliminated at the design stage. Designing quality into a product up front improves competitive advantage and reduces costs. Toyota's core competence in product design, for example, evidenced by its relatively low recall rates, gives its cars a competitive advantage. Finally, CAD enhances flexibility because it reduces the difficulty and lowers the cost of customizing a product to satisfy particular customers. In essence, computer-aided design brings to large-scale manufacturing one of the benefits of small-batch production—customized product design—but at far less cost. It also enhances an organization's ability to respond quickly to changes in its environment.[10]

Computer-Aided Materials Management

Computer-aided materials management (CAMM) An AMT that is used to manage the flow of raw materials and component parts into the conversion process.

Materials management, the management of the flow of resources into and out of the conversion process, is one of the most complex functional areas of an organization.[11] Computers are now the principal tool for processing the information that materials managers use for sound decision making, and computer-aided materials management is crucial to organizational effectiveness. **Computer-aided materials management (CAMM)** is an advanced manufacturing technique that is used to manage the flow of raw materials and component parts into the conversion process, to develop master production schedules for manufacturing, and to control inventory.[12] The difference between traditional materials management and the new computer-aided techniques is the difference between the so-called push and pull approaches to materials management.[13]

Traditional mass production uses the *push* approach. Materials are released from the input to the conversion stage when the production control system indicates that the conversion stage is ready to receive them. The inputs are *pushed* into the conversion process in accordance with a previously determined plan.

Computer-aided materials management makes possible the *pull* approach. The flow of input materials is governed by customer requests for supplies of the finished products, so the inputs are *pulled* into the conversion process in response to a pull from the output stage rather than a push from the input stage. Recall from Chapter 4 how VF Corporation, the manufacturer of Lee jeans, meets customer demand. As jeans sell out in stores, the stores issue requests by computer to Lee to manufacture different styles or sizes. Lee's manufacturing department then pulls in raw materials, such as cloth and thread, from suppliers as it needs them. If Lee were using the push approach, Lee would have a master plan that might say, "Make 30,000 pairs of style XYZ in May"; and at the end of the summer 25,000 pairs might remain unsold in the warehouse because of lack of demand.

CAMM technology allows an organization to increase integration of its input, conversion, and output activities. The use of input and output inventories (see Figure 10.1) allows the activities of each stage of the mass-production process to go on relatively independently. CAMM, however, tightly couples these activities. CAMM increases *task interdependence* because each stage must be ready to react quickly to demands from the other stages. CAMM increases technical complexity because it makes input, conversion, and output activities a continuous process, creating in effect a pipeline connecting raw materials to the customer. Because the high levels of task interdependence and technical complexity associated with CAMM require greater coordination, an organization may need to move toward an organic structure, which will provide the extra integration that is needed.

CAMM also helps an organization pursue a low-cost or differentiation strategy. The ability to control the flow of materials in the production process allows an organization to avoid the costs of carrying excess inventory and to be flexible enough to adjust to product or demand changes quickly and easily.

Just-in-Time Inventory Systems

Just-in-time (JIT) inventory system *An AMT that requires inputs and components needed for production to be delivered to the conversion process just as they are needed, not earlier and not later.*

Another advanced manufacturing technique for managing the flow of inputs into the organization is the just-in-time inventory system. Developed from the Japanese kanban system (a *kanban* is a card), a **just-in-time (JIT) inventory system** requires inputs and components needed for production to be delivered to the conversion process just as they are needed, neither earlier nor later, so that input inventories can be kept to a minimum.[14] Components are kept in bins, and as they are used up, the empty bins are sent back to the supplier with a request on the bin's card (kanban) for more components. Computer-aided materials management is necessary for a JIT system to work effectively because CAMM provides computerized linkages with suppliers—linkages that facilitate the rapid transfer of information and coordination between an organization and its suppliers.

In theory, a JIT system can extend beyond components to raw materials. A company may supply Ford or Toyota with taillight assemblies. The supplier itself, however, may assemble the taillights from individual parts (screws, plastic lenses, bulbs) provided by other manufacturers. Thus, the supplier of the taillight assembly could also operate a JIT system with its suppliers, which in turn could operate JIT systems with their suppliers. Figure 10.2 illustrates a just-in-time inventory system that goes from the customer, to the store, and then back through the manufacturer to the original suppliers.

A JIT system increases *task interdependence* between stages in the production chain. Traditional mass production draws a boundary between the conversion stage and the input and output stages and sequences conversion activities only. JIT systems break down these barriers and make the whole value creation process a single chain of sequential activities. Because organizational activities become a continuous process, *technical complexity* increases, in turn increasing the efficiency of the system.

At the same time, JIT systems bring flexibility to manufacturing. The ability to order components as they are needed allows an organization to widen the range of products it makes

Customer buys product

Store orders more product from manufacturer

Manufacturer signals suppliers and makes product to meet store's order

Suppliers signal their suppliers and produce to meet manufacturer's order

Other Suppliers and so on...

FIGURE 10.2   **Just-in-Time Inventory System.** The system is activated by customers making purchases.

and to customize products because it is not tied to one product by large inventories.[15] JIT, systems, thus, allow a modern mass-production organization to obtain the benefits of small-batch technology (flexibility and customization) with little loss of technical efficiency.

Like CAMM, JIT systems require an extra measure of coordination, and an organization may need to adopt new methods to manage this new technology. One of these, as we saw in Chapter 6, is to implement new strategies for managing relations with suppliers. Toyota, which owns a minority stake in its suppliers, periodically meets with its suppliers to keep them informed about new-product developments. Toyota also works closely with its suppliers to reduce the costs and raise the quality of input components, and it shares the cost savings with its suppliers.[16] Because owning a supplier can increase costs, many organizations try to avoid the need to integrate vertically. Long-term contracts with suppliers can create cooperative working relationships that have long-term benefits for both parties.

In sum, just-in-time inventory systems, computer-aided materials management, and computer-aided design increase technical complexity and task interdependence and, thus, increase the degree to which a traditional mass-production system operates like a continuous-process technology; they also increase efficiency and reduce production costs. The three advanced manufacturing techniques also give modern mass-production the benefits of small-batch production: heightened flexibility and ability to respond to customer needs and increased product quality. Together these techniques confer a low-cost and a differentiation advantage on an organization.

Now that we have looked at advanced techniques for coordinating the input and conversion stages, we can look at new developments inside the conversion stage. At the center of AMT's innovations of conversion processes is the creation of a system based on flexible workers and flexible machines.

Flexible Manufacturing Technology and Computer-Integrated Manufacturing

Traditional mass-manufacturing technology utilizes dedicated machines, which perform only one operation at a time. The production of many components, however, requires many sequential operations and a different type of machine—transfer machines. **Transfer machines** are a series of dedicated machines placed side by side, each of which performs one short operation on a component and then rapidly transfers the component to the next machine, where the next operation is performed. Some transfer machines can perform a different operation every two seconds. If 50 different operations are needed to produce a component, a transfer machine can turn out a complete part every 100 seconds.

Transfer machines A series of dedicated machines placed side by side.

Transfer machines increase *technical complexity* and make mass production more like continuous production. This benefit can reduce costs and increase quality, but the use of transfer machines does have a downside. Retooling a transfer machine is even more expensive than retooling a single dedicated machine. Moreover, when operations are sequentially interdependent, a change in one machine requires a change in all the others. This characteristic reduces flexibility and may increase the difficulty and raise the cost of using a transfer machine to make different kinds of products.

Flexible manufacturing technology An AMT that allows the production of many kinds of components at little or no extra cost.

Flexible manufacturing technology, in contrast, allows the production of many kinds of components at little or no extra cost. Each machine in a flexible manufacturing system is able to perform a range of different operations, and the machines in sequence are able to vary their operations so that a wide variety of different components can be produced. Flexible manufacturing technology combines the variety advantages of small-batch production with the low-cost advantages of continuous-process production. How is this achieved?

Computer-integrated manufacturing (CIM)

An AMT that controls the changeover from one operation to another by means of commands given to the machines through computer software.

In flexible manufacturing systems, the key factor that prevents the cost increases associated with changing operations is the use of a computer-controlled system to manage operations. **Computer-integrated manufacturing (CIM)** is an advanced manufacturing technique that controls the changeover from one operation to another by means of the commands given to the machines through computer software. A CIM system eliminates the need to physically retool machines. Within the system are a number of computer-controlled machines, each capable of automatically producing a range of components. They are controlled by a master computer, which schedules the movement of parts between machines in order to assemble different products from the various components that each machine makes.[17] Computer-integrated manufacturing depends on computers programmed to (1) feed the machines with components, (2) assemble the product from components and move it from one machine to another, and (3) unload the final product from the machine to the shipping area.

The use of robots is integral to CIM. A group of robots working in sequence is the AMT equivalent of a dedicated transfer machine. Unlike a dedicated transfer machine, however, each robot can be quickly programmed by software to perform different operations, and the costs of reprogramming robots are much lower than the costs associated with retooling dedicated transfer machines. Motorola's new cellular phone factory illustrates many of the advantages of robots and advanced manufacturing technology.

ORGANIZATIONAL INSIGHT

10.1 MOTOROLA'S FACTORY OF THE FUTURE

Motorola is one of America's oldest consumer electronics organizations. It developed the world's first car radio in 1930 and quickly entered the home audio and television market. In the 1970s, however, under pressure from the Japanese, it abandoned the home electronics market and entered the high-tech electronics sector. Today it is a world leader in communications technology, and the organization generates over $8 billion in revenue from the sales of cellular telephones, pagers, information networking systems, and automotive and industrial electronics.

Once again, however, Motorola is experiencing intense competitive pressure from both domestic and foreign competitors for control of the rapidly growing information technology sector. Hitachi, Panasonic, and Samsung already operate state-of-the art factories based on advanced manufacturing technology, and their low production costs make them fierce competitors. Motorola has had to figure out how to use AMT to its advantage.

Motorola decided to use AMT not only to increase technical efficiency but also to better meet the needs of customers. Using advanced manufacturing technology, Motorola has focused both product design and manufacturing on the customer. At Motorola, salespeople, not engineers, are empowered to direct the company's activities. The sales function is at the top of the organizational hierarchy, and the other functions serve its needs. What does this mean for the way the organization utilizes AMT?

Motorola created a "factory of the future" that is able to customize products to individual customer needs within hours. At a futuristic factory at Boynton Beach, Florida, Motorola can respond to a customer order for even one unit of a custom-designed pager within two hours. A salesperson in the field takes the customer's order for a pager that will operate on a specific frequency, be of a certain size, and contain one of a number of customized features. The salesperson electronically relays this information as a bar code to the factory. A computer scans the specifications and through software creates the circuit board design for the pager. The conversion process is handled by a series of computer-controlled robots. As the pager passes down the production line, each robot reads the bar code and performs the necessary operations. Each pager in the line can be different because CIM adapts the conversion process to the specific needs of each item. Finished products are electronically scanned and tested and are shipped to the customer.

Using AMT in this way is expensive. However, the ability to produce hundreds of different models customized to individual customers has given Motorola a strong competitive advantage and has allowed the company to charge a premium price for its products. Not surprisingly, customers like the flexibility of Motorola's approach and are willing to pay for it. Motorola firmly believes that successful organizations in the future will use AMT to integrate their production and delivery processes so that they too can respond directly to each customer.[18]

Sequential task interdependence is the basis for manufacturing any kind of product. However, the combination of flexible machines and computerization allows any given set of machines to perform many different sequences. In effect, a CIM system has the potential to act reciprocally and to produce a wide range of customized products.[19] It increases technical complexity. It allows an organization's resources to be used more efficiently because it quickens the pace of work and the speed of production. With computer-integrated manufacturing, the conversion of inputs becomes more like a continuous process instead of a mass-production process.

In sum, computer-integrated manufacturing, just-in-time inventory systems, computer-aided materials management, and computer-aided design give organizations the flexibility to make a variety of products, as well as different models of the same product, rapidly and cost-effectively. They break down the traditional barriers separating the input, conversion, and output stages of production; as a result, input, conversion, and output activities merge into one another. These four innovations in materials technology decrease the need for costly inventory buffers to protect conversion processes from disruptions in the environment. In addition, they increase product reliability because they increase automation and technical complexity.

ADVANCED MANUFACTURING TECHNOLOGY: INNOVATIONS IN KNOWLEDGE TECHNOLOGY

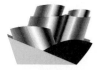

Knowledge technology
The skills and abilities of people individually and in groups.

Knowledge technology comprises the skills and abilities of people individually and in groups. Changes in materials technology have necessitated many changes in knowledge technology.

In traditional mass-production settings, knowledge technology centers on the establishment of procedures that lead to the efficient operation of dedicated machines. Generally, workers learn only the standard procedures necessary to complete a single task or operation. The amount of time needed to retrain these fixed workers to perform other tasks makes it difficult in the short run to retool a production line quickly or efficiently. Because workers' activities are sequentially linked by the production line, an alteration in the routines of any worker directly impacts the performance of all other workers, again making it difficult to change the way the technology operates. Moreover, workers in traditional mass-production settings are responsible only for performing the procedures associated with completing their task, not for the quality of the product that results from the task. Product quality is the responsibility of quality control personnel, who inspect the final product.

Clearly, traditional knowledge technology does not meet the needs of advanced materials techniques. The pull approach of a just-in-time inventory system, for example, means that the pace of work is controlled by need, not by a predetermined, preset schedule. Inventories are kept to a minimum, so workers must work to fill orders, and there is little room for error. Furthermore, workers must control the quantity and quality of their work because shortages or defects are immediately visible at the next stage of production. In addition, the use of flexible machines and computer-integrated manufacturing means that workers must perform complex, nonroutine tasks and quickly adjust their work routines to suit whatever task is needed.

The types of knowledge technology that AMT and traditional mass production require are quite different. With AMT, tasks are more complex because the range of work activities constantly increases as new products are introduced or old products are redesigned. The nonroutine nature of work activities in an AMT setting means that a better way of performing a task can often be found and the attempt to develop new procedures is ongoing. The high technical complexity associated with AMT creates a need for highly skilled workers. For all these reasons, the operation of advanced manufacturing technology requires the development of flexible workers and flexible work teams.

Flexible Workers

In an AMT setting, employees need to acquire and develop the skills to perform any of the tasks necessary for assembling a range of finished products.[20] A worker first develops the skills needed to accomplish one work task and then over time is trained to perform other tasks. Compensation is frequently tied to the number of different tasks that a person can perform. Each worker can substitute for any other worker. Thus, as the demand for components or finished products rises or falls, flexible workers can be transferred to the task most needed by the organization. In essence, AMT reduces the division of labor and allows each worker to become more broadly specialized in a number of skills. In contrast, in a traditional mass-production system, the division of labor is great, and the workers are narrowly specialized.

Both workers and the organization as a whole benefit from the use of advanced manufacturing techniques. The organization is able to respond quickly to changes in its environment. Performing more than one task cuts down on repetition, boredom, and fatigue and raises workers' incentives to improve product quality. When workers learn one another's tasks, they also learn how the different tasks relate to each other. This understanding often leads to new ways of combining tasks or to the redesign of a product to make its manufacture more efficient and less costly.

Flexible Work Teams

flexible work team *A group of workers who assume responsibility for performing all the operations necessary for completing a specified stage in the manufacturing process.*

One of AMT's most important contributions to modern technology is the concept of grouping workers into flexible work teams.[21] A **flexible work team** is a group of workers who assume responsibility for performing all the operations necessary for completing a specified stage in the manufacturing process. Production line workers who were previously responsible for only their own tasks are placed in groups and are jointly assigned responsibility for one stage of the manufacturing process. At Ford plants, for example, one work team is responsible for assembling the car transmission and sending it to the body assembly area, where the body assembly team is responsible for fitting it to the car body. A flexible work team is self-managed: The team members jointly assign tasks and transfer workers from one task to another as necessary.

Figure 10.3 illustrates the way in which flexible work teams perform their activities. Separate teams assemble different components and turn those components over to the final-product work team, which assembles the final product. Each team's activities are

FIGURE 10.3

The Use of Flexible Work Teams to Assemble Cars. Self-managed teams assemble brake systems, exhaust systems, and other components in accordance with the demands of the final-product team. Driven by customers demands, the final-product team assembles components to produce a car.

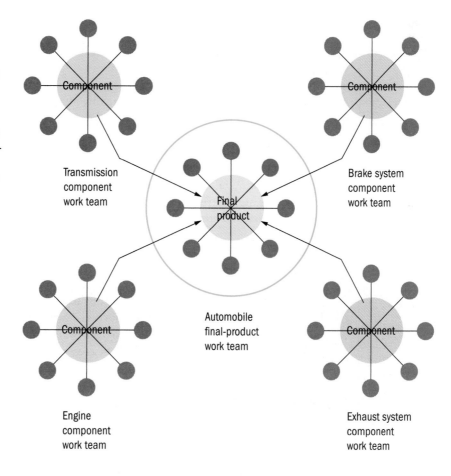

Transmission component work team

Brake system component work team

Final product

Automobile final-product work team

Engine component work team

Exhaust system component work team

● Team member

driven by demands that have their origins in customer demands for the final product. Thus, each team has to adjust its activities to the pull coming from the output side of the production process. The experience of Globe Metallurgical, Inc. illustrates many of the factors associated with the use of flexible work teams.

ORGANIZATIONAL INSIGHT

10.2 FLEXIBLE WORK TEAMS AT GLOBE

Globe Metallurgical, Inc. of Beverly, Ohio, and Selma, Alabama, was the first small company to win the Malcolm Baldridge National Quality Award. Globe makes specialty steel products and is one of the most successful organizations in its industry, surpassing its competitors in product quality, sales, and profit growth.

Globe's emergence as a leader in quality and particularly in its use of self-managed work teams came in an unusual way. In 1986, Globe wanted to introduce new, flexible work systems in order to raise profitability. When the unions refused to relax rigid work rules so that the new technology could be introduced, the company experienced a year-long strike. To continue operation, 10 managers and 35 salaried workers took control of two of Globe's furnaces (they closed three others). Lack of workers forced these 45 people to find new, more efficient ways to produce Globe's output.

With both managers and workers directly involved in production, many possibilities for improving the way the work was performed emerged. In the absence of work rules and job classifications specifying how the furnaces were to be operated, managers experimented with new ways to run them and within two weeks increased productivity by 20 percent. Every day brought new suggestions. It soon became obvious that productivity could be increased if welders, crane operators, furnace operators, forklift operators, stokers, furnace tappers, and tapper assistants worked cooperatively in teams. By trial and error, management discovered that a flexible work team of seven employees (one from each function), each of whom could do the others' jobs, could efficiently operate one furnace. Each team was put under the supervision of a team leader, who took responsibility for coordinating the team's work and schedules with those of other teams and with top management.

After the strike was over, Globe found that by using self-managed work teams it could operate all five furnaces with 120 employees (down from the 350 needed before the strike). The unions' fears about the shift to the new technology were justified: Flexible workers and flexible work teams resulted in a loss of jobs. For the employees who remained, however, Globe instituted a profit-sharing plan that allows workers to reap some of the benefits created by the new work system.[22] Globe continued to grow through the 1990s and is now the largest supplier of specialty metals in the United States.[23]

Flexible work teams are involved in more than just conversion or assembly activities. They also assume responsibility for controlling the quality of their outputs during production. Because a large, separate quality control function is no longer needed at the end of the production line, the use of work teams reduces costs.[24] The difference in the production methods used by Lexus, a division of Toyota, and Mercedes-Benz provides a dramatic example of the importance of quality control to work teams. Workers at Lexus are trained to solve assembly problems as they arise during production. A worker who spots a problem has the right to stop the production line, and together workers and managers find a solution for the problem before the line is started again. Thus, when a new car, such as the Lexus 400, is introduced, the production line may be continually starting and stopping as production begins. But gradually, as problems are solved, cars come off the production line with zero defects. At Lexus, management accepts the short-term losses in production time associated with AMT for long-term gains in product quality and reliability.

Mercedes-Benz, in contrast, operated a traditional mass-production system in the 1980s. Expecting mistakes to occur at each step of the assembly process, Mercedes-Benz employed a small army of quality control specialists whose job was to wait at the end of the production line to correct the problems that arose during manufacturing. Employing these people was very costly, and it has been estimated that Mercedes-Benz production costs were double those of Lexus. Not surprisingly, Daimler-Chrysler, as Mercedes-Benz is now known after its merger with Chrysler, moved in the 1990s to institute the new manufacturing methods in order to reduce costs. Already these are paying off as its costs have fallen while quality has remained high.

Quality control circles
Team meetings devoted to finding ways of improving productivity.

Flexible work teams are also responsible for devising ways to improve the efficiency of the manufacturing process. New ideas often originate in **quality control circles**, team meetings that bring members together specifically to discuss ways of improving productivity.[25] Moreover, the most experienced members of a team assume responsibility for training new members. All team members are often responsible for selecting new recruits whom they think will fit in with the team. In this way, a work-team culture emerges.

The managers' role in this system is not to monitor and supervise the work teams' activities but to facilitate team activities and do all they can to allow the teams to develop improved procedures. Since 1983, General Motors and Toyota have been cooperating in a joint venture that uses flexible work teams.

ORGANIZATIONAL INSIGHT

10.3 GM AND TOYOTA GIVE PLANT A NEW LEASE ON LIFE

In 1963, General Motors opened a car plant in Fremont, California, 35 miles east of San Francisco. From the outset, the plant was a loser. Productivity and quality were poor. Drug and alcohol abuse were widespread. Absenteeism was so high that hundreds of extra workers were employed to ensure that enough workers were on hand to operate the plant. Managers at the Fremont plant, as at all GM plants, constantly analyzed the worker-task relationship in order to design jobs to raise productivity. Workers strongly resisted these moves, and finally, seeing no hance of improvement, GM closed the plant in 1981.

In 1983, GM and Toyota announced a joint venture: They would cooperate to reopen the Fremont plant. GM wanted to learn how Toyota operated its production system, and Toyota wanted to see whether it could achieve its customary high level of productivity by using Japanese techniques with American workers. In 1984, the new organization, New United Motors Manufacturing Inc. (NUMMI), opened under the control of Japanese management. By 1986, productivity at NUMMI was higher than productivity at any other GM factory, and the plant was operating at twice the level it had operated at under GM management. Moreover, alcohol and drug abuse had virtually disappeared, and absenteeism had almost stopped. How had this miracle been achieved?

At the NUMMI factory, Toyota divided the workforce into 350 flexible work teams consisting of from five to seven people plus a team leader. Each worker can do the jobs of the other workers, and the workers regularly rotate jobs. In addition, all workers are taught procedures for analyzing jobs to improve the employee-task relationship. Team members design each team's jobs, time each other with stopwatches, and continually attempt to find better ways of performing the tasks. In the past, GM had employed 80 managers to perform this analysis. Now flexible work teams not only perform the analysis but also monitor product quality. What is the role of managers in the NUMMI factory? The manager's job is defined explicitly as providing shop-floor workers with support, not monitoring or supervising their activities.

Why do employees buy into this new system? NUMMI has a no-layoff policy; workers are given extensive training; and the use of flexible work teams gives workers, not managers, control over the production line. Apparently, most workers still consider assembly-line work a "lousy job"—but the best job they can expect to get. And in the new work system they at least have some control over what they do.[26]

In 1999, GM and Toyota announced new plans for the Freemont plant. For Toyota, it will build the 2000 model year Toyota Corolla, for GM a new sports utility vehicle. Clearly, the future looks bright indeed.[27]

Together, jointly specialized flexible workers and flexible work teams lead to *reciprocal task interdependence* within a team. These innovations in knowledge technology—that is, flexible workers and flexible work teams—are very important. Studies have found that when teams work effectively, the result is large increases in efficiency even when the materials technology remains unchanged. Thus, the use of flexible work teams has been called "group technology" because of its important effects on organizational performance.[28]

Although we have discussed innovations in knowledge and materials technology in the context of manufacturing organizations, it is important to note that these new methods have important applications in service organizations as well. McDonald's, for example, has consistently made use of many features of advanced manufacturing technology. It operates a sophisticated just-in-time delivery system to keep its foodstuffs fresh. It continuously improves the efficiency of its manufacturing process, and managers constantly search for new procedures to improve the quality of service delivered to customers. McDonald's also tries to maximize its response to customer needs by developing work procedures that allow it to switch quickly from one product line to another as customer demands change. Similarly, Wal-Mart operates one of the most sophisticated computerized warehousing and delivery systems of any manufacturing or service organization. All Wal-Mart stores are linked by satellite to regional distribution centers, which are able to restock the shelves of stores within days after notification.

MANAGING ADVANCED MANUFACTURING TECHNOLOGY

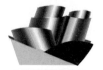

Managing the fit between the materials and knowledge components of AMT is a complex organizational process. Many elements of advanced manufacturing technology were either developed or refined by Japanese organizations. Toyota, Nissan, Matsushita, and Sony pioneered the development of new managerial techniques and organizational structures that allow AMT to be operated efficiently. In this section we focus on one of these techniques, total quality management, and then look at how organizations design their structures to effectively operate advanced manufacturing technology.

Total Quality Management

Total quality manage-ment (TQM) *A technique developed by W. Edwards Deming to continuously improve the effectiveness of flexible work teams.*

Total quality management (TQM) is a technique developed by W. Edwards Deming to improve the efficiency of flexible work teams. The broad goal of TQM is continuous improvement.[29] TQM aims to impress upon workers the importance of continuously improving the efficiency of the production process in order to reduce costs, increase quality, and reduce waste. Workers in a TQM system are expected to make suggestions for improving all aspects of the work process and are expected to share their specialized knowledge with management so that it can be communicated throughout the organization.[30] For example, new techniques and procedures can be programmed into the software that controls the production line so that they can be utilized by all work groups. Because TQM has received such attention, it is useful to examine it in detail. Deming's 14 points to guide TQM efforts are summarized in Table 10.1.[31]

TABLE 10.1
Deming's Principles of TQM

1. Create constancy of purpose toward improvement of product and service, with the aim of becoming competitive, staying in business, and providing jobs.
2. Adopt the new philosophy. We are in a new economic age. Western management must awaken to the challenge, learn its responsibilities, and take on leadership for change.
3. Cease dependence on mass inspection to achieve quality. Eliminate the need for inspection on a mass basis by building quality into the product in the first place,
4. End the practice of awarding business on price tag alone. Instead, minimize total cost.
5. Improve constantly and forever the system of production and service, to improve quality and productivity and thus constantly decrease costs.
6. Institute training on the job.
7. Institute leadership. The aim of leadership should be to help people, machines, and gadgets do a better job. Management leadership, as well as leadership of production workers, needs overhauling.
8. Drive out fear, so that everyone may work effectively for the company.
9. Break down barriers between departments. People in research, design, sales, and production must work as a team, to foresee problems in production and in use that may be encountered with the product or service.
10. Eliminate slogans, exhortations, and targets for the work force asking for zero defects and new levels of productivity. Such exhortations only create adversarial relationship. The bulk of the causes of low quality and low productivity belong to the system and thus he beyond the power of the work force.
11. (a) Eliminate work standards on the factory floor; substitute leadership.
    (b) Eliminate management by objective, management by numbers, and numerical goals; substitute leadership.
12. (a) Remove barriers that rob the hourly workers of their right to pride of workmanship. The responsibility of supervisors must be changed from sheer numbers to quality.
    (b) Remove barriers that rob people in management and in engineering of their right to pride of workmanship.
13. Institute a vigorous program of education and self-improvement.
14. Put everyone in the company to work to accomplish the transformation. The transformation is everybody's job.

Source: From *The Man Who Discovered Quality* by Andrea Gabor. Copyright © 1990 by Andrea Gabor. Reprinted by permission of Times Books, a division of Random House, Inc.

Quality is not just something that is turned out in the manufacturing department; it starts with the adoption of a philosophy of quality throughout an organization—quality not only in the things produced in the manufacturing department but also in the knowledge technology of every function. Deming emphasized that the commitment to quality has to exist at all levels. Each employee, from the CEO down to the shop-floor worker, is expected to reevaluate his or her role in the organization and take responsibility for improving the way a good or service is delivered to the customer. Quality in manufacturing might mean fewer defects per car. Quality in the customer service department might mean establishing long-term relationships with major customers. Quality in accounting might mean devising a bill that is easier for customers to read and that gives them more information about their account. An organization has to adopt the philosophy of TQM as a significant organizational norm and create an organizational culture based on the norms and values of TQM. Quality control circles are an important vehicle for the development of TQM norms both within and across functional areas.

Benchmarking *The practice of using the achievements of some other organization as a model of what an organization should strive for.*

One important activity in TQM is **benchmarking**, using the achievements of some other organization that is very successful in delivering quality as a model of what the organization can achieve. Managers and employees use significant indicators of the model organization's effectiveness as benchmarks and try to imitate and improve upon them. For example, two quality benchmarks for express delivery organizations such as DHL and Airborne Express are Federal Express's ability to guarantee overnight delivery of packages and its ability to track packages continuously from the time they leave the customer's hands.

Following the philosophy of TQM has radical effects on organizational structure. The idea behind TQM is to empower employees—that is, to make them personally responsible for devising efficient work procedures and for controlling the quality of their work. In an organization using TQM, control is achieved by mutual adjustment between workers (rather than by standardization) and by decentralization of authority to team members (rather than by centralization of authority in managers). McDonald's, Federal Express, Kmart, and Citibank all use TQM training programs that push authority as far down the hierarchy as possible and empower employees to do whatever it takes to deliver the highest-quality service to customers and solve problems on the spot.[32]

The use of TQM often reduces costs because better ways of designing, manufacturing, and delivering products to customers come to light when a focus on quality replaces a focus on cost. Among the TQM principles are calls to eliminate numerical targets, work quotas, and management by objectives, all of which force managers and workers to attend to the bottom line and not to the customer.

Recall from Chapter 5 the two kinds of values that organizational members share: **terminal values** (desired end states or outcomes); and **instrumental values** (desired modes of behavior). To achieve the goals of total quality management, the organization has to adopt quality and service as terminal values and develop instrumental values that help the organization achieve its terminal goals. First, it is necessary to drive out workers' fear that quality improvements and new work procedures will lead to layoffs. Second, it is necessary to remove barriers that prevent employees from taking pride in their workmanship, and it is necessary to give employees the autonomy and responsibility they need to perform their tasks spontaneously and cooperatively with others in the organization. Third, it is necessary to create a vigorous program of education and self-improvement to instill and develop new work values in employees.

TQM aims to break down communication barriers, not only between internal stakeholders but also between the organization and its external stakeholders, in order to increase cross-functional integration and provide new avenues for cooperation to improve quality. For example, a TQM organization strives to develop cooperative relationships with its suppliers and distributors so that continuous improvement of product quality becomes their goal, too. Ford, Motorola, General Motors, and other companies have taken steps to develop constructive long-term relationships with suppliers and distributors.[33] The use of new kinds of organizational structure, such as product team structure, and advanced information technologies, such as CAMM and CIM, facilitates integration inside and outside the organization. Xerox's efforts to instill a commitment to quality in its suppliers illustrates many of the principles of TQM.

ORGANIZATIONAL INSIGHT

10.4 XEROX AND TRIDENT TOOL: THE SEARCH FOR QUALITY

As we saw in Chapter 4, Xerox, its future threatened by intense Japanese competition, totally redesigned its structure to emphasize product quality and to allow itself to develop and introduce new products and processes quickly and successfully. Recognizing that the quality of its inputs was vital to ensuring the quality of its final products, Xerox began a program to improve input quality. The first step was to weed out troublesome suppliers. This process cut the number of Xerox suppliers from over 6,000 to less than 500. Xerox then created a detailed and rigorous set of specifications for its remaining suppliers to conform to. The specifications included on-time delivery and the virtual elimination of product defects. These requirements would allow Xerox to keep inventory levels low, to minimize costly reworking and repair, and to reduce the costs of quality control. Xerox, however, did not just hand the specifications to its suppliers and walk away. It embarked on a long-term program of TQM education to assist them with the development of new procedures that would strengthen their commitment to quality. The nature of this learning process is illustrated by Xerox's relations with Trident Tools.[34]

Trident Tools, which manufactures electromagnetic components, was founded in Rochester, New York, by Nick Juskiw, a former Xerox engineer. Like many other organizations, Trident had typically viewed quality not as a continuous process involving managers and workers at all stages of production but as an ingredient to be added at the end of the production line by the quality control department. To change this philosophy of production, Xerox first held a TQM seminar for the CEOs of its suppliers to teach them the meaning of TQM and how to develop TQM strategies in their organizations. Then Xerox organized TQM seminars for the top managers of its suppliers. Each organization was expected to appoint TQM managers who would be responsible for training other managers in TQM techniques. Juskiw at Trident, for example, required every manager and employee to undergo at least 21 hours of TQM training, and the organization annually spends 4 or 5 percent of its payroll on training—a very significant sum.

Learning the techniques of TQM paid off for Trident. Employees and managers who put the new techniques into practice achieved quick results. Employees from different departments soon saw that Trident's practice of having each department do its own ordering caused major communication and coordination problems between departments when new products were being developed. A team of 10 employees from four different departments met to create a more efficient ordering system. The new system reduced the number of steps from 26 to 12 and allowed each department to know what the others were doing. That change and others have produced enormous benefits for Trident. The company has received many long-term contracts from Xerox, and its future is assured. Trident has also reduced the time it needs to fill customer orders from 16 weeks to seven. In addition, Xerox engineers work closely with Trident engineers to design new components that Xerox needs for its future products, and beginning the TQM process at the design stage has cut the time for product development from five years to 16 months.

Xerox has forged such strategic alliances with all its suppliers, and the benefits of the TQM approach have been seen by all organizations in Xerox's network. Xerox has been so eager to spread the quality message that it has initiated seminars on TQM for business schools, so that their students who join organizations in the Rochester area will already be familiar with the TQM approach. In fact, TQM has become a core competence for the Rochester community—one that more and more organizations are seeking to exploit. In summary, the goal of TQM is to create a culture for quality, not just in the manufacturing department but in the organization as a whole. By unleashing and capturing the cooperation of workers, an organization can increase its effectiveness and better satisfy the needs of all its stakeholders. Xerox continued to pursue total quality management throughout the 1990s while many other companies had given up. Its managers remain committed to the approach, which continues to pay major dividends to the company.[35]

Organizational Structure and Advanced Manufacturing Technology

Several researchers have argued that to obtain the benefits associated with total quality management and advanced manufacturing technology an organization needs a structure that takes advantage of flexible workers and flexible manufacturing technology. AMT results in increased technical complexity, more complex tasks, and higher task interdependence.[36] As we discussed in Chapter 9, these factors typically cause an organization to adopt an organic structure, which facilitates the coordination of activities. The high level of coordination required to operate AMT increases the need for a complex structure and for complex integrating mechanisms.[37] Table 10.2 contrasts the structures of organizations that use traditional mass production and those that use AMT.

TABLE 10.2		
Structural Differences Between Organizations with Traditional Mass Production and Those with Advanced Manufacturing Technology		
Structural Characteristic	**Traditional Mass Production**	**Advanced Manufacturing Technology**
Hierarchy of authority	Relatively tall	Relatively flat
Decision making	Centralized	Decentralized
Control	Standardization	Mutual adjustment
Horizontal differentiation	Functional structure	Product team structure
Overall structure	Mechanistic	Organic

The relatively tall hierarchy and centralized decision making associated with mass production give way to a flatter structure in which authority is decentralized to give the flexible work teams more control over their activities. In an AMT setting, each team is expected to learn the best procedures for performing its tasks, and each team knows the standard of performance that it is expected to achieve. Mutual adjustment allows a work team to coordinate its activities, and team members together decide how to divide the work and coordinate their activities to improve team productivity. The extensive use of mutual adjustment is an important difference between AMT and mass production because it encourages workers to improve the work process and to take responsibility for the quality of their work.

AMT increases the need to remove functional barriers. Thus, at the organizational level in an AMT setting, the functional structure gives way to the product team structure. Cross-functional teams become an important integrating mechanism, and horizontal integration replaces rules, procedures, and the hierarchy of authority as the main means of control between functions. The move to an organic product team structure allows an organization operating with AMT to respond to the demands of its changing environment, increase its ability to produce a range of customized products, and utilize the skills and abilities of its workforce in a way that supports a philosophy of total quality management.

Some researchers question whether the majority of U.S. organizations that have introduced advanced manufacturing technology have designed the most appropriate structure for themselves. Researchers also question whether new philosophies such as TQM, developed in the Japanese context, can be successfully introduced into the United States, and if they can, in what ways they might need to be adapted for American use. They question, too, whether the Japanese have been obtaining the benefits of AMT because of their ability to exert control over a compliant workforce. To understand the way AMT affects the workforce, we need to look at the organizational culture and the values and norms that emerge when advanced manufacturing technology is employed to increase efficiency.

Advanced Manufacturing Technology and Organizational Culture

According to some researchers, Japanese culture and the Japanese work ethic play important roles in the successful use of AMT in Japan. Just-in-time systems and total quality management put great pressure on workers to perform at high speed. JIT reduces inventory to a minimum and speeds the pace of work. Some researchers have called TQM "management by stress." They point out that continuous improvement does not mean easier or more interesting work. Instead of relaxing the pace or giving workers time to learn new skills, some organizations remove workers from the production line as soon as labor-saving improvements are found. Those who remain work at least as quickly as before.[38]

Japanese workers tolerate high pressure at work because Japanese culture puts a high value on conformity, loyalty to the group, and duty to one's superior. In fact, as we saw in the opening case, Toyota, one of the first organizations to enjoy the increased productivity that results from the use of AMT, proposed to lay off 25 percent of its workforce when it was no longer needed. To secure agreement from its unions, Toyota was forced to agree to lifetime employment for the remaining workers and to guarantee them a share in the organization's profits. According to anecdotal evidence, however, Toyota established a "cruel work environment due to its tough work rules and extremely fast work pace, and an extremely large number of work injuries were reported."[39] A typical Toyota work shift lasts 11 hours, with two 10-minute breaks plus a lunch break.

Some researchers suggest that to encourage American workers to adopt AMT work practices, including TQM, it is necessary to transfer property rights to workers so that they will buy into the new set of organizational values. For example, it has been proposed that workers who are guaranteed long-term employment or promised monetary rewards for productivity improvements are likely to adopt new work practices at faster rates than workers without such incentives.[40] It has also been proposed that organizations that already invest in training workers will find the transition to advanced manufacturing technology easiest and will achieve the best results from the new technology.[41] It is not possible to simply change an organization's materials or knowledge technology and expect to reap the rewards of AMT. An organization has to change its culture (especially its ways of rewarding employees) to achieve the benefits offered by the new technology. As discussed in Chapter 9, sociotechnical systems theory offers some guidelines as to how this can be achieved.

Managerial Implications:
Advanced Manufacturing Technology

1. Study the tasks that employees are performing, and search for ways to increase the number and variety of their tasks.
2. Study the interactions among employees, and create work teams in which employees can learn one another's tasks and improve the procedures for performing their tasks.
3. Examine the feasibility of creating flexible work teams and delegating responsibility for production and quality to the teams.
4. Ensure that each team has access to the materials technology—computers and other machines—that it will need to implement the new work process effectively.
5. Seek to link the reward system to the new work process in order to increase employee motivation.
6. Implement a total quality management program to encourage employees to continuously improve work procedures, and link improvements in quality to the reward system.
7. Examine the organizational structure, and analyze its level of integration, centralization, and so forth, to ensure that it facilitates the adoption of advanced manufacturing technology. Redesign the structure as necessary.

ADVANCED INFORMATION TECHNOLOGY

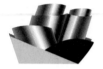

As just discussed, many of the advances in materials technology that have revolutionized the way organizations produce goods and services involve advances in information and computer-based technology. For example, computer-integrated manufacturing allows an organization to handle resource transfers efficiently, automatically smooths the work flow, and integrates work positions. However, rapid advances in the power of information technology are having a fundamental impact not just upon technology but upon all aspects of the way organizations operate.[42] Indeed, so important are these changes that many experts now argue that organizations that fail to adopt leading-edge information technology will rapidly lose out to those that do. Adoption of modern information technology has become a competitive imperative.[43]

Advanced information technology (AIT) comprises the computer- and communications-based technologies used to acquire, organize, store, manipulate, and transmit information to people and subunits both inside and outside the organization.[44] Advanced information technologies allow an organization to improve its handling and integration of the information-processing needs of all functions and divisions.[45] A computerized information system that integrates marketing and R&D with production, for example, would allow cross-functional teams to perform more effectively and would be as important as integrating workstations in a manufacturing setting.

One of an organization's or a function's major costs is the time that managers and employees spend gathering and processing information, making decisions, and solving problems. Advanced information technology reduces that time and those costs; its use enables managers and employees to make more productive use of their time and to use less of it to find solutions to problems. Three types of AIT are especially helpful: (1) teleconferencing systems, (2) information transfer and retrieval systems, and (3) personal information-processing systems.[46]

Teleconferencing systems enhance communication by reducing the need for face-to-face contact, thus saving time and money. Over 70 percent of management time is spent in meetings because face-to-face contact is usually necessary for resolving complex issues. Considerable time, however, is wasted in traveling to and setting up such meetings. Teleconferencing, the use of on-line television and video systems, provides a useful alternative to in-person attendance at meetings, especially in an era of global competition. Teleconferencing is used to link R&D laboratories and the home and foreign operations of international organizations. It is also used to link the various divisions of an organization or individual stores in a retail chain. To coordinate store activities, Wal-Mart uses teleconferencing to link store managers to each other and to Wal-Mart headquarters. Similarly, Mattel, the toy manufacturer, uses teleconferencing to train middle and lower-level managers and to keep in contact with its self-managed work groups.

Today, the increasing use of e-mail, the Internet, and the development of intranets or in-house communication networks are all speeding the flow of information in the organization. All these information transfer and retrieval systems are based on the use of networks of personal computers joined to each other and to a central computer that allows users to share files. Even when employees do not need to meet face-to-face, considerable time can be saved if computer-integrated information systems link the activities of different individuals, teams, departments, and managers involved in decision making. A major impediment to integration is the lack of communication among subunits. A system that directs information to where it is most needed and allows people to retrieve information in the form best suited to their needs saves time and improves the effectiveness of decision making. All kinds of organizations are able to take advantage of in-house communications networks as the following insight suggests.

A third type of AIT, personal information-processing and activity management systems, such as those provided by personal computers and personal communicators, also promotes the efficient use of individuals' time and effort. Southwestern Bell is test-marketing pocket telephones for use by physicians in hospitals. They would replace pagers and save the time the doctors spend looking for a telephone to answer their pager. Apple, Hitachi, and Sony have all developed personal communicators that are hand-held computers that act as recorders, paperless fax machines, and appointment books. The proliferation of personal computers has been driven by the realization that computers can enhance the quality and efficiency of many activities, such as writing, design, and calculation.

Personal computers are also at the foundation of networking computer systems that link personnel and standardize work activities across departments and throughout the organization. Networking systems and personal computers can reduce coordination costs because they allow tasks to be programmed and decision-making procedures to be specified in advance.

ORGANIZATIONAL INSIGHT

10.5 CAKEBREAD CELLARS GOES HIGH-TECH

At first glance, a small winery might seem like an unlikely candidate to use sophisticated new information technology to improve its effectiveness, but Cakebread Cellars, a specialty wine maker located in California's Napa Valley, is doing just that. Cakebread Cellars is known internationally for the quality of its wines. In order to keep its costs under control so that it can continue to improve product quality and protect the health of its vines, Cakebread Cellars recently moved to install advanced information technology. This technology has several different components.

First, because the quality of wine depends on how much water a vine receives and when, Cakebread installed at the root of each of its thousands of vines an electronic measuring device that monitors the water intake of each vine. The device also allows Cakebread to keep a lifetime record of the history of each vine in order to keep all the vines in peak condition.

Then information on all its thousands of vines is fed into a central computer, and via a complex computer software program, Cakebread's wine experts are able to monitor the vines and determine the optimum watering and feeding schedule. They can also pinpoint the right time to pick the grapes—the time when the grapes' sugar content is at its highest. Moreover, Cakebread is electronically linked to a local weather-forecasting service that can inform vintners quickly of any adverse weather conditions that might emerge during the harvesting period.

Once the grapes are picked, the monitoring process continues. Monitoring devices are placed in all the large wine fermentation vessels so that wine makers are able to study the fermentation process and monitor the progress of the wine. In this way they can seek to influence the taste of the final product by altering the length of the fermentation process or by making a decision to blend different varieties of wine to create the optimum product. Finally, the bottling process is also electronically monitored to ensure the quality of the final product. According to Cakebread's wine makers, AIT provides them with the information that allows them to make the final decisions that result in the production of a great wine as opposed to a good one. They must be right because in 1999, Cakebread's wines ranked seventh overrall in the United States in a survey of high-quality restaurants.[47]

Computers give the organization greater control over activities at lower levels in the hierarchy and promote the decentralization of authority to lower-level employees. For example, McDonald's authorized Compuadd Information Services Corporation to sell to all 8,800 McDonald's franchises a new type of touch-screen, order-recording, cash-register terminal to replace keyboard "skins" with preprinted buttons. The new terminals allow the introduction of new products without changing the skins, and they can be programmed to show only the food items that are available at a given time (breakfast items might not be available after 10 A.M.) together with their prices at that time.[48] Such customized computers reduce operator error and make it easier to program the work process and track the sales of items.

Increasing the ability of managers and employees to process information efficiently not only results in considerable cost savings but also increases the organization's responsiveness to customers' needs. In the past 20 years, for example, banks have invested over $200 billion in information technology to reduce operating costs by replacing human "paper shufflers" with computers. CitiCorp and NationsBank have saved hundreds of millions of dollars through their investment in advanced information systems. Advanced information systems have also enabled banks to handle more information so that they can increase the number of people they serve and offer them new products and services such as automated teller machines and personalized banking.[49] Similarly, utility companies have invested in personal computer networks that use improved software for billing and record keeping to track customers and respond to their requests.

Like advanced manufacturing technology, AIT can confer a competitive advantage on organizations by reducing their costs, by giving their products unique appeal, or by allowing them to respond flexibly and personally to their customers' needs. American Hospital Supply put terminals on customers' premises to make reordering easier. American Airlines and United Airlines made it possible for customers to use their personal computers to make reservations. All the large carmakers insist that their suppliers agree to adopt computerized information systems that allow information to be transferred and retrieved easily and without error.[50] So important have the new information technologies become in managing transfers of information between organizations that information and computer organizations such as Apple, Sony, Matsushita, Philips, and AT&T agreed in 1993 to form a joint venture and created a new organization, General Magic, to create the software that they all will use in the personal communicator industry. By creating an industry standard, these different organizations ensure that all of their products will be able to communicate with one another.

Chapter 8 discussed how managing the environment is becoming increasingly difficult as organizations extend their operations abroad and as competition increases in an industry. AIT can help an organization manage its environment in several ways. First, information systems such as global teleconferencing can help an organization to coordinate its domestic and foreign operations—a great help to organizations that outsource many of their functional activities to other global organizations. Computer information systems also facilitate the transfer of information between organizations and the coordination of interorganizational relations. For example, a shared networking information system permits close ties between the R&D departments of joint venture partners and also makes it easier to oversee the performance of joint ventures. At all levels—individual, departmental, organizational, and interorganizational—AIT enhances the value creation process and facilitates the management of both the organization and its environment. Consider how Amazon.com utilized both advanced information *and* manufacturing technology to create a competitive advantage.

Focus on New Information Technology: Amazon.com, Part 7

As we have seen throughout this book, Amazon.com has capitalized on new technological breakthroughs, particularly the development of the Internet, to develop a successful business-level strategy and create value for its customers. What is interesting, however, is that it has done this in a way that allows it to capitalize on advanced manufacturing technology as well.

Take the book-ordering process, for example. First, Amazon.com's customers use its Internet information system to find and select books in which they are interested; customers do the work. Essentially, what this means in terms of Figure 10.2 is that Amazon.com is utilizing a just-in-time inventory system. Once the customer buys a book, Amazon.com is then able to order the book directly from the publisher. Thus, it has to carry far less inventory than conventional bookstores, which results in huge cost savings. For example, Amazon.com turns its inventory 150 times a year versus four or five times for a regular bookstore.[51] Moreover, since Amazon.com is able to customize an order exactly to a customer's

requirements, unlike for example, a book-of-the-month club, which is only able to offer customers a small range of book selections, one can argue that its information systems essentially provide it with the advantages of flexible manufacturing technology discussed earlier—the ability to customize a product to the needs of each customer at little or no extra cost. Finally, as is discussed further in the chapter, its information systems permit the company to stay small and flexible. As we saw in Chapters 2 and 4, Amazon.com has decentralized control of all day-to-day operating activities to its employees, and it has a flat, functional structure that is cost-effective and that also permits a quick response to customer needs.

All in all, Amazon.com's innovative use of technology has allowed it to achieve a strategy-structure fit that has become a model for e-commerce business. And new technological developments such as streaming audio and video, which will allow customers to see a book's features and listen to authors discussing their work, can only enhance its competitive advantage.

IMPLICATIONS OF ADVANCED INFORMATION TECHNOLOGIES

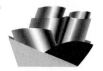

The revolution in information technology, such as is taking place at Amazon.com, is having a profound effect on the management of all organizations, whether they are Internet related or not. By improving the ability of managers to coordinate and control the activities of the organization, and by helping managers make more effective decisions, modern AIT has become a central component of any organization.

Information Systems and Organization Structure

Before the computer age, the main conduit that organizations used for gathering information was the management hierarchy. However, as discussed in Chapter 3, management hierarchies suffer from a number of deficiencies that impact negatively on the quality and timeliness of the information they can provide. Until the development of modern computer-based information systems, however, there was no viable alternative to hierarchy. Now there is, and the results have included the flattening of hierarchy and an increase in horizontal information flows both within and between organizations.[52]

FLATTENING ORGANIZATIONS.   By providing managers with high-quality, timely, and relatively complete information electronically, the new information technologies have reduced the need for tall management hierarchies. For example, consider the computer-based information system that T. J. Rodgers, CEO of Cypress Semiconductor, uses to help control his 1,500-employee organization. Rodgers requires each employee to maintain a list of 10 to 15 goals such as "meet with marketing for a new-product launch" or "make sure to check with customer X." Noted along with each goal is when it was agreed upon, when it is due to be finished, and so forth. This information is stored in a computer, and Rodgers claims that he can review the goals of all 1,500 employees in about four hours, which he does once a week![53] In an earlier age, Rodgers might have needed several managers to undertake such performance reviews. Thus, advanced information systems have reduced the need for hierarchy as a device to *control* the activities of the organization. In a similar vein, advanced information systems have also reduced the need for managers to *coordinate* and horizontally integrate the activities of the organization's different subunits. Information systems now coordinate the flow of production in an organization.

HORIZONTAL INFORMATION FLOWS.   Facilitated by the growth of three-tier, client-server computing architecture—personal computers, linked to a powerful server or mini-computer, linked to a mainframe computer—the last few years have seen the rapid expansion of organization-wide computer networks. Computer networks are now used as a primary conduit of information within many organizations. Both e-mail systems and the development of intranet software programs for sharing documents electronically, such as Lotus Notes, now owned by IBM, have accelerated this trend.

One of the major consequences of this development is an increase in horizontal information flows within organizations so that the development of organization-wide computer networks is breaking down the barriers—produced by differences in subunit orientations—that have traditionally separated departments and subunits.[54] Insofar as this is the case, the result should be an increase in integration, which can help to improve organizational performance. For example, faster product development and responsiveness to customers require managers to break down the barriers that have traditionally separated functional departments, and computer networks are a tool for doing this.[55]

Another consequence of advanced information technology's ability to speed the flow of horizontal communication has been the growth of outsourcing and the development of network organizations. To the degree that AIT can provide the required level of integration, activities that were previously performed in-house can now be handled outside. As an illustration of how AIT can promote product development, one has to look no further than the experience of Lotus Development Corporation, the company that developed Lotus Notes. In the early 1990s, using its own Notes technology, Lotus found that low-cost software writers in Asia and Europe could work almost concurrently with their counterparts in America, sharing documentation and communicating on a real-time basis. As a result, according to former CEO Jim Manzi, Lotus could release, say, a Japanese version of a new product within three or four weeks of its English language release, compared to the three-to-four-month time lag that existed before the adoption of Notes and before its takeover by IBM. Lotus was moving more and more toward outsourcing its software customization activities.[56]

Information Systems and Competitive Advantage

As noted earlier, the choice of an appropriate information technology can improve the competitiveness of an organization. Indeed, it is the search for competitive advantage that is driving the rapid development and adoption of AIT. For example, by reducing the need for hierarchy, modern information systems can reduce bureaucratic costs. One reason for this is that the adoption of AIT can reduce the number of managers required to coordinate and control organization activities. At one time, 13 layers of management lay between Eastman Kodak's general manager of manufacturing and the factory floor. Now, aided by information systems, the number of layers has been reduced to just four. Similarly, Intel has found that by increasing the sophistication of its information systems it has been able to cut the number of hierarchical layers in the organization from ten to five.

William Davidow and Michael Malone, coauthors of *The Virtual Corporation,* have described how AIT can be used to improve an organization's responsiveness to its customers—another source of competitive advantage. The essence of their argument is that information systems and technology are allowing companies to create *virtual products,* products that are customized to the needs of individual customers, without any extra-cost penalty. An example of this trend, the case of Motorola's factory of the future, was discussed in Organizational Insight 10.1, where we saw how Motorola is able to customize pagers to the needs of individual customers, and to do so at little extra cost. Another example of how advanced AIT can be used to produce virtual products and improve competitiveness is discussed in Organizational Insight 10.6 about Levi Strauss & Company.

10.6 LEVI'S DIGITAL JEANS

In 1994, Levi Strauss & Company began introducing a system that could change the face of apparel retailing. Levi's had long been aware that women often complained about the difficulty of finding off-the-rack jeans that fit properly. Now advances in information technology may be allowing Levi's to do something about it. Using the new technology, a sales clerk at an Original Levi's Store can use a personal computer and the customer's vital statistics to create what amounts to a digital blue jeans blueprint. A touch-screen software system leads a sales clerk through the fitting process and requires no special computer skills. The software allows for 4,224 possible combinations of four basic measurements: hips, waist, inseam, and rise. The sales clerk takes these coordinates by tape measure and enters them into the personal computer, along with other desired features such as color and style.

Once completed, a customer's order can be sent electronically to the company's factory in Mountain City, Tennessee, where the denim for the jeans will be cut to specification by a computer-driven cutting machine. The pieces are then tagged with bar codes and sent through the regular mass-production washing and sewing process. At the end of the assembly process, scanning equipment separates out the jeans, which are then sent to the store where they were ordered, or, if the customer prefers, by Federal Express to the customer's home.

The total additional cost to the customer is $10, well worth it according to one satisfied customer, Beth Gilmore, who paid $56 for a pair of digitally tailored Levi's from a store in Cincinnati. "I'm tall," she said. "In the past, there's always been a compromise—they're either too big or too little somewhere." Her digital jeans, in contrast, "fit like a glove.[57]"

Levi Strauss will not disclose how many jeans it has sold this way, but the company notes that sales of women's jeans at the Cincinnati store where the system is being tested rose by 300 percent compared with the prior year. By the end of 1995, the company was offering the service on an experimental basis to some 30 Original Levi Stores. Levi Strauss adopt the technology worldwide in the late 1990s and currently has over 30 locations operating in the United States. In 1999, it also experimented with a megastore in San Francisco that contains a hot tub in which customers can shrink their jeans to fit and afterward dry off in a waist-high glass booth that is filled with warm air.[58]

As this story suggests, properly implemented information systems can improve the ability of managers to coordinate and control organizational activities. Having said this, it must also be recognized that AIT is not always easy to implement within an organization, and once implemented it may still have its limitations. The final section looks at these two issues.

Problems Associated with Advanced Information Technology

There is evidence that implementing advanced information technology within organizations is no easy matter because of political opposition within organizations.[59] As just discussed, AIT can change the way in which an organization is managed by flattening hierarchies and encouraging horizontal, rather than vertical, information flows.

Many managers find these reengineering changes threatening, particularly if they suspect that their power and authority, or even their job security, may be impacted negatively by such changes.[60] Midlevel managers may worry that the adoption of computer-based management information systems may be followed by widespread management layoffs—as often happens. Thus, they will try to resist their implementation. Similarly, managers in charge of particular departments may worry that the adoption of a computer network, by encouraging horizontal information flows among managers deep within different departments, may limit their ability to control the flow of information into and out of the departments. If they perceive the resulting lack of control over information flows as impacting negatively upon their power, or even reengineering them out of a job, as well they might since control over information is a major source of power (see Chapter 14), then they may be tempted to try to block the implementation of AIT.[61]

One study found that managers who opposed the implementation of new information technology for political reasons adopted a number of tactics of counterimplementation, including (1) diverting resources from the project, (2) deflecting the goals of the project, (3) dissipating the energies of the project, and (4) neglecting the project with the hope that it would go away.[62] One way to overcome such attempts at counterimplementation is to link implementation of AIT with an organizational change program of the type that will be discussed in Chapter 13 of this book.

For all of its usefulness, AIT has its limitations. One potential problem is that with all of the enthusiasm for new information systems, electronic communication via a computer network and the like, a vital human element of communication might be lost. There are some kinds of information that cannot be aggregated and summarized by computer. Henry Mintzberg has noted that thick information is often required to coordinate and control an organization, that is, information rich in detail and color, far beyond that which can be quantified and aggregated by electronic means.[63] According to Mintzberg, such information must be dug out, on site, by people intimately involved with the phenomenon they wish to influence. Electronic information cannot substitute for thick information. For example, it would be wrong to make a judgment about a department's performance merely by "reading the numbers" provided by a computer report. Instead, the numbers should be used to alert managers to search for potential performance problems. The nature of these performance problems should then be explored in face-to-face visits with the members of the department, during which thick information can be gathered.

For similar reasons, electronic communication between individuals who are geographically dispersed, yet working together via a computer network, must be linked with regular face-to-face contact so that the human element of communication and cooperation is not lost. At Boeing, for example, the use of e-mail and video conferencing has not reduced the need to visit people at other sites; it has increased it. E-mail has facilitated the establishment of communication channels between people who previously would not communicate, which is an advantage, but direct visits are still required to cement any working relationships that evolve out of these electronic meetings. Finally, it is interesting to note that managers have been heard to complain that, for all of the benefits of internal e-mail or intranet systems, one of their drawbacks is that people spend a lot of time behind closed doors looking at computer screens and communicating electronically, and very little time interacting directly with other managers.[64] When face-to-face communication becomes rare in an organization, management decisions may suffer because of a lack of thick information, and value creation opportunities may be lost.

SUMMARY

New developments in manufacturing and information technology have changed the way organizations produce and develop goods and services and serve their customers. Advanced manufacturing technology has revolutionized mass production, making it more like small-batch and continuous-process technologies. All organizations can use total quality management to focus their input, conversion, and output activities more closely on the customer and find better ways of delivering goods and services to customers. Advanced information technology can improve the productivity of every function and enhance the flow of information within and between functions. An effective organization must exploit and manage the new technological environment to increase the value that the organization produces. Chapter 10 has made the following main points:

1. Traditional mass production relies on dedicated machines, fixed workers, standardized procedures, and the use of inventory buffers to make the work process predictable. The philosophy of mass production is guided by the need to reduce costs and increase technical efficiency. As a result, organizations operating a mass-production technology produce only a narrow range of standardized products.

2. When changing market conditions require an organization to rapidly introduce new products and customize products to suit customers, and keep costs low, a new, more flexible form of technology is needed.

3. Advanced manufacturing technology consists of innovations in materials technology and in knowledge technology that change the work process of traditional mass-production organizations.

4. Innovations in materials technology include computer-aided design, computer-aided materials management, just-in-time inventory systems, flexible manufacturing technology, and computer-integrated manufacturing.

5. Innovations in knowledge technology include flexible workers and flexible work teams.

6. Together, innovations in materials technology and in knowledge technology allow an organization to retain the technical efficiency gains from traditional mass production and act flexibly in response to changes in customer demands.

7. The proper fit between the materials and knowledge components of AMT is achieved through the design of the organization's structure and the development of a culture that encourages a commitment to quality.

8. Advanced information technology allows an organization to improve its handling and integration of the information-processing needs of all its functions. AIT systems increase organizational flexibility and the coordination of functions.

9. Advanced information technology affects organizational structure both vertically and horizontally. Vertically, it flattens the organizational hierarchy, reducing the need for managers. Horizontally, it increases the level of integration, something that can lead an organization to outsource some of its value creation functions.

10. Problems associated with advanced information technologies include political struggles that can arise between managers who seek to protect their interests, and the loss of thick information, which is vital to effective decision making.

DISCUSSION QUESTIONS

1. What are the main elements of mass-production technology? What kind of organizational structure and culture are you likely to find in a traditional mass-production organization?

2. Discuss how AMT and innovations in materials technology and in knowledge technology have increased task interdependence and the technical complexity of the work process. How have these innovations changed the structure of organizations operating a mass-production technology?

3. Under what conditions do flexible work teams function most effectively in organizations?

4. What are the main elements of total quality management? Outline the steps that are needed to establish a TQM system in a traditional mass-production setting.

5. In what ways can advanced information technologies impact organizational structure?

6. Find an organization and determine how new information technologies have affected the way the organization operates in the last decade.

ORGANIZATIONAL THEORY IN ACTION

PRACTICING ORGANIZATIONAL THEORY: BRINGING THE SALES FORCE ON-LINE

Form groups of three to five people and discuss the following scenario:

You are a group of sales managers of a major pharmaceutical company. You each supervise a group of 50 highly trained regional salespeople who visit HMOs and doctors to promote your company's products. You are now meeting to discuss what kind of advanced information technologies you could implement to better control the activities of salespeople in the field to improve national sales force effectiveness.

1. What potential benefits could AIT provide to improve your sales force effectiveness?
2. What specific kinds of AIT would you implement to obtain these benefits?
3. What potential problems might arise as you implement AIT?

MAKING THE CONNECTION #10

Find an example of an organization that has implemented one or more of the innovations in manufacturing or information technology. What innovation was it, how well has it worked, and what have been its effects on organizational structure and culture?

Analyzing the Organization: Design Module #10

This module continues your analysis of technology. It focuses on the extent to which your organization is or should be introducing elements of advanced manufacturing or information technology to increase its effectiveness.

ASSIGNMENT

1. Describe the philosophy behind the way in which your organization produces goods or services.

2. Judging from the goods or services that your organization produces, and the nature of its technology (which you identified in Design Module #9), identify the elements of advanced technology that are best suited to your organization's activities.

3. In what ways can advanced technologies help your organization increase its effectiveness in terms of efficiency, innovation, and stakeholder satisfaction?

4. Has your organization adopted any advanced kinds of technologies? Which ones? What success has it had as a result?

5. If you were selling the advantages of new technology to the managers of your organization, what would you tell them that it can do for them?

6. To what extent do you think the structure and culture of your organization are shaped by its technology? On the basis of your analysis of your organization's size, strategy, environment, and technology, indicate which factor you think is the most important contingency in explaining your organization's choice of structure and culture.

Cases for Analysis:
TOYOTA'S FLEXIBLE PRODUCTION SYSTEM

In 1956, Ohno Taiichi, a Toyota production engineer, came to the United States to visit automobile plants operated by Ford and General Motors in order to understand their mass-production methods. This visit convinced Taiichi that the manufacturing philosophy associated with mass production that had developed since the days of Henry Ford was flawed. He believed that U.S. factories' single-minded focus on the efficiency of the conversion process had actually reduced efficiency, increased costs, and lowered product quality. There were several reasons for these problems, and the solutions that Taiichi proposed jointly make up Toyota's flexible production approach to mass production.[65]

In traditional mass production, to take advantage of specialization and the division of labor, assembly-line workers perform only a single, fixed task rather than a variety of tasks. The assembly tasks are so routine and monotonous that workers become bored and frustrated, and the result is an increase in defects and a decrease in output quality. In contrast, workers in Toyota's flexible production system are thought of not as cogs in a machine but as a resource to be used to enhance organizational effectiveness. Toyota's workers are assigned to a task group or team. Each worker is required to learn all the tasks performed by the group. Workers are expected to find new and better ways of performing their tasks so that productivity can be continually improved. They are also required to take responsibility for monitoring and controlling the quality of their activities. (In the traditional system, quality control is the responsibility of people at the end of the assembly line.) Toyota's flexible work teams take advantage of employees' skills to reduce costs and improve quality; in return, workers are guaranteed lifetime employment, and their salary is linked to the profits of the company.

According to traditional mass-production philosophy, an organization produces a limited product line in massive quantities to gain the economies of scale that result from spreading the fixed costs of setting up specialized or dedicated equipment over as large a production run as possible. Ford, for example, had a dedicated machine that could produce only left-side doors. To reduce the unit cost of these doors, Ford made 50,000 of them at a time and held them in inventory until they were needed, increasing inventory costs. The use of dedicated machines makes it difficult for a company to switch production from one kind of product to another, to customize products, or to change models rapidly in response to competitors' product innovations.

Ohno Taiichi developed Toyota's capacity to produce a wide variety of products while using continuous-flow principles of mass production. Toyota designed machines on which the stamping dies could be changed quickly and easily. This new flexible manufacturing technology permitted Toyota to stamp out body parts in lot sizes as small as a few hundred. The ability to produce a wide variety of components meant that Toyota's flexible work teams could assemble a wide variety of products and that more than one model of car could be made on the same production line.

In traditional mass production, large inventories of parts and finished products are typically stockpiled to safeguard the conversion process from supply disruptions. To further protect the conversion process, American car companies vertically integrated and, thus, produced many of their own components. Like the use of dedicated machines, vertical integration and stockpiling raise costs and make it difficult for a company to change products in response to changes in customer demand. Toyota developed a different approach to managing its inputs. Toyota buys a minority stake in its suppliers and allows them to control their own activities, and it uses a just-in-time inventory system. Toyota's suppliers quickly produce components to order. The arrival of parts "just in time" for assembly not only minimizes the costs of carrying inventory but also allows Toyota to switch production rapidly to a different style or model of car as customer needs change.

Flexible work teams, flexible machines, and just-in-time inventory systems are at the heart of Toyota's flexible production system. Some theorists have described these refinements as a logical ex-

tension of Henry Ford's progressive manufacturing, and Ohno Taiichi once said that if Henry Ford was still alive he eventually would have done what Toyota has done.[66] In fact, Ford and General Motors have picked up many of these techniques from the Japanese, and many of their plants now use flexible manufacturing technology that is achieving levels of quality and performance similar to Toyota's.

1. What are the main elements of Toyota's flexible production system?

2. How does this production systems affect a company's strategy and structure?

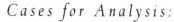

Cases for Analysis:
MANAGING MANUFACTURER-SUPPLIER RELATIONSHIPS

In the 1980s, the typical relationship between manufacturers and suppliers was conducted as follows: A manufacturer would first design the part that it needed itself using its own design engineers. It would then ask several suppliers to bid on producing the part and would normally choose the lowest-cost supplier. The development of advanced information technology has changed all this.

Recognizing that suppliers—the people who produce the parts—may be better positioned to design high-quality parts that can be produced at low cost, many manufacturers are letting their suppliers also design their own parts. Manufacturers electronically transmit to suppliers a description of the part that they need, early prototypes of the part, and specifications that the part will need to meet. A supplier then creates an in-house design team to both design and produce the part. Why are suppliers willing to incur the additional costs of designing the part for manufacturers? Because increasingly they are able to draw on the computer-aided design skills of their in-house designers so that they achieve economies of scale and scope in the design process. Moreover, if they satisfy the needs of a particular manufacturer, they are likely to become involved in a long-term relationship with that manufacturer, which can lead to big, long-term rewards. For example, Johnson Controls, a large supplier of automotive components for all the major car companies, set up a design studio to design a new generation of car seats for Chrysler's next line of midrange cars. So pleased was Chrysler with Johnson Controls' efforts that it ended a relationship with one of Johnson Controls' main rivals, Douglas & Lomason Company. Chrysler's platform teams are able to communicate continuously with Johnson's engineers using AIT so that, as Chrysler modifies the design of a new car, the implications of these changes for the design of the new seats can be continuously fed to Johnson's engineers.

Another striking way in which AIT can be used to coordinate relationships between a manufacturer and its suppliers occurs when a manufacturer needs to coordinate the activities of hundreds of suppliers to produce a final product. Boeing, for example, faced this task when it was designing its new 777 airplane. The 777 was the first plane that Boeing designed using computer-aided design technology. The airplane was literally designed through an AIT system that Boeing developed internally. Boeing then contracted with hundreds of different suppliers to both design and manufacture the 777's components and electronically linked up with its suppliers and made them a part of its AIT system. When Boeing made changes to the aircraft's design, it kept its suppliers informed through the AIT system, which showed them the implications of the design changes for the design of their respective parts. Similarly, if suppliers made a design change that affected Boeing and the other suppliers, they communicated this through the AIT system so that all parties involved had constant feedback and knowledge of the changes taking place. The result was that when the first 777 was actually assembled, all the pieces fitted together almost perfectly and the nose-to-tail measurement was off less than 23/1,000 of an inch. This was a big change from the old non-AIT system, where measurement could be off by a foot, necessitating a costly redesign process that often cost over $500 million. Although Boeing's AIT system cost over $1 billion to establish, it can now be used for all future design purposes.

1. What are the gains from using AIT to coordinate information between manufacturers and suppliers?

2. What might some of a manufacturer's problems or risks be in allowing suppliers to design its inputs?

REFERENCES

1. J. D. Thompson, *Organizations in Action* (New York: McGraw-Hill, 1967).

2. C. Edquist and S. Jacobsson, *Flexible Automation: The Global Diffusion of New Technology in the Engineering Industry* (London: Basil Blackwell, 1988).

2. Ibid.

4. M. Jelinek and J. D. Goldhar, "The Strategic Implications of the Factory of the Future," *Sloan Management Review*, 1984, vol. 25, pp. 29–37; G. I. Susman and J. W. Dean, "Strategic Use of Computer Integrated Manufacturing in the Emerging Competitive Environment," *Computer Integrated Manufacturing Systems*, 1989, vol. 2, pp. 133–138.

5. C. A. Voss, *Managing Advanced Manufacturing Technology* (Bedford, England: IFS Publications Ltd., 1986).

6. J. F. Krafcik, "Triumph of the Lean Production System," *Sloan Management Review*, Fall 1988, pp. 41–52.

7. Ibid.; M. T. Sweeney, "Flexible Manufacturing Systems—Managing Their Integration," in Voss, *Managing Advanced Manufacturing Technology*, pp. 69–81.

8. D. E. Whitney, "Manufacturing by Design," *Harvard Business Review*, July–August 1988, pp. 210–216.

9. "Microtechnology, Dropping Out," *The Economist*, 9 January 1993, p. 75.

10. F. M. Hull and P. D. Collins, "High Technology Batch Production Systems: Woodward's Missing Types," *Academy of Management Journal*, 1987, vol. 30, pp. 786–797.

11. R. H. Hayes and S. C. Wheelright, *Restoring Our Competitive Edge: Competing Through Manufacturing* (New York: Wiley, 1984).

12. C. A. Voss, "Managing Manufacturing Technology," in R. Wild, ed., *International Handbook of Production and Operations Management* (London: Cassel, 1989), pp. 112–121.

13. C. C. New and G. R. Clark, "Just-in-Time Manufacturing," Ibid., pp. 402–417.

14. S. M. Young, "A Framework for the Successful Adoption and Performance of Japanese Manufacturing Practices in the United States," *Academy of Management Review*, 1992, vol. 17, pp. 677–700.

15. A. Ansari and B. Modarress, *Just-in-Time Purchasing* (New York: The Free Press, 1990).

16. J. P. Womack, D. T. Jones, D. Roos, and D. Sammons, *The Machine That Changed the World* (New York: Macmillan, 1990).

17. H.-J. Warnecke and R. Steinhilper, "CIM, FMS, and Robots," in Wild, *International Handbook of Production and Operations Management*, pp. 146–173.

18. B. Avishai and W. Taylor, "Customers Drive a Technology-Driven Company: An Interview with George Fisher," *Harvard Business Review*, November–December 1989, pp. 106–114.

19. P. L. Nemetz and L. W. Fry, "Flexible Manufacturing Organizations: Implications for Strategy Formulation and Organizational Design," *Academy of Management Review*, 1988, vol. 13, pp. 627–638.

20. Young, "A Framework for the Successful Adoption and Performance of Japanese Manufacturing Practices in the United States."

21. R. Parthasarthy and S. P. Sethi, "The Impact of Flexible Automation on Business Strategy and Organizational Structure," *Academy of Management Review*, 1992, vol. 17, pp. 86–111; Voss, "Managing Manufacturing Technology."

22. B. Rayner, "Trial-by-Fire Transformation: An Interview with Globe Metallurgical's Arden C. Sims," *Harvard Business Review*, May–June 1992, pp. 117–129.

23. www.globemetallurgical.com, Annual Report, 1999.

24. Womack, Jones, Roos, and Sammons, *The Machine That Changed the World*.

25. J. McHugh and B. Dale, "Quality Circles," in Wild, *International Handbook of Production and Operations Research*, pp. 112–121.

26. "Return of the Stopwatch," *The Economist*, 23 January 1993, p. 69.

27. M. Nauman, "General Motors Committed to Freemont, Calif. Plant Shared with Toyota Corolla Sedans," *San Jose Mercury News*, 2 September 1999, p. 2.

28. J. Talmage and R. G. Hannam, *Flexible Manufacturing Systems in Practice* (New York: Marcel Dekker, 1988).

29. M. Walton, *The Deming Management Method* (New York: Perigee Books, 1990).

30. Young, "A Framework for Successful Adoption and Performance of Japanese Manufacturing Practices in the United States."

31. M. Walton, *The Deming Management Method*.

32. "How Does Service Drive the Service Company?" *Harvard Business Review*, November–December 1991, pp. 146–158.

33. "A Little Bit of Smarts, a Lot of Hard Work," *Business Week*, 30 September 1992, p. 70.

34. A. Gabor, "Rochester Focuses: A Community's Core Competences," *Harvard Business Review*, July–August 1991, pp. 116–126.

35. B. Witcher and R. Butterworth, "Hoshin Kanri: How Xerox Manages," *Total Quality Monthly*, June 1999, pp. 13–20.

36. R. F. Zammuto and E. J. O'Connor, "Gaining Advanced Manufacturing Technologies' Benefits: The Roles of Organizational Design and Culture," *Academy of Management Review*, 1992, vol. 4, pp. 701–728.

37. Nemetz and Fry, "Flexible Manufacturing Organizations."

38. S. M. Young and J. S. Davis, "Factories of the Past and Future: The Implications of Robotics on Workers and Management Accounting Systems," in D. Cooper and T. Hopper, eds., *Critical Accounts* (London: Macmillan, 1990), pp. 87–106.

39. Young, "A Framework for Successful Adoption and Performance of Japanese Manufacturing Practices in the United States," p. 686.

40. Ibid., p. 685.

41. Zammuto and O'Connor, "Gaining Advanced Manufacturing Technologies Benefits."

42. See (i) W. H. Davidow and M. S. Malone. *The Virtual Corporation* (New York: Harper Business, 1992); (ii) M. E. Porter, *Competitive Advantage* (New York: The Free Press, 1984).

43. Ibid.

44. See (i) R. I. Benjamin and J. Blunt, "Critical IT Issues: The Next Ten Years," *Sloan Management Review*, Summer 1992, pp. 7–19; (ii) W. H. Davidow and M. S. Malone, *The Virtual Corporation*.

45. G. P. Huber, "A Theory of the Effects of Advanced Information Technologies on Organizational Design, Intelligence, and Decision Making," *Academy of Management Review*, 1990, vol. 14, pp. 47–71.

46. R. F. Monger, *Mastering Technology* (New York: The Free Press, 1988).

47. www.cakebread.com, 1999.

48. T. Steinert-Threlkeld, "Compuadd to Supply McDonald's," *Dallas Morning News*, 20 October 1992, p. 2D.

49. "Banks and Technology," *The Economist*, 3 October 1992, pp. 21–23.

50. M. D. Hopper, "Rattling Sabre—New Ways to Compete on Information," *Harvard Business Review*, May–June 1990, pp. 118–125.

51. "Who's Writing the Book Business?" *Fast Company*, October-November, 1996, pp.132–133.

52. J. Fulk and G. DeSanctis, "Electronic Communication and Changing Organizational Forms," *Organizational Science*, 1995, vol. 6, pp. 337–349.

53. B. Dumaine, "The Bureaucracy Busters," *Fortune*, 17 June 1991, p. 46.

54. See, for example, W. H. Davidow and M. S. Malone. *The Virtual Corporation*.

55. P. Hinds and S. Kiesler, "Communication Across Boundaries: Work Structure and Use of Communications Technologies in a Large Organization," *Organizational Science*, 1995, vol. 6, pp. 373–393.

56. T. A. Stewart, "Managing in a Wire Company," *Fortune*, 11 July 1994, pp. 44–56.

57. W. H. Davidow and M. S. Malone, *The Virtual Corporation*, p. 168.

58. See (i) J. R. Meredith, "The Implementation of Computer Based Systems," *Journal of Operational Management*, October 1981; (ii) F. Turban, *Decision Support and Expert Systems: Managerial Perspectives* (New York: Macmillan, 1988), Chapter 16; (iii) R. J. Thierauf, *Effective Management and Evaluation of Information Technology* (London: Quorum Books, 1994).

59. T. H. Davenport, R. G. Eccles, and L. Prusak, "Information Politics," *Sloan Management Review*, Fall 1992, pp. 53–65.

60. J. Pfeffer, *Managing with Power* (Boston: Harvard Business School Press, 1992).

61. G. Dickson and J. C. Wetherby, "MIS Project Management: Myths, Opinions, and Realities," in W. McFarlin, ed., *Information Systems Administration* (New York: Holt, Rinehart, and Winston, 1993).

62. H. Mintzberg, *Mintzberg on Management: Inside our Strange World of Organizations* (New York: The Free Press, 1989).

63. T. A. Stewart, "Managing in a Wired Company," p. 54.

64. C. W. L. Hill, "Toyota: The Evolution of Toyota's Production System," in C. W. L. Hill and G. R. Jones, *Strategic Management: An Integrated Approach*, 2nd ed. (Boston: Houghton Mifflin, 1992).

65. J. F. Krafcik, "Triumph of the Lean Production System," pp. 41–52.

66. N. Templin and J. Cole, "Manufacturers Use Suppliers to Help Them Develop New Products," *Wall Street Journal*, 10 December 1994, pp. A1, A4.

Chapter 11

ORGANIZATIONAL BIRTH, GROWTH, DECLINE, and DEATH

Organizations that successfully carve out a niche in their environments so that they can attract resources (such as customers) face a series of problems in their struggle for growth and survival. The first problem is surviving the perils of organizational birth. Other problems arise as the organization grows; and, as the organization matures, the problems must be managed to prevent the onset of decline or death. This chapter examines the life cycle of an organization and three theories about how and when life cycle problems emerge and how they can be managed. It also looks at the consequences of the failure to manage the growth and maturing process. Managers who understand the factors that lead to organizational birth and growth, that influence maturity, and that cause decline and death will be able to change their organization's strategy and structure to increase its effectiveness and chances of survival.

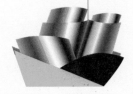

THE ORGANIZATIONAL LIFE CYCLE

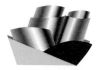

Organizational life cycle
A sequence of stages of growth and development through which organizations may pass.

Why do some organizations survive and prosper while others fail and die? Why do some organizations have the ability to manage their strategies, structures, and cultures to gain access to environmental resources while others fail at this task? To answer these questions, researchers have suggested that we need to understand the dynamics that affect organizations as they seek a satisfactory fit with their environment.[1] It has been suggested that organizations experience a predictable sequence of stages of growth and development: the **organizational life cycle**.

The four principal stages of the organizational life cycle are birth, growth, decline, and death (see Figure 11.1).[2] Organizations pass through these stages at different rates, and some do not experience every stage. Moreover, some companies go directly from birth to death without enjoying any growth if they do not attract customers or resources. Some organizations spend a long time in the growth stage, and many researchers have identified various substages of growth through which an organization must navigate. There are also substages of decline. Some organizations in decline take corrective action quickly and turn themselves around.

The way an organization manages the problems it confronts determines whether and when it will go on to the next stage in the life cycle and whether it will survive and prosper or fail and die. Each stage is examined in detail here.

ORGANIZATIONAL BIRTH

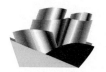

Entrepreneurs *People who recognize and take advantage of opportunities to use their skills and competences to create value.*

Organizations are born when individuals, called **entrepreneurs**, recognize and take advantage of opportunities to use their skills and competences to create value.[3] Michael Dell found a new way to market low-priced computers to customers through the mail. Debbi Fields developed a tasty, moist chocolate-chip cookie. Liz Claiborne exploited a niche in the women's

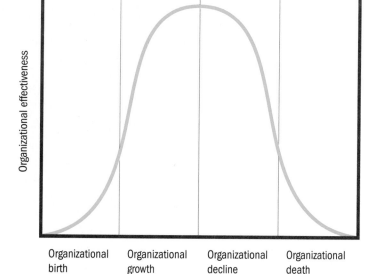

FIGURE 11.1

A Model of the Organizational Life Cycle. Organizations pass through these four stages at different rates, and some do not experience every stage.

Organizational effectiveness

Organizational birth   Organizational growth   Organizational decline   Organizational death

Stage of life cycle

clothing market—business attire for women. Dell, Fields, and Claiborne saw an opportunity to create value (for computer users, cookie lovers, and businesswomen), and each of them seized the opportunity by founding an organization to produce goods or services.[4] Dell Computer follows a low-cost business-level strategy: Dell's computers are less expensive than competitors' computers. Mrs. Fields Cookies follows a differentiation business-level strategy: The company produces a cookie for which customers are willing to pay a premium price.

Organizational birth, the founding of an organization, is a dangerous stage of the life cycle and is associated with the greatest chance of failure. The failure rate is high because new organizations experience the **liability of newness**—the dangers associated with being the first in a new environment.[5] This liability is great for several reasons.

Entrepreneurship is an inherently risky process. Because entrepreneurs undertake *new* ventures, there is no way to predict or guarantee success.[6] Entrepreneurs bear this uncertainty because they stand to earn potentially huge returns if their businesses take off. Much of the time, however, entrepreneurs make mistakes in judgment or planning, and the result is organizational death.[7]

A new organization is fragile because it lacks a formal structure to give its value creation processes and actions stability and certainty. At first everything is done by trial and error. An organizational structure emerges gradually, as decisions about procedures and technology are made. Eventually, for example, it may become clear that one manager should manage money coming in from customers (accounts receivable), another should manage money being paid out to suppliers (accounts payable), and another should obtain new accounts. But at first, in a new organization, the structure is in the mind of the founder; it is not formalized in a chart or a set of rules. The structure is flexible and responsive, allowing the organization to adapt and perfect its routines to meet the needs of its environment.

A flexible structure can be an advantage when it allows the organization to change and take advantage of new opportunities, but it can also be a disadvantage. A formal structure provides stability and certainty by serving as the organization's memory. Structure specifies an organization's activities and the procedures for getting them done. If such procedures are not written down, a new organization can literally forget the skills and procedures that made it successful. A formal structure provides an organization with a firm foundation from which to improve on existing procedures and develop new ones.[8]

Another reason why organizational birth is a dangerous stage is that conditions in the environment may be hostile to a new organization. Resources, for example, may be scarce or difficult to obtain because many established organizations are competing for them.

Organizational birth
The founding of an organization—a dangerous life cycle stage associated with the greatest chance of failure.

Liability of newness *The dangers associated with being the first in a new environment.*

Population ecology theory
A theory that seeks to explain the factors that affect the rate at which new organizations are born (and die) in a population of existing organizations.

A POPULATION ECOLOGY MODEL OF ORGANIZATIONAL BIRTH

Population of organizations *The organizations that are competing for the same set of resources in the environment.*

Population ecology theory seeks to explain the factors that affect the rate at which new organizations are born (and die) in a population of existing organizations.[9] A **population of organizations** comprises the organizations that are competing for the same set of resources in the environment. All the fast-food restaurants in College Station, Texas, constitute a population of restaurants that compete to obtain environmental resources in the form of dollars that students are willing to spend on food. IBM, Compaq, Dell, AST, Gateway, and the other personal computer companies constitute a population of organizations that are seeking to attract environmental resources in the form of dollars that consumers are willing to spend on personal computing. Different organizations within a population may choose to focus on dif-

Environmental niches
Particular sets of resources.

ferent **environmental niches**, or particular sets of resources. Dell Computer chose to focus on the mail-order niche of the personal computer environment; IBM and Compaq originally focused on the business niche; and Apple focused on the higher education niche.

Number of Births

Population density *The number of organizations that can compete for the same resources in a particular environment.*

According to population ecology theory, the availability of resources determines the number of organizations in a population. The amount of resources in an environment limits **population density**—the number of organizations that can compete for the same resources in a particular environment.[10] Population ecology theorists assume that growth in the number of organizational births in a new environment is rapid at first as new organizations are founded to take advantage of new environmental resources, such as dollars that people are willing to spend on personal computing (see Figure 11.2).[11]

Two factors account for the rapid birth rate. The first is that as new organizations are founded, there is an increase in the knowledge and skills available to generate similar new organizations. Many new organizations are founded by entrepreneurs who leave existing companies to set up their own companies. Many new computer companies were founded by people who left pioneering organizations such as Hewlett-Packard and IBM.

The second factor accounting for the rapid birth rate in a new environment is that when a new kind of organization is founded and survives, it provides a role model. The success of a new organization makes it relatively easy for entrepreneurs to found similar new organizations because success confers legitimacy, which will attract stakeholders. Fast-food restaurants, for example, were a relatively untested kind of organization until McDonald's proved their ability to attract resources in the form of customers. Entrepreneurs watched McDonald's create and succeed in the U.S. fast-food market and then imitated McDonald's by founding similar companies, such as Burger King and Wendy's. McDonald's became a U.S. institution, gave the population of fast-food organizations legitimacy, and allowed them to attract stakeholders such as customers, employees, and investors. Now fast food is taken for granted in many countries around the world.

FIGURE 11.2

Organizational Birth Rates over Time.
According to population ecology theory, the rate of birth in a new environment increases rapidly at first and then tapers off as resources become less plentiful and competition increases.

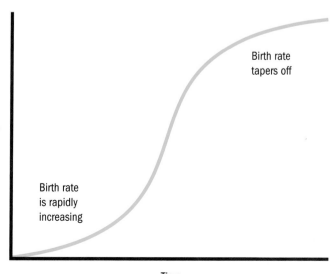

Birth rate tapers off

Number of Organizations

Birth rate is rapidly increasing

Time

Once an environment is populated with a number of successful organizations, the organizational birth rate tapers off (see the S-shaped curve in Figure 11.2).[12] Two factors work to decrease the rate at which organizations are founded. First, births taper off as the availability of resources in the environment for late entrants diminishes.[13] Companies that start first, such as McDonald's or Microsoft, have a competitive edge over later entrants because of first-mover advantages. **First-mover** advantages are the benefits an organization derives from being an early entrant into a new environment. They include customer support, a recognized brand name, and the best locations for new businesses such as restaurants. Latecomers enter an environment that is partially depleted of the resources that they need to grow. Investors, for example, are reluctant to lend money to new firms because their chances of survival in an established competitive environment are poor unless they can somehow discover and keep control of a new niche, as Dell Computer did. Similarly, the best managers and workers prefer to work in organizations that have established reputations and offer secure employment opportunities.

First-mover advantages
The benefits an organization derives from being an early entrant into a new environment.

The second factor that decreases the birth rate is the difficulty of competing with existing organizations for resources.[14] Potential entrepreneurs are discouraged from entering an industry or market because they understand that the larger the number of companies already competing for resources, the more difficult and expensive the resources will be to obtain. To obtain new customers, new companies may need to overspend on advertising or innovation, or they may need to reduce their prices too much. Moreover, existing companies may band together and make it very hard for new companies to enter the market. They may engage in collusion, agreeing (illegally) to set their prices at artificially low levels to drive new rivals out of an industry, or they may erect barriers to entry by investing heavily in advertising so that it is very expensive for new companies to enter the market.

Survival Strategies

Population ecologists have identified two sets of strategies that organizations can use to gain access to resources and enhance their chances of survival in the environment: (1) r-strategy versus K-strategy and (2) specialist strategy versus generalist strategy.

r-strategy A strategy of entering a new environment early.

K-strategy A strategy of entering an environment late, after other organizations have tested the water.

R-STRATEGY VERSUS K-STRATEGY. Organizations that follow an **r-strategy** are founded early in a new environment—they are early entrants. Organizations that follow a **K-strategy** are founded late—they are late entrants.[15] The advantage of an r-strategy is that an organization obtains first-mover advantages and has first pick of the resources in the environment. As a result, the organization is usually able to grow rapidly and develop skills and procedures that increase its chance of surviving and prospering. Organizations that follow a K-strategy are usually established in *other* environments and wait to enter a new environment until the uncertainty in that environment is reduced and the correct way to compete is apparent. These organizations then take the skills they have established in other environments and use them to develop effective procedures that allow them to compete with and often dominate organizations following the r-strategy.

The difference between r-strategy and K-strategy is evident in the situation that emerged in the personal computer industry. In 1977, Apple Computer founded the personal computer market by developing the Apple I. Other small companies quickly followed Apple's lead. Each of them pursued an r-strategy and developed its own personal computer. Many of these companies were successful in attracting resources, and the population of personal computer companies grew quickly. IBM, the dominant player in the mainframe computer market, realized the potential in the personal computer market. It adopted a K-strategy and moved to develop its own personal computer (based on Microsoft's MS-DOS operating system), which it introduced in 1981. The ability to put its massive resources to work in the new environment and to exploit its brand name gave IBM a competitive advantage. As the MS-DOS operating system became the industry standard, IBM drove many of the smaller r-strategists out of the market. IBM even threatened Apple Computer for a while, but Apple was able to hang on to its loyal customers and weather the storm of competition.

K-strategists can often outperform r-strategists when they are competing for the same environmental niche. Apple Computer, for example, focused its activities very heavily on the school and university markets for computers. IBM competed heavily in the business market. Thus, IBM primarily hurt competitors that were trying to occupy the business niche.

SPECIALIST STRATEGY VERSUS GENERALIST STRATEGY.   The difference between a specialist and a generalist strategy is defined by the breadth of the environmental niche—that is, the set of resources—for which an organization competes. Specialist organizations (or **specialists**) concentrate their skills to pursue a narrow range of resources in a single niche. Generalist organizations (or **generalists**) spread their skills thinly to compete for a broad range of resources in many niches.[16] By focusing their activities in one niche, specialists develop core competences that allow them to outperform generalists in that niche. Specialists are likely to offer customers much better service than the service offered by generalists, or they may be able to develop superior products because they invest all their resources in a narrow range of products. Intel, for example, invests all its resources in producing state-of-the-art microprocessors and does not bother with other kinds of electronic or computer components.

Specialists *Organizations that concentrate their skills to pursue a narrow range of resources in a single niche.*

Generalists *Organizations that spread their skills thinly to compete for a broad range of resources in many niches.*

Generalists can often outcompete specialists when there is considerable uncertainty in the environment and when resources are changing so that niches emerge and disappear continually. Generalists can survive in an uncertain environment because they have spread their resources thinly. If one niche disappears, they still have others in which to operate. If a specialist's niche disappears, however, there is a much higher chance of organizational failure and death.

Specialists and generalists often coexist in many environments. The reason for their coexistence is that successful generalists create the conditions that allow specialists to operate successfully.[17] Large department stores, for example, create a demand for different kinds of fashionable clothes. To meet that demand, boutiques set up and specialize in one kind of clothing, such as evening wear or sportswear.

The Process of Natural Selection

The two sets of strategies—specialist versus generalist and r versus K—give rise to four strategies that organizations can pursue: r-specialist, r-generalist, K-specialist, and K-generalist (see Figure 11.3).[18]

Early in an environment, as a niche develops and new resources become available, new organizations are likely to be r-specialists—organizations that move quickly to focus on serving the needs of particular customer groups. Many new organizations grow and prosper, as did Apple Computer. As they grow, they often become generalists and compete in new niches. While this is happening, however, K-generalists (usually the divisions or subsidiaries of large companies such as IBM or General Electric) move into the market and threaten the weakest r-specialist organizations. Eventually, the strongest r-specialists, r-generalists, and K-generalists dominate the environment by serving multiple market segments and by pursuing

FIGURE 11.3

Strategies for Competing in the Resource Environment

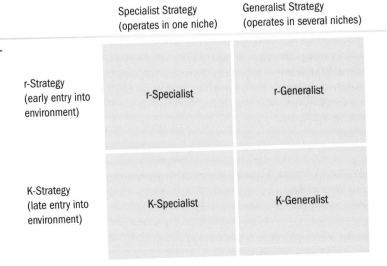

	Specialist Strategy (operates in one niche)	Generalist Strategy (operates in several niches)
r-Strategy (early entry into environment)	r-Specialist	r-Generalist
K-Strategy (late entry into environment)	K-Specialist	K-Generalist

a low-cost or differentiation strategy. Large companies, having chosen the K-generalist strategy, often create niches for new firms to enter the market, so K-specialists are founded to exploit the new market segments. In this way, generalists and specialists can coexist in an environment because they are competing for different sets of resources.

The early beginnings of the car industry provide a good example of this organizational birth process. The first car companies (such as Packard and Duesenberg) were small crafts operations that produced high-priced cars for small market segments. These companies were the original r-specialists. Then Henry Ford realized the potential for establishing a mass market via mass production, and he decided to pursue a K-generalist strategy by producing a low-priced, standardized car for the mass market. Similarly, at General Motors, Alfred Sloan was rapidly pursuing a K-generalist strategy based on differentiation. He positioned GM's different car divisions to serve the whole range of market segments, from low-price Chevrolets to high-price Cadillacs. The low price and variety of car models available eventually drove many of the small r-specialists out of business. GM and Ford, together with Chrysler, proceeded to dominate the environment. Many new small companies pursuing K-specialist strategies then emerged to serve specialist segments that these companies had left open. Luxury-car manufacturers such as Cord and Packard produced high-priced vehicles and prospered for a while, and foreign car manufacturers such as Rolls-Royce, Mercedes, and Bugatti were popular. In the 1970s, Japanese companies such as Toyota and Honda entered the U.S. market with a K-specialist strategy, producing cars much smaller than the vehicles that the Big Three were making. The huge popularity of these new cars gave the Japanese companies access to resources and allowed them to switch to a K-generalist strategy, directly threatening the Big Three. Thus, over time, new generations of organizations are born to take advantage of changes in the distribution of resources and the appearance of new niches.

New organizations are always emerging to take advantage of new opportunities. The driving force behind the population ecology model of organizational birth is **natural selection**, the process that ensures the survival of the organizations that have the skills and abilities that best fit with the environment.[19] Over time, weaker organizations, such as those with old-fashioned or outdated skills and competences or those that cannot adapt their procedures to fit with changes in the environment, are selected out of the environment and die. New kinds of organizations emerge and survive if they can stake a claim to an environmental niche. In the car industry, Ford was a more efficient competitor than the craft shops, which declined

Natural selection *The process that ensures the survival of the organizations that have the skills and abilities that best fit with the environment.*

and died because they lost their niche to Ford. In turn, Japanese companies, which continued to innovate their products and develop new skills, entered the U.S. car market. When customers selected Japanese cars because they wanted smaller, better-quality vehicles, U.S. carmakers were forced to imitate their Japanese competitors in order to survive.

Natural selection is a competitive process. New organizations survive if they can develop skills that allow them to fit with and exploit their environment. Entrepreneurship is the process of developing new capabilities that allow organizations to exploit new niches or find new ways of serving existing niches more efficiently. Over time, entrepreneurship leads to a continuous cycle of organizational birth as new organizations are founded to exploit new opportunities in the environment. Amazon.com offers a good illustration of this process.

Focus on New Information Technology:
Amazon.com, Part 8

Jeff Bezos was the first entrepreneur both to realize that the Internet could be used to effectively sell books and to act on the opportunity by establishing Amazon.com. As such he gave his company a first-mover advantage over rivals, which has been an important component of its strong position in the marketplace. Being early, Amazon.com was able to capture customer attention and keep their loyalty—45 percent of its business is repeat business. Moreover, Amazon.com's very success has made it difficult for new competitors to enter the market, and the birth rate into the industry has tapered off substantially.

First, new "unknown" competitors face the major hurdle of attracting customers to their Web sites rather than to Amazon.com's. Second, even "known" competitors such as Barnes & Noble and Borders, which have imitated Amazon.com's strategy and developed their own on-line bookstores, have faced the problem of attracting away Amazon.com's customer base and securing their position. Being late entrants, these organizations essentially followed a K-strategy, while Amazon.com followed an r-strategy, and this delay in going on-line has cost them dearly in the current highly competitive environment.

Indeed, the process of natural selection has been operating in the book-selling industry. As we have seen in earlier chapters, many small, specialized bookstores have been forced to close their doors. And even large bricks-and-mortar bookstores that may carry hundreds of thousands of books have been unable to compete with an on-line bookstore that can offer customers all 1.5 million books in print at a 10 percent price discount.

In the spring of 1999 a new round of competition took place in the book-selling industry when Amazon.com and its competitors announced a 50 percent discount off the price of new best-selling books in an attempt to keep and grow their market share. Amazon.com and its largest competitors, Barnes & Noble and Borders, are locked in a fierce battle to see who will dominate the book-selling industry in the new millennium.

THE INSTITUTIONAL THEORY
OF ORGANIZATIONAL GROWTH

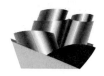

Organizational growth
The life cycle stage in which organizations develop value creation skills and competences that allow them to acquire additional resources.

If an organization survives the birth stage of the organizational life cycle, what factors affect its search for a fit with the environment? Organizations seek to obtain control over scarce resources to reduce the uncertainty they face. They can increase their control over resources by growing and becoming larger.

Organizational growth is the life cycle stage in which organizations develop value creation skills and competences that allow them to acquire additional resources. Growth allows an organization to increase its division of labor and specialization and, thus, develop a competitive advantage. An organization that is able to acquire resources is likely to generate surplus resources that allow it to grow further. Microsoft took the resources that it obtained from its popular MS-DOS system, for example, and used them to employ more computer programmers, who developed new software applications to bring in additional resources. In this way, Microsoft has grown from strength to strength.

Although largeness can increase an organization's chances of survival and stability, Microsoft and other companies do not usually pursue growth as an end in itself. Growth is a by-product of their ability to develop core competences that satisfy the needs of their stakeholders and so give them access to scarce resources.[20] **Institutional theory** studies how organizations can increase their ability to grow and survive in a competitive environment by satisfying their stakeholders.

Institutional theory A theory that studies how organizations can increase their ability to grow and survive in a competitive environment by satisfying their stakeholders.

New organizations suffer from the liability of newness, and many die because they do not develop the skills they need to attract customers and obtain scarce resources. To increase their survival chances as they grow, organizations must gain acceptability and legitimacy in the eyes of their stakeholders. Institutional theory argues that it is as important to study how organizations develop skills that increase their legitimacy in stakeholders' eyes as it is to study how they develop skills that increase their technical efficiency. Institutional theory also argues that to increase their chances of survival, new organizations adopt many of the rules and codes of conduct found in the institutional environment surrounding them.[21]

Institutional environment The set of values and norms in an environment that governs the behavior of a population of organizations.

The **institutional environment** is the set of values and norms that governs the behavior of a population of organizations. For example, the institutional environment of the banking industry comprises strict rules and procedures about what banks can and cannot do and penalties and actions to be taken against banks that break those rules. Banks that follow rules and codes of conduct are considered trustworthy and legitimate by stakeholders, such as customers, employees, and any group that controls the supply of scarce resources.[22] Banks that are considered legitimate are able to attract resources and improve their chances of survival. A new organization can strengthen its legitimacy by imitating the goals, structure, and culture of successful organizations in its population.[23]

Organizational Isomorphism

As organizations grow, they may copy one another's strategies, structures, and cultures and try to adopt certain behaviors because they believe doing so will increase their chances of survival. As a result, **organizational isomorphism**—the similarity among organizations in a population—increases. Three processes that explain why organizations become similar have been identified: coercive, mimetic, and normative isomorphism.[24]

Organizational isomorphism The similarity among organizations in a population.

COERCIVE ISOMORPHISM.
Isomorphism is said to be *coercive* when an organization adopts certain norms because of pressures exerted by other organizations and by society in general. As the dependence of one organization on another increases, the dependent organization is likely to become increasingly similar to the more powerful organization. Recall from Organizational Insight 10.4 how Xerox forced its suppliers to adopt TQM practices and develop work rules and procedures similar to those used by Xerox. Similarly, we discussed how the general public has put pressure on Wal-Mart and other organizations to boycott goods made by children in third-world countries. Coercive isomorphism also results when organizations are forced to adopt nondiscriminatory, equitable hiring practices because they are mandated by law.

MIMETIC ISOMORPHISM.
Isomorphism is *mimetic* when organizations intentionally imitate and copy one another to increase their legitimacy. A new organization is especially likely to imitate the structure and processes of successful organizations when the environment is very uncertain and the new organization is trying to find the structure, strategy, culture, and technology that will allow it to survive.[25] Because of mimetic

isomorphism, the similarity of a population of similar organizations, such as fast-food restaurants, increases along the lines suggested by the S-shaped curve in Figure 11.2.

McDonald's was the first organization to operate a national chain of fast-food restaurants. Ray Kroc, the man who orchestrated its growth, developed rules and procedures that were easy to replicate in every McDonald's restaurant. Standardization allowed the individual restaurants within the McDonald's organization to imitate one another, so that each part could reach the same high standards of performance. Entrepreneurs who later entered the fast-food industry saw how successful McDonald's was and imitated many of the techniques and procedures that McDonald's had developed. Thus, customers expect to see the same kinds of food on the menus of all fast-food restaurants, they expect certain standards of speed and cleanliness, and they expect to clear their own tables.

Although imitating the most successful organizations in a population increases efficiency and chances for success, there is a limit to how much a new organization should imitate an existing one. The first organization in the industry gains a first-mover advantage. If late arrivals model themselves too closely on the leader, customers might see no reason to try the newer restaurant. Each new organization needs to develop some unique competences to differentiate itself and define the niche where it has access to most resources. Wendy's principal claim to fame is that it can provide customers with a customized burger, unlike the McDonald's burger, which is totally standardized; and Burger King, unlike McDonald's, offers charbroiled instead of fried burgers.

NORMATIVE ISOMORPHISM. Isomorphism is *normative* when organizations come to resemble each other because over time they indirectly adopt the norms and values of other organizations in the environment. Organizations acquire norms and values in several ways. Managers and employees often move from one organization to another and bring with them the norms and values of their former employers. Many new telecommunications companies, for example, recruit managers from large companies such as AT&T and GTE. Similarly, Dell Computer recruits managers who know how to run a growing computer company because they have worked in one. Organizations also indirectly acquire norms and values through industry, trade, and professional associations. Through meetings and publications, these associations promote specific ideas to their members. Because of this indirect influence, organizations within an industry come to develop a similar view of the world.

Disadvantages of Isomorphism

Although organizational isomorphism can help new and growing organizations develop stability and legitimacy, it has some disadvantages.[26] First, organizations may learn ways to behave that have become outdated and no longer lead to organizational effectiveness. The pressure to imitate may reduce the level of innovation in the environment. For many years, for example, the Big Three U.S. carmakers were happy to imitate one another and produce big, fuel-inefficient cars. Innovations to reduce the costs of making a car or to significantly improve design, efficiency, and quality were few and slow in coming because no company took the lead. The entry of new companies from abroad was needed to show U.S. automakers that new manufacturing procedures could be developed.

An interesting example of the negative effects of imitation is evident in the way in which many U.S. companies started total quality management programs only to become disillusioned when TQM failed to have the desired effects. As this example suggests, imitation has to be backed by managerial commitment if organizations are to benefit from imitating others in their environment.

ORGANIZATIONAL INSIGHT

11.1 THE TOTAL QUALITY BANDWAGON

Xerox, Motorola, Harley-Davidson, and other U.S. companies have made total quality management work. In these organizations, which were under relentless competitive pressure from Japanese companies, committed management teams have institutionalized TQM principles and have developed norms and values that make quality the organization's number-one priority. Managers have spread the gospel of quality not only throughout their own organizations but also among their suppliers, and they have created an institutional environment in which quality is "job one," as Ford Motor Company proclaims in its advertisements. A commitment to TQM confers legitimacy on these companies, for customers are increasingly demanding quality and reliability in the products and services they buy. TQM also increases organizational effectiveness because it can significantly reduce costs.

Believing that they can increase efficiency and legitimacy simultaneously, thousands of other organizations have jumped on the TQM bandwagon. Many of these imitators, however, find that the quick gains they expected from TQM are not forthcoming and are not achieved easily. It is one thing to learn and recite TQM principles. It is another thing to make the long-term commitment of organizational resources required to obtain the benefits. Florida Power and Light, for example, started a TQM program but soon discontinued it because a new management team wanted to reduce costs more directly by reducing personnel rather than wait for reductions that would eventually result from a TQM program. Similarly, Douglas Aircraft adopted TQM but found the program in shambles when huge employee layoffs poisoned the good labor-management relations on which TQM depends.[27] As these companies found, simply copying other companies' organizational arrangements is not enough to obtain the benefits of innovations such as TQM. Adequate resources must be devoted to carrying out and following up on the program, and a long-term commitment is needed to see results. In the 1990s many companies have given up on TQM because of the commitment it requires, but those that have stayed the course, such as Xerox, discussed in the last chapter, have obtained important benefits in terms of cost savings and quality.

GREINER'S MODEL OF ORGANIZATIONAL GROWTH

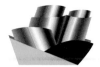

Institutional theory is one way to look at how the need to achieve legitimacy leads a growing organization to imitate the structure, strategy, and culture of successful organizations in its industry. If organizations do model themselves on one another in this way, it follows that both the imitators and the imitated encounter similar kinds of strategic and structural problems as they grow. Many organizational life cycle theorists believe that organizations encounter a predictable series of problems that must be managed if organizations are to grow and survive in a competitive environment. One of the best known of these life cycle models of organizational growth was developed by Larry Greiner in the 1970s (see Figure 11.4). Greiner's model proposes that an organization passes through five sequential growth stages during the course of organizational evolution and that each stage ends in a crisis due to a major problem that the organization encounters.[28] To advance from one stage to the next, an organization must successfully manage and solve the organizational problem associated with each crisis.

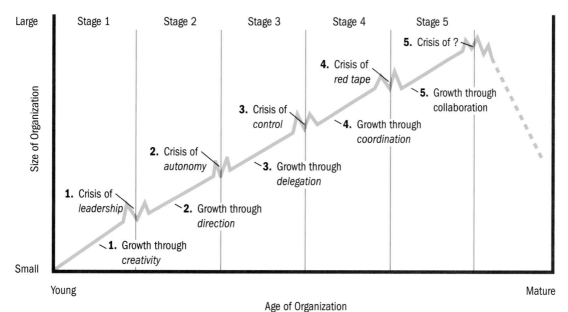

FIGURE 11.4   Greiner's Model of Organizational Growth.

Each stage that Greiner identified ends with a crisis that must be resolved before the organization can advance to the next stage. *Source:* Reprinted by permission of *Harvard Business Review*. An excerpt from, "Evolution and Revolution as Organizations Grow," by L. E. Greiner, July–August 1972, by the President and Fellows of Harvard College; all rights reserved.

Stage 1: Growth Through Creativity

Greiner calls the first stage in the growth cycle the creativity stage. In this stage (which includes the birth of the organization), entrepreneurs develop the skills and abilities to create and introduce new products for new market niches. As entrepreneurs create completely new procedures and adjust existing procedures, a great deal of organizational learning occurs. The organization learns which products and procedures work and continually adjusts its activities so that it can continue to expand. In this stage, innovation and entrepreneurship go hand in hand, as an organization's founders work long hours to develop and sell their new products with the hope of being rewarded by future profits. Compaq, for example, was started by some former Texas Instruments managers who designed a new computer from scratch and brought the first model to market in 18 months on a shoestring budget. In the creativity stage, the norms and values of the organization's culture, rather than the hierarchy and organizational structure, control people's behavior. The informal organization guides decision making and communication.

Once a new organization is up and running, a series of internal forces begins to change the entrepreneurial process. As the organization grows, the founding entrepreneurs confront the task of having to manage the organization, and they discover that management is a very different process from entrepreneurship. Management involves utilizing organizational resources to effectively achieve organizational goals. Thus, for example, in its manufacturing operations, management is confronted with the problem of making the production process more efficient. Early in the life of a new company, however, management is not likely to pay much attention to efficiency goals. Entrepreneurs are so involved in getting the organization off the ground that they forget the need to manage organizational resources efficiently. Similarly, they are so involved in providing customers with high-quality products that they ignore the costs involved. Thus, after securing a niche, the founding entrepreneurs are faced with the task of managing their organization, a task to which they are often not really suited and for which they lack the skills.

CRISIS OF LEADERSHIP.   Frequently, when an entrepreneur takes control of the management of the organization, significant problems arise that eventually lead to a *crisis of leadership*. CEO and founder Rod Canion, for example, had made Compaq a dominant force in the computer market. But when the price of computers tumbled in 1992, Compaq, a high-priced computer maker, lost its market niche. The firm's stock price plunged, and shareholders realized that the founding entrepreneur was not the best person to manage the company as it searched for a way to turn itself around. The board of directors replaced Canion with a professional manager, Ekhard Pfeiffer, who implemented a low-cost strategy that was very successful. However, in 1999 he lost his job because of his failure to successfully integrate Digital Equipment into Compaq after Compaq merged with this company. The way in which Steve Jobs was removed from the helm at Apple Computer shows how an organization must confront the crisis of leadership and replace entrepreneurs with managers.

ORGANIZATIONAL INSIGHT

11.2 THE CRISIS OF LEADERSHIP AT APPLE COMPUTER

On April 1, 1976, Stephen G. Wozniak and Steve Jobs formed Apple Computer Company in Menlo Park, California, with the proceeds of the sale of Jobs's Volkswagen and Wozniak's two programmable calculators. With the money they raised, and working out of Jobs's now-empty garage, they designed and built a single-board computer, which they called Apple I. By the end of the year, the demand for the computer was so high that the two founders could not handle the manufacturing needs. Lacking the funds to expand on their own, they formed an alliance with A. C. "Mike" Markkula, who invested $250,000, became chairman of the board, and directed Apple's first business plan. The Apple team proceeded to develop an improved computer, the Apple II. As sales took off for that machine, and more and more software applications were written, the fortunes of the company rose. In December 1980, every share of the initial share offering sold within minutes. By 1982, sales of Apple computers had reached $2 billion.

As the company grew, the structure of the top-management team changed quickly. Wozniak, interested in research, had no interest in managing the company. Jobs had an interest in both activities and in 1981 replaced Markkula as chairman and took over responsibility for Apple's strategic direction. At the same time, he was the product champion who pioneered the development of a new kind of Apple computer (the Macintosh), and he used considerable organizational resources to further its development. Jobs began to dominate Apple's top-management team and its decision making, especially after Wozniak left the company following a near-fatal plane crash.

By 1982, Jobs realized that he lacked the time and ability to both manage strategy and champion new-product development. He searched for someone to help him and fixed on John Sculley, PepsiCo's president and a known marketing expert. In 1983, Sculley became Apple's president and CEO and took over the responsibility for Apple's strategic growth and marketing plan. Jobs, as chairman, would oversee technical development. Together, the two would manage Apple's growth to become a mature company capable of dominating the industry.

However, things did not work out as planned. Jobs soon found that he missed the power that control over strategic decision making gave him. He started to oversee Sculley's activities and to intervene in corporate decision making whenever he felt it necessary. Moreover, in using resources to develop the Macintosh project, he stirred discontent among other Apple project teams, and the level of politics and conflict in the organization rose. Finally, by spreading his talents between management and research, Jobs caused delays in decision making, and the company lost its direction. By 1985, the board of directors realized that this situation could not go on and that the power battle at the top of the organization was hurting Apple's growth. They sided with Sculley, the professional manager, against Jobs, the founding entrepreneur. In 1985, Jobs was forced to resign after he lost the support of the board. Under Sculley, Apple prospered for some years. By 1993, however, low-cost competition was hurting Apple just as it hurt Compaq, and Sculley was forced out of Apple because the board of directors had lost confidence in his ability to lead the company through the new crisis it was experiencing. Although Apple continued to experience problems, its future looked increasingly bright after Steve Jobs once again assumed control of the company in 1998. Under his leadership Apple has developed innovative new products and is once again enjoying record sales and profits.

Stage 2: Growth Through Direction

The crisis of leadership ends with the recruitment of a strong top-management team to lead the organization through the next stage of organizational growth: growth through direction. The new top-management team takes responsibility for directing the company's strategy, and lower-level managers assume key functional responsibilities. In this stage, a CEO such as John Sculley at Apple chooses an organizational strategy and designs a structure and culture that allow the organization to meet its effectiveness goals as it grows. As we saw in Chapter 4, a functional or divisional structure is established to allow the organization to regain control of its activities, and decision making becomes more centralized. Then the adoption of formal, standardized rules and procedures allows each organizational function to better monitor and control its activities. Managers in production, for example, develop procedures to track cost and quality information, and the materials management function develops efficient purchasing and inventory control systems.

Often, growth through direction turns around an organization's fortunes and propels the organization up the growth curve to new levels of effectiveness, as happened at Apple and Compaq. As an organization continues to grow rapidly, however, the move to centralize authority and formalize decision making often leads to a new crisis.

CRISIS OF AUTONOMY.   With professional managers now running the show, many organizations experience a *crisis of autonomy*, which arises because the organization's creative people in departments such as R&D, product engineering, and marketing become frustrated by their lack of control over new-product development and innovation. The structure designed by top managers and imposed on the organization centralizes decision making and limits the freedom to experiment, take risks, and be internal entrepreneurs. Thus, the increased level of bureaucracy that comes in the growth-through-direction stage lowers entrepreneurial motivation. For instance, top-management approval may be needed to start new projects, and successful performance at low levels of the hierarchy may go unnoticed or at least unrewarded as the organization searches for ways to reduce costs. Entrepreneurs and managers in functional areas such as R&D begin to feel frustrated when their performance goes unrecognized and when top managers fail to act on their recommendations to innovate. Employees and managers feel lost in the growing organizational bureaucracy and become more and more frustrated with their lack of autonomy.

What happens if the crisis of autonomy is not resolved? Internal entrepreneurs are likely to leave the organization. In high-tech industries, entrepreneurs often cite frustration with bureaucracy as one of the main reasons they leave one company to start their own.[29] In the 1980s, for example, Eastman Kodak bought many small entrepreneurial companies to help increase Kodak's sales and profitability. Top Kodak managers then intervened in these companies and imposed centralized control over many of them. As a result, many of their managers left because they resented their loss of control and decision making. Similarly, when General Motors took over EDS, many of its top managers left after experiencing the crushing weight of GM's bureaucracy.

The departure of an organization's entrepreneurs not only reduces its ability to innovate but also creates new competitors in the industry. By not resolving the crisis of autonomy, an organization creates a major problem for itself and limits its ability to grow and prosper.[30]

Stage 3: Growth Through Delegation

To solve the crisis of autonomy, most organizations delegate authority to lower-level managers in all functions and link their increased control over organizational activities to a reward structure that recognizes their contributions. Thus, for example, managers and employees may receive bonuses and stock options that are directly linked to their performance. In essence, the growth-through-delegation stage allows the organization to strike a balance between the need for professional management to improve technical efficiency and the need to provide room for entrepreneurship so that the organization can innovate and find new ways of reducing costs or improving its products. We have already seen how Bill Gates at Microsoft delegates authority to small teams and creates a setting in which members can act entrepreneurially and control their own activities. Gates also rewards team members with stock options, and the most successful team members become highly visible stars of the organization. At the same time, however, Gates and his top-management team control the meshing of the activities of different teams to execute the company's long-term strategy. Gates designed Microsoft's structure to avoid the crisis of autonomy, and the organization has profited hugely from his forethought. Similarly, Ross Perot at EDS and John Sculley at Apple instituted stock options for managers to maintain the entrepreneurial spirit.

Thus, in the growth-through-delegation stage, more autonomy and responsibility are given to managers at all levels and functions. Moving to a product team structure or a multidivisional structure, for example, is one way in which an organization can respond to the need to delegate authority. These structures can reduce the time needed to get new products to market, improve strategic decision making, and motivate product or divisional managers to penetrate markets and respond faster to customer needs. At this stage in organizational growth, top managers intervene in decision making only when necessary. Growth through delegation allows each department or division to expand to meet its own needs and goals, and organizational growth often proceeds at a rapid pace. Once again, however, the organization's very success brings on another crisis: Explosive growth can cause top managers to feel that they have lost control of the company as a whole.

CRISIS OF CONTROL.   When top managers compete with functional managers or corporate-level managers compete with divisional managers for control of organizational resources, the result is a *crisis of control*. The need to resolve the crisis of autonomy by delegating authority to lower-level managers increases their power and control of organizational resources. Lower-level managers like this extra power because it is associated with prestige and access to valued rewards. If managers use this power over resources to pursue their own goals at the expense of organizational goals, the organization becomes less effective. Thus, power struggles over resources can emerge between top and lower-level managers. Sometimes during this power struggle top management tries to recentralize decision making and take back control over organizational activities. However, this action is doomed to failure because it brings back the crisis of autonomy. How does the organization solve the crisis of control so that it can continue to grow?

Stage 4: Growth Through Coordination

To resolve the crisis of control, as we saw in Chapter 3, an organization must find the right balance between centralized control from the top of the organization and decentralized control at the functional or divisional level. Top management takes on the role of coordinating different divisions and motivating divisional managers to take a companywide perspective. In many organizations, for example, divisions can cooperate and share resources in order to create new products and processes that benefit the organization as a whole. In Chapter 7, we saw how this kind of coordination is very important for companies pursuing a strategy of related diversification. If companies are growing internationally, coordination is even more important. Top functional managers and corporate headquarters staff must create the "matrix in the mind" that facilitates international cooperation between divisions and countries.

At the same time, corporate management must use its expertise to monitor and oversee divisional activities to ensure that divisions efficiently use their resources, and must initiate companywide programs to review the performance of the various divisions. To motivate managers and align their goals with those of the organization, organizations often create an internal labor market in which the best divisional managers are rewarded with promotion to the top ranks of the organization while the most successful functional-level managers gain control over the divisions. If not managed correctly, all this coordination and the complex structures to handle it will bring about yet another crisis.

CRISIS OF RED TAPE. Achieving growth through coordination is a complex process that has to be managed continuously if organizations are to be successful. When organizations fail to manage this process, they are plunged into a *crisis of red tape*. The number of rules and procedures increases, but this increased bureaucracy does little to increase organizational effectiveness and is likely to reduce it by stifling entrepreneurship and other productive activity. The organization becomes overly bureaucratic and relies too much on the formal organization and not enough on the informal organization to coordinate its activities. How can an organization cut itself free of all the confining red tape so that it can once again function effectively?

Stage 5: Growth Through Collaboration

In Greiner's model, growth through collaboration becomes the way to solve the crisis of red tape and push the organization up the growth curve. Growth through collaboration emphasizes "greater spontaneity in management action through teams and the skillful confrontation of interpersonal differences. Social control and self-discipline take over from formal control."[31] For organizations at this stage of the growth cycle, Greiner advocates the use of the product team and matrix structures, which, as we discussed in Chapter 4, many large companies use to improve their ability to respond to customer needs and introduce new products quickly. Developing the interpersonal linkages that underlie the "matrix in the mind" for managing global linkages is also a part of the collaborative strategy. Collaboration makes an organization more organic by making greater use of mutual adjustment and less use of standardization.

Changing from a mechanistic to an organic structure as an organization grows is a difficult task fraught with problems. We saw earlier how Chrysler and Xerox moved to a product team structure to streamline their decision making. This change was not made until *after* both companies had experienced huge problems with their structures—problems that increased costs, reduced product quality, and severely reduced their effectiveness. Indeed, both companies came close to bankruptcy.

Managerial Implications: Organizational Birth and Growth

1. Analyze the resources available in an environment to determine whether a niche to be exploited exists.
2. If a niche is discovered, analyze how the population of organizations currently in the environment will compete with you for the resources in the niche.
3. Develop the competences necessary to pursue a specialist strategy in order to attract resources in the niche.
4. Carefully analyze the institutional environment to learn the values and norms that govern the behavior of organizations in the environment. Imitate the qualities and actions of successful organizations, but be careful to differentiate your product from theirs to increase the returns from your specialist strategy.
5. If your organization survives the birth stage, recognize that it will encounter a series of problems as it grows and differentiates.
6. Recognize the importance of creating an effective top-management team and of delegating authority to professional managers in order to build a stable platform for future growth.
7. Then, following principles outlined in earlier chapters, manage the process of organizational design to meet each growth crisis as it emerges. Establish an appropriate balance between centralizing and decentralizing authority, for example, and between standardization and mutual adjustment.

ORGANIZATIONAL DECLINE AND DEATH

Before Xerox and Chrysler were able to adopt the kind of structure that allowed them to collaborate and regain their effectiveness, both companies had to shrink in size. Greiner's growth model shows organizations continuing to grow through collaboration until they encounter some new, unnamed crisis, but it is possible that an organization's growth path leads down, as shown by the direction of the dashed line in Figure 11.4. For many organizations, the next stage in the life cycle is not continued growth but organizational decline.

Greiner's model suggests that organizations at all stages of growth encounter problems—crises that will lead to organizational decline if they are not managed. **Organizational decline** is the life cycle stage that an organization enters when it fails to "anticipate, recognize, avoid, neutralize, or adapt to external or internal pressures that threaten the [its] long-term survival."[32] The liability of newness, for example, threatens young organi-

FIGURE 11.5

The Relationship Between Organizational Size and Organizational Effectiveness

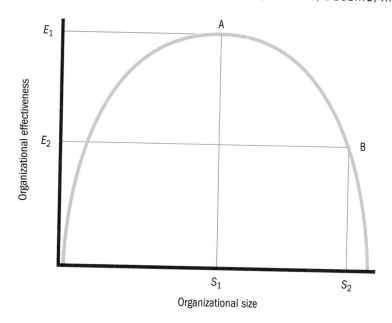

Organizational decline

The life cycle stage that an organization enters when it fails to anticipate, recognize, avoid, neutralize, or adapt to external or internal pressures that threaten its long-term survival.

zations, and the failure to develop a stable structure can cause early decline and failure. Similarly, in Greiner's model, the failure to adapt strategy and structure to suit changing conditions can result in crisis and failure. Regardless of whether decline sets in at the birth or the growth stage, it results in a decrease of an organization's ability to obtain resources from its stakeholders.[33] A declining company may be unable to attract financial resources from banks, customers, or human resources because the best managers or employees prefer to work for the most successful organizations.

Decline sometimes occurs because organizations grow too much.[34] The experience of Xerox, IBM, and Chrysler suggests that there is a tendency for organizations to grow past the point that maximizes their effectiveness. Figure 11.5 illustrates the relationship between organizational size and organizational effectiveness. The figure shows that organizational effectiveness is highest at point A, where effectiveness E_1 is associated with organizational size S_1. If an organization grows past this point—for example, to point S_2—effectiveness falls to E_2, and the organization ends up at point B.

Greiner's model assumes that managers have the ability to identify and solve organizational crises so that they can maintain the organization at point A. But suppose that managers cannot do this and that external and internal forces outside their control prevent the organization from growing. Suppose they lack the ability, motivation, and desire to manage the relationship between growth and effectiveness. Two factors that cause an organization to grow too much or to grow in ways that lead to organizational decline are organizational inertia and environmental changes.

Organizational Inertia

Organizational inertia

Forces inside an organization that make it resistant to change.

An organization may not easily adapt to meet changes in the environment because of **organizational inertia**—forces inside an organization that make it resistant to change. Greiner and other adaptation theorists focus on organizations' ability to change and adapt to new conditions in their environments. Population ecology theorists are more pessimistic, believing that organizations do not have the ability to quickly or easily change their strategy or structure to avoid decline. Instead, they believe that organizations are subject to considerable inertia, which prevents them from changing. Factors that can increase organizational inertia are risk aversion, the desire to maximize rewards, and an overly bureaucratic culture. When these factors operate together, the problems facing managers are greatly compounded.

RISK AVERSION.   As organizations grow, managers often become risk averse—that is, they become unwilling to bear the uncertainty associated with entrepreneurial activities.[35] As a result, the organization becomes increasingly difficult to change. Risk aversion may set in for several reasons. Managers' overriding concern may be to protect their positions; thus, they undertake relatively safe or inexpensive projects, so that if the projects fail, their burden of blame will be light. Managers might try to maximize the chance of success by pursuing projects that have already brought the organization success. Managers might institute bureaucratic rules and procedures that give close control over new ventures but also stifle innovation and entrepreneurship.

THE DESIRE TO MAXIMIZE REWARDS.   Research suggests that managers' desire for prestige, job security, power, and the strong property rights that bring large rewards is associated more with organizational size than with profitability.[36] Thus, managers may increase the size of the company to maximize their own rewards *even when* this growth reduces organizational effectiveness. The management teams of Goodyear Tire, Eastman Kodak, Greyhound, General Motors, and many other large organizations have been accused of pursuing their own goals at the expense of shareholders, customers, or other stakeholders. These management teams lacked any incentive to improve organizational effectiveness because they would not gain personally from doing so, and until recently there were no powerful stakeholders to discipline them and force them to streamline operations. The changes made at both Chrysler and Xerox, for example, came when new management teams took over. Similarly, a board revolt at GM finally forced managers to increase the rate of restructuring and downsizing.

OVERLY BUREAUCRATIC CULTURE.   As discussed in Chapter 5, in large organizations, property rights (such as salaries and stock options) can become so strong that managers spend all their time protecting their specific property rights instead of working to advance the organization's interests. Top managers, for example, resist attempts by subordinate managers to take the initiative and act entrepreneurially because subordinates who demonstrate superior skills and abilities may threaten the position of their managers and their managers' property rights.[37] Another bureaucracy-related problem is that, as C. Northcote Parkinson pointed out in Chapter 3, managers want to multiply subordinates, not rivals. To this end, managers limit the freedom of subordinates to protect their own positions. One way of limiting freedom is to establish a tall organizational hierarchy so that subordinates can be closely controlled and scrutinized. Another way is to develop a bureaucratic culture that emphasizes the status quo and the need for conformity to organizational procedures. Such a culture might be desirable in the armed forces, but it is not beneficial to a large company fighting for survival in an uncertain environment.

Although the behavior of managers is sometimes a major cause of organizational inertia and decline, it is important to realize that managers may not be deliberately trying to hurt the organization. Bureaucratization and risk aversion may creep up on organizations unexpectedly.

Changes in the Environment

Environmental changes that affect an organization's ability to obtain scarce resources may lead to organizational decline. The major sources of uncertainty in the environment are complexity, the number of different forces that an organization has to manage; dynamism, the degree to which the environment is changing; and richness, the amount of resources available in the environment (see Figure 6.2). The greater the uncertainty in the environment, the more likely it is that some organizations in a population, especially organizations affected by inertia, will go into decline.

Sometimes the niche that an organization occupies erodes and managers no longer have the incentive or ability to change strategy to improve the organization's access to resources. That is what happened to IBM when the demand for mainframe computers fell.[38] Sometimes the environment becomes poorer, and increased competition for resources threatens existing organizations that have not been managing their growth very effectively. Sometimes an "environmental jolt" changes the forces in the environment and precipitates an immediate crisis.[39] When the cold war ended, for example, the huge reduction in the size of government defense spending caused serious problems for large defense contractors such as General Dynamics and TRW. Both of them responded with downsizing that involved the layoffs of thousands of employees.

The combination of an uncertain, changing environment and organizational inertia makes it difficult for top management to anticipate the need for change and to manage the way organizations change and adapt to the environment. In Chapter 12, we examine how organizations can promote organizational learning, a process that facilitates changes and overcomes inertia. Here we discuss a model that charts the main stages of the decline process, just as Greiner's model charted the main stages of the growth process.

Weitzel and Jonsson's Model of Organizational Decline

Organizational decline occurs by degrees. William Weitzel and Ellen Jonsson have identified five stages of decline (see Figure 11.6).[40] At each stage except the dissolution stage, management action (shown by the dashed line in Figure 11.6) can reverse the decline.

STAGE 1: BLINDED. In the blinded stage, the first decline stage identified by Weitzel and Jonsson, organizations are unable to recognize the internal or external problems that threaten their long-term survival. The most common reason for this blindness is that organizations do not have in place the monitoring and information systems that they need to measure organizational effectiveness and identify sources of organizational inertia. Internal signals that indicate potential problems are excessive numbers of personnel, a slowdown in decision making, a rise in conflict between functions or divisions, and a fall in profits. At this stage, access to good information and an effective top-management team can prevent the onset of decline and allow the organization to maintain its pattern of growth. To avoid decline, managers need to monitor internal and external factors continuously so that they have the information to take timely corrective action. Taking action to correct problems at this stage and to reverse the decline process, however, does not necessarily mean that the organization will continue to grow. As General Dynamics' response to the slowdown in the defense industry suggests, a company may reorganize itself to use its existing resources more effectively.

FIGURE 11.6

Weitzel and Jonsson's Model of Organizational Decline. At each stage, action by management can halt the decline. *Source:* Adapted from "Decline in Organizations: A Literature Integration and Extension," by W. Weitzel and E. Jonsson, published in *Administrative Science Quarterly*. (c) 1989 Cornell University, 1989, Vol. 34, No. 1. Reprinted by permission.

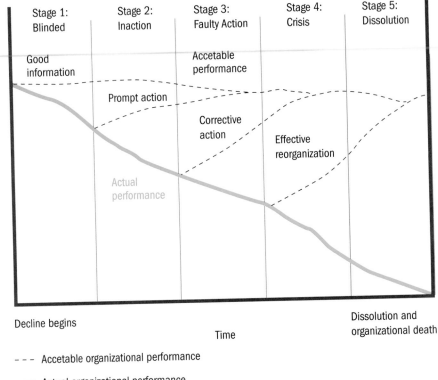

- - - Accetable organizational performance

⎯⎯ Actual organizational performance

ORGANIZATIONAL INSIGHT

11.3 GENERAL DYNAMICS GOES FROM WEAKNESS TO STRENGTH

In 1990, General Dynamics lost $578 million. In 1991, it made a profit of $305 million and its stock price tripled in 18 months. How has this major defense contractor (which specializes in making tactical aircraft, nuclear submarines, and armored vehicles) been able to avoid the problems brought on by the loss of resources in the environment as a result of the end of the cold war and drastic cuts in defense spending? The answer lies in the way the General Dynamics top-management team, led by William A. Anders, has been managing the decline process.

Faced with a lack of demand for its major products, General Dynamics has been selling off many of its $8.7 billion in assets and shrinking its operations to allow it to focus on four key areas: aircraft, submarines, armored vehicles, and space launch systems. The company downsized by laying off more than 25 percent of its workforce across its businesses. It then sold many of its assets to other companies. Those sales brought in over $1.2 billion to be distributed to shareholders or reinvested in core businesses. For example, General Dynamics sold its information technology unit for $184 million; it sold the Cessna aircraft unit to Textron for $600 million; and by the late 1990s it had sold its commercial aircraft components, materials service, electronics, ship management, and financial units, and its missile systems business.

Top managers realized that General Dynamics could not support all of its traditional activities in an environment in which resources were declining so rapidly. They responded quickly to the need to shrink and downsize, and they reorganized to focus more intently on the organization's core competences. Although the company has shrunk, shareholders, who have seen the value of their investments rise rapidly, view it as very effective. Clearly, this top-management team was not blinded by the first stages of organizational decline and has moved rapidly to adjust the organization to its new environment. It has positioned itself as a strong player in the global defense industry, and its performance increased steadily through the 1990s.[41]

STAGE 2: INACTION.   If an organization does not realize that it is in trouble in the blinded stage, its decline advances to the inaction stage. In this stage, despite clear signs of deteriorating performance, such as decreased sales or profits, top management takes little action to correct problems. This inaction may reflect managers' misinterpretation of information and belief that the situation reflects a short-term environmental change that the organization will weather. Inaction may also occur because managers are pursuing goals that benefit themselves at the expense of other stakeholders. Organizational inertia, too, may delay managers' response to the situation. Management may follow tried-and-true approaches to solve the organization's problems—approaches that may be inappropriate in the present situation.[42]

As the inaction stage progresses, as Figure 11.6 shows, the gap between acceptable performance and actual performance increases, and prompt action by managers is vital to reverse the decline. Managers may take steps to downsize by reducing the number of personnel, or they may scale back the scope of their operations. They may also change the organization's structure to overcome any organizational inertia that has set in as a result of the organization's large size or complex operations.

STAGE 3: FAULTY ACTION.   When managers fail to halt decline at the inaction stage, the organization moves into the faulty action stage. Problems continue to multiply despite corrective action. Managers may have made the wrong decisions because of conflict in the top-management team, or they may have changed too little too late because they feared that a major reorganization might do more harm than good. Often managers fear that radical change may threaten the way the organization operates and put the organization at risk.[43] For example, Rod Canion, Compaq's founder, could not bring himself to make the radical structural and strategy changes that were needed to turn the company around. After Ekhard Pfeiffer, the new CEO, took over, Compaq moved to a low-cost strategy and slashed its workforce by 35 percent, but by then Compaq was in stage 4, the crisis stage. Very often, an organization reaches the faulty-action stage because managers become overly committed to their present strategy and structure and fear changing them even though they are clearly not working to halt the decline.

STAGE 4: CRISIS.   By the time the crisis stage has arrived, only radical changes to an organization's strategy and structure can stop the decline and allow the organization to survive. An organization experiencing a crisis has reached a critical point in its history, and the only chance of recovery is a major reorganization. If managers wait until the organization reaches stage 4 before taking action, change is very difficult to achieve and must be drastic because organizational stakeholders are starting to dissolve or restrict their relationships with the organization.[44] The best managers may already have left because of fighting in the top-management team. Investors may be unwilling to risk lending their money to the organization. Suppliers may be reluctant to send the inputs the organization needs because they are worried about getting paid.

Very often by the crisis stage only a new top-management team can turn a company around. To overcome inertia, an organization needs new ideas so that it can adapt and change in response to new conditions in the environment.[45] Often the new organization that emerges from an effective reorganization resembles the old organization in name only.

STAGE 5: DISSOLUTION.   When an organization reaches the dissolution stage, it cannot recover, and decline is irreversible. At this point, the organization has lost the support of its stakeholders, and its access to resources shrivels as its reputation and markets disappear. If new leaders have been selected, they are likely to lack the organizational resources to institute a successful turnaround and develop new routines. The organization probably has no choice but to divest its remaining resources or liquidate its assets and enter bankruptcy proceedings. In either case, it moves into dissolution, and organizational death is the outcome.

As organizational death occurs, people's attachment to the organization changes. They realize that the end is coming and that their attachment to the organization is only temporary.[46] The announcement of organizational death signals to people that efforts to prevent decline have failed and that further actions by participants are futile. As the disbanding process begins, the organization severs its links to its stakeholders and transfers its resources to other organizations. Inside the organization, formal closing or parting ceremonies serve as a way of severing members' ties to the organization and focusing members on their new roles outside the organization.

The need to manage organizational decline is as great as the need to manage organizational growth. In fact, the processes of growth and decline are closely related to one another: The symptoms of decline often signal that a new path must be taken to allow the organization to grow successfully. As many large organizations have found, the solution to their problem may be to shrink and downsize and focus their resources on a narrower range of products and markets. If an organization cannot adapt to a changing environment, it generally faces organizational death.

Managerial Implications: Organizational Decline

1. To prevent the onset of organizational decline, continually analyze the organization's structure to pinpoint any sources of inertia that may have emerged as your organization has grown and differentiated.
2. Continually analyze the environment, and the niche or niches that your organization occupies, to identify changes in the amount or distribution of resources.
3. Recognize that because you are a part of the organization it may be difficult for you to identify internal or external problems. Call on other managers, members of the board of directors, and outside consultants to analyze the organization's current situation or stage of decline.
4. If you are the founder of the business, always keep in mind that you have a duty to your stakeholders to maximize the chances of your organization's survival and success. Be prepared to step aside and relinquish control if new leadership is required.

SUMMARY

Organizations have a life cycle consisting of four stages: birth, growth, decline, and death. They pass through these stages at different rates, and some do not experience every stage. To survive and prosper, organizations have to manage various internal and external forces. An organization must manage problems associated with its structure at critical points in its life cycle. If successfully managed, an organization continues to grow and differentiate. An organization must adapt to an uncertain and changing environment and overcome the organizational inertia that constantly threatens its ability to adapt to environmental changes. The fate of organizations that fail to meet these challenges is death. Their place is taken by new organizations, and a new cycle of birth and death begins. Chapter 11 has made the following main points:

1. Organizations pass through a series of stages as they grow and evolve. The four stages of the organizational life cycle are birth, growth, decline, and death.

2. Organizations are born when entrepreneurs use their skills and competences to create value. Organizational birth is associated with the liability of newness. Organizational birth is a dangerous stage because entrepreneurship is a risky process, organizational procedures are new and undeveloped, and the environment may be hostile.

3. Population ecology theory states that organizational birth rates in a new environment are very high at first but taper off as the number of successful organizations in a population increases.

4. The number of organizations in a population is determined by the amount of resources available in the environment.

5. Population ecologists have identified two sets of strategies that organizations can use to gain access to resources and to enhance their chances of survival: r-strategy versus K-strategy (r = early entry; K = late entry) and specialist strategy versus generalist strategy.

6. The driving force behind the population ecology model is natural selection, the process that ensures the survival of the organizations that have the skills and abilities that best fit with the environment.

7. As organizations grow, they increase their division of labor and specialization and develop the skills that give them a competitive advantage, which allows them to gain access to scarce resources.

8. Institutional theory argues that organizations adopt many of their routines from the institutional environment surrounding them in order to increase their legitimacy and chances of survival. Stakeholders tend to favor organizations that they consider trustworthy and legitimate.

9. A new organization can enhance its legitimacy by choosing the goals, structure, and culture that are used by other successful organizations in its populations. Similarity among organizations is the result of coercive, mimetic, and normative isomorphism.

10. According to Greiner's five-stage model of organizational growth, organizations experience growth through (a) creativity, (b) direction, (c) delegation, (d) coordination, and (e) collaboration. Each growth stage ends in a crisis that must be solved if the organization is to advance successfully to the next stage and continue to grow.

11. If organizations fail to manage the growth process effectively, the result is organizational decline, the stage an organization enters when it fails to anticipate, recognize, or adapt to external or internal pressures that threaten its survival.

12. Factors that can precipitate organizational decline include organizational inertia and changes in the environment.

13. Organizational decline occurs by degrees. Weitzel and Jonsson have identified five stages of decline: (a) blinded, (b) inaction, (c) faulty action, (d) crisis, and (e) dissolution. Managers can turn the organization around at every stage except the dissolution stage.

14. Organizational death occurs when an organization divests its remaining resources or liquidates its assets. As the disbanding process begins, the organization severs its links to its stakeholders and transfers its resources to other organizations.

DISCUSSION QUESTIONS

1. What factors influence the number of organizations that are founded in a population? How can pursuing a specialist strategy increase a company's chances of survival?

2. How does r-strategy differ from K-strategy? How does a specialist strategy differ from a generalist strategy? Use companies in the fast-food industry to provide an example of each strategy.

3. Why do organizations grow? What major crisis is an organization likely to encounter as it grows?

4. Why do organizations decline? What steps can top management take to halt decline and restore organizational growth?

5. What is organizational inertia? List some sources of inertia in a company such as IBM or General Motors.

6. Choose an organization or business in your city that has recently closed, and analyze why it failed. Could the organization have been turned around? Why or why not?

ORGANIZATIONAL THEORY IN ACTION

PRACTICING ORGANIZATIONAL THEORY:
GROWING PAINS

Form groups of three to five people and discuss the following scenario:

You are the top managers of a rapidly growing company that has been having great success in developing Web sites for large Fortune 500 companies. Currently, you employ over 150 highly skilled and qualified programmers, and to date you have operated with a loose, organic operating structure that has given them considerable autonomy. While this has worked, you are now experiencing problems. Performance is dropping because your company is fragmenting into different self-contained teams that are not cooperating and not learning from one another. You have decided that somehow you need to become more bureaucratic or mechanistic, but you recognize and wish to keep all the advantages of your organic operating approach. You are meeting to discuss how to make this transition.

1. What kind of crisis are you experiencing according to Greiner's model?
2. What kind of changes will you make to your operating structure to solve this crisis, and what will be the problems associated with implementing these changes?

MAKING THE CONNECTION #11

Find an example of an organization that is experiencing a crisis of growth or an organization that is trying to manage decline. What stage of the life cycle is the organization in? What factors contributed to its growth crisis? What factors led to its decline? What problems is the organization experiencing? How is top management trying to solve the problems?

Analyzing the Organization: Design Module #11

This module focuses on the way your organization is managing (a) the dynamics associated with the life cycle stage that it is in and (b) the problems it has experienced as it evolved.

ASSIGNMENT

Using the information at your disposal, answer the following questions.

1. When was your organization founded? Who founded it? What opportunity was it founded to exploit?

2. Describe the environment that the organization entered at its birth. How large was the organizational population? What resources were available to the new organization? Did it pursue an r-strategy or a K-strategy, a generalist or a specialist strategy?

3. How rapid was the growth of your organization, and what problems did it experience as it grew? Describe its passage through the growth stages outlined in Greiner's model. How did managers deal with the crisis that it encountered as it grew?

4. What stage of the organizational life cycle is your organization in now? What internal and external problems is it currently encountering? How are managers trying to solve these problems?

5. Has your organization ever shown any symptoms of decline? Did the organization become less effective as it grew? Did managers make systematic strategic errors? Did decision making become less effective?

6. How quickly were managers in the organization able to respond to the problem of decline? What changes did they make? Did they turn the organization around?

7. Given your analysis of the organization so far, what kinds of life cycle problems do you think your organization might encounter in the future? How well do you think managers will be able to deal with these problems?

Cases for Analysis:
THE BODY SHOP REACHES MIDDLE AGE

In 1976, Anita Roddick, a former flower child and the owner of a small hotel in southern England, had an idea. Rising sentiment against the use of animals in testing cosmetics and a wave of environmentalism that focused on "natural" products gave her the idea for a range of skin creams, shampoos, and lotions made from fruit and vegetable oils rather than animal products. Moreover, her products would not be tested on animals. Roddick began to sell her line of new products from a small shop she opened in Brighton, a seaside town in the south of England, and the results surpassed her wildest expectations. Her line of cosmetics was an instant success and customers were immediately attracted to it. Recognizing that she had discovered an unmet market niche for natural cosmetics, she moved quickly to take advantage of it. To speed the growth of her new organization in Britain and Europe she began to franchise the right to open stores called The Body Shop to sell her products. By 1993, there were over 700 of these stores around the world, with combined sales of over $250 million.

Although Roddick used franchising and alliances with other individuals and companies in Europe to grow her company, in her push to enter the U.S. market in the early 1990s she decided that her company would own (not franchise) its stores. Her rationale was that this would give her more control over U.S. operations and also allow her to retain a greater share of the profits. Forgoing the rapid expansion that franchising would have made possible was a costly mistake.

Large U.S. cosmetic companies such as Estée Lauder and entrepreneurs such as Leslie Wexner of The Limited were quick to see the opportunities that Roddick had opened up in this rapidly growing market segment. They moved fast to imitate her product lines and operating philosophy, emphasizing the "naturalness" of their products, and began to market their own natural cosmetics. For example, Estée Lauder brought out its Origins line of cosmetics, and Wexner opened the Bath and Body Works to sell his own line of natural cosmetics. Since most U.S. consumers were not familiar with The Body Shop's brand name, both these ventures have been very successful and have gained a large share of the market.

The competitive threat from imitators forced Roddick to quickly begin to franchise The Body Shop in the United States, and by 1995 over 250 stores had been opened. Although they have been successful, Roddick admits that the delay in opening them gave her competitors the opportunity to establish their own brand names and robbed her enterprise of the uniqueness that its products enjoy throughout Europe. The Body Shop has not enjoyed the success that it expected in the United States and she has come under increasing pressure from investors who are concerned that The Body Shop's flat sales signaled the start of a decline in the company's fortunes. In 1998, new CEO Patrick Gournay took control of the company to try to head it back on the right path, and by 1999 he seemed to be succeeding as sales and profits both increased.

1. What mistakes did Roddick make over time?

2. What strategies should Roddick have adopted to grow her company successfully?

REFERENCES

1. R. E. Quinn and K. Cameron, "Organizational Life Cycles and Shifting Criteria of Effectiveness: Some Preliminary Evidence," *Management Science*, 1983, vol. 29, pp. 33–51.
2. I. Adizes, "Organizational Passages: Diagnosing and Treating Life Cycle Problems of Organizations," *Organizational Dynamics*, 1979, vol. 8, pp. 3–25; D. Miller and P. Freisen, "Archetypes of Organizational Transitions," *Administrative Science Quarterly*, 1980, vol. 25, pp. 268–299.
3. F. H. Knight, *Risk, Uncertainty, and Profit* (Boston: Houghton Mifflin, 1921); I. M. Kirzner, *Competition and Entrepreneurship* (Chicago: University of Chicago Press, 1973).
4. H. G. Manne, *Insider Trading and the Stock Market* (New York: The Free Press, 1966).
5. A. Stinchcombe, "Social Structure and Organizations," in J. G. March, ed., *Handbook of Organizations* (Chicago: Rand McNally, 1965), pp. 142–193.
6. J. A. Schumpeter, *The Theory of Economic Development* (Cambridge, MA: Harvard University Press, 1934).
7. H. Aldrich, *Organizations and Environments* (Englewood Cliffs, NJ: Prentice Hall, 1979).
8. R. R. Nelson and S. Winter, *An Evolutionary Theory of Economic Change* (Cambridge, MA: Harvard University Press, 1982).
9. M. T. Hannan and J. H. Freeman, *Organizational Ecology* (Cambridge, MA: Harvard University Press, 1989).
10. G. R. Carroll, "Organizational Ecology," *Annual Review of Sociology*, 1984, vol. 10, pp. 71–93; G. R. Carroll and M. Hannan, "On Using Institutional Theory in Studying Organizational Populations," *American Sociological Review*, 1989, vol. 54, pp. 545–548.
11. Aldrich, *Organizations and Environments*.
12. J. Delacroix and G. R. Carroll, "Organizational Foundings: An Ecological Study of the Newspaper Industries of Argentina and Ireland," *Administrative Science Quarterly*, 1983, vol. 28, pp. 274–291; Carroll and Hannan, "On Using Institutional Theory in Studying Organizational Populations."
13. Ibid.

14. M. T. Hannan and J. H. Freeman, "The Ecology of Organizational Foundings: American Labor Unions, 1836–1975," *American Journal of Sociology*, 1987, vol. 92, pp. 910–943.

15. J. Brittain and J. Freeman, "Organizational Proliferation and Density Dependent Selection," in J. Kimberly and R. Miles, eds., *Organizational Life Cycles* (San Francisco: Jossey-Bass, 1980), pp. 291–338; Hannan and Freeman, *Organizational Ecology*.

16. G. R. Carroll, "The Specialist Strategy," *California Management Review*, vol. 3, pp. 126–137; G. R. Carroll, "Concentration and Specialization: Dynamics of Niche Width in Populations of Organizations," *American Journal of Sociology*, 1985, vol. 90, pp. 1262–1283.

17. Carroll, "Concentration and Specialization."

18. M. Lambkin and G. Day, "Evolutionary Processes in Competitive Markets," *Journal of Marketing*, 1989, vol. 53, pp. 4–20; W. Boeker, "Organizational Origins: Entrepreneurial and Environmental Imprinting at the Time of Founding," in G. R. Carroll, *Ecological Models of Organization* (Cambridge, MA: Ballinger, 1987), pp. 33–51.

19. Aldrich, *Organizations and Environments*, p. 27.

20. J. Pfeffer and G. R. Salancik, *The External Control of Organizations* (New York: Harper and Row, 1978).

21. J. Meyer and B. Rowan, "Institutionalized Organizations: Formal Structure as Myth and Ceremony," *American Journal of Sociology*, 1977, vol. 83, pp. 340–363; B. E. Ashforth and B. W. Gibbs, "The Double Edge of Organizational Legitimation," *Organization Science*, 1990, vol. 1, pp. 177–194.

22. L. G. Zucker, "Institutional Theories of Organization," *Annual Review of Sociology*, 1987, vol. 13, pp. 443–464.

23. B. Rowan, "Organizational Structure and the Institutional Environment: The Case of Public Schools," *Administrative Science Quarterly*, 1982, vol. 27, pp. 259–279; P. S. Tolbert and L. G. Zucker, "Institutional Sources of Change in the Formal Structure of Organizations: The Diffusion of Civil Service Reform, 1880–1935," *Administrative Science Quarterly*, 1983, vol. 28, pp. 22–38.

24. P. DiMaggio and W. Powell, "The Iron Cage Revisited: Institutional Isomorphism and Collective Rationality in Organizational Fields," *American Sociological Review*, 1983, vol. 48, pp. 147–160.

25. J. Galaskiewicz and S. Wasserman, "Mimetic Processes Within an Interorganizational Field: An Empirical Test," *American Sociological Review*, 1983, vol. 48, pp. 454–479.

26. Ashforth and Gibbs, "The Double Edge of Organizational Legitimation."

27. J. Mathews and P. Katel, "The Cost of Quality," *Newsweek*, 7 September 1992, pp. 48–49.

28. This section draws heavily on L. E. Greiner, "Evolution and Revolution as Organizations Grow," *Harvard Business Review*, July–August 1972, pp. 37–46.

29. A. C. Cooper, "Entrepreneurship and High Technology," in D. L. Sexton and R. W. Smilor, eds., *The Art and Science of Entrepreneurship* (Cambridge, MA: Ballinger, 1986), pp. 153–168; J. R. Thorne and J. G. Ball, "Entrepreneurs and Their Companies," in K. H. Vesper, ed., *Frontiers of Entrepreneurial Research* (Wellesley, MA: Center for Entrepreneurial Studies, Babson College, 1981), pp. 65–83.

30. G. R. Jones and J. E. Butler, "Managing Internal Corporate Entrepreneurship: An Agency Theory Perspective," *Journal of Management*, 1992, vol. 18, pp. 733–749.

31. Greiner, "Evolution and Revolution as Organizations Grow," p. 43.

32. W. Weitzel and E. Jonsson, "Decline in Organizations: A Literature Integration and Extension," *Administrative Science Quarterly*, 1989, vol. 34, pp. 91–109.

33. K. S. Cameron, M. U. Kim, and D. A. Whetten, "Organizational Effects of Decline and Turbulence," *Administrative Science Quarterly*, 1987, vol. 32, pp. 222–240; K. S. Cameron, D. A. Whetten, and M. U. Kim, "Organizational Dysfunctions of Decline," *Academy of Management Journal*, 1987, vol. 30, pp. 126–138.

34. G. R. Jones, R. Kosnik, and J. M. George, "Internationalization and the Firm's Growth Path: On the Psychology of Organizational Contracting," in R. W. Woodman and W. A. Pasemore, *Research in Organizational Change and Development* (Greenwich, CT: JAI Press, 1993).

35. A. D. Chandler, *The Visible Hand* (Cambridge, MA: Belknap Press, 1977); H. Mintzberg and J. A. Waters, "Tracking Strategy in an Entrepreneurial Firm," *Academy of Management Journal*, 1982, vol. 25, pp. 465–499; J. Stopford and L. T. Wells, *Managing the Multinational Enterprise* (London: Longman, 1972).

36. A. A. Berle and C. Means, *The Modern Corporation and Private Property* (New York: Macmillan, 1932); K. Williamson, "Profit, Growth, and Sales Maximization," *Economica*, 1966, vol. 34, pp. 1–16.

37. R. M. Kanter, *When Giants Learn to Dance: Mastering the Challenges of Strategy* (New York: Simon and Schuster, 1989).

38. L. Greenhalgh, "Organizational Decline," in S. B. Bacharach, ed., *Research in the Sociology of Organizations* (Greenwich, CT: JAI Press, 1983), pp. 231–276.

39. A. Meyer, "Adapting to Environmental Jolts," *Administrative Science Quarterly*, 1982, vol. 27, pp. 515–537.

40. Weitzel and Jonsson, "Decline in Organizations."

41. "Defence Contractor Reports Earnings Up 14.5 Percent," *Business News*, 29 October 1999, p. 3.

42. W. H. Starbuck, A. Greve, and B. L. T. Hedberg, "Responding to Crisis," in C. F. Smart and W. T. Stansbury, eds., *Studies in Crisis Management* (Toronto: Butterworth, 1978), pp. 111–136.

43. M. Hannan and J. Freeman, "Structural Inertia and Organizational Change," *American Sociological Review*, 1984, vol. 49, pp. 149–164; D. Miller, "Evolution and Revolution: A Quantum View of Structural Change in Organizations," *Journal of Management Studies*, 1982, vol. 19, pp. 131–151.

44. Weitzel and Jonsson, "Decline in Organizations," p. 105.

45. B. L. T. Hedburg, P. C. Nystrom, and W. H. Starbuck, "Camping on Seesaws, Prescriptions for a Self-Designing Organization," *Administrative Science Quarterly*, 1976, vol. 21, pp. 31-65; M. L. Tushman, W. H. Newman, and E. Romanelli, "Convergence and Upheaval: Managing the Steady Pace of Organizational Evolution," *California Management Review*, 1986, vol. 29, pp. 29–44.

46. R. I. Sutton, "The Process of Organizational Death," *Administrative Science Quarterly*, 1987, vol. 32, pp. 542–569.

Chapter 12

DECISION MAKING and ORGANIZATIONAL LEARNING

Organizations have to continually improve the way decisions are made so that managers and employees can learn new, more effective ways to act inside the organization and, thus, better manage the external environment. This chapter first examines several models of decision making that describe how managers make decisions. Second, the chapter discusses the nature of learning and how managers can promote organizational learning to improve the quality of their decision making. Third, several factors, such as the operation of cognitive biases that reduce the level of organizational learning and result in poor decision making, are discussed. Finally, some techniques that managers can use to overcome these problems and, thus, open the organization up to new learning are examined.

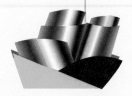

ORGANIZATIONAL DECISION MAKING

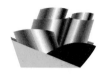

Organizational decision making *The process of responding to a problem by searching for and selecting a solution or course of action that will create value for organizational stakeholders.*

Programmed decisions *Decisions that are repetitive and routine.*

Nonprogrammed decisions *Decisions that are novel and unstructured.*

In previous chapters, we have discussed how an organization and its managers design a structure and a culture that match the organization's environment; choose a technology to convert inputs into outputs; and choose a strategy to guide the use of organizational skills and resources to create value. In making these choices, organizations are making decisions. Indeed, everything that an organization does involves a decision of some kind. Clearly, an organization is not only a value creation machine but a decision-making machine as well. At every level and in every subunit, people continuously make decisions, and how well they make them determines how much value their organization creates.

Organizational decision making is the process of responding to a problem by searching for and selecting a solution or course of action that will create value for organizational stakeholders. Whether the problem is to find the best inputs, to decide on the right way to provide a service to customers, or to figure out how to deal with an aggressive competitor, managers must in each case decide what to do. In general, managers are called upon to make two kinds of decisions: programmed and nonprogrammed.

Programmed decisions are repetitive and routine. Rules, routines, and standard operating procedures can be developed in advance to handle them.[1] Many of the routines and procedures for selecting appropriate solutions are formalized in an organization's rules and standard operating procedures and in the values and norms of its culture.

Nonprogrammed decisions are novel and unstructured. No rules, routines, or standard operating procedures can be developed to handle them. Solutions must be worked out as problems arise.[2] Nonprogrammed decision making requires much more search activity and mutual adjustment by managers to find a solution than does programmed decision making. For example, nonroutine research and development is based on nonprogrammed decision making by researchers who continually experiment to find solutions to problems. Similarly, the creation of an organization's strategy involves nonprogrammed decision making by managers who experiment to find the best way to use an organization's skills and resources to create value and who never know in advance whether they are making the right decision.

Nonprogrammed decision making forces managers to rely on judgment, intuition, and creativity to solve organizational problems; they cannot rely on rules and standard operating procedures to provide nonprogrammed solutions. *Nonprogrammed decisions* lead to the creation of a new set of rules and procedures that would allow organizational members to make appropriate *programmed* decisions.

All organizations have to develop the capacity to make both programmed and nonprogrammed decisions. Programmed decision making allows an organization to increase its efficiency and reduce the costs of making goods and services. Nonprogrammed decision making allows the organization to adapt to its environment and to generate new ways of behaving so that it can effectively exploit and manipulate its environment. Programmed decision making provides stability and increases predictability. Nonprogrammed decision making allows the organization to change and adapt itself so that it can deal with unpredictable events. In the next section, we examine several models of organizational decision making.

MODELS OF ORGANIZATIONAL DECISION MAKING

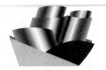

Early models of decision making portrayed decision making as a rational process in which all-knowing managers make decisions that allow organizations to adjust perfectly to the environment in which they operate.[3] Newer models recognize that decision making is an inherently uncertain process in which managers grope for solutions that may or may not lead to outcomes favorable to organizational stakeholders.

The Rational Model

According to the *rational model*, decision making is a straightforward, three-stage process (see Figure 12.1).[4] In stage 1, managers identify problems that need to be solved. The managers of an effective organization, for example, spend a great deal of time analyzing all aspects of their organization's specific and general environments to identify conditions or problems that call for new action. To achieve a good fit between an organization and its environment, they must analyze the environment and recognize the opportunities or threats it presents. In stage 2, managers individually or collectively seek to design and develop a list of alternative solutions and courses of action to the problems they have identified. They study ways to exploit the organization's skills and resources to respond to opportunities and threats. In stage 3, managers compare the likely consequences of each alternative and decide which course of action offers the best solution to the problem they identified in stage 1.

Under what "ideal" circumstances can managers be sure that they have made a decision that will maximize stakeholders' satisfaction? The ideal situation is one in which there is no uncertainty: Managers know *all* the courses of action open to them. They know the *exact* effects of all alternatives on stakeholders' interests. They are able to use the *same* set of *objective* criteria to evaluate each alternative. And they use the *same* decision rules to rank each alternative and, thus, can make the *one* best or right decision—the decision that will maximize the return to organizational stakeholders.[5] Do such conditions exist? If they did, managers could always make decisions that would perfectly position their organizations in the environment to acquire new resources and make the best use of existing resources.

This ideal state is the situation assumed by the rational model of organizational decision making. The rational model ignores the ambiguity, uncertainty, and chaos that typically plague decision making. Researchers have criticized as unrealistic or simplistic three assumptions underlying the rational model: (1) the assumption that decision makers have all the information they need; (2) the assumption that decision makers are smart; and (3) the assumption that decision makers agree about what needs to be done.

INFORMATION AND UNCERTAINTY.   The assumption that managers are aware of all alternative courses of action and their consequences is unrealistic. In order for this assumption to be valid, managers would need access to all the information necessary to make a decision, would need to collect information about every possible situation the organization might encounter, and would need accurate knowledge about the likelihood

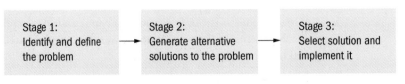

FIGURE 12.1

The Rational Model of Decision Making. This model ignores the uncertainty that typically plagues decision making.

| Stage 1: | Stage 2: | Stage 3: |
| Identify and define the problem | Generate alternative solutions to the problem | Select solution and implement it |

of each situation's occurring.[6] Clearly, collecting all this information would be very expensive, and the *information costs* associated with this model would be exorbitant.[7]

The assumption that it is possible to collect all the information needed to make the best decision is also unrealistic.[8] Because the environment is inherently uncertain, every alternative course of action and its consequences cannot be known. Furthermore, even if it were possible to collect information to eliminate all uncertainty, the costs of doing so would be as great as, or greater than, any potential profit the organization could make from selecting the best alternative. Thus, nothing would be gained from the information.

Suppose a fast-food company thinks that some new kind of sandwich has the potential to attract large numbers of new customers. According to the rational model, to identify the right kind of sandwich, the company would do extensive market research, test different kinds of sandwiches with different groups of customers, and evaluate all alternatives. The cost of adequately testing *every* alternative for *all* possible different groups of customers, however, would be so high that it would swallow up any profit the new sandwich might generate from increased sales. The rational model ignores the fact that organizational decision making always takes place in the midst of uncertainty, which poses both an opportunity and a threat for an organization.

MANAGERIAL ABILITIES.   The rational model assumes that managers possess the intellectual capability not only to evaluate all the possible alternative choices but to select the best solution. In reality, managers have only a limited ability to process the information required to make decisions, and most do not have the time to act as the rational model demands.[9] The intelligence required to make a decision according to the rational model would exceed any one manager's mental abilities and necessitate the employment of an enormous number of managers. The rational model ignores the high level of *managerial costs*.

PREFERENCES AND VALUES.   The rational model assumes that different managers have the same preferences and values and that they will use the same rules to decide on the best alternative. The model also assumes that managers agree about what are the most important organizational goals. These "agreement assumptions" are unrealistic.[10] In Chapter 2, we discussed how managers in different functions are likely to have different subunit orientations that lead them to make decisions that favor their own interests over those of other functions, other stakeholders, or the organization as a whole.

To sum up, the rational model of decision making is unrealistic because it rests on assumptions that ignore the information and managerial problems associated with decision making. The Carnegie model and other newer models take these problems into consideration and provide a more accurate picture of how organizational decision making takes place.

The Carnegie Model

In an attempt to describe the realities of the decision-making process more accurately, researchers introduced into decision-making theory a new set of assumptions that has come to be called the *Carnegie model*.[11] Table 12.1 summarizes the differences between the Carnegie and the rational models of decision making. The Carnegie model recognizes the effects of satisficing, bounded rationality, and organizational coalitions.

SATISFICING.   In an attempt to explain how organizations avoid the costs of obtaining information, the Carnegie model suggests that managers engage in **satisficing**, limited information searches to identify problems and alternative solutions.[12] Instead of searching for all possible solutions to a problem, as the rational model suggests, managers resort to satisficing—that is, they decide on certain criteria that they will use to evaluate possible

Satisficing *Limited information searches to identify problems and alternative solutions.*

TABLE 12.1
Differences Between the Rational and the Carnegie Models of Decision Making

Rational Model	Carnegie Model
Information is available	Limited information is available
Decision making is costless	Decision making is costly (e.g., managerial costs, information costs)
Decision making is "value free"	Decision making is affected by the preferences and values of decision makers
The full range of possible alternatives is generated	A limited range of alternatives is generated
Solution is chosen by unanimous agreement	Solution is chosen by compromise, bargaining, and accomodation between organizational coalitions
Solution chosen is best for the organization	Solution chosen is satisfactory for the organization

acceptable solutions.[13] The criteria automatically limit the set of possible alternatives. The managers then select one alternative from the range of alternatives that they have generated. Thus, satisficing involves a much less costly information search and puts far less of a burden on managers than does the rational model.

BOUNDED RATIONALITY.   The rational model assumes that managers possess the intellectual capacity to evaluate all possible alternatives. The Carnegie model assumes that managers are limited by **bounded rationality**—a limited capacity to process information. The fact that they have limited information-processing capacity, however, does not mean that managers will take the first acceptable solution they are offered.[14] Managers can improve their decision making by sharpening their analytical skills. Managers can also use technology like computers to improve their decision-making skills.[15] Thus, bounded rationality in no way implies lack of ability or motivation. The Carnegie model recognizes that much of decision making is subjective and relies on managers' prior experiences, beliefs, and intuition.

Bounded rationality A limited capacity to process information.

ORGANIZATIONAL COALITIONS.   The rational model ignores the variation in managers' preferences and values and the impossibility of developing decision rules that allow different managers to evaluate different alternatives in the same way. The Carnegie model, in contrast, explicitly recognizes that the preferences and values of managers differ and that conflict between managers and different stakeholder groups is inevitable.[16] However, this fact does not mean that the organization has to bear the costs of forcing managers to agree to use the same criteria to make decisions.

The Carnegie model views an organization as a coalition of different interests, in which decision making takes place by compromise, bargaining, and negotiation between managers from different functions and areas of the organization. Any solution chosen meets the approval of the dominant coalition, the collection of managers or stakeholders who have the power to select a solution and commit resources to implement it.[17] Over time, as interests change, the makeup of the dominant coalition changes and so does decision making. The Carnegie model recognizes that decision making is not a neutral process with objective decision rules but a process during which managers formulate decision rules as they pursue their goals and interests.

To sum up, the Carnegie model recognizes that decision making takes place in an uncertain environment where information is often incomplete and ambiguous. It also recognizes that decisions are made by people who are limited by bounded rationality, who satisfice, and who form coalitions to pursue their own interests. The Carnegie model offers a more accurate description of how decision making takes place in an organization than does the rational model. Yet Carnegie-style decision making is rational because managers act intentionally to find the best solution to reach their desired goal, despite uncertainty and disagreement over goals. The response of Jack Welch, CEO of General Electric, to the question of whether GE should continue to make its own washing machines or buy machines made by other companies illustrates decision making in accordance with the Carnegie model.

ORGANIZATIONAL INSIGHT

12.1 SHOULD GE MAKE OR BUY WASHING MACHINES?

In 1993, General Electric's CEO, Jack Welch, faced a major decision. GE's appliance division, maker of well-known products such as dishwashers, ranges, refrigerators, and washing machines, was fighting declining profitability; and Appliance Park, GE's complex of factories near Louisville, Kentucky, which employed 10,000 of the company's 22,000 workers, was losing a substantial amount of money. The washing machine operations, technologically outdated, were contributing significantly to this loss, and Welch had to evaluate two alternative courses of action proposed by his corporate staff: Should GE spend $70 million and make a major investment in new technology to bring the washing machine operations up-to-date so that GE could compete into the twenty-first century, or should GE close down its washing machine operations and buy from another manufacturer washing machines that it would sell under its own brand name?

To evaluate each alternative, Welch and his managers tried to decide which one would lead to the better long-term outcome for the organization. They used criteria such as manufacturing costs, quality, profitability, and product development costs to evaluate each alternative. One of the factors that GE was most concerned about was whether the unions in its Appliance Park operations would agree to flexible work arrangements that would reduce labor costs. There had already been significant job losses, and GE managers had been sitting down with the unions to hammer out a new work agreement that would allow the corporation to evaluate its future labor costs. Using information on future labor costs and internal forecasts of future product development and manufacturing costs, Welch and his team tried to assess whether the investment would lead to a profit. At the same time, corporate executives talked to companies like Maytag and Whirlpool to determine what it would cost GE to have them make a washing machine according to GE specifications.[18]

If GE could buy another manufacturer's washing machine for less than it would pay to make its own, then it seemed to make sense to choose the less costly alternative. However, GE's managers had to evaluate the effects of other factors. For example, if GE stopped making washing machines, it would lose a core competence in washing machine production that it would be unable to recover. Suppose the company that GE chose as its supplier failed to live up to its agreement and put only its old technology into the machines it supplied GE, or suppose it produced for GE machines that were much lower in quality than the machines it produced for itself. GE would be at the mercy of its suppliers. On the other hand, suppose the unions reneged on the contract and refused to cooperate after GE had made the investment in modernizing the washing machine plant.

The situation was further complicated by appliance division managers who were lobbying for the investment because it would protect their jobs and the jobs of 1,500 workers. The division managers championed the advantages of the investment for improving the competitive advantage of the division. Corporate managers, however, had to evaluate the potential return of the investment to the entire organization.

Jack Welch and his managers had a very difficult time evaluating the pros and cons of each alternative. Because of uncertainty, they could not accurately predict the consequences of any decision they made and had to rely on their knowledge of and experience in the appliance market. In the summer of 1993, they decided that GE would make the investment and continue to produce its own washing machines. A new line of modern washing machines became available in 1994, and improved models have been introduced every year since as consumers have responded well to the new appliances. In 1999, GE opened a $5 million reliability Growth Test Centre and it tripled the amount it spends on research and development in 1999 to produce appliances that never break down and that "delight" its customers.[19]

The Incrementalist Model

In the Carnegie model, satisficing and bounded rationality drastically reduce the number and complexity of alternatives that need to be analyzed. According to the *incrementalist model* of organizational decision making, managers select alternative courses of action that are only slightly, or incrementally, different from those used in the past, thus lessening their chances of making a mistake.[20] Often called the science of "muddling through," the incrementalist model implies that managers rarely make major decisions that are radically different from decisions they have made before.[21] Instead, they correct or avoid mistakes through a succession of incremental changes, which eventually may lead to a completely new course of action. During the muddling-through process, organizational goals and the courses of action for achieving them may change, but they change very slowly so that corrective action can be taken if things start to go wrong.

The incrementalist model is very different from the rational model. According to the rational model, an all-knowing decision maker weighs every possible alternative course of action and chooses the best solution. According to the incrementalist model, managers, limited by lack of information and lack of foresight, move cautiously one step at a time to limit their chances of being wrong.

The Unstructured Model

The incrementalist approach works best in a relatively stable environment where managers can accurately predict movements and trends. In an environment that changes suddenly or abruptly, the incrementalist approach might prevent managers from changing quickly enough to meet new conditions, thus causing the organization to go into decline. The *unstructured model* of organizational decision making, developed by Henry Mintzberg and his colleagues, describes how decision making takes place when uncertainty is high.[22]

The unstructured model recognizes the incremental nature of decision making and how decision making takes place in a series of small steps that collectively add up to a major decision over time. Incremental decisions are made within an overall decision-making framework consisting of three stages—identification, development, and selection—that are similar to the stages shown in Figure 12.1. In the identification stage, managers develop routines to recognize problems and to understand what is happening to the organization. In the development stage, they search for and design alternatives to solve the problems they have defined. Solutions may be new plans or modifications of old plans as in the muddling-through approach. Finally, in the selection stage, managers use an incremental selection process—judgment and intuition, bargaining, and to a lesser extent formal analysis (typical of the rational model)—to reach a final decision.[23]

In the unstructured model (unlike the incrementalist model), whenever organizations encounter roadblocks, they rethink their alternatives and go back to the drawing board. Thus, decision making is not a linear, sequential process but a process that may evolve unpredictably in an unstructured way. For example, decision making may be constantly interrupted because uncertainty in the environment alters managers' interpretations of a problem and, thus, casts doubt on the alternatives they have generated or the solutions they have chosen. The managers must then generate new solutions and find new strategies that help the organization adapt to and modify its environment.

Mintzberg's approach emphasizes the unstructured nature of incremental decision making: Managers make decisions in a haphazard, intuitive way, and uncertainty forces them to constantly adjust to find new ways to behave in the constantly changing situation. The organization tries to make the best decisions it can, but uncertainty forces it to adopt an unstructured way of making decisions. Thus, the unstructured model tries to explain how organizations make nonprogrammed decisions, and the incrementalist model tries to explain how organizations improve their programmed decisions over time.

The Garbage Can Model

The view of decision making as an unstructured process is taken to its extreme in the *garbage can model* of organizational decision making.[24] This model turns the decision-making process around and argues that organizations are as likely to start making decisions from the *solution side* as from the *problem side*. In other words, decision makers may propose solutions to problems that do not exist; they create a problem that they can solve with solutions that are already available.

Garbage can decision making arises in the following way: An organization has a set of solutions, or skills, with which it can solve certain problems—for example, how to generate new customers, how to lower production costs, or how to innovate products. Possessing these skills, the organization seeks ways to use them, so managers create problems, or decision-making opportunities, for themselves. Suppose a company has skills in making custom-designed furniture. The head of the marketing department persuades the company president that the organization should exploit these skills by expanding internationally. Thus, a new problem—how to manage international expansion—is created because of the existence of a solution—the ability to make superior custom-designed furniture.

While an organization is encountering new problems of its own making, it is also trying to find solutions to problems it has identified in its environment or in its internal operations. To further complicate the decision-making process, different coalitions of managers may champion different alternatives and compete for resources to implement their own chosen solutions. Thus, decision making becomes like a "garbage can" in which problems, solutions, and the preferences of different individuals and coalitions all mix together and contend with one another for organizational attention and action. In this situation, an organization becomes an organized anarchy in which the selection of alternatives depends on which coalition's or manager's definition of the situation holds sway at the moment.[25] Chance, luck, and timing are important determinants of what the organization decides to do, because the problem that is currently the major source of uncertainty facing the organization has the best chance of being dealt with. Outcomes for the organization become more uncertain than usual, and decision making becomes fluid, unpredictable, and even contradictory.

The reality of decision making in organizations is clearly a far cry from the process described by the rational model. Instead of benefiting from the wisdom of all-knowing managers generating all possible solutions and agreeing on the best one so that decisions can be programmed over time, real organizations are forced to make unprogrammed decisions in an unstructured, garbage-can-like way in order to deal with the uncertainty of the environment that surrounds them.

Summary

Decision making drives the operation of an organization. At the core of every organization is a set of decision-making rules and routines that brings stability and allows the organization to reproduce its structure, activities, and core competences over time. These routines provide the organization with a memory and provide managers with programmed solutions to problems, which in turn increase organizational effectiveness.[26] However, as we saw in Chapter 11, routines also can give rise to inertia. If an organization gets in a rut and cannot make decisions that allow it to change and adapt to and modify its environment, it may fail and die. To prevent this from happening, managers need to encourage organizational learning.

THE NATURE OF ORGANIZATIONAL LEARNING

Because decision making takes place in an uncertain environment, it is not surprising that many of the decisions that managers and organizations make are mistakes and end in failure. Others, of course, allow the organization to adapt to the environment and to succeed beyond managers' wildest dreams. Organizations survive and prosper because managers make the right decisions—sometimes through skill and sound judgment, sometimes through chance and good luck. For decision making to be successful over time, organizations must improve their ability to learn new behaviors and unlearn inefficient old ones. One of the most important processes that helps managers to make better nonprogrammed decisions, decisions that allow them to adapt to, modify, and change the environment to increase an organization's chances of survival, is organizational learning.[27] **Organizational learning** is the process through which managers seek to improve organization members' desire and ability to understand and manage the organization and its environment so that they can make decisions that continuously raise organizational effectiveness.[28]

Today organizational learning is a vital process for organizations to manage because of the rapid pace of change affecting every organization. As previous chapters have discussed, organizations are racing to develop new and improved core competences that can give them a competitive advantage. They are fighting to respond to the low-cost competitive challenges from foreign organizations. They are searching for every opportunity to use advanced materials technology and information systems to more effectively pursue their strategies and manage their structures. Indeed, the increasing tendency of organizations to experiment with restructuring and reengineering that occurred in the 1990s was motivated by managers' realization that they had to learn new ways to operate more efficiently if they were to survive. Consequently, managers must understand how organizational learning occurs and the factors that can promote and impede it.

Types of Organizational Learning

In studying organizational learning, James March has proposed that two principal types of organizational learning strategies can be pursued: exploration and exploitation.[29] **Exploration** involves organizational members searching for and experimenting with new kinds or forms of organizational activities and procedures to increase effectiveness. Learning that involves exploration might involve finding new ways of managing the environment—such as experimenting with the use of strategic alliances and network organizations—or inventing new kinds of organizational structures for managing organizational resources—such as product team structures and cross-functional teams.

Exploitation involves organizational members learning ways to refine and improve existing organizational activities and procedures in order to increase effectiveness. Learning that involves exploitation might entail implementing a total quality management program to promote the continuous refinement of existing operating procedures, or developing an improved set of rules to more effectively perform specific kinds of functional activities. Exploration is, therefore, a more radical learning process than exploitation although both are important in increasing organizational effectiveness.[30]

A **learning organization** is an organization that purposefully designs and constructs its structure, culture, and strategy so as to enhance and maximize the potential for organizational learning (explorative and exploitative) to take place.[31] How do managers create a learning organization, one capable of allowing its members to appreciate and respond quickly to changes taking place around it? By increasing the ability of employees, at every level in the organization, to question the way an organization currently performs its activities and to experiment with new ways to act to increase effectiveness.

Levels of Organizational Learning

In order to create a learning organization, managers need to encourage learning at four levels: individual, group, organizational, and interorganizational[32] (Figure 12.2). Some principles for creating a learning organization at each level have been developed by Peter Senge and are discussed next.[33]

Organizational learning
The process through which managers seek to improve organization members' capacity to understand and manage the organization and its environment so that they can make decisions that continuously raise organizational effectiveness.

Exploration *Organizational members' search for and experimentation with new kinds or forms of organizational activities and procedures.*

Exploitation *Organizational members' learning of ways to refine and improve existing organizational and procedures.*

Learning organization
An organization that purposefully designs and constructs its structure, culture, and strategy so as to enhance and maximize the potential for organizational learning to take place.

FIGURE 12.2

Levels of Organizational Learning. To create a learning organization, managers must use systems thinking and recognize the effects of one level of learning on another.

INDIVIDUAL.   At the individual level, managers need to do all they can to facilitate the learning of new skills, norms, and values so that individuals can increase their own personal skills and abilities and thereby help build the organization's core competences. One noted researcher in organizational learning, Peter Senge, has argued that for organizational learning to occur each person in an organization needs to develop a sense of *personal mastery*, by which he means that organizations should empower individuals and allow them to experiment and create and explore what they want. The goal is to give employees the opportunity to develop an intense appreciation for their work that translates into a distinctive competence for the organization. As part of attaining personal mastery, and to give employees a deeper understanding of what is involved in a particular activity, organizations need to encourage employees to develop and use complex *mental models* that challenge them to find new or better ways of performing a task. To give an analogy, a person might mow the lawn once a week and treat this as a chore that has to be done. However, suppose the person decides to study how the grass grows and to experiment with cutting the grass to different heights and using different fertilizers and watering patterns. Through this study, he or she notices that cutting the grass to a certain height and using specific combinations of fertilizer and water promote thicker growth and fewer weeds, resulting in a better-looking lawn that needs less mowing. What had been a chore may become a hobby and the personal mastery achieved from the new way of looking at the task may become a source of deep personal satisfaction. This is the message behind Senge's first principle for developing a learning organization—namely, organizations must encourage each of their individual members to develop a similar commitment and attachment to their jobs so that they will develop a taste for experimenting and risk taking.[34]

A learning organization can encourage employees to form complex mental models and develop a sense of personal mastery by providing them with the opportunity to assume more responsibility for their decisions. This can be done in a variety of different ways. Employees might be cross-trained so that they can perform many different tasks, and the knowledge that they gain may give them new insight into how to improve work procedures. On the other hand, perhaps a specific task that was performed by several different workers can be redesigned or reengineered so that one worker, aided by an advanced information system, can perform the complete task. Again, the result may be an increase in the level of organizational learning as the worker finds new ways to get the job done. Recall that one of the aims of reengineering is to fundamentally rethink basic business processes. Reengineering is about promoting organizational learning.

GROUP.   At the group level, managers need to encourage learning by promoting the use of various kinds of groups—such as self-managed groups or cross-functional teams—so that individuals can share or pool their skills and abilities to solve problems. Groups allow for the creation of synergism—the idea that the whole is much more than the sum of its parts—which can enhance performance. In terms of Thompson's model of task interdependence discussed in Chapter 9, for example, the move from a pooled, to a sequential, to a reciprocal form of task interdependence will increase the potential for synergism and group-level learning because group members have more opportunity to interact and learn from one another over time. "Group routines" and "shared pools of collective meaning" that enhance group effectiveness may develop from such group interactions.[35] Senge refers to this kind of learning as *team learning*, and he argues that team learning is more important than individual-level learning in promoting organizational learning because most important decisions are made in subunits such as groups, functions, and divisions.

The ability of teams to bring about organizational learning was unmistakable when Toyota revolutionized the work process in the former GM factory discussed in Organizational Insight 10.3. Large performance gains were achieved in the factory when Toyota's managers created work teams and empowered team members to take over the responsibility for measuring, monitoring, and controlling their own behavior to find ways to continuously increase performance. The power of teams to bring about organizational learning is also revealed in another of Toyota's attempts to increase effectiveness. In the late 1980s, Toyota decided that in the future the most efficient way to produce cars would be to build fully roboticized factories embodying the latest, most advanced manufacturing technology. As a result, when it built its most recent manufacturing plant in Kyoto, Toyota's engineers focused on perfecting the plant's materials technology, and workers were simply an appendage to the machines. By the mid-1990s, however, it had become clear to Toyota's managers that the new technology had not produced the large performance gains that they had expected. Why? According to Toyota, the new factories had eliminated the opportunity for team learning; workers were neither asked nor expected to contribute their ideas for improving efficiency. Computers are only as good as the people who program them, and programmers were not the ones working on the production line. Toyota has since junked its fully roboticized factories, and in its new factories it has made sure that people in teams can contribute their knowledge and skills to increase effectiveness.

ORGANIZATION.   At the organizational level, managers can promote organizational learning through the way they create an organization's structure and culture. An organization's structure can be designed to inhibit or facilitate intergroup communication and problem solving, and this affects team members' approach to learning. Mechanistic and organic structures, for example, encourage different approaches to learning. The design of a mechanistic structure seems likely to facilitate exploitative learning, while the design of an organic structure seems more likely to facilitate explorative learning. Indeed, organizations need to strike a balance between a mechanistic and an organic structure in order to take advantage of both types of learning.

Culture, too, is likely to be an important influence on learning at the organizational level. Another of Senge's principles for designing a learning organization emphasizes the importance of *building shared vision*, by which he means building the ongoing frame of reference or mental model that all organizational members use to frame problems or opportunities and that binds them to an organization. At the heart of this vision is likely to be the set of terminal and instrumental values and norms that guide behavior in a particular setting and that affect the way people interact with individuals and groups outside an organization, that is, organizational culture. Thus, yet another important aspect of organizational culture is its ability to promote or inhibit organizational learning and change.

Indeed, in a recent study of 207 companies, John Kotter and James Heskett distinguished between adaptive cultures and inert cultures in terms of their ability to facilitate organizational learning.[36] **Adaptive cultures** are those that value innovation and encourage and reward experimenting and risk taking by middle and lower-level managers. **Inert cultures** are those that are cautious and conservative, do not value middle and lower-level managers taking such action, and, indeed, may actively discourage such behavior. According to Kotter and Heskett, organizational learning is higher in organizations with adaptive cultures because managers can quickly introduce changes in the way the organization operates that allow the organization to adapt to changes occurring in the environment. This does not occur in organizations with inert cultures. As a result, organizations with adaptive cultures are more likely to survive in a changing environment and, indeed, should have higher performance than organizations with inert cultures—exactly what Kotter and Heskett found among the 207 companies that they examined.

INTERORGANIZATIONAL. Organizational structure and culture not only establish the shared vision or framework of common assumptions that guide learning inside an organization but also determine how learning takes place at the interorganizational level. For example, organizations with organic, adaptive cultures are more likely to actively seek out new ways to manage interorganizational linkages with other organizations while mechanistic, inert cultures are slower to recognize or to take advantage of new kinds of linkage mechanisms.

In general, interorganizational learning is important because organizations can improve their effectiveness by copying and imitating each other's distinctive competences. The last chapter discussed how mimetic, coercive, and normative processes encourage organizations to learn from each other in order to increase their legitimacy, but this can also increase their effectiveness. In the automobile industry, for example, Japanese car manufacturers came to the United States after World War II to learn U.S. manufacturing methods and took this knowledge back to Japan where they improved upon it. This process was then reversed when struggling U.S. carmakers went to Japan to learn about the advances that Japanese carmakers had pioneered, took this knowledge back to the United States, and improved upon it.

Similarly, organizations can encourage explorative and exploitative learning by cooperating with their suppliers and distributors to find new and improved ways of handling inputs and outputs. Strategic alliances and network organizations provide useful vehicles for increasing the speed at which new learning takes place because they open up the organization to the environment and give organizational members new opportunities to experiment and find new ways to increase effectiveness.

In fact, Senge's fifth principle of organizational learning, *systems thinking*, emphasizes that in order to create a learning organization, managers must recognize the effects of one level of learning on another. Thus, for example, there is little point in creating teams to facilitate team learning if an organization does not also take steps to give its employees the freedom to develop a sense of personal mastery. Similarly, the nature of interorganizational learning is likely to be affected by the kind of learning going on inside an organization.

By encouraging and promoting organizational learning at each of these four levels—that is, by looking at organizational learning as a system—managers can create a learning organization that facilitates an organization's quick response to the changes in the environment that are constantly taking place around it. To enhance an organization's ability to create value, managers need to promote both explorative and exploitative learning and then use this learning in ways that will promote organizational effectiveness. Managers need to recognize, however, that empowering workers, allowing teams to take control of their own activities, and creating an organic, adaptive organization all expose an organization to risk. Risk increases because the explorative learning that takes place may disrupt taken-for-granted routines and assumptions so that managers have to carefully manage the changes taking place (an issue discussed in Chapter 13). On the other hand, very often the problem is not too *much* learning taking place but too *little*. Several factors may impede organizational learning, and when this happens the quality of decision making falls and effectiveness suffers. The nature of these factors is discussed in the following section.

FACTORS AFFECTING ORGANIZATIONAL LEARNING

An interesting model that illustrates several factors that may *reduce* the level of organizational learning over time has been developed by Paul C. Nystrom and William H. Starbuck. This model illustrates how problems may arise that prevent an organization from learning and adapting to its environment and that, therefore, cause an organizational crisis to emerge.[37] Nystrom and Starbuck define a crisis as any situation that seriously threatens an organization's survival.

According to Nystrom and Starbuck, as organizations learn to make decisions, they develop rules and standard operating procedures that facilitate programmed decision making. If an organization achieves success by using its standard procedures, this success may lead to complacency and deter managers from searching for and learning from new experiences.[38] Thus, past (successful) learning can inhibit new learning and lead to organizational inertia. If programmed decision making drives out nonprogrammed decision making, the level of organizational learning drops. Blindness and rigidity in organizational decision making may then set in and lead to a full-blown crisis.

Managers often discount warnings that problems are impending and do not perceive that crises are developing. Even if they notice, they may attribute the source of the problems to temporary disturbances in the environment and implement what Nystrom and Starbuck call "weathering-the-storm strategies," such as postponing investments, downsizing the workforce, or centralizing decision making and reducing the autonomy of people at low levels in the organization. Managers adopt this incrementalist approach to decision making because sticking to what they know is much safer than setting off in new directions (explorative learning) where consequences are unknown. Managers continue to rely on the information obtained from their existing operating routines to solve problems—information that does not reveal the real nature of the problems they are experiencing.

Another reason why past learning inhibits new organizational learning is that managers' mind-sets or cognitive structures shape their perception and interpretation of problems and solutions. A **cognitive structure** is the system of interrelated beliefs, preferences, expectations, and values that a person uses to define problems and events.[39] In an organization, cognitive structures reveal themselves in plans, goals, stories, myths, and jargon. Cognitive structures shape the way a CEO or members of the top-management team make decisions, and they predetermine what managers perceive as opportunities and threats in the environment. Two managers (or two top-management teams), for example, might perceive the same "objective" environment very differently because of differences in their cognitive structures.

Cognitive structure The system of interrelated beliefs, preferences, expectations, and values that a person uses to define problems and events.

A classic example of how cognitive structure influences decision making occurred after World War II, when Sears, Roebuck and Montgomery Ward were planning their post-war strategies. The top-management team at Sears believed that there would be a boom in consumer spending after the war and that the environment was very favorable for large-scale investment and expansion. Managers at Sears set out to establish a nationwide store system to take advantage of the anticipated surge in demand. Managers at Montgomery Ward interpreted the environment differently. They believed that consumers would save their money. Consequently, Montgomery Ward's postwar expansion program was much smaller and less ambitious than Sears's program. After the war, consumer spending boomed, and the environment became richer and richer. Sears could take advantage of this change in the environment, but Montgomery Ward could not. As a result, Sears grew to become the dominant retailer of the 1960s.

Just as top managers' cognitive structures can produce successful learning, they can also cause a crisis. During the early 1990s, for example, Sears was unable to respond to the challenges posed by the new retailing environment because it relied on past learning to make new business decisions (an incrementalist approach to decision making). Sears's decisions have been shown to be inferior to those made by Wal-Mart, for example, whose top-management team has made the best predictions about customer demands for low-cost retailing in the 1980s and 1990s. Why do top managers often cling to outdated ideas and use inappropriate cognitive structures to interpret events and problems—something that leads to faulty learning? It is useful to look at some factors that distort managers' perceptions and flaw organizational learning and decision making.

Organizational Learning and Cognitive Structures

As noted earlier, cognitive structures are the systems of beliefs, preferences, expectations, and values that develop over time and predetermine a person's responses to and interpretations of situations. When a manager confronts a problem, his or her cognitive structure shapes the interpretation of the information at hand; that is, the manager's view of a situation is shaped by prior experience and customary ways of thinking—by the manager's mind-set.[40] That view, however, might be distorted.

Over many years, for example, the cognitive structures of IBM's top managers reinforced the idea that organizations needed mainframe computers to handle their information-processing needs. IBM, therefore, sought to develop core competences in the design, manufacture, and servicing of mainframe computers. When personal computers came along, IBM viewed them as machines suitable only for managers' personal information-processing needs or as a way of linking managers to a mainframe. IBM did not regard personal computers as an alternative to the mainframe because its managers were fixated on the idea that mainframes, and only mainframes, could satisfy organizations' information-processing needs. When major advances in software and microchip technology allowed personal computers to handle and store increasing volumes of information, IBM managers discounted these developments. The company searched for better ways to tie PCs into mainframes through networking, and it worked to improve the network capabilities of mainframe computers by developing new operating languages such as UNIX.

The cognitive structures of IBM managers led to a misinterpretation or undervaluing of new information. IBM's managers discounted the threat that PCs posed and continued to operate as if mainframe computers would dominate the market forever. When events proved their view of the environment to be distorted, it was too late to take corrective action. IBM was in crisis. The board of directors brought in a new CEO, Lou Gerstner, hop-

FIGURE 12.3

The Distortion of Organizational Decision Making by Cognitive Biases. Cognitive dissonance and other cognitive biases affect managers' information-processing abilities and distort managers' interpretation of a problem.

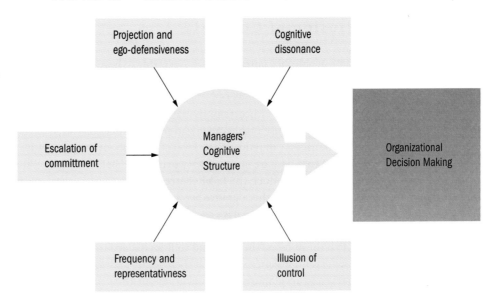

Types of Cognitive Biases

Cognitive biases Factors that systematically bias cognitive structures and affect organizational learning and decision making.

Researchers have identified several factors that lead managers to develop a cognitive structure that causes them to misperceive and misinterpret information. These factors are called **cognitive biases** because they systematically bias cognitive structures and affect organizational learning and decision making. As Figure 12.3 shows, cognitive biases affect the way managers process information. Cognitive dissonance, illusion of control, and several other cognitive biases that influence organizational learning and decision making are discussed next and are illustrated by an examination of IBM's problems in changing its strategy and structure in the 1990s.[41]

Cognitive Dissonance

Cognitive dissonance The state of discomfort or anxiety that a person feels when there is an inconsistency between his or her beliefs and actions.

Cognitive dissonance is the state of discomfort or anxiety that a person feels when there is an inconsistency between his or her beliefs and actions. According to cognitive dissonance theory, decision makers try to maintain consistency among their images of themselves, their attitudes, and their decisions.[42] Managers seek or interpret information that confirms and reinforces their beliefs, and they ignore information that does not. Managers also tend to seek information that is only incrementally different from the information they already possess and that, therefore, supports their established position.

Cognitive dissonance theory explains why managers tend to misinterpret the real threats facing an organization and attempt to muddle through even when it is clear to many observers that the organization is in crisis. The operation of this cognitive bias might help account for the faulty learning and decisions of IBM's top managers during the 1980s. Whenever they received outside information suggesting that PC research was threatening the viability of mainframes, they discounted the information and relied on information that they generated to support their view of mainframes. The desire to reduce cognitive dissonance pushes managers to adopt flawed incremental solutions even when they are wrong.

Illusion of Control

Some people, like entrepreneurs, seem able to bear high levels of uncertainty; others prefer the security associated with working in established organizations. Regardless of one's tolerance for ambiguity, however, uncertainty is very stressful. When an organization's environment or future is uncertain, managers do not know whether they have made the right choices, and considerable organizational resources are often at stake. Research has shown that managers can reduce their level of stress about uncertainty by strengthening their perception that they are in control of a situation.[43] Belief in one's personal ability to control uncertainty can reduce the level of stress one feels. However, as a manager's perception of control increases, the cognitive bias known as illusion of control alters his or her perceptions.

Illusion of control A cognitive bias that causes managers to overestimate the extent to which the outcomes of an action are under their personal control.

Illusion of control is a cognitive bias that causes managers to overestimate the extent to which the outcomes of an action are under their personal control and the extent to which they possess the skills and abilities needed to manage uncertainty and complexity.[44] In uncertain situations in which their ability and competence are really being tested, managers may develop irrational beliefs about their personal ability to manage uncertainty. They may, for example, overestimate their ability to use their skills in new ventures and embark on a huge acquisition program. Soon, however, they encounter problems and realize that they lack the ability to manage the more complex organization effectively.

Very frequently, when top managers lose control, they try to centralize authority in the mistaken belief that centralization will increase their control and allow them to turn the situation around. Because their perception of control is an illusion, the organizational crisis deepens. IBM, for example, finally established a PC division to produce and market personal computers. But the division never got the autonomy it needed to devise a strategy that would have allowed it to compete successfully with the clone makers and respond to the frequent price cutting and discounting characteristic of the personal computer industry. Managers in the PC division were constantly overseen by IBM's top managers, who believed that they alone had the ability to control the division's strategy. Because they were blinded by the illusion of control, no organizational learning was taking place; the PC division's managers were unable to respond quickly to the moves of its competitors and were unable to develop a long-term strategy to give the division a strong competitive advantage.

It is not uncommon for a strong CEO or the members of an entrenched top-management team to develop the illusion that only they have the ability to manage the uncertainty facing the organization and to lead the organization to success even when it is in crisis. The way in which two former CEOs of Nissan held onto the reins of power for many years is another example of the tendency of powerful people—that is, those who control organizational resources—to fall victim to the illusion of control.

ORGANIZATIONAL INSIGHT

12.2 NISSAN'S TOP-HEAVY MANAGEMENT STYLE

In 1980, Nissan Motor Company was poised to reap the returns from a decade of investment in new technology. Its U.S. sales had steadily increased, and in 1975 it had surged past Volkswagen to be the number-one importer of cars to the United States. By 1980, Nissan held 5.5 percent of the U.S. market. Then, between 1980 and 1990, when the overall Japanese share of the U.S. market increased from 17.7 to 28 percent,

Nissan's share slipped to 4.7 percent. What went wrong? What had derailed Nissan and left Toyota and Honda the undisputed Japanese leaders in the United States? The answer lies in Nissan's top-management team's approach to learning and decision making.

Until 1985, Nissan was run by Katsuji Kawamata, a conservative former banker. Kawamata surrounded himself with yes-men. His successor was Takashi Ishihara, a former accountant. Ishihara's domineering style of management led to clashes with both managers and employees. Under both Kawamata and Ishihara, decision making at Nissan became increasingly centralized and bureaucratic so that they could control the kind of learning taking place. Both men attempted to put their stamp on every part of Nissan's global operations.[45] Both appointed top-management teams that were totally loyal to them, and they ruled by committee, using the top-management team to make a joint decision about every significant issue facing the company. The result was a series of strategic errors that cost Nissan its lead in the U.S. market. For example, both leaders used the top-management team to pick a prototype for each new car being developed. The haggling that resulted as team members tried to reach a consensus destroyed all creativity in design and resulted in a new model only marginally different from the old model.

Other examples of poor learning and decision making included the misguided name change from Datsun to Nissan in 1981 to satisfy the egos of top-management team members, and the failure to recognize and respond to the needs of the different segments of the car market and to produce minivans and family sedans, which were increasingly becoming the cars of choice. At the same time, costs were rising as top management made a series of expensive investment decisions that resulted from a series of power struggles between factions within the top-management team.

By 1985, the cumulative effects of a decade of centralized decision making from Nissan's bureaucratic headquarters in Japan were apparent to both inside and outside stakeholders. A shift in the power structure resulted in the installation of Yutaka Kume, an engineer, as president of Nissan. He moved immediately to change the company's decision-making process. Top management no longer made all the decisions. One top manager was given control of each car and was made solely responsible for the success of the venture. Control of operations in the United States was decentralized to Nissan's U.S. headquarters, and U.S. design teams were allowed direct input on the shape of the cars intended for the American market. The result of Kume's attempts to create a learning organization was a series of spectacular successes when Nissan introduced its new line of minivans, the Quest, in 1991 and its new small sedan, the Altima, in 1992. By 1993, the Altima had become the best-selling small sedan in the United States.

Frequency and Representativeness

Frequency *A cognitive bias that deceives people into assuming that extreme instances of a phenomenon are more prevalent than they really are.*

Frequency and representativeness are tendencies that often lead people to misinterpret information.[46] **Frequency** is a cognitive bias that deceives people into assuming that extreme instances of a phenomenon are more prevalent than they really are. Suppose purchasing managers have had a particularly bad experience with a supplier that has been shipping them large quantities of defective goods. Because of severe manufacturing problems caused by the defective parts, the managers decide to sever relations with that supplier. The frequency bias may cause them to become very fearful of relying on other suppliers for their inputs. They may instead decide to vertically integrate their operations so that they control their inputs, even though vertical integration will increase costs. Although there is no rational reason to believe that a new supplier will be as bad as, or worse than, the rejected supplier, the managers jump to an expensive solution to avoid the risk, and faulty learning has occurred.

Representativeness *A cognitive bias that leads managers to form judgments based on small and unrepresentative samples.*

Representativeness is a cognitive bias that leads managers to form judgments based on small and unrepresentative samples. Exposure to a couple of unreliable suppliers, for example, prompts managers to generalize and believe that all suppliers are untrustworthy and unreliable, again leading to faulty learning.

Frequency and representative biases can also work in the opposite direction. A company that has great success with a new product may come to believe that this product is the wave of the future and devote all its resources to developing a new product line for which there actually is little demand. Federal Express, for example, believed that the demand for international express delivery would increase dramatically as companies became increasingly global. It came to this conclusion because it had been receiving more and more requests for international delivery. Federal Express, thus, decided to invest a huge amount of resources to buy and operate a fleet of planes and overseas facilities to handle global express delivery. The decision was a disaster. The volume of express packages shipped to Europe turned out to be only half of that shipped in the United States, and the cost of operating the new global structure was enormous. After major losses, Federal Express decided to form strategic alliances with foreign delivery companies to deliver the mail (rather than go it alone), and this new strategy has been successful. As this example shows, a bad decision can be made because a CEO and top-management team overgeneralize from a limited range of knowledge and experience.

Projection and Ego-Defensiveness

Projection *A cognitive bias that allows managers to justify and reinforce their own preferences and values by attributing them to others.*

Projection is a cognitive bias that allows managers to justify and reinforce their own preferences and values by attributing them to others.[47] Suppose a top-management team is dominated by managers who are threatened by a deteriorating economic situation and doubt their ability to manage it. Feeling threatened and powerless, the team may accuse other lower-level managers of being unable to control the situation or of lacking the ability or desire to do so. Thus, top managers project their own feelings of helplessness onto others and blame them. This situation arose at IBM in 1991 when CEO John Akers, realizing the enormity of IBM's problems, publicly denounced IBM's managers as being lazy and useless. Obviously, when projection starts to operate, it can become self-reinforcing: Everybody blames everybody else, and the culture of the organization deteriorates.

Ego-defensiveness *A cognitive bias that leads managers to interpret events in such a way that their actions appear in the most favorable light.*

Ego-defensiveness also affects the way managers interpret what is happening in the organization. **Ego-defensiveness** is a cognitive bias that leads managers to interpret events in such a way that their actions appear in the most favorable light. If an organization is employing more and more managers but profitability is not increasing, managers may emphasize that they are positioning the organization for future growth by putting in place the infrastructure to support future development. Ego-defensiveness results in little organizational learning, and faulty decision making ultimately leads to a manager's replacement.

Escalation of Commitment

The bias toward escalation of commitment is another powerful cause of flawed learning and faulty decision making.[48] According to the Carnegie model of decision making, managers generate a limited number of alternative courses of action, from which they choose one that they hope will lead to a satisfactory (if not optimum) outcome. But what happens if they choose the wrong course of action and experience a negative outcome, such as when Federal Express found itself losing enormous amounts of money as a result of its international express delivery venture? A logical response to a negative outcome would be a reevaluation of the course of action. Research, however, indicates that managers who have made an investment in a mistake tend to persist in the same behavior and increase their commitment to it even though it is leading to poor returns and organizational ineffectiveness. **Escalation of commitment** is a cognitive bias that leads managers to remain committed to a losing course of action and refuse to admit that they have made a mistake, perhaps because of ego-defensiveness or because they are gripped by the illusion of control. In later decision making, they try to correct and improve on their prior (bad) decision rather than acknowledge that they have made a mistake and turn to a different course of action. At Federal Express, for example, the CEO realized the error and quickly moved to redeploy resources to make the international express delivery venture viable, and he succeeded.

Escalation of commitment A cognitive bias that leads managers to remain committed to a losing course of action and refuse to admit that they have made a mistake.

At IBM, in contrast, managers' commitment to mainframe computers escalated even though the market for mainframes was shrinking. Top managers at IBM refused to redeploy significant organizational resources to develop skills in servers and PCs. They continued to invest resources to improve mainframes and tried to maintain them as the technology of the future. IBM spent billions of dollars to improve the storage and information-processing capacity of mainframe computers instead of spending money to recruit software experts who could either develop new skills that would allow IBM to compete directly with Microsoft or find new ways to exploit IBM's existing skills and resources.

The bias toward escalation of commitment is clearly reinforced by an incrementalist approach to decision making. Managers prefer to modify existing decisions to make them fit better with new conditions rather than to work out new solutions. Although this method of decision making may work in stable environments, it is disastrous when technology or competition is rapidly changing.

The net effect of all of the cognitive biases is that managers lose their ability to see new problems or situations clearly and to devise new responses to new challenges, and the level of learning falls. The flawed decision making that results from these biases hampers an organization's ability to adapt and modify its environment. By hampering organizational learning, biased decision making threatens an organization's ability to grow and survive. What can an organization do to develop a less incremental and more unstructured approach to decision making? How can it make managers receptive to learning new solutions and to challenging the assumptions they use to make decisions? Nystrom and Starbuck argue that when organizational learning and decision making is seriously affected by out-of-date or wrong cognitive structures, only radical actions can correct the situation and bring the organization back on the path to success.[49] Research has suggested several steps that managers and organizations can take to raise the level of organizational learning and improve the quality of their decision making.

IMPROVING DECISION MAKING AND LEARNING

Organizational inertia and cognitive biases make it difficult to promote organizational learning and maintain the quality of organizational decision making over time. How can managers avoid using inappropriate routines, beliefs, and values to interpret and solve problems? There are several ways in which an organization can overcome the effect of cognitive biases and promote organizational learning. It can implement strategies for organizational learning, increase the breadth and diversity of the top-management team, use devil's advocacy and dialectical inquiry to evaluate proposed solutions, and develop a collateral organizational structure.

Strategies for Organizational Learning

Managers have to continuously unlearn old ideas and constantly test their decision-making skills by confronting errors in their beliefs and perceptions. Three ways in which they can stimulate the unlearning of old ideas (and the learning of new ones) are by listening to dissenters, by converting events into learning opportunities, and by experimenting.[50]

LISTENING TO DISSENTERS.   To improve the quality of decision making, top managers can make it their policy to surround themselves with people who hold different and often opposing points of view. They can try to collect new information to evaluate the new interpretations and alternatives generated by dissenters.

Unfortunately, research has shown that top managers do not listen carefully to their subordinates and tend to surround themselves with yes-men who distort the information they provide, enhancing good news and suppressing bad news.[51] Moreover, because of bounded rationality, managers may be reluctant to encourage dissent because dissent will increase the amount of information they have to process.

CONVERTING EVENTS INTO LEARNING OPPORTUNITIES.   Nystrom and Starbuck discuss one unidentified company that appointed a "Vice President for Revolutions," whose job was to step in every four years and shake up the organization by transferring managers and reassigning responsibilities so that old, taken-for-granted routines were reexamined and people could bring new points of view to various situations. It did not make much difference what specific changes were made. The objective was to make them large enough so that people were forced to make new interpretations of situations. After each shake-up, productivity increased for two years and then declined for the next two, until the organization was shaken up again.[52]

More generally, an organization needs to design and manage its structure and culture—in ways that were discussed earlier—so that managers are motivated to find new or improved responses to a situation. Total quality management, for example, is based on the idea of making people responsible for continuously reexamining their jobs to see whether improvements that result in increased quality and productivity can be made. Similarly, as noted earlier, different kinds of organizational structure (e.g., mechanistic or organic) can encourage or discourage organizational learning.

An interesting study conducted in California when hospitals were jolted by a doctor's strike shows the influence of organizational culture in decision making. The study found that responses by hospitals to this crisis were strongly influenced by the way in which each hospital typically made decisions in uncertain situations.[53] Hospitals that had organic structures characterized by decentralized decision making and that frequently redesigned their structures were accustomed to both learning and unlearning. As a result, these hospitals dealt with the strike much better than did hospitals with centralized, mechanistic structures and a formalized, programmed approach to decision making.

EXPERIMENTING.   To encourage explorative learning, organizations must encourage experimenting, the process of generating new alternatives and testing the validity of old ones. Experimenting can be used to improve both incremental and garbage can decision-making processes. To test new ways of behaving, such as new ways to serve customers or to manufacture a product, managers can run experiments that deviate only slightly from what the organization is currently doing. Or, taking a garbage can approach, managers can brainstorm and come up with new solutions that surprise even themselves. Managers who are willing to experiment avoid overcommitment to previously worked-out solutions, reduce the likelihood of misinterpreting a situation, and can learn from their failures.

NATURE OF THE TOP-MANAGEMENT TEAM.   The way the top-management team is constructed and the type of people who are on it affect the level of organizational learning.[54] There are various ways to construct a top-management team, and each has different implications for the processing of information, organizational learning, and the quality of decision making.[55] Figure 12.4 shows two top-management configurations, each of which has different implications for the level of learning taking place. In the wheel configuration, organizational learning is decreased because managers from the different functions report separately to the CEO. Rather than coordinate their own actions as a team, they send all information to the CEO, who processes this information, arrives at a decision, and communicates the decision back to the top managers. Research suggests that the wheel works best when problems are simple and require minimal coordination among top team members.[56] When problems are complex and nonprogrammed decision making is required, the wheel configuration slows organizational learning because all coordination takes place through the CEO.

In the circle configuration, top managers from different functions interact with each other and with the CEO. That is, they function as a team—something that promotes team and organizational learning. Research has suggested that the circle works best for complex problems requiring coordination among group members to arrive at a solution. The circle design solves complex problems much more quickly than the wheel arrangement because communication around the circle takes less time and there is more opportunity for team and organizational learning among all top managers.[57]

FIGURE 12.4

Types of Top-Management Teams

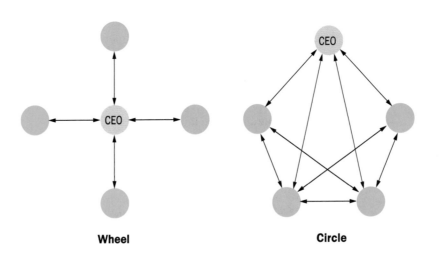

Wheel   **Circle**

The level and quality of organizational learning and decision making by the top-management team are also a function of the personal characteristics and backgrounds of team members.[58] An organization that draws its top-management team from many different industries and different functional backgrounds can promote organizational learning and decision making. Diversity in the top-management team also exposes managers to the implications and consequences of many alternative courses of action. Such exposure may cause managers to examine their own expectations and assumptions more closely.

At IBM, for example, members of the top-management team had been promoted from within the organization. There were no outsiders to propose credible alternative courses of action and, thus, to force IBM's top managers to examine their assumptions. By contrast, Coca-Cola was concerned that its top managers' lack of international experience could hurt the organization's emerging global strategy. To provide new direction, three foreign managers were appointed to its top-management team, and one of them, Roberto Goizueta, became the new CEO.

It has been found that the most learning takes place when there is considerable heterogeneity among team members and when managers from different functions have an opportunity to express their views. When managers bring different information and viewpoints to bear on a problem, the organization can avoid **groupthink**, the conformity that emerges when like-minded people reinforce one another's tendencies to interpret events and information in similar ways.[59] It has also been found that top-management teams function most effectively when their membership is stable and there is not too much entry into or departure from the team.[60] When team membership is stable, group cohesiveness increases and promotes communication among members and improved decision making.[61]

Groupthink *The conformity that emerges when like-minded people reinforce one another's tendencies to interpret events and information in similar ways.*

Designing and managing the top-management team to promote organizational learning is a vital task for a CEO.[62] Often an organization picks as CEO the person who has the functional and managerial background needed to deal with the most pressing issues facing the organization. Caterpillar, General Motors, and Xerox all picked as CEOs managers who had extensive experience in international business because the organizations' major problems all centered on the challenge of meeting global competition. For example, as head of European operations at GM, Jack Smith quickly turned around the performance of GM's European operations and rapidly introduced cost-saving innovations into the manufacturing and design processes.[63]

Sometimes the only way to promote organizational learning is to change the CEO or the top-management team. Although an organization might retain the rare top manager who has dissented from prevailing beliefs and perceptions, removing top managers can be the quickest way to erase organizational memory and programmed decision making, so that the organization can develop new routines. Thus, for example, IBM's board of directors ousted John Akers and installed as CEO Louis Gerstner, the former CEO of RJR Nabisco, who had no previous experience in the computer industry. The board's rationale seemed to be that IBM needed a new person with new views and new solutions to turn the organization around and lead it out of crisis.

Devil's Advocacy and Dialectical Inquiry

Devil's advocacy and dialectical inquiry are also ways of overcoming cognitive biases and promoting organizational learning.[64] Figure 12.5 shows how these strategies differ from one another and from the rational approach to decision making. The goal of both is to improve decision making.

FIGURE 12.5

How Devil's Advocacy and Dialectical Inquiry Alter the Rational Approach to Decision Making. Devil's advocacy and dialectical inquiry improve decision making by making managers aware of several possible solutions to a problem and by encouraging the analysis of the pros and cons of each proposed solution before a final decision is made.

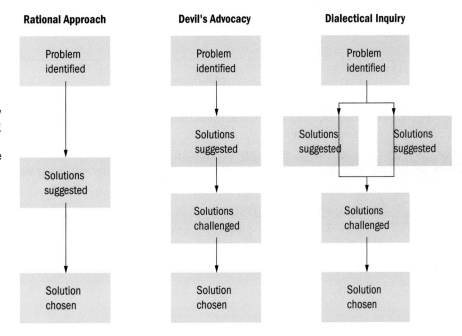

Devil's advocate *A person who is responsible for critiquing ongoing organizational learning*

An organization that uses devil's advocacy institutionalizes dissent by assigning a manager or management team the role of devil's advocate. The **devil's advocate** is responsible for critiquing ongoing organizational learning and for questioning the assumptions the top-management team uses in the decision-making process. For example, 3M makes excellent use of devil's advocacy. At 3M, product managers submit proposals for a new product to a product development committee composed of top managers. The committee acts as devil's advocate. It critiques the proposal and challenges assumptions (such as the estimated size of the market for the product or its cost of manufacturing) in order to improve the plan and verify its commercial viability. 3M directly attributes its product development successes to the use of devil's advocacy.

An organization that uses dialectical inquiry creates teams of decision makers. Each team is instructed to generate and evaluate alternative scenarios and courses of action and then recommend the best one. After hearing each team's alternatives, all of the teams and the organization's top managers sit down together to cull the best parts of each plan and synthesize a final plan that offers the best chance of success.

Collateral Organizational Structure

Finally, an organization can attempt to improve learning and decision making by establishing a *collateral organizational structure*—that is, an informal organization of managers that is set up parallel to the formal organizational structure to "shadow" the decision making and actions of managers in the formal organization.[65] Managers in the formal structure know that their decisions are being evaluated by others and become used to examining the assumptions that they use to test alternatives and arrive at a solution. An organization establishes a collateral structure to improve the organization's ability to learn and adjust to new situations, and to enhance its ability to make decisions in an unstructured way. A collateral organizational structure allows an organization to maintain its capacity for change at the same time that it maintains its stability.

1. Try to guard against blindness and rigidity in decision making, be on the lookout for new problems, and be open to new solutions.

2. Develop a questioning attitude, and never discount warnings that problems are impending.

3. Analyze the cognitive structures through which you and your subunit define problems. Question whether these beliefs or values reflect the realities of the situation.

4. Examine your decision making to determine whether cognitive biases are affecting the quality of your decisions.

5. To protect the quality of your decision making, develop strategies to enhance organizational learning. For example, listen to your opponents, experiment with new solutions, encourage diversity, and use dialectical inquiry.

SUMMARY

The problems that companies such as General Motors, IBM, and Federal Express are experiencing are a warning about the need to encourage organizational learning so that organizations have the ability to continuously adapt to and modify their environments. Strategy and structure are the tools that an organization uses to fashion its future; the decisions about strategy and structure that an organization makes now will determine its fate for years to come. Too often, managers view strategy and structure as given and unchangeable and not as things to be experimented with and altered to move the organization forward. When strategy and structure are seen as something to be protected or hidden behind, they become a source of organizational inertia that eventually may bring an organization to its knees. Managers need to understand the way in which an organization's current strategy and structure can constrain organizational learning, and they need to understand how cognitive biases can affect learning and distort the decision-making process. Chapter 12 has made the following main points:

1. Organizational decision making is the process of responding to a problem by searching for and selecting a solution or course of action that will create value for organizational stakeholders.

2. Managers make two basic types of decisions: programmed and nonprogrammed. Programmed decisions provide an organization with stability and increase efficiency. Nonprogrammed decisions allow an organization to adapt to changes in its environment and find solutions to new problems.

3. The rational model of decision making outlines how decision making takes place when there is no uncertainty. It ignores the effects of information costs and managerial costs.

4. Newer models of decision making recognize the effects of uncertainty, information, bounded rationality, satisficing, and bargaining by coalitions on the decision-making process. The Carnegie, incrementalist, unstructured, and garbage can models provide a more realistic picture of how organizational decision making takes place.

5. Organizational learning is the process through which managers seek to improve organization members' desire and ability to understand and manage the organization and its environment so that they can make decisions that continuously raise organizational effectiveness. There are two main kinds of learning—explorative and exploitative—and both are necessary to raise the quality of decision making.

6. The routines and procedures that an organization uses to make programmed decisions can cause organizational inertia. When programmed decision making drives out nonprogrammed decision making, the level of organizational learning drops. To encourage organizational learning, managers can act at the individual, group, organizational, and interorganizational levels.

7. Cognitive structures (sets of interrelated beliefs, preferences, expectations, and values) affect the way managers interpret the problems facing an organization and shape the way they make decisions.

8. Cognitive biases may distort the way managers process information and make decisions. Common cognitive biases include cognitive dissonance, the illusion of control, frequency and representativeness, projection and ego-defensiveness, and escalation of commitment.

9. There are several ways in which an organization can counter the effect of cognitive biases and raise the level of learning and decision making. It can implement strategies for organizational learning, increase the breadth and diversity of the top-management team, use devil's advocacy and dialectical inquiry to evaluate proposed solutions, and develop a collateral organizational structure.

DISCUSSION QUESTIONS

1. What are the critical differences between the rational and the Carnegie approaches to decision making? What are the critical differences between the incrementalist and the garbage can models? Which models best describe how decision making takes place in (a) a fast-food restaurant and (b) the research and development laboratory of a major drug company?

2. What is organizational learning? In what ways can managers promote the development of organizational learning by acting at various levels in the organization?

3. What are cognitive structures, and where do they come from? How do cognitive biases affect organizational learning and the quality of decision making? How has IBM suffered from cognitive biases?

ORGANIZATIONAL THEORY IN ACTION

PRACTICING ORGANIZATIONAL THEORY:
STORE LEARNING

Form groups of three to five people and discuss the following scenario:

You are a group of top managers of a major clothing store who are facing a crisis. Your establishment has been the leading clothing store in your city for 15 years. In the last three years, however, two other major clothing store chains have opened up in your city and they have steadily been attracting away your customers—your sales are down 30 percent. To find out why, you have been surveying some of your former customers and have learned that they perceive, for whatever reason, that your store is just not keeping up with changing fashion trends and new forms of customer service. In examining the way your store operates, you have come to realize that over time the 10 buyers who purchase the clothing and accessories for your store have been increasingly buying from the same set of clothing suppliers and have become reluctant to try new ones. Moreover, your salespeople rarely, if ever, make suggestions for changing the way your store operates. Your goal is to shake up store employees and turn around store performance.

1. Devise a program to increase the level of organizational learning.
2. In what specific ways can you promote organizational learning at all levels?

MAKING THE CONNECTION #12

Find an example of an organization that has been trying to change the way it makes decisions or increase its level of learning. Why is the organization making these changes? What is it doing to stimulate new learning?

Analyzing the Organization: Design Module #12

This module focuses on organizational decision making and learning and on the way your company has changed its strategy and structure over time. To answer these questions, you will need the information you collected in Design Module #11 on organizational growth and decline.

ASSIGNMENT

1. Given the changes your organization has made to its strategy and structure over time, which of the decision-making models best characterizes the way it makes decisions?

2. At what hierarchical level does responsibility for nonprogrammed decision making seem to lie in your organization? How would you characterize the approach of the CEO or top-management team? What problems do you see with the way your company makes decisions?

3. Characterize your organization's ability to learn over time. Evaluate its capacity to adapt itself to and modify the environment. What factors seem to promote or impede learning?

4. What crises has your organization experienced? How and why did they arise? How were they resolved?

5. Can you pinpoint any cognitive biases that may have affected the way managers made decisions or influenced their choice of strategy or structure? What was the effect of these cognitive biases?

6. What techniques does your organization use to promote organizational learning and improve the quality of decision making?

Cases for Analysis:
ENCOURAGING LEARNING AT BAXTER INTERNATIONAL

Baxter International is a global health care products company. From 1970 until 1990, Baxter, like other health care companies, enjoyed annual growth rates of over 20 percent. In such a rich environment, top managers had been happy to decentralize decision-making authority to the heads of the various divisions and let managers in these divisions decide how to allocate funds to promote specific research and development projects. Managers in each division were also rewarded on the basis of the performance of their individual divisions. As a result of these factors, they confined their energies to their division and did not take a company-wide view.

The problems with such a division-focused approach to decision making became obvious in the 1990s when the global health care environment became very competitive because of a combination of factors such as cheap generic drugs; government control of drug prices; the emergence of powerful buyers, such as HMOs, that demanded lower prices; and increased competition from new biotechnology companies. All these factors put pressure on health care companies like Baxter to find ways both to reduce costs and to speed the rate of new-product development. However, to its chagrin, Baxter found that it did not have in place a culture for innovation that would allow managers to make the decisions that would enable the company to respond quickly to these pressures.

The problem facing Baxter's CEO Vernon R. Loucks, Jr., was how to stimulate organizational learning and increase Baxter's managers' desire and ability to understand and manage the organization and its environment so that they could make the decisions that would continually raise organizational performance. Specifically, realizing that Baxter's main problem was that divisional managers only made decisions with their own division in mind, how could he get them to take an organization-wide view to encourage them to experiment with new ways of creating value?

Loucks recognized that he did not have much time to change Baxter's culture. A wave of merger activity was sweeping across the industry as companies sought to protect their position. He de-

cided on a radical move. To change the managers' mind-set he would totally change the way they were rewarded. Instead of rewarding them based on the performance of their divisions, in the future they would be rewarded based on an increase in the stock price of the whole company. Moreover, top managers would be required to buy seven times their annual salary in company stock, and middle managers would also be rewarded with stock options linked to company performance.[66]

The change in the reward system precipitated a complete change in Baxter's managers' approach to decision making and learning. They began to experiment with new kinds of strategies and structures, and they started to take an organization-wide approach to decision making. At their regular meetings divisional heads started to challenge each others' decisions and the assumptions on which the decisions were made. They also began to realize that each of them possessed a stock of knowledge that could potentially be useful to the other divisions, and they now had the incentive (through the new reward system) to cooperate with other divisions to capitalize on that knowledge. Inside each division and between divisions, employees started to become involved in teams to discuss these new ideas and develop new interdivisional projects. As a result, when any manager now makes a proposal to invest resources for a specific project, managers at all levels engage in a spirited debate and subject it to rigorous evaluations, since they see that their own "money" is at stake.

Baxter's managers' new "systems viewpoint" and their mind-set, which allows them to see the company and not just their individual division, have resulted in enormous synergies being reaped at Baxter as the divisions learn to share their skills and resources. Cash flow and profits have increased fivefold, and the company's share price has doubled since 1990—rewarding managers for their new approach and reinforcing their desires to further promote and develop the new learning approach that has changed Baxter's culture.[67]

1. What problems was Baxter International experiencing?

2. How did the company try to solve these problems?

REFERENCES

1. H. A. Simon, *The New Science of Management Decision* (New York: Harper and Row, 1960), p. 206.
2. Ibid.
3. S. Keiser and L. Sproull, "Managerial Response to Changing Environments: Perspectives on Sensing from Social Cognition," *Administrative Science Quarterly*, 1982, vol. 27, pp. 548–570; G. T. Allison, *The Essence of Decision* (Boston: Little, Brown, 1971).
4. Simon, *The New Science of Management Decision.*
5. H. A. Simon, *Administrative Behavior* (New York: Macmillan, 1945).
6. Ibid.; J. G. March and H. A. Simon, *Organizations* (New York: Wiley, 1958).
7. J. G. March, "Bounded Rationality, Ambiguity, and the Engineering of Choice," *Bell Journal of Economics*, 1978, vol. 9, pp. 587–608.
8. J. G. March, "Decision Making Perspective," in A. Van De Ven and W. Joyce, eds., *Perspectives on Organizational Design and Behavior* (New York: Wiley, 1981), pp. 205–252.
9. Simon, *Administrative Behavior.*
10. R. M. Cyert and J. G. March, *A Behavioral Theory of the Firm* (Englewood Cliffs, NJ: Prentice Hall, 1963).
11. P. D. Larkey and L. S. Sproull, Advances in Information Processing in Organizations, vol. 1 (Greenwich, CT: JAI Press, 1984), pp. 1–8.
12. March and Simon, *Organizations.*
13. H. A. Simon, *Models of Man* (New York: Wiley, 1957); A. Grandori, "A Prescriptive Contingency View of Organizational Decision Making," *Administrative Science Quarterly*, 1984, vol. 29, pp. 192–209.
14. Simon, *The New Science of Management Decision.*
15. H. A. Simon, "Making Management Decisions: The Role of Intuition and Emotion," *Academy of Management Executives*, 1987, vol. 1, pp. 57–64.
16. Cyert and March, *A Behavioral Theory of the Firm.*
17. Ibid.
18. Z. Schiller, "GE's Appliance Park: Rewire, or Pull the Plug?" *Business Week*, 8 February 1993, p. 30.
19. J. Ward, "GE Center Makes Things Fail so It Can Make Them Better," *The Courier Journal*, 12 September 1999, p. 1.
20. C. E. Lindblom, "The Science of Muddling Through," *Public Administration Review*, 1959, vol. 19, pp. 79–88.
21. Ibid., p. 83.
22. H. Mintzberg, D. Raisinghani, and A. Theoret, "The Structure of Unstructured Decision Making," *Administrative Science Quarterly*, 1976, vol. 21, pp. 246–275.
23. Ibid., p. 257.
24. M. D. Cohen, J. G. March, and J. P. Olsen, "A Garbage Can Model of Organizational Choice," *Administrative Science Quarterly*, 1972, vol. 17, pp. 1–25.
25. Ibid.
26. G. P. Huber, "Organizational Learning: The Contributing Processes and the Literature," *Organizational Science*, 1991, vol. 2, pp. 88–115.
27. B. Hedberg, "How Organizations Learn and Unlearn," in W. H. Starbuck and P. C. Nystrom, eds., *Handbook of Organizational Design*, vol. 1 (New York: Oxford University Press, 1981), pp. 1–27.

28. P. M. Senge, *The Fifth Discipline: The Art and Practice of the Learning Organization* (New York: Doubleday, 1990).
29. J. G. March, "Exploration and Exploitation in Organizational Learning," *Organizational Science*, 1991, vol. 2, pp. 71–87.
30. T. K. Lant and S. J. Mezias, "An Organizational Learning Model of Convergence and Reorientation," *Organizational Science*, 1992, vol. 5, pp. 47–71.
31. M. Dodgson, "Organizational Learning: A Review of Some Literatures," *Organizational Studies*, 1993, vol. 14, pp. 375–394.
32. A. S. Miner and S. J. Mezias, "Ugly Duckling No More: Pasts and Futures of Organizational Learning Research," *Organizational Science*, 1990, vol. 7, pp. 88–99.
33. P. Senge, *The Fifth Discipline.*
34. P. Senge, "The Leader's New Work: Building Learning Organizations," *Sloan Management Review*, Fall 1990, pp. 7–23.
35. Miner and Mezias, "Ugly Ducking No More."
36. J. P. Kotter and J. L. Heskett, *Corporate Culture and Performance* (New York: The Free Press, 1992).
37. P. C. Nystrom and W. H. Starbuck, "To Avoid Organizational Crises, Unlearn," *Organizational Dynamics*, 1984, vol. 12, pp. 53–65.
38. Y. Dror, "Muddling Through—Science or Inertia?" *Public Administration Review*, 1964, vol. 24, pp. 103–117.
39. Nystrom and Starbuck, "To Avoid Organizational Crises, Unlearn."
40. S. T. Fiske and S. E. Taylor, *Social Cognition* (Reading, M: Addison-Wesley, 1984).
41. See G. R. Jones, R. Kosnik, and J. M. George, "Internalization and the Firm's Growth Path: On the Psychology of Organizational Contracting," in R. W. Woodman and W. A. Pasemore, eds., *Research in Organizational Change and Development*, vol. 7 (Greenwich, CT: JAI Press, 1993), pp. 105–135, for an account of the biases as they operate during organizational growth and decline.
42. L. Festinger, *A Theory of Cognitive Dissonance* (Stanford, CA: Stanford University Press, 1957); E. Aaronson, "The Theory of Cognitive Dissonance: A Current Perspective," in L. Berkowitz, ed., *Advances in Experimental Social Psychology*, 1969, vol. 4, pp. 1–34.
43. J. R. Averill, "Personal Control over Aversive Stimuli and Its Relationship to Stress," *Psychological Bulletin*, 1973, vol. 80, pp. 286–303.
44. E. J. Langer, "The Illusion of Control," *Journal of Personality and Social Psychology*, 1975, vol. 32, pp. 311–328.
45. K. L. Miller, L. Armstrong, and J. B. Treece, "Will Nissan Get It Right This Time?" *Business Week*, 20 April 1992, pp. 82–87.
46. A. Tversky and D. Kahneman, "Judgment Under Uncertainty: Heuristics and Biases," *Science*, 1974, vol. 185, pp. 1124–1131.
47. R. De Board, *The Psychoanalysis of Organizations* (London: Tavistock, 1978).
48. B. M. Staw, "The Escalation of Commitment to a Course of Action," *Academy of Management Review*, 1978, vol. 6, pp. 577–587; B. M. Staw and J. Ross, "Commitment to a Policy Decision: A Multi-Theoretical Perspective," *Administrative Science Quarterly*, 1978, vol. 23, pp. 40–64.
49. Nystrom and Starbuck, "To Avoid Organizational Crises, Unlearn."
50. Ibid.
51. L. Porter and K. Roberts, "Communication in Organizations," in M. Dunnette, ed., *Handbook of Industrial and Organizational Psychology* (Chicago: Rand McNally, 1976).

52. Nystrom and Starbuck, "To Avoid Organizational Crises, Unlearn."

53. A. D. Meyer, "Adapting to Environmental Jolts," *Administrative Science Quarterly*, 1982, vol. 27, pp. 515–537; A. D. Meyer, "How Ideologies Supplant Formal Structures and Shape Responses to Environments," *Journal of Management Studies*, 1982, vol. 7, pp. 31–53.

54. D. C. Hambrick, *The Executive Effect: Concepts and Methods for Studying Top Managers* (Greenwich, CT: JAI Press, 1988).

55. D. G. Ancona, "Top-Management Teams: Preparing for the Revolution," in J. S. Carroll, ed., *Applied Social Psychology and Organizational Settings* (Hillsdale, NJ: Lawrence Erlbaum Associates, 1990).

56. M. Shaw, "Communications Networks," in L. Berkowitz, ed., *Advances in Experimental Social Psychology*, vol. 1 (New York: Academic Press, 1964).

57. Ibid.

58. S. Finkelstein and D. C. Hambrick, "Top-Management Team Tenure and Organizational Outcomes: The Moderating Role of Managerial Discretion," *Administrative Science Quarterly*, 1990, vol. 35, pp. 484–503.

59. I. L. Janis, *Victims of Groupthink*, 2nd ed. (Boston: Houghton Mifflin, 1982).

60. K. M. Eisenhardt and C. B. Schoonhoven, "Organizational Growth: Linking Founding Team, Strategy, Environment, and Growth Among U.S. Semiconductor Ventures, 1978–1988," *Administrative Science Quarterly*, 1990, vol. 35, pp. 504–529; L. Keck and M. L. Tushman, "Environmental and Organizational Context and Executive Team Structure," *Academy of Management Journal*, 1993, vol. 36, pp. 1314–1344.

61. A. J. Lott and B. E. Lott, "Group Cohesiveness and Interpersonal Attraction: A Review of Relationships with Antecedent and Consequent Variables," *Psychological Bulletin*, 1965, vol. 14, pp. 259–309.

62. D. L. Helmich and W. B. Brown, "Successor Type and Organizational Change in the Corporate Enterprise," *Administrative Science Quarterly*, 1972, vol. 17, pp. 371–381; D. C. Hambrick and P. A. Mason, "Upper Echelons: The Organization as a Reflection of Its Top Managers," *Academy of Management Journal*, 1984, vol. 9, pp. 193–206.

63. R. F. Vancil, *Passing the Baton* (Boston: Harvard Business School Press, 1987).

64. C. Schwenk, "Cognitive Simplification Processes in Strategic Decision Making," *Strategic Management Journal*, 1984, vol. 5, pp. 111–128.

65. D. Rubenstein and R. W. Woodman, "Spiderman and the Burma Raiders: Collateral Organization Theory in Practice," *Journal of Applied Behavioral Science*, 1984, vol. 20, pp. 1–21; G. R. Bushe and A. B. Shani, *Parallel Learning Structures: Increasing Innovations in Bureaucracies* (Reading, MA: Addison-Wesley, 1991).

66. V. R. Loucks, Jr., "Business World: An Equity Cure For Managers," *Wall Street Journal*, 26 September 1995, p. 19.

67. "Baxter Receives the Grand Prix Quebecois de la Qualite," Canada Newswire, 30 September 1999, p. 1

Chapter 13

MANAGING INNOVATION
and CHANGE

Today, as never before, organizations are facing an environment that is changing rapidly, and the task facing managers is to help organizations respond and adjust to the changes taking place. This chapter discusses how organizations can manage the process of innovation and change to stay ahead in today's competitive environments. First, it examines the different types of change that organizations can pursue and the problems associated with overcoming obstacles to change that produce organizational inertia. The chapter then focuses on one important type of change, technological change, and examines how organizations can manage the innovation process to promote the development of new products.

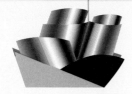

WHAT IS ORGANIZATIONAL CHANGE?

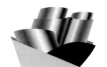

Organizational change
The process by which organizations move from their present state to some desired future state to increase their effectiveness.

Organizational change is the process by which organizations move from their present state to some desired future state to increase their effectiveness. The goal of planned organizational change is to find new or improved ways of using resources and capabilities in order to increase an organization's ability to create value and improve the returns to its stakeholders.[1] An organization in decline may need to restructure its resources to improve its fit with the environment. IBM and General Motors, for example, experienced falling demand for their products in the 1990s and have been searching for new ways to use their resources to improve their performance and attract customers back. On the other hand, even a thriving organization may need to change the way it uses its resources so that it can develop new products or find new markets for its existing products. Wal-Mart, Target, Blockbuster Video, and Toys "R" Us, for example, have been moving aggressively to expand their scale of operations and open new stores to take advantage of the popularity of their products. In the last decade, over half of all Fortune 500 companies have undergone major organizational changes to allow them to increase their ability to create value.

Targets of Change

Planned organizational change is normally targeted at improving performance at one or more of four different levels: human resources, functional resources, technological capabilities, and organizational abilities.

HUMAN RESOURCES.   Human resources are an organization's most important asset. Ultimately, an organization's distinctive competences lie in the skills and abilities of its employees. Because these skills and abilities give an organization a competitive advantage, organizations must continually monitor their structures to find the most effective way of motivating and organizing human resources to acquire and use their skills. Typical kinds of change efforts directed at human resources include (1) new investment in training and development activities so that employees acquire new skills and abilities; (2) socializing employees into the organizational culture so that they learn the new routines on which organizational performance depends; (3) changing organizational norms and values to motivate a multicultural and diverse workforce; (4) ongoing examination of the way in which promotion and reward systems operate in a diverse workforce; and (5) changing the composition of the top-management team to improve organizational learning and decision making.

FUNCTIONAL RESOURCES.   As discussed in previous chapters, each organizational function needs to develop procedures that allow it to manage the particular environment it faces. As the environment changes, organizations often transfer resources to the functions where the most value can be created. Crucial functions grow in importance, while those whose usefulness is declining shrink. An organization can improve the value that its functions create by changing its structure, culture, and technology. The change from a functional to a product team structure, for example, may speed the new-product development process. Alterations in functional structure can help provide a setting in which people are motivated to perform. The change from traditional mass production to a manufacturing operation based on self-managed work teams often allows companies to increase product quality and productivity if employees can share in the gains from the new work system.

TECHNOLOGICAL CAPABILITIES.   Technological capabilities give an organization an enormous capacity to change itself in order to exploit market opportunities. The ability to develop a constant stream of new products or to modify existing products so that they continue to attract customers is one of an organization's core competences. Similarly, the ability to improve the way goods and services are produced in order to increase their quality and reliability is a crucial organizational capability. At the organizational level, an organization has to provide the context that allows it to translate its technological competences into value for its stakeholders. This task often involves the restructuring of organizational activities. IBM, for example, has recently moved to change its organizational structure to better capitalize on its technological strengths. Previously, it had been unable to translate its technical capabilities into commercial opportunities because its structure did not provide divisions with the freedom to compete independently.

ORGANIZATIONAL CAPABILITIES.   Through the design of organizational structure and culture an organization can harness its human and functional resources to exploit technological opportunities. Organizational change often involves changing the relationships between people and functions in order to increase their ability to create value. Changes in structure and culture take place at all levels of the organization and include changing the routines an individual uses to greet customers, changing work group relationships, improving integration between divisions, and changing corporate culture by changing the top-management team.

Because these four levels at which change can take place are obviously interdependent, it is often impossible to change one without changing another. Suppose an organization invests resources and recruits a team of scientists who are experts in a new technology—for example, biotechnology. If successful, this human resource change will lead to the emergence of a new functional resource and a new technological capability. Top management will be forced to reevaluate its organizational structure and the way it integrates and coordinates its other functions to ensure that they support its new functional resources. Exploiting the new resources may require a move to a product team structure. It may even require downsizing and the elimination of functions that are no longer central to the organization's mission.

The incremental changes that an organization makes to its strategy and structure can add up over time to a major change in the nature of an organization. For example, Greyhound Corporation used profits from its bus operations to pursue a strategy of unrelated diversification. Over many years, it gradually acquired companies in many other businesses such as financial services and consumer product companies like Dial Corporation. Then, in 1987, after many years of poor operating results and a damaging nationwide strike, Greyhound decided to sell off its bus operations and focus on consumer products. Over time, the company completely transformed itself by a series of incremental changes.

Managing organizational change is one of management's most difficult and challenging tasks. There is little evidence that Greyhound's top managers had a vision of what they wanted the company to become: They had no plan to take a bus company and turn it into a consumer products company. They simply reacted to the company's declining situation and tried to manage problems as they arose. To understand the process of change it is useful to examine various types of change that organizations can pursue.

Types of Change

Evolutionary change
Change that is gradual, incremental, and specifically focused.

Revolutionary change
Change that is sudden, drastic, and organization-wide.

In general, change falls into two broad categories: **evolutionary change**, which is gradual, incremental, and specifically focused; and **revolutionary change**, which is sudden, drastic, and organization-wide.[2] As the name suggests, evolutionary change involves not a drastic or sudden change in the basic nature of an organization's strategy and structure but the constant attempt to incrementally improve, adapt, and adjust strategy and structure to better match the changes in the environment that are taking place.[3] Total quality management is a type of change process through which organizations attempt to manage incremental improvements in the way work gets done.

While evolutionary change involves the attempt to increase the effectiveness of the way an organization currently operates, revolutionary change involves the attempt to find new ways to be effective. Revolutionary change is more likely to result in a dramatic shift that involves a whole new way of doing things, new goals, and a new structure. An organization can employ one of several approaches to implementing revolutionary change to bring about quick results: reengineering, restructuring, or innovation.

REENGINEERING.   As discussed in Chapter 4, reengineering involves the rethinking and redesign of business processes to increase organizational effectiveness.[4] Instead of focusing on an organization's functions, the managers of a reengineered organization make business processes the focus of attention. Organizations that take up reengineering deliberately ignore the existing arrangement of tasks, roles, and work activities. They start the reengineering process with the customer (not the product or service) and ask the question, How can I reorganize the way we do our work, our business processes, to provide the best-quality, lowest-cost goods and services to the customer? Frequently, when companies ask this question, they realize that there are more effective ways to organize their activities. For example, after reengineering, a business process that once involved members of 10 different functions working sequentially to provide goods and services might be performed by one or a few people at a fraction of the cost.

Reengineering and TQM are highly interrelated and complementary. After revolutionary reengineering has taken place and the question, What is the best way to provide customers with the goods or services they require? has been answered, evolutionary TQM takes over with its focus on How can we now continue to improve and refine the new process and find better ways of managing task and role relationships? Successful organizations examine both questions simultaneously and continuously attempt to identify new and better processes for meeting the goals of increased efficiency, quality, and customer responsiveness. At the Eastman Chemical Company, for example, the TQM process began with a major reengineering that decentralized authority for business processes to teams of managers low in the organization and reduced the number of levels in the hierarchy to four. Change through reengineering requires managers to go back to the basics and pull apart each step in the work process to identify a better way to coordinate and integrate the activities necessary to provide customers with goods and services.

RESTRUCTURING.   Restructuring is a second form of revolutionary change that organizations often undergo because of rapidly deteriorating performance. As noted in Chapter 3, there are two basic steps to restructuring: (1) an organization reduces its level of differentiation and integration by eliminating divisions, departments, or levels in the hierarchy and (2) an organization *downsizes* by reducing the number of its employees to reduce operating costs. For example, when William F. Malec took over as head of the federally administered Tennessee Valley Authority, the TVA had over 14 levels in its hierarchy and 37,000 employees, and its customers had been experiencing an average increase in their utility rates of over 10 percent per year. Describing his organization as a top-heavy bureaucracy, Malec quickly moved to slash costs and restructure the company. Within three years, he had reduced the number of levels in the hierarchy to nine and the number of employees to 18,500.

Change in the relationships between divisions or functions is common in restructuring. For example, IBM, in an effort to cut development costs and speed cooperation among its engineers, created a new division to take control of the production of microprocessors and memory systems. This restructuring move took engineers from IBM's 13 divisions and grouped them together in a brand-new headquarters in Austin, Texas to increase their effectiveness.

There are many reasons why restructuring becomes necessary and why an organization may need to downsize its operations. Sometimes a change in the environment occurs that cannot be foreseen; for example, a shift in technology may make the company's products obsolete, or a worldwide recession may reduce the demand for its products. Sometimes an organization has excess capacity because customers no longer want the goods and services it provides because they are outdated or offer poor value for the money. Sometimes organizations downsize because over time they have grown too tall and bureaucratic and operating costs have become much too high. Sometimes organizations restructure even when they are in a strong position simply to stay on top.

All too often companies are forced to downsize and lay off employees because they have *not* continually monitored the way they operate (their basic business processes) and made the incremental changes to their strategies and structures that would allow them to contain costs and adjust to changing conditions. Paradoxically, because they have not paid attention to the need to reengineer themselves, they are forced into a position where restructuring becomes the only way they can survive and compete in an increasingly competitive environment.

Innovation *The process by which organizations use their skills and resources to develop new goods and services or to develop new production and operating systems so that they can better respond to the needs of their customers.*

INNOVATION.   **Innovation** is the process by which organizations use their skills and resources to develop new goods and services or to develop new production and operating systems so that they can better respond to the needs of their customers.[5] Innovation can result in spectacular success for an organization. Apple Computer changed the face of the computer industry when it introduced its personal computer; Honda changed the face of the small motor-bike market when it introduced small 50cc motorcycles; Mary Kay cosmetics changed the nature of the way cosmetics are sold when it introduced its at-home cosmetics parties and personalized style of selling; Toyota revolutionized the car production system to increase product quality; and Chrysler's adoption of a new operating system, the product team structure, was an innovation that many other car companies have copied.

Although innovation brings about change, it is also associated with a high level of risk because the outcomes of research and development activities are often uncertain.[6] It has been estimated that only 12 to 20 percent of R&D projects result in products that get to market.[7] Thus, although innovation can lead to change of the sort that organizations want—the introduction of profitable new technologies and products—it can also lead to the kind of change that they want to avoid—technologies that are inefficient and products that customers don't want. For example, Synergen, the biotechnology company, was riding high on the promise of its new drug Antril as an effective treatment for severe blood infections. Less than nine months later, tests of the drug had revealed that it had no promise and Synergen was forced to lay off 375 people or about 60 percent of its Boulder, Colorado workforce.[8]

Of all the kinds of revolutionary change, innovation has the best prospects for long-term success but also the greatest risks. The way in which organizations can manage the innovation process to increase the chance of successful learning taking place is discussed in detail later in the chapter.

FORCES FOR AND RESISTANCES TO ORGANIZATIONAL CHANGE

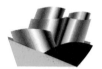

Why do organizations need to change the way they perform their activities? Because the forces in the environment in which they operate are constantly changing and they must adapt to these changes in order to survive.[9] At the same time, however, there are many sources of resistance to change in organizations that make it difficult to respond to these forces for change. The nature of these forces and resistances to change is discussed next.

Forces for Change

As discussed in previous chapters, there are many forces in the environment that impact on an organization, and recognizing the nature of these forces is one of a manager's most important tasks.[10] If managers are slow to respond to these forces, the organization will lag behind its competitors and its effectiveness will be lower (Figure 13.1).

COMPETITIVE FORCES.   Organizations constantly strive to obtain a competitive advantage over other organizations.[11] Competition is a force for change because organizations must attempt to match or exceed their competitors on at least one of the dimensions of competitive advantage: efficiency, quality, innovation, or customer responsiveness.[12] To lead on the dimension of efficiency, for example, an organization must constantly adopt the latest forms of technology, such as computerized manufacturing, as they become available.

FIGURE 13.1

Forces for and Resistances to Change

Forces for Change	Resistances to Change
Competitive Forces	Organizational Level • Structure • Culture • Strategy
Economic Forces	
Politcal Forces	Functional Level • Differences in Subunit Orientation • Power and Conflict
Global Forces Demographic Forces	
Social Forces	Group Level • Norms • Cohesiveness • Groupthink
Ethical Forces	
	Individual Level • Cognitive Biases • Uncertainty and Insecurity • Selective Perception and Retention • Habit

Adopting new technology normally involves an organization changing task relationships also, as workers have to learn new skills or techniques to operate new technologies. To lead on the dimension of innovation and obtain a technological edge over competitors, a company must possess skills in managing the process of innovation, a type of change discussed later. The ability to manage organizational change is central to the ability to obtain *and* sustain a competitive advantage in an environment in which different organizations compete for the most important resource of all: customers.

ECONOMIC, POLITICAL, AND GLOBAL FORCES.   Economic, political, and global forces continually affect organizations and force them to change how and where they produce goods and services. Economic and political unions between countries are becoming an increasingly important force for change.[13] In North America, the North American Free Trade Agreement (NAFTA) has paved the way for cooperation between Canada, the United States, and Mexico. Many organizations in these countries have taken advantage of NAFTA to find new markets for their products and new sources of inexpensive labor and inputs to assemble their products.

The European Union, an alliance of European countries formed after the end of World War II to reduce conflict and destructive competition between Germany, France, and Britain, has grown to include over 20 countries, as organizations seek to exploit the advantages of large, protected markets for their products. Japan and other fast-growing Asian countries such as Malaysia, Thailand, and China, recognizing how these economic unions protect their members and create barriers against foreign competitors, have moved to increase their presence in foreign countries. For example, many Japanese companies have opened new manufacturing plants within the United States and Mexico, and in European countries such as Spain and the United Kingdom, so that they can share the advantages of economic and political union. Toyota, Honda, and Nissan, for example, have all opened large car plants in England to supply cars to the rest of the countries in the European Union. These firms have taken advantage of low labor costs in England (compared to France, Germany, or Japan), and their products are no longer subject to foreign tariffs because they are produced *inside* the union and not exported from Japan. Similarly, the countries of the Pacific Rim such as Japan, Thailand, Taiwan, Malaysia, and Singapore all face the problem of how to develop an economic union of their own as the world divides into three distinct economic spheres—North America, Europe, and Asia. In the near future trade among countries inside these three spheres is expected to be many times as great as trade between spheres.

The rise of low-cost foreign competitors, the development of new technology that can erode a company's competitive advantage, and the failure to exploit low-cost sources of inputs abroad can all doom an organization that does not change and adapt to the realities of the global marketplace.[14] Other global challenges facing organizations include the need to change an organization's structure to allow expansion into foreign markets, and the need to adapt to the nature of different national cultures.[15]

DEMOGRAPHIC AND SOCIAL FORCES.   Changes in the composition of the workforce and the increasing diversity of employees have presented organizations with many challenges and opportunities.[16] Increasingly, changes in demographic characteristics of the workforce have led managers to change their styles of managing employees and to learn how to effectively understand, supervise, and motivate minority and female organizational members.[17] Managers have had to abandon the stereotypes they may have unwittingly used in making promotion decisions; to accept the importance of equity in the recruitment and promotion of new hires; and to appreciate the needs of "baby busters," who often desire a lifestyle that better balances work and leisure. As more and more women enter the workforce, companies have to accommodate the needs of dual-career and single-parent families, to provide child care, and to allow their members to adopt work schedules that allow them to manage work-life linkages.[18]

ETHICAL FORCES.   Just as it is important for an organization to take steps to change in response to changing demographic and social forces, it is also important for an organization to take steps to promote ethical behavior in the face of increasing governmental, political, and social demands for more responsible and honest corporate behavior.[19] Many companies, for example, have created the role of ethics officer, a person to whom employees can turn to report ethical lapses by an organization's managers or workers and for advice on difficult ethical questions and dilemmas. Similarly, organizations are trying to promote ethical behavior by giving employees more direct access to important decision makers and by protecting whistle-blowers who turn the organization in when they perceive ethical problems with managers' behavior. Many organizations need to make changes to allow managers and workers at all levels to report unethical behavior so that an organization can move quickly to eliminate such behavior and protect the general interests of its members and customers.[20] Similarly, if organizations operate in countries that pay little attention to human rights or to the well-being of organizational members, they have to learn how to change these standards and to protect their foreign employees.

The forces of change bombard organizations from all sides. The number and variety of forces for change suggest that effective organizations must be agile enough to adjust to these forces. However, several forces internal to an organization make it resistant to change and, thus, threaten its very survival.

In the 1990s many of America's best known (and formerly strongest and most successful) companies, such as DEC, GM, IBM, Ford, Chrysler, Kodak, TWA, Macy's, Texas Instruments, and Westinghouse, have seen their fortunes decline. Some companies, such as Macy's and TWA, have gone bankrupt; some, such as Westinghouse and DEC, are still in deep trouble; and some, such as GM and IBM, seem to have reversed their decline and started a recovery. How did such former powerhouses become so ineffective? The main explanation for such decline is almost always an organization's inability to change in response to changes in its environment such as increased competition. Research suggests that one of the main reasons for some organizations' inability to change is organizational inertia, a condition in which organizations are resistant to change (see Chapter 11). This resistance, in turn, lowers an organization's effectiveness and chances of survival.[21] Resistances to change that cause inertia are found at the organization, subunit, group, and individual levels[22] (Figure 13.1).

Organization-Level Resistances to Change

Many forces inside an organization make it difficult for an organization to change in response to changing conditions in its environment.[23]

ORGANIZATIONAL STRUCTURE.   An organization's structure can be an obstacle to change. When an organization creates an organizational structure, it creates a stable pattern of task relationships that affects the way people behave. Over time, an organizational structure becomes self-maintaining—that is, people come and go, but the task relationships go on forever. Thus, organizational structure becomes resistant to change. Changing organizational structure is not easy to do. Change disrupts taken-for-granted expectations, and people often react negatively to it. This is one reason why some researchers prefer a revolutionary approach to change.

Recall that mechanistic structures are characterized by tall hierarchies, centralized decision making, and the standardization of behavior through rules and procedures. In contrast, organic structures are flat, decentralized, and rely on mutual adjustment between people to get the job done.[24] Which type of structure is likely to be the most resistant to change? Mechanistic structures are, because people are programmed to act in certain ways and have not developed the capacity to adjust their behavior to changing conditions. In an organic structure, the extensive use of mutual adjustment and decentralized authority allows workers to develop skills that enable them to be creative and responsive and to find solutions for new problems. Because mechanistic structures typically develop as an organization becomes larger, the failure to maintain the ability to act in an organic way is a principle source of inertia, especially in large organizations.

ORGANIZATIONAL CULTURE. The values and norms in an organization's culture are another source of resistance to change. Just as role relationships result in a series of stable expectations between people, so values and norms cause people to behave in predictable ways. If organizational change disrupts taken-for-granted values and norms and forces people to change what they do and how they do it, an organization's culture will cause resistance to change. For example, many organizations develop conservative values that support the status quo and make managers reluctant to search for new ways to compete. As a result, if the environment changes and a company's products become obsolete, the company has nothing to fall back on and failure is likely.[25] Also, if property rights become too strong, both managers and employees may work to prevent any change that might threaten their position inside the organization. Once established, norms and values tend to persist despite attempts to modify or uproot them, and again sometimes only revolutionary change is strong enough to modify an organization's culture.

ORGANIZATIONAL STRATEGY. An organization's strategy can be an obstacle to change. As noted earlier, the escalation of commitment bias may cause managers to stick with a course of action even if it is not working. One researcher, Danny Miller, has noted the tendency for organizations to continue to pursue a strategy that brought success in the past long after the strategy has ceased to create value. He calls this tendency of successful companies to bring about their own downfall the Icarus paradox. Recall the story of Icarus, whose father made him a pair of feathered wings held together by wax. Able to fly like a bird, Icarus soared toward the sun. The heat of the sun softened the wax that held the feathers together, the wings fell apart, and Icarus fell to his doom.[26] The moral for organizations is that they have to pay attention to their environment and not make avoidable mistakes that have dire consequences. Digital Equipment, General Motors, and IBM are three organizations that to varying degrees have fallen victim to the Icarus paradox. Each one failed to recognize changes in its competitive environment and suffered a rude awakening.

Subunit-Level Obstacles to Change

As at the organization level, important obstacles to change exist at the subunit level.

DIFFERENCES IN SUBUNIT ORIENTATION. Differences in subunit orientation are another major resistance to change and source of organizational inertia. Recall that different functions and divisions of an organization often see the source of a problem differently because they see an issue or problem primarily from their own viewpoint. Like top managers or divisional managers, functional managers may lobby for their own interests and try to influence the change process so that change benefits them. If declining sales is the problem that must be solved, what changes should the organization make? The sales function may lobby for an increase in the size of the sales budget and the hiring of more salespeople. R&D might lobby for more money for new-product development. Manufacturing might lobby for new low-cost machinery so that the organization can obtain a low-cost advantage. It is easy to see how different viewpoints can be an obstacle to change.

A high level of task interdependence among functions also makes change difficult to achieve because a change in one function can affect all the other functions. The more interdependent functions are, the more complicated the change process. Moreover, the higher the organizational level at which the change is made, the more likely is the change to have repercussions throughout the organization.

POWER AND CONFLICT.   As will be discussed in detail in Chapter 14, change usually benefits some people, functions, or divisions at the expense of others. When change causes power struggles and organizational conflict, an organization is likely to resist it.[27] Suppose, for example, that a change in purchasing practices will help materials management achieve its goal of reducing input costs but will harm manufacturing's ability to reduce manufacturing costs. While materials management will push for the change, manufacturing will resist it. The conflict between the two functions will slow down the process of change and perhaps prevent it from occurring.

If powerful functions can prevent change from occurring, an organization will not change. It is this kind of resistance that many large companies have experienced. At IBM, for example, managers in the mainframe computer division were the most powerful in the corporation. To preserve their established prestige and power in the organization, mainframe managers fought off attempts to redirect IBM's resources to produce the personal computers or minicomputers that customers wanted. This failure to change in response to customer demands severely reduced IBM's speed of response to its competitors with the result that IBM lost billions of dollars in the 1990s. Only in the late 1990s did IBM learn to manage the new competitive environment.

Group-Level Resistances to Change

Much of an organization's work is performed by groups, and several group characteristics can produce resistance to change.

GROUP NORMS.   Many groups develop strong informal norms that specify appropriate and inappropriate behaviors and govern the interactions among group members. Often change alters task and role relationships in a group, and when it does it will disrupt group norms and the informal expectations that group members have of one another. As a result, members of a group may resist change because a whole new set of norms may have to be developed or adapted to meet the needs of the new situation.

GROUP COHESIVENESS.   The level of group cohesiveness, that is, the attractiveness of a group to its members, affects group performance. Although some level of cohesiveness promotes cooperation and group performance, too much cohesiveness may reduce performance because it stifles opportunities for the group to change and adapt. A highly cohesive group may resist attempts by management to change what it does or even who is a member of the group. Group members may also unite to preserve the status quo and to protect their interests at the expense of other groups.

GROUPTHINK AND ESCALATION OF COMMITMENT.   As discussed in Chapter 12, groupthink is a pattern of faulty decision making that occurs in cohesive groups when members discount negative information in order to arrive at a unanimous agreement. The escalation of commitment bias (also covered in Chapter 12) worsens this situation because even when group members realize that the decision they made is wrong they still pursue it because they are now committed to it. If these group processes are operating, it will make it very difficult to change a group's behavior. Also, the more important the group's activities are to the organization (the top-management team's activities are *very* important, for example) the more impact these processes will have on organizational performance.

Individual-Level Resistances to Change

The final source of resistance to change occurs at the level of individual organizational members.[28]

COGNITIVE BIASES.   The cognitive biases discussed in Chapter 12 can influence individual managers' perception of a situation and cause them to interpret the situation in ways that benefit themselves. Cognitive biases distort managers' perception of why change is necessary and what should be done. They also strengthen the organizational and functional obstacles discussed previously.

UNCERTAINTY AND INSECURITY.   People tend to resist change because of the uncertainty, insecurity, and stress it may bring.[29] Change brings with it uncertainty because, for example, workers might be given new tasks, role relationships may be reorganized, some workers might lose their jobs, and some people might benefit at the expense of others. Researchers have found that workers' resistance to the uncertainty and insecurity surrounding change can cause organizational inertia. Absenteeism and turnover can increase as change takes place, for example, and workers may become uncooperative, attempt to delay or slow down the change process, and otherwise passively resist the change in an attempt to "squash" it.

SELECTIVE PERCEPTION AND RETENTION.   People's perceptions play a major role in determining work attitudes and behaviors. There is a general tendency for people to selectively perceive information that is consistent with their existing views of their organizations. Thus, when change takes place in organizations, workers tend to focus only on how it will personally affect them or their function or division; if they perceive few benefits they may reject the purpose behind the change. As a result, it can be difficult for an organization to develop a common platform to promote change across an organization and to get people to see the need for change in the same way.

HABIT.   Habits, people's preferences for familiar actions and events, are also an important source of resistance to change. Some researchers have suggested that habits are hard to break because people have a built-in tendency to return to their original behaviors, which is a tendency that prevents change. Suppose a supervisor tries to reintroduce a rule that has been allowed to lapse, such as the rule that employees must arrive at work on time. For a while, people arrive promptly at the designated hour, but gradually, in the absence of any reminders by the supervisor, they relax and no longer worry if they are late. We all know how difficult it is to break personal habits. It is also difficult to break organizational

FIGURE 13.2

Lewin's Force Field The-
ory of Change

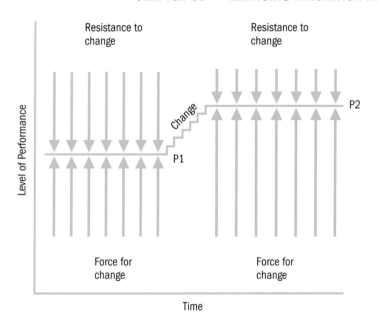

habits and follow new routines. Individuals' resistance to change is another source of organizational inertia and a major obstacle to organizational change.

Lewin's Force Field Theory of Change

There is a wide variety of forces that make an organization resistant to change just as there
is a wide variety of forces that push organizations to change. One researcher, Kurt Lewin,
developed the *force field theory,* which demonstrates how these two forces always oppose
each other and how an organization is *balanced* at any time between these two opposing
forces.[30] When these forces are in balance, the organization is in a state of inertia and does
not change. To get an organization to change, managers must adopt a change strategy to
increase the forces for change, *reduce* the resistances to change, or do both simultaneously.

Lewin's theory is demonstrated in Figure 13.2. An organization at level P1 is in balance because the forces to change just equal the resistances to change. However, managers
have determined that the organization should strive to achieve a future performance level
of P2. To get to P2, managers must *increase* the pressures for change (represented by the
longer up arrows), *reduce* resistances to change (represented by the shorter down arrows),
or both. If they succeed in pursuing any of the three strategies, the organization will change
and move to point P2, and the organization will reach the desired performance level.

A MODEL OF ORGANIZATIONAL CHANGE

A model of the change process that helps managers plan their change efforts is discussed
next. In the model, managers first evaluate the organization's current situation and decide
where they would like the organization to be in the future (its desired performance level).
They then manage the change process to overcome obstacles to change to reach the desired future situation (see Figure 13.3). These steps are discussed next.[31]

FIGURE 13.3

A Model of Organizational Change

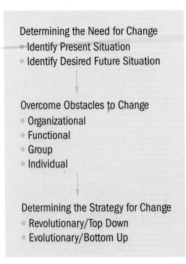

FIGURE 13.3

A Model of Organizational Change

Determining the Need for Change
- Identify Present Situation
- Identify Desired Future Situation

Overcome Obstacles to Change
- Organizational
- Functional
- Group
- Individual

Determining the Strategy for Change
- Revolutionary/Top Down
- Evolutionary/Bottom Up

Determining the Need for Change

To determine the need for change, managers must identify problems that need to be solved (stage 1 of the rational approach to decision making). Frequently, the need for change is recognized because somebody in the organization perceives a gap between desired performance and actual performance. Many pressures cause organizations to reevaluate their current situation. Changes in competitive conditions, such as the emergence of global competitors, can cause an organization to reevaluate its use of resources. The introduction of superior products and technologies by competitors is a clear indication that an organization needs to restructure its resources. In Chapter 11, we explored the crises that organizations encounter as they grow and decline; these crises, too, are pressures for change.

One indication of the need for change is a decline in organizational performance as measured by factors such as sales revenues or profitability. Most organizations compare their performance to the performance of their competitors. Even when performance is lagging, however, it is likely to be difficult for managers to make an accurate assessment of their real situations. One reason for this difficulty is the effect of cognitive biases, which may cause managers to paint a rosy picture of organizational performance or to blame the environment for poor performance. Another reason is that organizational performance does not necessarily follow the path of the solid line in Figure 13.4, declining steadily over time. Deteriorating performance is not always obvious.

Frequently, performance varies up and down as managers work to correct a situation but then declines suddenly, propelling the organization into a crisis. The dashed line in Figure 13.4 portrays that type of performance. Managers, for example, may restrict investment in research and development or in marketing to boost short-term returns, but eventually the long-term implication of their actions becomes obvious to customers and shareholders. By the time the organization realizes that it is lagging behind its competitors, it is in a very inferior position and has to move quickly to change the way it uses its resources to initiate a turnaround.

To diagnose an organization's current situation, researchers have proposed that top managers establish programs for periodically reviewing their organization and its environment.[32] In this way they can forecast the future and decide on their future ideal situation. However, as discussed in the last chapter, an organization's past influences its future. To allow for new learning, organizations need to institutionalize dissent and provide a framework in which managers can unlearn past behaviors so that they can experiment with new approaches. Thus, making decisions about the ideal future state is also an ongoing process: The future is created by the flow of decision making, that stems from organizational learning.

FIGURE 13.4

How Organizational Per-
formance Way Vary over
Time

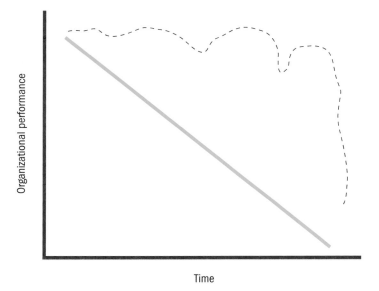

Time

Clearly, determining the need for change and managing change are complex decision-making processes. Managers generate a number of alternative scenarios that they
think will allow them to reach their desired future state. They then focus on the alternative that seems to offer the best or most satisfactory chance of success. At this point managers have a choice about how to proceed. They can adopt either an evolutionary or a
revolutionary approach to managing change.[33]

Managers who choose an evolutionary approach make incremental changes to organizational strategy and structure. Managers who choose a revolutionary approach make
drastic changes to organizational strategy and structure, as noted earlier. Instead of making changes one by one, they wait until change is really necessary and then make all the
changes simultaneously. Some researchers claim that because the effects of changing strategy and structure are always very uncertain, it might always be best or least risky to wait
until change is really needed and then use a revolutionary approach and totally sweep
away prior learning to ease the process of unlearning.[34] One reason why researchers advocate a revolutionary approach to change is the importance of overcoming the organizational inertia produced by the various obstacles to change discussed earlier.

Determining the Strategy for Change

Together, people's tendency to follow routines unthinkingly and the tendency of an organization's structure and culture to perpetuate the use of existing routines constitute
formidable obstacles to change. Given these obstacles, organizations must choose between
evolutionary and revolutionary change. An organization that pursues revolutionary change
adopts a *top-down change strategy*. The organization waits until it believes that the costs of not
changing exceed the costs of overcoming organizational inertia and then introduces its
master plan for change. Generally, a top-down strategy calls for intervention at a high
level of the organization. Suppose an organization decides to reduce the number of its operating divisions and downsize its corporate staff. Top management instructs the divisions
to restructure their resources and abilities and reexamine the way they operate in order
to improve effectiveness. The plan for change then continues down the organization, as
each level moves to change its structures to suit the new realities and top managers provide functional managers with new goals and priorities.

Top-down change often involves a massive dislocation of organizational task and reporting relationships. It emphasizes finding solutions for problems as they arise and adopting

an unstructured approach to decision making to allow managers to experiment and find new ways to organize. Very often, as in the company with the "Vice President for Revolutions" discussed in Chapter 12, top managers may know the ultimate goal that they want to achieve—for example, raising the rate of product development or reducing costs—but they leave the specific steps necessary to achieve these goals to be worked out as the change process unfolds. The uncertainty surrounding revolutionary change is very great. However, according to Jack Welch, CEO of General Electric, it is often the only way in which an organization can overcome the inertia that threatens efforts to restructure a company.

ORGANIZATIONAL INSIGHT

13.1 JACK WELCH'S APPROACH TO CHANGE

Jack Welch has been making drastic changes to General Electric's structure and strategy since he took over as CEO in 1981. Concerned about the ponderous way in which GE made decisions and the huge bureaucracy that permeated all aspects of its operations, Welch has been constantly trying to shake up his company and put the responsibility for decision making as far down in the organization as he can. Among other changes, he has eliminated GE's strategic business unit (SBU) structure, in which a team of SBU executives took responsibility for making decisions for the divisions inside their SBU. Now the heads of divisions make operational decisions and report directly to Welch, who uses a very simple yardstick to evaluate divisional performance: Is the division either first or second in terms of market share in its industry? If it is not, then Welch's policy is to divest the division and allow the top-management team of some other company to restructure its resources.

In discussing his model of change, Welch has said that he is firmly convinced that incremental change does not work for the kinds of large-scale restructuring efforts that GE has gone through. He has found that if change is not "revolutionary enough then the bureaucracy can beat you."[35] His philosophy is that the expectations and habits that people have developed as a result of their positions in an organization can derail any attempts as a "soft change approach." People like the status quo, and the stress of change causes them to react negatively to any change in their routines. Welch believes that the changing of organizational structure, which forces a change in task relationships, must precede any appeal to people to change the way they behave and learn new behaviors, because otherwise they will lapse back into the old ways. Thus, his approach at GE has been to change structure first. The structural change produces a cultural change, which in turn changes norms, values, and people's orientation toward the organization.

One program that Welch pushes whenever he makes a change is called "Work-Out." After a change has taken place, GE employees from all levels in the organization act together to find new and better ways of working. The program reinforces the idea that once change has taken place, people must change. As Welch puts it, "Take out the layers. Pull up the weeds. Scrape off the rust."[36] His goal is for GE to run as a learning machine in which boundaries between jobs, between positions in the hierarchy, and between divisions are eliminated so that the best work practices can be shared throughout the organization and new ideas can be translated quickly into practice.

Welch believes that despite GE's enormous size, his revolutionary approach to breaking down barriers and simplifying organizational structure has had a significant effect on his company. Analysts agree. They have watched GE's transformation from the bureaucratic monolith it was in 1980 to the collection of competitive businesses it is today.

In contrast to revolutionary change, evolutionary change depends on a *bottom-up change strategy*. Managers perceive that the uncertainty associated with organizational change is best managed through an incremental process in which managers continually make adjustments to their strategy and structure. Managers using a bottom-up strategy prepare the organization for change by involving managers and employees at all levels in discussions about the need for change and the need to identify the problems facing the organization. Top management guides these change efforts and ties them in with overall corporate objectives. Total quality management, for example, is used to bring about evolutionary change.

Managers at each level in the organization acknowledge the problems they are experiencing, recommend ways to solve them, and proceed to implement their solutions. Because bottom-up change takes place over a longer period than top-down change, many potential problems or dislocations associated with the change effort can be anticipated. Moreover, the involvement of both managers and employees often breaks down people's resistance to change and makes everyone more amenable to searching for new solutions. The bottom-up strategy facilitates unstructured decision making.

The continuous and gradual nature of evolutionary change appears to give it an advantage over the revolutionary approach. Evolutionary change facilitates organizational learning and allows the organization to respond to a changing environment. The principal argument against a bottom-up approach is that it may fail to overcome organizational inertia and, thus, fail to bring about change. In practice, however, it appears that organizations that are accustomed to change and that have institutionalized mechanisms for promoting organizational learning can overcome organizational inertia. Paradoxically, the organizations that are easiest to change are those that are most used to change because change is a basic element of their organizational learning process. Organizations that experience the greatest difficulty and greatest costs of changing are those that rarely restructure themselves. When these organizations decide to change, they have to adopt a revolutionary approach in order to overcome inertia and unlearn previous behaviors.

Managerial Implications: Organizational Change

1. Develop a set of criteria that can be used to evaluate whether change is necessary. Continually evaluate organizational performance against these criteria, and update these criteria as organizational performance improves.
2. Carefully evaluate the obstacles to change that will arise as you change organizational policies and procedures. Work out strategies for dealing with these obstacles, and incorporate those strategies into your plan for change.
3. Whenever possible, use a bottom-up change strategy. Involve people at all levels in the change process, and keep them informed about how the change will affect them.
4. Recognize that change is easiest to manage when the organization and its members are used to change. Consider using a total quality management program as a way of keeping the organization attuned to the need for change.
5. Always use the criteria that you defined at the beginning of the change process to evaluate the effects of your change efforts.

INNOVATION AND TECHNOLOGICAL CHANGE

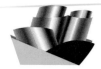

As noted earlier, *innovation* is the development of *new* products (goods and services) or the development of *new* production and operating systems (including new forms of organizational structure.) In this section, the relationship between innovation and technological change is examined. The next section then discusses how to create an organizational setting that fosters innovation and entrepreneurship.

As discussed in Chapter 9, *technology* refers to the skills, knowledge, experience, body of scientific knowledge, tools, machines, and equipment that are used in the design, production, and distribution of goods and services. Technology is central to the operations and products of most organizations. Consequently, technological change can have major implications for managers and their organizations—and at present the world is characterized by a rapid rate of technological change.[37]

Quantum technological change *A fundamental shift in technology that revolutionizes products or the way they are produced.*

Generally speaking, there are two types of technological change: quantum change and incremental change. **Quantum technological change** refers to a fundamental shift in technology that revolutionizes products or the way in which they are produced. Recent examples of quantum changes in technology include the development of the first personal computers, which revolutionized the computer industry, and the development of genetic engineering techniques (biotechnology), which are promising to revolutionize the treatment of illness by replacing conventional pharmaceutical compounds with genetically engineered medicines. New products or operating systems that incorporate a quantum technological improvement are referred to as **quantum innovations**. The introduction in 1971 of Intel's 4004 microprocessor, the first "computer on a chip" ever produced, is an example of a quantum product innovation. Quantum innovations are likely to cause major changes in an environment and to increase uncertainty because it forces organizations to change the way they operate.

Quantum innovations *New products or operating systems that incorporate quantum technological improvements.*

Incremental technological change *Technological change that represents a refinement of some base technology.*

Incremental technological change refers to technological change that represents a refinement of some base technology, and **incremental innovations** refer to products or operating systems that incorporate those refinements. For example, since 1971, Intel has produced a series of improvements of its original 4004 microprocessor. These subsequent improvements include the 8088, 8086, 286, 386, 486, and Pentium chips. Similarly, flexible manufacturing, robots, and TQM are examples of incremental innovations. They improved the quality of cars and forced U.S. carmakers to make major organizational changes in response to conditions in the new competitive environment.[38]

Incremental innovations *Products or operating systems that incorporate refinements of some base technology.*

As one might expect, quantum innovations are relatively uncommon. As Philip Anderson and Michael Tushman note, "At rare and irregular intervals in every industry, innovations appear that command a decisive cost or quality advantage and that strike not at the margins of the profits and the outputs of existing firms, but at their foundations and their very lives."[39] Anderson and Tushman call these kinds of quantum innovations "technological discontinuities," and in their model of innovation, a technological discontinuity sets off an era of ferment (see Figure 13.5) in which there is intense competition among companies in an industry to develop the design that will become the dominant model for others to copy—just as Intel's chips are the dominant design in the microprocessor industry.

After the dominant design emerges, the next period of the technology cycle involves an era of incremental change and innovation in which companies compete to elaborate on the base technology. Most companies spend most of their time engaged in incremental product innovation. For example, every time a car company redesigns a basic model, it is engaged in incremental product innovation, but this is nevertheless a very competitive

FIGURE 13.5

The Technology Cycle.
Source: "Technological Discontinuities and Dominant Designs: A Cyclical Model of Technological Change," by P. Anderson and M. L. Tushman, published in *Administrative Science Quarterly*, 1990, 35. Reprinted by permission of *Administrative Science Quarterly* (c) 1990 Cornell University.

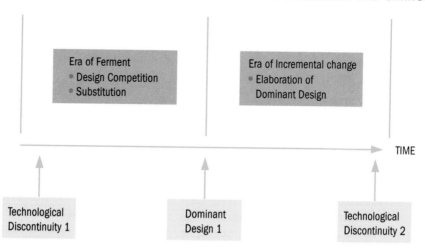

process. At some point, however, a second technological discontinuity may occur, which starts the whole process again.

The innovations that result from quantum and incremental technological change are all around us. Microprocessors, personal computers, cellular phones, pagers, personal digital assistants, word processing software, on-line information services, computer networks, camcorders, compact disc players, videocassette players, and the genetically engineered medicines produced by biotechnology either did not exist a generation ago or were considered to be exotic and expensive products. Now these products are commonplace, and they are being continually improved all the time. Organizations whose managers helped develop and exploit these new technologies have often reaped enormous gains. They include many of the most successful and rapidly growing organizations today: Compaq Computer (personal computers), Microsoft (computer software), Intel (microprocessors), America Online (on-line information services), Cisco Systems (computer networking equipment), Motorola (microprocessors, cellular phones, and pagers), Sony (camcorders and compact discs), Matsushita (videocassette recorders), and Amgen (biotechnology).

However, although some organizations have benefited from technological change, other have seen their markets threatened. The competitive decline of mainframe and midrange computer companies, such as IBM and Digital Equipment Corporation, is a direct reflection of the rise of the personal computer. Traditional telephone companies the world over have seen their market dominance threatened by new companies offering cellular telephone service. And the decline of once-dominant consumer electronics companies such as RCA can be directly linked to their failure to develop new products such as videocassette recorders and compact disc players.

Technological change is, thus, both an opportunity and a threat—it is both *creative and destructive.*[40] It helps create new product innovations that managers and their organizations can exploit, but at the same time these new innovations can harm or even destroy demand for older, established products. Thus, for example, the development of the microprocessor by Intel has helped create a host of new-product opportunities, including personal computers, but at the same time it has destroyed demand for older products. Conventional typewriters, for instance, have been largely replaced by the combination of personal computers and word processing software—putting typewriter companies out of business in the process. Similarly, Amazon.com has changed the nature of industry competition through its technological innovations.

Focus on New Information Technology:
Amazon.com, Part 9

Jeff Bezos's use of the Internet to sell books can probably be regarded as a quantum innovation in this industry. However, innovation at Amazon.com has not stopped here, and Bezos and his top-management team have engaged in a series of incremental innovations to grow and expand Amazon.com's core competences as an on-line retailer.

Although Bezos initially chose to focus on selling books, he soon realized that Amazon.com's information technology could be used to sell other kinds of products, so he began to search for products that could be sold profitably over the Internet. First, he realized CDs were a natural product extension to offer customers, and Amazon.com announced its intention of becoming the "earth's biggest book *and* music store." Then Amazon.com opened a hol-iday gift store to entice customers to send books and CDs as presents and began to offer a gift-wrapping service as well as launching a free electronic greeting card service to announce the arrival of the Amazon.com gift. Finally, realizing the popularity of on-line auctions, Bezos moved to enter this market by purchasing Live-bid.com, the Internet's only provider of live on-line auctions. Then in 1999 Bezos entered into an agreement with Sotheby's, the famous auction house.

As a result of these incremental innovations to Amazon.com's business, Bezos has transformed his company from "on-line book seller" to "leading Internet product provider." The company's share price boomed as investors realized that Amazon.com was poised to become the leading on-line retailer—the Sears of the Internet.

MANAGING THE INNOVATION PROCESS

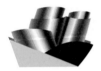

How should managers control the innovation process in organizations such as pharmaceutical and high-tech companies like Amazon.com in order to raise the level of both quantum and incremental innovation? There are several related methods and techniques that managers can use to promote innovation. These methods are often necessary because the resistances to change discussed earlier also affect the process of innovation. For example, different functions may be differently affected by the kinds of technological changes taking place, and managers may even fail to recognize new opportunities because of the existence of cognitive biases.

Stage-Gate Development Funnel

One of the common mistakes that managers often make in managing the innovation process is trying to fund too many development projects at any one point in time. The result is to spread limited financial, functional, and human resources too thinly over too many different projects. As a consequence, no single project is given the resources that are required to make it succeed and the level of successful innovation falls.

Given the nature of this problem, it is necessary for managers to develop a structured process for evaluating different new-product development proposals and deciding which to support and which to reject. A common solution to this problem is to implement a stage-gate development funnel[41] (Figure 13.6). The purpose of a **stage-gate funnel** is to establish a structured and coherent innovation process that both improves control over the product development effort and forces managers to make choices among competing new-product development projects so that resources are not spread too thinly over too many projects.

The funnel has a wide mouth (stage 1) in order to initially promote innovation by encouraging as many new-product ideas as possible. Companies establish a wide mouth by creating incentives for employees to come up with new-product ideas. Some organizations

Stage-gate funnel A technique used to improve control over innovation and new-product development.

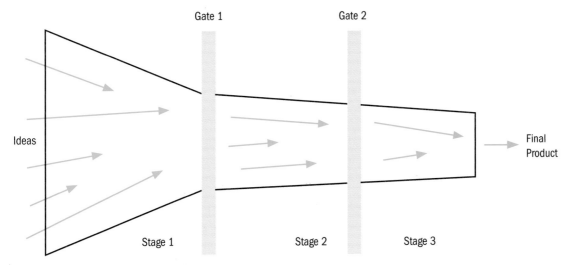

FIGURE 13.6   **A Stage-Gate Development Funnel**

run "bright ideas" programs, which reward employees for submitting new-product ideas that eventually make it through the development process. Others allow research scientists to devote a certain amount of work time to their own projects. For example, Hewlett-Packard and 3M have a 15 percent rule: 15 percent of a research scientist's workweek can be devoted to working on a project of his or her own choosing. Ideas may be submitted by individuals or by groups.

These new-product ideas are then written up in the form of a brief new-product development proposal and submitted to a cross-functional team of managers who evaluate the proposal at gate 1. At gate 1, the proposal is reviewed in terms of its fit with the strategy of the organization and its technical feasibility. Proposals that are consistent with the strategy of the organization and judged technically feasible will be passed on to stage 2; the rest will be turned down (although the door is often left open for reconsidering the proposal at a later date).

The primary goal in stage 2 is to draft a detailed new-product development plan that specifies all of the relevant information required to make a decision about whether to go ahead with a full-blown product development effort. Included in the new-product development plan should be factors such as strategic and financial objectives, an analysis of market potential, a list of desired product features, a list of technological requirements, a list of financial and human resource requirements, a detailed development budget, and a time line that contains specific milestones (e.g., dates for prototype completion and final launch). This plan is normally drafted by a cross-functional team of managers who spend considerable time in the field with customers trying to understand their needs.

Once completed, the plan is reviewed by a senior management committee at gate 2. Here the review focuses on a detailed look at the new-product development plan and considers whether the proposal is attractive given its market potential, and viable given the technological, financial, and human requirements of actually developing the product. This review should be made in light of all other product development efforts being undertaken by the organization. One goal at this point is to ensure that limited technical, financial, and human resources are used to their maximum effect.

At gate 2, projects are either rejected, sent back for revision, or allowed to proceed to the development phase (stage 3). The stage 3 development effort can last anywhere from six months to ten years depending on the industry and product type. For example, some electronics products have development cycles of six months, and it takes three to five years to develop a new car, about five years to develop a new jet aircraft, and as much as ten years to develop a new medical drug.

Using Cross-Functional Teams and a Product Team Structure

As just noted, establishing cross-functional teams is a critical element in any structured new-product development effort.[42] Although successful innovation begins in the R&D function, the way the activities of the R&D department are coordinated with the activities of other functions is crucial.[43] Figure 13.7 identifies the many functions necessary for successful innovation. In addition to R&D, they include product engineering, process engineering, materials management, manufacturing, and marketing.

Because those different groups usually have different orientations and attitudes, coordinating their activities is difficult. The link between R&D and the product and process engineering groups, for example, is vital to the conversion of research results into a product that is designed efficiently and can be produced cheaply. R&D scientists, however, may complain that the potential of "their" new product is being sacrificed if the engineers tinker with its design to make production either easy or cheap. In turn, engineering may feel that R&D is too emotionally committed to the product and has lost sight of the market in its pursuit of technical excellence.

Both R&D and engineering also need to coordinate with manufacturing to ensure that the new product can be made cost-effectively and reliably. A link with marketing will ensure that the product possesses the features and qualities that customers need and want and that R&D resources are not being spent to create or improve a product that customers do not want. Marketing may discover, for example, that customers are not willing to pay the price that the organization will be forced to charge for the product. This marketing information may conflict with R&D's and engineering's views about producing a high-quality product even at a high price.

FIGURE 13.7

Innovation as a Cross-Functional Activity. Successful innovation depends on the coordination of the activities of the research and development department with the activities of other departments.

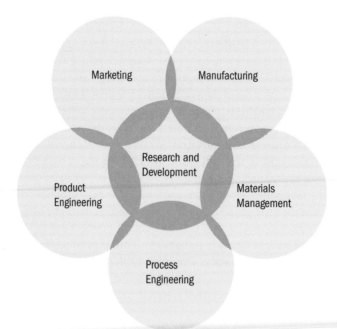

Marketing, engineering, and manufacturing personnel need to be core members of successful new-product development teams. The term *core members* refers to a nucleus of three to six people who bear primary responsibility for the product development effort. In addition to core members, others typically work on the project as the need arises, but it is the core members who stay with the project from inception to completion of the development effort. To ensure that core members are not distracted by other development projects, they are usually assigned to only one development project at a time. In addition, for particularly important new-product development projects, core members may be taken out of their regular functional role for the duration of the project and assigned to work on the project full-time.

Many organizations have been unable to manage the functional linkages necessary for successful product innovation, and the results have often been disastrous. A list of innovative products for which there was little demand includes the RCA laser disc player, the Kodak photo CD player, and the cost-ineffective supersonic *Concorde* airliner. In Chapter 4, we discussed various structures that organizations can use to manage activities in conditions of great uncertainty. Two of them, product team structure and matrix structure, are especially suitable for managing innovation in high-tech organizations. Both of these structures focus on creating cross-functional teams to pursue new-product development from the concept and design stage, through manufacturing, to the marketing and sales stage. These structures allow each function to develop an understanding of the problems and interests of the other functions, and they reduce communication problems. Decentralizing authority to the team also forces team members to cooperate and develop a shared understanding of the project.

Even though a product team structure facilitates innovation and the new-product development process, it is often not sufficient to solve the coordination problem. Many organizations use additional integrating mechanisms to facilitate innovation: team leaders and project champions, "skunk works," new venture divisions, and joint ventures.

Team Leadership

Although establishment of a cross-functional product development team may be a necessary condition for successful innovation, it is not a sufficient condition. If a cross-functional team is to succeed, it must have the right kind of leadership, and it must be managed in an effective manner.[44]

One important consideration is to have a team leader who can rise above his or her functional background and take a cross-functional view. Another issue is how much power and authority should be given to the team leader. Here a distinction can be made between lightweight and heavyweight team leaders.[45] A **lightweight team leader** is a midlevel functional manager who has lower status than the head of a functional department. The lightweight team leader is not given control over human, financial, and functional resources. Rather, he or she remains under the control of functional department heads. If the lightweight leader wants access to those resources, he or she must pursue the heads of functional departments to allocate resources to him or her for a period of time. This arrangement weakens the power and authority of the team leader, for he or she is subservient to the heads of functional departments. The result can be limited cross-functional coordination. Still, this arrangement might be appropriate in those cases in which minor modifications of an existing product are all that is required.

A **heavyweight team leader** is a manager who has higher status within the organization (e.g., a senior functional manager or someone from a general management background). The heavyweight team leader is given primary control over key human, financial,

Lightweight team leader *A midlevel functional manager who has lower status than the head of a functional department.*

Heavyweight team leader *A senior functional manager or someone from a general management background who has higher status within the organization.*

and technical resources for the duration of the project. This allows the heavyweight leader to lay first claim to key resources and, if necessary, to override the wishes of the heads of the functions. For example, the heavyweight leader may be able to insist that a certain marketing and engineering manager be assigned full-time to the project, even if the heads of the engineering and marketing departments are not in favor of this assignment. This power gives the heavyweight team leader a much greater chance of assembling a cross-functional team capable of successfully developing a new product. Researchers who study this issue argue that heavyweight team leaders make most sense in the case of important new-product development efforts.[46]

Product champions

People who take "ownership" of a project, solve problems as they occur, smooth over disputes among team members, and provide leadership to the team.

Heavyweight team leaders often function as **product champions**—the people who take "ownership" of the project, solve problems as they occur, smooth over disputes among team members, and provide leadership to the team. However, sometimes the product champion is not formally appointed and emerges informally during the innovation process. The way in which Don Frey, a product champion at Ford, worked with Lee Iacocca to develop the Ford Mustang in the early 1960s illustrates the importance of the product champion role.

ORGANIZATIONAL INSIGHT

13.2 CHAMPIONING THE MUSTANG

Don Frey, an R&D engineer, was a product champion at Ford Motor Company. At Ford's R&D laboratories, Frey was assigned to projects that seemed new and interesting, but he never got to talk to customers and never got involved in operational decision making about what to offer the customer and how much new developments would cost. As a result, for many years, he and other R&D engineers worked on products that never got to market. Frustrated by the lack of payoff from his work, Frey began to question the utility of a corporate R&D laboratory that was so far removed from operations and the market. In 1957, he moved from R&D to head the passenger car design department, where he would be closer to market operations. In this new position, Frey was much closer to the customer and directed the energies of his department to producing innovations that customers wanted and were willing to pay for.

Frey soon concluded that in the automobile business the best R&D was incremental: Year by year a car was improved to meet customer demands. He also saw how important it was to use customer complaints as a guide for investing R&D resources to get the most benefit. Equipped with this new perspective on innovation, he was made a member of Ford's top planning committee in 1961, and he became interested in developing a new car for the emerging "sporty car segment."

Frey and his staff saw the possibility of designing a car for this segment, and Frey began championing the development of a product. Ford, however, had just lost a fortune on the Edsel and was reluctant to start a new car. Because there was no corporate support for Frey's ideas, all of the early engineering and styling of what became the Mustang was carried out with bootleg funds—that is, funds earmarked for one project but used for something else. By 1962, Frey and his team had produced the first working prototype of the Mustang and believed they had a winner. Top management in general and Henry Ford II in particular were not impressed and offered no support, still fearing the new car might turn out to be another Edsel.

Luckily for the Mustang team, Lee Iacocca became vice president and general manager of Ford in 1962, and he bought into the Mustang concept. Believing that the Mustang would be a huge success, Iacocca risked his reputation to convince top management to back the idea. In the fall of 1962, after much pressure, funds to produce the car were allocated. With Frey as product champion, the Mustang was completed from approval to market in only 18 months. When the Mustang was introduced in 1964, it was an instant success, and over 400,000 Mustangs were sold.

Frey went on to champion other innovations in Ford vehicles, such as disc brakes and radial tires. Reflecting on his experiences as a product champion, he offered some "coaching tips" for future product champions: Innovation can start anywhere and from small beginnings, and product champions must be prepared to use all the skill they have to pull people and resources together and to resist top managers and financial experts who use numbers to kill new ideas.[47] As Frey's experiences suggest, innovation is a risky business, and product champions have to go out on a limb to take on the disbelievers.

Skunk Works and New Venture Divisions

Skunk works *A task force—a temporary team—created to expedite new-product design and to promote innovation.*

A **skunk works** is a task force, a temporary team, that is created to expedite new-product design and to promote innovation by coordinating the activities of functional groups.[48] The task force consists of members of the engineering and research departments and other support functions, such as marketing, and is assigned to other facilities, often at a location away from the rest of the organization. This setting provides the opportunity for the intensive face-to-face interactions necessary to generate successful innovation. Together, the members of the task force "own the problem" and become internal entrepreneurs, or **intrapreneurs**, people inside an organization who are responsible for the success or failure of the project. Thus, a skunk works is an island of innovation and provides a large organization with a small-organization-type setting in which team members have the opportunity and motivation to bring a new product to market quickly. Ford created a skunk works to develop the new Mustang that was introduced in 1993.

Intrapreneurs *Enrepreneurs inside an organization who are responsible for the success or failure of a project.*

Hewlett-Packard, 3M, and other organizations have also recognized the advantages of a small-organization-type atmosphere for fostering entrepreneurship in their employees. Thus, as viable new product developments occur in the corporate R&D laboratories, these organizations create a **new venture division**, a new division that is allocated a complete set of value-creating functions to manage a project from beginning to end.[49] Unlike a skunk works, which is dissolved when the product is brought to market, a new venture division assumes full responsibility for the commercialization of the product and is normally an independent division. Project members become the heads of the division's functions and are responsible for managing the functional structure created to bring the new product to market.

New venture division *A new division that is allocated a complete set of value-creating functions to manage a project from beginning to end.*

Establishing the balance of control between the division and the corporate center can become a problem in a new venture division. As the new division absorbs more and more resources to fulfill its mission, the corporate center may become concerned about the commercial success of the project. If corporate managers begin to intervene in the division's activities, divisional managers begin to lose their autonomy, and the division's entrepreneurial attitude may start to decline. Thus, managing a new venture division is a difficult process that requires considerable organizational skill.

Joint ventures between two or more organizations, discussed in Chapter 6, are another important means of managing high-tech innovation. A joint venture allows organizations to combine their skills and technologies and pool their resources to embark on risky R&D projects. A joint venture is similar to a new venture division in that a new organization is created in which people can work out new procedures that lead to success.

Creating a Culture for Innovation

Organizational culture also plays an important role in shaping and promoting innovation. Values and norms can reinforce the entrepreneurial spirit and allow an organization to respond quickly and creatively to a changing environment. As we saw in Chapter 5, three factors that shape organizational culture are organizational structure, people, and property rights (see Figure 5.2).

ORGANIZATIONAL STRUCTURE.   Because organizational structure influences the way people behave, creating the right setting is important to fostering intrapreneurship. Several factors can stunt innovation and reduce the ability of an organization to introduce new products as it grows.

Increasing organizational size may slow innovation. As organizations grow, decision making slows down. Decisions have to be made through established channels in a sizable hierarchy, and a thriving bureaucracy may stifle the entrepreneurial spirit. As an organization becomes more bureaucratic, people may become more conservative and unwilling to take risks, and those most willing and able to innovate may become discouraged and leave the organization.

As organizations age, they tend to become less flexible and less innovative.[50] Relatively old, inflexible organizations may fail to notice new opportunities for new products because of what one writer has described as "the inability of many traditional mature firms to anticipate the need for productive change and their resistance to ideas advanced by creative people."[51] In addition, it is difficult for people to remain entrepreneurial throughout their careers. Thus, as organizations and their personnel age, there may be an inherent tendency for both to become more conservative.

With organizational growth comes complexity, and an increase in vertical and horizontal differentiation may hurt innovation. An increase in hierarchical levels makes it hard for employee entrepreneurs to exercise meaningful authority over projects. They may be under the constant scrutiny of upper-level managers who insist on signing off on projects. Similarly, when the skills and knowledge needed for innovation are spread across many subunits and functions, it is difficult for a product manager or product champion to coordinate the innovation process and secure the resources needed to bring a project to fruition.[52]

To promote innovation, organizations need to adopt a structure that can overcome those problems. Organic structures based on norms and values that emphasize lateral communication and cross-functional cooperation tend to promote innovation. Matrix and product team structures possess these organic characteristics and provide the autonomy for people to make their own decisions. In addition, many organizations use the informal organization to overcome obstacles presented by the formal structure. Such organizations give their employees wide latitude to act outside formal task definitions and to work on projects where they think they can make a contribution. Hewlett-Packard and 3M informally grant employees the right to use organizational resources to work on projects of their own choosing. Sony allows its scientists to move from project to project and to select a team to work on where they feel they can make the best contribution. Apple and Microsoft confer on their top R&D scientists the title "research fellow" and give them the autonomy and resources to decide how to put their skills to best use. When a research fellow's research leads to a promising new product development, a project team is established.

PEOPLE.   The culture of innovation in high-tech organizations is fostered by the characteristics of employees themselves. In many research settings, people cooperate so closely on product development that they become increasingly similar to one another. They buy into the same set of organizational norms and values and, thus, are able to communicate well with each other. In turn, organizational members select new members who buy into the same set of values, so that time a recognizable culture that promotes communication and the flow of new ideas emerges. However, an organization needs to guard against too much similarity in its scientists, lest they lose sight of new or emerging trends in the industry. IBM scientists, for example, fixated on improving mainframe computers and ignored signs that customers wanted better personal computers, not more sophisticated mainframes. To maintain a capacity to innovate successfully, a high-tech organization must strive to maintain diversity in its scientists and to allow them to follow divergent paths. The uncertainty associated with innovation makes it important for people to be adaptable and open to new ideas. One way to encourage flexibility and open-mindedness is to recruit people who are committed to innovation but who travel along different pathways to achieve it.

PROPERTY RIGHTS.   The uncertainty associated with innovation makes it difficult for managers to evaluate the performance of highly skilled R&D scientists. Managers cannot watch scientists to see how well they are performing. Often their performance can be evaluated only over a long time period—perhaps years. Moreover, innovation is a complex, intensive process that demands skills and abilities inherent in the scientist, not in the organization. When scientists come up with a new idea, it is relatively easy for them to take it and establish their own organizations to exploit the benefits from it. Indeed, much technological innovation occurs in new organizations founded by scientists who have left large organizations to branch out on their own. Given these issues, strong property rights are needed to align the interests of R&D scientists with the interests of the organization.[53]

An organization can create career paths for its R&D employees and demonstrate that success is closely linked to future promotion and rewards. Career paths can be established not only inside the R&D function but also between R&D and general management functions. Inside the R&D function, successful scientists can be groomed to lead future R&D projects. After some years in R&D, however, many scientists move to take control of manufacturing operations or to assume other management responsibilities. Because of the experience they gained in various functions, these managers are in a position to ensure that future R&D activities are aligned with customer needs and to serve as project managers.

Strong property rights can also be created if an organization ties individual and group performance to large monetary premiums. Innovative employees should receive bonuses and stock options that are proportional to the increase in profitability that can be attributed to their efforts. Making employees owners in the organization will discourage them from leaving the organization and will provide them with a strong incentive to perform well. Many successful high-tech organizations, such as Merck and Apple, do this; and one in five of Microsoft's employees is a millionaire as a result of the organization's policy of giving stock options to employees. The last thing that Bill Gates wants is for his best employees to leave and found their own organizations that then compete with Microsoft!

By focusing on property rights, people, and structure, an organization can create a culture in which norms and values foster innovation and the search for excellence in new-product development.

Managerial Implications: Innovation

1. Research and development activities must be integrated with the activities of the other functions if the innovation process is to be successful.
2. Employees must be given autonomy and encouraged to use organizational resources to facilitate the continuous development of new products and processes.
3. A stage-gate product development funnel, cross-functional teams, appropriate team leadership, a skunk works, and new venture divisions should be created to provide a setting that encourages entrepreneurship.
4. Top management must create a culture that supports innovation and that recognizes and rewards the contributions of organizational members—for example, by linking rewards directly to performance.

SUMMARY

Managing the process of innovation and change to enhance organizational effectiveness is a central challenge facing managers and organizations today. An increasing rate of technological change and an increase in global competition are the two forces that are putting enormous pressure on organizations to find new and better ways of organizing their activities to increase their ability to create value. Chapter 13 has made the following major points:

1. Organizational change is the process by which organizations move from their present state to some desired future state to increase their effectiveness. The goal of planned organizational change is to find new or improved ways to use resources and abilities to increase the organization's ability to create value for its stakeholders.

2. In general, the two main types of change are evolutionary change (such as total quality management), which is gradual, incremental, and specifically focused, and revolutionary change, which is sudden, drastic, and often organization-wide (such as reengineering, restructuring, and innovation).

3. Forces for change include competition; economic, political, and global pressures; demographic and social forces; and ethical issues. Resistances or obstacles to change are found at the organizational, functional, group, and individual levels.

4. The first step in planned organizational change is to identify the need for change. Managers must then decide on the desired future state of the organization and manage the process of change to overcome obstacles to reaching that future state.

5. Managers can adopt a revolutionary, top-down approach to change or an evolutionary, bottom-up approach. Frequently, to overcome organizational inertia, managers must use a revolutionary approach. When organizations are used to change, an evolutionary approach may be more practical.

6. Innovation is the development of new products or new production and operating systems (including new forms of organizational structures). There are two types of innovations: quantum innovations, which are the result of quantum shifts in technology, and incremental innovations, which result from the refinements to an existing technology. Technological change that results in quantum innovations can create opportunities for an organization to introduce new products, but it can also be a threat since it can increase the level of competition.

7. There are a number of techniques that managers can use to help promote innovation. These include using a stage-gate development funnel, using cross-functional teams and a product team structure, establishing strong team leadership, making use of skunk works and new venture divisions, and creating a culture for innovation.

DISCUSSION QUESTIONS

1. What are the major forces and resistances to change? How does Lewin suggest that organizations should manage the change process?

2. How do evolutionary change and revolutionary change differ? Under what conditions might managers choose one approach or the other? What would you recommend for IBM?

3. What is the relationship between quantum and incremental change?

4. What steps would you take to create (a) a structure and (b) a culture congenial to innovation in a high-tech organization?

ORGANIZATIONAL THEORY IN ACTION

PRACTICING ORGANIZATIONAL THEORY: MANAGING CHANGE

Break up into groups of three to five people and discuss the following scenario:

You are a group of top managers of one of the Big Three carmakers. Your company has been experiencing increased competition from other carmakers whose innovations in car design and manufacturing methods have allowed them to produce cars that are higher in quality and lower in cost than yours. You have been charged with preparing a plan to change the company's structure to allow you to compete better, and you have decided on two main changes. First, you plan to reengineer the company and move from a multidivisional structure (in which each division produces its own range of cars) to one in which cross-functional product teams become responsible for developing new car models that will be sold by all the divisions. Second, you have decided to implement a total quality management program to raise quality and decentralize decision-making authority to the teams and make them responsible for achieving higher quality and lower costs. Thus, the changes will disrupt role relationships at both the divisional and functional levels.

1. Discuss the nature of the obstacles at the divisional, functional, and individual levels that you will encounter in implementing this new structure. Which do you think will be the most important obstacles to overcome?

2. Discuss some ways you can overcome obstacles to change to help your organization move to its desired future state.

MAKING THE CONNECTION #13

Find an example of an organization that has been going through a major kind of organizational change. What kind of change is it? Why is the organization making the change? What is its change strategy? Why did it choose this change strategy?

Analyzing the Organization: Design Module #13

This module focuses on the extent to which your organization has been involved in major change efforts recently and on its approach to promoting innovation.

1. Does *revolutionary* or *evolutionary* better describe the changes that have been taking place in your organization? What types of change (such as restructuring) has your organization been most involved in? How successful have these change efforts been?
2. With the information that you have at your disposal, discuss (a) the forces for change, (b) obstacles to change, and (c) the strategy for change that your organization has adopted.
3. With what kind of innovation (quantum or incremental) has your organization been most involved?
4. In what ways, if any, has your organization sought to manage the innovation process and alter its structure or culture to increase its capacity to develop new products or services?

Cases for Analysis:
BIG CHANGES AT BOEING

In October 1990, the Boeing Corporation committed itself to developing an all new wide-bodied, 400-seat commercial jet aircraft, the Boeing 777. Competition is fierce in the passenger jet aircraft business. Boeing's managers recognized that they had to change the way the company operated in order to find a way to simultaneously reduce costs, increase quality, and design a new aircraft that its customers would want.

Boeing began to change the process when it moved to a product team structure and created cross-functional design teams to develop its new aircraft. Engineering and production employees were put together in scores of teams, each of which was given the responsibility of developing a specific portion of the new plane and making it easy to manufacture. Boeing also brought 18 major suppliers into the 777 program to consult with project engineers in order to rectify any problems that might arise in production ahead of time, thereby reducing the need for costly design changes late in the development cycle. The suppliers became informal members of the team that became most committed to raising quality and finding ways to keep costs low.

To build a plane that was designed with customer requirements in mind, Boeing also invited eight U.S. and foreign airlines to help them design the aircraft. The group included United, which launched the program with orders for 32 planes, American, Delta, British Airways, and Japan Air Lines. For almost a year, technical representatives from these airlines took up residence in Boeing's Seattle facility and met with the engineering staff assigned to the 777 project. Making customers an integral part of the innovation process was a dramatic change for Boeing, which hitherto had always been very secretive about its design work.

The input from the eight carriers had a major effect on the design of the new 777. The eight airlines demanded a fuselage that was wider than rivals McDonnell Douglas and Airbus models so that they could pack another 30 or so seats onto the aircraft. The result was an aircraft 5 inches wider than the McDonnell Douglas MD-11 and 25 inches wider than the Airbus A-330. The airlines also wanted a plane in which the galleys and lavatories could be quickly relocated almost anywhere within the plane, so Boeing designed a plane whose interior can be completely reconfigured in three to four hours, with one, two, or three classes depending on a carrier's market of the moment. American Airlines, in particular, wanted the 777 to have an option for folding wingtips so that the plane could utilize the same airport space as American's DC-10s and 767s. Boeing devised a way of folding 22 feet of each wing, leaving a parked 777 with roughly the same wingspan as a DC-10 or 767.

In another major change for Boeing, the 777 was the first airliner to be designed entirely by computer. Boeing's engineers innovated a state-of-the-art, three-dimensional, computer-aided design technology to engineer and test parts in virtual space. The new system dramatically cut back on the need for expensive mock-ups and design changes and cut down on development time. Indeed, the 777 was the first commercial jet aircraft ever built without a full-sized mock-up. Preassemblies were first created and put together in virtual space on a computer screen to make sure that every component fit. When components didn't fit, they were redesigned on the computer until they did, and only then were real parts and subassemblies manufactured.

The success of its new innovation process was demonstrated when the first 777 took off only four years later from Boeing's Everett, Washington, production facility. The four-year development time for the 777 represented a triumph for Boeing; the typical development time for jet aircraft is at least six years. Moreover, by the time the 777 took off, Boeing already had 150 firm orders for the plane, and airlines had taken out options on another 150 planes. This kind of advanced ordering is a sure sign that Boeing had innovated an aircraft that customers wanted. By changing its technology and operating system, Boeing had succeeded in raising the speed of new-product innovation and developing a new product that its customers wanted.

1. Chart the major steps that Boeing took to encourage innovation and new-product development.

2. How easy would it be for other organizations to follow Boeing's is lead?

REFERENCES

1. M. Beer, *Organizational Change and Development* (Santa Monica, CA: Goodyear, 1980); J. I. Porras and R. C. Silvers, "Organization Development and Transformation," *Annual Review of Psychology*, 1991, vol. 42, pp. 51–78.

2. D. Miller, "Evolution and Revolution: A Quantum View of Structural Change in Organizations," *Journal of Management Studies*, 1982, vol. 19, pp. 11–151; D. Miller, "Momentum and Revolution in Organizational Adaptation," *Academy of Management Journal*, 1980, vol. 2, pp. 591–614.

3. C. E. Lindblom, "The Science of Muddling Through," *Public Administration Review*, 1959, vol. 19, pp. 79–88; P. C. Nystrom and W. H. Starbuck, "To Avoid Organizational Crises, Unlearn," *Organizational Dynamics*, 1984, vol. 12, pp. 53–65.

4. M. Hammer and J. Champy, *Reengineering the Corporation* (New York: Harper Collins, 1993).

5. R. A. Burgelman and M. A. Maidique, *Strategic Management of Technology and Innovation* (Homewood, IL: Irwin, 1988).

6. G. R. Jones and J. E. Butler, "Managing Internal Corporate Entrepreneurship: An Agency Theory Perspective," *Journal of Management*, 1992, vol. 18, pp. 733–749.

7. E. Mansfield, J. Rapaport, J. Schnee, S. Wagner, and M. Hamburger, *Research and Innovation in the Modern Corporation* (New York: Norton, 1971).

8. "Synergen Inc.," *Wall Street Journal*, 2 August 1994, p. B6.

9. C. Argyris, R. Putman, and D. M. Smith, *Action Science* (San Francisco: Jossey-Bass, 1985).

10. R. M. Kanter, *The Change Masters: Innovation for Productivity in the American Corporation* (New York: Simon & Shuster, 1984).

11. C. W. L. Hill and G. R. Jones, *Strategic Management: An Integrated Approach* (Boston: Houghton Mifflin, 1995).

12. Ibid.

13. C. W. L. Hill, *International Business* (Chicago: Irwin, 1997).

14. C. A. Bartlett and S. Ghoshal, *Managing Across Borders* (Boston: Harvard Business School, 1989).

15. C. K. Prahalad and Y. L. Doz, *The Multinational Mission: Balancing Local Demands and Global Vision* (New York: The Free Press, 1987).

16. D. Jamieson and J. O'Mara, *Managing Workforce 2000: Gaining a Diversity Advantage* (San Francisco: Jossey-Bass, 1991).

17. S. Jackson and Associates, *Diversity in the Workplace: Human Resource Initiatives* (New York: The Guilford Press, 1992).

18. T. H. Cox and S. Blake, "Managing Cultural Diversity: Implications for Organizational Competitiveness," *Academy of Management Executives*, August 1991, pp. 49–52.

19. W. H. Shaw and V. Barry, *Moral Issues in Business*, 6th ed. (Belmont, CA: Wadsworth, 1995).

20. T. Donaldson, *Corporations and Morality* (Englewood Cliffs, NJ: Prentice Hall, 1982).

21. M. Hannan and J. Freeman, "Structural Inertia and Organizational Change," *American Sociological Review*, 1989, vol. 49, pp. 149–164.

22. L. E. Greiner, "Evolution and Revolution as Organizations Grow," *Harvard Business Review*, July–August 1972, pp. 37–46.

23. R. M. Kanter, *When Giants Learn to Dance: Mastering the Challenges of Strategy* (New York: Simon and Shuster, 1989).

24. T. Burns and G. M. Stalker, *The Management of Innovation* (London: Tavistock, 1961).

25. P. R. Lawrence and J. W. Lorsch, *Organization and Environment* (Boston: Harvard Business School Press, 1972).

26. D. Miller, *The Icarus Paradox: How Exceptional Companies Bring About Their Own Downfall* (New York: Harper-Collins, 1990); D. Miller, "The Architecture of Simplicity," *Academy of Management Review*, 1993, vol. 1, pp. 116–138.

27. J. P. Kotter and L. A. Schlesinger, "Choosing Strategies for Change," *Harvard Business Review*, March/April 1979, pp. 106–114.

28. R. Likert, *The Human Organization* (New York: McGraw Hill, 1967).

29. C. Argyris, *Personality and Organization* (New York: Harper & Row, 1957).

30. This section draws heavily on K. Lewin, *Field Theory in Social Science* (New York: Harper & Row, 1951).

31. R. Beckhard and R. T. Harris, *Organizational Transitions: Managing Complex Change* (Reading, MA: Addison-Wesley, 1987); W. L. French and C. H. Bell, *Organizational Development* (Englewood Cliffs, NJ: Prentice Hall, 1990).

32. March and Simon, *Organizations*.

33. D. Miller, "Evolution and Revolution: A Quantum View of Structural Change in Organizations," *Journal of Management Studies*, 1982, vol. 19, pp. 131–151.

34. Ibid.; D. Miller and P. Freisen, "Momentum and Revolution in Organizational Adaptation," *Academy of Management Journal*, 1980, vol. 23, pp. 591–614.

35. "Jack Welch's Lessons for Success," *Fortune*, 25 January 1993, pp. 86–93.

36. Ibid.

37. R. D'Aveni, *Hyper-Competition* (New York: The Free Press, 1994).

38. P. Engardio and N. Gross, "Asia's High-Tech Quest: Can the Tigers Compete Worldwide?" *Business Week*, 7 December 1992, pp. 126–130.

39. P. Anderson and Michael L. Tushman, "Technological Discontinuities and Dominant Designs: A Cyclical Model of Technological Change," *Administrative Science Quarterly*, 1990, vol. 35, pp. 604–633; quoting J. Schumpeter, *Capitalism, Socialism, and Democracy* (New York: Harper Brothers, 1942).

40. The concept of creative destruction goes back to the classic work of J. A. Schumpeter, *Capitalism, Socialism, and Democracy* (New York: Harper Brothers, 1942).

41. K. B. Clark and S. C. Wheelwright, *Managing New Product and Process Development* (New York: The Free Press, 1993).

42. A. Griffin and J. R. Hauser, "Patterns of Communication Among Marketing, Engineering, and Manufacturing," *Management Science*, 1992, vol. 38, pp. 360–373; R. K. Moenaert, W. E. Sounder, A. D. Meyer, and D. Deschoolmeester, "R&D-Marketing Integration Mechanisms, Communication Flows, and Innovation Success," *Journal of Production and Innovation Management*, 1994, vol. 11, pp. 31–45.

43. R. A. Burgelman and M. A. Maidique, *Strategic Management of Technology and Innovation* (Homewood, IL: Irwin, 1988).

44. G. Barczak and D. Wileman, "Leadership Differences in New Product Development Teams," *Journal of Product Innovation Management*, 1989, vol. 6, pp. 259–267; E. F. McDonough and G. Barczak, "Speeding Up New Product Development: The Effects of Leadership Style and Source of Technology," *Journal of Product Innovation Management*, 1991, vol. 8, pp. 203–211; K. B. Clark and T. Fujimoto, "The Power of Product Integrity," *Harvard Business Review*, November–December 1990, pp. 107–119.

45. K. B. Clark and S. C. Wheelwright, *Managing New Product and Process Development* (New York: The Free Press, 1993).

46. Ibid.

47. D. Frey, "Learning the Ropes: My Life as a Product Champion," *Harvard Business Review*, September–October 1991, pp. 46–56.

48. M. A. Maidique and R. H. Hayes, "The Art of High Technology Management," *Sloan Management Review*, Winter 1984, pp. 18–31.

49. R. A. Burgelman, "Designs for Corporate Entrepreneurship in Established Firms," *California Management Review*, 1984, vol. 26, pp. 154–166.

50. H. Mintzberg and J. A. Waters, "Tracking Strategy in an Entrepreneurial Firm," *Academy of Management Journal*, 1982, vol. 25, pp. 465–499; P. Strebel, "Organizing for Innovation over an Industry Life Cycle," *Strategic Management Journal*, 1987, vol. 8, 117–124.

51. R. M. Kanter, *The Change Masters* (New York: Simon and Schuster, 1983).

52. G. R. Jones and J. E. Butler, "Managing Internal Corporate Entrepreneurship: An Agency Theory Perspective," *Journal of Management*, 1992, vol. 18, pp. 733–749.

53. Ibid.

C h a p t e r 1 4

ORGANIZATIONAL CONFLICT, POWER, and POLITICS

This chapter focuses on the social and interpersonal processes that affect the way managers make decisions and the way organizations operate. Specifically, it examines the causes, nature, and consequences of organizational conflict, power, and politics. First, the nature of organizational conflict, its sources, and the way it arises between stakeholders and subunits are examined. Second, the mechanisms by which managers and stakeholders can obtain power and use that power to influence decision making and resolve conflict in their favor are analyzed. Third, the way in which individuals and subunits can engage in organizational politics in order to enhance their control over decision making and obtain the power that increases their share of organizational resources is described.

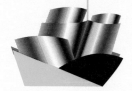

WHAT IS ORGANIZATIONAL CONFLICT?

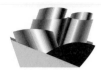

As noted in Chapter 1, an organization consists of different groups of stakeholders, each of which contributes to the organization in return for rewards. Stakeholders cooperate with one another to jointly contribute the resources an organization needs to produce goods and services. At the same time, however, stakeholders compete with one another for the resources the organization generates from these joint activities.[1] To produce goods and services, an organization needs the skills and abilities of managers and employees, the capital provided by shareholders, and the inputs provided by suppliers. Inside and outside stakeholders, such as employees, management, and shareholders, however, compete over their share of the rewards and resources that the organization generates.

To grow and survive, an organization must manage both cooperation and competition among stakeholders. As Figure 14.1 suggests, each stakeholder group has its own goals and interests, which overlap somewhat with those of other groups because all stakeholders have a common interest in the survival of the organization. But stakeholders' goals and interests are not identical, and conflict arises when one group pursues its own interests at the expense of other groups. **Organizational conflict** is the clash that occurs when the goal-directed behavior of one group blocks or thwarts the goals of another.

Organizational conflict
The clash that occurs when the goal-directed behavior of one group blocks or thwarts the goals of another.

Because the goals, preferences, and interests of stakeholder groups differ, conflict is inevitable in organizations.[2] Although conflict is often perceived as something negative, research suggests that some conflict is good for an organization and can improve organizational effectiveness. Beyond some point (point A in Figure 14.2), however, extreme conflict among stakeholders can hurt organizational performance.[3]

Why is some conflict good for an organization? Conflict can be beneficial because it can overcome organizational inertia and lead to organizational learning and change. When conflict within an organization or conflict between an organization and elements in its environment arises, the organization and its managers must reevaluate their view of the world. As we saw in Chapter 12, conflict between different managers or between different stakeholder groups can improve decision making and organizational learning by revealing new ways of looking at a problem or the false or erroneous assumptions that distort decision making. For example, conflict at General Motors between the board of directors and top managers about the slow speed at which top managers were restructuring the company caused a radical change in managerial attitudes. A new top-management team was appointed to increase the pace of change and to overcome GM's conservative ap-

FIGURE 14.1

Cooperation and Competition Among Organizational Stakeholders

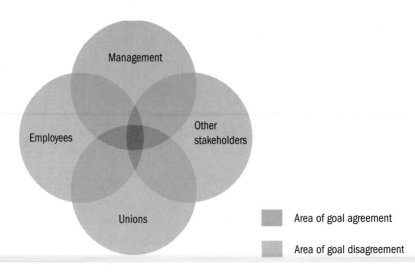

FIGURE 14.2

The Relationship Between Conflict and Organizational Effectiveness. Research suggests that there is an optimal level of conflict within an organization. Beyond that point (point A), conflict is likely to be harmful.

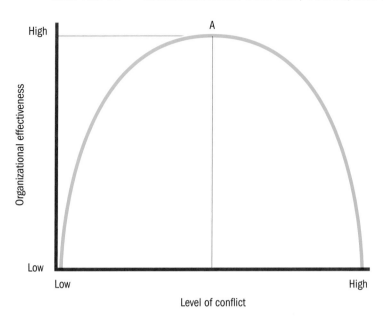

proach. Similarly, conflict among divisional managers at Digital Equipment resulted in a major change in organizational focus—from a purely engineering focus to a more market-oriented focus. It also resulted in the removal of CEO Kenneth H. Olsen, who was seen as a major source of the problem.

The conflict that arises when different groups perceive the organization's problems in different ways and are willing to act on their beliefs is a built-in defense against the organizational inertia produced by a top-management team whose members have the same vision of the world. In short, conflict can improve decision making and allow an organization to make better use of its resources to create value.[4]

Beyond a certain point, however, conflict stops being a force for good and becomes a cause of organizational decline. Suppose, for example, conflict among managers (or among other stakeholders) becomes chronic, so that managers cannot agree about organizational priorities or about how best to allocate resources to meet organizational needs. In this situation, managers spend all their time bargaining and fighting, and the organization gets so bogged down in the process of decision making that actual decisions become few and far between. In a somewhat vicious cycle, the slow and ponderous decision making that is characteristic of organizations in decline leads to even greater conflict because the consequences of failure are so great. An organization in trouble spends a lot of time making decisions—time that it cannot afford because it needs to adapt quickly to turn itself around. Thus, although some conflict can jolt an organization out of inertia, too much conflict can cause organizational inertia: As different groups fight for their own positions and interests, they fail to arrive at a consensus, and the organization drifts along, going from bad to worse.[5]

Many analysts claim that both GM and IBM faced this difficult situation. Top managers knew they had to make radical changes to their organization's strategy and structure, but they could not do so because different groups of managers lobbied for their own interests and for cutbacks to fall on other divisions. Conflict among divisions and the constant fight to protect each division's interests resulted in a slow rate of change and worsened the situation. In both companies, the boards of directors removed the CEOs and brought in newcomers who they hoped would overcome opposition to change and develop a strategy that would promote organizational interests, not just the interests of any particular group.

On balance, then, organizations need to be open to conflict, to recognize its value both in helping to identify problems and in contributing to the generation of alternative solutions that improve decision making. Conflict can promote organizational learning. However, in order to exploit the functional aspects of conflict and avoid the dysfunctional effects, managers must learn how to control it. Louis R. Pondy developed a useful model of organizational conflict. Pondy first identifies the sources of conflict and then examines the stages of a typical conflict episode.[6] His model provides many clues about how to control and manage conflict in an organization.

PONDY'S MODEL OF ORGANIZATIONAL CONFLICT

Pondy views conflict as a process that consists of five sequential episodes or stages, as summarized in Figure 14.3. No matter how or why conflict arises, managers can use Pondy's model to interpret and analyze a conflict situation and take action to resolve it—for example, by redesigning the organization's structure.

Stage 1: Latent Conflict

In the first stage of Pondy's model, *latent conflict*, no outright conflict exists; however, the potential for conflict to arise is present, though latent, because of the way an organization operates. According to Pondy, all organizational conflict arises because vertical and horizontal differentiation leads to the establishment of different organizational subunits with different goals and often different perceptions of how best to realize those goals. In business enterprises, for example, managers in different functions or divisions can generally agree

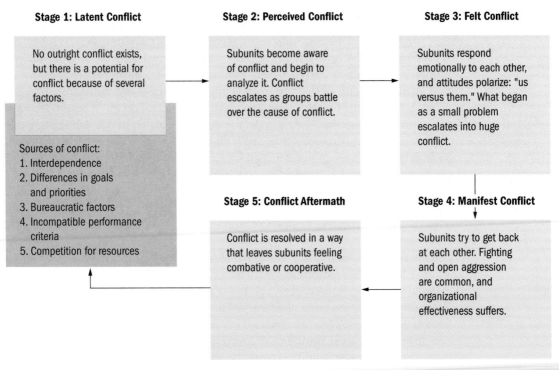

FIGURE 14.3   Pondy's Model of Organizational Conflict

about the organization's central goal, which is to maximize the organization's ability to create value in the long run. But they may have different ideas about how to achieve this goal: Should the organization invest resources in manufacturing to lower costs or in research to develop new products? Five potential sources of conflict among subunits have been identified: subunits' interdependence, subunits' differing goals, bureaucratic factors, incompatible performance criteria, and competition for resources.[7]

INTERDEPENDENCE. As organizations differentiate, each subunit develops a desire for autonomy and begins to pursue goals and interests that it values over the goals of other subunits or of the organization as a whole. Because the activities of different subunits are interdependent, subunits' desire for autonomy leads to conflict among groups. Eventually, each subunit's desire for autonomy comes into conflict with the organization's desire for coordination.

In terms of James D. Thompson's model of technology, discussed in Chapter 9, the move from pooled to sequential to reciprocal task interdependence among people or subunits increases the degree to which the actions of one subunit directly affect the actions of others.[8] When task interdependence is high, conflict is likely to occur at the individual, functional, and divisional levels. If it were not for interdependence, there would be no potential for conflict to occur among organizational subunits or stakeholders.[9]

DIFFERENCES IN GOALS AND PRIORITIES. Differences in subunit orientation affect the way each function or division views the world and cause each subunit to pursue different goals that are often inconsistent or incompatible. Once goals become incompatible, the potential for conflict arises because the goals of one subunit may thwart the ability of another to achieve its goals. As we discussed in Chapter 12, top managers often have different goals and priorities that may cause conflict in the decision-making process. The way in which the CEO and chief operating officer of Eastman Kodak fought over plans for reorganizing the company shows how differences in goals can lead to organizational conflict.

ORGANIZATIONAL INSIGHT

14.1 CONFLICT CAUSES SLOW CHANGE AT KODAK

Eastman Kodak, whose ubiquitous little yellow film boxes have long been a part of the American scene, has been experiencing declining performance for years. As with IBM and General Motors, Kodak was slow to react to the threat of competition in its central business, and a ponderous decision-making style has stifled its attempts to restructure its activities. In the early 1990s, CEO Kay Whitmore, a Kodak veteran, was reluctant to make the drastic changes that Kodak needed to regain its competitiveness. Although Kodak's management had repeatedly tried to turn the company's fortunes around, nothing had really worked, and the company's share price had been declining steadily for years.

Thus, in 1993, investors on Wall Street were delighted to hear about the appointment of Christopher Steffen as Kodak's new chief operating officer. Steffen had a reputation as a "turnaround artist" who performed miracles at Chrysler and Honeywell, and news of his appointment sent Kodak's stock price up by 17 percent. Investors thought that an outsider would finally bring a breath of fresh air and fresh ideas to Kodak's inbred top-management team. Investors, were, therefore, shocked when Steffen announced his resignation from the company less than a week after his appointment, citing "differences with the company's approach to problem solving."[10]

Apparently he and CEO Whitmore had very different ideas about how to restructure the company and the speed at which restructuring should be done. Steffen reportedly wanted to institute a massive cost-cutting regime, including large layoffs. He proposed a revolutionary change strategy and wanted to implement it right away. Whitmore, pursuing Kodak's traditional consensus approach to decision making, wanted much slower, evolutionary change, even though this approach had failed in the past. In short, Steffen and Whitmore came into conflict over the company's priorities. As in the past, Kodak's entrenched management team had the power to carry the day and resist attempts by Steffen and stockholders to change the way the company operated. Stockholders reacted to Steffen's departure by sending the company's share price down by over 10 percent, but within months the price shot back up when Whitmore was ousted by a concerned board of directors and replaced by the chairman of Motorola, George Fisher. Fisher has brought about many changes that Kodak so badly needed, but Kodak's performance and stock price have still not achieved the levels that both he and the board had hoped for. On January 1, 2000, a new CEO, Dan Carp, took over the company. His goal? To continue to shrink Kodak's size by 20 percent or 20,000 employees, and to expand its push into electronic imaging.[11]

BUREAUCRATIC FACTORS. The way in which task relationships develop in organizations can also be a potential source of conflict. Over time, conflict can occur because of status inconsistencies among different groups in the organization's bureaucracy. A classic type of bureaucratic conflict occurs between staff and line functions.[12] A *line function* is directly involved in the production of the organization's outputs. In a manufacturing company, manufacturing is the line function; in a hospital, doctors are the line function; and in a university, professors are the line function. *Staff functions* advise and support the line function and include functions such as personnel, accounting, and purchasing. In many organizations, people in line functions come to view themselves as the critical organizational resource and people in staff functions as secondary players. Acting on this belief, the line function constantly uses its supposedly lofty status as the producer of goods and services to justify putting its interests ahead of the other functions' interests. The result is conflict.[13]

INCOMPATIBLE PERFORMANCE CRITERIA. Sometimes conflict arises among subunits not because their goals are incompatible but because the organization's way of monitoring, evaluating, and rewarding different subunits brings them into conflict. Production and sales can come into conflict when, to achieve the goal of increased sales, the sales department asks manufacturing to respond quickly to customer orders—an action that raises manufacturing costs. If the organization's reward system benefits sales personnel (who get higher bonuses because of increased sales) but penalizes manufacturing (which gets no bonus because of higher costs), conflict will arise.

The way an organization designs its structure to coordinate subunits can affect the potential for conflict. The constant conflict among divisions at CS First Boston shows how incompatible reward systems can produce conflict.

14.2 HOW REWARDS PRODUCED CONFLICT AT CS FIRST BOSTON

CS First Boston, a large American investment bank, was formed by the merger of two smaller banks: First Boston (based in New York) and Crédit Suisse (based in London). From the beginning, the two divisions of the new bank were at odds. Although the merger was formed to take advantage of synergies in the growing transatlantic investment banking business, the divisions could never cooperate with one another, and managers in both were fond of openly criticizing the banking practices of their peers to anybody who would listen.

As long as the performance of one unit of the bank did not affect the other, the lack of cooperation between them was tolerated, although analysts pointed out that the loss in synergy from the arrangement kept CS First Boston out of the top league of investment banks. In the 1990s, however, the performance of the European unit began to affect the American unit, and conflict started to build. First Boston made record profits from issuing and trading fixed-income debt securities, and its managers were expecting hefty bonuses. However, those bonuses were not paid. Why? The London arm of the organization had made huge losses, and although the losses were not the fault of the Boston-based bank, the corporation's top managers decided not to pay bonuses to their U.S. employees because of the losses from Europe.

This inequitable decision, punishing U.S. employees for an outcome that they could not control, led to considerable conflict in the organization. Relations between the U.S. and European arms of the bank became even more strained; the divisions began fighting with top management; and when employees decided that the situation would not change in the near term, they began to leave CS First Boston in droves. Many senior managers left for competitors, such as Merrill Lynch and Goldman Sachs. With the organization in disarray, top managers faced the job of trying to restore cooperative relations.[14] Clearly, redesigning the reward system so that it does not promote conflict between divisions should be one of their major priorities.[15]

COMPETITION FOR SCARCE RESOURCES.   Conflict would never be a problem if there was always an abundance of resources for subunits to use. When resources are scarce, as they always are, choices about resource allocation have to be made, and subunits have to compete for their share.[16] Divisions fight to increase their share of funding because the more funds they can obtain and invest, the faster they can grow. Similarly, at the functional level there can be conflict over the amount of funds to allocate to sales or to manufacturing or to R&D to meet organizational objectives. Thus, to increase access to resources, functions promote their interests and importance often at one another's expense.

Together, these five factors have the potential to cause a significant level of conflict in an organization. At stage 1, however, the conflict is latent. The potential for conflict exists, but conflict has not yet surfaced. In complex organizations with high levels of differentiation and integration, the potential for conflict is especially great. The subunits are highly interdependent and have different goals and complicated reward systems, and the competition among them for organizational resources is intense. Managing organizational conflict to allocate resources to where they can produce the most value in the long run is very difficult.

Stage 2: Perceived Conflict

The second stage of Pondy's model, *perceived conflict*, begins when a subunit or stakeholder group perceives that its goals are being thwarted by the actions of another group. In this stage, each subunit begins to define why the conflict is emerging and to analyze the events that have led up to it. Each group searches for the origin of the conflict and constructs a scenario that accounts for the problems that it is experiencing with other subunits. The manufacturing function, for example, may suddenly realize that the cause of many of its production problems is defective inputs. When production managers investigate, they discover that materials management always buys inputs from the lowest-cost sources of supply and makes no attempt to develop the kind of long-term relationships with suppliers that can raise the quality and reliability of inputs. Materials management reduces input costs and improves this function's bottom line, but it raises manufacturing costs and worsens that function's bottom line. Not surprisingly, manufacturing perceives materials management as thwarting its goals and interests.

Normally at this point the conflict escalates as the different subunits or stakeholders start to battle over the cause of the problem. To get materials management to change its purchasing practices, manufacturing complains about materials management to the CEO and whomever else will listen. Materials management is likely to dispute the charge that its purchase of low-cost inputs leads to inferior quality. Instead, it attributes the problem to manufacturing's failure to provide employees with sufficient training to operate new technology and dumps responsibility for the quality problems back in manufacturing's lap. Even though both functions share the goal of superior product quality, they attribute the poor quality to very different causes.

Stage 3: Felt Conflict

At the *felt conflict stage*, subunits in conflict quickly develop an emotional response toward each other. Typically, each subunit closes ranks and develops a polarized us-versus-them mentality that puts the blame for the conflict squarely on the other subunit. As conflict escalates, cooperation between subunits falls, and so does organizational effectiveness. It is difficult to speed new-product development, for example, if research and development, materials management, and manufacturing are fighting over quality and final product specifications.

As the different subunits in conflict battle and argue their point of view, the conflict escalates. The original problem may be relatively minor, but if nothing is done to solve it, the small problem will escalate into a huge conflict that becomes increasingly difficult to manage. If the conflict is not resolved now, it quickly reaches the next stage.

Stage 4: Manifest Conflict

In the *manifest conflict stage* of Pondy's model, one subunit gets back at another subunit by attempting to thwart its goals. Manifest conflict can take many forms. Open aggression between people and groups is common. There are many stories and myths in organizations about board-room fights in which managers actually come to blows as they seek to promote their interests. Infighting in the top-management team is very common as managers seek to promote their own careers at the expense of others'. When Lee Iacocca was at Ford Motor Company, for example, and Henry Ford II decided to bring in the head of

General Motors as the new Ford CEO, Iacocca engineered the downfall of the new CEO within one year in order to promote his own rise to the top. Eventually, Iacocca lost the battle: Henry Ford forced Iacocca out because he feared that Iacocca would usurp his power.

A very effective form of manifest conflict is *passive aggression*—frustrating the goals of the opposition by doing nothing. Suppose there is a history of conflict between sales and production. One day, sales desperately needs a rush order for an important client. What might the manager of production do? One strategy is to informally agree to the sales department's request but then do nothing. When the head of sales comes banging on the door, the production manager says innocently, "Oh, you meant last Friday. I thought you meant this Friday."

In general, once conflict is manifest, organizational effectiveness suffers because coordination and integration between managers and subunits break down. Managers need to do all they can to prevent conflict from reaching the manifest stage, for two reasons: because of the breakdown in communication that is likely to occur and because of the aftermath of conflict.

Stage 5: Conflict Aftermath

Sooner or later, organizational conflict is resolved in some way, often by the decision of some senior manager. And sooner or later, if the sources of the conflict have not been resolved, the disputes and problems that caused the conflict arise again in another context. What happens when the conflict reappears depends on how it was resolved the first time. Suppose that sales comes to production with a new request. How are sales and production likely to behave? They probably will be combative and suspicious of each other and will find it hard to agree on anything. But suppose that sales and marketing had been able to solve their earlier dispute amicably and were able to agree on the need to respond flexibly to the needs of an important customer. The next time sales comes along with a special request, how is production likely to react? The production manager will probably have a cooperative attitude, and both parties will be able to sit down and work out a joint plan that suits the needs of both functions.

Every episode of conflict leaves a *conflict aftermath* that affects the way both parties to the conflict perceive and react to future conflict episodes. If a conflict is resolved before it gets to the manifest conflict stage, then the aftermath will promote good future working relationships. If conflict is not resolved until late in the process, or is not resolved at all, the aftermath will sour future working relationships, and the organizational culture will be poisoned by permanently uncooperative relationships. Managers at First Boston, for example, made it a point of honor to denigrate their colleagues in the other divisions of the organization. They went out of their way to be uncooperative and they are still doing so.

MANAGING CONFLICT: CONFLICT RESOLUTION STRATEGIES

Because organizational conflict can rapidly escalate and sour an organization's culture, managing organizational conflict is an important priority.[17] An organization must balance the need to have some "good" conflict (which overcomes inertia and allows new organizational learning) with the need to prevent "good" conflict from escalating into "bad conflict" (which causes a breakdown in coordination and integration between functions and divisions). In this section, we look at a few conflict resolution strategies designed to help organizations manage organizational conflict. Later in the chapter, we look at organizational politics as another way of managing organizational conflict when the stakes are high and when divisions and functions can obtain power to influence organizational outcomes in their favor.

The method an organization chooses to manage conflict depends on the source of the problem. At CS First Boston, the problem was an inequitable reward system that penalized one subunit for the poor performance of another. To solve this problem, CS First Boston's management needs to remove the source of the conflict by changing the way its reward systems operate—that is, by devising an equitable reward system. At Eastman Kodak, the source of the conflict was top managers' fight to protect their positions and property rights, and the conflict was resolved only by changing the top-management team. These examples suggest the two strategies that managers are likely to use to resolve conflict: changing an organization's structure to reduce or eliminate the cause of the conflict or trying to change the attitudes of individuals or the individuals themselves.[18]

Acting at the Level of Structure

Because task interdependence and differences in goals are two major sources of conflict, altering the level of differentiation and integration to change task relationships is one way to resolve conflict. An organization might change from a functional structure to a product division structure in order to remove a source of conflict among manufacturing managers who are unable to control the overhead costs associated with different kinds of products. As we saw in Chapter 4, moving to a product structure makes it much easier to assign overhead costs to different product lines. Similarly, if product managers are finding it difficult to convince departments to cooperate to speed product development, the move to a product team structure, in which different functional managers are assigned permanently to a product line, will remove the source of the problem.

If divisions are battling over resources, corporate managers can increase the number of integrating roles in the organization and assign top managers the responsibility for solving conflicts between divisions and for improving the structure of working relationships.[19] In general, increasing the level of integration is one major way in which organizations can manage the problem of differences in subunit goals. To resolve potential conflict situations, organizations can increase their use of liaison roles, task forces, teams, and integrating mechanisms (see Figure 2.3).

Another way to manage conflict is to make sure that the design of an organization's hierarchy of authority is in line with its current needs. As an organization grows and differentiates, the chain of command lengthens, and the organization is likely to lose control of its hierarchy. This loss of control can be a major source of conflict when people are given the responsibility for making decisions but lack the authority to do so because a manager above them must sign off on every move they make. Flattening the hierarchy, so that authority relationships are clearly defined, and decentralizing authority can remove a major source of organizational conflict. One major source of such conflict occurs when two or more people, departments, or divisions compete for the same set of resources. This situation is likely to be disastrous because decision making is impossible when different people claim the right to control the same resources. For this reason, the military and some other organizations have established very clear lines of authority; there is no ambiguity about who reports to whom and who has control of what resources.

Good organizational design should result in the creation of an organizational structure that minimizes the potential for organizational conflict. However, because of inertia, many organizations fail to manage their structures and change them to suit the needs of a changing environment. As a result, conflict increases and organizational effectiveness falls.

Acting at the Level of Attitudes and Individuals

Differences in goals and in beliefs about the best way to achieve organizational goals are inevitable because of differences between functions and divisions. One way to harness conflict between subunits and prevent the polarization of attitudes that results during the stage of felt conflict in Pondy's model is to set up a procedural system that allows parties in conflict to air their grievances and hear other groups' points of view. Committees or teams, for example, can provide a forum in which subunits in dispute can meet face-to-face and directly negotiate with one another. In this way, subunits can clarify the assumptions they are using to frame the problem, and they can develop an understanding of one another's motives. Very often the use of a procedural system reveals that the issue in dispute is much smaller than was previously thought and that the positions of the parties are more similar than anyone had realized.

Attitudinal structuring

A process designed to influence the attitudes of the opposing party and to encourage the perception that both parties are on the same side and want to solve a dispute amicably.

A procedural system is especially important in managing industrial conflicts between managers and unions. When a union exists, formal procedures govern the resolution of disputes to ensure that the issue receives a fair hearing. Indeed, an important component of bargaining in labor disputes is **attitudinal structuring**—a process designed to influence the attitudes of the opposing party and to encourage the perception that both parties are on the same side and want to solve a dispute amicably.[20] Thus, strikes become the last resort in a long process of negotiation.

Often an organization engages a *third-party negotiator* to moderate a dispute between subunits or stakeholders.[21] The third-party negotiator can be a senior manager who occupies an integrating role or an outside consultant employed because of his or her expertise in solving organizational disputes. The negotiator's role is to prevent the polarization of attitudes that occurs during the felt conflict stage and, thus, prevent the escalation to manifest conflict. Negotiators are skilled in managing organizational conflict so as to allow new learning to take place. Often the negotiator supports the weaker party in the dispute to make sure that both sides of the argument get heard.

Another way of managing conflict through attitude change is by the exchange and rotation of people among subunits to encourage groups to learn each other's points of view. This practice is widespread in Japan. Japanese organizations continually rotate people from function to function so that they can understand the problems and issues facing the organization as a whole.[22]

When attitudes are difficult to change because they have developed over a long period of time, the only way to resolve a conflict may be to change the people involved. This can be done by permanently transferring employees to other parts of the organization, promoting them, or firing them. We have already seen that top-management teams are often replaced to overcome inertia and change organizational attitudes. Analysts attribute a large part of the conflict at CS First Boston to the attitudes of a few key top managers who needed to be removed.

An organization's CEO is an important influence on attitudes in a conflict. The CEO personifies the values and culture of the organization, and the way the CEO acts affects the attitudes of other managers directly. As head of the organization, the CEO also has the ultimate power to resolve conflict among subunits. A strong CEO actively manages organizational conflict and opens up a debate, allowing each group to express its views. The strong CEO can then use his or her power to build a consensus for a resolution and decision and can motivate subunits to cooperate to achieve organizational goals. In contrast, a weak CEO can actually increase organizational conflict. When a CEO fails to manage the bargaining and negotiation process among subunits, the strongest subunits (those with the most power) are encouraged or allowed to fight for their goals at the expense of other subunits. A weak CEO produces a power vacuum at the top of the organization, enabling the strongest members of the organization to compete for control. As consensus is lost and infighting becomes the order of the day, conflict becomes destructive.

Managerial Implications: Conflict

1. Analyze the organizational structure to identify potential sources of conflict.
2. Change or redesign the organizational structure to eliminate the potential for conflict whenever possible.
3. If conflict cannot be eliminated, be prepared to intervene quickly and early in the conflict to find a solution.
4. Choose a way of managing the conflict that matches the source of the conflict.
5. Always try to achieve a good conflict aftermath so that cooperative attitudes can be maintained in the organization over time.

WHAT IS ORGANIZATIONAL POWER?

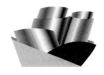

Organizational power
The ability of one person or group to overcome resistance by others to resolve conflict and achieve a desired objective or result.

The presence of a strong CEO is important in managing organizational conflict. Indeed, the relative power of the CEO, the board of directors, and other top managers is important in understanding the outcome of a conflict—that is, the organization's decision about how to allocate its resources. To understand how and why organizational conflict is resolved in favor of different subunits and stakeholders, we need to look closely at the issue of power.

What is power, and what is its role in organizational conflict? According to most researchers, **organizational power** is the mechanism through which conflict gets resolved, and it can be defined as the ability of one person or group to overcome resistance by others to achieve a desired objective or result.[23] More specifically, organizational power is the ability of A to cause B to do something that B would not otherwise have done.[24] Thus, when power is used to resolve conflict, the element of coercion exists. Actors with power can bring about outcomes they desire over the opposition of other actors.

The possession of power is an important determinant of the kind of decisions that resolve a conflict—for example, decisions concerning the allocation of resources or the assignment of responsibility between managers and subunits.[25] When decisions are made through bargaining between organizational coalitions, the relative power of the various coalitions to influence decision making is what determines how conflicts get resolved and which subunits benefit from the decision-making process.

Thus, conflict and power are intimately related. Conflict is caused by the existence of different individuals or groups that need to cooperate to achieve organizational objectives but must compete for organizational resources and have different individual or group goals and priorities. When a situation arises that causes these groups to compete for resources, conflict emerges. When the issue is sufficiently important, individuals and groups use their power to influence decision making and obtain outcomes that favor them.

SOURCES OF ORGANIZATIONAL POWER

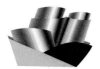

If people, groups, and divisions engage in activities to gain power within an organization, where do they get it from? What gives one person or group the power to influence, shape, or control the behavior of others? To answer these questions, we must recognize the sources of power in an organization. Figure 14.4 identifies seven of them; they are examined next.

Authority

Authority, power that is legitimized by the legal and cultural foundations on which an organization is based, is the ultimate source of power in an organization.[26] The power of the president of the United States, for example, is based on the Constitution of the United States, which specifies the rights and obligations of the president and the conditions under which that person can seek or be removed from office. In a similar way, authority in an organization derives from the organization's legal charter, which allows shareholders, through the board of directors, to grant a CEO the formal power, or authority, to use organizational resources to create value for shareholders. In turn, the CEO has the right to grant authority to other top managers in the organization, and they have the right to confer it on their subordinates.

People who join an organization accept the legal right of the organization to control their behavior. In exercising authority, a manager exercises a legal right to control resources, including human resources. The way in which authority is distributed depends on the organizational setting. As discussed in Chapter 3, in organizations that are centralized, authority is retained by top managers. In organizations that are decentralized, authority is delegated to those lower in the hierarchy, who are then held responsible for the way they use organizational resources. When authority is centralized, there is generally less scope for people to engage in behaviors aimed at gaining power. Because top managers keep power among themselves, it is difficult for coalitions to form. In such centralized organizations, however, a culture often develops in which people become afraid to take responsibility for decisions or to initiate new action for fear they will overstep their authority and be censured by top management. Instead, subordinates ingratiate themselves with top management in the hope of receiving favor, and they compete to curry favor with their superiors.

FIGURE 14.4

Sources of Organizational Power. All functions and divisions gain power from one or more of these sources.

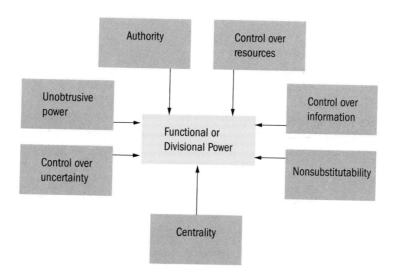

Thus, the effectiveness of decision making in a centralized organization can be reduced as managers surround themselves with yes-men and few important decisions get made.

Frequently, managers negotiate the limits of their authority among themselves, and more senior managers give authority to subordinates by making a conscious decision to decentralize. Sometimes, however, a subordinate who is active or competitive can indirectly take away a superior's authority by gradually assuming more and more of the supervisor's duties and responsibilities. The result, over time, is that even though the superior has legitimate authority, the subordinate has the real power. Superiors who are aware that this indirect seizure of authority can happen may take steps to prevent it. They may make a point of exercising their authority to show subordinates that they possess it, or they may insist on the display of certain rituals or symbols of their power—such as a big office and a personal secretary.

One of the classic ways in which superiors hold onto power is by restricting the information they give to subordinates to make a decision. If a manager gives out too much information, the subordinate will know as much as the manager does, and power over the subordinate will be lost. As a result of this fear, managers hoard information and do not share it with subordinates. However, if managers withhold too much and subordinates cannot make decisions, managers are likely to become overburdened, and the quality of decision making in the organization declines.

Managers have to realize that there is a difference between the decentralization of authority and the loss of authority: Decentralizing authority to a subordinate does not necessarily reduce a manager's authority because the manager continues to bear the responsibility for whatever decisions the subordinate makes. Thus, when subordinates make decisions that have important consequences, the responsibility and authority of the superior also increase. If subordinates fail, however, the manager also bears the consequences. If the failure is big enough, the decision to decentralize can result in the loss of power—that is, the loss of the official position that carries the authority in the organization.

As noted elsewhere, *empowerment* is the deliberate decentralization of authority to encourage subordinates to assume responsibility for organizational activities.[27] The goal of empowerment is to give subordinates wide latitude to make decisions and, thus, motivate them to make best use of their skills to create value. In an organization that decentralizes authority and empowers employees, all organizational members can gain authority as the organization prospers and attracts more resources. Employees who assume more authority and responsibility often demand more rights from the organization, such as higher salaries, increased job security, or bonuses tied to organizational performance.

Empowerment is also important at the corporate divisional level. As we have seen, in some organizations the corporate center is reluctant to delegate authority to the divisional level and prefers to centralize decision making. The problem with this choice is that divisional managers become afraid to experiment and to initiate new action even though they are close to a problem and have more information and knowledge about it than corporate managers have. Thus, divisions become unable to devise strategies that allow them to capitalize on opportunities in the environment, and both divisional performance and organizational performance suffer. For this reason, Jack Welch, CEO of General Electric, and many other CEOs deliberately empower divisional managers and make them responsible for their divisions' ultimate success in the marketplace. Welch believes that it is impossible to manage a company as large and diverse as GE unless managers at the divisional level and below have the authority and responsibility to innovate and make decisions. At GE, the corporate center's primary role is to make resource allocation decisions for the whole organization, and divisional managers know that GE's policy is to divest any division that is not number one or number two in its market.

Control over Resources

Power is not a fixed quantity. Managers who make decisions and perform actions that benefit the organization can increase their power. Just as an organization's power grows as the organization controls more and more resources in its environment, power within an organization also comes from the control of resources.[28] To survive, organizations require resources such as capital, human skills, raw materials, and customers. If a resource is particularly critical for an organization, the individual or subunit that has control over that resource has a good deal of power. At a company like Merck, for example, the R&D skills and knowledge necessary to produce new drugs are a critical resource. Given this fact, who has the most power at Merck? The answer is senior scientists, because they possess the knowledge on which the success of the organization depends. Similarly, at companies that rely heavily on the success of their marketing efforts, like Coca-Cola or McDonald's, the marketing department has considerable power because it is the department that can attract customers—the critical scarce resource.

Money or capital is, in a way, the ultimate organizational resource because money buys other resources. This small fact explains the ultimate power of top managers. Legally, they control the allocation of money in the organization and, thus, control its future. Recall from Organizational Insight 12.1 the make-or-buy decision that General Electric faced as it contemplated the future of its washing machine operations. Jack Welch's ultimate power was his ability to decide whether to give the appliance division the money it needed to modernize its technology.

The ability to *allocate* financial resources, however, is not the only source of a manager's or subunit's power. The ability to generate financial resources is also an important source of power.[29] The power of top managers at Merck rests in their ability to allocate R&D funds to various projects. The scientists, however, are the ones who invent the drugs that generate future revenues for the company, and their ability to generate resources gives them supreme power in the organization. In a multidivisional company, the divisions that generate revenues from customers have considerable power. In a university setting, the most powerful departments are ones such as engineering, chemistry, and agriculture, which generate the most revenues because they attract millions of dollars for sponsored research. At many schools, athletics programs and alumni groups have considerable power because of their ability to generate revenues.

Control over Information

Information can be a very important and scarce organizational resource. Access to strategic information and the control of the information flow to, from, and between subunits are sources of considerable power in the decision-making process.[30] It is possible to shape the views of others by carefully tailoring the information they receive. Andrew Pettigrew, in a study of the decision to buy a certain kind of computer system at a department store, showed how Jim Kenny, the head of management services, was able to influence the behavior of other senior managers by controlling the flow of information to them. Kenny was able to act as a gatekeeper. Pettigrew observed, "By sitting at the junction of the communications channels between his subordinates, the manufacturers, and the board, Kenny was able to exert biases in favor of his own demands and at the same time feed the board negative information about the demands of his opponents."[31] Even in the face of strong opposition by other managers, Kenny was able to resolve the conflict in his favor by controlling the information used to evaluate alternatives. In conflicts, senior managers have been known to deliberately manipulate other managers by supplying them with information that causes them to make bad decisions, so that in the contest for power in the organization they lose out to managers with better performance records.[32]

The control of information is the source of the power of many people or subunits in specialized roles.[33] The power of doctors in a hospital or mechanics in a garage stems from their ability to control specific knowledge and information. People who consult an expert have to take that person's word on trust or else get a second opinion. Similarly, functions may have power because they control the information and knowledge that are necessary to solve organizational problems. Researcher Michael Crozier found that maintenance engineers in the French tobacco-processing plants he was investigating enjoyed an inordinate amount of power despite their low status in the organizational hierarchy.[34] The reason for their power was that the principal problem in the company's routine mass production technology was machine breakdown. The maintenance engineers were the only people who knew how to repair the machines, and they had systematically used this knowledge to develop a considerable power base in the organization. Moreover, they jealously guarded their knowledge, refusing to write down repair procedures or share them with others, realizing that if they did so they would undermine their power. All subunits possess some expert information and knowledge, but the functions or divisions that control critical information have the most power.

Nonsubstitutability

If no one else can perform the tasks that a person or subunit performs, that person or subunit is nonsubstitutable. Only it can provide resources that another subunit or the organization wants. The maintenance engineers at the French tobacco plant had made themselves nonsubstitutable: Only they could reduce one of the major uncertainties facing the plant—machine breakdown. As a result of their nonsubstitutability, they exerted considerable power.[35]

Centrality

As we saw previously, Jim Kenny had power because he could control information flows and was central to the decision-making process. In his role as manager of information services, he could provide others with information that reduced the uncertainty they were experiencing about orders or accounts. Similarly, the subunits that are most central to resource flows have the ability to reduce the uncertainty facing other subunits.[36] Often an organization's strategy is a crucial determinant of which subunit is central in an organization. In a company, such as Coca-Cola, which is driven by marketing, other subunits—product development, manufacturing, sales—depend on the information collected by the marketing department. The marketing department is central because it supplies a resource that all the other functions need: knowledge about customers and their future needs. R&D is not central at Coca-Cola because it responds to the needs of other functions—for example, to the marketing function's decision that the company should develop "clear" Coke, a quickly passing fad. In a biotechnology company such as Amgen, whose differentiation strategy depends on R&D, R&D becomes the central function, and marketing shapes its behaviors to suit the needs of R&D.

Control over Uncertainty

A subunit that can actually control the principal sources of uncertainty or the contingencies facing the organization has significant power.[37] The R&D function in a biotechnology organization is powerful because the major source of uncertainty is whether the organization can discover safe, new drugs. In a hospital, doctors have power because only they have the ability to diagnose and treat patient problems, the main source of uncertainty for a hospital.

Over time, as the contingencies facing an organization change, some subunits rise in power, while the power of others whose services are no longer so valuable falls.[38] In business organizations after World War II, for example, the main source of uncertainty was the need to manufacture products fast enough to meet the demand for consumer goods that had built up during the war years. Manufacturing became the most important subunit during the postwar period, and many CEOs came from the manufacturing department. Then, during the 1960s, with manufacturers producing at full capacity, companies' main contingency became the need to sell their products, and marketing rose in prominence. With the 1970s came recession. Companies diversified to compete in new industries, and accounting and finance became the powerful organizational function. Thus, the power of subunits rises and falls as their ability to cope with organizational uncertainties changes.

Unobtrusive Power: Controlling the Premises of Decision Making

Another important source of power is the power of the dominant coalition—that is, the coalition that has the most power to control the decision-making process so that the decisions made in a conflict situation favor the interests of the coalition. When different subunits share similar interests, they often join together in a coalition to increase their power to pursue their common goals. The enhanced power of the coalition is then brought to bear on the decision-making process against coalitions that are pursuing different goals. The power flowing from the ability to control the premises behind decision making is called *unobtrusive power* because others are generally not aware that the coalition is shaping their perceptions or interpretations of a situation.[39]

The power of a coalition lies in its ability to control the assumptions, goals, norms, or values that managers use to judge alternative solutions to a problem. As a result of unobtrusive power, many alternatives that some parties in a conflict might like to evaluate are ruled out because they do not fit with the ruling coalition's view of the situation. Thus, even before decision making starts, the coalition in power has ensured that the decision that is eventually made will support its interests.

An example will clarify how unobtrusive power can work. Profits can be increased in two basic ways: by expanding sales revenues or by decreasing costs. If sales and marketing form the dominant coalition in an organization, then the option of cutting costs receives little attention, and decision making focuses on how the organization should invest its resources to increase sales. Conversely, when production is in the power seat, the goal of investing resources in new advanced machinery to reduce costs is likely to be an important factor influencing the selection of a course of action.

A specific coalition's ability to resolve conflict in its favor depends on which coalition has the balance of power in the organization. Organizational power is a dynamic concept, and organizational strategy can change quickly as the balance of power shifts from one coalition to another.[40]

USING POWER: ORGANIZATIONAL POLITICS

Organizational politics
Activities taken within organizations to acquire, develop, and use power and other resources to obtain one's preferred outcomes in a situation in which there is uncertainty or disagreement about choices.

Given the size of the benefits that can be gained by managers who use organizational power to resolve conflicts in their favor, it is not surprising that managers want to acquire as much power as they can and then use it to get what they want. **Organizational politics** comprises, in the words of Jeffrey Pfeffer, "activities taken within organizations to acquire, develop, and use power and other resources to obtain one's preferred outcomes in a situation in which there is uncertainty or disagreement about choices."[41] To get conflicts resolved in their favor, individuals, subunits, and coalitions must often engage in political activity and behavior to enhance the power and influence they have. Even if organizational members or subunits have no personal desire to play politics, they still must understand how politics operates because sooner or later they will come up against a master player of the political game. In such situations, apolitical managers (those who do not engage in politics) get all the tedious assignments or the responsibility for projects that do little to enhance their career prospects. Astute political managers get the visible and important projects that bring them into contact with powerful managers and allow them to build up their own power base, which they can use to enhance their chances of promotion.

Tactics for Playing Politics

To understand the political component of organizational life, we need to examine the political tactics and strategies that individuals and subunits use to increase their chances of winning the political game. The reward for success is a greater share of organizational resources. Individuals and subunits can use many political tactics to obtain the power to achieve their goals and objectives. Primarily, they must develop the skills and abilities to enhance not only their legitimate authority (theirs by virtue of their role in the organization) but also the power they derive from all the other sources of power.

INCREASING INDISPENSABILITY.   One prime political tactic that an individual or subunit can use to increase power is to become indispensable to the organization. Indispensability can be achieved by an increase in nonsubstitutability or an increase in centrality.

Increasing Nonsubstitutability.   Wily managers deliberately engage in behaviors and actions that make them nonsubstitutable.[42] They may develop specialized organizational skills, such as knowledge of computers, that allow them to solve problems for other managers. They may specialize in an area of increasing concern to the organization—such as international trade regulations, pollution control, or health and safety—so that they eventually are in a position to control a crucial contingency facing the organization. Individuals and subunits that use these tactics are often called in to solve problems as they arise, and the ability to come up with solutions increases their status and prestige.

Increasing Centrality.   Managers can increase their indispensability by making themselves more central to an organization. They can deliberately accept responsibilities that bring them into contact with many functions or with many managers so that they can enhance their personal reputation and that of their function. By being central, they may also enhance their ability to obtain information that they can use to make themselves and their functions nonsubstitutable. By being able to reduce the uncertainty experienced by others—for example, by obtaining and supplying information or by helping out on rush projects—they make others dependent on them. Then, in return for their help, they can request favors (such as access to privileged information) from other people and groups and feed this information to other managers, who in turn become obligated to them and who share even more information. Following this process, politically astute managers cultivate both people and information and are able to build within the organization a personal network of contacts that they can use to pursue personal goals such as promotion, and functional goals such as increasing the supply of scarce resources.

ASSOCIATING WITH POWERFUL MANAGERS.

Another way to obtain power is by attaching oneself to powerful managers who are clearly on their way to the top. By supporting a powerful manager and making oneself indispensable to that person, it is possible to rise up the organizational ladder with that person. Top managers often become mentors to aspiring lower-level managers because planning for the managerial succession is an important organizational task of top managers.[43] CEOs typically promote their friends, not their enemies. Managers who have taken the initiative to develop skills that make them stand out from the crowd and who are central and nonsubstitutable have the best chance of being selected as protégés by powerful managers who are seeking people to groom as their successors.

To identify the powerful people in an organization, it is necessary to develop skills in sensing who has power. A politically savvy manager figures out who are the key people to cultivate and what are the best ways to get their attention. Indicators of power include an individual's personal reputation and ability to (1) influence organizational decision-making outcomes, (2) control significant organizational resources, and (3) display symbols of prestige and status such as access to the corporate jet or limousine.[44]

A secondary way to form an attachment with powerful people is to take advantage of common ties such as graduation from the same school or university or similarity in socioeconomic background. Recall from Chapter 5 on organizational culture that top managers typically select as associates or successors other managers who are like themselves. They do so because they believe that shared norms and values are evidence of reliability or trustworthiness. Not surprisingly, then, it is not uncommon for managers to go to considerable lengths to look and behave like their superiors and to imitate or copy the habits or preferences of a senior person. Imitation has been called the sincerest form of flattery, and flattery is never wasted on those in power. The more powerful the person, the more he or she is likely to appreciate it.

BUILDING AND MANAGING COALITIONS.

Forming a coalition of different interests, stakeholders, individuals, and subunits around some common issue is a political tactic that a manager can use to obtain the power to resolve a conflict in her or his favor. Coalitions are often built around a trade-off: A supports B on an issue of interest to B in return for B supporting A on an issue of interest to A. Coalitions can be built through many levels in an organization, between various functions or divisions, and between important external or internal stakeholders. It is very important, for example, for top-level managers to build personal relationships with powerful shareholders or with members of the board of directors. Many of the most intense political contests occur at this level because the stakes are so high. The CEO needs the support of the board in any contest with members of the top-management team. Without it, the CEO's days are numbered. At General Motors, Robert Stempel lost the support of the board and was replaced by Jack Smith, who had gained the support of the board because of the success of his European restructuring efforts.

Building alliances with important customers is another valuable tactic, as is developing long-term relationships with the officers of the banks and other financial institutions from which a company obtains its capital. The more external linkages top managers can develop, the more chips they have to put on the table when the political game gets rough. Similarly, the ability to forge inside alliances with the managers of the most important subunits provides aspiring top managers with a power base that they can use to promote their personal agendas. In the game of organizational politics, having a lot of friends greatly enhances one's claim to power in the organization.

Skills in coalition building are important to success in organizational politics because the interests of parties to a coalition change frequently, as the environment changes. To maintain the coalition's consensus, the coalition has to be actively managed. Co-optation is a particularly important tool in coalition management. Recall from Chapter 6 that co-optation is a strategy that allows one subunit to overcome the opposition of a second subunit by involving it in decision making. Giving an opponent a place on an important committee or an important managerial role in solving organizational problems makes the opponent part of the coalition, with rights to share in the rewards from the outcome of the political decision-making process.

INFLUENCING DECISION MAKING.   Perhaps the most important political tactic a manager, group, division, or coalition can pursue to acquire, increase, and use power is to influence the politics of decision making. Possessing and using power (as a result of increasing indispensability, associating with powerful people, and knowing how to build and manage coalitions) is not the only skill needed to play politics. Knowing how and when to use power is equally important. As we saw earlier, the use of power to influence decision making is most effective when the power is unobtrusive. If other managers and coalitions become aware that they are being manipulated, they are likely to oppose the interests of the coalition doing the manipulating—or at least to insist that any decisions that are made also favor their interests. This is the thought behind the notion that a person who uses power loses it: Once the opposition realizes that a manager is using power to influence a decision in his or her favor, opponents will start to lobby for their interests and try to protect their claims to the resource at stake.

Two tactics for controlling the decision-making process so that the use of power seems to be legitimate—that is, in the organization's interests and not in the pursuit of self-interest or self-promotion—are controlling the agenda and bringing in an outside expert.[45]

Controlling the Agenda.   Managers and coalitions like to be on, and particularly in control of, committees so that they can control the agenda or business of the committee. By controlling the agenda, they are able to control the issues and problems to be considered by important decision makers. Thus, a coalition of powerful managers can prevent consideration of any issue that they do not support by not putting it on the agenda. In this way conflict remains either latent or in the felt stage because the opposition does not get the chance to air its view on problems or solutions. The ability to control the agenda is similar to the ability to control the premises of decision making. Both tactics limit the alternatives considered in the decision-making process.

Bringing In an Outside Expert.   When a major conflict exists, such as when top managers are deciding how to change or restructure the organization, all managers and coalitions know that individuals and groups are fighting for their interests and perhaps for their political survival. Every subunit manager wants the axe to fall on other subunits and wants to try to benefit from whatever change takes place. Self-interested managers and coalitions, knowing that the solution they want will be perceived by other subunits as politically motivated, are eager to legitimize their position, and so they often bring in an outside expert who is considered to be neutral. The supposedly objective views of the expert are then used to support the position of the coalition in power.

In some cases, however, the experts are not neutral at all but have been coached by the coalition in power and know exactly what the coalition's view is so that they can develop a favorable scenario. When this scenario is presented to the groups in conflict, the "objectivity" of the expert's plan is used to sway decision making in favor of the coalition in power. The opposition is outgunned and accepts the inevitable.

In sum, there are many tactics that individuals, managers, subunits, and coalitions can use to obtain power and play organizational politics. The success of attempts to influence and control decision making to resolve conflicts in a certain way depends on individuals' ability to learn the political ropes and hone their political skills.

The Costs and Benefits of Organizational Politics

Organizational politics is an integral part of decision making in an organization. Coalitions form to control the premises behind decision making, to lobby for their interests, and to resolve organizational conflict in their own favor. Because the stakes are high—the control of scarce resources like promotions and budgets—politics is a very active force in most organizations. When we look to see what strategy or structure an organization chooses, we need to recognize the role that politics plays in these choices. It can improve the choices and decisions that an organization makes, but it can also produce problems and promote conflict if it is not managed skillfully. If, for example, different coalitions continually fight about resource allocation decisions, more time is likely to be spent in making decisions than in implementing the decisions that are made. As a result, organizational effectiveness suffers.

To manage organizational politics and gain its benefits, an organization must establish a balance of power in which alternative views and solutions can be offered and considered by all parties and dissenting views can be heard (see Figure 14.5). It is also important for the balance of power to shift over time toward the party that can best manage the uncertainty and contingencies facing the organization. An organization that confers power on those who help it the most can take advantage of the political process to improve the quality of organizational decision making. By allowing managers to use their power to advance their future objectives, and to form coalitions that compete for support for their agendas, an organization can improve the quality of decision making by encouraging useful and productive debate about alternatives. Thus, politics can improve organizational effectiveness if it results in resource allocation decisions that produce more value.

FIGURE 14.5

Maintaining a Balance of Power

A. Power Balance. Decisions result from bargaining between subunits, which improves the quality of organizational decision making.

B. Power Imbalance. Decisions are made in the interests of one subunit. As a result, the quality of decision making may decline.

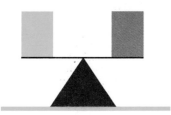

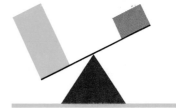

▢ Subunit A
▧ Subunit B

An organization's ability to obtain the benefits of politics depends on the assumption that power flows to those who can be of most help to the organization. This assumption means that unsuccessful managers lose power to successful managers and that there is a constant movement of power in the organization as an individual's or a group's power ebbs and flows. Suppose, however, that the top-management team in power becomes entrenched and is able to defend its power and property rights against its opponents even though the performance of the organization is faltering. Suppose a top-management team has institutionalized its power by occupying all important roles on organizational committees and by carefully selecting supporters for top organizational roles. Suppose the CEO occupies the role of board chair so that he or she can dominate the board of directors. In this situation, top management can use its power to fend off shareholders' attempts to restructure the organization to make better use of organizational resources. Similarly, top management, far from encouraging dissent among promising middle managers, might deny them promotion or decision-making power. By doing this, top management encourages the departure of those who threaten top management's dominant position. In this situation, the power that the top-management team has obtained as a result of its ability to control the distribution of property rights threatens organizational performance and survival.[46] Power holders are notoriously reluctant to give up the positions that give them the right to allocate resources and enrich themselves. CEOs in particular rarely give up their positions voluntarily, as the following example illustrates.

ORGANIZATIONAL INSIGHT

14.3 LIFE AT THE TOP

In the last decade, the number of CEOs who have been removed by coups by boards of directors has been steadily increasing. GM's Robert Stempel; Kenneth Olsen, founder and president of Digital Equipment; John Akers, CEO of IBM; James D. Robinson, CEO of American Express; Rod Canion and Edward Pfieffer, both CEOs of Compaq, as well as the former heads of Goodyear, Tenneco, and Hartmarx, have all been forced out by boards of directors annoyed at deteriorating performance and the slow rate of organizational change and restructuring.[47]

In all of these cases, the CEO and others on the top-management team had been reluctant to hand the reins of power over to others who might be better suited to lead company turnarounds. Although some part of their reluctance may have stemmed from their overestimation of their turnaround skills and abilities (the illusion-of-control bias, discussed in Chapter 12), most of their reluctance stemmed from unwillingness to give up their hold on the property rights that accompany high office in an organization. In addition to the control of monetary rewards that run into millions of dollars a year and stock options that run into millions more, many CEOs become used to the lifestyle at the top. Chauffeured cars, private planes, and company houses and ranches make the top-management team of large companies the aristocracy of the corporate class. No wonder they go to considerable lengths to preserve the power necessary to defend their property rights. For example, disgruntled shareholders of DWG Corporation recently took Victor Posner, the principal shareholder and chairman, to court to complain about his practice of giving himself a hefty salary, distributing outrageous bonuses (to himself and his family), and sticking the company with bills for his personal expenses.[48]

Because of such uses and abuses of organizational power, large institutional shareholders have called for changes in laws—changes that will increase shareholders' rights to monitor and discipline top managers. Traditionally, CEOs have picked the board directors, and staging a coup to remove the CEO has been difficult.[49] Now shareholders are beginning to demand a much greater say in the appointment of outside directors. Shareholders also want the organization's salary and rewards committee (which sets the salary of the CEO and other top managers) to be staffed by outside directors, who may be less inclined than insiders to reward poor performance or grant large stock options to managers of companies whose performance is declining. In these ways, stakeholders can create a more equitable balance of power at the top of the organization—one that prevents any stakeholder group from running the company in its own interests and allows power to flow to the individuals or subunits that can best manage the uncertainty the organization faces.

When the balance of power between stakeholders or subunits does not force the allocation of resources to where they can best create value, organizational effectiveness suffers. When powerful managers can suppress the views of those who oppose their interests, debate becomes restricted, checks and balances fade, bad conflict increases, and organizational inertia increases. Today in organizations, as we have seen, there is increasing support for measures that would increase the power of stakeholders to remove inefficient top-management teams and CEOs who pay themselves exorbitant salaries that often are not tied to organizational performance. Thus, ultimately, whether power and politics benefit or harm an organization is a function of the balance of power between organizational stakeholders.

Managerial Implications: Power and Politics

1. Recognize that politics is a fact of organizational life, and develop the skills to understand how politics shapes organizational decision making.

2. Develop a personal power base to influence decision making, and use it to prevent political managers or groups from pursuing their interests at the expense of organizational interests.

3. To obtain power, try to associate with powerful managers and find a powerful mentor, make yourself central and nonsubstitutable, develop personal skills so that you can reduce uncertainty for other subunits or for the organization, seek membership on committees that will give you access to information, and obtain control of organizational resources.

4. Seek to maintain a power balance between individuals or subunits in an organization in order to preserve the quality of organizational decision making.

SUMMARY

Managing conflict, power, and politics is one of an organization's major priorities because these factors determine which decisions the organization makes and, therefore, ultimately, its survival. Chapter 14 has made the following main points:

1. Organizational conflict is the clash that arises when the goal-directed behavior of one group blocks or thwarts the goals of another.

2. Conflict can be functional if it overcomes organizational inertia and brings about change. However, too high a level of conflict can reduce the level of coordination and integration between people and subunits and reduce organizational effectiveness.

3. The five stages of Pondy's model of organizational conflict are latent conflict, perceived conflict, felt conflict, manifest conflict, and the conflict aftermath.

4. There are five sources of conflict between subunits: interdependence, differences in goals and priorities, bureaucratic factors, incompatible performance criteria, and competition for scarce resources.

5. Conflict resolution strategies are used to manage organizational conflict and to prevent it from becoming destructive. Two important strategies are acting at the level of structure to change task relationships and acting at the level of attitudes and individuals to change the attitudes of the parties or the parties themselves.

6. Organizational power is the ability of one actor or stakeholder to overcome resistance by other actors and achieve a desired objective or result.

7. The main sources of power available to managers and subunits are authority, control over resources, control over information, nonsubstitutability, centrality, control over uncertainty or contingencies, and unobtrusive power.

8. Organizational politics comprises activities carried out within organizations to acquire, develop, and use power and other resources to obtain one's preferred outcomes.

9. Tactics that individuals and subunits can use to play politics include increasing indispensability, associating with powerful managers, building and managing coalitions, controlling the agenda, and bringing in an outside expert.

10. Using power to play organizational politics can improve the quality of decision making if the people who have the power are those who can best serve the needs of the organization. However, if top managers have the ability to control and hoard power and entrench themselves in the organization, the interests of other organizational stakeholders may be jeopardized as decisions are made to serve top management's personal interests. Thus, there needs to be a balance of power among organizational stakeholders.

DISCUSSION QUESTIONS

1. Why and under what conditions can conflict be good or bad for an organization? Would you expect a higher level of conflict in a mechanistic or an organic structure? Why?

2. You have been appointed to manage a large R&D laboratory. You find a high level of conflict among scientists in the unit. Why might this conflict be arising? How will you try to resolve it?

3. Why is it important to maintain a balance of power among different groups of organizational stakeholders?

4. What is unobtrusive power? Why is it so important?

5. How can the design of the organization's structure and culture give some subunits more power than others?

6. Discuss how you, as manager of the R&D function in a cosmetic products company, might try to increase your power and the power of your subunit to control more resources in a battle with marketing and manufacturing.

ORGANIZATIONAL THEORY IN ACTION

PRACTICING ORGANIZATIONAL THEORY: MANAGING CONFLICT

Form groups of three to five people and discuss the following scenario:

You are a group of top managers of a large, well-established pharmaceutical company that has made its name by pioneering innovative new drugs. Intense competition from other companies in the pharmaceutical industry, plus increasing government pressure to reduce the price of drugs, has put pressure on you to find ways to reduce costs and speed product development. In addition, the emergence of large health maintainance organizations (HMOs) and other large buyers of drugs has made marketing drugs much more difficult, and marketing managers are demanding an increased say in which drugs should be developed and when. To respond to these pressures, you have decided to create cross-functional teams composed of people from R&D, marketing, finance, and top management to evaluate the potential of new drug products and to decide if they should be pursued.

1. How will the change in structure affect the relative power of the different functions?
2. How likely is conflict to occur because of these changes, and what will be the source of the conflict?
3. What can you do to help manage the conflict process to make the new operating system work as you hope it will?

MAKING THE CONNECTION #14

Find an example of a conflict occurring between the managers, or between the managers and other stakeholders, of a company. What is the source of the conflict? How are managers using their power to influence the decision-making process?

Analyzing the Organization: Design Module #14

This module focuses on conflict, power, and politics in your organization.

ASSIGNMENT

1. What do you think are the likely sources of conflict that may arise in your organization? Is there a history of conflict among managers or among stakeholders?

2. Analyze the sources of power of the principal subunits, functions, or divisions in the organization. Which is the most central subunit? Which is the most nonsubstitutable subunit? Which one controls the most resources? Which one handles the main contingencies facing the organization?

3. Which subunit is the most powerful? Identify any ways in which the subunit has been able to influence decision making in its favor.

4. Describe any political contests that have taken place in the organization in recent years. Has organizational politics been used to resolve any conflicts among organizational stakeholders? If so, describe the incident.

5. Do you think that the organization has a political culture? Why or why not?

6. To what degree are the organization's strategic and operational decisions affected by conflict and politics?

Cases for Analysis:
MARTHA STEWART TAKES ON TIME

In the 1990s, Martha Stewart, the well-known interior decorator, gardener, and general "lifestyle expert," has been building an extensive empire of magazines, books, television shows, and videos to communicate her vision of the good life to the American public. Despite the fact that she created these various communications products, however, Martha Stewart Living Enterprises, which manages them, is a division of Time Warner Turner, the largest entertainment company in the world, and Martha Stewart is an employee of Time Warner Turner.

As the popularity of her entertainment franchise increased in the 1990s, Stewart began to demand more say in the running of the division and a greater share in its profits. At first, Time Warner executives were happy to give her most of what she wanted. Beyond her cash salary of $400,000 a year she receives extensive bonuses, a $40,000 clothing allowance, and a loan of $2 million to buy a vacation home in East Hampton, a fashionable Long Island, New York, retreat.[50] They also gave her creative control of her division and promised her a 15 percent equity stake in the business so that she could share in the profits as they grew during the 1990s.

These changes have not been sufficient to satisfy her demands for more power and control over the Martha Stewart division, however. Reportedly, she wants a 40 percent equity stake in the division and complete control over both creative content and the development and marketing of all future products from her division. In other words, she wants to run Martha Stewart Enterprises as if it were a totally self-contained division.

Her demands for more power over the division have brought her into conflict with the Time Warner executives who are responsible for overseeing its operations. These managers, who were not involved in the original negotiations, are much less willing to accede to her demands, believing that she has already been offered a fair share of the division's profits. Moreover, they note that she is also being paid lavishly through her salary and bonuses. Martha Stewart, on the other hand, argues that all the growth in the division has been the result of her efforts so she deserves a bigger share of the pie.[51]

In 1996, unable to get Time Warner's managers to agree to her demands, she began to threaten that she would move to another entertainment company and create a new Martha Stewart company. She contacted companies such as Conde Nast, the publisher of such magazines as *Gourmet* and *Conde Nast Traveler*, and began exploring the idea of moving her empire to these companies if Time Warner Turner would not give her what she wanted. These moves enraged Time Warner executives who felt that her new demands were outrageous. Continuing to put pressure on Time Warner, Stewart announced in the summer of 1996 that she was contemplating a leveraged buyout of the division in which she, with financial backers, would buy it from Time Warner and take it private. In 1999, Martha Stewart did take her company public in an IPO. Its share price doubled overnight and her activites now include magazines, books, a syndicated television show, a line of merchandise for the home, and an Internet site.[52]

1. What were the causes of conflict between Martha Stewart and Time?

2. How would you go about trying to resolve this conflict?

REFERENCES

1. T. Burns, "Micropolitics: Mechanism of Institutional Change," *Administrative Science Quarterly*, 1961, vol. 6, pp. 257–281.

2. J. G. March, "The Business Firm as a Coalition," *Journal of Politics*, 1962, vol. 24, pp. 662–678.

3. L. Coser, *The Functions of Social Conflict* (New York: The Free Press, 1956); S. P. Robbins, *Managing Organizational Conflict: A Non-Traditional Approach* (Englewood Cliffs, NJ: Prentice Hall, 1974).

4. J. McCann and J. R. Galbraith, "Interdepartmental Relationships," in P. C. Nystrom and W. H. Starbuck, eds., *Handbook of Organizational Design*, vol. 2 (New York: Oxford University Press, 1981), pp. 60–84.

5. A. C. Amason, "Distinguishing the Effects of Functional and Dysfunctional Conflict and Strategic Decision Making: Resolving a Paradox for Top Management Teams," *Academy of Management Review*, 1996, vol. 39, pp. 12–148.

6. The following discussion draws heavily on these sources: L. R. Pondy, "Organizational Conflict: Concepts and Models," *Administrative Science Quarterly*, 1967, vol. 2, pp. 296–320; R. E. Walton and J. M. Dutton, "The Management of Interdepartmental Conflict: A Model and Review," *Administrative Science Quarterly*, 1969, vol. 14, pp. 62–73.

7. J. D. Thompson, "Organizational Management of Conflict," *Administrative Science Quarterly*, 1960, vol. 4, pp. 389–409; K. Thomas, "Conflict and Conflict Management," in M. D. Dunnette, ed., *The Handbook of Industrial and Organizational Psychology* (Chicago: Rand McNally, 1976).

8. J. D. Thompson, *Organizations in Action* (New York: McGraw-Hill, 1967).

9. J. A. Litterer, "Conflict in Organizations: A Reexamination," *Academy of Management Journal*, 1966, vol. 9, pp. 178–186.

10. A. Miller, S. Nayyar, and S. Sevante, "Picture This Executive Battle," *Newsweek*, 10 May 1993, p. 54.

11. "Kodak Forms 15-member Senior Management Team," *Business Wire*, 14 October 1999.

12. M. Dalton, "Conflicts Between Staff and Line Managerial Officers," *American Sociological Review*, 1950, vol. 15, pp. 342–351.

13. P. R. Lawrence and J. R. Lorsch, *Organization and Environment* (Homewood, IL: Irwin, 1967).

14. "CS First Boston: All Together Now?" *The Economist*, 10 April 1993, p. 90.

15. M. Siconolfi, "CS First Boston's Hennessy to Relinquish Top Posts," *Wall Street Journal*, 3 July 1996, p. C1.

16. Coser, *The Functions of Social Conflict*.

17. R. H. Miles, *Macro Organizational Behavior* (Santa Monica, CA: Goodyear, 1980).

18. This discussion draws heavily on E. H. Nielsen, "Understanding and Managing Intergroup Conflict," in P. R. Lawrence, L. B. Barnes, and J. W. Lorsch, *Organizational Behavior and Administration* (Homewood, IL: Irwin, 1976).

19. Lawrence and Lorsch, *Organization and Environment*.

20. R. E. Walton and R. B. McKersie, *A Behavioral Theory of Labor Negotiations: An Analysis of a Social Interaction System* (New York: McGraw-Hill, 1965).

21. R. E. Walton, "Third-Party Roles in Interdepartmental Conflict," *Industrial Relations*, 1967, vol. 7, pp. 29–43.

22. W. G. Ouchi, *Theory Z: How American Business Can Meet the Japanese Challenge* (Reading, MA: Addison-Wesley, 1981).

23. R. M. Emerson, "Power-Dependence Relations," *American Sociological Review*, 1962, vol. 27, pp. 31–41; J. Pfeffer, *Power in Organizations* (Boston: Pitman, 1981).

24. R. A. Dahl, "The Concept of Power," *Behavioral Science*, 1957, vol. 2, pp. 210–215.

25. M. Gargiulo, "Two-Step Leverage: Managing Constraint in Organizational Politics," *Administrative Science Quarterly*, 1993, vol. 38, pp. 1–19.

26. M. Weber, *The Theory of Social and Economic Organization* (New York: The Free Press, 1947).

27. J. A. Conger and R. N. Kanungo, "The Empowerment Process: Integrating Theory and Practice," *Academy of Management Review*, 1988, vol. 13, pp. 471–481.

28. G. R. Salancik and J. Pfeffer, "The Bases and Uses of Power in Organizational Decision Making," *Administrative Science Quarterly*, 1974, vol. 19, pp. 453–473; J. Pfeffer and G. R. Salancik, *The External Control of Organizations: A Resource Dependence View* (New York: Harper and Row, 1978).

29. Salancik and Pfeffer, "The Bases and Uses of Power in Organizational Decision Making."

30. A. M. Pettigrew, "Information Control as a Power Resource," *Sociology*, 1972, vol. 6, pp. 187–204.

31. A. M. Pettigrew, *The Politics of Organizational Decision Making* (London: Tavistock, 1973), p. 191.

32. C. Perrow, *Organizational Analysis: A Sociological View* (Belmont, CA: Wadsworth, 1970).

33. D. Mechanic, "Sources of Power of Lower-Level Participants in Complex Organizations," *Administrative Science Quarterly*, 1962, vol. 7, pp. 349–364.

34. M. Crozier, *The Bureaucratic Phenomena* (Chicago: University of Chicago Press, 1964).

35. D. J. Hickson, C. R. Hinings, C. A. Lee, R. E. Schneck, and J. M. Pennings, "A Strategic Contingencies Theory of Intraorganizational Power," *Administrative Science Quarterly*, 1971, vol. 16, pp. 216–227.

36. Ibid.

37. Ibid.

38. Pfeffer, *Power in Organizations*, Ch. 3.

39. S. Lukes, *Power: A Radical View* (London: MacMillan, 1974).

40. Pfeffer, *Power in Organizations*, pp. 115–121.

41. Ibid., p. 7.

42. Hickson, Hinings, Lee, Schneck, and Pennings, "A Strategic Contingencies Theory of Intraorganizational Power."

43. E. E. Jennings, *The Mobile Manager* (New York: McGraw-Hill, 1967).

44. J. R. P. French, Jr., and B. Raven, "The Bases of Social Power," in D. Cartwright and A. F. Zander, eds., *Group Dynamics* (Evanston, IL: Row Peterson, 1960), pp. 607–623.

45. This discussion draws heavily on J. Pfeffer, *Power in Organizations*, Ch. 5.

46. O. E. Williamson and W. G. Ouchi, "The Markets and Hierarchies Program of Research: Origins, Implications, Prospects," in A. E. Van De Ven and W. F. Joyce, eds., *New Perspectives on Organizational Design and Behavior* (New York: Wiley, 1981), pp. 347–406.

47. S. Stewart, "The King Is Dead," *Fortune*, 11 January 1993, pp. 34–40.

48. "Is Victor Posner Off His Leash?" *Business Week*, 30 December 1991, p. 39.

49. A. Franham, "How to Stage a Coup," *Fortune*, 11 January 1993, p. 41.

50. P. M. Reilly, "The Best Revenge," *Wall Street Journal*, 19 April 1996, p. A1.

51. P. L. Brown, "For Martha-Holics, It's Marathon Season," *The New York Times*, 25 November 1995, p. C1.

52. K. Goff, "The Muscle Behind Martha," *The Ottawa Citizen*, 21 October 1999, p. 1.

CASE 1

United Products, Inc. ——————————— JEFFREY C. SHUMAN

Having just returned from lunch, George Brown, president of United Products, Inc., was sitting in his office thinking about his upcoming winter vacation—in a few days, he and his family would be leaving from Boston to spend three weeks skiing on Europe's finest slopes. His daydreaming was interrupted by a telephone call from Hank Stevens, UPI's general manager. Mr. Stevens wanted to know if their two o'clock meeting was still on. The meeting had been scheduled to review actions UPI could take in light of the company's sluggish sales and the currently depressed national economy. In addition, Brown and Stevens were to go over the financial results for the company's recently completed fiscal year—they had just been received from UPI's auditors. Although it had not been a bad year, results were not as good as expected, and this, in conjunction with the economic situation, had prompted Mr. Brown to reappraise the plans he had for the company for the upcoming year.

COMPANY HISTORY

United Products, Inc., established in 1941, was engaged in the sales and service of basic supply items for shipping and receiving, production and packaging, research and development, and office and warehouse departments. Mr. Brown's father, the founder of the company, recognized the tax advantages in establishing separate businesses rather than trying to consolidate all of his operations in one large organization. Accordingly, over the years, the elder Mr. Brown had created new companies and either closed down or sold off older companies as business conditions seemed to warrant. As of the mid-1960s, his holdings consisted of a chain of four related sales distribution companies covering the geographic area from Chicago eastward.

In 1967, feeling it was time to step aside and turn over active control of the business to his sons, the elder Mr. Brown recapitalized and restructured his companies, merging some and disposing of others. When the restructuring process was completed, he had set up two major companies. United Products, Inc., was to be run by his youngest son, George Brown, with its headquarters in Massachusetts, while his other son, Richard Brown, was to operate United Products Southeast, Inc., headquartered in Florida.

Although the Brown brothers occasionally worked together and were on each other's board of directors, the two companies operated on their own. As George Brown explained, "Since we are brothers, we often get together and discuss business, but the two are separate companies and each files its own tax return."

During 1972, United Products moved into new facilities in Woburn, Massachusetts. From this location it was thought that the company would be able to serve its entire New England market area effectively. "Our abilities and our desires to expand and improve our overall operation will be enhanced in the new specially designed structure containing our offices, repair facilities, and warehouse," is how George Brown viewed the role of the new facilities. Concurrent with the move, the company segmented the more than 3500 different items it carried into eight major product categories:

1. Stapling machines. Manual and powered wire stitchers, carton stitchers, nailers, hammers, and tackers
2. Staples. All sizes and types (steel, bronze, monel, stainless steel, aluminum, brass, etc.) to fit almost all makes of equipment
3. Stenciling equipment and supplies. Featuring Marsh hand and electric machines, stencil brushes, boards, and inks
4. Gummed tape machines. Hand and electric, featuring Marsh, Derby, and Counterboy equipment
5. Industrial tapes. Specializing in strapping, masking, cellophane, electrical, cloth, nylon, and waterproof tapes made by 3M, Mystik, Behr Manning, and Dymo
6. Gluing machines. Hand and electric
7. Work gloves. All sizes and types (cotton, leather, neoprene, nylon, rubber, asbestos, and so on)
8. Marking and labeling equipment

In a flyer mailed to United Products' 6000 accounts announcing the move to its new facilities, the company talked about its growth in this fashion:

Jeffrey C. Shuman, Ph.D., Associate Professor of Management, Bentley College, Waltham, MA. Reprinted with permission.

	11/30/71	11/30/72	11/30/73
Current assets	$ 862,783	$ 689,024	$ 937,793
Other assets	204,566	774,571	750,646
Current liabilities	381,465	223,004	342,939
Net worth	685,884	750,446	873,954
Sales	n.a.*	2,830,000	3,450,000

Statement of financial condition, November 30, 1973:

Cash on hand	$ 46,961	Accounts payable	$ 321,885
Accounts receivable	535,714	Notes payable	20,993
Merchandise in inventory	352,136		
Prepaid insurance, interest, taxes	2,980		
Current assets	$ 937,791	Current liabilities	$ 342,878
Fixtures and equipment	$ 42,891	Retained earnings	$ 471,655
Motor vehicles	49,037	Capital stock	519,800
Land and buildings	658,768	Surplus	354,154
Total assets	$ 1,688,487	Total liabilities	$ 1,688,487

* n.a.: Not available.

EXHIBIT 1   Selected Financial Information, United Products, Inc.

Here we grow again—thanks to you—our many long-time valued customers ....

Time and circumstances have decreed another United Products transPLANT—this time, to an unpolluted garden-type industrial area, ideally located for an ever-increasing list of our customers. Now, in the new 28,000-square-foot plant with enlarged offices and warehouse, we at UNITED PRODUCTS reach the peak of efficiency in offering our customers the combined benefits of maximum inventories, accelerated deliveries, and better repair services.

By 1974, the company had grown to a point where sales were $3.5 million (double that of four years earlier) and 34 people were employed. Results for 1973 compared to 1972 showed a sales increase of 22 percent and a 40 percent gain in profits. Exhibit 1 contains selected financial figures for 1971, 1972, and 1973, in addition to the fiscal 1973 balance sheet.

COMPETITION

George Brown indicated that UPI does not have clearly defined rivals against whom it competes head-on with respect to all of its 3,500-plus items:

> It is hard to get figures on competition, since we compete with no one company directly. Different distributors carry lines that compete with various of our product lines, but there is no one company that competes against us across our full range of products.

On a regular basis, Mr. Brown receives Dun & Bradstreet's Business Information Reports on specific firms with which he competes. Mr. Brown feels that since the rival firms are, like his own firm, privately held, the financial figures reported are easily manipulated and therefore are not a sound basis on which to devise strategies and plans. Exhibit 2 contains comparative financial figures for two competing companies, and Exhibit 3

	East Coast Supply Co., Inc.—Sales $1 Million		
	Fiscal December 31, 1971	Fiscal December 31, 1972	Fiscal December 31, 1973
Current assets	$ 88,555	$ 132,354	$ 163,953
Other assets	16,082	18,045	27,422
Current liabilities	41,472	47,606	74,582
Net worth	63,165	102,793	116,793

Statement of financial condition, December 31, 1973:

Cash	$ 42,948	Accounts payable	$ 39,195
Accounts receivable	86,123	Notes payable	27,588
Merchandise in inventory	34,882	Taxes	7,799
Current assets	$ 163,953	Current liabilities	$ 74,582
Fixtures and equipment	$ 15,211	Capital stock	$ 10,000
Deposits	12,211	Retained earnings	106,793
Total assets	$ 191,375	Total liabilities and net worth	191,375

	Atlantic Paper Products, Inc.—Sales $6 Million		
	June 30, 1970	June 30, 1971	June 30, 1972
Current assets	$884,746	$1,243,259	$1,484,450
Other assets	93,755	101,974	107,001
Current liabilities	574,855	520,572	1,120,036
Net worth	403,646	439,677	471,415
Long-term debt	0	384,984	

EXHIBIT 2   Financial Information on Rival Firms

contains D&Bs description of their operations, along with D&B's comments about two other firms operating in UPI's New England market area.

MANAGEMENT PHILOSOPHY

When Mr. Brown took over UPI in 1967 at the age of 24, he set a personal goal of becoming financially secure and developing a highly profitable business. With the rapid growth of the company, he soon realized his goal of financial independence and in so doing began to lose interest in the company. "I became a rich person at age 28 and had few friends with equal wealth who were my age. The business no longer presented a challenge, and I was unhappy with the way things were going."

After taking a ten-month "mental vacation" from the business, George Brown felt he was ready to return to work. He had concluded that one way of proving himself to himself and satisfying his ego would be to make the company as profitable as possible. However, according

East Coast Supply Co., Inc.
Manufactures and distributes pressure-sensitive tapes to industrial users throughout New England area on 1/10 net 30-day terms. Thirty-four employed including the officers, 33 here. Location: Rents 15,000 square feet on first floor of two-story building in good repair. Premises are orderly. Nonseasonal business. Branches are located at 80 Olife Street, New Haven, Connecticut, and 86 Weybosset Street, Providence, Rhode Island.
Atlantic Paper Products, Inc.
Wholesales paper products, pressure-sensitive tapes, paper specialties, twines, and other merchandise of this type. Sales to industrial accounts and commercial users on 1/10 net 30-day terms. There are about 1,000 accounts in eastern Massachusetts, and sales are fairly steady throughout the year. Employs 60, including officers. Location: Rents 130,000 square feet of floor space in a six-story brick, mill-type building in a commercial area on a principal street. Premises orderly.
The Johnson Sales Co.
Wholesales shipping room supplies, including staplings and packing devices, marking and stencil equipment. Sells to industrial and commercial accounts throughout the New England area. Seasons are steady. Terms are 1/10 net 30 days. Number of accounts not learned; 15 are employed including the owner. Location: Rents the first floor of a two-story yellow brick building in good condition. Housekeeping is good.
Big City Staple Corp.
Wholesales industrial staples, with sales to 2,000 industrial and commercial firms, on 1/10 net 30-day terms. Territory mainly New Jersey. Employs ten including the officers. Seasons steady and competition active. Location: Rents 5,000 square feet in one-story cinder block and brick structure in good condition; premises in neat order. Located on well-traveled street in a commercial area.

EXHIBIT 3   Descriptions of Major Competitors

to Mr. Brown, "The company can only grow at approximately 20 percent per year, since this is the amount of energy I am willing to commit to the business."

In 1974, at age 31, Mr. Brown described his philosophical outlook as "very conservative" and surmised that he ran UPI in much the same way as his 65-year-old father would have. In describing his managerial philosophy and some of the operating policies he had established, he said:

> I am very concerned about making UPI a nice place to work. I have to enjoy what I'm doing and have fun at it at the same time. I cannot make any more money, since I'm putting away as much money as I can. The government won't allow me to make more money, since I already take the maximum amount.
>
> I like to feel comfortable, and if we grow too quickly, it could get out of hand. I realize that the business won't grow to its potential, but why should I put more into it? ... The company could grow, but why grow? Why is progress good? You have to pay for everything in life, and I'm not willing to work harder....
>
> Another thing ... I am a scrupulously honest businessman, and it is very hard to grow large if you're honest. There are many deals

> that I could get into that would make UPI a lot of money, but I'm too moral a person to get involved ....
>
> To me, happiness is being satisfied with what you have. I've got my wife, children, and health. Why risk these for something I don't need? I don't have the desire to make money, because I didn't come from a poor family; I'm not hungry.
>
> I have never liked the feeling of owing anything to anyone. If you can't afford to buy something, then don't. I don't like to borrow any money and I don't like the company to borrow any. All of our bills are paid within fifteen days. I suppose I've constrained the business as a result of this feeling, but it's my business. The company can only afford to pay for a 20-percent growth rate, so that's all we'll grow.

ORGANIZATIONAL STRUCTURE

Upon returning to the company from his "mental vacation" in 1971, George Brown realigned UPI's organizational structure as shown in Exhibit 4 (the company does not have a formal organizational chart; this one is drawn from the case researcher's notes). With

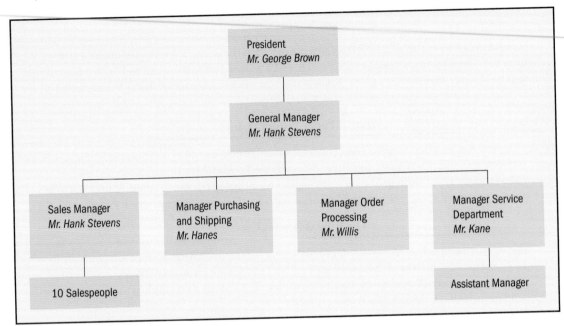

EXHIBIT 4 UPI Organization Chart, December 1974

respect to the way his company was organized, he remarked:

> We have to have it on a functional basis now. We are also trying something new for us by moving to the general manager concept. In the past when I was away, there was no one with complete authority; now my general manager is in charge in my absence.

In discussing the new structuring of the organization, Mr. Brown was quick to point out that the company had not established formalized job descriptions. "Job descriptions are not worth anything. My people wear too many hats, and besides, we're too small to put it in writing." At present the company employs thirty-four people, including Mr. Brown.

Mr. Brown is quick to point out that he has never had a personnel problem. "All my people enjoy working here." He believes that "nobody should work for nothing" and has therefore established a personal goal of seeing to it that no one employed by UPI makes less than $ 10,000 per year. Mr. Brown commented on his attitude toward his employees:

> The men might complain about the amount of responsibility placed on them, but I think it's good for them. It helps them develop to their potential. I'm a nice guy who is interested in all of my people. I feel a strong social obligation to my employees and have developed very close relationships with all of them. My door is always open to them no matter what the problem may be. I make it a policy never to yell at anyone in public; it's not good for morale. Maybe it's part of my conservative philosophy, but I

want everyone to call me Mr Brown, not George. I think it's good for people to have a Mr Brown. Although I want to run a nice friendly business, I have learned that it's hard to be real friends with an employee. You can only go so far. Employers and employees cannot mix socially; it just doesn't work out over the long run.

This is not your normal business. I am very approachable; I don't demand much and I allow an easy, open dialogue with my employees. Seldom do I take any punitive action. I'm just not a hard-driving tough guy .... I'm an easygoing guy.

It would take much of the enjoyment out of the business for me to come in here and run this place like a machine.[1]

I find it hard to motivate the company's salespeople. Since we have so much trouble finding good, capable people, I'm not likely to fire any that I have. This situation makes it hard for me to put pressure on them to produce.

The bonus system, if you want to call it that, is, I guess, what you'd call very arbitrary. I have not set up specific sales quotas, or targeted goals for my inside people, so, as a result, I base my bonus decisions on my assessment of how well I feel an employee performed during the past year.

Recently, I've given some thought to selling the company. I could probably get around $3–$4 million for it. If I did that, I'm not sure what I would do with my time. Besides my family and UPI, there is not much that I am interested in. A couple of years ago, when I took my extended vacation, I got bored and couldn't wait to get back to the company.

---

[1] *When the case researcher arrived at the plant one afternoon, he observed Mr. Brown running around the office deeply involved in a water fight with one of his office girls. By the way, he lost.*

UPI'S PLANNING PROCESS

George Brown claims to be a firm believer in planning. "I find myself spending more and more time planning for the company. Currently, I'm averaging about 50 percent of my time and I see this increasing." As he described it, the planning process at United Products is really a very loose system:

> We have no set way as to how we do the planning. Basically, the process is directed at ways of increasing the profitability of the company. I look at the salespeople's performance on a weekly and monthly basis and use this information in the development of the plans. Since we have a very informal planning process, we only forecast out one year at most. The company's plans are reevaluated each month and, if necessary, new plans are set. Only on rare occasions have we ever planned beyond one year. However, I think the current economic and political situation may force us to develop plans that cover a two-year period.
>
> I am familiar with commonly accepted theory about planning systems, but I do not feel it is necessary for UPI to institute, in a formal manner, any of those I've read about. We perform many of the activities advocated in the planning models, but we do them in a relaxed, casual fashion. For example, I am a member of many organizations connected with my business and receive industry newsletters on a regular basis. In addition, I receive input from friends and business associates both inside and outside my line of business. Since we do not have a formal process, planning tends to be a continuous process at UPI.

Although goals are not formally developed and written down, Mr. Brown said he established targets for the company to achieve in the areas of sales, profits, and organizational climate:

1. Increase sales volume by 20 percent per year.
2. Increase gross profit margin 0.5 to 1 percent per year.
3. Make UPI a friendly place to work.

Mr. Brown feels that the company has been able to grow at about 20 percent a year in the past and should be able to realize that level in the future. In addition, he believes that sales growth is a necessary evil: "Those companies that don't grow are swallowed up by the competition, and besides, given the amount of energy I'm willing to exert, I think 20 percent is a reasonable level of growth."

In the area of profits, the company actually sets no specific targeted figures other than simply an increase in the gross profit margin (as already stated). Mr. Brown observed:

> We do not set a goal because we would not have a way of measuring it. I have no way of knowing how much money I am mak-

ing until the end of the year, without spending considerable time and effort.

When asked about UPI's strengths and weaknesses, Mr. Brown indicated that the company had four areas of strength:

1. The number of different products carried.
2. The quality of its employees, particularly salespeople.
3. The absence of any debt.
4. Purchasing capabilities.

The major weakness he viewed was an inability to get and train new personnel—primarily in the area of sales.

SALES FORCE

UPI's salespeople are not assigned a sales quota for the year, but rather are evaluated based on Mr. Brown's assessment of the particular salesperson's territory and initiative. He feels his salespeople make more than those of his competitors. Several of UPI's ten salespeople have earned as much as $40,000 in a single year. All salespeople are compensated on a straight, sliding-scale, commission basis calculated as follows:

> 8 percent for the first $180,000 in sales
> 7 percent for the next $60,000
> 6 percent for the next $60,000
> 5 percent for all sales over $300,000

Mr. Brown is pleased with the sales success of his company and feels that United Products' greatest strength is its ability to "sell anything to anybody." Still, he perceives UPI's main problem as finding good salespeople. "There just aren't good salespeople around and this is a problem because salespeople are the lifeblood of our business."

UPI'S MANAGEMENT TEAM

At the time of the company's reorganization, Hank Stevens was brought in as general manager and assistant to the president. Over the past several years, Mr. Stevens's areas of responsibility have grown to an extent where they now comprise approximately 80 percent of the activities that were formerly done by Mr. Brown. As a result, George Brown sometimes finds himself with little to do and often works only five hours per day. As he described it:

> Hank's discretionary power has increased steadily since he arrived here—partly as a result of the extent of responsibility I've placed on him and partly due to his aggressiveness. As it now stands, he makes almost all of the daily operating decisions for the company, leaving me with only the top-management decisions. Let's be

realistic … there just aren't that many top-management decisions that have to be made here in the course of a day. A lot of the time, I walk around the plant checking on what other people are doing and, I guess, acting as a morale booster.

When asked about the management capabilities of Hank Stevens, Mr. Brown responded by saying, "Hank probably feels that he is working at a very fast pace, but when you evaluate the effectiveness of his actions, he is actually moving forward at what I would consider to be a very slow pace. However, everything else considered, Hank is the best of what is around. I guess if I could find a really good sales manager, I would add him to the company and relieve Hank of that area of responsibility."

Hank Stevens

Hank Stevens, 32, joined UPI at the time of the reorganization in 1970 after having graduated from a local university with a B.S. in economics. As general manager, Mr. Stevens's responsibilities include planning, purchasing, and sales management, as well as involvement in other decisions that affect UPI's policies. Mr. Stevens feels that he has been fortunate in that "ever since I came to UPI, I've reported to the president and in essence have had everyone else reporting to me."

When asked about the goals of UPI, Mr. Stevens responded, "As I see it, we have goals in three major areas: profitability, sales level, and personal relationships." In discussing his own personal goals, Hank explained that he hoped the organization would grow and that, as a result, he would be able to grow along with it. Since Mr. Stevens works so closely with Mr. Brown, he has given considerable thought to his boss's business philosophy:

> I feel that George's business philosophy is unique. I guess the best way to describe it is to say that above all he is a businessman. Also, he has very high moral values and as a result of that he is extremely honest and would never cheat anybody. Actually, the company would probably look better financially if it was run by someone who didn't operate with the same values as George.

When asked about the sales force at UPI, Mr. Stevens commented, "When a new salesman starts with the company, he does so with full salary. After a period of about two years, we change him over to a commission basis." As has always been the case, UPI concentrated its sales efforts on large customers. Mr. Stevens noted that "on the average the company processes approximately 105 orders per day, with an average dollar value per order of roughly $132. It's not that we won't write small orders, we just don't solicit business from small accounts. It just makes more sense to concentrate on the larger accounts."

Jim Hanes

Jim Hanes, 24, has been with UPI for over six years and during that time has worked his way up from assistant service manager to his current position as the number-three man in the company—manager of purchasing and shipping. Jim is responsible for the front office, repair work, and the warehouse. He feels that his reporting responsibility is approximately 60 percent to Mr. Stevens and 40 percent to Mr. Brown. "Since I have responsibility for all merchandise entering and leaving the company, I get involved with both Hank and George, and therefore I guess I report to both of them."

In talking about where he would go from his present position, he explained:

> I guess the next step is for me to become a salesman so that I can broaden my background and move up in the company. However I am a little worried; I don't think the salespeople in our company are given the right sales training. As the system works now, a new salesman is assigned to work with an experienced salesperson for about six weeks—after which time he is given his own territory. Perhaps if our sales manager had had more experience as a salesman, he would handle the training differently.

In commenting on his understanding of Mr. Brown's philosophy, Jim summed up his position: "George is a very open person. I think he is too honest for a businessman. He certainly gives his people responsibility. He gives you the ball and lets you run with it. I don't think enough planning is done at UPI. At most, it appears that we look ahead one year, and even then what plans are developed are kept very flexible."

UPI'S CORPORATE STRATEGY

When asked about UPI's current strategy, Mr. Brown responded that "the company is presently a distributor in the industrial packaging equipment, shipping supplies, and heavy-duty stapling equipment business. In the past when we've wanted to grow, we have either added new lines of merchandise or added more salespeople, or both. For example, this past year I got the idea to create what I call a contract sales department. It is a simple concept. I took one man, put him in an office with a telephone and a listing of the Fortune top 1000 companies, and told him to call and get new business. You would be surprised at how easy it was to pick up new accounts."

Mr. Stevens looks at UPI as being in the distribution and shipping of packaging supplies business. "In order for UPI to reach the goals that have been set, we have to sell more products. That is, we can grow by adding new salespeople, adding more product lines, purchasing more effectively, and undertaking more aggressive sales promotion."

Mr. Brown believes that UPI should try to maximize the profit on every item sold. To do this the company tries to set its prices at a level that is approximately 10 percent above the competition. Mr. Brown explained his pricing philosophy:

> I don't understand why people are afraid to raise prices. If you increase the price, you will pick up more business and make more money. That allows you to keep the volume low and still make more money. In addition, although the customer may pay more, he gets more. The higher price allows me to provide top-notch service to all my customers.

In his view, UPI is an innovative company. "Until very recently we were always innovating with new products and new applications. Now I think it's again time that we started to look for additional new and exciting products."

Brown was aware that UPI's strategic emphasis on service, together with his business philosophy, had resulted in UPI's organization being larger than it had to be, given the level of business. Mr. Brown explained the reasoning behind this condition. "I know the organization is bigger than it has to be. We could probably handle three times the present volume of business with our present staff and facility. I think it's because of my conservative attitude: I've always wanted the organization to stay a step ahead of what is really needed. I feel comfortable with a built-in backup system and therefore I am willing to pay for it."

In December 1974, Mr. Brown talked optimistically about the future. He felt that sales should reach the $6–$7 million range by 1978. "Looked at in another way, we should be able to grow at 20–25 percent per year without any particular effort." He went on to say:

> I want to grow and therefore I am making a concerted effort. I am constantly looking for possible merger avenues or expansion possibilities. I do not want to expand geographically. I would rather control that market area we are now in.
>
> I recently sent a letter to all competitors in New England offering to buy them out. Believe it or not, no one responded.
>
> I do not see any problems in the future. The history has been good; therefore, why won't it continue to be?
>
> Growth is easy. All I have to do is pick up a new line and I've automatically increased sales and profits. Basically we are distributors, and we operate as middlemen between the manufacturers and users. In light of what has been happening in the market, I feel that supply and demand will continue to be a problem. Therefore, I am giving serious thought to integrating vertically and becoming a manufacturer. This will guarantee our supply.[2]

> Actually, I don't want to do the manufacturing. I think it would be better if I bought the manufacturing equipment and then had someone else use it to make my products.

THE FUTURE

Nevertheless, after reviewing with his accountant the results for the just-completed fiscal year, Mr. Brown was concerned about UPI's future course. "I know changes have to be made for next year as a result of this year, but I'm not sure what they should be." Mr. Brown continued:

> I think this next year is going to be a real bad year. Prices will probably fall like a rock from the levels they reached during 1974 and as a result those items that would have been profitable for the company aren't going to be, and we have much too large an inventory as it is. It isn't easy to take away customers from the competition. As a result of this, I feel we have to step up our efforts to get new lines and new accounts. Recently, I've given some thought to laying off one or two people for economic reasons, but I'm not sure. I will probably give raises to all employees even though it's not a good business decision, but it's an ingrained part of my business philosophy.

When asked if he had informed his employees of his concern about the future, Mr. Brown referred to the minutes of a sales meeting that had been held in November 1974:

> … Mr. Brown then presided at the meeting, and announced that Al King had won the coveted "Salesman of the Month" award. This was a "first" for our Al, and well deserved for his outstanding sales results in October. Congratulations and applause were extended to him by all present. The balance of the meeting was then spent in a lengthy, detailed discussion, led by Mr. George Brown, of the general, overall picture of what the future portends in the sales area as a result of the current inflationary, recessionary, and complex competitive conditions prevailing in the economy.

The gist of the entire discussion can be best summarized as follows:

1. Everyone present must recognize the very real difficulties that lie ahead in these precarious economic times.
2. The only steps available to the salespeople and to the company for survival during the rough period ahead are as follows:
   a. Minimize contacts with existing accounts.
   b. Spend the majority of time developing new accounts on the less competitive products, and selling new products to established accounts.

---

[2] *Refer to Exhibit 5, which contains minutes of a United Products sales meeting held at the end of 1973.*

Mr. Brown presided at the meeting. His opening remarks highlighted the extraordinary times our country and our company are going through as far as the general economy and the energy crisis are concerned, and the extraordinary effects of these unusual crises on people and businesses, including our company and our sources of supply.

He thanked all present for the many thoughtful, considered, and excellent suggestions that they had offered in writing as to how the salespeople and their company might best handle the gasoline crisis without incurring an undue loss of sales and profits, and still maintain the high standards of service to which UNITED PRODUCTS' thousands of satisfied customers are accustomed.

The whole situation, according to Mr. Brown, boils down to a question of supply and prices. Mr. Brown reported that on his recent trip to the Orient, there were very few companies that wanted to sell their merchandise to us—rather, THEY WANTED TO BUY FROM US MANY OF THE ITEMS WE NORMALLY BUY FROM FOREIGN COMPANIES, i.e., carton-closing staples, tape, gloves, et cetera . . . and at inflated prices!!! The Tokyo, Japan, market is so great that they are using up everything they can produce—and the steel companies would rather make flat steel than the steel rods that are used for making staples. A very serious problem exists, as a result, in the carton-closing staple field not only in Japan, but also in Europe and America.

Mr. Brown advised that every year the company's costs of operating increase just as each individual's cost of living goes up and up yearly. Additional personnel, increased group and auto insurance premiums, increased Social Security payments, new office equipment and supplies, new catalogues, "Beeper system" for more salespeople—all of these costs accumulate and result in large expenditures of money. Manufacturers cover their increased operating costs by pricing their products higher—but to date, UNITED PRODUCTS has never put into their prices the increased costs resulting from increased operating expenses. Last year, the 3 percent increase that the company needed then was put into effect by many of you. HOWEVER, in order for the company to realize that additional profit, this 3 percent price increase had to be put into effect ACROSS THE BOARD . . . all customers . . . all items!

That Did Not Happen!!!

Mr. Brown advised that UNITED PRODUCTS got LAMBASTED when all of the sources of supply started to increase their prices. When SPOTNAILS, for example, went up 10 percent, the salespeople only increased their prices 7 percent. We did *not get the 3 percent price increase above the manufacturers' price increase*—and we needed it then and need it even more NOW.

Eliminating the possibility of cutting commissions, there are three possible solutions for the problem and how to get this much needed and ABSOLUTELY IMPERATIVE additional 3 percent PRICE INCREASE ACROSS THE BOARD to cover the constantly growing operating costs for running a successful, progressive-minded and growing business whose high standards of service and performance are highly regarded by customers and sources of supply alike, namely:

a. A 3 percent increase on all items to all customers across the board

b. A surcharge on all invoices or decrease in discounts allowed off LIST

c. A GCI charge (government cost increase) on all invoices

Considerable discussion regarding these three possibilities resulted in the following conclusions concerning the best method for obtaining this special 3 percent ACROSS THE BOARD PRICE INCREASE, as follows:

a. A new PRICE BOOK should be issued with all new prices to reflect not only the manufacturers' new increased prices, but in addition the 3 percent UNITED PRODUCTS PRICE INCREASE. All of the salespeople agreed that it would be easier to effect the additional 3 percent price increase if the 3 percent was "built in" on their price book sheets.

b. This new PRICE BOOK will be set up in such a way that prices will be stipulated according to quantity of item purchased . . . with no variances allowed. WITH NO EXCEPTIONS, the price of any item will depend on the quantity a customer buys.

c. Some items will continue to be handled on a discount basis—but lower discounts in order to ascertain that UNITED PRODUCTS is getting its 3 percent price increase.

d. Until these new PRICE BOOKS are issued, all salespeople were instructed to proceed IMMEDIATELY to effect these 3 percent price increases.

EXHIBIT 5 Minutes of UPI's Sales Meeting, December 5, 1973

Ten New Accounts Contest

Seven of our ten salespeople won a calculator as a result of opening up 10 new accounts each ... a total of 70 NEW ACCOUNTS for our company!!! However, both Mr. Brown and Mr. Stevens confessed that the dollar volume amount stipulated in the contest had been set ridiculously low, as a "feeler" to determine the success and effectiveness of such a contest. All the salespeople voiced their approval of all of the contests offered to them—and agreed that they had enjoyed many excellent opportunities of increasing their personal exchequers.

New Customer Letters

Mr. Brown again reminded all present that we have an excellent printed letter, which is available for sending to every new customer—and urged all to take advantage of this service by the office personnel by clearly indicating on their sales and order slips "NEW CUSTOMER." The procedure is but another step towards our goal of becoming more and more professional in our approach with our customers.

New Catalogs

Mr. Brown advised that by the first of the new year, hopefully, all our hard-cover catalogues with their new divider breakdowns will be ready for hand-delivering to large accounts. These catalogues cost the company over $5 and should only be distributed by hand to those customers who can and will make intelligent and effective use of them.

Excessive Issuance of Credits

As a result of a detailed study made by Mr. Brown of the nature and reasons for the ever-increasing number of credits being issued, he instructed all of the salespeople to follow these procedures when requesting the issuing of CREDITS:

a. Issue the CREDIT at the right time.

b. Do not sell an item where it is not needed.

c. NEVER PUT "NO COMMENT" for the reason why merchandise is being returned. EVERY CREDIT MUST HAVE A REASON FOR ITS ISSUANCE.

The ever-increasing number of CREDITS being issued is extremely costly to the company: (1) new merchandise comes back 90-plus days after it has been billed, and frequently, if not always, is returned by the customer FREIGHT COLLECT; (2) CREDIT 9-part forms, postage for mailing, and extra work for both the Bookkeeping and Billing and Order Processing Departments mean higher expenses for the Company. More intelligent, considered and selective selling, plus greater care on the part of the Order Processing personnel, according to Mr. Brown, could easily eliminate a large percentage of these CREDITS.

---

3. Concentrate on and promote our new items.

4. Mr. Brown and inside management are making and will continue to make every concerted effort to find new products and new lines for the coming year.

In preparation for his meeting with Hank Stevens, Mr. Brown had drawn up a list of activities to which Hank should address himself while running UPI during George's upcoming vacation. Mr. Brown believed that upon his return from Europe his activities at UPI would be increasing as a result of the problems caused by the uncertain economic conditions. The first item on the list was a possible redefinition of UPI's marketing strategy. Mr. Brown now believed that UPI would have

to be much more liberal with respect to new products considered for sale. "I'm not saying we are going to get into the consumer goods business, but I think we need to give consideration to handling consumer products that require no service and that carry a high-profit-margin factor for the company."

As he sat at his desk thinking about possible changes he could make in UPI's planning process, Mr. Brown was convinced that if he hadn't done some planning in the past, the situation would be more drastic than it was. Yet at the same time, he wasn't sure that a more structured and formalized planning process would put UPI in any better position to face the more difficult times that he saw ahead.

CASE 2

The Paradoxical Twins: Acme and Omega Electronics ——————— JOHN F. VEIGA

PART I

In 1955, Technological Products of Erie, Pennsylvania was bought out by a Cleveland manufacturer. The Cleveland firm had no interest in the electronics division of Technological Products and subsequently sold to different investors two plants that manufactured printed circuit boards. One of the plants, located in nearby Waterford, Pennsylvania, was renamed Acme Electronics, and the other plant, within the city limits of Erie, was renamed Omega Electronics, Inc. Acme retained its original management and upgraded its general manager to president. Omega hired a new president, who had been a director of a large electronics research laboratory, and upgraded several of the existing personnel within the plant.

Acme and Omega often competed for the same contracts. As subcontractors, both firms benefited from the electronics boom of the early 1960s and both looked forward to future growth and expansion. Acme had annual sales of $10 million and employed 550 people. Omega had annual sales of $8 million and employed 480 people. Acme was consistently more effective than Omega and regularly achieved greater net profits, much to the chagrin of Omega's management.

Inside Acme

The president of Acme, John Tyler, credited his firm's greater effectiveness to his managers' abilities to run a "tight ship." He explained that he had retained the basic structure developed by Technological Products because it was most efficient for high-volume manufacture of printed circuits and their subsequent assembly. Tyler was confident that had the demand not been so great, its competitor would not have survived. "In fact," he said, "we have been able to beat Omega regularly for the most profitable contracts, thereby increasing our profits." Acme's basic organization structure is shown in Exhibit 1. People were generally satisfied with their work at Acme; however, some of the managers voiced the desire to have a little more latitude in their jobs. One manager characterized the president as a "one-man band." He said, "While I respect John's ability, there are times when I wish I had a little more information about what is going on."

This case was developed from material gathered from the two firms by Dr. John F. Veiga. All names and places have been disguised.

Inside Omega

Omega's president, Jim Rawls, did not believe in organization charts. He felt that his organization had departments similar to Acme's, but he thought the plant was small enough that things such as organization charts just put artificial barriers between specialists who should be working together. Written memos were not allowed, since, as Jim expressed it, "the plant is small enough that if people want to communicate, they can just drop by and talk things over." Other members of Omega complained that too much time was wasted "filling in" people who could not contribute to the problem solving. As the head of the mechanical engineering department expressed it, "Jim spends too much of his time and mine making sure everyone understands what we're doing and listening to suggestions." A newer member of the industrial engineering department said, "When I first got here, I wasn't sure what I was supposed to do. One day I worked with some mechanical engineers and the next day I helped the shipping department design some packing cartons. The first months on the job were hectic, but at least I got a real feel for what makes Omega tick." Most decisions of any significance were made by the management team at Omega.

PART II

In 1966, the integrated circuits began to cut deeply into the demand for printed circuit boards. The integrated circuits (I.C.), or "chips," were the first step into microminiaturization in the electronics industry. Because the manufacturing process for I.C.'S was a closely guarded secret, both Acme and Omega realized the potential threat to their futures and both began to seek new customers aggressively. In July 1966, one of the major photocopy manufacturers was looking for a subcontractor to assemble the memory unit for its new experimental copier. The projected contract for the job was estimated to be $5–$7 million in annual sales. Both Acme and Omega were geographically close to this manufacturer and both had submitted highly competitive bids for the produc-

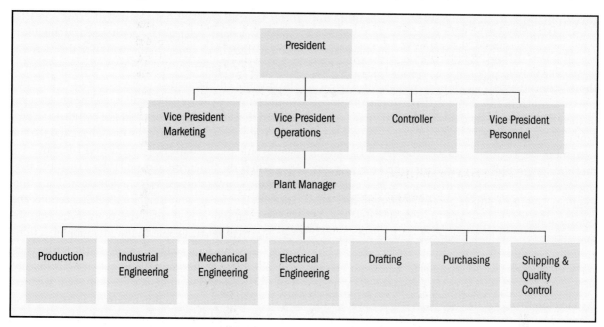

EXHIBIT 1   Acme Electronics Organization Chart

tion of one hundred prototypes. Acme's bid was slightly lower than Omega's; however, both firms were asked to produce one hundred units. The photocopy manufacturer told both firms that speed was critical because their president had boasted to other manufacturers that they would have a finished copier available by Christmas. This boast, much to the designer's dismay, required pressure on all subcontractors to begin prototype production before final design of the copier was complete. This meant that Acme and Omega would have at most two weeks to produce the prototypes or delay the final copier production.

PART III

Inside Acme

As soon as John Tyler was given the blueprints (Monday, July 11, 1966), he sent a memo to the purchasing department requesting them to move forward on the purchase of all necessary materials. At the same time, he sent the blueprints to the drafting department and asked that they prepare manufacturing prints. The industrial engineering department was told to begin methods design work for use by the production department foremen. Tyler also sent a memo to all department heads and executives indicating the critical time constraints of this job and how he expected everyone to perform as efficiently as they had in the past. On Wednesday, July 13, purchasing discovered that a particular component

used in the memory unit could not be purchased or shipped for two weeks because the manufacturer had shut down for summer vacations. The head of purchasing was not overly concerned by this obstacle, because he knew that Omega would face the same problem. He advised Tyler of this predicament, who in turn decided that Acme would build the memory unit except for the one component and then add that component in two weeks. Industrial engineering was told to build this constraint into their assembly methods. On Friday, July 15, industrial engineering notified Tyler that the missing component would substantially increase the assembly time if it was not available from the start of assembly. Mr. Tyler, anxious to get started, said that he would live with that problem and gave the signal to go forward on the assembly plans. Mechanical engineering received manufacturing prints on Tuesday, July 12, and evaluated their capabilities for making the chassis required for the memory unit. Because their procedure for prototypes was to get estimates from outside vendors on all sheet metal work before they authorized in-house personnel to do the job, the head of mechanical engineering sent a memo to the head of drafting requesting that vendor prints be drawn up on the chassis and that these prints then be forwarded to purchasing, which would obtain vendor bids. On Friday, July 15, Mr. Tyler called the head of mechanical engineering and asked for a progress report on the chassis. He was advised that mechanical engineering was waiting for vendor estimates before they moved forward.

Mr. Tyler was shocked by the lack of progress and demanded that mechanical engineering begin building those "damn chassis." On Monday, July 18, Mr. Tyler received word from the shipping department that most of the components had arrived. The first chassis were sent to the head of production, who began immediately to set up an assembly area. On Tuesday, July 19, two methods engineers from industrial engineering went out to the production floor to set up the methods to be used in assembly. In his haste to get things going, the production foreman ignored the normal procedure of contacting the methods engineers and set up what he thought would be an efficient assembly process. The methods engineers were very upset to see assembly begin before they had a chance to do a proper layout. They told the foreman they had spent the entire weekend analyzing the motions needed and that his process was very inefficient and not well balanced. The methods engineers ordered that work be stopped until they could rearrange the assembly process. The production foreman refused to stop work. He said, "I have to have these units produced by Friday and already I'm behind schedule."

The methods engineers reported back to the head of industrial engineering, who immediately complained to the plant manager. The plant manager sided with the production foreman and said, "John Tyler wants these units by Friday. Don't bother me with methods details now. Once we get the prototypes out and go into full production, then your boys can do their thing." As the head of industrial engineering got off the phone with the plant manager, he turned to his subordinates and said, "If my boss doesn't think our output is needed, to hell with him! You fellows must have other jobs to worry about, forget this one." As the two methods engineers left the head industrial engineer's office, one of them said to the other, "Just wait until they try to install those missing components. Without our methods, they'll have to tear down the units almost completely."

On Thursday, July 21, the final units were being assembled, although the process was delayed several times as production waited for chassis from mechanical engineering to be completed. On Friday, July 22, the last units were finished while John Tyler paced around the plant. Late that afternoon, Tyler received a phone call from the head designer of the photocopier manufacturer, who told Tyler that he had received a call on Wednesday from Jim Rawls of Omega. He explained that Rawls's boys had found an error in the design of the connector cable and had taken corrective action on their prototypes. He told

Tyler that he checked out the design error and that Omega was right. Tyler, a bit overwhelmed by this information, told the designer that he had all of the memory units ready for shipment and that as soon as they received the missing component, on Monday or Tuesday, they would be able to deliver the final units. The designer explained that the design error would be rectified in a new blueprint he was sending over by messenger and that he would hold Acme to the delivery date on Tuesday.

When the blueprint arrived, Tyler called the production foreman in to assess the damages. The alterations in the design would call for total disassembly and the unsoldering of several connections. Tyler told the foreman to put extra people on the alterations first thing on Monday morning and to try to finish the job by Tuesday. Late Tuesday afternoon the alterations were finished and the missing components were delivered. Wednesday morning, the production foreman discovered that the units would have to be torn apart again to install the missing components. When John Tyler was told this, he "hit the roof." He called industrial engineering and asked if they could help out. The head of industrial engineering told Tyler that his people would study the situation and get back to him first thing in the morning. Tyler decided to wait for their study because he was concerned that tearing apart the units again could weaken several of the soldered contacts and increase their potential rejection. Thursday, after several heated debates between the production foreman and the methods engineers, John Tyler settled the argument by ordering that all units be taken apart again and the missing component installed. He told shipping to prepare cartons for delivery on Friday afternoon. On Friday, July 29, fifty prototypes were shipped from Acme without final inspection. John Tyler was concerned about his firm's reputation, so he waived the final inspection after he personally tested one unit and found it operational. On Tuesday, August 2, Acme shipped the last fifty units.

Inside Omega

Jim Rawls called a meeting on Friday, July 8, that included department heads to tell them about the potential contract they were to receive. He told them that as soon as he received the blueprints, work could begin. On Monday, July 11, the prints arrived and again the department heads met to discuss the project. At the end of the meeting, drafting had agreed to prepare manufacturing prints while industrial engineering and production would begin methods design. On Wednesday, July 13, at a progress report session, purchasing indicated a particular component would not be available for two weeks, when the manufacturer reopened from summer vacation shutdown. The head of electrical engineering suggested using a possible substitute component, which was made in Japan, containing all of the necessary characteristics. The head of industrial engineering promised to have the methods engineers study the assembly methods to see if the unit could be produced in such a way that the missing component could be installed last.

The head of mechanical engineering raised the concern that the chassis would be an obstacle if they waited for vendor estimates and he advised the group that his people would begin production even though it might cost more. On Friday, July 15, at a progress report session, industrial engineering reported that the missing component would increase the assembly time substantially. The head of electrical engineering offered to have one of his engineers examine the missing component specifications and said he was confident that the Japanese component would work. At the end of the meeting, purchasing was told to order the Japanese components.

On Monday, July 18, a methods engineer and the production foreman formulated the assembly plans, and production was set to begin on Tuesday morning. On Monday afternoon, people from mechanical engineering, electrical engineering, production, and industrial engineering got together to produce a prototype just to ensure that there would be no snags in production. While they were building the unit, they discov-

ered an error in the connector cable design. All of the engineers agreed, after checking and rechecking the blueprints, that the cable was erroneously designed. People from mechanical engineering and electrical engineering spent Monday night redesigning the cable and on Tuesday morning, the drafting department finalized the changes in the manufacturing prints. On Tuesday morning, Jim Rawls was a bit apprehensive about the design changes and decided to get formal approval. Rawls received word on Wednesday from the head designer of the photocopier firm that he could proceed with the design changes as discussed on the phone. On Friday, July 22, the final units were inspected by quality control and were then shipped.

PART IV: RETROSPECT

Ten of Acme's final memory units were ultimately defective, while all of Omega's units passed the photocopier firm's tests. The photocopier firm was disappointed with Acme's delivery delay and incurred further delays in repairing the defective Acme units. However, rather than give the entire contract to one firm, the final contract was split between Acme and Omega, with two directives added: (1) Maintain zero defects and (2) reduce final cost. In 1967, through extensive cost-cutting efforts, Acme reduced its unit cost by 20 percent and was ultimately awarded the total contract.

CASE 3

Continental Can Company of Canada, Ltd. ———————— PAUL R. LAWRENCE

revised by John P. Kotter

By the fall of 1963, Continental Can Company of Canada had developed a sophisticated control system for use in its plants. This control system, begun in the years following World War II, stressed competition within the company as well as against other companies in the industry. Within its division at Continental, the can manufacturing plant at St. Laurent, Quebec, had become a preferred site for production management trainees as a result of its successful use of control systems. According to a division training executive:

The St. Laurent people look at the controls as tools. They show trainees that they really work. The French-Canadian atmosphere

is good too. In a French-Canadian family everything is open and aboveboard. There are no secrets. Trainees can ask anyone anything and the friendliness and company parties give them a feel for good employee relations.

PRODUCTS, TECHNOLOGY, AND MARKETS

Continental Can Company of Canada in 1963 operated a number of plants in Canada. The principal products of the St. Laurent plant were Open Top food cans, bottle caps and crowns, steel pails, and general line containers. Of these, Open Top cans constituted the largest group. They were manufactured for the major packers of vegetable products—peas, beans, corn, and tomatoes—and for the soup manufacturers. Beer and soft drink cans were a growing commodity, and large quantities of general line containers of many different configurations were produced to hold solvents, paints, lighter fluids, waxes, antifreeze, and so on. Several styles of steel pails of up to five-gallon capacity were also produced to hold many specialized products.

Most of the thousands of different products, varying in size, shape, color, and decoration, were produced to order. Typical lead times between the customer's order and shipment from the plant were two to three weeks in 1963, having been reduced from five and one-half weeks in the early 1950s, according to St. Laurent plant executives.

Quality inspection in the can manufacturing operation was critical, as the can maker usually supplied the closing equipment and assisted in or recommended the process to be used in the final packing procedure. In producing Open Top food cans, for example, the can body was formed, soldered, and flanged at speeds exceeding 400 cans per minute. After the bottom, or end unit, was assembled to the body, each can was air tested to reject poor double seams or poor soldering or plate inclusions that could cause pinholes. Both side seams and double seams underwent periodic destruction testing to ensure that assembly specifications were met. Although a number of measuring devices were used in the process, much of the inspection was still visual, involving human inspection and monitoring. The quality of the can also affected the filling and processing procedure: It had to withstand internal pressures from expansion of the product as it was heated, and then it had to sustain a vacuum without collapsing when it was cooled. Costly claims could result if the container failed in the field and the product had to be withdrawn from store shelves.

Almost all of the containers required protective coatings inside and out, and the majority were decorated. The coating and decorating equipment was sophisticated and required sizable investment. This part of the operation was unionized, and the lithographers, or pressmen, were among the highest paid of the various craftsmen in the plant.

"Continental Can Co." by Paul R. Lawrence. Copyright © 1977 by the President and Fellows of Harvard College. Harvard Business School case 478-017. This case prepared by C. Bourke under the direction of John P. Kotter, is based on a case originally written by Paul R. Lawrence. This case was prepared as the basis for class discussion rather than to illustrate either effective or ineffective handling of an administrative situation. Reprinted by permission of the Harvard Business School.

Most of the key equipment was designed and developed by the parent organization over many years. The St. Laurent plant spends substantial sums each year to modernize and renovate its equipment. Modernization and the implementation of new techniques to increase speed, reduce material costs, and improve quality were a necessity as volume increased. Over the years, many of the small-run, handmade boxes and pails were discontinued and the equipment scrapped. Other lines were automated and personnel were retrained to handle the higher mechanical skills and changeovers required. In spite of these changes, however, according to a general foreman, a production worker of the 1940s could return in 1963 and not feel entirely out of place. Many of the less skilled machine operators were required to handle several tasks on the higher-speed equipment. In general, most of the jobs in the plant were relatively unskilled and highly repetitive and gave the worker little control over method or pace. The die makers, who made and repaired the dies, the machine repairmen, and those who made equipment setup changes between different products were considered the most highly skilled.

All production workers below the rank of assistant foreman were unionized; however, there had never been a strike at the plant. Wages were high compared to other similar industries in the Montreal area. The union was not part of the Master Agreement that governed all other plants in Canada and most of the plants in the United States, but management made every effort to apply equality to this plant. Output standards were established for all jobs, but no bonus was paid for exceeding standards.

The metal can industry was relatively stable with little product differentiation. The St. Laurent plant to some extent shipped its products throughout Canada, although transportation costs limited its market primarily to eastern Canada. While some of the customers were large and bought in huge quantities (between 300 and 500 million cans), many were relatively small and purchased a more specialized product.

THE PLANT ORGANIZATION

Plant Management

Andrew Fox, the plant manager at St. Laurent since 1961, had risen from an hourly worker through foreman up to plant manufacturing engineer in the maintenance end of the business. He had developed an intimate first-hand knowledge of operations and was frequently seen around the plant, a cigar clenched between his teeth.

As plant manager, Fox had no responsibility for sales or research and development activities. In fact, both Fox and the district sales manager in his area had separate executives to whom they reported in the division headquarters, and it was in the superior of these executives that responsibility for both sales and production first came together.

Fox commented about the working relationships at the St. Laurent plant:

> You will see that frequently two managers with different job titles are assigned responsibility for the same task. [He implied that it was up to them to work out their own pattern of mutual support and cooperation.] However I don't have to adhere strictly to the description. I may end up asking a lot more of the man at certain times and under certain conditions than is ever put down on paper. In effect, the staff[1] runs the plant. We delegate to the various staff department heads the authority to implement decisions within the framework of our budget planning. This method of handling responsibility means that staff members have to be prepared to substantiate their decisions. At the same time, it gives them a greater sense of participation in and responsibility for plant income. We endeavor to carry this principle into the operating and service departments. The foreman is given responsibility and encouraged to act as though he were operating a business of his own. He is held responsible for all results generated in his department and is fully aware of how any decisions of his affect plant income.
>
> Our division personnel counsel and assist the plant staff, and the plant staff counsel and assist the department foreman. Regular visits are made to the plant by our division manager and members of his staff. The principal contact is through the division manager of manufacturing and his staff, the manager of industrial engineering, the manager of production engineering, and the manager of quality control. [There was no division staff officer in production control.]
>
> However, the onus is on the plant to request help or assistance of any kind. We can contact the many resources of Continental Can Company, usually on an informal basis. That is, we deal with other plant managers directly for information when manufacturing problems exist, without going through the division office.
>
> Each member of the staff understands that we, as a plant, have committed ourselves through the budget to provide a stated amount of income, and regardless of conditions that develop,

this income figure must be maintained. If sales are off and a continuing trend is anticipated, we will reduce expenses wherever possible to retain income. Conversely, if we have a gain in sales volume, we look for the complete conversion of the extra sales at the profit margin rate. However, this is not always possible, especially if the increase in sales comes at a peak time when facilities are already strained.

Fox was assisted by Robert Andrews, the assistant plant manager. Andrews, promoted from quality control manager in 1961, was responsible for all manufacturing operations within the plant. Andrews appeared more reserved than Fox, talked intently, and smiled easily while working with the persons who reported to him. Fifteen salaried supervisors reported to Andrews and helped him control the three-shift operation of the plant and its 500 hourly workers. (During peak periods in the summer, the plant employed as many as 800 people; most of the additional workers were the sons and daughters of plant employees.)

> ANDREWS Our foremen have full responsibility for running their departments: quality conditions of equipment, employee relations, production according to schedule, control of inventory through accurate reporting of spoilage and production, and cost control. He is just as accountable for those in his department as the plant manager is for the entire plant.

Andrews added that supervisory positions carried a good deal of status. Each supervisor had a personal parking spot and office and was expected to wear white shirts.[2] Andrews spoke of these symbols as an important aspect of the supervisor's position of authority. "He is no longer the best man with the wrench—he is the man with the best overall supervisory qualification."

Production Control

Al Whitelaw, the production control manager, had worked all of his eighteen years with Continental Can at the St. Laurent plant. He was responsible for planning and controlling plant inventories and production schedules to meet sales requirements consistent with efficient utilization of facilities, materials, and manpower. Whitelaw spoke quickly and chain-smoked cigarettes. According to him the main task of his job was "...to try to achieve the maximum length of run without affecting service or exceeding inventory budgets."

---

[1] *The personnel reporting directly to Fox. The organization chart (see Exhibit 1) was prominently displayed on the wall of the lobby. See Exhibit 2 for other information on personnel.*

[2] *The plant manager, management staff, foremen, and clerks in the office all wore white shirts and ties but no coats. The union president (a production worker) wore a white shirt but no tie. All other personnel wore colored sports shirts.*

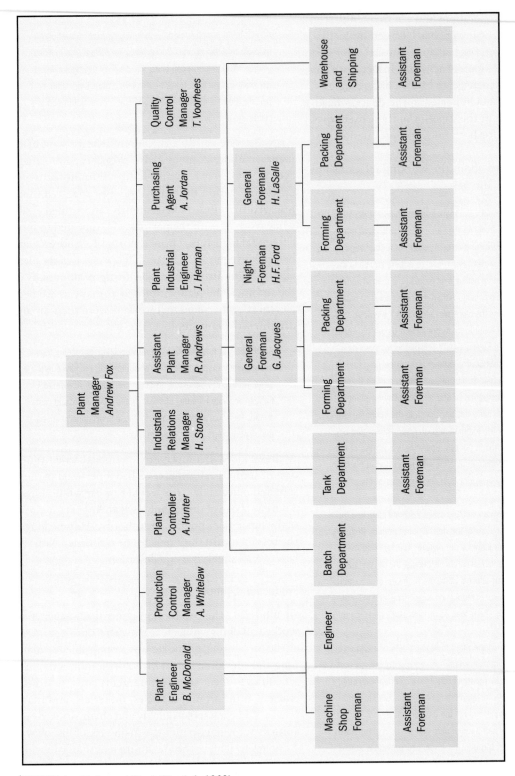

EXHIBIT 1 St. Laurent Plant (March 1, 1963)

Name, Position	Approximate Age	Approximate Length of Service		College Education
		St. Laurent	CCC	
Andrew Fox, Plant Manager	40–45	8	18	None
Robert Andrews, Assistant Plant Manager	35	3	8	Agricultural engineering
A. Hunter, Plant Controller	50	15	23	None
A. Whitelaw, Production Control Manager	45	18	18	None
Harold Stone, Industrial Relations Manager	45–50	5	29	None
Joe Herman, Plant Industrial Engineer	30–35	1	10	Engineering
Tom Voorhees, Quality Control Manager	30	5	5	Engineering in Netherlands
G. E. Jacques, General Foreman	45–50	25	25	None
Henri LaSalle, General Foreman	50	18	18	None
L. G. Adams, District Sales Manager	45–50	18	18	None

EXHIBIT 2   Information About Certain Personnel

Whitelaw was assisted by a scheduler for each major operating department and by clerks to service the schedulers. The schedulers worked closely with the department foremen in the plant and were in frequent telephone contact with the sales offices. Whitelaw commented: "We in production control are the buffer between sales and operating people."

To facilitate their work, Whitelaw and Andrews headed biweekly production control meetings, each lasting about one hour. Fox, the plant manager, was a frequent observer. These meetings were attended by the two general foremen. Each production foreman and the production control scheduler working for his depart-ment came to the meeting at a prearranged time, and when their turn came, they reported on operations in their department and on problems they were encountering. Most of the questions, as well as instructions given in the meeting, came from Andrews. It was also he who usually dismissed one foreman/scheduler pair and called on the next. Questions from Andrews or Whitelaw were seldom clearly addressed to either the foreman or the scheduler. They were answered more frequently by the scheduler than the foreman, and often a scheduler would supplement comments made by the foreman. Generally, the schedulers were younger but spoke with more self-assurance than the foremen.

In these meetings, there were frequent references to specific customers, their needs, complaints, and present attitudes toward Continental Can. Both Whitelaw and Andrews tended to put instructions and decisions in terms of what was required to satisfy some particular customer or group of customers.

A recent meeting involving a foreman, Maurice Pelletier, and the scheduler for his department, Dan Brown, is illustrative of the process. It was observed that while Dan presented the status report Maurice shook his head in disagreement without saying anything. Dan was discussing his plan to discontinue an order being processed on a certain line on Friday to shift to another order and then to return to the original order on Tuesday.

> ANDREWS I don't think your plan makes much sense. You go off on Friday and then on again Tuesday.
>
> MAURICE [to Dan] Is this all required before the end of the year? [This was asked with obvious negative emotional feeling and then followed by comments by both Andrews and Whitelaw.]
>
> DAN Mind you—I could call sales again.
>
> WHITELAW I can see the point, Dan. It is sort of nonsensical to change back after so short a run.
>
> MAURICE This would mean our production would be reduced all week to around 300 instead of 350. You know it takes four hours to make the changeover.
>
> DAN But the order has been backed up.
>
> ANDREWS It is backed up only because their [sales] demands are unreasonable.
>
> DAN They only asked us to do the best we can.
>
> ANDREWS They always do this. We should never have put this order on in the first place.
>
> MAURICE If you want to we could... [Makes a suggestion about how to handle the problem.]
>
> ANDREWS Production-wise, this is the best deal [Agreeing with Maurice's plan.]
>
> DAN Let me look at it again.
>
> ANDREWS Production-wise, this is best; make the changeover on the weekend.
>
> WHITELAW [Summarizes; then to Dan] The whole argument is the lost production you would have.
>
> MAURICE It'll mean backing up the order only one day.
>
> ANDREWS [After another matter in Maurice's department has been discussed and there is apparently nothing further, Andrews turns to Dan and smiles.] It's been a pleasure, Dan.
>
> [Dan then returned the smile weakly and got up to leave, somewhat nervously.]

As Whitelaw left the conference room after the meeting he was heard to comment:

> Danny got clobbered as you could see. I used to stand up for him, but he just doesn't come up here prepared. He should have the plans worked out with his foreman before they come up.

When discussing his job, Whitelaw frequently commented on how he thought a decision or problem would affect someone else in the plant:

> If all you had to do was manage the nuts and bolts of production scheduling and not worry about the customer or how people were going to react, this would be the easiest job in the whole plant. You could just sit down with a paper and pencil and lay it out the best way. But because the customer is so important and because you've got to look ahead to how people are going to react to a given kind of schedule, it makes the whole job tremendously complicated. It isn't easy!

Other Personnel and Functions

Hunter, the plant accountant, reported directly to the plant manager, although he was functionally responsible to the division controller. The major tasks for Hunter's department were the development and application of many thousands of individual product costs and the coordination of the annual sales and income budget, developed by the responsible operating and staff groups. Explaining another of his duties, Hunter noted:

> We are the auditors who see that every other department is obeying rules and procedures. It is our responsibility to know all that is in the instruction manuals. There are twelve volumes of general instructions and lots of special manuals.

Joe Herman, the plant industrial engineer, explained the responsibilities of his department:

> We're active in the fields of time study, budgetary control, job evaluation, and methods improvement. Our company is on a standard cost system—that is, all our product costs are based on engineered standards, accurately measuring all labor, direct and indirect, and material that is expended in the manufacture of each and every item we make in our plants. All the jobs in the St. Laurent plant, up to and including the foremen, have been measured and standards set. However, all our standards are forwarded to division, which checks them against standards in use at other plants. There are companywide benchmarks for most standards, since most of the machinery is the same in other Continental Can plants.

Herman noted that the budgeted savings from methods improvement was approximately $600,000 for the year, and he expected to exceed that by a substantial amount.

Harold Stone, the industrial relations manager, was proud that the St. Laurent plant had never experienced a strike and that formal written grievances were almost unheard of. Stone ran training programs and monitored safety, absenteeism, and turnover data. The St. Laurent plant had an outstanding record in these areas. Stone attributed this to the high wages and fringe benefits of the plant. He also maintained campaigns on housekeeping and posted slogans and comments, in both French and English, on job security and industrial competition. Also, he was responsible for the display of a five-foot chart on an easel near the main entrance that showed the manufacturing efficiency rating (actual production cost versus standard cost) of the previous month for each of the Continental Can Company plants and their standing within the division.

Regarding Continental Can's personnel policy, Stone stated:

> We believe that it is important that the supervisor and the employee understand each other, that they know what the other person thinks about business, profit, the importance of satisfying the customer, and any other aspect of business. We also believe that rapport between the supervisor and the employee can be improved in the social contacts that exist or that can be organized. For this reason, we sponsor dances, bowling leagues, golf days, fishing derbies, picnics, baseball leagues, supervision parties, management weekends, and many unofficial get-togethers. Over many years we have been convinced that these activities really improve management-labor relations. They also provide a means for union and management to work closely together in organizing and planning these events. These opportunities help provide a mutual respect for the other fellow's point of view.

It was Stone's responsibility to maintain the confidential file in connection with Continental's performance appraisal program for salaried employees. Procedures for handling the program were spelled out in one of the corporate manuals. Two forms were completed annually. One called for a rating of the employee by his supervisor, first on his performance of each of his responsibilities outlined in the Position Analysis Manual and then on each of twelve general characteristics such as cooperation, initiative, job knowledge, and delegation. In another section, the supervisor and the appraised employee were jointly required to indicate what experience, training, or self-development would improve the performance or prepare for the advancement of the employee prior to the next appraisal. The appraisal was to be discussed between the supervisor and the employee; the latter was required to sign the form, and space was given for any comments he or she might want to make. The second form was not shown to the employee. It called for a rating on overall performance, an indication of promotability, and a listing of potential replacements. It was used for manpower planning, and after comments by the supervisor of the appraiser, it was forwarded to the division office.

MANAGERIAL PRACTICES

Managing with Budgets

Management at the St. Laurent plant coordinated their activities through a number of informal, as well as scheduled, meetings. Impromptu meetings of two or more members of management were frequent, facilitated by the close proximity of their offices. Among the formal meetings, the most important was the monthly discussion of performance against the budget. This meeting was attended by all of the management staff as well as production supervisors. Other regularly scheduled meetings included the production control meeting (twice weekly) and the plant cost reduction committee meetings.

In discussing the budget, Fox explained that the manufacturing plant was organized as a profit center. Plant income was determined by actual sales, not a transfer price. Therefore, income was adversely affected when sales failed to come up to the forecast on which the budget was based and when sales prices were reduced to meet competition. Fox also explained that sales managers also have their incentives based on making or exceeding the budget and that their forecasts had tended to be quite accurate. Overoptimism regarding one group of products had usually been offset by underestimation of sales of other products. However, because no adjustment was permitted in budgeted profit when sales income was below forecast, the fact that sales were running 3 percent below the level budgeted for 1963 was forcing the plant to reduce expenses substantially in order to equal or exceed the profit budgeted for the year.

When asked whether the budget was a straightjacket or if there were some accounts that left slack for reducing expenses in case sales fell below forecast, Fox replied:

> We never put anything in the budget that is unknown or guessed at. We have to be able to back up every single figure in the budget. We have to budget our costs at standard, assuming that we can operate at standard. We know we won't all the time. There will be errors and failures, but we are never allowed to budget for them.

Hunter agreed with Fox, stating, "In this company there is very little opportunity to play footsy with the figures."

Fox conceded that there were some discretionary accounts like overtime and outside storage that involved arguments with the division. For example, "I might ask for $140,000 for overtime. The division manager will say $130,000, so we compromise at $135,000." As far as cost-reduction projects are concerned, Fox added that "... we budget for more than the expected savings. We might have $ 100,000 in specific projects and budget for $150,000."

Fox went on to note that equipment repairs and overhauls could be delayed to reduce expenses. But even the overhaul schedule was included as part of the budget, and any changes had to be approved at the division level.

Robert Andrews complained that the budget system didn't leave much room for imagination. He felt that overly optimistic sales estimates were caused by the salespeople being fearful of sending a pessimistic estimate up to the division. These estimates, according to Andrews, were a major source of manufacturing inefficiency.

Andrews was asked whether he was concerned about increasing production volume, and he replied:

> We have standards. So long as we are meeting the standards, we are meeting our costs and we do not worry about increasing production. We don't tell the foreman that he needs to get more goods out the door. We tell him to get rid of the red in his budget. I'm content with a 100 percent performance. I'd like 105 percent, but if we want more production it is up to industrial engineering to develop methods changes.

Andrews talked about the necessary skills for a foreman:

> The foreman should be good at communications and the use of available control procedures. The foreman is expected to communicate effectively with all plant personnel, including staff heads. Our control procedures are easy to apply. In each department there is an engineered standard for each operation covering labor, materials, and spoilage. Without waiting for a formal statement from accounting, a foreman can analyze his performance in any area and take corrective action if necessary. Then he receives reports from accounting to assist him in maintaining tight cost control. One is a daily report that records labor and spoilage performance against standard. The monthly report provides a more detailed breakdown of labor costs, materials and supplies used, and spoilage. It also establishes the efficiency figure for the month. This report is discussed at a monthly meeting of all my supervisors. Generally, the plant industrial engineer and a member of the accounting staff are present. Each foreman explains his variances from standard and submits a forecast for his next month's performance.

The Bonus Plan

Andrew Fox indicated that the budget was also used in rewarding employees of Continental Can. The incentive for managers was based on performance of the plant compared to budget. According to Fox:

> The bonus is paid on the year's results. It is paid as a percentage of salary to all who are eligible—the ones on the organization chart (see Exhibit 1). There are three parts to it—one part is based on plant income, one on standards improvement or cost cutting, and the third on operating performance. We can make up to 20 percent by beating our plant income target and 25 percent on cost reduction and operating efficiency together. But we have to make 90 percent of our budgeted income figure to participate in any bonus at all. I think we have the 25 percent on efficiency and cost reduction pretty well sewn up this year If we go over our budgeted income, we can get almost 35 percent bonus.

In years past, St. Laurent managers had made about 10 percent of their salaries from the bonus. The improved performance was the result of a change in the design of the bonus plan. Hunter explained the effect of the change:

> At one time the bonus plan was based on departmental results and efficiency. Under this there was a tendency for the departments to work at cross-purposes, to compete rather than cooperate with each other. For the last seven or eight years, the emphasis has been on the plant, not the department. The latest plan is geared not only to the attainment of budgeted cost goals, but also to the attainment of budgeted income. This is consistent with the attention we are placing on sales. I think the company was disturbed by what they sensed was a belief that those at the plant level can't do much about sales. Now we are trying to get the idea across that if we make better cans and give better service, we will sell more.

FOREMEN AND PRODUCTION WORKERS

General Foremen

Guillaume Jacques and Henri LaSalle were the general foremen on two of the three shifts. They described their jobs as working closely with both the assistant plant manager and the production control manager, but more with the latter. Jacques and LaSalle were asked how they balanced employee satisfaction with the requirements of the budget. Jacques commented:

> Management not only asks me to meet the budget, but to do better. So you've got to make the worker understand the importance of keeping under budget. I get them in the office and explain that if we don't meet the budget, we'll have to cut down somewhere else. It is mathematical. I explain all this to them; management has given me a budget to meet, I need them for this, they need

me to give them work. We work like a team. I try to understand them. All supervisors work under tension. Myself, I ask the men to go out to have a beer with me, to go to a party. It relaxes them from our preoccupations. Right now, for example, there is this party with the foremen coming up. At these gatherings it is strictly against the rules to talk about work. These things are necessary.

LaSalle explained that while foremen have a copy of the budget for their department, the workers see only a machine operating standard. The standard was set so that if he works the machine at full capacity, he achieves 110 percent of standard. LaSalle told of his way of handling workers:

Well, there is usually some needling when a man is down below standard. He's told, "Why don't you get to be part of the crew?" It doesn't hurt anything...you only get a good day's work out of people if they are happy. We strive to keep our people happy so they'll produce the standard and make the budget. We try to familiarize them with what is expected of them. We have targets set for us. The budget is reasonable, but it is not simple to attain. By explaining our problems to the workers, we find it easier to meet the budget.

Foremen

Most of the foremen were aware of, and accepted, the necessity of keying their activities to the work standards and budgets. One young, and purportedly ambitious, foreman commented about this job:

What I like about this department is that I am in charge. I can do anything I like as long as I meet the budget. I can have that machine moved—send it over there—as long as I have a good reason to justify it. The department, that's me. I do all the planning and I'm responsible for results. I'm perfectly free in the use of my time [gives examples of his different arrival times during the past week and the fact that he came in twice on Saturday and once on Sunday for short periods].

While other foremen expressed dislike for some of the pressures inherent in their jobs, there was general satisfaction. One notable exception was a foreman with many years' service, who said:

We have a meeting once a month upstairs. They talk to us about budgets, quality, etc. That's all on the surface; that's b–s–. It looks good. It has to look good but it is all bull. For example, the other day a foreman had a meeting with the workers to talk about quality. After that an employee brought to his attention a defect in some products. He answered, "Send it out anyway," and they had just finished talking to us about quality.

Foremen tended to view the production worker as irresponsible and interested, insofar as his job is concerned, only in his paycheck and quitting time. One foreman said, "We do all the work; they do nothing." Even an officer of the union, speaking about the workers, commented:

They don't give a damn about the standards. They work nonchalantly, and they are very happy when their work slows up. If the foreman is obliged to stop the line for two minutes, everyone goes to the toilet. There are some workers who do their work conscientiously, but this is not the case with the majority.

Workers

Several of the production workers expressed feelings of pressure, although others declared that they were accustomed to their work and that it did not bother them. One said:

Everyone is obsessed with meeting the standards—the machine adjuster, the foreman, the assistant foreman. They all get on my nerves.

One old-timer clearly differentiated the company, which he considered benevolent, from his foreman:

I can understand that these men are under tension just as we are. They have meetings every week. I don't know what they talk about up there. The foremen have their standards to live up to. They're nervous. They don't even have a union like us. So if things go bad, well, that's all. They make us nervous with all this. But there's a way with people. We don't say to a man, "Do this, do that." If we said, "Would you do this?" it is not the same thing. You know a guy like myself who has been here for 35 years knows a few tricks. If I am mad at the foreman, I could do a few little things to the machine to prevent it from keeping up with standards and no one would know.

While some workers stated they would work for less money if some of the tension were relieved, the majority were quite content with their jobs.[3]

ENFORCING THE BUDGET

By November 1963, sales for the year had fallen below expectations and the management bonus was in jeopardy as a result.

One day in early November there was an unusual amount of activity in the accounting section. Fox came into the area frequently, and he and Hunter from time to time would huddle with one of the accountants over some figures. Hunter explained that the extra activity was in response to a report on the October results that had been issued about a week before.

---

[3] In a Harvard Business School research study of twelve plants in the United States and Canada, the St. Laurent plant workers ranked highest of the twelve plants in job satisfaction.

Fox decided to schedule a joint meeting of the management staff and the line organization to go over the October results. This was a departure from the usual practice of having the groups in separate meetings. Prior to the meeting Fox outlined what he hoped to accomplish in the meeting:

> Those figures we got last week showed that some of the accounts did what they were expected to do, some did more, and some did a good deal less. The thing we have to do now is to kick those accounts in the pants that are not making the savings they planned to make. What we've been doing is raising the expected savings as the time gets shorter. It may be easy to save 10 percent on your budget when you've got six months; but with only six weeks, it is an entirely different matter. The thing to do now is to get everybody together and excited about the possibility of doing it. We know how it can be done. Those decisions have already been made. It's not unattainable even though I realize we are asking an awful lot from these men. You see, we are in a position now where just a few thousand dollars one way or the other can make as much as 10 percent difference in the amount of bonus the men get. There is some real money on the line. It can come either from a sales increase or an expense decrease, but the big chunk has to come out of an expense decrease.

Fox did not feel there would be a conflict in the meeting about who is right and who is wrong:

> We never fight about the budget. It is simply a tool. All we want to know is what is going on. There are never any disagreements about the budget itself. Our purpose this afternoon is to pinpoint those areas where savings can be made, where there is a little bit of slack, and then get to work and pick up the slack.

Fox talked about his style of handling cost and people problems:

> When budgeted sales expenses get out of line, management automatically takes in other accounts to make up the losses. We'll give the department that has been losing money a certain period of time to make it up. Also, anytime anybody has a gain, I tell them I expect them to maintain that gain.
>
> The manager must make the final decisions and has to consider the overall relationships. But there are some things I can't delegate—relations with sales, for example. The manager and not production control, must make the final decisions.
>
> Larry Adams, the sales manager in our district, feels that the budget gets in the way of the customer's needs. He thinks the budget dominates the thinking and actions around here. Maybe he's right. But I have to deal with the people and problems here.
>
> The manager must be close to his people. I take a daily tour of the plant and talk to the people by name. My practice as a manager is to follow a head-on approach. I don't write many memos. When I have something to say I go tell the person or persons right away. That's why I'm holding a meeting this afternoon.

Bob Andrews commented on the methods used to pick up the projected savings:

> When you have lost money in one sector you have to look around for something else that you can "milk" to make up the difference. But we don't ask for volunteers; we do the "milking." Those guys just have to do what we say. How much we can save pretty much depends on how hard the man in the corner office wants to push on the thing. I mean, if we really wanted to save money, we probably could do it, but it would take a tremendous effort on everybody's part and Fox would really have to crack the whip.

Because of Fox's comments on relationships with sales, Larry Adams, the district sales manager, was asked about his feelings on working with the production people at the St. Laurent plant:

> The budget comes to dominate people's thinking and influence all their actions. I'm afraid even my salesmen have swallowed the production line whole. They can understand the budget so well they can't understand their customers. And the St. Laurent plant boys are getting more and more local in their thinking with this budget. They're not thinking about what the customer needs today or may need tomorrow; they just think about their goddamned budget.
>
> If the customer will not take account of your shortcomings, and if you can't take account of the customer's shortcomings, the two of you will eventually end up at each other's throats. That's what this budget system has built into it. Suppose, for example, you want to give a customer a break. Say he has originally planned for a two-week delivery date, but he phones you and says he really has problems and if you possibly could he would like about four days knocked off that delivery date. So I go trotting over to the plant, and I say, "Can we get it four days sooner?" Those guys go out of their minds, and they start hollering about the budget and how everything is planned just right and how I'm stirring them up. They get so steamed up I can't go running to them all the time, but only when I really need something in the worst way. You can't let those plant guys see your strategy, you know. It is taking an awful lot out of a guy's life around here when he has to do everything by the numbers.

SPECIAL BUDGET MEETING

The meeting was held in the conference room at 4:00 P.M. Fox and Hunter sat at the far end of the table, facing the door, with an easel bearing a flip chart near them. The chart listed the projected savings in budgeted expenses for November and December, account by account. The group of about 30 arranged themselves at the table so that, with only a couple of exceptions, the management staff personnel and general foremen sat closest to Fox and Hunter and the foremen and assistant foremen sat toward the foot of the table.

Fox opened the meeting and declared that performance against the budget for October would first be reviewed, followed by discussion of the November and December projections. He stated rather emphatically that he was "disappointed" in the October performance. Although money had been saved, it represented good performance in some areas but rather poor performance in others. Fox declared that the gains made in the areas where performance had been good must be maintained and the weak areas brought up.

He then turned the meeting over to Hunter, who reviewed the October results, reading from the report, which everyone had in front of him. Where performance was not good, he called on the individual responsible for that area to explain. The typical explanation was that the original budgeted figure was unrealistic and that the actual amount expended was as low as it could possibly be under the circumstances. Fox frequently broke into the explanation with a comment like, "Well, that is not good enough" or, "Can you possibly do better for the rest of the year?" or, "I hope we have that straightened out now." When he sat down, the person giving the explanation was invariably thanked by Hunter.

Next, Hunter, followed by Whitelaw, commented on the sales outlook for the remainder of the year. They indicated that for two months as a whole sales were expected to be about on budget. After asking for questions and getting one from a foreman, Fox said:

> Well now, are there any more questions? Ask them now if you have them. Everybody sees where we stand on the bonus, I assume. Right?

Fox then referred to the chart on plant expense savings and began to discuss it, saying:

> The problem now is time. We keep compressing the time and raising the gain [the projected savings for the year had been raised $32,000 above what had been projected in October]. You can only do that so long. Time is running out, fellows. We've got to get on the stick.

Several times Fox demanded better upward communication on problems as they came up. Referring to a specific example, he said:

> This sort of thing is absolutely inexcusable. We've got to know ahead of time when these mix-ups are going to occur so that we can allow for and correct them.

As Hunter was covering manufacturing efficiency projections for November, he addressed Andrews:

> Now we have come to you, Bob. I see you're getting a little bit more optimistic on what you think you can do.

Andrews replied:

> Yes, the boss keeps telling me I'm just an old pessimist and I don't have any faith in my people. I'm still a pessimist, but we are

doing tremendously. I think it's terrific, fellows [pointing to a line graph]. I don't know whether we can get off the top of this chart or not, but at the rate this actual performance line is climbing, we might make it. All I can say is, keep up the good work.... I guess I'm an optimistic pessimist.

During the discussion of projected savings for December in the equipment maintenance account, Hunter commented:

> Where in the world are you fellows going to save $8000 more than you originally said you would save?

Jones responded:

> I'd just like to say at this point to the group that it would be a big help if you guys would take it easy on your machines. That's where we are going to save an extra $8000—simply by only coming down to fix the stuff that won't run. You're really going to have to make it go as best you can. That's the only way we can possibly save the kind of money we have to save. You have been going along pretty well, but all I've got to say is I hope you can keep it up and not push those machines too hard.

Although Jones spoke with sincerity, a number of foremen sitting near the door exchanged sly smiles and pokes in the ribs.

Fox concluded the meeting at about 5:30, still chewing on his cigar:

> There are just a couple of things I want to say before we break up. First, we've got to stop making stupid errors in shipping. Joe [foreman of shipping], you've absolutely got to get after those people to straighten them out. Second, I think it should be clear, fellows, that we can't break any more promises. Sales is our bread and butter. If we don't get those orders out in time, we'll have no one but ourselves to blame for missing our budget. So I just hope it is clear that production control is running the show for the rest of the year. Third, the big push is on now! We sit around here expecting these problems to solve themselves, but they don't! It ought to be clear to all of you that no problem gets solved until it's spotted. Damn it, I just don't want any more dewy-eyed estimates about performance for the rest of the year. If something is going sour, we want to hear about it. And there's no reason for not hearing about it! [Pounds the table, then voice falls and a smile begins to form.] It can mean a nice penny in your pocket if you can keep up the good work. That's all I've got to say. Thank you very much.

The room cleared immediately, but Whitelaw lingered on. He reflected aloud on the just-ended meeting:

> I'm afraid that little bit of advice there at the end won't make a great deal of difference in the way things work out. You have to play off sales against production. It's built into the job. When I attend a meeting like that one and I see all those production people with their assistants and see the other staff managers with their assistants, and I hear fellows refer to corporate policy that dictates

and supports their action at the plant level, I suddenly realize that I'm all alone up there. I can't sit down and fire off a letter to my boss at the division level like the rest of those guys can do. I haven't got any authority at all. It is all based strictly on my own guts and strength. Now Bob is a wonderful guy—I like him and I have a lot of respect for him—but it just so happens that 80 percent of the time he and I disagree. He knows it and I know it; I mean it's nothing we run away from; we just find ourselves on opposite sides of the question, and I'm dependent upon his tact and good judgment to keep us from starting a war.

Boy, it can get you down—it really can after a while, and I've been at it for—God—20 years. But in production control you've got to accept it—you're an outcast. They tell you you're cold, that you're inhuman, that you're a bastard, that you don't care about anything except your schedule. And what are you going to say? You're just going to have to swallow it because basically you haven't got the authority to back up the things you know need to be done. Four nights out of five I am like this at the end of the day—just completely drained—and it comes from having to fight my way through to try to get the plant running as smoothly as I can.

And Andrews up there in that meeting. He stands up with his chart and he compliments everybody about how well they are doing on efficiency. You know, he says, "Keep up the good work,"

and all that sort of stuff. I just sat there—shaking my head. I was so dazed you know; I mean I just keep saying to myself, "What's he doing? What's he saying? What's so great about this?" You know if I could have, I'd have stood up and said, "Somebody go down to my files in production control and pick out any five customer orders at random—and letters—and bring them back up here and read them—at random, pick any five." You know what they would show? Broken promises and missed delivery dates and slightly off-standard items we've been pushing out the door here. I mean, what is an efficient operation? Why the stress on operating efficiency? That's why I just couldn't figure out why in the world Andrews was getting as much mileage out of his efficiency performance as he was. Look at all the things we sacrifice to get that efficiency. But what could I do?

In early 1964, the report being sent by Fox to the division would show that profits for 1963 had exceeded the amount budgeted and that operating efficiency and cost reduction had both exceeded the budget by a comfortable margin, despite the fact that sales had fallen about 3 percent below budget. This enabled the managers and supervisors at the St. Laurent plant to attain the salary bonuses for which they had been striving.

CASE 4

TRW Systems Group (A and B Condensed) — PAUL H. THOMPSON

revised by Joseph Seher and John P Kotter

HISTORY OF TRW INC. AND TRW SYSTEMS GROUP*

TRW Inc. was formed in 1957 by the merger of Thompson Products, Inc., and the Ramo-Wooldridge Corporation. Thompson Products, a Cleveland-based manufacturer of auto and aircraft parts, had provided $500,000 to help Simon Ramo and Dean Wooldridge get started in 1953. Ramo-Wooldridge Corporation grew quickly by linking itself with the accelerating ICBM program sponsored by the Air Force. After winning the contract for the technical supervision of the ICBM program, R-W gradually expanded its capabilities to include advance planning for future ballistic weapons systems and space technology and by providing technical advice to the Air Force.

R-W was considered by some industry specialists to be a quasi-government agency. In fact, some of its competitors in the aerospace industry resented R-W's opportunities for auditing and examining their operations.

Because of this close relationship with the Air Force, RW was prohibited from bidding on hardware contracts. This prevented the company from competing for work on mainframes or on assemblies. In 1959, after the merg-

Copyright © 1976 by the President and Fellows of Harvard College. Harvard Business School case 476-117. This case was prepared by Joseph A. Seher under the direction of John P. Kotter. It is a condensation of the A and B cases originally written by Paul H. Thompson under the direction of Gene W. Dalton. This case was prepared as the basis for class discussion rather than to illustrate either effective or ineffective handling of an administrative situation. Reprinted by permission of the Harvard Business School.

In its brief history, this part of TRW, Inc. had had several names: The Guided Missiles Division of Ramo-Wooldridge, Ramo-Wooldridge Corporation, Space Technology Laboratories (S.T.L.), and most recently, TRW Systems Group. Frequently used abbreviations of TRW Systems Group are TRW Systems and Systems Group.

er with Thompson, TRW decided that the hardware ban was too great a liability and moved to free the Systems Group from its limiting relationship with the Air Force.

The Air Force was reluctant to lose the valued services of the Systems Group. But it agreed to a solution that called for the creation by the Air Force of a nonprofit organization, the Aerospace Corporation, to take over the advance planning and broad technical assistance formerly given by the Systems Group. TRW agreed to recruit, from its own personnel, a staff of top technicians to man Aerospace, and in 1960, about 20 percent of Systems' professional people went over to Aerospace.

The Systems Group had to undergo a difficult transition from serving a single customer to a competitive organization. The change involved worrying about marketing and manufacturing and dealing with different types of contracts. Previously, Systems had worked on a cost-plus-fixed-fee basis, but now worked on incentive contracts rewarding performance and specified delivery dates, while penalizing failures.

Systems thrived in the new competitive arena (see Exhibit 1), winning a number of important contracts. Nestled in the sunny southern California region at Redondo Beach, the Systems Group worked in a free and open atmosphere. According to an article in *Fortune*, Systems' competitive advantage was its professional personnel:

> S.T.L. is headed by 38-year-old Rube Mettler, who holds the title of president of the subsidiary. A Ph.D. from Caltech, he served with Hughes Aircraft, and was a consultant at the Pentagon before coming to Ramo-Wooldridge in 1955, where he made his mark directing the Thor program to completion in record time. Of his technical staff of 2100, more than 35 percent hold advanced degrees, and despite their youth they average eleven years of experience per man; in other words, most of them have been in the space industry virtually since the space industry began. They are housed mostly in a group of four long, low buildings for research, engineering, and development in the campus-like Space Center at Redondo Beach. Some of them are occupied in the various labs for research in quantum physics, programming, and applied mathematics, intertial guidance and control, etc.; others simply sit in solitude in their offices and think, or mess around with formulas on the inevitable blackboard. But typically, the materialization of all this brainpower is accomplished in one medium-sized manufacturing building called FIT (Fabrication, Integration, and Testing), which has but 800 employees all told. FIT has a high bay area to accommodate its huge chamber for simulating space environment and other exotic testing equipment.[1]

	June 1960	February 1963
Customers	8	42
Contracts	16	108
Total personnel	3,860	6,000
Technical staff	1,400	2,100
Annual sales rate	$63 million	$108 million

EXHIBIT 1 Comparative Profile of TRW Systems Group

THE AEROSPACE INDUSTRY

Observers have described the industry in which Systems competed as a large job shop subject to frequent changes. T. C. Miller and L. P. Kane, experts on the aerospace industry, described it as follows:

> Because of rapid changes in technology, in customer requirements, and in competitive practices, product lines in the aerospace industry tend to be transitory. The customers' needs are finite and discrete .... Although the aerospace industry as a whole has grown steadily during the last decade, the fluctuations of individual companies underscore the job-shop nature of the defense work. Aerospace industry planners must be constantly aware of the possibility of cancellation or prolongation of large programs.[2]

The rapid changes and temporary nature of the programs had several effects on companies within the industry. Sales and profits fluctuated with the number and size of contracts the company had; the level of activity in the company fluctuated, which meant hiring and later laying off large numbers of employees; and each plant went from full utilization of physical facilities to idle capacity.

The fluctuations resulted in a highly mobile work force that tended to follow the contracts, moving from a company that had finished a contract to one that was beginning a new contract. But the employees were highly trained and could find other jobs without difficulty. Miller and Kane pointed out:

> The industry's ratios of technical employment to total employment and of technical employment to dollar volume of sales are higher than those in any other industry. Moreover, 30 percent of all persons privately employed in research and development are in the aerospace industry.[3]

[2] T. C. Miller, Jr., and L. P. Kane, "Strategies for Survival in the Aerospace Industry," *Industrial Management Review*, Fall 1965, pp. 22–23.
[3] Ibid., p. 20.

[1] *Fortune*, February 1963, p. 95.

TRW Systems tried to minimize these fluctuations and their effects by limiting the size of a contract for which they might compete. They would rather have had ten $10 million contracts than one $100 million contract; also they had a policy of leasing a certain portion of their facilities in order to maintain flexibility in their physical plant.

In pursuing a conscious policy of growth, they competed for many contracts. By winning a reasonable number of these contracts, the company grew; and when one contract ran out, there were others always starting up. As a result, between 1953 and 1963 Systems did not have a single major layoff.

Another characteristic of the industry was the complexity of the products being produced. There were thousands of parts in a space rocket and they had to interrelate in numerous subtle ways. If one part didn't come up to specifications, it might harm hundreds of others. Since the parts and systems were so interdependent, the people in the various groups, divisions, and companies who made and assembled the parts were also highly interdependent. These interdependencies created some organizational problems for the companies in the industry, which forced them to develop a new type of organization called the matrix organization.

TRW SYSTEMS' ORGANIZATION

Exhibit 2 shows an organization chart for TRW in 1963 with the various functional divisions and the offices for program management (the word *project* is often used interchangeably for *program*). These different systems interrelated in what was called a matrix organization. The relationship between program offices and the functional divisions was a complex one, but can best be explained in a simple fashion by noting that instead of setting up, for example, a systems engineering group for the Atlas missile and another separate systems group for the Titan missile program, all the systems engineers were assigned organizationally to the Systems Division. This Systems Division was one of five technical divisions, each staffed with MTS (Members Technical Staff) working in a particular functional area. The various program offices coordinated the work of all the functional groups working on their particular programs and, in addition, handled all relationships with the contracting customer. It will be noted that the program offices were, formally, on the same organizational level as the functional divisions.

The engineers in these functional divisions were formally responsible to the director of their division, but they might also have a "dotted line" responsibility to a program office. For example, an electrical engineer would be responsible to his manager in the Electronics Division even though he might spend all of his time working for the Atlas program office. While working on the program he would report to the Atlas program director through one of his assistants.

Functional Organization

Each functional division served as a technology center and focused on the disciplines and skills appropriate to its technology. Generally, a number of operations managers reported to the division manager, each of whom was in charge of a group of laboratories dealing with similar technologies. The laboratory directors who reported to the operation managers were each responsible for a number of functional departments that were organized around technical specialties. The engineers in these laboratory departments were the people who performed the actual work on program office projects.

Program Office Organization

A program manager maintained overall management responsibility for pulling together the various phases of a particular customer project. His office was the central location for all project-wide activities such as the project schedule, cost and performance control, system planning, system engineering, system integration, and contract and major subcontract management. Assistant project managers were appointed for these activities as warranted by the size of the project.

The total project effort was divided into subprojects, each project being assigned to a specific functional organization according to the technical specialty involved. The manager of the functional organization appointed a subproject manager with the concurrence of the project manager. The subproject manager was assigned responsibility for the total subproject activity and was delegated management authority by the functional division management and by the assistant project manager to whom he reported operationally for the project. The subproject manager was a full-time member of the project organization, but he was not considered a member of the project office; he remained a member of his functional organization. He was accountable for performance in his functional specialty to the manager of his functional area, usually a

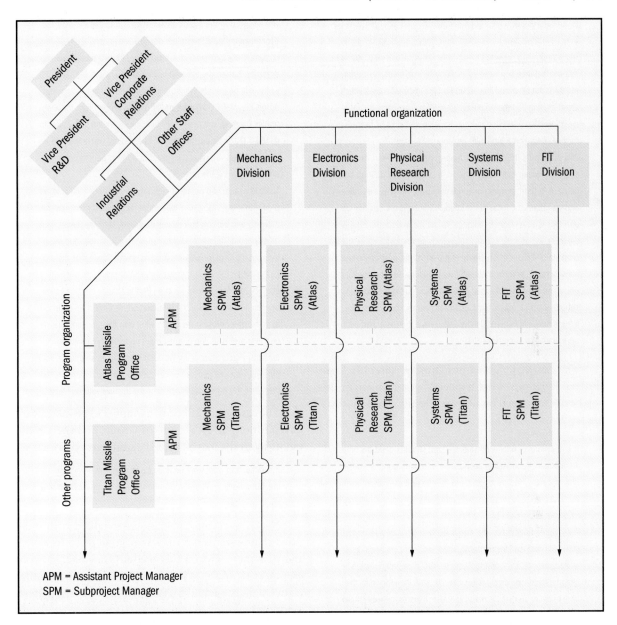

EXHIBIT 2   Organization Chart, 1963

APM = Assistant Project Manager
SPM = Subproject Manager

laboratory manager. The functional manager was responsible for the performance evaluation of the subproject manager. The subproject manager thus represented both the program office and his functional area and was responsible for coordinating the work of his subproject with the engineers within the functional area. Normally each functional area was involved in work on several projects simultaneously. One manager defined the subproject manager's responsibility this way:

The subproject manager is a prime mover in this organization, and his job is a tough one. He is the person who brings the program office's requirements and the lab's resources together to produce a subsystem. He has to deal with the pressures and needs of both sides of the matrix and is responsible for bringing a subsystem together. He has to go to the functional department managers to get engineers to work on his project, but about all he can say is, "Thanks for the work you've done on my subproject." But he does have program office money as a source of power, which the functional managers need to fund their operations. The technical managers are strong people. They are not "yes" men; they have their own ideas about how things ought to be done. You do not want them to be "yes" men either. Otherwise, you've lost the balance you need to make sure that technical performance is not sacrificed for cost and schedule expediencies, which are of great importance to the program office. The functional managers are also interested in long-range applications of the work they are doing on a particular project.

This often puts the subproject manager in a real bind; he gets caught between conflicting desires. It is especially difficult because it is hard for him not to identify with the program office because that's the focus of his interest. But he is paid by the lab and that is also where he must go to get his work done. If he is smart he will identify with his subsystem and not with either the program office or the lab. He must represent the best course for his subproject, which sometimes means fighting with the program office and the departments at different times during the life of the subproject. If he reacts too much to pressures from either side, it hurts his ability to be objective about his subproject, and people will immediately sense this.

The casewriter asked Jim Dunlap, Director of Industrial Relations, what happened when an engineer's top bosses disagreed on how he should spend his time. He replied:

> The decisions of priority on where a man should spend his time are made by Rube Mettler because he is the only common boss. But, of course, you try to get them to resolve it at a lower level. You just have to learn to live with ambiguity. It's not a structured situation. It just can't be.
>
> You have to understand the needs of Systems Group to understand why we need the matrix organization. There are some good reasons why we use a matrix. Because R&D-type programs are finite programs—you create them, they live, and then they die—they have to die or overhead is out of line. Also, there are several stages in any project. You don't necessarily need the same people on the project all the time. In fact, you waste the creative people if they work until the end finishing it up. The matrix is flexible. We can shift creative people around and bring in the people who are needed at various stages in the project. The creative people in the functions are professionals and are leaders in their technical disciplines. So the functional relationship helps them to continue to improve their professional expertise. Also, there is a responsiveness to all kinds of crises that come up. You sometimes have thirty days to answer a proposal—so you can put together a team of guys from everywhere. We're used to temporary systems; that's the way we live.
>
> Often an engineer will work on two or three projects at a time and he just emphasizes one more than others. He's part of two systems at the same time.

The key word in the matrix organization is interdependency. Matrix means multiple interdependencies. We're continually setting up temporary systems. For example, we set up a project manager for the Saturn project with twenty people under him. Then he would call on people in systems engineering to get things started on the project. Next he might call in people from the Electronics Division, and after they finish their work the project would go to FIT [Fabrication, Integration, and Testing] where it would be manufactured. So what's involved is a lot of people coming in and then leaving the project.

> There is a large gap between authority and responsibility and we plan it that way. We give a man more responsibility than he has authority and the only way he can do this job is to collaborate with other people. The effect is that the system is flexible and adaptive, but it's hard to live with. An example of this is that the project manager has no authority over people working on the project from the functional areas. He can't decide on their pay, promotion, or even how much time they'll spend on his project as opposed to some other project. He has to work with the functional heads on these problems. We purposely set up this imbalance between authority and responsibility. We design a situation so that it's ambiguous. That way people have to collaborate and be flexible. You just can't rely on bureaucracy or power to solve your problems.

The casewriter talked to a number of people in various positions at TRW Systems Group, and their comments about the matrix could be summarized as follows:

> It is difficult to work with because it's flexible and always changing, but it does work; and it's probably the only organization that could work here.

Nearly everyone the casewriter talked with indicated that Systems Group was a "good place to work" and that they enjoyed the freedom they had. However, one critic of the system, a member of the administrative staff, presented his complaints about the system as follows:

> People think this is a country club. It's a college campus atmosphere. Top management thinks everyone is mature and so they let them work as if they were on a college campus. They don't have rules to make people come to work on time or things like that. Do you know that 60–70 percent of the assigned parking spaces are empty at 8:30 A.M.? Personnel did a study of that—people are late. It's a good place to work for people who want complete freedom. But people abuse it. They don't come to work on time; they just do what they want around here. Its very democratic here. Nobody is telling you what to do and making all the decisions, but it can border on anarchy.
>
> The management philosophy is that everybody will work harmoniously and you don't need a leader. But I think there has to be leadership, some one person who's responsible.

The casewriter than asked the question, "Isn't the project engineer responsible?" and the reply was:

> The project engineer is a figurehead—in many cases he doesn't lead. I know one project engineer who provides no leadership at all. Besides, the matrix is constantly agitating. It's changing all the time, so it's just a bucket of worms. You never know where you stand. It's like ants on a log in a river and each one thinks he's steering—when none of them are. It's true that the top-level managers can make this philosophy work on their level. But we can't on our level. Let me give you an example. Mettler says he wants everything microfilmed, but he doesn't tell others to let me do it. I have responsibility but no authority in the form of a piece of paper or statement that I can do it. I just can't walk into some guy's empire and say I'm here to microfilm all of your papers. It's like an amoeba, always changing so you never know where your limits are or what you can or can't do.

As a contrasting view, one of the laboratory heads felt that the lack of formal rules and procedures was one of the strengths of the organization. He commented:

> This is not a company characterized by a lot of crisp orders and formal procedures. Quite honestly, we operate pretty loosely as far as procedures, etc., are concerned. In fact, I came from a university environment, but I believe there's more freedom and looseness of atmosphere around here than there was as a faculty member. I think if you have pretty average people, you can have a very strict line type of organization and make it work, and maybe that's why we insist on being different. You see, I think you can also have a working organization with no strict lines of authority if you have broader-gauged people in it. I like to think that the individuals in the company are extremely high caliber and I think there is some evidence to support that.

Another manager supported the matrix organization with the following comments:

> The people around here are really committed to the job. They'll work 24 hours a day when it is necessary, and sometimes it's necessary. I was on a team working on a project proposal a few months ago and during the last week of the proposal there were people working here around the clock. We had the secretaries come in on different shifts and we just stayed here and worked. I think that Mettler makes this matrix organization work. It's a difficult job but people have faith that Mettler knows what he's doing so they work hard and it comes out all right.

EVOLUTION OF CAREER DEVELOPMENT

In 1962, TRW Systems Group began a management development program called Career Development. Jim Dunlap, the Director of Industrial Relations, had responsibility for this program along with his other duties in Industrial Relations (see Exhibit 3).

Early History of Career Development (1957–1965)

"What are we doing about management development?" Simon Ramo was asked in 1957. Ramo replied: "We don't believe in management development. We hire bright, intelligent people and we don't plan to insult their intelligence by giving them courses in courage."

In 1961, as Systems was trying to expand its customer base and cope with its new competitive environment, Rube Mettler became President. Mettler asked a consulting firm for advice on how best to make the transition to a competitive firm. "Systems needs men with experience in business management," the consultants said. "You will have to hire experienced top-level administrators from outside the firm. There aren't any here." Mettler agreed with them about needing top-level administrators. "But we'll develop our own people," Mettler added. Mettler confided in others that he feared that a manager with experience in another organization would have to unlearn a lot of bad habits before he could be successful at TRW.

Mettler put Dunlap in charge of the development program at TRW. Mettler made it clear to Dunlap that he wanted a task-oriented, dynamic development program to fit the special needs of the Systems Group.

Dunlap felt he needed assistance to implement the kind of program Mettler wanted. "The one thing I did was to entice Shel Davis to come into Industrial Relations," commented Dunlap. "He impressed me as a restless, dynamic, creative sort of guy." Davis had worked in a line position in one of TRW's other divisions.

With the help of an outside consultant, Dunlap and Davis began to design a development program. Early in 1962, forty top managers were interviewed about what they felt was needed. One manager characterized the feelings of the entire group: "We need skills in management. Every time a new project starts around here, it takes half of the project schedule just bringing people on board. If we could have a quicker start-up, we'd finish these projects on time."

Dunlap, Davis, and the consultant went to work on a plan to fit these specific needs. Dunlap set up a two-day offsite meeting to discuss their plans and recommendations with some of the top managers. At the meeting, Dunlap and Davis talked about two, relatively new, applied behavioral science techniques (called team development and T-groups) as ways of meeting the needs of managers.[4] Dave Patterson was there and was impressed by this approach. Patterson had recently been appointed head of a new project and asked for their assistance: "I have a new team and I'm ready to hold a team-building meeting next week. Can you arrange it?"

Shel Davis, along with a consultant, held an off-site team development session for Patterson. After the meeting, Patterson's project group improved its working relationships with manufacturing. The success of this experiment became well known throughout the company. Mettler asked Patterson what effect the meeting had had. "It saved us six weeks on the program. About a million bucks," Patterson replied. This impressed people.

Late in 1962 Davis and Dunlap prepared a "white paper" on possible approaches in career development and sent it to the top seventy people. Most of the managers responded that TRW should improve its skills in three areas: communications and interpersonal skills, business management skills, and technical skills. Davis described the conversation he and Dunlap had with Mettler.

> Jim and I talked with Mettler about the kind of program we wanted in the company and what we did and didn't want to do. As it turned out, we were in agreement with Mettler on almost every issue. For example, we decided not to make it a crash effort but to work at it and to take a lot of time making sure people understood what we wanted to do and that they supported it. We also decided to start at the top of the organization rather than at the bottom. During these discussions, they decided to call the training effort Career Development rather than organizational development or management development because Mettler didn't want to give the impression that they were going to concentrate on administrative training and neglect technical training.

Shortly after the white paper came out, Shel Davis and Jim Dunlap began to invite people to T-groups run by professionals outside of TRW. About twelve people took advantage of this opportunity between January and May of 1963. Ten of the twelve later reported that it was a "great experience." As a result, Mettler continued to support Dunlap and Davis, telling them, "Try

things—if they work, continue them; if they don't, modify them, improve them, or drop them."

In April 1963, Davis and Dunlap decided to hold a team development meeting for the key people in Industrial Relations. The two men felt that once employees at the Systems Group started going to T-groups there would be a growing demand for "Career Development" activities, which the IR group would be asked to meet. The team development session, they felt, would help train the IR staff to meet this demand.

Dunlap and Davis next decided to run some T-groups themselves within TRW. Dunlap argued for limiting this effort to twenty people. Davis wanted forty, saying, "Hell, let's go with it. Let's do too much too fast and then it will really have an effect on the organization. Otherwise, it might not be noticed." Dunlap and Davis eventually decided to run four T-groups of ten people each.

The chain of events following that activity was later described by Frank Jasinski, who became Director of Career Development in 1964:

> After that things really started to move. There was a strong demand for T-group experience. But we didn't just want to send people through labs like we were turning out so many sausages. We wanted to free up the organization, to seed it with people who had been to T-groups. The T-groups were to be just the beginning of a continuing process.
>
> This continuing process was in several stages and developed over the three-year period. Maybe I can describe it in terms of one manager and his work group. First, the manager volunteered to go to a T-group (we have kept the program on a voluntary basis). Before he went to the T-group, there was a pre-T-group session where the participants asked questions and got prepared for the T-group experience. Then they went through the T-group.
>
> After the T-group, there were three or four sessions where the T-group participants got together to discuss the problems of applying the T-group values back home. After the manager had been through the T-group, some of the members of his work group could decide to go to a T-group. The next stage was when the manager and his group decided they wanted to undertake a team development process where they could work on improving intragroup relations, that is, how they could be more effective as a team. Following a team development effort could be an interface meeting. This is the kind Alan East had. It seems Alan's department, Product Assurance, was having trouble getting along with a number of different departments in the organization. Alan felt if they were going to do their job well they had to be able to work effectively with these other groups. So he got three or four of his peo-

---

[4] *Team development (or team building) refers to a development process designed to improve the performance and effectiveness of people who work together. Laboratory T-groups (training groups) is a form of experiential learning away from the normal environment. Using unstructured groups, participants attempt to increase their sensitivity to their own and others' behavior as well as factors that hinder group interaction and effectiveness.*

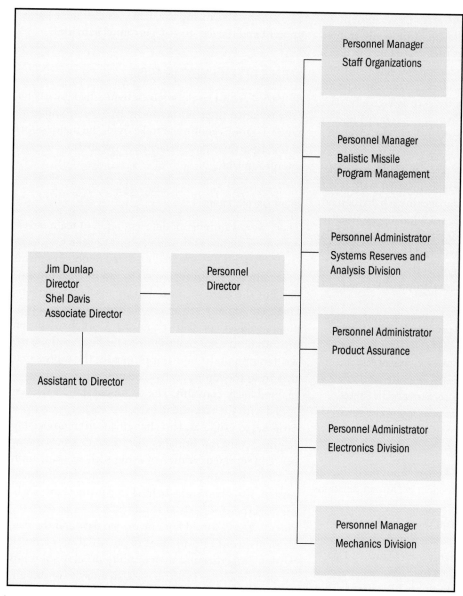

EXHIBIT 3   Industrial Relations

ple together with the key people from five or six other departments and they worked on the interdepartmental relationship. Still another type of meeting that is similar is the intergroup meeting. If two groups just can't get along and are having difficulties, they may decide to hold an off-site meeting and try to work on the problems between them.

We also started doing some technical training and business management training. As with all of our training, we try to make it organic: to meet the needs of the people and the organization. We tend to ask, "What is the problem?" Specific skills training may

not be the answer. For example, a manager calls us and says he wants his secretary to have a review course in shorthand because she is slipping in her ability to use it. We might say, "Let's talk about it; maybe her shorthand is slipping because she doesn't use it enough and maybe she wants more challenging work. Why don't we get together with you and your secretary and discuss it?" We have held several meetings with bosses and their secretaries to improve boss-secretary relationships. When they understand each other better, the secretary is more willing to help her boss and she is also in a better position to do so.

Such a large increase in Career Development activities required a rapid build-up of uniquely trained personnel. This problem was met in part by the use of outside consultants. Systems Group was able to interest a number of the national leaders in T-group-type activities to act as consultants, to serve as T-group trainers, and to work with the divisions on team-building activities. By December 1964, they had built up a staff of nine outside consultants.[5]

For the program to work on a day-to-day basis, they felt a need to build a comparable internal staff. It was decided that the personnel manager in each division not only would be responsible for traditional personnel activities but would also be an internal consultant on Career Development activities. Lynn Stewart, one of the outside consultants working with the Systems Group, described how TRW obtained a group of trained personnel managers:

> Systems Group needed to build some internal change agents, which meant expanding the Industrial Relations effort. It required the development of the skills of people in Industrial Relations, especially the personnel managers. They were able to retool some of the people in Industrial Relations by sending them to T-groups. Some were not able to make the transition. They were transferred or fired. All of this was done to provide a staff that could service the needs created when people returned from T-groups.

In December 1964, Jim Dunlap announced that he had been promoted to Vice President of Human Relations for TRW Inc. and would be moving to Cleveland. He also announced that Shel Davis would succeed him as Director of Industrial Relations. (Exhibit 4 presents an organization chart of Industrial Relations as of January 1965).

A number of the personnel managers became concerned about the future of Industrial Relations. They knew Shel Davis had openly referred to the day-to-day personnel activities as "personnel crap," and they wondered what changes he would make. One personnel manager expressed this feeling when he said, "There were some undertones of a threat in Jim's leaving which might break the balance of prudence and loose Shel upon the group, forcing us to work exclusively on Career Development and to neglect our day-to-day personnel responsibilities."

By summer, 1966, however, most of the people in Industrial Relations felt that Shel Davis had adjusted to his role as Director of Industrial Relations and was doing a good job of balancing the demands of Career Development and the day-to-day personnel activities.

CAREER DEVELOPMENT IN 1966

By 1966, Career Development activities had greatly increased since their initiation in 1963 (see Exhibit 5). While T-groups continued to be used, the major effort of the department was in facilitating team building and intergroup labs.

Team Development

There were a number of different types of team development activities. One was an effort to get a new team started faster. TRW repeatedly created temporary teams to accomplish recurring tasks. The tasks were quite similar, but the team membership changed considerably. One example was a team established to prepare a proposal to bid on a particular contract. More than a dozen organizations would contribute to the final product: the written proposal. On major proposals, the representatives from the administrative and nontechnical areas remained fairly constant. The technical staff, however, varied with the task and usually was entirely new from proposal to proposal. This changing team membership required constant "bringing up to speed" of new members and repeated creation of a smoothly working unit. As the new team came together, a team development session, usually off-site, helped to get the team working together sooner and would save time in the long run. A session would last one or two days and the participants would try to identify potential problems in working together and then begin to develop solutions for such problems. Lynn Stewart, an outside consultant, described a team development session for a launch team:

> TRW has a matrix organization so that any one man is a member of many systems simultaneously. He has interfaces with many different groups. In addition, he is continually moving from one team to another, so they need team development to get the teams off to a fast start. On a launch team, for example, you have all kinds of people who come together for a short time. There are project directors, manufacturing people, the scientists who designed the experiments, and the men who launch the bird. You have to put all of those men together into a cohesive group in a short time. At launch time they can't be worrying about an organizational chart and how their respective roles change as preparation for the launch progresses. Their relationships do change over time, but they should work that through and discuss it beforehand, not when the bird is on the pad. The concept of the

---

[5] *This group consisted of senior professors at some of the largest business schools in the country and nationally recognized private consultants.*

A. Industrial Relations

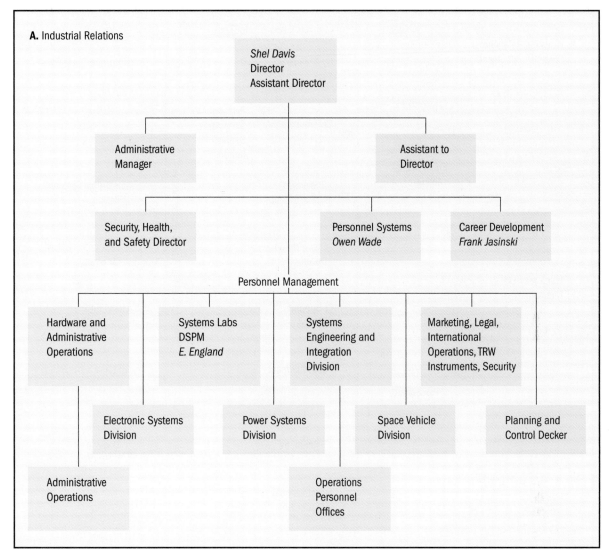

EXHIBIT 4

organization is that you have a lot of resources and you need to regroup them in different ways as customers and contracts change. You can speed up the regrouping process by holding team development sessions.

Another type of team development activity was one with an ongoing group. Typically, the manager would come to the personnel manager in his division and express an interest in team development for his group. If both agreed it would be beneficial, they would begin to plan such a session. First, an effort would be made to identify an agenda for the one- or two-day off-site meetings. This would be developed in one of two ways. The personnel manager or the consultant could interview, on an individual basis, all the people who would be at-

tending the session to identify problem areas on which they needed to work. He would then summarize the problems identified in his interviews and distribute this summary to the participants a day or two before the session was held. Another method sometimes used to develop an agenda was to get all of the participants together on-site for two or three hours several days before the off-site meeting. The participants would then be divided into subgroups and would identify problem areas to work on. At the extended off-site staff meeting, the intention was that the group would be task-oriented, addressing itself to the question, "How can we improve the way our groups work together?" They would look at how the group's process got in the way of the group's

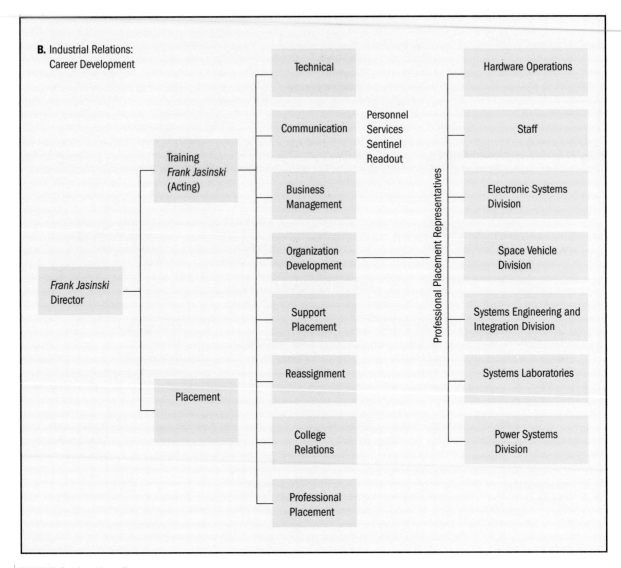

B. Industrial Relations:
Career Development

EXHIBIT 4 (continued)

performance. The manager of the group would conduct the meeting, but the personnel manager and an outside consultant would be there to help the group by observing and raising issues that the group should look at. There had been a number of similar team development sessions at TRW, and the people involved felt that they had been worthwhile in that they had improved the group's effectiveness.

Another type of team development activity that was carried out on a continuous basis was the critiquing of the many meetings held in the organization. The casewriter sat in on a staff meeting of the Industrial Relations Department that was attended by the personnel managers and key people in the staff groups of Personnel Systems and Career Development. The purpose of the meeting was to plan the projects to be undertaken by Personnel Systems and Career Development throughout the remainder of the year. This included a discussion of what projects the personnel managers would like undertaken and a priority listing as to which were most important. Owen Wade, Director of Personnel Systems, led the discussion during the first hour and a half of the meeting while the group discussed projects for Personnel Systems. Frank Jasinski, Director of Career Development, led the discussion in the last hour of the meeting, in which projects for Career Development were discussed. Near the end of the meeting the following discussion took place:

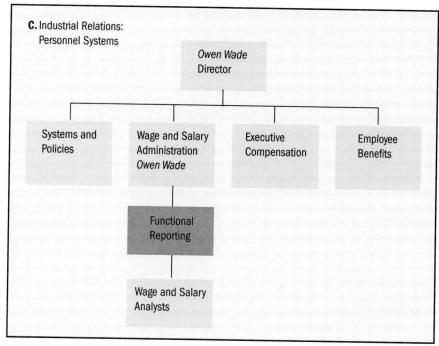

C. Industrial Relations: Personnel Systems

EXHIBIT 4 (continued)

SHEL DAVIS We only have ten minutes left so we had better spend some time on a critique of the meeting. Does anyone have any comments?

ED (Personnel Manager) We bit off more than we could chew here. We shouldn't have planned to do so much.

DON (Personnel Manager) I felt we just floated from 10:30 to 10:45. We got through with Frank and his subject and then nothing was done until the break.

BOB (Personnel Manager) Why didn't you make that observation at 10:30, Don, so we could do something about it? Do you feel intimidated about making a process observation?

DON No. I felt like I was in the corner earlier. But not after making this observation. Besides, I did say earlier that we weren't doing anything and should move on, but I guess didn't say it loud enough for people to hear me.

ED Don, that is the first time you've made a process observation in six months. I wish you'd make more of them.

SHEL I think Owen's presentation was very good because he had estimated the number of man-weeks of work required for each of the projects. Frank's presentation was less effective because his didn't have that.

JASINSKI I have a question on the manpower requirements. I spent seven or eight hours preparing for this meeting in setting priorities on all the projects we had listed and then it wasn't followed up in this meeting. [Two or three people echoed support for this statement.]

BOB I thought we were asked to do too much in preparing for this meeting. It was just too detailed and too much work, so I rebelled and refused to do it.

WADE (Director of Personnel Systems) Well, from my point of view on the staff side of the fence, I feel pressured and as if I'm asked to do too much. The personnel managers have a very different set of rules. You don't plan as much as we have to and I think you should plan more.

One of the participants commented that a large number of the meetings at TRW were critiqued in a similar manner.

Intergroup and Interface Labs

As a result of the nature of the work at TRW and of the matrix organization, there was a great deal of interaction between the various groups in the organization. Sometimes this interaction was characterized by conflict; the Career Development staff began to work on ways to help groups deal with this conflict. One such effort, the first interface lab, developed out of an experience of Alan East, Director of Product Assurance. Mr. East commented on his experience:

> I came to Product Assurance from a technical organization, so I knew very little of what Product Assurance was about. First, I tried to find out what our objectives were. I talked to our supervisors,

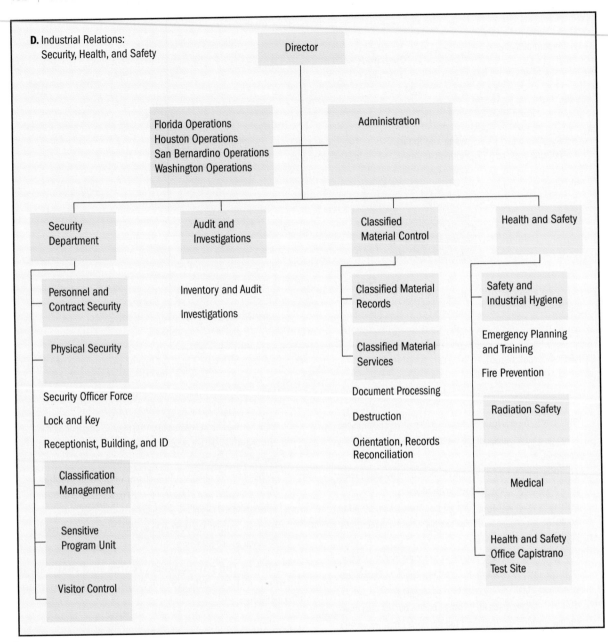

D. Industrial Relations:
Security, Health, and Safety

Director

Florida Operations
Houston Operations
San Bernardino Operations
Washington Operations

Administration

Security Department

Audit and Investigations

Classified Material Control

Health and Safety

Personnel and Contract Security

Inventory and Audit

Investigations

Classified Material Records

Safety and Industrial Hygiene

Physical Security

Emergency Planning and Training

Fire Prevention

Security Officer Force

Lock and Key

Receptionist, Building, and ID

Classified Material Services

Document Processing

Destruction

Orientation, Records Reconciliation

Radiation Safety

Classification Management

Sensitive Program Unit

Medical

Visitor Control

Health and Safety Office Capistrano Test Site

EXHIBIT 4   (continued)

and I found there was a lack of morale. They thought they were second-class citizens. They were cowed by the domineering engineers and they felt inferior. I decided one of the problems was that people outside Product Assurance didn't understand us and the importance of our job. I concluded that that was easy to solve: We'd educate them. So, we set out to educate the company. We decided to call a meeting, and we drew up an agenda. Then, as an afterthought, I went to see Shel Davis to see if he had some ideas on how to train people. But he just turned it around. He got me to see that rather than educating them, maybe we could find

out how they really saw us and why. Well, we held an off-site meeting and we identified a lot of problems between Product Assurance and the other departments. After the meeting, we came back and started to work to correct those problems.

After East's successful interface meeting, the idea caught hold and similar meetings were held by other groups. Harold Nelson, the Director of Finance, held an interface meeting between four members of his department and a number of departments that had frequent contact with Finance. The purpose of the meeting was to get feedback on how Finance was seen by others in the organization. Commenting on the effectiveness of the meeting, Nelson added, "They were impressed that we were able to have a meeting, listen to their gripes about us, and not be defensive. The impact of such meetings on individuals is tremendous. It causes people to change so these meetings are very productive."

Del Thomas, a participant in the interface meeting with Finance, represented another department. Thomas observed that, prior to the meeting, his group felt Finance was too slow in evaluating requests and that Nelson and his subordinates "... were too meticulous, too much like accountants." Thomas felt the meeting improved the performance of Finance:

I think Harold [Nelson] got what he was looking for, but he may have been surprised there were so many negative comments. I think there are indications that the meeting has improved things. First, Harold is easier to get ahold of now. Second, since the meeting, Harold brought in a new man to evaluate capital expenditures, and he's doing a top job. He's helpful, and he has speeded up the process. I think the atmosphere of the whole Finance group is changing. They are starting to think more of "we the company" and less of "us and them."

EVALUATION OF THE CAREER DEVELOPMENT EFFORT

Jim Dunlap, the Vice President for Human Relations, was asked to evaluate the effect of Career Development on TRW Systems. Dunlap pulled two studies from his desk drawer. The first, a report by a government official titled "Impulse for Openness," noted in its summary:

It is not our intention, nor certainly that of TRW Systems, to imply that either the company reorganization or the physical progress is solely the result of the Career Development program, but it does appear that the program had a substantial impact on the success of the company. The data shown completes the picture of changes in the company during the period under discussion. Employment at 6000 in 1962 and over 11,000 in March 1966 will most likely double by the end of this year. Sales more than tripled between 1962 and 1965. Professional turnover decreased from 17.1 percent in 1962 to 6.9 percent in March 1966. The average for the aerospace industry in this area of California is approximately 20 percent.

Also, Dunlap revealed the results of a study by a professional organization to which many of Systems Group employees belong. It took a survey of all of its members, asking them to rank fifty-four firms in the aerospace industry on six different factors. The respondents ranked TRW Systems first in "desirability as an employer," seventh for "contribution to aerospace," and second in "salary."

Dunlap also added his personal comments on the efforts of the Career Development program:

It's very hard to make an evaluation of the program and say it has saved us "X" million dollars. But there are several indications that it has been effective. Turnover is down significantly and I've heard a lot of people say, "I stayed at TRW because of the Career Development activities." Some people make more definite claims for the program. Dave Patterson says our Team Development Process saved us $500,000. Rube Mettler is convinced the program has improved our skills so that we've won some contracts we wouldn't have gotten otherwise. I believe it has improved our team performance. All of our proposal teams spend two days of team building before they start on the proposal. Every program starts with an off-site team development lab. They help build a team esprit de corps, and it creates an openness so they are better able to solve problems.

A number of employees were willing to discuss their attitudes toward the Career Development program. Denis Brown, a member of the administrative staff, and a participant in the activities of Career Development, felt the program was valuable. Denis noted:

They took the OGO launch crew off-site and improved their effectiveness. Well, a launch is very tense, and if one guy is hostile toward another, it may mean a failure that costs $20 million. I don't know how much they spent on Career Development, but say it's a quarter of a million dollars. If one man improves his relationship with another and it saves a launch and $20 million, you've made it back many times over. The company feels it is a good thing, and it has worked well, so they'll continue it.

Jim Whitman, a subproject manager, had high praise for Career Development. Whitman credited the program for making groups more effective in communicating and working with one another. Recounting his own experiences, Whitman added that the program led to better collaboration and working conditions between the design engineer and the fabrication engineer.

But other employees were less enthusiastic. John Ward, a member of a program office, discussed his participation in Career Development activities. Ward felt that some of the off-site sessions were "rather grueling affairs, particularly when you are the center of attention." But Ward added that the session he attended was valuable:

In my opinion, the reason it was worthwhile is that under the pressure of work people cannot—I use the word cannot when I should say will not—take the time to sit down and discuss some very

Activities	1963		1964		1965	
	Courses	Attendees	Courses	Attendees	Courses	Attendees
Orientation	49	627	32	369	32	1,146
Colloquia	51	3,060	31	5,580	7	1,525
Invited lectures	2	800	4	1,600	—	—
Evening courses	12	261	17	438	16	651
Staff education	—	767	—	1,066	—	1,166
Technical courses	—	—	3	97	6	377
Internal leadership laboratories (T-groups)	1	45	4	104	4	151
External leadership laboratories (T-groups)	—	20	—	17	—	27
Team development meetings	—	—	4	76	44	671

EXHIBIT 5 Career Development Activities, 1963–1965

basic issues to get the air cleared. Even in a small group people tend to wear blinders. You think about your own problems because you have so many of them, so you tend to build up a fence to keep some of the other fellow's problems from getting through. He talks about them but you don't hear them; you don't get the significance of what he's trying to tell you. But if you go away with instructions that people are not to bother you unless it is really important, you create an environment where there is time to work out some of these things.

One member of the administrative staff, Dan Jackson, had very different views on Career Development. Jackson noted:

> Idealistically, it's a good thing. If in the real world people lived that way, were open and sincere and could tell each other their feelings without getting hurt, it would be excellent. But people just aren't that way in the real world. The people who are enthusiastic about this—Mettler, Hesse, Davis, etc.—are at a level in the company where they can practice this. They're just dealing with other vice presidents and top-level people. But down on my level it won't work. We've got to produce things down here and people just aren't responsible and we can't just be nice to people all the time. We have to get some work done.
>
> I think that the trainers at the lab live that way and that's all right, but they tend to be frustrated head-shrinkers. They want

to be psychiatrists, but they don't have the training—so they do sensitivity training. Its kind of like running a therapy group. I think the techniques they use are pretty good, like having one group inside talking and one group on the outside observing, but the people running it aren't well enough trained. They may be the best that are available, but they are not good enough. Frankly, I think these trainers are really just trying to find out their own problems, but they do it by getting mixed up in other people's problems.

Jackson continued, observing that participation in these activities was not completely voluntary:

> Oh, it's voluntary, but you are kind of told you had better go. You aren't fired if you don't, but there's pressure put on you to go. One of our Ph.D.'s walked out after two days at a T-group. I don't think it has hurt his career but people know he took a walk. He just felt it was a sin, morally wrong, what was going on up there.

While Jackson seemed to express the most negative attitudes toward Career Development, there was a widely circulated story about a man who had suffered a nervous breakdown after attending a T-group. Jim Dunlap was asked to comment on the incident:

> Yes, one group had a traumatic experience, or as they say, "cracked up." Very early in the program we decided that the people in per-

sonnel should go to a T-group so they'd understand what we were going to do. I asked this fellow if he'd like to go. He took it as an order and he went. But I was only asking him to go. If I'd known more about him, I wouldn't have asked him if he wanted to go. But I just saw him at work and he seemed to be getting along all right, although I knew that he didn't enjoy his job. He wanted to get into education. But I didn't know he was having troubles at home and that things weren't going very well for him in general. He was just kind of holding himself together as best he could. He

went to the T-group and it caused him to start thinking about his situation and he fell apart; he had a nervous breakdown. After the T-group was over he went home, but he didn't go to work. He stayed home for a week or two. Finally, he decided he needed help and began to see a psychiatrist. Apparently that was just what he needed because he then decided to get that job in education, which he liked very much. He seems to have solved his problems, so everything has turned out for the best. But it scared the hell out of us at the time.

C A S E   5

Texana Petroleum Corporation

JAY W. LORSCH, PAUL R. LAWRENCE,
AND JAMES A. GARRISON

During the summer of 1966, George Prentice, the newly designated Executive Vice President for domestic operations of the Texana Petroleum Corporation, was devoting much of his time to thinking about improving the combined performance of the five product divisions reporting to him (see Exhibit 1). His principal concern was that corporate profits were not reflecting the full potential contribution that could result from the close technological interdependence of the raw materials utilized and produced by these divisions. The principal difficulty, as Prentice saw it, was that the division general managers reporting to him were not working well together:

As far as I can see, the issue is, Where do we make the money for the corporation? Not, How do we beat the other guy? Nobody is communicating with anybody else at the general manager level. In fact, they are telling a bunch of secrets around here.

RECENT CORPORATE HISTORY

The Texana Petroleum Corporation was one of the early major producers and marketers of petroleum products in southwestern United States. Until the early 1950s, Texana had been almost exclusively in the business of processing and refining crude oil and selling petroleum

products through a chain of company-operated service stations in southwestern United States and in Central and South America. By 1950, company sales had risen to approximately $500 million, with accompanying growth in profits. About 1950, however, Texana faced increasingly stiff competition at the retail service station level from several larger national petroleum companies. As a result, sales volume declined sharply during the early 1950s, and by 1955 sales had fallen to only $300 million and the company was operating at just above the break-even point.

At this time, because of his age, Roger Holmes, who had been a dominant force in the company since its founding, retired as President and Chief Executive Officer. He was replaced by Donald Irwin, 49, who had been a senior executive with a major chemical company. William Dutton, 55, was appointed Chairman of the Board to replace the retiring Board Chairman. Dutton had spent his entire career with Texana. Prior to his appointment as Chairman, he had been Senior Vice President for Petroleum Products, reporting to Holmes.

Irwin and Dutton, along with other senior executives, moved quickly to solve the problems facing Texana. They gradually divested the company's retail outlets and abandoned the domestic consumer petroleum markets. Through both internal development and acquisition they expanded and rapidly increased the company's involvement in the business of processing petroleum for chemical and plastics products. In moving in this direction, they were rapidly expanding on initial moves made by Texana in 1949, when the company built its first chemical processing plant and began marketing these products. To speed the company's growth in these areas, Irwin and Dutton selected aggressive general managers for each division and gave them a large degree of freedom in decision making. Top management's major requirement was that each division general manager create a growing division with a satisfactory return on investment capital. By 1966, top management had reshaped the company so that in both the domestic and foreign markets it was an integrated producer of chemicals and plastic materials. In foreign operations the company continued to operate service stations in Latin America and in Europe. This change in direction was successful, and by 1966 company sales had risen to $750 million, with a healthy rise in profit.

In spite of this success, management believed that there was a need for an increase in return on invested capital. The financial and trade press, which had been generous in its praise of the company's recovery, was still critical of the present return on investment, and top management shared this concern. Dutton, Irwin, and Prentice were in agreement that one important method of increasing profits was to take further advantage of the potential cost savings that could come from increased coordination between the domestic operating divisions, as they developed new products, processes, and markets.

DOMESTIC ORGANIZATION, 1966

The product divisions' reports to Mr. Prentice represented a continuum of producing and marketing activities from production and refining of crude oil to the marketing of several types of plastics products to industrial consumers. Each division was headed by a general manager. While there was some variation in the internal organizational structure of the several divisions, they were generally set up along functional lines (manufacturing, sales, research and development). Each division also had its own controller and engineering activities, although these were supported and augmented by the corporate staff. While divisions had their own research effort, there was also a Central Research Laboratory at the corporate level, which carried on longer-range research of a more fundamental nature that was outside the scope of the activities of any of the product divisions.

The *Petroleum Products Division* was the remaining nucleus of the company's original producing and refining

activities. It supplied raw materials to the Polymer and Chemicals Division and also sold refining products under long-term contracts to other petroleum companies. In the early and mid-1950s, this division's management had generated much of the company's revenue and profits through its skill in negotiating these agreements. In 1966, top corporate management felt that this division's management had accepted its role as a supplier to the rest of the corporation and that there were harmonious relations between it and its sister divisions.

The *Polymer and Chemicals Division* was developed internally during the late 1940s and early 1950s as management saw its share of the consumer petroleum market declining. Under the leadership of Seymour Knoph (who had been General Manager for several years) and his predecessor (who in 1966 was Executive Vice President-Administration), the division had rapidly developed a line of chemical and polymer compounds derived from petroleum raw materials. Most of the products of this division were manufactured under licensing agreement or were materials with formulations that were well understood. Nevertheless, technical personnel in the division had developed an industrywide reputation for their ability to develop new and improved processes. Top management of the division took particular pride in this ability. From the beginning, the decisions of what products to manufacture were based to a large extent upon the requirements of the Molded and Packaging Products Divisions. However, Polymer and Chemicals Division executives had always attempted to market these same products to external customers and had been highly successful. These external sales were extremely important to Texana, since they assured a large enough volume of operation to process a broad product line of polymer chemicals profitably. As the other divisions had grown, they had required a larger proportion of the division's capacity, which meant that Polymer and Chemicals Division managers had to reduce their commitment to external customers.

The *Molded Products Division* was also an internally developed division, formed in 1951. Its products were a variety of molded plastic products ranging from toys and household items to automotive and electronic parts. This division's major strengths were its knowledge of molding technology and particularly its marketing ability. While it depended upon the Polymer and Chemicals Division for its raw materials, its operations were largely independent of those of the Packaging Products and Building Products Divisions.

The *Packaging Products Division* was acquired in 1952. Its products were plastic packaging materials, including

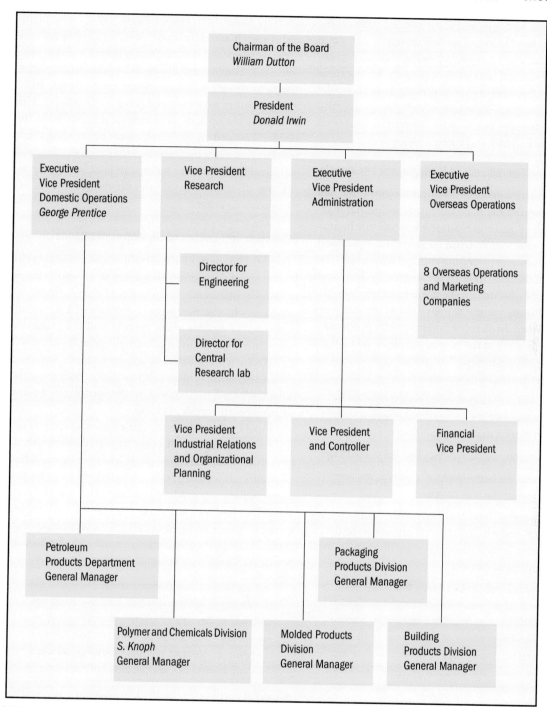

EXHIBIT 1   Texana Petroleum Company—Partial Organization Chart, 1966

films, cartons, bottles, etc. All of these products were marketed to industrial customers. Like the Molded Products Division, the Packaging Division depended on the Polymer and Chemicals Division as a source of raw materials but was largely independent of other end-product divisions.

The *Building Products Division* was acquired in 1963 to give Texana a position in the construction materials market. The division produced a variety of insulation roofing materials and similar products and marketed them to the building trade. It was a particularly attractive acquisition for Texana because, prior to the acquisition, it had achieved some success with plastic products for insulation and roofing materials. Although the plastic products accounted for less than 20 percent of the total division sales in 1965, plans called for these products to account for over 50 percent of division sales in the next five years. Its affiliation with Texana gave this division a stronger position in plastic raw materials through the Polymer and Chemicals Division.

Selection and Recruitment of Management Personnel

The rapid expansion of the corporation into these new areas had created the need for much additional management talent, and top management had not hesitated to bring new men in from outside the corporation, as well as to advance promising younger men inside Texana. Most managers, in both the internally developed and acquired divisions, had spent their careers inside the division, although some top division managers were moved between divisions or into corporate positions.

In speaking about the type of people he had sought for management positions, Donald Irwin described his criteria in a financial publication:

> We don't want people around who are afraid to move. The attraction of Texana is that it gives the individual responsibilities that aren't diluted. It attracts the fellow who wants a challenge.

Another corporate executive described Texana managers:

> It's a group of very tough-minded, but considerate, gentlemen with an enormous drive to get things done.

Another manager, who had been with Texana for his entire career, and who considered himself to be different from most Texana managers, described the typical Texana manager as follows:

> Texana attracts a particular type of person. Most of these characteristics are personal characteristics rather than professional ones. I would use terms such as cold, unfeeling, aggressive, and extremely competitive, but not particularly loyal to the organization. He is loyal to dollars, his own personal dollars. I think this is part of the communication problem. I think this is done on purpose. The selection process leads in this direction. I think this is so because of contrast with the way the company operated ten years ago. Of course, I was at the plant level at that time. But today the attitude I have described is also in the plants. Ten years ago, the organization was composed of people who worked together for the good of the organization because they wanted to. I don't think this is so today.

Location of Division Facilities

The Petroleum Products, Polymer and Chemicals, and Packaging Products Divisions had their executive offices located on separate floors of the Texana head-quarters building in the Chicago "Loop." The plants and research and development facilities of these divisions were spread out across Oklahoma, Texas, and Louisiana. The Molded Products Division had its headquarters, research and development facilities, and a major plant in an industrial suburb of Chicago. This division's other plants were at several locations in the Middle West and on the East Coast. The Building Products Division's headquarters and major production and technical facilities were located in Fort Worth, Texas. All four divisions shared sales offices in major cities from coast to coast.

Evaluation and Control of Division Performance

The principal method of controlling and evaluating the operations of these divisions was the semiannual review of division plans and the approval of major capital expenditures by the executive committee.[1] In reviewing performance against plans, members of the executive committee placed almost sole emphasis on the division's actual return on investment against budget. Corporate executives felt that this practice, together with the technological interdependence of the divisions, created many disputes about transfer pricing.

In addition to these regular reviews, corporate executives had frequent discussions with division executives about their strategies, plans, and operations. It had been difficult for corporate management to strike the proper balance in guiding the operations for the divisions. This problem was particularly acute with regard to the Polymer and Chemicals Division because of its central place in the corporation's product line. One corporate staff member explained his view of the problem:

> This whole matter of communications between the corporate staff and the Polymer and Chemicals Division has been a fairly difficult problem. Corporate management used to contribute immensely to this by trying to get into the nuts and bolts area within the Polymer and Chemicals organization, and this created serious criticisms; however I think they have backed off in this matter

A second corporate executive, in discussing this matter for a trade publication report, put the problem this way:

> We're trying to find the middle ground. We don't want to be a holding company, and with our diversity we can't be a highly centralized corporation.

---

[1] *The executive committee consisted of Messrs. Dutton, Irwin, and Prentice, as well as the vice president of research, the executive vice president of administration, and the executive vice president of foreign operations.*

Executive Vice President—Domestic Operations

In an effort to find this middle ground, the position of Executive Vice President—Domestic Operations was created in early 1966, and George Prentice was the first to hold the position. Prior to this change, there had been two Senior Domestic Vice Presidents—one in charge of the Petroleum and Polymer and Chemicals Divisions and the other in charge of the end-use divisions. Mr. Prentice had been Senior Vice President in charge of the end-use divisions before the new position was created. He had held that position for only two years, having come to it from a highly successful marketing career with a competitor.

At the time of his appointment, one press account described Mr. Prentice as "hard-driving, aggressive, and ambitious—an archetype of the self-actuated dynamo Irwin has sought out."

Shortly after taking his new position, Prentice described the task before him:

> I think the corporation wants to integrate its parts better and I am here because I reflect this feeling. We can't be a bunch of entrepreneurs around here. We have got to balance discipline with entrepreneurial motivation. This is what we were in the past, just a bunch of entrepreneurs and if they came in with ideas we would get the money, but now our dollars are limited, and especially the Polymer and Chemical boys haven't been able to discipline themselves to select from within ten good projects. They just don't seem to be able to do this, and so they come running in here with all ten good projects, which they say we have to buy, and they get upset when we can't buy them all.
>
> This was the tone of my predecessors [Senior Vice Presidents]. All of them were very strong on being entrepreneurs. I am going to run it different[ly]. I am going to take a marketing and capital orientation. As far as I can see, there is a time to compete and a time to collaborate, and I think right now there has been a lack of recognition in the Polymer and Chemicals executive suite that this thing has changed.

Other Views of Domestic Interdivisional Relations

Executives within the Polymer and Chemicals Division, in the end-use divisions, and at the corporate level shared Prentice's view that the major breakdown in interdivisional relations was between the Polymer and Chemicals Division and the end-use divisions. Executives in the end-use divisions made these typical comments about the problem:

> I think the thing we have got to realize is that we are wedded to the Polymer and Chemicals Division whether we like it or not. We are really tied up with them. And just as we would with any outside supplier or with any of our customers, we will do things to maintain their business. But because they feel they have our business wrapped up they do not reciprocate in turn. Now let me emphasize that they have not arbitrarily refused to do the things that we are requiring, but there is a pressure on them for investment projects and we are low man on the pole. And I think this could heavily jeopardize our chances for growth.
>
> I would say our relationships are sticky, and I think this is primarily because we think our reason for being is to make money, so we try to keep Polymer and Chemicals as an arm's length supplier. For example, I cannot see, just because it is a Polymer and Chemicals product, accepting millions of pounds of very questionable material. It takes dollars out of our pocket, and we are very profit-centered.
>
> The big frustration, I guess, and one of our major problems, is that you can't get help from them [Polymer and Chemicals]. You feel they are not interested in what you are doing, particularly if it doesn't have a large return for them. But as far as I am concerned this has to become a joint-venture relationship, and this is getting to be real sweat with us. We are the guys down below yelling for help. And they have got to give us some relief.
>
> My experience with the Polymer and Chemicals Division is that you cannot trust what they say at all, and even when they put it in writing you can't be absolutely sure that they are going to live up to it.

Managers within the Polymer and Chemicals Division expressed similar sentiments:

> Personally, right now I have the feeling that the divisions' interests are growing further apart. It seems that the divisions are going their own ways. For example, we are a polymer producer but the molding division wants to be in a special area, so that means they are going to be less of a customer to us, and there is a whole family of plastics being left out that nobody's touching, and this is bearing on our program .... We don't mess with the Building Products Division at all, either. They deal in small volumes. Those that we are already making we sell to them; those that we don't make we can't justify making because of the kinds of things we are working with. What I am saying is that I don't think the corporation is integrating, but I think we ought to be, and this is one of the problems of delegated divisions. What happens is that an executive heads this up and goes for the place that makes the most money for the division, but this is not necessarily the best place from a corporate standpoint.
>
> We don't have as much contact with sister divisions as I think we should. I have been trying to get a liaison with guys in my function but it has been a complete flop. One of the problems is that I don't know who to call on in these other divisions. There is no table of organization, nor is there any encouragement to try and get anything going. My experience has been that all of these operating divisions are very closed organizations. I know guys up the line will say that I am nuts about this. They say to just call

over and I will get an answer. But this always has to be a big deal, and it doesn't happen automatically, and it hurts us.

The comments of corporate staff members describe these relationships and the factors they saw contributing to the problem:

Right now I would say there is an iron curtain between the Polymer and Chemicals Division and the rest of the corporation. You know, we tell our divisions they are responsible, autonomous groups, and the Polymer and Chemicals Division took it very seriously. However, when you are a three-quarter-billion-dollar company, you've got to be coordinated or the whole thing is going to fall apart—it can be no other way. The Domestic Executive Vice President thing has been a big step forward to improve this, but I would say it hasn't worked out yet.

The big thing that is really bothering [the Polymer and Chemicals Division] is that they think they have to go develop all new markets on their own. They are going to do it alone independently, and this is the problem they are faced with. They have got this big thing, that they want to prove that they are a company all by themselves and not rely upon packaging or anybody else.

Polymer and Chemicals Division executives talked about the effect of this drive for independence of the divisional operating heads on their own planning efforts:

The Polymer and Chemicals Division doesn't like to communicate with the corporate staff. This seems hard for us, and I think the [recent major proposal] was a classic example of this. That plan, as it was whipped up by the Polymer and Chemicals Division, has massive implications for the corporation both in expertise and in capital. In fact, I think we did this to be a competitive one-up on the rest of our sister divisions. We wanted to be the best-looking division in the system, but we carried it to an extreme. In this effort, we wanted to show that we had developed this concept completely on our own .... Now I think a lot of our problems with it stemmed from this intense desire we have to be the best in this organization.

Boy, a big doldrum around here was shortly after Christmas (1965) when they dropped out a new plant, right out of our central plan, without any appreciation of the importance of this plant to the whole Polymer and Chemicals Division's growth .... Now we have a windfall and we are back in business on this new plant. But for a while things were very black and everything we had planned and everything we had built our patterns on were out. In fact, when we put this plan together it never really occurred to us that we were going to get it turned down, and I'll bet we didn't even put the plans together in such a way as to really reflect the importance of this plant to the rest of the corporation.

A number of executives in the end-use divisions attributed the interdivisional problems to different management practices and assumptions within the Polymer and Chemicals Division. An executive in the packaging division made this point:

We make decisions quickly and at the lowest possible level, and this is tremendously different from the rest of Texana. I don't know another division like this in the rest of the corporation.

Look at what Sy Knoph has superfluous to his operation compared to ours. These are the reasons for our success. You've got to turn your guys loose and not breathe down their necks all the time. We don't slow our people down with staff. Sure, you may work with a staff, the wheels may grind, but they sure grind slow.

Also, we don't work on detail like the other divisions do. Our management doesn't feel they need the detail stuff. Therefore, they're [Polymer and Chemical] always asking us for detail which we can't supply. Our process doesn't generate it and their process requires it, and this always creates problems with the Polymer and Chemicals Division. But I'll be damned if I am going to have a group of people running between me and the plant, and I'll be goddamned if I am going to clutter up my organization with all the people that Knoph has got working for him. I don't want this staff, but they are sure pushing it on me.

This comment from a Molding Division manager is typical of many about the technical concerns of the Polymer and Chemicals Division management:

Historically, even up to the not-too-distant past, the Polymer and Chemicals Division was considered a snake pit as far as the corporate people were concerned. This was because the corporate people were market-oriented and Polymer and Chemicals Division was technically run and very much a manufacturing effort. These two factors created a communication barrier, because to really understand the Polymer and Chemicals Division problems, they felt that you had to have a basic appreciation of the technology and all the interrelationships.

Building on this strong belief, the Polymer and Chemicals Division executives in the past have tried to communicate in technical terms, and this just further hurt the relationship, and it just did not work. Now they are coming up with a little bit more business or commercial orientation, and they are beginning to appreciate that they have got to justify the things they want to do in a business or commercial orientation, and they are beginning to appreciate that they have got to justify the things they want to do in a business sense rather than just a technical sense. This also helps the problem of maintaining their relationships with the corporation as most of the staff is nontechnical; however, this has changed a little bit in that more and more technical people have been coming on and this has helped from the other side.

They work on the assumption in the Polymer and Chemicals Division that you have to know the territory before you can be an effective manager. You have got to be an operating guy to contribute meaningfully to their problems. However, their biggest problem is this concentration on technical solutions to their problems. This is a thing that has boxed them in the most trouble with the corporation and the other sister divisions.

These and other executives also pointed to another source of conflict between the Polymer and Chemicals Division and other divisions. This was the question of whether the Polymer and Chemicals Division should develop into a more independent marketer, or whether it should rely more heavily on the end-use divisions to "push" its products to the market.

Typical views of this conflict are the following comments by end-use division executives:

The big question I have about Polymer and Chemicals is, What is their strategy going to be? I can understand them completely from a technical standpoint—this is no problem. I wonder what is the role of this company? How is it going to fit into what we and others are doing? Right now, judging from the behavior I've seen, Polymer and Chemicals could care less about what we are doing in terms of integration of our markets or a joint approach to them.

I think it is debatable whether the Polymer and Chemicals Division should be a new product company or not. Right now we have an almost inexhaustible appetite for what they do and do well. As I see it, the present charter is fine. However, that group is very impatient, aggressive, and they want to grow, but you have got to grow within guidelines. Possibly the Polymer and Chemicals Division is just going to have to learn to hang on the coattails of the other divisions, and do just what they are doing now, only better. I think the future role of the Polymer and Chemicals Division is going to be, at any one point in time for the corporation, that if it looks like a product is needed, they will make it . . . . They are going to be suppliers because I will guarantee you that if the moment comes and we can't buy it elsewhere, for example, then I darn well know they are going to make it for us regardless of what their other commitments are. They are just going to have to supply us. If you were to put the Polymer and Chemicals Division off from the corporation, I don't think they would last a year. Without their huge captive requirements, they would not be able to compete economically in the commercial areas they are in.

A number of other executives indicated that the primary emphasis within the corporation on return on in-

vestment by divisions tended to induce, among other things, a narrow, competitive concern on the part of the various divisional managements. The comment of this division executive was typical:

As far as I can see, we [his division and Polymer and Chemicals] are 180 degrees off on our respective charters. Therefore, when Sy Knoph talks about this big project, we listen nicely and then we say, "God bless you, lots of luck," but I am sure we are not going to get involved in it. I don't see any money in it for us. It may be a gold mine for Sy, but it is not for our company; and as long as we are held to the high profit standards we are, we just cannot afford to get involved. I can certainly see it might make good corporate sense for us to get it, but it doesn't make any sense in terms of our particular company. We have got to be able to show the returns in order to get continuing capital, and I just can't on that kind of project. I guess what I am saying is that under the right conditions we could certainly go in but not under the present framework; we would just be dead in terms of dealing with the corporate financial structure. We just cannot get the kinds of returns on our capital that the corporation has set to get new capital. In terms of the long run, I'd like very much to see what the corporation has envisioned in terms of a hookup between us, but right now I don't see any sense in going on. You know my career is at stake here, too.

Another divisional executive made this point more succinctly:

Personally, I think a lot more could be done from a corporate point of view and this is frustrating. Right now, all these various divisions seem to be viewed strictly as an investment by the corporate people. They only look at us as a banker might look at us. This hurts us in terms of evolving some of these programs because we have relationships that are beyond financial relationships.

The remarks of a corporate executive seemed to support this concern:

One of the things I worry about is, Where is the end of the rope on this interdivisional thing? I'm wondering if action really has to come from just the division. You know, in this organization, when they decide to do something new it has always been a divisional proposal—they were coming to us for review and approval. The executive committee ends up being a review board; not us, working downward. With this kind of pattern, the talent of the corporate people is pretty well seduced into asking questions and determining whether a thing needs guidelines. But I think we ought to be the idea people as well, thinking about where we are going in the future, and if we think we ought to be getting into some new area, then we tell the divisions to do it. The stream has got to work both ways. Now it is not.

CASE 6

Bob's Appliances ——————————————— GARETH R. JONES

Form groups of three or four people and appoint one member as the spokesperson who will communicate your findings to the whole class when called upon by the instructor. Then, discuss the following scenario:

Bob's Appliances sells and services household appliances such as washing machines, dishwashers, ranges, and refrigerators. Over the years, the company has developed a good reputation for the quality of its customer service, and many local builders patronize the store. Recently, however, a series of new appliance retailers, including Circuit City and REX, have opened stores that also provide numerous appliances. In addition to appliances, however, to attract more customers these stores also carry a complete range of consumer electronics products like televisions, stereos, and computers. The owner of Bob's Appliances, Bob Lange, has decided that

if he is to stay in business he must widen his product range and compete directly with the chains.

In 1996, he decided to build a new 20,000-square-foot store and service center, and he is currently in the process of hiring new employees to sell and service the new line of consumer electronics. Because of his company's increased size, however, Lange is not sure of the best way to organize the employees. Currently, he uses a functional structure in which employees are divided into sales, purchasing and accounting, and repair. Bob is wondering, however, whether selling and servicing consumer electronics is so different from selling and servicing appliances that he should move to a product structure (see Exhibit 1) and create separate sets of functions for each of his two lines of business.

You are a team of local consultants whom Bob has called in to advise him as he makes this crucial choice. Which structure would you choose? Why?

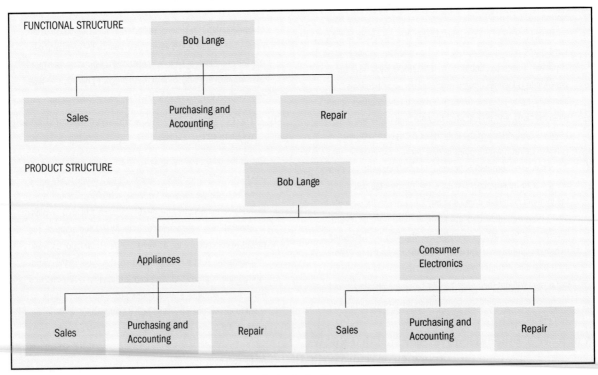

EXHIBIT 1   Functional Structure and Product Structure for Bob's Appliance

CASE 7

Mega-Zoinks Records ——————————— DAVID LOREE

Mega-Zoinks Records began ten years ago as a small, independent recording label for several hard-rock bands in Dallas, Texas. Its founder, Ian Westberry, had long been connected to the club scene in Dallas and

actually distributed the first single (of many) of his own band— TurboHead—through Mega-Zoinks Records. For several years, Mega-Zoinks Records capitalized on its strengths by focusing all of its attention on the hard-rock niche of the music industry, but several associates continued to prod Ian to record and distribute music of other tastes.

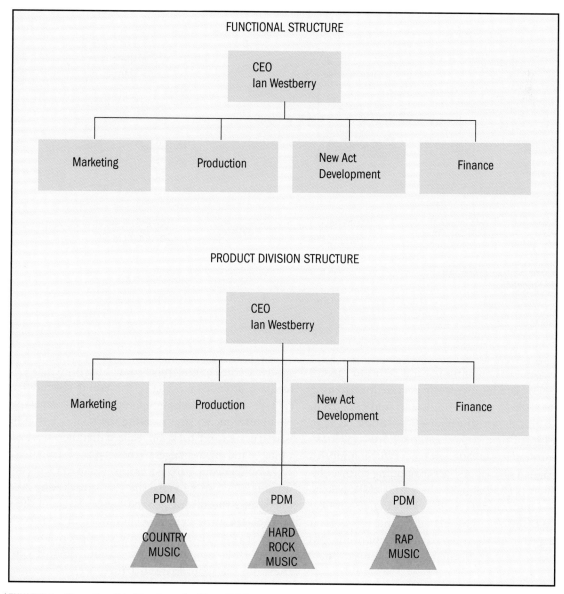

EXHIBIT 1 Three Possible Structures for Mega-Zoinks

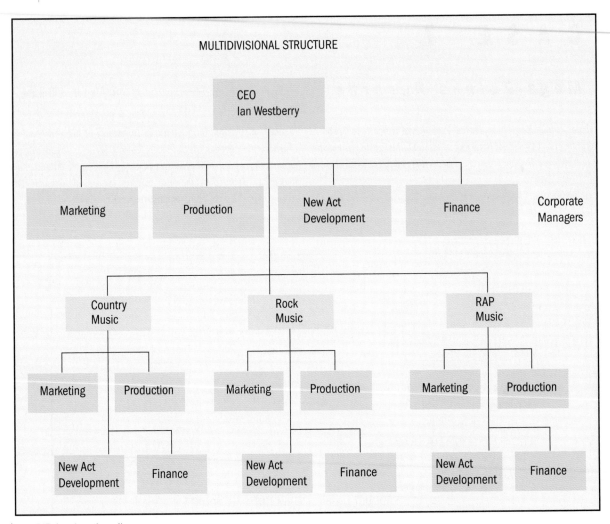

MULTIDIVISIONAL STRUCTURE

EXHIBIT 1 *(continued)*

The combination of his natural desire to "grow" the company and his increasing distaste for listening to the same three guitar chords over and over again led Ian to branch out. The phone rang steadily as soon as word spread that Mega-Zoinks Records was looking for musical acts of different types. Within months, Ian had signed several new acts, including country favorites such as The Twigg Brothers and FiddleSlickers, and emerging rap stars such as Dr. Dog, Dr. B.I.G., and Dr. B.I.G. Dog (all unrelated). While it was great to be steeped in all these different veins of music, Ian found himself facing his first real "organizational" challenge.

He seemed to remember something from a class he regularly attended years ago—something about different types of structures being appropriate in different types of circumstances. After locating the textbook that he vowed never to sell back, Ian realized that there were advantages and disadvantages to these types of structures.

Consider your team as a group of management consultants (who also didn't sell their books back) who need to consider the advantages and disadvantages of these types of structures in light of Ian's situation, and decide which structure would be most appropriate (see Exhibit 1). Be prepared to discuss and support your choice for the appropriate structure.

CASE 8

W. L. Gore & Associates, Inc. ——————— FRANK SHIPPER
AND CHARLES C. MANZ

On July 26, 1976, Jack Dougherty, a newly minted M.B.A. from the College of William and Mary bursting with resolve, dressed in a dark blue suit, reported for his first day at W. L. Gore & Associates. He presented himself to Bill Gore, shook hands firmly, looked him in the eye, and said he was ready for anything.

What happened next was one thing for which Jack was not ready. Gore replied, "That's fine, Jack, fine. Why don't you look around and find something you'd like to do." Three frustrating weeks later he found that something, dressed in jeans, loading fabric into the mouth of a machine that laminated the company's patented Gore-Tex membrane to fabric. By 1982, Jack had become responsible for all advertising and marketing in the fabrics group. This story was part of the folklore that was heard over and over about W. L. Gore. By 1991, the process was slightly more structured. New associates took a journey through the business before settling into their own positions, regardless of the position for which they were hired. A new sales associate in the Fabric Division might spend six weeks rotating through different areas before concentrating on sales and marketing. Among other things, he or she might learn how Gore-Tex fabric was made, what it could and could not do, how Gore handled customer complaints, and how it made investment decisions.

Anita McBride related her early experience at W. L. Gore & Associates this way:

> Before I came to Gore, I had worked for a structured organization. I came here, and for the first month it was fairly structured because I was going through training and this is what we do and this is how Gore is and all of that, and I went to Flagstaff for that training. After a month I came down to Phoenix, and my sponsor said, "Well, here's your office, and here's your desk," and walked away. And I thought, "Now what do I do," you know? I was waiting for a memo or something, or a job description. Finally, after another month, I was so frustrated I felt, "What have I gotten myself into?"

Frank Shipper, Franklin P. Perdue School of Business, Salisbury State University and Charles C. Manz, College of Business, Arizona State University. Reprinted with permission.

> And so I went to my sponsor and I said, "What the heck do you want from me? I need something from you." And he said, "if you don't know what you're supposed to do, examine your commitment, and opportunities."

BACKGROUND

W. L. Gore & Associates evolved from the late Wilbert L. Gore's experiences personally, organizationally, and technically. He was born in Meridian, Idaho, near Boise, in 1912. By age six, he claimed he had become an avid hiker in the Wasatch Mountain Range in Utah. In those mountains, at a church camp, he met Genevieve (called Vieve by everyone), his future wife. In 1935, they got married, which was, in their eyes, a partnership—a partnership that lasted a lifetime.

He received both a bachelor of science degree in chemical engineering in 1933 and a master of science degree in physical chemistry in 1935 from the University of Utah. He began his professional career at American Smelting and Refining in 1936; moved to Remington Arms Company in 1941; and moved once again to E. I. Du Pont de Nemours in 1945, where he held positions of research supervisor and head of operations research. While at Du Pont, he worked on a team to develop applications for polytetrafluoroethylene, frequently referred to as PTFE in the scientific community and known as Teflon by consumers. On this team, Wilbert Gore, called Bill by everyone, felt a sense of excited commitment, personal fulfillment, and self-direction. He followed the development of computers and transistors and believed that PTFE had the ideal insulating characteristics for use with such equipment.

He tried a number of ways to make a PTFE-coated ribbon cable, without success. A breakthrough came in his home basement laboratory. He was explaining the problem to his son, Bob. Bob saw some PTFE sealant tape made by 3M and asked his father, "Why don't you try this tape?" His father then explained to his son, "Everyone knows you cannot bond PTFE to itself." So, Bob went on to bed.

Bill Gore remained in his basement lab and proceeded to try what everyone knew would not work.

About 4:00 A.M., he woke his son, waving a small piece of cable around and saying excitedly, "It works, it works." The following night, father and son returned to the basement lab to make ribbon cable coated with PTFE.

For the next four months, Bill Gore tried to persuade Du Pont to make a new product—PTFE-coated ribbon cable. By this time in his career, Bill Gore knew some of the decision makers at Du Pont. After he had talked to a number of them, it became clear that Du Pont wanted to remain a supplier of raw materials and not a fabricator.

Bill began to discuss with his wife the possibility of starting their own insulated wire and cable business. On January 1, 1958, their wedding anniversary, they founded W. L. Gore & Associates, which they viewed as another partnership. The basement of their home served as their first facility. After finishing dinner on their anniversary, Vieve turned to her husband of 23 years and said, "Well, let's clear up the dishes, go downstairs, and get to work."

Bill Gore was 45 years old with five children to support when he left Du Pont. He left behind a career of 17 years and a good and secure salary. To finance the first two years of the business, they mortgaged their house and took $4000 from savings. All of their friends cautioned them against taking the risk.

The first few years were rough. In lieu of salary, some of their employees accepted room and board in the Gore home. At one point, eleven employees were living and working under one roof. Then came the order from the city of Denver's water department that put the company on a profitable footing. One afternoon, Vieve answered a phone call while sifting PTFE powder. The caller indicated that he was interested in the ribbon cable, but wanted to ask some technical questions and so asked for the product manager. Vieve explained that Bill was out running some errands at the moment. Next, the caller asked for the sales manager and, finally, the president. Vieve explained that they were also out. The caller became outraged and hollered, "What kind of company is this anyway?" With a little diplomacy, the Gores eventually secured an order for $100,000. This order put the company over the hump and it began to take off.

W. L. Gore & Associates continued to grow and develop new products primarily derived from PTFE, including its best-known product, Gore-Tex. In 1986, Bill Gore died while backpacking in the Wind River Mountains of Wyoming. Before he died, however, he had become chairman and his son, Bob, president. Vieve remained as the only other officer, secretary-treasurer.

THE OPERATING COMPANY

W. L. Gore & Associates was a company without titles, hierarchy, or any of the conventional structures associated with enterprises of its size. The titles of president and secretary-treasurer were used only because they were required by the laws of incorporation. In addition, Gore did not have a corporate-wide mission or code of ethics statement; nor did it require or prohibit business units from developing such statements for themselves. Thus, the associates of some business units who felt a need for such statements had developed them. The majority of business units within Gore did not have such statements. When questioned about this issue, one associate stated, "The company belief is that (1) its four basic operating principles cover ethical practices required of people in business and (2) it will not tolerate illegal practices." Gore's management style was often referred to as "unmanagement." The organization had been guided by Bill's experiences on teams at Du Pont and had evolved as needed.

For example, in 1965, W. L. Gore & Associates was a thriving and growing company with a facility on Paper Mill Road in Newark, Delaware, with about 200 employees. One warm Monday morning in the summer, Bill Gore was taking his usual walk through the plant. All of a sudden he realized he did not know everyone in the plant. The team had become too big. As a result, the company established a policy that no facility would have over 150 to 200 employees. Thus was born the expansion policy of "Get big by staying small." The purpose of maintaining small plants was to accentuate a close-knit and interpersonal atmosphere.

By 1991, W. L. Gore & Associates consisted of forty-four plants worldwide with over 5300 associates. In some cases, the plants were clustered together on the same site, as in Flagstaff, Arizona, with four plants on the same site. Twenty-seven of those plants were in the United States and seventeen were overseas. Gore's overseas plants were located in Scotland, Germany, France, Japan, and India.

PRODUCTS

The products that W. L. Gore made were organized into eight divisions—electronic, medical, waterproofing fabrics, fibers, industrial filtration, industrial seals, coatings, and microfiltration.

The electronic products division produced wire and cable for various demanding applications in aerospace, defense, computers, and telecommunications. The wire and cable products had a reputation for unequaled reliability. Most of the wire and cable was used where conventional cables could not operate. For example, Gore wire and cable assemblies were used in the space shuttle Columbia because they would stand the heat of ignition and the cold of space. Gore wire was used in the moon vehicle shuttle that scooped up samples of moon rocks, and Gore's microwave coaxial assemblies opened new horizons in microwave technology. On Earth, the electrical wire products helped make the world's fastest computers possible because electrical signals could travel through them at up to 90 percent of the speed of light. Because of the physical properties of the Gore-Tex material used in their construction, the electronic products were used extensively in defense systems, electronic switching for telephone systems, scientific and industrial instrumentation, microwave communications, and industrial robotics. Reliability was a watchword for all Gore products.

In medical products, reliability was literally a matter of life and death. Gore-Tex-expanded PTFE was an ideal material used to combat cardiovascular disease. When human arteries were seriously damaged or plugged with deposits that interrupt the flow of blood, the diseased portions could often be replaced with Gore-Tex artificial arteries. Gore-Tex arteries and patches were not rejected by the body, because the patient's own tissues grew into the grafts' open porous spaces. Gore-Tex vascular grafts came in many sizes to restore circulation to all areas of the body. They had saved limbs from amputation and saved lives. Some of the tiniest grafts relieved pulmonary problems in newborns. Gore-Tex was also used to help people with kidney disease. Associates were developing a variety of surgical reinforcing membranes, known as Gore-Tex cardiovascular patches, which could literally mend broken hearts, by patching holes and repairing aneurysms.

Through the waterproof fabrics division, Gore technology had traveled to the top of the world on the backs of renowned mountaineers. Gore-Tex fabric was waterproof and windproof, yet breathable. Those features had qualified Gore-Tex fabric as essential gear for mountaineers and adventurers facing extremely harsh environments. The PTFE membrane blocked wind and water but allowed sweat to escape. That made Gore-Tex fabric ideal for anyone who worked or played hard in foul weather. Backpackers had discovered that a single lightweight Gore-Tex fabric shell would replace a poplin jacket and a rain suit and dramatically outperform both. Skiers, sailors, runners, bicyclists, hunters,

fishermen, and other outdoor enthusiasts had also become big customers of garments made of Gore-Tex fabric. General sportswear and women's fashion footwear and handwear of Gore-Tex fabric were as functional as they were beautiful. Boots and gloves, both for work and recreation, were waterproof thanks to Gore-Tex liners. Gore-Tex was even becoming government issue for many military personnel. Wet suits, parkas, pants, headgear, gloves, and boots kept the troops warm and dry on foul-weather missions. Other demanding jobs also required the protection of Gore-Tex fabric because of its unique combination of chemical and physical properties.

The Gore-Tex fiber products, like the fabrics, ended up in some tough places. The outer protective layer of NASA's spacesuit was woven from Gore-Tex fibers. Gore-Tex fibers were in many ways the ultimate in synthetic fibers. They were impervious to sunlight, chemicals, heat, and cold. They were strong and uniquely resistant to abrasion.

Industrial filtration products, such as Gore-Tex filter bags, reduced air pollution and recovered valuable solids from gases and liquids more completely than alternatives; they also did it more economically. They could make coalburning plants smoke-free, contributing to a cleaner environment.

The industrial seals division produced joint sealant, a fixable cord of porous PTFE that could be applied as a gasket to the most complex shapes, sealing them to prevent leakage of corrosive chemicals, even at extreme temperature and pressure. Steam valves packed with Gore-Tex valve stempacking never leaked and never needed to be repacked.

The coatings division applied layers of PTFE to steel castings and other metal articles by a patented process. Called Fluoroshield protective coatings, this fluorocarbon polymer protected processing vessels in the production of corrosive chemicals.

Gore-Tex microfiltration products were used in medical devices, pharmaceutical manufacturing, and chemical processing. These membranes removed bacteria and other microorganisms from air or liquids, making them sterile.

FINANCIAL INFORMATION

W. L. Gore was a closely held private corporation. Financial information was as closely guarded as proprietary information on products and processes. Eighty percent of the stock was held by the Gore family and veteran associates, 10 percent by current associates, and 10 percent by others.

According to Shanti Mehta, an associate, Gore's return on assets and equity ranked it among the top 5 percent of major companies. According to another source, W. L. Gore & Associates was working just fine by any financial measure. It had had twenty-seven straight years of profitability and positive return on equity. The compounded growth rate for revenues at W. L. Gore over the past twenty years had been over 18 percent, discounted for inflation.[1] In 1969, total sales were $6 million; in 1982, $125 million; in 1983, $160 million; in 1985, $250 million; in 1987, $400 million; in 1988, $426 million; and in 1989, $600 million. This growth had largely been financed without debt.

ORGANIZATIONAL STRUCTURE

Bill Gore wanted to avoid smothering the company in thick layers of formal "management." He believed they stifled individual creativity. As the company grew, he knew a way had to be devised to help new people get started and to follow their progress. This was seen as particularly important when it came to compensation. W. L. Gore & Associates developed what it called the "sponsor" program to meet those needs. When people applied to W. L. Gore, they were initially screened by personnel specialists, as in most companies. For those who met the basic criteria, there were interviews with other associates. Before a person was hired, an associate must have agreed to be that person's sponsor. The sponsor was to take a personal interest in the new associate's contributions, problems, and goals. The sponsor was both a coach and an advocate. The sponsor tracked the new associate's progress, helping and encouraging, dealing with weaknesses, and concentrating on strengths. Sponsoring was not a short-term commitment. All associates had sponsors and many had more than one. When individuals were hired, they had a sponsor in their immediate work area. If they moved to another area, they also had a sponsor in that work area. As associates' responsibilities grew, they could acquire additional sponsors.

Because the sponsoring program looked beyond conventional views of what made a good associate, some anomalies occurred in the hiring practices. Bill Gore proudly told the story of "a very young man" of 84 who walked in, applied, and spent five very good years with the company. The individual had thirty years of experience in the industry before joining Gore. His other associates had no problems accepting him, but the personnel computer did. It insisted his age was 48.

An internal memo by Bill Gore described three kinds of sponsorship and how they might work:

1. The sponsor who helps a new associate get started on the job. Also, the sponsor who helps a present associate get started on a new job (starting sponsor).
2. The sponsor who sees to it that the associate being sponsored gets credit and recognition for contributions and accomplishments (advocate sponsor).
3. The sponsor who sees to it that the associate being sponsored is fairly paid for contributions to the success of the enterprise (compensation sponsor).

A single sponsor could perform any one or all three kinds of sponsorship. A sponsor was a friend and an associate. All the supportive aspects of the friendship were also present. Often (perhaps usually) two associates sponsored each other as advocates.

W. L. Gore & Associates had been described not only as unmanaged, but also as unstructured. Bill Gore referred to the structure as a lattice organization. A lattice structure is portrayed in Exhibit 1. The characteristics of this structure were:

1. Direct lines of communication—person-to-person—with no intermediary.
2. No fixed or assigned authority.
3. Sponsors, not bosses.
4. Natural leadership defined by followership.
5. Objectives set by those who must "make them happen."
6. Tasks and functions organized through commitments.

The structure within the lattice was described by the people at Gore as complex and had evolved from interpersonal interactions, self-commitment to group-known responsibilities, natural leadership, and group-imposed discipline.

Bill Gore once explained this structure by saying, "Every successful organization has an underground lattice. It's where the news spreads like lightning, where people can go around the organization to get things done." Another description of what was occurring within the lattice structure was constant cross-area teams—the equivalent of quality circles going on all the time. When a puzzled interviewer told Bill he was having trouble understanding how planning and accountabil-

---

[1] *By comparison, only eleven of the two hundred largest companies in the Fortune 500 have had positive ROE each year from 1970–1988, and only two other companies missed only one year. The revenue growth rate for these thirteen companies was 5.4 percent compared to 2.5 percent for the entire Fortune 500.*

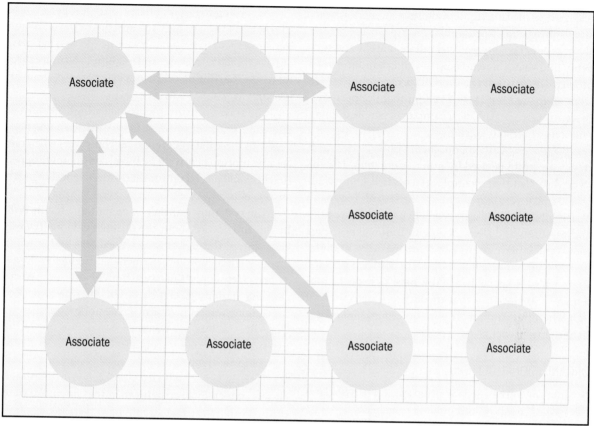

EXHIBIT 1   The Lattice Structure

ity worked, Bill replied with a grin, "So am I. You ask me how it works—it works every which way."

The lattice structure did have some similarities to traditional management structures. For instance, a group of thirty to forty associates who made up an advisory group met every six months to review marketing, sales, and production plans. As Bill Gore has conceded, "The abdication of titles and rankings can never be 100 percent."

The lattice structure was not without its critics. As Bill Gore stated, "I'm told from time to time that a lattice organization can't meet a crisis well because it takes too long to reach a consensus when there are no bosses. But this isn't true. Actually, a lattice, by its very nature, works particularly well in a crisis. A lot of useless effort is avoided because there is no rigid management hierarchy to conquer before you can attack a problem."

The lattice had been put to the test on a number of occasions. For example, in 1975, Dr. Charles Campbell, the University of Pittsburgh's senior resident, reported that a Gore-Tex arterial graft had developed an aneurysm. An aneurysm is a bubble-like protrusion that

is life-threatening. If it continued to expand, it would explode. Obviously, this kind of problem had to be solved quickly and permanently.

Within only a few days of Dr. Campbell's first report, he flew to Newark to present his findings to Bill and Bob Gore and a few other associates. The meeting lasted two hours. Bill Hubis, a former policeman who had joined Gore to develop new production methods, had an idea before the meeting was over. He returned to his work area to try some different production techniques. After only three hours and twelve tries, he had developed a permanent solution. In other words, in three hours, a potentially damaging problem to both patients and the company was resolved. Furthermore, Hubis's redesigned graft went on to win widespread acceptance in the medical community. By 1991, it dominated the market with a 70 percent share.

One critic, Eric Reynolds, founder of Marmot Mountain Works Ltd. of Grand Junction, Colorado, and a major Gore customer, said, "I think the lattice has its problems with the day-to-day nitty-gritty of getting things done on time and out the door. I don't think Bill realizes how the lattice system affects customers. I mean, after you've established a relationship with someone about product quality, you can call up one day and suddenly find that someone new to you is handling your problem. It's frustrating to find a lack of continuity." He went on to say, "But I have to admit that I've personally seen at Gore remarkable examples of people coming out of nowhere and excelling."

Bill Gore was asked a number of times if the lattice structure could be used by other companies. His answer was, "No. For example, established companies would find it very difficult to use the lattice. Too many hierarchies would be destroyed. When you remove titles and positions and allow people to follow whomever they want, it may very well be someone other than the person who has been in charge. The lattice works for us, but it's always evolving. You have to expect problems." He maintained that the lattice system worked best when put in place in start-up companies by dynamic entrepreneurs.

ORGANIZATIONAL CULTURE

In addition to the sponsor program, Gore associates were asked to follow four guiding principles:

1. Try to be fair.
2. Use your freedom to grow.
3. Make your own commitments, and keep them.
4. Consult with other associates before taking any action that may hurt the reputation or financial stability of the company.

The four principles were often referred to as fairness, freedom, commitment, and discretion. The last principle was also often referred to as the waterline principle. The terminology was drawn from an analogy to ships. If someone poked a hole in a boat above the waterline, the boat would be in relatively little real danger. But if someone poked a hole below the waterline, the boat would be in immediate danger of sinking.

In practice, the fourth principle provided associates with a great deal of discretion. For example, W. L. Gore had no travel policy, no request for travel forms, no prohibition against first-class travel, and no expense reports. The associate called an internal travel consultant and gave the individual his or her requirements. All tickets issued to Gore travelers were accompanied by a note that stated, "The normal coach fare is X, you've saved Y." Upon return, the associate could file a travel investment report and be reimbursed for his or her savings investment.

According to Debbie Sharp, "Very few people take advantage of this. It's only the infrequent travelers who sometimes get carried away. If we see expenses that stand out, we'll call the traveler and ask him to be more careful next time. But no one ever pays money back on an investment report."

The travel consultant also had a high amount of discretion. For example, W. L. Gore had been doing business with three different rental car companies when one became more expensive. The travel consultant dropped that firm and picked up another without checking with anyone else.

The operating principles were put to a test in 1978. By this time, word about the qualities of Gore-Tex was being spread throughout the recreational and outdoor markets. Production and shipment had begun in volume. At first, a few complaints were heard. Next, some of the clothing started coming back. Finally, a great deal of the clothing was being returned. The trouble was that the Gore-Tex was leaking. Waterproof fabric was one of the two major properties responsible for Gore-Tex's success. The company's reputation and credibility were on the line.

Peter W. Gilson, who led Gore's fabric division, said, "It was an incredible crisis for us at that point. We were really starting to attract attention, we were taking off—and then this." In the next few months, Peter and some of his associates made a number of those below-the-waterline decisions. First, the researchers determined that certain oils in human sweat were clogging the pores in Gore-Tex and altering the surface tension of the membrane, allowing water to pass through. They also discovered that a good washing could restore the waterproof property. At first, this solution, known as the "Ivory Snow Solution," was accepted.

A single letter from "Butch," a mountain guide in the Sierras, changed the company's position. Butch wrote how he had been leading a group and, "My parka leaked and my life was in danger." As Gilson said, "That scared the hell out of us. Clearly, our solution was no solution at all to someone on a mountaintop." All of the products were recalled. As Gilson said, "We bought back, at our own expense, a fortune in pipeline material. Anything that was in the stores, at the manufacturers, or anywhere else in the pipeline."

In the meantime, Bob Gore and other associates set out to develop a permanent fix. One month later, a second generation Gore-Tex had been developed. Gilson told dealers that if at any time a customer returned a leaky parka, they should replace it and bill the company. The replacement program cost Gore roughly $4 million.

One thing that might strike an outsider was the informality and amount of humor in the Gore organization. One of the most common words heard in meetings was "bullshit!" In contrast, other commonly heard words were "responsibilities" and "commitments." This was an organization that seemed to take what it did very seriously, but its members did not take themselves too seriously.

Gore, for a company of its size, had a very short organizational pyramid. The pyramid consisted of Bob Gore, the late Bill Gore's son, as president, and Vieve, Bill Gore's widow, as secretary-treasurer. All the other members of the Gore organization were referred to as associates. Words such as *employees, subordinates,* and *managers* were taboo in the Gore culture.

Gore did not have any managers, but it did have many leaders. Bill Gore described in an internal memo the kinds of leadership and the role of leadership:

1. The associate who is recognized by a team as having a special knowledge or experience (for example, this could be a chemist, computer expert, machine operator, salesman, engineer, lawyer). This kind of leader gives the team guidance in a special area.

2. The associate the team looks to for coordination of individual activities to achieve the agreed-on objectives of the team. The role of this leader is to persuade team members to make the commitments necessary for success (commitment seeker).

3. The associate who proposes necessary objectives and activities and seeks agreement and team consensus on objectives. This leader is perceived by the team membership as having a good grasp of how the objectives of the team fit in with the broad objective of the enterprise. This kind of leader is often also the "commitment-seeking" leader.

4. The leader who evaluates relative contributions of team members (in consultation with other sponsors) and reports these contribution evaluations to a compensation committee. This leader may also participate in the compensation committee on relative contribution and pay and reports changes in compensation to individual associates. This leader is then also a compensation sponsor.

5. The leader who coordinates the research, manufacturing, and marketing of one product type within a business, interacting with team leaders and individual associates who have commitments regarding the product type. These leaders are usually called product specialists. They are respected for their knowledge and dedication to their products.

6. Plant leaders who help coordinate activities of people within a plant.

7. Business leaders who help coordinate activities of people in a business.

8. Functional leaders who help coordinate activities of people in a "functional" area.

9. Corporate leaders who help coordinate activities of people in different businesses and functions and who try to promote communication and cooperation among all associates.

10. Intrapreneuring associates organize new teams for new businesses, new products, new processes, new devices, new marketing efforts, and new or better methods of all kinds. These leaders invite other associates to "sign to" for their project. It is clear that leadership is widespread in our lattice organization and that it is continually changing and evolving. The situation that leaders are frequently also sponsors should not [blur the fact] that these are different activities and responsibilities. Leaders are not authoritarians, managers of people, or supervisors who tell us what to do or forbid us doing things; nor are they "parents" to whom we transfer our own self-responsibility. However, they do often advise us of the consequences of actions we have done or propose to do. Our actions result in contributions, or lack of contribution, to the success of our enterprise. Our pay depends on the magnitude of our contributions. This is the basic discipline of our lattice organization.

Many other aspects were arranged along egalitarian lines. The parking lot did not have any reserved parking spaces except for customers and the handicapped. There was only one area in each plant in which to eat. The lunchroom in each new plant was designed to be a focal point for employee interaction. As Dave McCarter of Phoenix explained, "The design is no accident. The lunchroom in Flagstaff has a fireplace in the middle. We want people to like to be here." The location of the plant was also no accident. Sites were selected based on transportation access, a nearby university, beautiful surroundings, and climate appeal. Land cost was never a primary consideration. McCarter justified the selection by stating, "Expanding is not costly in the long run. The loss of money is what you make happen by stymieing people into a box."

Not all people functioned well under such a system, especially initially. For those accustomed to a more structured work environment, there were adjustment problems. As Bill Gore said, "All our lives most of us have been told what to do, and some people don't know how to respond when asked to do something—and have the very real option of saying no—on their job. It's the new associate's responsibility to find out what he or she can do for the good of the operation." The vast majority of the new associates, after some initial floundering, adapted quickly.

For those who required more structured working conditions and could not adapt, Gore's flexible workplace was not for them. According to Bill, for those few, "It's an unhappy situation, both for the associate and the sponsor. If there is no contribution, there is no paycheck."

As Anita McBride, an associate in Phoenix, said, "It's not for everybody. People ask me, Do we have turnover? And, yes, we do have turnover. What you're seeing looks like utopia, but it also looks extreme. If you finally figure the system, it can be real exciting. If you can't handle it, you've got to go—probably by your own choice, because you're going to be so frustrated."

Associates had also encountered criticism from outsiders who had problems with the idea of no titles. Sarah Clifton, an associate at the Flagstaff facility, was being pressed by some outsiders as to what her title was. She made one up and had it printed on some business cards—SUPREME COMMANDER. When Bill Gore learned what she did, he loved it and recounted the story to others.

In rare cases, an associate "is trying to be unfair," in Bill's own words. In one case, the problem was chronic absenteeism and in the other the individual was caught stealing. "When that happens, all hell breaks loose," said Bill Gore. "We can get damned authoritarian when we have to."

Over the years, Gore & Associates faced a number of unionization drives. The company neither tried to dissuade an associate from attending an organizational meeting nor retaliated when fliers were passed out. Each attempt was unsuccessful. None of the plants had been organized to date. Bill believed no need existed for third-party representation under the lattice structure. He asked the question, "Why would associates join a union when they own the company? It seems rather absurd."

Overall, the associates appeared to have responded positively to the Gore system of unmanagement and unstructure. Bill estimated the year before he died that "the profit per associate is double" that of Du Pont.

ASSOCIATE DEVELOPMENT

Ron Hill, an associate in Newark, said W. L. Gore "will work with associates who want to advance themselves." Associates were offered many in-house training oppor-

tunities. Most were technical and engineering-focused because of the type of organization W. L. Gore was, but the company also offered in-house programs in leadership development. In addition, the company had cooperative programs with associates to obtain training through universities and other outside providers in which Gore picked up most of the educational costs for the associates. The emphasis in employee development, as in many parts of W. L. Gore, was that the associate must take the initiative.

COMPENSATION

Compensation at W. L. Gore & Associates took three forms—salary, bonus, and an Associates' Stock Option Program (ASOP).[2] Entry-level salary was in the middle of the range for comparable jobs. According to Sally Gore, daughter-in-law of the founder, "We do not feel we need to be the highest paid. We never try to steal people away from other companies with salary. We want them to come here because of the opportunities for growth and the unique work environment." Associates' salaries were reviewed at least once a year and more commonly twice a year. The reviews were conducted by a compensation team for most workers in the facility in which they worked. The sponsors for all associates acted as their advocates during this review process. Before meeting with the compensation committee, the sponsor checked with customers or whomever used the results of the person's work to find out what contributions had been made. In addition, the evaluation team considered the associate's leadership ability and willingness to help others develop to their fullest.

Besides salaries, W. L. Gore had a bonus and ASOP profit-sharing plan for all associates. The bonus consisted of 15 percent of the company's profits distributed among all associates twice a year. In addition, the firm bought company stock equivalent to 15 percent of the associates' annual income and placed it in an (ASOP) retirement fund. Thus, an associate became a stockholder after being at Gore for one year. Bill wanted all associates to feel they were the owners.

The principle of commitment was seen as a two-way street. W. L. Gore & Associates tried to avoid layoffs. Instead of cutting pay, which was seen at Gore as disastrous to morale, the company used a system of temporary transfers within a plant or cluster of plants and voluntary layoffs.

---

[2] Gore's ASOP is similar legally to an ESOP (Employee Stock Option Plan). Gore simply does not use the word employee in any of its documentation.

RESEARCH AND DEVELOPMENT

Research and development, like everything else at Gore, were unstructured. There was no formal research and development department. Yet the company held over 150 patents, although most inventions were held as proprietary or trade secrets. Any associate could ask for a piece of raw PTFE, known as a silly worm, with which to experiment. Bill Gore believed all people had it within themselves to be creative.

The best way to understand how research and development worked was to see how inventiveness had previously occurred at Gore. By 1969, the wire and cable division was facing increased competition. Bill Gore began to look for a way to straighten out the PTFE molecules. As he said, "I figured out that if we ever could unfold those molecules, get them to stretch out straight, we'd have a tremendous new kind of material." He thought that if PTFE could be stretched, air could be introduced into its molecular structure. The result would be greater volume per pound of raw material without affecting performance. Thus, fabricating costs would be reduced and the profit margins would be increased. Going about this search in a scientific manner, Bill Gore and his son, Bob, heated rods of PTFE to various temperatures and then slowly stretched them. Regardless of the temperature or how carefully they stretched them, the rods broke.

Working alone late one night in 1969 after countless failures, Bob, in frustration, yanked at one of the rods violently. To his surprise, it did not break. He tried it again and again with the same results.

The next morning, Bob demonstrated his breakthrough to his father, but not without some drama. As Bill Gore recalled, "Bob wanted to surprise me so he took a rod and stretched it slowly. Naturally, it broke. Then he pretended to get mad. He grabbed another rod and said, 'Oh the hell with this,' and gave it a pull. It didn't break—he'd done it." The new arrangement of molecules changed not only the wire and cable division, but also led to the development of Gore-Tex and what is now the largest division at Gore plus a host of other products.

Initial field-testing of Gore-Tex was conducted by Bill and Vieve in the summer of 1970. Vieve made a hand-sewn tent out of patches of Gore-Tex. They took it on their annual camping trip to the Wind River Mountains in Wyoming. The very first night in the wilderness, they encountered a hail storm. The hail tore holes in the top of the tent, but the bottom filled up like a bathtub from the rain. As Bill Gore stated, "At least we knew from all the water that the tent was waterproof. We just needed to make it stronger, so it could withstand hail."

The second largest division began on the ski slopes of Colorado. Bill was skiing with his friend Dr. Ben Eiseman of the Denver General Hospital. As Bill Gore told the story, "We were just about to start a run when I absentmindedly pulled a small tubular section of Gore-Tex out of my pocket and looked at it. 'What is that stuff?' Ben asked. So I told him about its properties. 'Feels great,' he said,' What do you use it for?' 'Got no idea,' l said. 'Well give it to me,' he said,' and I'll try it in a vascular graft on a pig.' Two weeks later, he called me up. Ben was pretty excited. 'Bill,' he said 'I put it in a pig and it works. What do I do now?' I told him to get together with Pete Cooper in our Flagstaff plant, and let them figure it out." Now hundreds of thousands of people throughout the world walk around with Gore-Tex vascular grafts.

Every associate was encouraged to think, experiment, and follow a potentially profitable idea to its conclusion. For example, at a plant in Newark, Delaware, a machine that wrapped thousands of yards of wire a day was designed by Fred L. Eldreth, an associate with a third-grade education. The design was done over a weekend. Many other associates had contributed their ideas through both product and process breakthroughs.

Even without a research and development department, innovations and creativity worked very well at Gore & Associates. The year before he died, Bill Gore claimed, "The creativity—the number of patent applications and innovative products—is triple" that of Du Pont.

MARKETING STRATEGY

Gore's marketing strategy was based on making the determination that it could offer the best valued products to a marketplace, that people in that marketplace appreciated what it manufactured, and that Gore could become a leader in that area of expertise. The operating procedures used to implement the strategy followed the same principles as other functions at Gore.

First, the marketing of a product revolved around a leader who was referred to as a product champion. According to Dave McCarter, "You marry your technology with the interests of your champions, as you've got to have champions for all these things no matter what. And that's the key element within our company. Without a product champion you can't do much anyway, so it is individually driven. If you get a person interested in a particular market or a particular product for the marketplace, then there is no stopping them."

Second, a product champion was responsible for marketing the product through commitments with sales representatives. Again according to McCarter, "We have no quota system. Our marketing and our salespeople make their own commitments as to what their forecasts are. There is no person sitting around telling them that that is not high enough, you have to increase it by 10 percent, or whatever somebody feels is necessary. You are expected to meet your commitment, which is your forecast, but nobody is going to tell you to change it.... There is no order of command, no chain involved. These are groups of independent people who come together to make unified commitments to do something, and sometimes when they can't make those agreements ... you may pass up a marketplace, ... but that's OK because there's much more advantage when the team decides to do something."

Third, the sales representatives were on salary. They were not on commission. They participated in the profit sharing and ASOP plans in which all other associates participated.

As in other areas of Gore, the individual success stories came from diverse backgrounds. McCarter related one of these success stories as follows:

> I interviewed Sam one day. I didn't even know why I was interviewing him actually. Sam was retired from AT&T After twenty-five years, he took the golden parachute and went down to Sun Lakes to play golf. He played golf a few months and got tired of that. He was selling life insurance.
>
> I sat reading the application; his technical background interested me.... He had managed an engineering department with 600 people. He'd managed manufacturing plants for AT&T and had a great wealth of experience at AT&T He said, "I'm retired. I like to play golf, but I just can't do it every day so I want to do something else. Do you have something around here I can do?" I was thinking to myself, this is one of these guys I would sure like to hire, but I don't know what I would do with him.
>
> The thing that triggered me was the fact that he said he sold insurance and here is a guy with a high degree of technical background selling insurance. He had marketing experience, international marketing experience. So the bell went off in my head that we were trying to introduce a new product into the marketplace that was a hydrocarbon leak protection cable. You can bury it in the ground and in a matter of seconds it could detect a hydrocarbon (gasoline, etc.). I had a couple of other guys working on it who hadn't been very successful with marketing it. We were having a hard time finding a customer
>
> Well, I thought that kind of a product would be like selling insurance. If you think about it, why should you protect your tanks? It's an insurance policy that things are not leaking into the environment. That has implications, big-time monetary. So, actually, I said, "Why don't you come back Monday? I have just the thing for you." So he did. We hired him; he went to work, a very energetic guy. Certainly a champion of the product, he picked right up on it, ran with it single-handed.... Now it's a growing business. It certainly is a valuable one, too, for the environment.

In the implementation of its marketing strategy, Gore relied on cooperative and word-of-mouth advertising. Cooperative advertising was especially used to promote Gore-Tex fabric products, which were sold through a number of clothing manufacturers and distributors, including Apparel Technologies, Lands' End, Austin Reed, Timberland, Woolrich, North Face, Grandoe, and Michelle Jaffe. Gore engaged in cooperative advertising because the associates believed positive experiences with any one product would carry over to purchases of other and more Gore-Tex fabric products. Apparently, this strategy was paying off. Richard Zuckerwar, president of the Grandoe Corporation, said about his company's introduction of Gore-Tex gloves, "Sports activists have had the benefit of Gore-Tex gloves to protect their hands from the elements.... With this handsome collection of gloves ... you can have warm, dry hands without sacrificing style."

The power of informal marketing techniques extended beyond consumer products. According to McCarter, "In the technical end of the business, company reputation probably is most important. You have to have a good reputation with your company." He went on to say that without a good reputation, a company's products would not be considered seriously by many industrial customers. In other words, the sale was often made before the representative called. Gore had been very successful using its marketing strategies to secure a market leadership position in a number of areas ranging from waterproof outdoor clothing to vascular grafts.

ACKNOWLEDGMENTS

A number of sources were especially helpful in providing background material for this case. The most important sources were the W. L. Gore associates who generously shared their time and viewpoints about the company. We especially appreciate the input received from Anita McBride, who spent hours with us sharing her personal experiences as well as providing many resources, including internal documents and videotapes. In addition, Trish Hearn and Dave McCarter added much to this case by sharing their personal experiences and ensuring that the case accurately reflected the Gore company and culture.

REFERENCES

Aburdene, Patricia, and John Nasbitt. *Reinventing the Corporation.* New York: Warner Books, 1985.

Angrist, S. W. "Classless Capitalists," *Forbes,* May 9, 1983, pp. 123–24.

Franlesca, L. "Dry and Cool," *Forbes,* August 27, 1984, p. 126. "The Future Workplace," *Management Review,* July 1986, pp. 22–23.

Hoerr, J. "A Company Where Everybody Is the Boss," *Business Week,* April 15, 1985, p. 98.

Levering, Robert. *The 100 Best Companies to Work for in America.*

McKendrick, Joseph. "The Employees as Entrepreneur," *Management World,* January 1985, pp. 12–13.

Milne, M. J. "The Gorey Details," *Management Review,* March 1985, pp. 16–17.

Posner, B. G. "The First Day on the Job," *Inc.,* June 1986, pp. 73–75.

Price, Kathy. "Firm Thrives Without Boss," *AZ Republic,* February 2, 1986.

Rhodes, Lucien. "The Un-Manager," *Inc.,* August 1982, p. 34.

Simmons, J. "People Managing Themselves: Un-Management at W. L. Gore Inc.," *Journal for Quality and Participation,* December 1987, pp. 14–19.

Trachtenberg, J. A. "Give Them Stormy Weather," *Forbes,* March 24, 1986, pp. 172–74.

Ward, Alex. "An All-Weather Idea," *The New York Times Magazine,* November 10, 1985, sec. 6.

Weber, Joseph. "No Bosses. And Even 'Leaders' Can't Give Orders," *Business Week,* December 10, 1990, pp. 196–97.

"Wilbert L. Gore," *Industry Week,* October 17, 1983, pp. 48–49.

CASE 9

Three Roads To Innovation ——————— RONALD A. MITSCH

Innovation is important to most companies, but it is our lifeblood at 3M. We like to keep innovation coming from all directions: by developing new technologies and new applications for them, by assessing customer needs, and by anticipating market trends in all areas in which we operate.

That presents a considerable management challenge. How do you develop all those channels for innovation and keep them open? How do you turn innovation into product successes? How do you ensure that those processes are going on, day in and day out, year in and year out?

One thing 3M discovered is that innovation does not just happen unless you make sure people know it is a top priority—and then provide them with enough freedom and resources to make it work. It certainly is not going to happen without top management's commitment to innovation as a key ingredient in the company's overall business strategy and planning.

Journal of Business Strategy, *Sept/Oct 1990, pp. 18–21. Reprinted with permission of Faulkner & Gray, Inc., 11 Penn Plaza, New York, NY 10001, 800-535-8403.*

Finally, it will not happen without a continuing reassessment of the barriers to innovation that tend to develop over time, despite management's best efforts. To keep abreast of the pace of technological change in the global marketplace, this company needs to continually enhance the prospects for successful innovation. Ultimately, the goal of innovation must be continued quality growth.

One of 3M's best-known examples of quality growth is also a classic case of how the company nurtures one channel of innovation: the development of new technologies and new applications for existing technologies.

3M scientist Arthur Fry had the freedom and found the resources in the company to develop Post-it brand Notes. At the time, he was working on a bookshelf-arranger tape. While doing research for this project, he came up with the idea for a removable, sticky-backed bookmarker as he was singing in a church choir.

Fry began devoting more of his time to the sticky-backed pieces of paper and less and less time to the bookshelf tape, especially when he realized that the former promised to open up a whole new channel of communication. No one complained, because 3M has a company policy that encourages researchers to use 15 percent of their time on projects of their own choosing.

The adhesive Fry used was developed by another scientist, Spencer Silver, in 3M's corporate research laboratories. It was a technology available to Fry and to any other researcher in the company.

At one point, Post-it Notes faced the possibility of an early demise when an initial market test failed. But management sponsors gave it a second life. They personally took the product into the field to see how customers responded.

Freedom, sharing of technologies, and management sponsorship are all essential ingredients of the lab-to-market channel of innovation. These elements have been institutionalized in the 3M culture.

In the company's formative years, 3M's president, William L. McKnight, established policies and philosophies that have withstood the test of more than six decades. He was convinced that new product development and diversification were important to the company's continued growth. McKnight established a practice of promotion from within, encouraged individual initiative, and gave people room to grow on the job.

He also believed that failure is not fatal. Freedom to make honest mistakes is a good general policy, but it is particularly applicable to innovation. No person likes to fail, but it does happen occasionally when a company wants to grow by sponsoring new products and taking risks. The important thing is, one mistake is not a ticket to oblivion.

Out of McKnight's philosophies have developed policies like the 15 percent option, management sponsorship, and a dual-ladder system of promotion. Laboratory employees can advance up a technical ladder, as well as a management ladder, and continue with their first love—research and development.

McKnight's philosophies have been passed on from one management level to another, from one generation to another. But more recent managements have also set strategies to reinforce the innovation philosophy.

NURTURING NEW PRODUCTS

To ensure that the company's early pattern of growth through innovative new products continues, a quantifiable new products target has become part of 3M's financial goals. *The company aims to achieve at least 25 percent of its growth each year through new products developed within the last five years.* Every

operating unit and its people are evaluated on their ability to reach this goal. To encourage innovation, 3M, in the past decade, has increased the ratio of spending on R&D from 4.6 percent of sales to 6.5 percent.

3M continues to expand and build on two dozen core technologies, which provide a rich source of new products. From the company's nonwoven technology have come oil sorbents; from adhesives, a new class of foam-backed tapes that can replace mechanical fasteners; from fluorochemicals, a new line of carpet stain release treatments; and from the company's oldest technology, abrasives, a line of microabrasives for finishing and polishing high-tech components.

3M does research and development on three levels. Division laboratories develop products and technologies for specific markets, doing shorter-term research for the most part. Sector laboratories work on technologies and applications the divisions will need three to ten years from now. Corporate laboratories conduct basic research that may not lead to products for ten to twenty years.

Sharing technologies and these laboratory resources across the company is of prime importance. Whereas products belong to individual operating units, technologies belong to anyone in the company who needs them. Both formal and informal forums allow technical people from all of the company's divisions and corporate and sector laboratories to share information.

Innovation is recognized in many ways. Two examples: The Golden Step program honors cross-functional teams that introduce successful new products. The Carleton Society, a hall of fame for 3M scientists, honors those who have made long-range contributions to 3M's product and technological leadership. All of these steps nurture the lab-to-market channel.

Yet, the lab-to-market channel is only one route to innovation from which the company derives its growth. Equally important are assessing customer needs and anticipating market trends. All three are increasingly intertwined and essential to innovation.

From 3M's standpoint, one of the critical issues facing the company is to continually focus activities throughout the corporation to produce quality growth. Each of our operating units is encouraged to spend more time in planning and setting priorities for product development based on customer needs and expectations.

The question is, How do we balance priority setting with a climate of freedom? Prioritizing and providing freedom to innovate cannot be trade-offs; both are needed.

Contrary to what one might think, we have found that prioritizing not only enhances productivity and the flow of the products but also affords individual researchers more time for projects of their own choosing.

Once the priorities are in place, the second critical challenge is to develop the products and bring them to market as quickly as possible. The idea is to overcome time-consuming delays and roadblocks built into traditional new product development schedules. Product development often has moved from laboratory to market in sequential order. Process development, marketing, manufacturing, packaging, and other functions become involved step-by-step. But by having all functions involved from the start, development time can be compressed dramatically.

After priorities are established, cross-functional teams are empowered by management to design and develop a product that will meet customer expectations. Several 3M divisions have set up cross-functional action teams to address their most important new product challenges.

The Occupational Health and Environmental Safety Division cut its product development time in half through this process. It substantially increased the number of major new products introduced through action teams consisting of laboratory, marketing, manufacturing, engineering, quality, packaging, and financial people.

Each team is led by a product champion, someone who believes strongly in the value of the project and is committed to making it successful. Each team also has a management sponsor who serves as a cheerleader, helps get access to needed resources, and helps teams stay on track.

A third critical issue for the 1990s is the need to satisfy customer expectations. Staying close to customers is a 3M tradition that dates back to McKnight. He believed in going into the back shops of factories to see how the company's products were being used and to get ideas for new products. The vertical organizational structure he set up has made it easy to keep 3M operating units small enough so that people, from top management on down, get to know their customers.

In the 1990s, 3M is adding some new twists to this practice. The company's divisions are doing more involved market research to pinpoint present and future customer needs. The goal is to reemphasize a long-standing tradition of regularly sending lab people into the field to help keep research focused on high-priority projects that meet customer expectations.

Cross-functional teams work closely with customers. For example, many of 3M's carpet treatments and many of its tape closures for disposable diapers were developed either in joint efforts or in close consultation with carpet-fiber makers and diaper makers.

A recent addition to 3M's line of data cartridges for off-line storage of computer data illustrates how innovation occurs in response to changing customer needs and expectations.

The company's Data Storage Products Division found that with equipment and usage changing, one computer maker needed a cartridge that operated in environmental temperature extremes, another wanted to reduce friction in tape handling, and a third needed better acoustic noise properties.

A multifunctional team developed a new line of cartridges that not only met those challenges but also operated at higher speeds. Other data cartridge users, as well as the three customers seeking special features, are benefiting from this new product line.

Another major channel of innovation—anticipating market trends—also requires the organization to stay close to the customer.

Studying industry trends and talking to customers of our X-ray films made it clear that electronic diagnostic equipment was the wave of the future. That knowledge prompted the development of one of the company's most recent new products—the 3M Laser Imager for electronic medical imaging.

The Laser Imager "writes" digital signals from CAT scanners and other electronic diagnostic equipment onto a proprietary 3M film. It gives doctors a high-quality, hard-copy image of the scanner information that they had never had before.

Development of the Laser Imager drew on existing 3M imaging, materials, and hardware technologies. The high-priority effort eventually brought together a team from five different laboratories from the United States and abroad, as well as outside optical suppliers.

The project was initiated by management, but it was the persistence and diligence of the team that proved to be the driving force once the project began.

FAILURE IS NOT FATAL

If we gain a lot from each successful program at 3M, we also learn as much or more from every failure. For example, we tried to market a line of suntan lotions that adhered to the skin without being sticky; it protected the skin even after a thirty-minute swim. There was nothing wrong with the product's performance; however, we were not successful in the marketplace. The suntan lotions were competing against the products of well-established competitors who offered broad lines of well-known skin care products.

The experience reinforced our traditional wisdom that keeping one foot in a "comfort zone" enables us to compete more successfully. So we try to leverage our existing marketing strengths as often as we can when we embark on new products.

But we also learned never to give up too easily. Some astute laboratory people kept working on the sun-tan lotion technology and came up with a successful insect repellent.

Failures often turn into successes. A few years ago, a group of researchers working on adaptations of 3M's nonwoven fibers discovered that when very large fibers were made from polyvinyl chloride in a particular way, the end result is very curly fibers. At first, no one had any idea what to do with these curly fibers.

The project seemed doomed. But a few researchers continued thinking of potential uses for this fiber. Someone thought of putting a backing on the fibers; someone else realized curly fibers trap dirt and can be easily cleaned. The team eventually developed the line of Nomad brand floor mats, a valuable addition to the company's line of building maintenance products.

So we continue to leverage our cultural and technological strengths while giving a new emphasis to setting priorities, assessing the importance of individual programs, and focusing on those with major impact on the business.

We want each of our operating units to have a viable technology and product vision of the future. But we also want to keep those products coming that arise out of the curiosity and skill of our researchers.

CASE 10

The Lincoln Electric Company —————— ARTHUR SHARPLIN

People are our most valuable asset. They must feel secure, important, challenged, in control of their destiny, confident in their leadership, be responsive to common goals, believe they are being treated fairly, have easy access to authority and open lines of communication in all possible directions. Perhaps the most important task Lincoln employees face today is that of establishing an example for others in the Lincoln organization in other parts of the world. We need to maximize the benefits of cooperation and teamwork, fusing high technology with human talent, so that we here in the USA and all of our subsidiary and joint venture operations will be in a position to realize our full potential. [George Willis, CEO, The Lincoln Electric Company]

The Lincoln Electric Company is the world's largest manufacturer of arc welding products and a leading producer of industrial electric motors. The firm employs 2400 workers in two U.S. factories near Cleveland and an equal number in eleven factories located in other countries. This does not include the field sales force of more than 200. The company's U.S. market share (for arc welding products) is estimated at more than 40 percent.

The Lincoln incentive management plan has been well known for many years. Many college management texts make reference to the Lincoln plan as a model for achieving higher worker productivity. Certainly, the firm has been successful according to the usual measures.

James F. Lincoln died in 1965, and there was some concern, even among employees, that the management system would fall into disarray, that profits would decline, and that year-end bonuses might be discontinued. Quite the contrary. Twenty-four years after Lincoln's death, the company appears as strong as ever. Each year, except the recession years 1982 and 1983, has seen high profits and bonuses. Employee morale and productivity remain very good. Employee turnover is almost nonexistent except for retirements. Lincoln's market share is stable. The historically high stock dividends continue.

A HISTORICAL SKETCH

In 1895, after being "frozen out" of the depression-ravaged Elliott-Lincoln Company, a maker of Lincoln-designed electric motors, John C. Lincoln, took out his second patent and began to manufacture his improved motor. He opened his new business, unincorporated, with $200 he had earned redesigning a motor for young Herbert Henry Dow, who later founded the Dow Chemical Company.

Started during an economic depression and cursed by a major fire after only one year in business, the company grew, but hardly prospered, through its first quarter century. In 1906, John C. Lincoln incorporated the business and moved from his one-room fourth-floor factory to a new three-story building he erected in east Cleveland. He expanded his work force to thirty, and sales grew to over $50,000 a year. John preferred being an engineer and inventor rather than a manager, though, and it was to be left to another Lincoln to manage the company through its years of success.

In 1907, after a bout with typhoid fever forced him from Ohio State University in his senior year, James F. Lincoln, John's younger brother, joined the fledgling company. In 1914, he became active head of the firm, with the titles of general manager and vice president. John remained president of the company for some years but became more involved in other business ventures and in his work as an inventor.

One of James Lincoln's early actions was to ask the employees to elect representatives to a committee that would advise him on company operations. This "advisory board" has met with the chief executive officer every two weeks since that time. This was only the first of a series of innovative personnel policies that have, over the years, distinguished Lincoln Electric from its contemporaries.

The first year the advisory board was in existence, working hours were reduced from fifty-five per week, then standard, to fifty hours a week. In 1915, the company gave each employee a paid-up life insurance policy. A welding school, which continues today, was begun in 1917. In 1918, an employee bonus plan was attempted. It was not continued, but the idea was to resurface later.

The Lincoln Electric Employees' Association was formed in 1919 to provide health benefits and social activities. This organization continues today and has assumed several additional functions over the years. In 1923, a piecework pay system was in effect, employees got two weeks paid vacation each year, and wages were adjusted for changes in the Consumer Price Index. Approximately 30 percent of the common stock was set aside for key employees in 1914. A stock purchase plan for all employees was begun in 1925.

The board of directors voted to start a suggestion system in 1929. The program is still in effect, but cash awards, a part of the early program, were discontinued several years ago. Now, suggestions are rewarded by additional "points," which affect year-end bonuses.

The legendary Lincoln bonus plan was proposed by the advisory board and accepted on a trial basis in 1934.

The first annual bonus amounted to about 25 percent of wages. There has been a bonus every year since then. The bonus plan has been a cornerstone of the Lincoln management system, and recent bonuses have approximated annual wages.

By 1944, Lincoln employees enjoyed a pension plan, a policy of promotion from within, and continuous employment. Base pay rates were determined by formal job evaluation, and a merit-rating system was in effect.

In the prologue of James F. Lincoln's last book, Charles G. Herbruck writes regarding the foregoing personnel innovations:

> They were not to buy good behavior. They were not efforts to increase profits. They were not antidotes to labor difficulties. They did not constitute a "do-gooder" program. They were expression of mutual respect for each person's importance to the job to be done. All of them reflect the leadership of James Lincoln, under whom they were nurtured and propagated.

During World War II, Lincoln prospered as never before. By the start of the war, the company was the world's largest manufacturer of arc welding products. Sales of about $4 million in 1934 grew to $24 million by 1941. Productivity per employee more than doubled during the same period. The navy's Price Review Board challenged the high profits. And the Internal Revenue Service questioned the tax deductibility of employee bonuses, arguing they were not "ordinary and necessary" costs of doing business. But the forceful and articulate James Lincoln was able to overcome the objections.

Certainly since 1935 and probably for several years before that, Lincoln productivity has been well above the average for similar companies. The company claims levels of productivity more than twice those for other manufacturers from 1945 onward. Information available from outside sources tends to support these claims.

COMPANY PHILOSOPHY

James F. Lincoln was the son of a Congregational minister, and Christian principles were at the center of his business philosophy. The confidence that he had in the efficacy of Christ's teachings is illustrated by the following remark taken from one of his books:

> The Christian ethic should control our acts. If it did control our acts, the savings in cost of distribution would be tremendous. Advertising would be a contact of the expert consultant with the customer. In order to give the customer the best product available when all of the customer's needs are considered. Competition would then be in improving the quality of products and increasing

efficiency in producing and distributing them, not in deception, as is now too customary. Pricing would reflect efficiency of production; it would not be a selling dodge that the customer may well be sorry he accepted.

There is no indication that Lincoln attempted to evangelize his employees or customers—or the general public for that matter. Neither the chairman of the board and chief executive, George Willis, nor the president, Donald F. Hastings, mention the Christian gospel in their recent speeches and interviews. The company motto, "The actual is limited, the possible is immense," is prominently displayed, but there is no display of religious slogans, and there is no company chapel.

Attitude Toward the Customer

James Lincoln saw the customer's needs as the raison d'être for every company. "When any company has achieved success so that it is attractive as an investment," he wrote, "all money usually needed for expansion is supplied by the customer in retained earnings. It is obvious that the customer's interests, not the stockholder's, should come first." In 1947 he said, "Care should be taken...not to rivet attention on profit. Between 'How much do I get?' and 'How do I make this better, cheaper, more useful?' the difference is fundamental and decisive." Willis, too, ranks the customer as management's most important constituency. This is reflected in Lincoln's policy to "at all times price on the basis of cost and at all times keep pressure on our cost..." Lincoln's goal, often stated, is "to build a better and better product at a lower and lower price." "It is obvious," James Lincoln said, "that the customer's interests should be the first goal of industry."

Attitude Toward Stockholders

Stockholders are given last priority at Lincoln. This is a continuation of James Lincoln's philosophy: "The last group to be considered is the stockholders who own stock because they think it will be more profitable than investing money in any other way." Concerning division of the largess produced by incentive management, he wrote, "The absentee stockholder also will get his share, even if undeserved, out of the greatly increased profit that the efficiency produces."

Attitude Toward Unionism

There has never been a serious effort to organize Lincoln employees. While James Lincoln criticized the labor movement for "selfishly attempting to better its position at the expense of the people it must serve," he still had kind words for union members. He excused abuses of union power as "the natural reactions of human beings to the abuses to which management has subjected them." Lincoln's idea of the correct relationship between workers and managers is shown by this comment: "Labor and management are properly not warring camps; they are parts of one organization in which they must and should cooperate fully and happily."

Beliefs and Assumptions About Employees

If fulfilling customer needs is the desired goal of business, then employee performance and productivity are the means by which this goal can best be achieved. It is the Lincoln attitude toward employees, reflected in the following comments by James Lincoln, that is credited by many with creating the success the company has experienced:

> The greatest fear of the worker, which is the same as the greatest fear of the industrialist in operating a company, is the lack of income....The industrial manager is very conscious of his company's need for uninterrupted income. He is completely oblivious, evidently, of the fact that the worker has the same need.
>
> He is just as eager as any manager is to be part of a team that is properly organized and working for the advancement of our economy....He has no desire to make profits for those who do not hold up their end in production, as is true of absentee stockholders and inactive people in the company.
>
> If money is to be used as an incentive, the program must provide that what is paid to the worker is what he has earned. The earnings of each must be in accordance with accomplishment.
>
> Status is of great importance in all human relationships. The greatest incentive that money has, usually, is that it is a symbol of success....The resulting status is the real incentive....Money alone can be an incentive to the miser only.
>
> There must be complete honesty and understanding between the hourly worker and management if high efficiency is to be obtained.

LINCOLN'S BUSINESS

Arc welding has been the standard joining method in shipbuilding for decades. It is the predominant way of connecting steel in the construction industry. Most industrial plants have their own welding shops for maintenance and construction. Manufacturers of tractors and all kinds of heavy equipment use arc welding extensively in the manufacturing process. Many hobbyists have their own welding machines and use them for making metal items such as patio furniture and barbecue pits. The popularity of welded sculpture as an art form is growing.

While advances in welding technology have been frequent, arc welding products, in the main, have hardly changed. Lincoln's Innershield process is a notable exception. This process, described later, lowers welding cost and improves quality and speed in many applications. The most widely used Lincoln electrode, the Fleetweld 5P, has been virtually the same since the 1930s. The most popular engine-driven welder in the world, the Lincoln SA-200, has been for at least four decades a gray-colored assembly including a four-cylinder continental "Red Seal" engine and a 200-ampere direct-current generator with two current-control knobs. A 1989 model SA-200 even weighs almost the same as the 1950 model, and it certainly is little changed in appearance.

The company's share of the U.S. arc welding products market appears to have been about 40 percent for many years. The welding products market has grown somewhat faster than the level of industry in general. The market is highly price-competitive, with variations in prices of standard items normally amounting to only a percent or two. Lincoln's products are sold directly by its engineering-oriented sales force and indirectly through its distributor organization. Advertising expenditures amount to less than three-fourths of a percent of sales. Research and development expenditures typically range from $10 million to $12 million, considerably more than those of competitors.

The other major welding process, flame welding, has not been competitive with arc welding since the 1930s. However, plasma arc welding, a relatively new process that uses a conducting stream of superheated gas (plasma) to confine the welding current to a small area, has made some inroads, especially in metal tubing manufacturing, in recent years. Major advances in technology that will produce an alternative superior to arc welding within the next decade or so appear unlikely. Also, it seems likely that changes in the machines and techniques used in arc welding will be evolutionary rather than revolutionary.

Products

The company is primarily engaged in the manufacture and sale of arc welding products—electric welding machines and metal electrodes. Lincoln also produces electric motors ranging from one-half horsepower to 200 horsepower. Motors constitute about 8 to 10 percent of

total sales. Several million dollars have recently been invested in automated equipment that will double Lincoln's manufacturing capacity for 1/2- to 20-horsepower electric motors.

The electric welding machines, some consisting of a transformer or motor and generator arrangement powered by commercial electricity and others consisting of an internal combustion engine and generator, are designed to produce 30 to 1500 amperes of electrical power. This electrical current is used to melt a consumable metal electrode with the molten metal being transferred in superhot spray to the metal joint being welded. Very high temperatures and hot sparks are produced, and operators usually must wear special eye and face protection and leather gloves, often along with leather aprons and sleeves.

Lincoln and its competitors now market a wide range of general-purpose and specialty electrodes for welding milled steel, aluminum, cast iron, and stainless and special steels. Most of these electrodes are designed to meet the standards of the American Welding Society, a trade association. They are thus essentially the same in size and composition from one manufacturer to another. Every electrode manufacturer has a limited number of unique products, but these typically constitute only a small percentage of total sales.

Welding electrodes are of two basic types. The first is coated "stick" electrodes, usually 14 inches long and smaller than a pencil in diameter, which are held in a special insulated holder by the operator, who must manipulate the electrode in order to maintain a proper arc width and pattern of deposition of the metal being transferred. Stick electrodes are packaged in 6- to 50-pound boxes. The second type is coiled wire, ranging in diameter from 0.035 to 0.219 inch, which is designed to be fed continuously to the welding arc through a "gun" held by the operator or positioned by automatic positioning equipment. The wire is packaged in coils, reels, and drums weighing from 14 to 1000 pounds and maybe solid or flux-cored.

Manufacturing Processes

The main plant is in Euclid, Ohio, a suburb on Cleveland's east side. The layout of this plant is shown in Exhibit 1. There are no warehouses. Materials flow from the half-mile-long dock on the north side of the plant through the production lines to a very limited storage and loading area on the south side. Materials used in each workstation are stored as close as possible to the workstation. The administrative offices, near

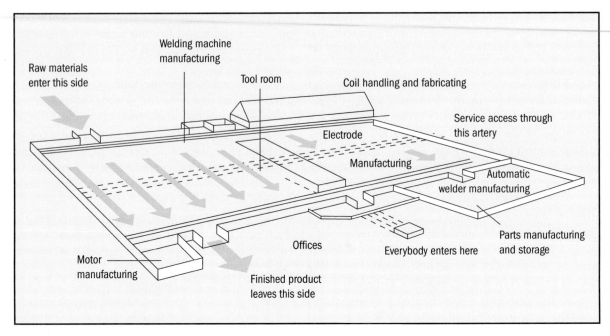

EXHIBIT 1   Main Factory Layout

the center of the factory, are entirely functional. A corridor below the main level provides access to the factory floor from the main entrance near the center of the plant. *Fortune* magazine recently declared the Euclid facility one of America's ten best-managed factories, and compared it with a General Electric plant also on the list:

> Stepping into GE's spanking new dishwasher plant, an awed supplier said, is like stepping "into the Hyatt Regency." By comparison, stepping into Lincoln Electric's 33-year-old, cavernous, dimly lit factory is like stumbling into a dingy big-city YMCA. It's only when one starts looking at how these factories do things that similarities become apparent. They have found ways to merge design with manufacturing, build in quality, make wise choices about automation, get close to customers, and handle their work forces.

A new Lincoln plant, in Mentor, Ohio, houses some of the electrode production operations, which were moved from the main plant.

Electrode manufacturing is highly capital intensive. Metal rods purchased from steel producers are drawn down to smaller diameters, cut to length and coated with pressed-powder "flux" for stick electrodes, or plated with copper (for conductivity) and put into coils or spools for wire. Lincoln's Innershield wire is hollow and filled with a material similar to that used to coat stick electrodes. As mentioned earlier, this represented a major innovation in welding technology when it was introduced. The company is highly secretive about its electrode production processes, and outsiders are not given access to the details of those processes.

Lincoln welding machines and electric motors are made on a series of assembly lines. Gasoline and diesel engines are purchased partially assembled, but practically all other components are made from basic industrial products—for example, steel bars and sheets and bar copper conductor wire.

Individual components, such as gasoline tanks for engine-driven welders and steel shafts for motors and generators, are made by numerous small "factories within a factory." The shaft for a certain generator, for example, is made from raw steel bar by one operator who uses five large machines, all running continuously. A saw cuts the bar to length, a digital lathe machines different sections to varying diameters, a special milling machine cuts a slot for the keyway, and so forth, until a finished shaft is produced. The operator moves the shafts from machine to machine and makes necessary adjustments.

Another operator punches, shapes, and paints sheet metal cowling parts. One assembles steel laminations onto a rotor shaft, then winds, insulates, and tests the rotors. Finished components are moved by crane operators to the nearby assembly lines.

Worker Performance and Attitudes

Exceptional worker performance at Lincoln is a matter of record. The typical Lincoln employee earns about twice as much as other factory workers in the Cleveland area. Yet the company's labor cost per sales dollar in 1989, 26 cents, is well below industry averages. Worker turnover is practically nonexistent except for retirements and departures by new employees.

Sales per Lincoln factory employee currently exceed $150,000. An observer at the factory quickly sees why this figure is so high. Each worker is proceeding busily and thoughtfully about the task at hand. There is no idle chatter. Most workers take no coffee breaks. Many operate several machines and make a substantial component unaided. The supervisors are busy with planning and record-keeping duties and hardly glance at the people they "supervise." The manufacturing procedures appear efficient—no unnecessary steps, no wasted motions, no wasted materials. Finished components move smoothly to subsequent workstations.

ORGANIZATION STRUCTURE

Lincoln has never allowed development of a formal organization chart. The objective of this policy is to ensure maximum flexibility. An open-door policy is practiced throughout the company, and personnel are encouraged to take problems to the persons most capable of resolving them. Once, Harvard Business School researchers prepared an organization chart reflecting the implied relationships at Lincoln. The chart became available within the company, and present management feels that it had a disruptive effect. Therefore, no organization chart appears in this report.

Perhaps because of the quality and enthusiasm of the Lincoln work force, routine supervision is almost nonexistent. A typical production foreman, for example, supervises as many as 100 workers, a span of control that does not allow more than infrequent worker-supervisor interaction.

Position titles and traditional flows of authority do imply something of an organizational structure, however. For example, the vice president, sales, and the vice president, electrode division, report to the president, as do various staff assistants such as the personnel director and the director of purchasing. Using such implied relationships, it has been determined that production workers have two or, at most, three levels of supervision between themselves and the president.

PERSONNEL POLICIES

As mentioned earlier, it is Lincoln's remarkable personnel practices that are credited by many with the company's success.

Recruitment and Selection

Every job opening is advertised internally on company bulletin boards, and any employee can apply for any job so advertised. External hiring is permitted only for entry-level positions. Selection for these jobs is done on the basis of personal interviews—there is no aptitude or psychological testing. Not even a high school diploma is required—except for engineering and sales positions, which are filled by graduate engineers. A committee consisting of vice presidents and supervisors interviews candidates initially cleared by the personnel department. Final selection is made by the supervisor who has a job opening. Out of over 3500 applicants interviewed by the personnel department during a recent period, fewer than 300 were hired.

Job Security

In 1958, Lincoln formalized its guaranteed continuous employment policy, which had already been in effect for many years. There have been no layoffs since World War II. Since 1958, every worker with over two years of longevity has been guaranteed at least thirty hours per week, forty-nine weeks per year.

The policy has never been so severely tested as during the 1981–1983 recession. As a manufacturer of capital goods, Lincoln's business is highly cyclical. In previous recessions the company was able to avoid major sales declines. However, sales plummeted 32 percent in 1982 and another 16 percent the next year. Few companies could withstand such a revenue collapse and remain profitable. Yet, Lincoln not only earned profits, but no employee was laid off and year-end incentive bonuses continued. To weather the storm, management cut most of the nonsalaried workers back to thirty hours a week for varying periods of time. Many employees were reassigned, and the total work force was slightly reduced through normal attrition and restricted hiring. Many employees grumbled at their unexpected misfortune, probably to the surprise and dismay of some Lincoln managers. However, sales and profits—and employee bonuses—soon rebounded and all was well again.

Performance Evaluations

Each supervisor formally evaluates subordinates twice a year using the cards shown in Exhibit 2. The employee performance criteria—"quality," "dependability," "ideas and cooperation," and "output"—are considered to be independent of each other. Marks on the cards are converted to numerical scores, which are forced to average 100 for each evaluating supervisor. Individual merit-rating scores normally range from 80 to 110. Any score over 110 requires a special letter to top management. These scores (over 110) are not considered in computing the required 100-point average for each evaluating supervisor. Suggestions for improvements often result in recommendations for exceptionally high performance scores. Supervisors discuss individual performance marks with the employees concerned. Each warranty claim is traced to the individual employee whose work caused the defect. The employee's performance score may be reduced, or the worker may be required to repay the cost of servicing the warranty claim by working without pay.

Compensation

Basic wage levels for jobs at Lincoln are determined by a wage survey of similar jobs in the Cleveland area. These rates are adjusted quarterly in accordance with changes in the Cleveland area wage index. Insofar as possible, base wage rates are translated into piece rates. Practically all production workers and many others—for example, some forklift operators—are paid by piece rate. Once established, piece rates are never changed unless a substantive change in the way a job is done results from a source other than the worker doing the job.

In December of each year, a portion of annual profits is distributed to employees as bonuses. Incentive bonuses since 1934 have averaged about 90 percent of annual wages and somewhat more than after-tax profits. The average bonus for 1988 was $21,258. Even for the recession years 1982 and 1983, bonuses averaged $13,998 and $8557, respectively. Individual bonuses are proportional to merit-rating scores. For example, assume the amount set aside for bonuses is 80 percent of total wages paid to eligible employees. A person whose performance score is 95 will receive a bonus of 76 percent (0.80×0.95) of annual wages.

Vacations

The company is shut down for two weeks in August and two weeks during the Christmas season. Vacations are taken during these periods. For employees with over twenty-five years of service, a fifth week of vacation may be taken at a time acceptable to superiors.

Work Assignment

Management has authority to transfer workers and to switch between overtime and short time as required. Supervisors have undisputed authority to assign specific parts to individual workers who may have their own preferences due to variations in piece rates. During the 1982–1983 recession, fifty factory workers volunteered to join sales teams and fanned out across the country to sell a new welder designed for automobile body shops and small machine shops. The result—$10 million in sales and a hot new product.

Employee Participation in Decision Making

Thinking of participative management usually evokes a vision of a relaxed, nonauthoritarian atmosphere. This is not the case at Lincoln. Formal authority is quite strong. "We're very authoritarian around here," says Willis. James F. Lincoln placed a good deal of stress on protecting management's authority. "Management in all successful departments of industry must have complete power," he said. "Management is the coach who must be obeyed. The men, however, are the players who alone can win the game." Despite this attitude, there are several ways in which employees participate in management at Lincoln.

Richard Sabo, assistant to the chief executive officer, relates job enlargement/enrichment to participation. He said, "The most important participative technique that we use is giving more responsibility to employees. We give a high school graduate more responsibility than other companies give their foremen." Management puts limits on the degree of participation that is allowed, however. In Sabo's words:

> When you use "participation," put quotes around it, because we believe that each person should participate only in those decisions he is most knowledgeable about. I don't think production employees should control the decisions of the chairman. They don't know as much as he does about the decisions he is involved in.

The advisory board, elected by the workers, meets with the chairman and the president every two weeks to discuss ways of improving operations. As noted earlier, this board has been in existence since 1914 and has contributed to many innovations. The incentive bonuses, for example, were first recommended by this committee. Every employee has access to advisory board members, and answers to all advisory board suggestions are promised by the following meeting. Both Willis and Hastings are quick to point out, though, that the advisory board only recommends actions. "They do not have

Increasing Quality

This card rates the QUALITY of work you do.

It also reflects your success in eliminating errors and in reducing scrap and waste.

QUALITY

This rating has been done jointly by your department head and the Inspection Department in the shop and with other department heads in the office and engineering.

Increasing Dependability

This card rates how well your supervisors have been able to depend upon you to do those things that have been expected of you without supervision.

It also reflects your ability to supervise yourself including your work safety performance, your orderliness, care of equipment, and the effective use you make of your skills.

DEPENDABILITY

This rating has been done by your department head.

Increasing Ideas & Cooperation

This card rates your cooperation, ideas and initiative.

IDEAS & COOPERATION

Increasing Output   Days
Absent

This card rates HOW MUCH PRODUCTIVE WORK you actually turn out. It also reflects your willingness not to hold back and recognizes your attendance record.
New ideas and new methods are important to your company in our continuing effort to reduce costs, increase output, improve quality, work safely and improve our relationship with our customers. This card credits you for your ideas and initiative used to help in this direction.

It also rates your cooperation—how you work with others as a team. Such factors as your attitude toward supervision, co-workers and the company, your efforts to share knowledge with others, and your cooperation in installing new methods smoothly, are considered here.

OUTPUT

This rating has been done jointly by your department head and the Production Control Department in the shop and with other department heads in the office and engineering.

EXHIBIT 2   Merit Rating Cards

direct authority," Willis says, "and when they bring up something that management thinks is not to the benefit of the company, it will be rejected."

Under the early suggestion program, employees were awarded one-half of the first year's savings attributable to their suggestions. Now, however, the value of suggestions is reflected in performance evaluation scores, which determine individual incentive bonus amounts.

Training and Education

Production workers are given a short period of on-the-job training and then placed on a piecework pay system. Lincoln does not pay for off-site education, unless very specific company needs are identified. The idea behind this latter policy, according to Sabo, is that everyone cannot take advantage of such a program, and it is unfair to expend company funds for an advantage to which there is unequal access. Recruits for sales jobs, already college graduates, are given on-the-job training in the plant followed by a period of work and training at one of the regional sales offices.

Fringe Benefits and Executive Perquisites

A medical plan and a company-paid retirement program have been in effect for many years. A plant cafeteria, operated on a break-even basis, serves meals at about 60 percent of usual costs. The Employee Association, to which the company does not contribute, provides disability insurance and social and athletic activities. The employee stock ownership program has resulted in employee ownership of about 50 percent of the common stock. Under this program, each employee with more than two years of service may purchase stock in the corporation. The price of these shares is established at book value. Stock purchased through this plan may be held by employees only. Dividends and voting rights are the same as for stock that is owned outside the plan. Approximately 75 percent of the employees own Lincoln stock.

As to executive perquisites, there are none—crowded, austere offices, no executive washrooms or lunchrooms, and no reserved parking spaces. Even the top executives pay for their own meals and eat in the employee cafeteria. On one recent day, Willis arrived at work late due to a breakfast speaking engagement and had to park far away from the factory entrance.

FINANCIAL POLICIES

James F. Lincoln felt strongly that financing for company growth should come from within the company—through initial cash investment by the founders, through retention of earnings, and through stock purchases by those who work in the business. He saw the following advantages of this approach:

1. Ownership of stock by employees strengthens team spirit. "If they are mutually anxious to make it succeed, the future of the company is bright."
2. Ownership of stock provides individual incentive because employees feel that they will benefit from company profitability.
3. "Ownership is educational." Owners-employees "will know how profits are made and lost; how success is won and lost.... There are few socialists in the list of stock-holders of the nation's industries."
4. "Capital available from within controls expansion." Unwarranted expansion would not occur, Lincoln believed, under his financing plan.
5. "The greatest advantage would be the development of the individual worker. Under the incentive of ownership, he would become a greater man."
6. "Stock ownership is one of the steps that can be taken that will make the worker feel that there is less of a gulf between him and the boss.... Stock ownership will help the worker to recognize his responsibility in the game and the importance of victory."

Until 1980, Lincoln Electric borrowed no money. Even now, the company's liabilities consist mainly of accounts payable and short-term accruals.

The unusual pricing policy at Lincoln is succinctly stated by Willis: "At all times price on the basis of cost and at all times keep pressure on our cost." This policy resulted in the price for the most popular welding electrode then in use going from 16 cents a pound in 1929 to 4.7 cents in 1938. More recently, the SA-200 welder, Lincoln's largest-selling portable machine, decreased in price from 1958 through 1965. According to Dr. C. Jackson Grayson of the American Productivity Center in Houston, Texas, Lincoln's prices increased only one-fifth as fast as the Consumer Price Index from 1934 to about 1970. This resulted in a welding products market in which Lincoln became the undisputed price leader for the products it manufactures. Not even the major Japanese manufacturers, such as Nippon Steel for welding electrodes and Osaka Transformer for welding machines, were able to penetrate this market.

Substantial cash balances are accumulated each year preparatory to paying the year-end bonuses. The bonuses totaled $54 million for 1988. The money is invested in short-term U.S. government securities and certificates of deposit until needed. Financial statements are shown in Exhibit 3. Exhibit 4 shows how company revenue was distributed in the late 1980s.

	1979	1980	1981	1982	1983	1984	1985	1986	1987
Balance Sheets									
Assets:									
Cash	2	1	4	1	2	4	2	1	7
Bonds & CDs	38	47	63	72	78	57	55	45	41
N/R & A/R	42	42	42	26	31	34	38	36	43
Inventories	38	36	46	38	31	37	34	26	40
Prepayments	1	3	4	5	5	5	7	8	7
Total CA	121	129	157	143	146	138	135	116	137
Other assets†	24	24	26	30	30	29	29	33	40
Land	1	1	1	1	1	1	1	1	1
Net buildings	22	23	25	23	22	21	20	18	17
Net M&E	21	25	27	27	27	28	27	29	33
Total FA	44	49	53	51	50	50	48	48	50
Total assets	189	202	236	224	227	217	213	197	227
Claims:									
A/P	17	16	15	12	16	15	13	11	20
Accrued wages	1	2	5	4	3	4	5	5	4
Accrued taxes	10	6	15	5	7	4	6	5	9
Accrued div.	6	6	7	7	7	6	7	6	7
Total CL	33	29	42	28	33	30	31	27	40
LT debt		4	5	6	8	10	11	8	8
Total debt	33	33	47	34	41	40	42	35	48
Common stock	4	3	1	2	0	0	0	0	2
Ret. earnings	152	167	189	188	186	176	171	161	177
Total SH equity	156	170	190	190	186	176	171	161	179
Total claims	189	202	236	224	227	217	213	197	227
Income Statements									
Net Sales	374	387	450	311	263	322	333	318	368
Other income	11	14	18	18	13	12	11	8	9
Income	385	401	469	329	277	334	344	326	377
CGS	244	261	293	213	180	223	221	216	239
Selling, G&A‡	41	46	51	45	45	47	48	49	51
Incentive bonus	44	43	56	37	22	33	38	33	39
IBT	56	51	69	35	30	31	36	27	48
Income taxes	26	23	31	16	13	14	16	12	21
Net income	30	28	37	19	17	17	20	15	27

*Column totals may not check and amounts less than $500,000 (0.5) are shown as zero, due to rounding.
†Includes investment in foreign subsidiaries, $29 million in 1987.
‡includes pension expense and payroll taxes on incentive bonus.

EXHIBIT 3   Condensed Comparative Financial Statements (in Millions of Dollars)*

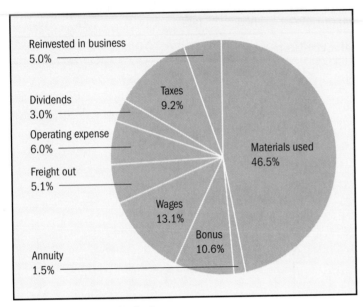

EXHIBIT 4   Revenue Distribution

HOW WELL DOES LINCOLN SERVE ITS STAKEHOLDERS?

Lincoln Electric differs from most other companies in the importance it assigns to each of the groups it serves. Willis identifies these groups, in the order of priority ascribed to them, as (1) customers, (2) employees, and (3) stockholders.

Certainly the firm's customers have fared well over the years. Lincoln prices for welding machines and welding electrodes are acknowledged to be the lowest in the marketplace. Quality has consistently been high. The cost of field failures for Lincoln products was recently determined to be a remarkable 0.04 percent of revenues. The "Fleetweld" electrodes and SA-200 welders have been the standard in the pipeline and refinery construction industry, where price is hardly a criterion, for decades. A Lincoln distributor in Monroe, Louisiana, says that he has sold several hundred of the popular AC-225 welders, which are warranted for one year, but has never handled a warranty claim.

Perhaps best served of all management constituencies have been the employees. Not the least of their benefits, of course, are the year-end bonuses, which effectively double an already average compensation level. The foregoing description of the personnel program further illustrates the desirability of a Lincoln job.

While stockholders were relegated to an inferior status by James F. Lincoln, they have done very well indeed. Recent dividends have exceeded $11 a share and

earnings per share have approached $30. In January 1980, the price of restricted stock, committed to employees, was $117 a share. By 1989, the stated value, at which the company will repurchase the stock if tendered, was $201. A check with the New York office of Merrill Lynch, Pierce, Fenner, and Smith at that time revealed an estimated price on Lincoln stock of $270 a share, with none being offered for sale. Technically, this price applies only to the unrestricted stock owned by the Lincoln family, a few other major holders, and employees who have purchased it on the open market. Risk associated with Lincoln stock, a major determinant of stock value, is minimal because of the small amount of debt in the capital structure, because of an extremely stable earnings record, and because of Lincoln's practice of purchasing the restricted stock whenever employees offer it for sale.

A CONCLUDING COMMENT

It is easy to believe that the reason for Lincoln's success is the excellent attitude of the employees and their willingness to work harder, faster, and more intelligently than other industrial workers. However, Sabo suggests that appropriate credit be given to Lincoln executives, whom he credits with carrying out the following policies:

1. Management has limited research, development, and manufacturing to a standard product line designed to meet the major needs of the welding industry.

2. New products must be reviewed by manufacturing and all producing costs verified before being approved by management.

3. Purchasing is challenged not only to procure materials at the lowest cost, but also to work closely with engineering and manufacturing to assure that the latest innovations are implemented.

4. Manufacturing supervision and all personnel are held accountable for reduction of scrap, energy conservation, and maintenance of product quality.

5. Production control, material handling, and methods engineering are closely supervised by top management.

6. Management has made cost reduction a way of life at Lincoln, and definite programs are established in many areas, including traffic and shipping, where tremendous savings can result.

7. Management has established a sales department that is technically trained to reduce customer welding costs. This sales approach and other real customer services have eliminated nonessential frills and resulted in long-term benefits to all concerned.

8. Management has encouraged education, technical publishing, and long-range programs that have resulted in industry growth, thereby assuring market potential for the Lincoln Electric Company.

Sabo writes, "It is in a very real sense a personal and group experience in faith—a belief that together we can achieve results which alone would not be possible. It is not a perfect system and it is not easy. It requires tremendous dedication and hard work. However, it does work and the results are worth the effort."

CASE 11

Beer and Wine Industries: Bartles & Jaymes ———————————— PER V. JENSTER

INTRODUCTION

At the end of 1986, Bartles & Jaymes conquered the number one position in the wine cooler industry after coming in second to California Coolers since this product hit the consumer goods market. Going into 1987, Bartles & Jaymes and its corporate parent, Ernest & Julio Gallo Winery, were faced with the task of maintaining this market position and increasing sales of its newest product—the wine cooler.

HISTORY OF THE FIRM

Ernest and Julio Gallo Winery, the world's largest, began in 1938 at a tragic point in the brothers' lives. They had just inherited their father Joseph's vineyard after he shot his wife, reportedly chased Ernest and Julio with a shotgun, and committed suicide. Suddenly they were faced with operating the vineyard where they grew up and had gone to work upon completing their education

Professor Per V. Jenster, IMD, Lausanne, Switzerland. Reprinted with permission.
The author gratefully acknowledges the assistance of students Morlon Bell, Michele Goggins, and Mary Kay, as well as the support provided by the McIntire Foundation. Copyright © 1987.

(high school for Julio and junior college for Ernest). The business of growing grapes was all they knew. Joseph Gallo, an immigrant from Italy, came to Modesto, California, and began his small grape-producing company. The fledgling company survived Prohibition due to the fact that the government allowed wine production for medicinal and religious use. The Depression dealt the small company a somewhat more devastating blow. It was at this company low point that Joseph decided on such a dramatic solution to his problems. Though he may have solved his problems, Joseph left his relatively young sons a burden of responsibility and decision making. Shortly after their parents' deaths, Prohibition was repealed and the brothers decided to move from grape growing to wine producing. With two pamphlets on wine making from the local public library and less that $6000 in hand, the ambitious Gallos began their empire.

Gallo's climb to its dominant position in the wine industry (see Exhibit 1) began slowly. In the 1930s and 1940s, Ernest developed his acute marketing sense and Julio cultivated and refined his wine-making expertise. Initially they sold their product in bulk to bottlers on the East Coast, but in 1938 they decided it would be more profitable to bottle the wine under a Gallo label. In the 1950s, Gallo greatly increased its success with a high-alcohol, low-price product called Thunderbird. This product became exceptionally popular on skid rows and increased Gallo's profitability, but it may have done irreparable damage by saddling Gallo with a "gutter" image. In the 1960s and early 1970s, Gallo's image, not sales, was further tarnished by the "pop-wine" craze of which it was a leader with such products as Boone's Farm and Spanada wines. In the mid-1970s, Ernest Gallo became conscious of and concerned about the fact that even though it had formidable sales, it also had a "brownbag," jug-wine image. At that time, the company decided to attempt to upgrade its image and at the same time maintain its market share and sales. As part of this attempt, it began to produce premium table wines such as Zinfandel, Sauvignon Blanc, Ruby Cabernet, and French Colombard. This push to improve its image continued to be a dominating theme for Gallo.

E. & J. Gallo Winery	26.1%
Seagram & Sons	8.3
Canandaigua Wine	5.4
Brown-Forman	5.1
National Distillers	4.0
Heublein	3.7
Imports	23.4
All others	24.0

Source: From *Advertising Age,* March 24, 1986. Reprinted with permission of Crain Communications, Inc.

EXHIBIT 1 **1985 Share of U.S. Wine Market**

As Gallo grew, it not only developed its wine sales but became extensively vertically integrated. It had divisions in virtually every step of the wine-producing process. The brothers owned one of the largest intrastate trucking companies in California, which was used to haul wine, grapes, raw materials, sand, lime, etc. Gallo was the only wine producer that made its own bottles, and its Midcal Aluminum Company supplied it with screw tops. Unlike most other wine producers, Gallo took an active role in the marketing of its products. Typical wineries would turn their products over to independent distributors who represented several producers

and expected the distributor to get the product to the consumer. These distributors, on the other hand, felt their job consisted of taking orders and making deliveries. Gallo owned many of its distributors, and the independent distributors it used had to be willing to submit to Gallo's regimentation. Gallo was known to "encourage" its independent distributors to exclusively distribute Gallo products. Ten years ago, the Federal Trade Commission took offense at this, charging Gallo with unfair competition and forcing Gallo to sign a consent order. In 1984, the FTC removed the order due to the fact that the wine industry had become more competitive.

In its fifty-year history, Gallo developed an extensive product line. It had products geared toward the low-priced, jug-wine market (Carlo Rossi, Chablis Blanc, etc.). It also had a replete category of premium wines, selling more than any competitor, but growth in this market was limited due to the fact that Gallo did not have snob appeal. In 1984, Gallo entered the wine cooler category (a carbonated drink with half white wine and half citrus juice) with its Bartles & Jaymes wine cooler. Gallo followed the lead of such industry innovators as California Cooler, Sun Country Coolers, etc., which fit well with its strategy of building market share through skillful marketing and sales, but not introducing inventive new products. Bartles & Jaymes was marketed in 12-ounce green bottles similar to those used for Michelob beer and aimed at a more sophisticated consumer than its competitors. To help promote this upgraded image, Gallo tried to distance itself from Bartles & Jaymes, and many consumers did not know that Gallo wine was used to make the coolers. In the summer of 1986, Bartles & Jaymes took over the number one position in the wine cooler market with a share of 22.1 percent.

With that initial $6000, some ingenuity, a little luck, and a lot of spunk, the Gallo brothers built the world's preeminent wine dynasty. Because Gallo was a private, tightly held company, there was no public financial data, but it was estimated that it had annual sales of $1 billion and yearly earnings of $50 million. In comparison, Joe E. Seagram and Sons, the second largest winery, had revenues of $350 million and lost money on its best-selling table wines in 1985.

BACKGROUND ON KEY EXECUTIVES

E. & J. Gallo was a private company owned and operated by the Gallo brothers, Ernest and Julio. Julio, the 77-year-old president of the firm, and Ernest, chairman of the board at 78, ran their company in a very dichotomous manner. Julio was in charge of producing the wine and Ernest marketed and distributed it. They operated in their separate worlds and often did not have daily contact. It seemed to be a game—Julio trying to produce more than Ernest could sell and Ernest trying to sell more than Julio could produce. But the game apparently worked and provided the company with good returns.

Julio, the more easygoing of the two, described himself as a "farmer at heart." He spent much of his time in the fields and overseeing the wine making. Though definitely not a pushover, Julio was not the hard-core, intense businessman that his brother Ernest was. Ernest ruled over the company and usually made the final decisions. He was characterized as being polite, but blunt. He could not bear to relinquish power and control, and it was at his insistence that everything about the operations of the firm was kept secret. He could be a very demanding, driving boss, and when asked about the secret to Gallo's success, he remarked it was a "constant striving for perfection in every aspect of our business."

A looming concern, though not openly addressed or dealt with at Gallo, was the brothers' advancing age. Julio seemed to be training and grooming his son, Robert, and his son-in-law, James Coleman, in his area of expertise. Ernest, on the other hand, had no heir apparent. Two of his sons, David and Joseph, worked with him, but neither was viewed as having the ability to take over their father's job. Joseph was felt to give uneven decisions, and David was described as "occasionally bizarre." The firm had many intelligent, able, top-level executives, but they had no power to make decisions and predominantly strove to please Ernest. The deaths of Ernest and Julio, which were inevitable, could prove to be devastating for the firm.

INTERNAL OPERATIONS

Because Gallo was so tightly held and secretive, it was hard to determine how and why things were done the way they were—maybe only Ernest knew. A few loyal senior managers ran the divisions of the vertically integrated firm and reported to Ernest. He had a hand in all major decisions and procedures and went so far as to help write a 300-page, very detailed training manual for sales representatives. Gallo was so secretive that at times even its own employees did not know what was happening. According to Diana Kelleher, former marketing manager at Gallo, "I never saw a profit-and-loss statement; Ernest wouldn't tell anyone the cost of raw materials, overhead, or packaging."

INDUSTRY HISTORY, AND ANALYSIS

It would be difficult to pinpoint exactly when the wine cooler industry emerged. Three separate events were cited to mark the beginning of this prosperous industry. In 1977, Joseph Bianchi, owner of Bianchi Vineyards, observed people at a summer party mixing Seven-Up with wine. In 1981, Thomas Steid, owner of Canada Dry/Graf's Bottling Company, formulated his own wine cooler recipe. The event that was commonly viewed as the beginning of this industry stemmed from the concoction of Michael M. Crete and R. Stuart Bewley produced by California Cooler.

Crete and Bewley's drink was initially served in 1972, to their friends. Little did they know that this new refresher would be a huge success a decade later. Batches of white wine and fruit juice were mixed in a beer barrel and served from a plastic hose. Labels were stuck on by hand and an average workday consisted of bottling 100 to 150 cases. As this product was marketed in the early 1980s, sales began to increase steadily. This campaign spurred national attention toward the new market.

At the point of the cooler's entry, other sectors of the beverage industry were experiencing declining sales. The wine industry had experienced declining table wine sales for two years in a row at the beginning of the 1980s. Likewise, the beer industry was faced with declining sales. It was costing both industries more in advertising to keep their regular customers. Several factors caused such a response in the consumer market. First, drunken driving laws and the crackdown on drinking that they spurred led to more awareness about the negative effects of alcohol. Public interest groups such as MADD (Mothers Against Drunk Driving) played a key role in changing the consumer's perceptions of drinking. Second, there was growing concern for fitness. As the health-conscious consumers grew in number, the tendency to indulge in alcoholic beverages declined. Third, the raising of the legal drinking age presented obstacles to increasing sales. Since younger adults consumed a significant percentage of the alcohol sold, the change in age cut out some sales originally anticipated by beer and wine producers. Fourth, the lobbying to remove liquor advertising from television showed wineries and breweries as the villains in society.

In view of societal factors, a method was needed to help the alcohol industries survive. Thus, an alternative to beer and wine appeared to be the solution in the eyes of Crete and Bewley. They saw the potential and seized the opportunity to capitalize on the venture. To achieve a successful outcome, however, the product had to be positioned properly. The wine cooler was a fruity-tasting, slightly cloudy beverage made from chablis, blended citrus-pineapple juice, fructose, and a slight amount of carbonation. Its targeted consumers were young adults from legal drinking age to 34 years old, both male and female. The cooler was marketed in the same manner as beer, particularly its "coldbox," refrigerator bottling. It was to be less of an elitist drink than wine. It contained more alcohol than beer but less alcohol than wine.

For the wine cooler industry to succeed, several characteristics had to be present. Taste was an important factor to provide a basis for differentiation between products. Points of difference were sought to make individual brands stand out, by varying fruit flavors, packaging, or advertising techniques. Another major characteristic was merchandising, which was relevant to the success of any consumer market. In the wine industry particularly, price was the key to merchandising. It could be extremely difficult for competitors to come up with original ideas to differentiate their product, so most relied on price to help them capture a reasonable percentage of the market.

Several viewpoints have been given about wine coolers. The single-service focus was the major thrust of the cooler's marketing plan. It could be carried easily (exactly like beer) and did not concentrate heavily on the jug mentality of wineries. Coolers also cut across beverage boundaries by "touting the fizz of soft drinks, the popularity of white wine, the freshness of citrus juice, plus a bit of fructose to satisfy the sweet tooth." The cooler fit the desires of the current pluralistic consumer society. It was viewed as "wine for the common man" because it appealed to the beer drinker who wanted a little more alcohol, the wine drinker who wanted a little less, the calorie- and taste-conscious, and the first-time wine drinkers put off by the snobbery of the wine elite. The marketing module appeared to contain all the elements of success— "a firm product identity; a well-defined package and price image; a powerful distribution channel that stressed cold-box merchandising to capitalize on its 'cool' perception and enhance its full price and profit positioning; and advertising that communicated a refreshing message to the public." This segment showed second-generation development. Three trends were cited in the existing industry. One trend focused on the low alcohol content of approximately 6 percent. This aspect was probably influenced by the anti–drunk driving campaigns. Sales of coolers were said to have been spurred by this concern. Another trend was geared toward its thirst-quenching characteristic. Its refreshing health perspective was the focus of the last trend. Coolers were professed to be healthful since they contained half citrus juice.

The wine cooler industry appeared particularly attractive because the product offered high margins and a low base with no capital requirements. It generated better gross dollar margins than beer or wine. The expected annual growth rate was projected to be 13 percent until 1993. The expected growth rate in 1986 was 69 percent. Cooler sales were estimated to account for 17 percent to 20 percent of total wine sales in 1986 as compared to only 1 percent in 1984.

In 1986, the cooler industry was faced with various trends in the beverage world. First, it was reported that Americans were drinking more soft drinks (April 1986). The alcohol industry was still faced with overall declines, but the wine industry was better situated than the beer industry due to the success of the wine cooler. It was predicted that the wine cooler industry would soon be viewed separately from the wine industry. The second area of concern involved the steadily increasing cost of competing. The fight for wholesale and retail distribution was intensifying. This led marketers to cut prices to acquire more shelf space and visibility. Also, coupons were used to increase distribution. As of August 1986, the dollar level was low and the investment spending was high.

The wine cooler industry consisted of approximately forty producers and 154 individual labels during the summer of 1986. Because of the high barriers to entry, competition from other segments, particularly the breweries and wineries, did not appear to be substantial. Since the beer and wine markets were mature, the success achieved in the wine cooler industry caused them to take a second look at this area for potential profits. Even though breweries and wineries experienced decreasing sales, only a small portion was attributed to the boom in the wine cooler industry. The soft-drink industry, on the other hand, proved to be a minor problem for coolers due to increased consumption by consumers. The effect of the competition was not significantly shown in the sales figures for coolers, but the potential loomed in the background. Experts raised questions concerning cooler sales. Declines were predicted based on a speculated consumer interest in a variety of flavored drinks. Were coolers a fad or a new and growing industry?

COMPETITION

When California Cooler began peddling its wine cooler, the competition was sparse and far from formidable. Initially, the cost of entry into the new market was relatively low. But by the first quarter of 1986, the world's largest winery, brewery, and distillery were all vying for the top spot and all three were holding fat bankrolls. The cost of entry into the market had risen to $10 million just for advertising. Cooler marketers and industry observers were confident this category would continue to grow steadily for the next few years. It was estimated that sixty to sixty-five million cases of coolers—including malt-based coolers—would have been sold by the end of 1987, up from forty-one million cases in 1985. In 1987, more than 150 kinds of wine coolers were competing with the top seven coolers, which controlled about 90 percent of the market—E. & J. Gallo Winery's Bartles & Jaymes, Brown-Forman Corporation's California Cooler, Canandaigua Wine Company's Sun Country, Joseph Victori Wines' Calvin Cooler, Stroh Brewery Company's malt-based White Mountain cooler, and Joe E. Seagram and Sons' Premium and Golden coolers. (See Exhibit 2.)

Bartles & Jaymes

By October 1986, Gallo's Bartles & Jaymes wine cooler was the largest-selling cooler in the nation, with a 22.1 percent market share. Its standing was quite remarkable in light of Bartles & Jaymes' relatively narrow product line. Gallo produced only one flavor of wine cooler (6 percent alcohol). This clear, less sweet cooler came in sleek 12-ounce green bottles like those of imported beers and was available in the standard four-pack.

Two key factors, advertising and distribution, differentiated the industry leader from its competitors. In 1986, Gallo budgeted $30 million for advertising expenditures for Bartles & Jaymes (see Exhibit 3). The majority of this money was spent on an ad campaign in which Gallo chose to distance its cooler from the parent corporation by creating fictional proprietors named Frank Bartles and Ed Jaymes, who sat on their front porch while Frank delivered low-key, comical monologues about the product. An advertiser with the Bartles & Jaymes campaign said, "Most of the competition was using youthful music and showing young people doing all the predictable things. We thought that if we got into all those clichés, we'd get lost." This was all part of a cold, hard-edged effort on Gallo's part to maintain a sense of warm, down-home, folksy legitimacy around the TV

	1986*	1985
1. Bartles & Jaymes	22.1%	17.5%
2. California Cooler	18.0	26.8
3. Sun Country	13.1	11.7
4. White Mountain	12.4	7.5
5. Calvin Cooler	8.3	6.5
6. Seagram's Golden	6.9	—
7. Seagram's Premium	5.5	9.3
8. Dewey Stevens	2.8	—
9. 20/20	2.5	3.7
10. La Croix	1.5	1.9

Source: From Impact Databank, 1986. Reprinted by permission of M. Shanken Communications, Inc.
*Estimate.

EXHIBIT 2 Top 10 Cooler Brands Share of the Market

spots that obviously had many Americans believing there really were a Frank Bartles and an Ed Jaymes.

Some observers, including a few of Gallo's competitors, were not as amused by Gallo's marketing strategy as most of America seemed to be. Tom Gibbs, director of marketing for California Coolers, saw the ads as downright deceptive. "Yuppies are not Gallo drinkers, so they (Gallo) have tried to disassociate their names from this market." Mr. Gibbs said the public did not know Frank and Ed were not on the level and believed consumers would turn away from the product if they knew the truth. He claimed his company had done interviews after which people quit drinking Bartles & Jaymes once they

Bartles & Jaymes	$30,000,000
Seagram's	30,000,000
California Cooler	25,000,000
Dewey Stevens	20,000,000
Sun Country	20,000,000
White Mountain	12,000,000
Calvin Cooler	10,000,000

Source: From *Advertising Age,* March 24, 1986. Reprinted with permission of Crain Communications, Inc.

EXHIBIT 3 1986 Advertising Budgets

learned it was a Gallo product—a name, he says, "people equate with jug wines."

Jon Fredrikson, an industry analyst with San Francisco-based wine industry consultants Gomberg, Fredrikson & Associates, said the public might react negatively if the truth got out on a widespread basis, but added that wasn't likely.

Aileen Fredrikson, also with Gomberg, said the campaign had the dual effect of helping beer drinkers relate to the wine cooler market. "Young people can always be convinced to try something once," she said, "but this may be a way to get hard-core beer drinkers to try it, since it's two good ole boys selling it."

The channel of distribution chosen by Gallo was the second key factor in differentiating Bartles & Jaymes from its competitors. Unlike other wine cooler producers who distributed their products through beer distributors, Bartles & Jaymes used Gallo's extensive wine distributorship. Ernest Gallo handpicked each of these distributors and then planned strategies with them down to the last detail, analyzing traffic patterns in every store in the district and the number of Gallo cases each should stock. Ernest Gallo encouraged distributors to hire a separate sales force to sell his products alone. He also tried to persuade distributors to sell his wine exclusively.

California Cooler

Stuart Bewley and Michael Crete were partners who founded California Cooler Company, Stockton, California, just five years ago. The two childhood friends created the product when they started filling washtubs at beach parties with their special mixture—half white wine and half citrus juice. In September 1985, Brown-Forman, a Louisville-based distiller, bought out the segment leader California Cooler for $63 million in cash plus millions more in incentive payments based on future sales.

California Coolers contained 6 percent alcohol and came in a variety of flavors including tropical, Orange, and the original citrus flavor. Crucial to California Cooler's initial success was that it was marketed more as a beer than as a wine. From the beginning, Crete and Bewley wanted a quality package, and from their beer-drinking days, they felt nothing beat a Heineken bottle. So they packaged California Cooler in a green-tinged, twist-top, short-neck bottle, added a gold foil top, and sold it in four-packs for under $4. This, they figured, might draw some beer drinkers. Subsequently, to counter competition, California Cooler introduced several new packages, including 2-liter bottles, 198-milliliter bottles, and, in some areas, quarter and half barrels.

In another important step, they left the natural fruit pulp in the bottle and stressed it on the label. California Cooler was thus further removed from the clear, sipping wine category. California Cooler hoped to get the younger, natural-thinking consumers. The product was positioned as an informal, mainstream American drink, targeted toward males and females from 18 to 35 years of age.

Once the company broke even in early 1983, the co-founders began looking for an advertising agency to help broaden sales from its northern California base. Its only advertising up until that point was a spot radio jingle sung to the tune of the Beach Boys' hit "California Girls." The new advertising campaign positioned California Cooler not as a beer, not as a wine, but "beyond ordinary refreshment." These ads were funny put-downs by outsiders who were slightly envious of the hot tubs, health food fetishes, and all-around casual lifestyles of Californians—including their namesake drink, California Cooler. Other ads featured young people and 1960s rock 'n roll. Brown-Forman Corporation spent over $20 million on this ad campaign in 1986, yet still lost its top standing to Bartles & Jaymes. In 1986, California Cooler had an 18.0 percent market share, down from 26.8 percent in 1985 (see Exhibit 2).

Unlike Bartles & Jaymes, California Coolers were distributed by beer distributors, not wine wholesalers. The founders of California Cooler wanted their cooler to be in the "cold box" or refrigerator of a sales account. They felt the movement in beverages was out of the cold box, not the racks. Beer distributors were chosen because they typically had more accounts than their wine counterparts; beer distributors carried fewer products compared to the huge portfolios of wine wholesalers; and as "good ole boys," beer distributors represented their informal product better. More recently, though, to counter Gallo's tremendous distribution strength, California Cooler tried to take advantage of Brown-Forman's distribution muscle—it handled the popular Jack Daniels whiskey—and worked at broadening the overall market for coolers.

Sun Country

Sun Country coolers, produced by Canandaigua Wine, were the third-largest-selling wine coolers, with a 13.1 percent market share. Sun Country coolers were very similar to California Coolers: Both contained 6 percent alcohol; both retained the fruit pulp, which gave them a cloudy appearance; both were available in citrus, tropical, and orange flavors; and both were packaged in green bottles and sold in convenient four-packs or 2-liter bottles.

To help differentiate their product, Canandaigua expanded Sun Country's product line to include two new flavors, cherry and peach. They also pumped up advertising with a $25 million budget and celebrity spokespeople, including Charo, Cathy Lee Crosby, and The Four Tops. The ads targeted both men and women between the ages of 21 and 34.

Canandaigua also hoped to capitalize on exports of Sun Country, already available in Canada, Japan, South Africa, and the United Kingdom. As of 1986, about 600,000 of ten million cases were exported.

White Mountain

Recognizing the appeal of wine coolers, several brewers entered the market with malt-based products. As of 1986, only Stroh's White Mountain cooler showed any real success and significant sales. White Mountain cooler had a market share of 12.4 percent, up from 7.5 percent in 1985. The majority of its sales came from states where it had a tax and distribution advantage over wine coolers. Several states like Pennsylvania, White Mountain's leading market, barred the sale of wine-based products in supermarkets and other food stores.

White Mountain cooler bore a closer resemblance to beer than to wine. It was derived from malt, but unless the consumers looked closely at the label or the advertising they wouldn't know it, and that was how the brewer wanted it. Rather than attempt to create a market for a subcategory of malt-based coolers, which could be misconstrued as a flavored beer, the brewers simply sold their products as "coolers," taking advantage of the imagery of the winebased products. White Mountain's label said it was an "alcohol beverage with natural fruit juices" and 5 percent alcohol content by weight.

White Mountain cooler was packaged in 12-ounce bottles and sold in six-packs like beer. Stroh's had over a $12 million ad budget behind White Mountain, targeting mainly 21- to 40-year-olds. Stroh's also distributed its cooler through its existing beer distributors.

Seagram

Joe E. Seagram & Sons produced both Seagram's Premium and Seagram's Golden wine coolers. Combined, these two coolers made up 12.4 percent of the market. Seagram's coolers were a clear liquid, not cloudy like those of Sun Country and California Cooler. They came in 12-ounce glass bottles and were available in four-packs. Unlike the industry leaders, Bartles & Jaymes and California Cooler, which contained 6 percent alcohol, Seagram's coolers had just 4 percent alcohol. The Premium cooler came in a variety of flavors, including citrus, peach, wild berry, and apple cranberry.

Seagram's original ads for the Premium cooler were fast-paced scenes of young people playing outdoor sports, with energetic background music. The cooler ad was intentionally like a beer commercial because Seagram's was aiming its product at beer drinkers and encouraging them to switch. Though men consumed 80 percent of the beer sold, they tended to be skeptical of coolers. But since women consumed almost four times as much beer as wine, Seagram's hoped that women who switched would encourage men to join them.

The citrus-based Premium wine cooler did not receive the market leverage observers had expected. As a result, the company then backed Golden wine coolers, a new line, with a $25 million ad campaign. The campaign starred "Moonlighting" star Bruce Willis, who played the same roguish character he portrayed on the hit ABC-TV series. These ads were once again targeted toward women between the ages of 21 and 35.

Seagram's also introduced a new product into the market—Seagram's Golden Spirits. It was the first line of spirit-based drinks modeled after the wine cooler. It was sold in four-packs of 375-milliliter bottles that closely resembled the Golden wine cooler. The line's four flavors—Mandarin Vodka, Peach Melba Rum, Spiced Canadian (whiskey) and Sunfruit Gin—each contained 5.1 percent alcohol. These flavors were proprietary; consumers could not replicate them in their homes.

The spirit coolers were expected to appeal more to men and to an older audience than wine coolers did. "They're positioned somewhat more serious," said Thomas McInerney, executive VP-marketing, Seagram Distillers. "They are not being given the beach-party image of wine coolers."

Calvin

Calvin Cooler, produced by New York based Joseph Victori Wines, was the fifth-largest-selling cooler. The company broke into early dominance in New York City, thanks to a state law that allowed only New York state liquor products to be sold in grocery stores, when its cooler hit the market in 1984. As of 1986, Calvin Cooler had an 8.3 percent market share and distributed nearly six 6 million cases to every state but South Dakota.

However, the cooler still sat behind competitors with stronger distribution channels and two or three times Calvin's $10 million ad budget.

Calvin coolers came in a full line of flavors, including raspberry, one of its most popular flavors. The product was available in both four-packs and 2-liter bottles.

Dewey Stevens

Dewey Stevens Premium Light, produced by Anheuser-Busch, was the first product of its kind. The wine cooler was sold in four-packs of 12-ounce bottles, each containing 4 percent alcohol and only 135 calories. Most wine coolers contained 5 percent to 6 percent alcohol and more than 200 calories. Dewey Stevens contained no artificial sweeteners; Anheuser-Busch cut the calories by cutting its wine content and adding water.

The ad campaign for the cooler made an appeal to active, young women and placed emphasis on the product's lower calorie content.

SELECTED REFERENCES

William Dunn, "Coolers Add Fizz to Flat Wine Market," *American Demographics* (March 1986), pp. 19–20.

Scott Hume, "Drop in Consumption a Sour Note for Industries," *Advertising Age*, April 7, 1986, p. 23.

J. D. Stacy, "The Wine Cooler Phenomenon," *Beverage World* (December 1984), pp. 49–50.

Patricia Winters, "Predict Big Chill for Wine Coolers," *Advertising Age*, August 11, 1986, p. 23.

CASE 12

Bennett's Machine Shop, Inc. ——— ARTHUR SHARPLIN

"This won't even be a one-page month," said Pat Bennett. "Worst month we've ever had." Pat was the owner of Bennett's Machine Shop, an automotive engine rebuilder in Lake Charles, Louisiana. He went on to explain what he meant by a "one-page month": "We write each engine job order on one line of a 32-line yellow legal pad. Last year, we figured out that a breakeven point was about sixty engines a month. If we have three pages in a month, we have really made some money. A single page? We should have gone fishing."

Bennett's engine sales for July 1987 were $57,000, down from $80,000 to $90,000 a year earlier. Pat said, "We install about 40 percent of the engines we rebuild, at about $1250 a shot. The carryouts average about $750. So I don't expect sales in August to even reach $30,000."

Pat saw his problem as "too little sales to support the overhead cost." He said, "Because of this, we have a day-to-day cash flow problem." After receiving his July financial statement from the accountant, Pat had laid off all the office help (a secretary/bookkeeper and a clerk/parts runner). Pat had released four mechanics and a helper earlier in the year.

Pat himself had been spending most of his time on a tool modification and sharpening contract with Boeing of Louisiana, Inc. (BLI). Bennett's had begun doing this work in February 1987, shortly after Boeing opened its new Louisiana facility, where Air Force KC-135 tankers (a variation of the Boeing 707) were reworked. In July, Boeing had begun returning Bennett's invoices, with a rubber-stamped note that they exceeded the $75,000 contract amount. By mid-August, unpaid billings to Boeing totaled over $60,000. Pat said, "I've cut about everything I can cut and sold about as much as I can sell. I even took out a second mortgage on my condo. If Boeing doesn't pay pretty soon, or a miracle doesn't happen in the machine shop, we're going to be history." The appendix contains excerpts from an interview with Pat Bennett conducted in mid-September 1987.

COMPANY BACKGROUND

In 1972, Pat Bennett earned a bachelor of science degree in mechanical engineering at McNeese University in Lake Charles. Recalling his senior year, Pat said, "I knew then I would not stick with my engineering career. Besides going through just a real burnout, I already had this machine shop idea. There were just three automotive machine shops in Lake Charles. And all the operators were in their late fifties. I knew there would be an excellent opportunity for a new shop in just a few years."

After graduation, Pat took a job with a chemical plant contractor as a designer/draftsman. The contract was completed in six months and Pat's employer offered him a chance to move to St. Louis. Instead, he quit and hired on at a local Cities Service plant as a "field engineer." Since all he actually did at the plant was drafting, Pat felt he had been misled. He stuck out his one-year contract—all except the last four hours. Pat said, "On the 365th day when the boss went to lunch, I said 'goodbye' to the man sitting beside me, took just the drafting equipment I could hold in my hand, and walked out the back door." Pat's impetuosity cost him the one week of vacation pay he had accumulated.

For the next year (1974–75), Pat commuted sixty miles to Beaumont, Texas, where he worked for Stubbs-Overbeck, Inc., a petroleum refinery engineering firm. According to Pat, this was "my first real engineering job." He explained:

> My first day on the job, they fired the civil engineer. I was sitting there feeling inadequate, worrying what my assignment would be and if I would remember how to do it. I heard the office manager ask two other guys, "Who are we going to get to run the theodolite (a sophisticated surveying instrument) so the design crew can get going?" I got their attention and timidly said, "I know how to run a theodolite." They questioned why a mechanical engineer would know how to do that. I told them I had worked for a civil engineer while in college.

At about the same time, Pat bought a boring bar (a tool used to recondition cylinders in engine blocks) from a farmer for $50. He also sold his wife's washer and dryer for $100 to get the down payment on a valve grinding machine, the other piece of equipment required for the most rudimentary engine rebuilder. At night and on weekends, Pat rebuilt engines in a six-by-eight-foot shack next to the trailer house where he lived with his wife, Cheryl. Customers gave Pat money to buy parts, and he charged them only for his labor.

Pat told of his big entrepreneurial decision:

> I worked ten hours in Beaumont and drove an hour each way in addition to the time I spent doing engines. The drive just got too dangerous. I was sleepy most of the time and kept dozing at the wheel. Finally, one morning on the way to work I almost ran off the road. I had to pull over and sleep and didn't get to work until 9:30. When I got home that evening, Cheryl and I talked it over and decided I should quit my job and try the machine shop business full-time.

Pat rented a small Quonset hut as his first shop, paying the owner $75 for the month he used it. Then he moved to a stall in a service station about a block from the trailer park. There, his rent was one-third of all labor charges. The service station owner made additional profit on engine parts. Pat said, "I could not get any discount on parts. I had no business license. We did not even have a name. But the fellow who ran the service station bought parts at jobber prices."

Near the end of 1975, a local garage owner asked Pat if he would split the rent on a larger building the garage owner was considering. Pat would pay $150 of the $400 monthly rent. Pat agreed, and the arrangement lasted about two years. During that time Pat hired a helper (a pre-med student) and bought a cylinder head grinder and two other specialized machines (all on credit).

In 1977, Pat incorporated his business as Bennett's Machine Shop, Inc. and moved it to a rented building on Prien Lake Road, a busy commercial street. Sales and profits continued to expand through 1979, when his landlady, whom Pat had nicknamed "The Iron Maiden," ordered him to move because of the growing pile of used engines and parts next to the shop building. The shop flooded frequently anyway, and the fire department had complained about the oily rinse water Bennett's discharged into the city storm drains. Pat said, "I told the Iron Maiden that this was about as clean as it was going to get and made plans to move."

"I arranged to borrow $80,000 from Gulf National Bank," said Pat, adding, "I found a two-acre lot on the old Chennault air base for $57,000. I built a 4000-square-foot building with the other $23,000 plus $3000 I had saved." Bennett's Machine Shop moved to the new location in December 1979.

Pat said, "The first year we really had any extra money was 1981. We bought eleven pieces of property. We put 20 percent down on all of it and borrowed the rest, about $80,000." That year and the next, Pat added 6000 square feet to the machine shop and built another shop building, all without borrowing. In 1981, Bennett's began to do "over-the-fender" work for the first time, installing engines and some minor general repair work. At about this time, Pat and Cheryl bought a "real house" in nearby Westlake and moved from their mobile home. By 1985, Pat had bought a new condominium in Lake Charles and a 38-foot cabin cruiser. Cheryl was using the Westlake home as a cat sanctuary, and the sixty cats she had taken in required much of her time. Pat had collected twenty-two "muscle cars" and his personal car was a 1984 Jaguar XJS coupe.

"Then we made our big blunder," said Pat. "I thought it was time to open a new location, not to rebuild engines, but to install them. We bought the back half of an old Dodge dealership on Ryan Street [about three miles from Bennett's Machine Shop]. A Firestone tire store was in the front. Cheryl often reminds me how stupid it was to think I could run the business long-distance."

Pat opened the new shop as Lake Charles Motor Exchange, Inc. He assigned four of his people there. He said, "For fourteen months, I pumped money into the new operation." Pat closed the Ryan Street location and sold the facility—he said at a $25,000 profit—in March 1986. "I never realized how personalized the business was," said Pat. He added, "By the way, we proved it again this summer, while I was fooling with Boeing. Things really got out of hand."

OPERATIONS

In late 1987, Bennett's Machine Shop was involved in three types of work: engine rebuilding, "over-the-fender" work, and tool sharpening and modification (the Boeing contract). Exhibit 1 shows the layout of Bennett's facilities.

Engine Rebuilding

Rebuilding engines is highly technical work. "The heart of it," said Pat, "is don't let the customer talk you into skipping the machine work. You've got to start with an empty, bare block." An actual case will illustrate the steps involved.

On August 9, 1987, Thomas Winkles, maintenance manager for a local dry cleaning firm and a personal friend of Pat's, ordered a "1974 250 Chevy short block." (A "short block" is a basic engine core, without the cylinder head, oil pan, oil pump, and several other parts that can be reused. These accounted for about 20 percent of the engines Bennett sold.) Pat felt Winkles was qualified to install the engine. "Otherwise," Pat said, "I would have questioned the customer to make sure the job could be done right. Replacing an engine is major surgery. It must not be done by amateurs."

Pat recorded the order on the yellow legal pad mentioned earlier and checked the Four-Star Engine Catalog (published by a national engine rebuilder) for casting numbers of 250-cubic-inch 1974 Chevrolet engines. He found there were two. Notes Pat had made in the catalog revealed that one used a straight and the other an offset starter motor. After having Winkles look to see which he had, Pat wrote the distinguishing feature, "straight starter," above the record on the legal pad.

Pat told the "teardown man," Lac Xuan Huyn, that he had added an order to the list. That day, Lac checked the order record and located the appropriate used engine among the several thousand piled here and there around the shop. (To augment the supply of exchange engines from previous jobs, Bennett bought some from a traveling used-engine dealer and from individuals who called or came by from time to time.) Lac disassembled the engine, distributing parts to the crankshaft grinding area (crankshaft, pistons, and connecting rods) and the headwork area (cylinder heads). Lac placed the block near the two cleaning machines—which work like large dishwashers but use caustic soda (lye) instead of regular detergent. He put the camshaft in a wood box. The contents of the box were shipped periodically to Cam-Recon, a shop in Houston, Texas, for regrinding. Bolts and valve pushrods were placed in appropriate bins. The oil pan and timing cover were set aside for reuse on this or another engine. And certain parts, mostly sheet metal items such as rocker-arm covers, were discarded.

Bennett's machinists were responsible for checking the legal pad record of orders and making sure parts were available for jobs listed there. There were no written procedures, about this or anything else, and the machinists often failed to verify parts availability. Still, the system worked about as intended for the Winkles engine. Dale LeBlanc, who operated the cylinder boring machines, checked to see that the correct pistons and rings were on hand. He found that the ring set was not in stock. Curtis Manuel, who ground crankshafts and sized connecting rods, located a crankshaft for the engine—as usual, not the one Lac had just delivered. Curtis checked the crankshaft with a micrometer to see how far he would have to grind it and then confirmed that he had all main and connecting rod bearings, in the correct undersizes. Byron Woods, the assembler, checked the parts bins for the following items: gasket set, oil pump, matched camshaft and crankshaft gears, camshaft, camshaft bearings, and valve lifters. No gasket set was in stock. Dale and Byron, separately, called a Bennett's supplier in Houston and ordered needed parts, confirming that parts would arrive by bus or UPS the next day.

Dale washed the engine block in one of the cleaning machines. He then took the block to the cylinder boring area and "magnafluxed" it. This involves sprinkling iron filings over unmachined surfaces and placing a large electromagnet at strategic points. Any crack

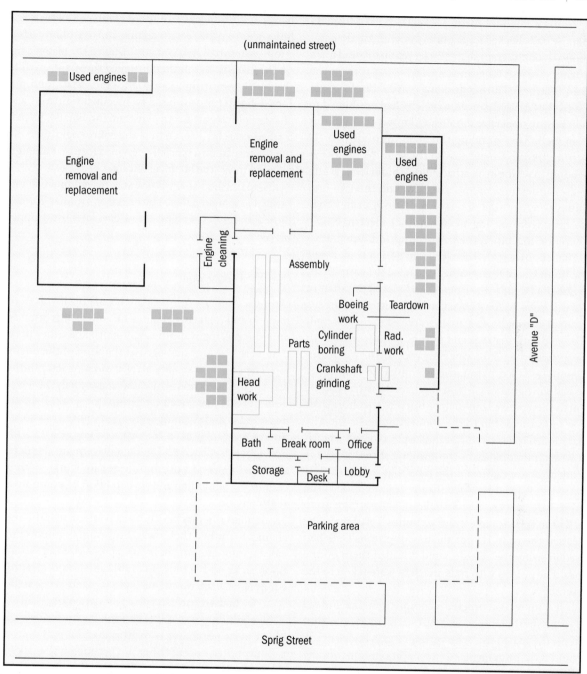

EXHIBIT 1   Layout of Bennett's Facilities

would have been indicated by a string of concentrated iron filings. None existed. Dale selected a box of six 0.030-inch oversize 250 Chevrolet pistons. After measuring one of the pistons with a micrometer, he proceeded to bore the cylinders, to 0.001 inch larger than the piston size, manually checking cylinder diameters with a hand-held "bore gauge" after each cut. He visu-

ally inspected each cylinder for cracks. Then the block was placed in a "honing tank," where, in a bath of number 2 jet fuel, the cylinders were honed to 0.002–0.003 inch beyond the piston size. Dale cleaned the engine again, this time finishing with a steam cleaner. Finally, he sprayed the cylinder walls with light oil and delivered the block to the assembly area.

Still on August 9, Curtis Manuel cleaned the crankshaft he had checked for Winkles's engine. He then positioned it on the crankshaft grinder set up to grind main bearing journals (the shiny surfaces that turn in the main bearings). During grinding, Curtis carefully observed the "Arnold gauge," which he had positioned to indicate the undersize dimension, in ten-thousandths of an inch. After grinding the main journals to 0.010 inch undersize, Curtis moved the shaft to the other grinding machine in an adjacent room and left it set up to do connecting rod journals (Pat said the two machines were located across a wall from each other "to keep from having to rig another electric box"). There, he machined the connecting rod journals to 0.020 inch undersize. The whole operation took about one hour. Curtis then cleaned and oiled the crankshaft, as Dale had done for the block, and placed the shaft in a plastic tube. It, too, was taken to the assembly area.

Not through yet, Curtis searched the waist-high pile of connecting rods and pistons at his work station for six Chevrolet 250 connecting rods. Unsure of his selection, he called Byron, the assembler, to help verify he had the right ones. Byron confirmed Curtis's choice. Curtis then pressed out each piston pin (the short shaft that joins the piston to the connecting rod). Then he placed each rod in a rod vise and, using a torque wrench (a wrench that indicates the amount of twisting force being applied), tightened the nuts that secure the rod cap. Next, Curtis measured the inside dimension at the crankshaft end of each rod. Finding all measurements to be within specifications (plus or minus 0.0005 inch), he cleaned the rods. He got the box of pistons Dale had used in sizing the cylinders and installed them on the rods. The pistons with rods attached were taken to the assembly area.

If Winkles had ordered a complete engine, instead of just a short block, Scott McConathy or Martin Simmons, the machinists who recondition cylinder heads, would have been involved. Reconditioning a cylinder head mainly consists of resizing the valve guides, grinding valves and valve seats, and regrinding the cylinder head surface. After these operations, the cylinder head is cleaned, reassembled, and painted.

At about 3:00 P.M., Byron finished his previous job and began assembling the Winkles engine. He visually checked each cylinder for cracks. Then he painted the surfaces of the block that would be exposed to oil with "Cast Blast," a grey paint that seals cast iron surfaces and minimizes sludge buildup. Byron also painted the exterior surfaces of the block the appropriate original color.

Next, he installed the plugs in the block, which seal holes required for certain casting and machining operations. After that, he manually installed the piston rings on the pistons. Byron then installed the major parts in the block—bearings, camshaft, crankshaft, and pistons—tightening all bolts to specified tightness and checking each part for free movement. Finally, he performed a careful inspection of the entire engine, recording the results on a specially designed form—kiddingly referred to as "the birth certificate."

The finished short block was placed in a bag and banded to a small pallet. The next day, Thomas Winkles picked up his new engine. A few days later, he dropped his old one by Bennett's.

Over-the-Fender Work

Over-the-fender work at Bennett's mainly involved removing and replacing engines. Of course, this often required replacing water hoses, V-belts, and other items that were worn or damaged at the time of the engine job. The engine warranty (12,000 miles or six months) was conditioned upon an exhaust gas analysis, which often revealed the need for carburetor work. Radiator disassembly and cleaning were also required as a condition of warranty, even for carryout engines. In addition to work related to engine replacement, Bennett's accepted general automobile repair work, such as carburetor rebuilding and air-conditioning component replacement.

Unlike the machinists already discussed, the mechanics furnished their own hand tools. Bennett's provided testing equipment, hoists, a pressurized air system, floor jacks and stands, hydraulic lifts, and cleaning equipment. Each mechanic had a separate work stall.

"We had a terrible, terrible parts situation," said Pat. "The situation was so out of control, I was actually looking at parts purchases as overhead and not as a profit producer. Items were either not getting on the tickets, or not getting on the cars." To solve this, Pat assigned one mechanic, his best, as checker, to make sure every part put on each car was on the respective invoice. He also closed all charge accounts with parts suppliers, requiring mechanics to come to Pat or his shop coordinator, Jack Beard, to get a check for any parts purchase. "Now we've got some control over it," said Pat.

Bennett's kept an inventory of common engine filters, ignition components, vacuum hoses and fittings, and nuts and bolts. Mechanics were required to order and pick up other required parts. Pat said, "We don't stock any radiator hoses, belts, or water pumps because there are just too many different ones."

Richard Hardesty, one of the mechanics Pat had laid off in July, leased one of the company's three buildings and the equipment in it to do general automotive repair, engine installations, and exhaust system repairs. Pat explained, "Our whole objective was to get the payroll down. Payroll taxes are a burden. And the $675 lease payment will come in handy. I was able to rent the building to Richard so cheaply because we don't owe anything on it."

Tool Sharpening and Modification

Boeing's operations in Lake Charles involved a great deal of drilling and reaming, especially of rivet holes in the skins of the KC-135s. Many screwed fasteners required countersunk holes to preserve a flush exterior surface. The thousands of drill bits, reamers, and countersinks used by Boeing required frequent modifications and/or sharpening. There were also numerous occasions when specialized tools such as reamer extensions had to be made, modified, or repaired. When Boeing had trouble locating a local supplier for these services, Pat Bennett volunteered to do the work and negotiated a single-source supply contract with Boeing procurement.

Gearing up to do this highly technical work consumed most of Pat's energy and time from February to August 1987. A 1000-square-foot area of the machine shop building was enclosed and modified to house the tool work. A large horizontal lathe, a cylindrical grinder, two form-relief grinders, two tool and cutter grinders, and a drill bit sharpening machine were purchased and installed in the temperature-controlled enclosure. To find these machines, Pat traveled to Wichita, Cincinnati, Dallas, and Houston.

Boeing was on an extremely tight schedule on its own contract with the air force and there were frequent emergencies, often involving innovative solutions to unique problems. For example, Pat stayed up all one night sharpening and resharpening a special cobalt drill bit then being used to drill through a titanium alloy engine mount. Much experimentation was required on this and other jobs, and Pat worked many nights and weekends to solve problems.

Generally, Pat Bennett picked up the tools to be modified at the Boeing plant, a few hundred yards from the machine shop, and returned them there. Because of a Boeing procedure, the tools only needing sharpen-

ing were picked up at a Boeing warehouse at the Lake Charles Port, four miles away. Each batch of tools to be serviced was accompanied by a work order providing instructions for the work to be done. For nonstandard modifications, Pat frequently had to call or visit the supervisor who wrote the order and get clarification of the instructions.

Five machinists, three on days and two on evenings, were hired to do the Boeing work. Two only sharpened drill bits, while the others did the work on countersinks, reamers, and special tools. James Smith, the machinist Pat charged with quality control for the Boeing contract, did most of the particularly innovative operations. For example, James designed and made a number of torque wrench extensions that allowed tightening nuts that were not directly accessible.

Pat personally trained the machinists to do the repetitive operations. "The most difficult operation to perfect," said Pat, "was grinding the flutes of a piloted reamer so that they would cut. We were finally able to do it on a German form-relief grinder. Everything on it was written in German. We couldn't read any of the buttons except the one which said 'halt.'" The machine came to be used solely for grinding the cutting edges on piloted reamers. A large magnifying glass was installed so the machinist could see the tiny flutes. With his left hand, the machinist would orientate one of the six flutes on a reamer. Then, with his right hand, he would move the grinding head into the reamer flute and back, grinding the tiny cutting edge at precisely ten degrees. This was repeated on each of the six flutes. Because of the exactness required, the grinding wheel had to be reshaped daily with a diamond "dresser."

Drill bit sharpening is a fairly standard operation, although the Boeing specification added some complexity. Bennett's drill bit sharpening machine was hardly state-of-the-art, requiring several manual manipulations of each bit sharpened. Still, sharpening each bit took only about forty-five seconds.

The two-way form-relief grinder used to sharpen countersinks was almost completely automatic. Once the machinist orientated a countersink to be ground, the machine did the rest. This took about four minutes per countersink.

A great deal of skill was required to set up each of the operations described and especially to do the custom tool making. But, according to Pat, a person of average dexterity could learn any of the repetitive jobs in a day or two.

PERSONNEL

In late 1987, Bennett's employed sixteen people in addition to Pat and Jack Beard, the shop coordinator. There were five machinists and a radiator repairman in the automotive machine shop, five mechanics in the service department, and five machinists in the tool grinding shop.

Jack Beard had been with Bennett's four years. He was about 29 years old. A hard worker, Jack often spent ten hours a day at the shop, including every Saturday—except during hunting season, when Jack and Byron, an assembler, alternated Saturdays. On a weekend in August, Jack rebuilt the engine in a Chevrolet Citation he had just bought. The following Monday, he told Pat, "I can see how they have such a hard time getting any motors built. There is only one air hose, tools are scattered everywhere, and the place is filthy dirty."

Pat observed that Jack was right. He had tried several ways to get the workers to keep the shop clean, at one point assigning each person "just one little area" to clean. "Nothing worked," said Pat, "so that morning I just pulled the main breaker. When everything shut down and the men came to see why, I told them I would restore the power when the shop was clean." Pat said two of the "main culprits" came in to punch in on the time clock—they were on piece rates—so they would be paid for doing the cleaning. Pat objected to paying them "for cleaning up a mess they had a big part in creating," and they both quit. Asked how he replaced the men, Pat replied, "They weren't worth replacing."

The automotive machinists, Lac, Dale, Curtis, Scott, Martin, and Byron, were mentioned earlier. None had been automotive machinists when Bennett hired them, although Curtis had taken a regular machinist course at a local trade school. Lance Hammack, the radiator repairman, also learned his trade at Bennett's. He had been a welder. "It is much easier to teach a person a new trade than to get a person who already knows a trade to change bad work habits," said Pat.

Lac, a Vietnamese, was hired in 1985. Pat said, "He had to bring an interpreter to apply for the job, he could speak so little English. But his attitude—he just seemed so eager. He learned very rapidly. Meticulous. Pays attention to detail. Terribly dependable. I don't know that he ever missed a day—never even asks for time off."

Dale, Curtis, Martin, and Lance had all been with Bennett's less than six months. Dale had been a construction worker before Pat hired him. "Couldn't even read a micrometer," said Pat. "He had some kind of hangup about reading the dial. I got him a micrometer with a digital readout and three days later he was oper-ating the cylinder boring machine." Curtis knew how to run a lathe when he was hired. "So we put him on our crankshaft grinder," said Pat. (The two machines have similarities but are far from identical.) Martin had been a paint and body technician before Pat hired him. "He turns out the prettiest paint jobs on cylinder heads you ever saw," Pat kidded. Martin worked most Saturdays, in addition to full days during the week. Radiator work was not a full-time job at Bennett's, so Lance helped out in the office, drove the delivery truck, and did other tasks.

Scott and Byron had been hired about four years earlier, Scott right out of high school, Byron off the unemployment line. According to Pat, Scott had a strong interest in cars. "He was easy to train, always thinking," said Pat. "I could just give him a few pointers and he would go with it. He is very thorough. I don't have to check anything he tells me. He doesn't mind staying late during the week, but he likes his Saturdays off." Pat said that Scott did almost all the "really difficult head jobs—the overhead cams, heads that need new valve seats." Byron, young and unskilled, had started doing engine "teardowns." "Most machinists are too proud to do that," said Pat. "They think that is the low-class job in the shop. Byron was so easygoing. There was nothing he wouldn't try to learn if you needed him to do it."

Next Byron had mastered the cylinder-boring machine. Pat told how Byron got his next job: "I was grinding the crankshafts at that time. You should have seen me—an Extendaphone on my belt and a Sony Walkman under by shirt. People thought the Walkman was part of the machine. But I was grooving, listening to 'fifties' music while I watched the cranks go round and round." Pat's wife, Cheryl, was "acting secretary" (the regular secretary had left due to illness) at the time. She quit after Pat threw a can of blue engine paint at her, so he had to take over the office. Another man, later fired for suspected theft, took over the boring machine, and Byron moved to the crankshaft grinder, relieving Pat. "That was a major accomplishment for Byron," Pat said. "He had never even run a lathe." Byron stayed with that job until March 1987, when he started assembling engines.

The five mechanics were Ronnie Smith, Tim "Tamale" Authemont, Kenneth Thornton, Clyde Brown, and Kevin "Goat" Gauthreaux. Ronnie, in his fourth year at Bennett's, was responsible for inspecting and test driving every vehicle repaired, regardless of who did the work. He also did mechanic work himself—all the carburetor work, certain diesel-to-gasoline conversions, and most of the computer checks. But Ronnie refused to do engine replacements in front-wheel-drive cars. Tim was a helper, supervised and paid by Ronnie. Tim had been with Bennett's over two years, but had worked as Ronnie's helper only about six months.

Kenneth Thornton was the longest-tenured employee Pat had, having hired on eight years earlier, when the shop was on Prien Lake Road. He did most of the engine replacements on front-wheel-drive cars, certain diesel-to-gasoline conversions, and regular repair work.

Clyde and Kevin had worked at Bennett's only a couple of months. Both did all kinds of engine replacements as well as a wide range of other mechanic work. Both were in their early thirties, married, with children. Pat said, "I am really impressed with their attitudes. Unlike many mechanics, they are not afraid of this new generation of cars—mostly transverse-engined, fuel-injected, and computer-controlled."

The machinists who did the tool work were James Smith (Ronnie's brother), James McManus, Craig McMichael, John Shearer, and Billy Lambert. James Smith had worked on and off for Bennett's for about five years, doing various construction jobs. He had hired on full-time in March 1987. Pat said, "In the early weeks of the Boeing job, I was running that German form-relief grinder while James was building the room around me." As the Boeing work had begun to increase, Pat taught James to run the grinder. Pat said, "I would run it on the weekends, he'd do it during the week." James had paid his own way to go with Pat and locate other machines to buy.

James McManus and Billy worked evenings. Craig and John worked days. James and Craig did reamers and countersinks. Billy and John sharpened drill bits. All four were in their early twenties. Pat recruited James and Craig through Sowela Tech, a local vo-tech school, and James continued as a co-op student there. John's father, who worked at the Boeing port warehouse, had recommended his unemployed son to Pat one day as Pat picked up an order. John had later recommended Billy.

The automotive machinists, except for Curtis (who operated the crankshaft grinder), were paid on a piece-rate basis, so much for each type of operation and each model of engine. Each had an established hourly rate as well, which was applied to other than normally assigned work. Curtis was paid on an hourly basis.

The mechanics were paid a combination of piece rates, commissions, and hourly rates. Piece rates applied to engine replacements. Most other automotive work was done on a commission basis—each mechanic got one-half of all labor charges that mechanic generated. Hourly rates were paid for warranty work that was not the mechanic's fault. Pat said, "We don't do like the dealerships and guarantee the mechanics a weekly minimum."

The machinists who did the tool grinding were all paid by the hour. At first, Pat set the machinists' wages according to the Boeing pay scale. But when Boeing tried to hire some of his people, he hiked the rate by about 40 percent. "I pay James Smith more than the rest," said Pat, "but he and I have an agreement that he doesn't get any overtime pay when he works over forty hours."

Jack Beard, the shop coordinator, and Lance Hammack, the radiator repairman, were also paid by the hour.

Bennett's provided limited fringe benefits. There was a group health plan, paid entirely by the employees. Several chose not to participate. Each employee received six paid holidays each year (after a ninety-day waiting period) and a one-week paid vacation each year after the first. Bennett's paid all uniform costs per employee over one dollar a day, although workers were not required to wear them. "I also let the men work on their personal and family cars in the shop after hours and on weekends," said Pat.

MARKETING

Exhibit 2 provides demographic and economic data for Bennett's market area.

Sprig Street, where Bennett's was located, was "off the beaten path and far from the business district," according to Pat. He said, "The best thing about the location is it's one block outside the city limits. No one bothers us out here, no matter how messy it gets." It was messy. Except for concrete areas, grass and weeds were everywhere. Piles of greasy used engines were here and there—even next to the street behind the facility. Inside the machine shop building, half the space was occupied by stacks—no, piles—of engines and useless remnants of others long deceased. Individual blocks, heads, and other parts, as well as several derelict cars, littered the property, especially around the edges of driveways and other concrete areas. Everywhere there was grease and oil. Two large pitch-coated septic tanks and a stack of rusting metal shelves added confusion. A dingy, although lighted, 3-by-4-foot sign near the lobby and office area announced "Bennett's Machine Shop—Engine Rebuilding."

	Lake Charles	Calcasieu Parish (County)	Southwest Louisiana*	State of Louisiana	United States
Population, 7/80	77,400	167,223	259,809	4,206,000	226,546,000
Per capita income, 1985	$10,183	$10,224	$8,806	$10,741	$12,772
Change in *real* per capita income, 1980–85 (percent change for period)	1.2	1.3	1.6	2.3	2.8
Work force employed in manufacturing, 3/87 (percent)	7.4	17.3	16.2	11.2	18.8
Work force employed in construction, 3/87 (percent)	8.7	9.4	9.0	6.2	3.0
Land area (square miles)	27	1,082	5,083	44,521	3,539,289

*Southwest Louisiana Parishes—Allen, Beauregard, Calcasieu, Cameron, and Jefferson Davis.

EXHIBIT 2 **Geographic and Demographic Data**

Thirty-second television spots featuring Pat Bennett ran throughout the year at a cost of about $350 per month. A feature article written by Pat appeared in the American Press, the local paper, once a month, at a cost of $114 per month. Once a year, when business was slow, a Bennett's supplement would be distributed with the 48,000-circulation newspaper. The cost was $1600 for each distribution. The supplement offered discounts, good for two months with presentation of the flyer, on reconditioned engines—$50 on carryouts, $100 on installations. "The first time we did this, two years ago," said Pat, "we had to shut down and just answer the phones and take orders for two days. We sold twenty-eight engines, almost a whole page, that time."

A form letter was sent to engine customers, thanking them for the business and asking for referrals to other prospective customers. Once a year, during the local festival called "Contraband Days," Bennett's subscribed to a radio advertising special. A thirty-second spot was run sixty times during a ten-day period at a cost of $450. Pat said, "I've never seen a sale directly related to radio advertising. We did it one time, and they hounded us the next year till I agreed to do it."

Bennett's major competitors for engine sales were Dimick Supply Company, 100,000 Auto Parts, and Hi-Lo Auto Parts. None of these did installations and all bought their engines from large remanufacturers. No local automobile service shop other than Bennett's specialized

in rebuilt engines, although most bought and installed them from time to time. Periodically, Pat Bennett checked the prices competitors charged for engines, often by simply calling and asking. He also kept current catalogs and price sheets for the engine remanufacturers who supplied Bennett's competitors. "We get their catalogs because we're a jobber," Pat said, "and sometimes we sell truck engines we buy from others—because the risk is so high if a truck engine fails."

Asked where he set his prices relative to the competition, Pat replied, "We make sure we're a little under everybody except Hi-Lo. They sell almost nothing but short blocks remanufactured in Texas. They are ridiculously low."

Pat said the quality of all the engines was about the same. "But if you have a problem with a Four-Star or a Roadrunner (the brands sold by Bennett's competitors) you bought from, say, Dimick," Pat said, "you have to take it out and wait for them to send it back to Texas. And they normally don't help you with labor." In contrast, he said, a Bennett's customer who has problems "can just bring the car to my front gate, and it's taken care of—if it's within warranty and hasn't been overheated or run out of oil." Pat complained, "Carryout customers will go to somebody else if there is just a $20 difference. It bothers me that customers will bring us their car if anything goes wrong, expecting us to fix it free. They wouldn't think of doing this at Hi-Lo or Dimick." He explained that parts-and-labor warranties, in general, only apply to situations where the labor is supplied by the vendor. "Sometimes," said Pat, "a customer will even call me for advice about some trouble with an engine he bought from a parts house. I tell him to call the parts house."

Mechanic labor at Bennett's was based on the time estimates in the Chilton Flat-Rate Manual (a book that gives estimated times to do all kinds of repair operations for most automobiles and light trucks), priced at $30 per hour. Most good mechanics can beat the flat-rate times significantly, more so on some types of work than on others. Bennett's priced most parts, other than engines, at locally competitive retail. The local parts houses gave Bennett's a 20 percent discount off retail. "List" prices, usually about 40 percent above retail, are shown on parts house invoices. Pat said, "If we think the list price is fair and the customer is unlikely to check with a parts house, we often use list instead of retail."

For the Boeing work, prices were set according to contract. Drill bit sharpening was at so much per item. The other operations were done by the hour. At first, Boeing allowed Bennett's to charge very profitable prices. After the work had totaled about $137,000, Boeing audited Bennett's costs and revised the prices downward, by more than 50 percent. The audit was conducted by Boeing's vendor cost analysis (VCA) group and involved many lengthy meetings with four different teams of auditors. In fact, Bennett's initial contract was apparently so remunerative that Boeing assigned a "security investigator" who asked many questions implying possible collusion between Pat and various Boeing officials.

Boeing held up payment on past invoices while pressure was exerted on Bennett's to reprice previously submitted invoices at the VCA-determined rates. Pat refused to do that and successfully insisted that the invoices be paid as submitted. Pat did decide to accept the VCA prices during month-to-month renewals of the contract, while Boeing made plans to let the work out for bids. Meanwhile, Pat was trying to decide how to bid the work. He was making money at the new rates. Profits on the earlier contract had more than paid for all his machines. So he was tempted to bid even a little below the VCA numbers. But he knew Boeing was having trouble finding other vendors with even minimal competence to do the work. And he had served Boeing faithfully, and at great cost to his other business, for several difficult months.

FINANCE

Exhibits 3 and 4 give financial summaries for Bennett's Machine Shop, Inc. For ten years, Pat Bennett had employed a local accounting firm, Management Ser-

vices, Inc., to keep financial records, prepare financial statements and sales and income tax returns, submit business license applications, and so forth. During the 1987 tax season, Bennett's was not able to get Management Services to prepare the usual monthly profit and loss statements. Pat explained, "They said they couldn't get to it. So I changed to a real CPA firm in the Lakeside Plaza Building—and that was worse. This guy had less time than Management Services did for us. When he finally, after sixty days, got the first month done, he asked me to come in at nine o'clock one day. I got there at 9:15, and nobody except the secretary was at work. I passed him on the sidewalk with his briefcase and his three-piece suit. That's the last time I saw him."

After firing his new accountant, Pat talked with Dorothy McConathy, who had been assigned his work at Management Services, and asked whom he could get to do his bookkeeping. Pat said, "Dorothy had already told her boss she was going to quit when she got one more account on the side. She already had two, so she agreed to keep my books and gave Management Services notice."

After buying the boring bar when he first started rebuilding engines in 1972, Pat never directly contributed any more equity funds to the business. Equipment vendors furnished financing for most of the machines Pat bought. When Pat started to buy a used crankshaft grinder, which he found at a shop in Plaquemines Parish, he approached the bank that handled his checking account. Pat had taken out a few small personal loans at the bank, but the loan officer who had approved them was gone at the time. The bank president refused to loan Pat the $6400 he needed to buy the machine.

"I got my little file from him and went over to the new American Bank of Commerce," said Pat. "There, I was a total stranger, but I got the loan." Three years later, Pat needed the $80,000 loan to buy the Chennault property. "American Bank of Commerce wouldn't make a decision," said Pat, "so I went back to Gulf National. My friend Lloyd Rion, the loan officer who was gone that day three years earlier, was there. He gave me the money, and I moved our checking account back." The loan was a ten-year, fixed-rate loan at 10 percent interest.

From 1980 to 1985, Pat took out several ninety-day loans to make additions to the shop facilities. The bank allowed him to roll the loans over once. "Those were super productive years. We never had any money problems," said Pat.

	Fiscal Year 1985*	Fiscal Year 1986*	Fiscal Year 1987*	4 Mos. 1988**
Revenue				
Automotive	926,243	1,091,890	971,950	140,131
Aircraft Tool	0	0	13,318	140,679
Total revenue	926,243	1,091,890	985,268	280,810
Expenses				
Direct costs				
Materials	456,828	570,372	504,811	64,939
Labor	248,833	316,164	271,858	53,693
Freight	0	0	0	1,031
Total direct costs	705,661	886,536	776,669	119,663
Gross profit	220,582	205,354	208,599	161,147
G & A expenses				
Advertising	10,697	15,831	17,828	1,193
Depreciation	33,550	42,240	29,220	7,359
Equipment leasing	5,680	950	1,657	0
Insurance	23,100	39,298	35,528	11,359
Interest	22,060	24,044	26,504	8,841
Miscellaneous	4,867	7,205	7,020	4,438
Office labor	6,815	11,420	13,300	3,961
Office supplies	5,883	7,015	6,458	2,129
Professional fees	3,696	8,373	6,622	1,175
Taxes	5,623	4,852	5,926	245
Utilities and telephone	15,871	30,767	27,933	8,830
Total G & A expenses	137,842	191,995	177,996	49,530
Net Income	82,740	13,359	30,603	111,617
Withdrawals***	(61,500)	(53,389)	(70,755)	(17,109)
Earnings reinvested	21,240	(40,030)	(40,152)	94,508

*Fiscal years end April 30 of years shown.

**May–August 1988.

***Includes funds to pay income taxes. The corporation is taxed as a partnership/proprietorship under Subchapter S of the Internal Revenue Code.

EXHIBIT 3 Bennett's Machine Shop, Inc., Income Statements

	1985	1986	1987	1988*
Assets				
Current assets				
Cash	11,698	1,206	3,475	5,385
A/R, trade	0	1,255	16,662	65,436
N/R, stkhdr.	0	22,568	22,568	22,569
Inventory	37,548	45,436	45,436	45,436
Total c/a	49,246	70,465	88,141	138,826
Fixed assets				
Furniture & equip.	205,292	165,886	193,432	212,209
Buildings	305,657	155,657	155,657	155,657
Total depr.	510,949	321,543	349,089	367,866
Less accu. depr.	(133,559)	(134,067)	(143,834)	(155,081)
Net depr. assets	377,390	187,476	205,255	212,785
Land	126,418	90,000	90,000	90,000
Total fixed assets	503,808	277,476	295,255	302,785
Other assets				
Deposits	492	342	342	342
Total assets	553,546	348,283	383,738	441,953
Liabilities and Capital				
Current liabilities				
A/P, trade & other	12,727	25,062	29,407	31,242
N/P, current	103,160	16,385	60,299	57,775
Accrued payroll, taxes, interest	0	0	3,223	1,571
Total c/1	115,887	41,447	92,929	90,588
Long-term liabilities				
Notes payable	266,720	175,897	200,052	166,099
Stockholders' equity				
Common stock	10,000	10,000	10,000	10,000
Retained earnings	160,939	120,909	80,757	175,265
Total capital	170,939	130,909	90,757	185,265
Total liabilities and capital	553,546	348,253	383,738	441,952

* August 31, 1988.

EXHIBIT 4   Bennett's Machine Shop, Inc., Balance Sheets, April 30

When Pat bought the Ryan Street shop in 1985, which he sold fourteen months later, the seller financed the whole $180,000, for ten years at 10–14 percent variable rate. "That's when our trouble started," said Pat. "We loaded up the company with operating loans— a $25,000 three-year loan, a $24,000 five-year loan, and another three-year loan for $12,000, all from Calcasieu Marine Bank. I also let the work force run up to twenty-two people. It was a real runaway situation."

Pat described 1986 as "one helluva bad year." "That's when we could have used some input from the bookkeeper," said Pat. "I didn't realize that payroll and the taxes related to it were having such a devastating effect. We had almost the same sales as in 1984. Just the increase in payroll-based taxes was $70,000. What really ticked me off was that I had to figure this out and show him (the bookkeeper)." Pat had to refinance the ten-year loan on the Chennault property. "I put off laying off the extra people from January to August," said Pat. "That cost me another $40,000 and made me have to redo the loan." Bennett's showed a $12,000 profit in November that year. Pat said, "It was our first three-page month in a long time. I was scared to death. If we had not made a profit with that kind of sales, I didn't know what else to do." On the way to a New Year's Eve party, Pat made himself a promise: "I will not go through another year like that." A friend asked, "What are you going to do to prevent that—as if you have some control over it?" "I'm going to work my tail off," Pat replied.

The machinery to do the Boeing work was all financed with $37,000 in ninety-day notes at Calcasieu Marine. There were no other financial crises until August, when Boeing was holding up payment and engine sales collapsed. Pat was able to sell enough assets to meet the payroll and pay operating expenses, but he was unable to pay maturing loans. So Pat mortgaged his condominium and consolidated the three term loans into one $45,000 five-year mortgage. Boeing paid its account up to date in early September, and Pat paid off the $37,000 in ninety-day notes.

Until 1987, all the loans mentioned above were in Pat's and Cheryl's personal names, although entered on the company books and sometimes secured by company assets. The $45,000 mortgage loan from Calcasieu Marine was put in the company name, "So we could deduct the interest under the new tax law," according to Pat. But Pat and Cheryl had to personally endorse the note and sign continuing guaranty agreements with the bank.

APPENDIX: EXCERPTS FROM INTERVIEW WITH PAT BENNETT

Q: *What is your main objective for this year?*

A: *I guess the goal we're all in business for is to make it profitable, and it hasn't been for the past two years. We've had a real bad downward trend. We might not make a real big profit this year, but I hope we can stop the downward trend and turn it around. That would be a major accomplishment.*

Q: *What about the longer term?*

A: *I would like the business to be successful to the point that I would have some freedom to do some of the things I want to do. Travel some, sports in the winter—before I get decrepit. Until recently, I dreamed of having a nicer shop near the downtown area, but that seems out the window now.*

Q: *Can you be a little more specific about what the business would have to do to satisfy you?*

A: *If we got back to where net profit, including my total compensation, was $70,000–$100,000 a year—and we've been there— I would think that was okay.*

Q: *Do you mean in ten years? Twenty years?*

A: *I'm not really that patient a person. I mean in the next two to three years. That is very obtainable.*

Q: *Do you think about twenty-five years from now, when you will be almost sixty-five?*

A: *No.*

Q: *Do you feel responsible to make the business support anyone else but you and Cheryl, in the long or short term?*

A: *Sure, I probably have more loyalty to some of those guys than I should.*

Q: *Which ones? Or do you mean all of the workers?*

A: *I mean as a whole. My dad was a union man his entire life. We grew up with the idea that the company had to provide benefits— medical care, retirement, vacations, days off. Retirement is a big thing Dad always talked about. He always talked about the days before Roosevelt, when there wasn't any Social Security, not much to look forward to.*

Q: *Do the workers look out for your interests?*

A: *Sometimes I think they do. But on days like today I wonder.*

Q: *What happened today?*

A: *Everybody screwed up. Jack has trouble ordering anybody to do anything. Someday he's got to learn he isn't "one of the gang" anymore. Dale loaded the wrong engine on a customer truck. Lance spent the whole day chasing his tail, pretending to go get parts. One of my good customers asked for his car at 1:00—and it wasn't out until 4:00. Know what I'm going to do? I'm moving my desk right out to the middle of the shop, right by the boring bars. They'll be nervous with me watching every move. But I'm going to get this mess under control. [Within three weeks, Pat had built a six-by-eight-foot office in the center of the shop near the assembly area. It had one-way windows so that Pat could observe the machinists but could not be seen by them.]*

Q: What major changes in the business do you foresee?

A: More diversity. Wait! I mean more diversification. We've had all the diversity we can stand.

Q: What do you mean by diversification?

A: There still are several areas of the engine business that are untouched in Lake Charles. I just did a catalog so we'll be ready to do the parts house business. The closest production shops are in Baton Rouge and Houston, both over two hours away. We've got the whole west side of the state. And the crack repair business, cylinder head cracks mainly, is just untapped. I visited a big diesel shop in Houston that does this. The

whole system, really nothing more than a big fire-bricked oven, would cost only a couple of thousand dollars. This is an especially good business with today's thin-wall castings on engines. There are tremendous numbers of heads thrown away. A plain old six-cylinder Chevrolet head is $400 new, bare. I also think we have a good opportunity in the aircraft industry—the tool work, a heat-treating facility. And Boeing is about to certify us for "level II" work, allowing us to make parts which stay on the plane. No more gravy train—we'll have to bid everything. Level II will also let us bid on the work for the big Strategic Petroleum Reserve. They have to send their work eighty miles to New Iberia.

C A S E   1 3

Southwest Airlines

For more than three years, seemingly endless rounds of litigation had thwarted the plan to launch a new Texas airline, to be known as Southwest Airlines. The Texas Aeronautics Commission approved the application in 1968, but legal challenges by incumbent airlines facing new competition for the first time in decades stretched the proceedings all the way to the Texas Supreme Court, which unanimously ruled in Southwest's favor on May 13, 1970.

When the U.S. Supreme Court upheld the Texas court ruling in December, Southwest's founders believed the courtroom battles lay behind them. However, the delays and litigation nearly wrecked Southwest's finances. The company had long since exhausted its original $543,000 in capital, but was able to continue the litigation only because its attorney, determined not to lose, agreed to absorb the legal costs himself.

The lawyer was Herb Kelleher, a transplanted New Jersey native who came to San Antonio to practice law. Kelleher had first been introduced to the idea of creating a new airline by his client, Rollin King, who had an idea that a commercial airline serving Texas's three largest markets might be able to make money. To illustrate his idea, King drew a triangle on a cocktail napkin, with the corners representing the Texas cities of Dallas, Houston, and San Antonio. Initially, Kelleher was skeptical, but as the discussion progressed, so did his interest.

Southwest Airlines, Spirit, *June, 1996. Reprinted courtesy of Southwest Airlines* Spirit.

By one account, Kelleher's ultimate resolve was cemented with the words, "Rollin, you're crazy. Let's do it." Kelleher agreed to do the initial legal work for a 25 percent discount, but he wound up doing much of the work for free.

In exploring the feasibility of the project, Kelleher's research turned up some intriguing aspects of King's seemingly outlandish idea. Kelleher knew that the Civil Aeronautics Board, the federal regulatory body that had jurisdiction over the airlines, had not authorized the creation of a new major airline since before World War II. Indeed, the major function of the CAB was to prevent competition. But the CAB's jurisdiction extended only to interstate airlines—those with routes extending across state lines. By flying only within the state of Texas, Southwest might be able to avoid CAB jurisdiction.

In fact, a precedent existed. In California, Pacific Southwest Airlines (PSA) had flown for years as an intrastate airline. By avoiding the suffocating regulation of the CAB, PSA was able to offer low fares and frequent flights and had achieved great popularity with its customers. With the stimulus of competition, the California airline market had become the most highly developed in the world. Why couldn't Texas support the same kind of service?

On the competitive front, King and Kelleher were familiar with the sorry state of air service in Texas. Fares were high, flights were often late, and schedules frequently were dictated by the availability of aircraft after flying more lucrative, longer-haul flights where the CAB-regulated airlines made their real money. Short-haul, intrastate service was merely an afterthought, existing primarily as a tail-end segment of a longer flight coming in from New York or Minneapolis, for example.

Kelleher concluded that Texas was ripe for an airline that would focus on the intrastate passenger, offering good, reliable service at a reduced fare and on a schedule designed to meet the needs of local travelers rather than passengers coming in from far-off points.

After three years of litigation, Southwest still had no airplanes, no management team, no employees, and no money. But when the U.S. Supreme Court ruled in its favor, the founders quickly went to work and hired M. Lamar Muse as Southwest's president in January 1971. Muse was a wily veteran of the airline business, trained as an accountant, but possessed the brash and daring temperament of an entrepreneur.

With the certificate from the Texas Aeronautics Commission as Southwest's only valuable asset and its bank account down to $142, Muse somehow managed to raise $1.25 million through the sale of promissory notes. For his management team, Muse put together a group of industry veterans, most of whom had either retired from or been cut loose by old-line airlines. Muse is reported to have claimed that all the top people he hired had been fired by other airlines. "I figured the other airlines were doing such a lousy job that anybody they fired had to be pretty good."

As luck would have it, a slow market caused Boeing to have three new 737-200 aircraft sitting on the tarmac. Southwest recognized the 737 as the perfect aircraft for the mission it had in mind. The 737's modern, fuel-efficient, twin engine configuration would allow highly reliable, efficient, and economical operation in Texas' short-haul intrastate markets. Boeing executives accommodated the cash-strapped Texans by agreeing to finance 90 percent of the cost of the new planes—unheard-of terms for such desirable aircraft.

With airplanes secured and crews hired, Southwest's long-awaited inaugural flight finally seemed at hand. But the entrenched airlines hadn't quit. First, they asked the CAB to exercise its jurisdiction to block the new competition in Texas. The CAB declined to interfere, throwing out the complaints by Braniff and Texas International on June 16, 1971—just two days before Southwest's first scheduled flight. Within hours, lawyers for Braniff and Texas International won a restraining order from a friendly district judge in Austin, banning Southwest from beginning service.

Southwest's leaders were simultaneously outraged and crestfallen. For more than three years, they had fought and won the legal battles. Now, on the eve of seeing their dream come to fruition, they faced the prospect of starting all over.

Kelleher, having left his San Antonio law office without a toothbrush or change of clothes, was in Dallas when he heard of the Austin judge's restraining order. An already rumpled-looking Kelleher headed to Austin, hitching a ride on a proving flight of one of Southwest's new and brightly painted red, orange, and desert-gold 737s. In Austin, Kelleher located Texas Supreme Court Justice Tom Reavely, the man who had written the court's unanimous 1970 opinion authorizing Southwest to fly. Kelleher persuaded Reavely to convene an extraordinary session of the Supreme Court the next day.

Kelleher worked through the night to prepare his papers and arguments for the court. The next day, June 17, 1971, sleepless and wearing the same well-worn suit, he appeared before the full Supreme Court, asking again that Southwest be allowed to take flight.

Finally, the phone in Muse's office rang. It was Kelleher. The Supreme Court not only had heard the arguments, it already had ruled. The district court's restraining order was thrown out. Southwest was free to start service the next day.

"What do I do if the sheriff shows up tomorrow with another restraining order?" Muse asked.

"Leave tire tracks on his back," Kelleher replied.

As 1973 began, Southwest had operated for a year and a half without approaching profitability. Start-up capital, including proceeds of a 1971 stock offering, was almost depleted. A fourth aircraft had been acquired, but it had to be sold to raise cash. Almost miraculously, the schedule had been maintained when Southwest employees, under the leadership of vice president Bill Franklin, invented the "ten-minute turnaround," enabling a plane to be fully unloaded and reloaded in ten minutes at the gate. With the increased productivity from the ten-minute turnaround, Southwest's management found that three planes could do the work of four. Thus was borne one of the precepts of Southwest's success—a plane doesn't make money sitting on the ground.

Still, cash was dwindling, and profitability remained a mere dream. The Dallas-Houston run was doing okay, but loads on the Dallas-San Antonio route were poor, draining the airline of its remaining cash. Muse decided to try a bold move. On January 22, 1973, he cut fares in half, to $13, on the Dallas-San Antonio route—every seat, every flight, no restrictions. What followed was one of the most widely reported and publicly watched conflicts in the history of the airline industry.

Braniff struck back, running full-page ads announcing a "Get Acquainted" fare of $13 between Dallas and Houston. Braniff's plan meant that Southwest would surely go broke if it matched the $13 fare between Dallas and Houston, Southwest's only profitable route.

Southwest's leaders frantically searched for a response. Even if they had known at the time that Braniff and Texas International ultimately would be convicted of federal criminal antitrust violations for their tactics, it would have provided little solace. The judicial system's ultimate judgment was years away. Insolvency was only days away.

The spark of inspiration that saved Southwest from certain liquidation finally came. The airline would give anybody who paid the full $26 fare a bottle of premium liquor—Chivas Regal, Crown Royal, or Smirnoff. But passengers could pay the $13 fare if they preferred.

Southwest vice president Franklin was dispatched to get a truckload of liquor delivered to the airport. To accommodate nondrinkers, Southwest vice president Jess Coker located a stash of leather ice buckets that hadn't sold well at Christmas and bought thousands of them. Somebody asked if it would be legal. Muse said to let Kelleher take care of that.

Muse then decided to write his company's reply to Braniff, which would be carried in Southwest's own full-page ads. After Kelleher removed the profanities and polished up Muse's initial draft, the ad ran under the headline "Nobody's going to shoot Southwest out of the sky for a lousy $13."

Suddenly, public attention was riveted on the air war over Texas. It became front-page news, the lead story on television and radio. For two months, Southwest was the largest liquor distributor in Texas. It was a defining moment, one in which people decided their allegiances for a lifetime.

The overwhelming response to Southwest's underdog crusade produced the first quarterly profit in the company's history and made 1973 Southwest's first profitable year.

"Tell the mayor that Southwest Airlines will be the best partner the city of Chicago ever had," Kelleher is saying into the telephone. It is November 1991, and Kelleher's face betrays a hint of tension and excitement as he makes his pitch to one of the mayor's closest advisers. For years, Southwest's efforts to expand in Chicago were stymied because of the unavailability of gate facilities at Midway Airport.

Southwest had grown beyond its Texas roots. With the passage of the federal Airline Deregulation Act of 1978, the end of the CAB's stranglehold on competition in interstate markets was assured. Southwest promptly became an interstate airline, flying first from Houston to New Orleans in January 1979. Although expansion out of Dallas's Love Field was limited by a 1979 congressional enactment known as the Wright Amendment, named for then-Congressman Jim Wright, who represented Fort Worth and sought to protect the growth of Dallas-Fort Worth International Airport, Southwest nonetheless found abundant opportunities for expansion outside Texas.

Kelleher had moved from the role of lawyer to executive, first becoming acting president in 1978 when Muse resigned after a disagreement with the board of directors, and then becoming full-time president and chief executive officer in September 1981 when Howard Putman resigned to become president of Braniff. Expansion in the West had proved highly successful, although not free of competitive challenges. Using Phoenix as the major base for its westward push, Southwest penetrated most of the major markets in California and the southwestern United States during the eighties and early nineties.

But Chicago had been a particularly frustrating situation. Although Southwest offered forty-three flights out of its four overcrowded gates, the demand existed for many more flights, to more destinations. Southwest could not expand to meet the demand because all remaining gates were leased—mostly to hometown favorite Midway Airlines. However, rumors now were swirling that Midway Airlines was about to shut down. Southwest had attempted to obtain leases on some of the gates in return for a cash payment and/or loan that might allow Midway

Airlines to remain open. But Midway had transferred leases on all the gates to Northwest Airlines, in anticipation of an acquisition of the entire airline by Northwest. When Northwest announced on November 13, 1991, that it was abandoning plans to acquire the airline, Midway barely had enough cash to finish out the day.

Kelleher desperately wanted access to the Midway gates, which would now sit empty if Midway Airlines shut down. Although the lease belonged to Northwest, Jim Parker, Southwest's creative General Counsel, knew of a loophole—the city retained the right to permit another airline to use the gates any time they were not being used by the primary tenant. If Midway shut down that night, as seemed likely, Parker reasoned there was no way Northwest could occupy all of Midway's gates by the next day. Kelleher arranged a 9 o'clock meeting the next morning in Chicago between Southwest's representatives and top advisers to Mayor Richard M. Daley.

When Southwest's delegation arrived at their Chicago hotel at 1:00 A.M., live TV reports from Midway Airport were confirming the shutdown of Midway Airlines. While Southwest's lawyers planned their strategy that night, the airline's Facilities and Technical Services departments swung into action, diverting deliveries and pulling computer equipment, back-wall signage, podium inserts, and hold-room chairs from other cities throughout the system, and shipped them to Chicago. Everyone knew that time was of the essence.

The entire city of Chicago was concerned about the shutdown of Midway Airlines. Not only were 4300 employees thrown out of work, but serious concern existed about the future of Midway Airport itself, a longtime economic engine of the southside of Chicago. When Southwest's representatives met with the city's leaders at 9:00 A.M., they told the mayor's aides that Southwest Airlines was prepared to spend at least $20 million for the development and promotion of the airport and commit to a program of substantial expansion at Midway Airport if the city would exercise its authority to assure Southwest access to the facilities necessary to effect its growth plan. Negotiations continued throughout the day, as Southwest lawyers pointed to the airline's financial stability, record of developing underutilized airports, outstanding record of customer satisfaction, excellent employee relations, and commitment to community involvement as rea-

sons why the city should choose Southwest over any competitor as its partner for the redevelopment of Midway Airport.

The people of Chicago didn't know much about Southwest Airlines, but apparently they were impressed. At mid-afternoon, the mayor's press aide entered the negotiating room and asked, "You guys have a deal yet? The mayor is having a press conference at 3:30." A letter of agreement and press release were quickly hammered out, and the deal was done.

Taking a side trip on his way into the press conference, Parker called Calvin Phillips, his contact from the Facilities Department, who had arrived in Chicago along with a dedicated band of volunteers from the Technical Services Department.

"Where's the equipment?" Parker hurriedly inquired.

"It's in Chicago, in a warehouse near the airport."

"We have a letter of agreement. Let's go."

"What if somebody from the department of aviation or Northwest tries to stop us?"

"Tell them to talk to the mayor," Parker replied.

When Mayor Daley announced Southwest Airlines as Chicago's new partner for the redevelopment of Midway Airport, a reporter inquired when he could expect to see some sign of Southwest's growth at the airport. A Southwest spokesman stepped forward, "If you go to the airport, you can see it right now." Daley beamed as reporters scurried for the door to head to the airport. News reports that night were filled with pictures of Midway Airport in transition, with Southwest workers toiling through the night to install Southwest signage and equipment at gate after gate.

A meeting was arranged the next day between representatives of Southwest and Northwest, the titular leaseholder.

"How far have your troops advanced?" the Northwest representative asked.

"I think they stopped at the edge of the A Concourse," Parker replied.

A deal ultimately was negotiated, whereby Northwest relinquished its claim to the former Midway Airlines gates and the city of Chicago entered into a direct lease with Southwest, assuring Southwest's ability to expand in Chicago and the Midwest.

Kelleher sits in his windowless office, contemplating his company's upcoming expansion into Florida. It is January 1996, and Southwest Airlines is approaching the twenty-fifth anniversary of that day in 1971 when

Kelleher told Muse to leave tire tracks on the sheriff's back, if necessary.

Southwest's fleet has grown from three 737-200s to more than 220 modern Boeing 737 aircraft. So strong is Southwest's loyalty to the 737 that it is the only major U.S. airline with an all-Boeing fleet. The little airline that had to ask for 90 percent financing from Boeing in 1971 has served as the launch customer for three new models of the 737: the 737-300, now the workhorse of the fleet, the 737-500, and the upcoming 737-700, which will be delivered in 1997.

Since recording its first profit in 1973, Southwest is about to report its twenty-third consecutive year of profitability. The halls and walls of Southwest's headquarters are filled with mementos of employee celebrations and accomplishments. The "Triple Crown" trophy sits proudly in the lobby, commemorating Southwest's unparalleled record of having the best on-time performance record, fewest mishandled bags, and fewest customer complaints, according to U.S. Department of Transportation consumer reports for four consecutive years. Southwest has become so successful that a 1993 U.S. Department of Transportation study described Southwest Airlines as "the principal driving force behind dramatic fundamental changes" in the U.S. airline industry.

The walls also include mementos of other innumerable achievements—the 1993 book by Robert Levering and Milton Moskowitz naming Southwest Airlines one of the ten best companies to work for in America; the Air Transport World designation of Southwest as "Airline of the Year" for 1991; the *Condé Nast Traveler* magazine recognition of Southwest as the safest airline in the world for its accident-free history; the 1994 *Fortune* magazine cover with a zany picture of Kelleher and the caption, "Is Herb Kelleher America's Best CEO?"

But Kelleher is intense, uncharacteristically humorless, as he contemplates his company's upcoming expansion into Florida, a market he has coveted for more than a decade. He knows the competition will be intense, and his mind flashes back to past battles. Florida in 1996 bears striking similarities to California in 1989. Air fares are high, intrastate service poor, and the geography of the state lends itself to a need for high-frequency, low-fare, reliable air service between major metropolitan areas. In California, Southwest's one-time role model, PSA, and its in-state competitor, Air Cal, long ago lost their way and were swallowed up by megacarriers who cared little for short-haul intrastate

markets, leaving a vacuum that Southwest gladly filled. Southwest's friendly low-fare service was quickly embraced by Californians with such enthusiasm that Southwest soon carried a majority of California's intrastate passengers.

The West Coast had become intensely competitive, however. United, the largest airline in the world, targeted Southwest as an unwanted intruder, and articulated a goal of eliminating, or at least slowing, Southwest's expansion. To this end, United created its own "airline within an airline," designed to offer low fares and fly largely in markets served by Southwest. In anticipation of the massive resources that could be thrown into the battle by United, an airline many times Southwest's size, Southwest had acquired Salt Lake City–based Morris Air, and launched a major expansion of its own into the Northwest.

After fifteen months of competition, though, Southwest seemed to be at least holding its own. Despite a huge influx of new competitive service, Southwest's California traffic was actually up. United officials were no longer maintaining even a pretense that the effort to erode Southwest's base of loyal customers had been successful. To the contrary, Southwest was about to report its most profitable year ever.

Suddenly, a Southwest executive interrupts Kelleher's concentration. "Herb, you're not going to believe what one of our customers just told us."

"What?"

"Guess what happens if you pick up your phone and call 1-800-SOUTHWEST?"

"You mean 1-800-I FLY SWA. That's our reservations number."

"I know. But guess what happens if you call 1-800-SOUTHWEST?"

Kelleher walks over to his telephone and dutifully dials the number. The answer comes after four rings.

"Shuttle by United reservations. This is Todd."

"What?" Kelleher exclaims in dismay.

"May I help you?"

"Uh. No, thanks."

After a moment of stunned silence, Kelleher explodes in laughter. The world's largest airline has been reduced to impersonating Southwest in an attempt to hold onto its West Coast passengers. An exquisite look of satisfaction settles over Kelleher's face as the laughter subsides.

A moment later, the look of intensity is back.

"Let's talk about Florida."

CASE 14

Blockbuster Entertainment in 1996 ————————————————— GARETH R. JONES

In 1995 the Blockbuster Entertainment Corporation (BEC) was bought by Viacom, one of the fastest-growing entertainment companies in the United States, and became one of that company's principal business divisions. Blockbuster started life in the video-rental industry in 1986 with nineteen stores; by 1993 it had more than 2,400 stores in the United States and more than 1,000 stores abroad, making it the biggest video-rental store chain in the world; by 1995 it had more than 4,513 stores located in the United States and around the world. In 1986 Blockbuster experienced a loss of $2.9 million on sales of $20 million. By 1992 sales and net income were $1.2 billion and $142 million, respectively, and its after-tax profits in 1993 and 1994 exceeded $250 million.[1] In the same period, the company's stock price has risen from an average of $.75 in 1986 to a high of $30 by October 1993 (despite four 2-for-1 stock splits), and in 1990 the stock was added to the S&P 500 Index.[2] How did the company achieve this remarkable performance, and what are the core competences that motivated Viacom to pay $8.4 billion for Blockbuster?

BLOCKBUSTER'S HISTORY

David Cook, the founder of Blockbuster, formed David P. Cook & Associates, Inc., in 1978 to offer consulting and computer services to the petroleum and real estate industries. He created programs to analyze and evaluate oil and gas properties and to compute oil and gas reserves.[3] When oil prices began to decline in 1983 due to the breakdown of the Organization of Petroleum Exporting Countries (OPEC) cartel, his business started to decline and Cook began evaluating alternative businesses in which he could apply his skills. He decided to exit his current business by selling his company and to enter the video-rental business based on a concept for a video superstore. He opened his first Superstore, called Blockbuster Video, in October 1985 in Dallas, Texas.[4]

Cook developed his idea for a video superstore by analyzing the trends in the video industry that were occurring at that time. During the 1980s the number of

This case is intended to be used as a basis for class discussion rather than as an illustration of either effective or ineffective handling of the situation. This case was prepared by Gareth R. Jones. Texas A & M University. Copyright © Gareth R. Jones, 1996, 1997.

households that owned VCRs was increasing rapidly (see Exhibit 1) and, consequently, so were the number of video-rental stores set up to serve their needs.

In 1983, 7,000 video-rental stores were in operation; by 1985 there were 19,000, and by 1986 there were more than 25,000, of which 13,000 were individually owned.[5] These mom-and-pop video stores generally operated for only a limited number of hours, offered customers only a limited selection of videos, and were often located in out-of-the-way strip shopping centers. These small stores often charged a membership fee in addition to the tape rental charge. Generally, customers brought an empty video box to the video-store clerk, who would exchange it for a tape if it was available—a procedure that was often time-consuming, particularly at peak times such as evenings and weekends.

Cook realized that as VCRs became more widespread and the number of film titles available steadily increased, customers would begin to demand a larger and more varied selection of tides from video stores. Moreover, they would demand more convenient store locations and quicker instore service than mom-and-pop stores could offer. He realized that the time was right for the development of the next generation of video stores, and he used this opportunity to implement his video superstore concept, which is still the center of Blockbuster's strategy.[6]

THE VIDEO SUPERSTORE CONCEPT

There are several components to Cook's superstore concept. First, Cook decided that in order to give his video superstores a unique identity that would appeal to customers; the stores should be highly visible, stand-alone structures, rather than part of a shopping center. In addition, his superstores were to be large—between 3,800 and 10,000 square feet—well lit, and brightly colored. (For example, each store has a bright blue sign with *Blockbuster Video* displayed in huge yellow letters.) Each store would have ample parking and would be located in the vicinity of a large urban population to maximize potential exposure to customers.

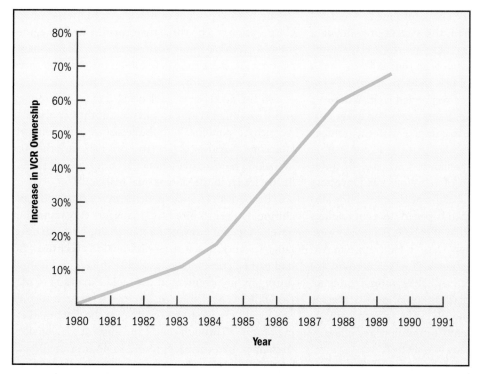

Source: Blockbuster 10-K reports.

| EXHIBIT 1 | VCR Penetration in U.S. Households, 1980–1991 |

Second, each superstore was to offer a wide variety of tapes, such as adventure, children's, instructional, and video-game titles. Believing that movie preferences differ in different locations, Cook decided to have each store offer a different selection of between 7,000 and 13,000 film titles organized alphabetically in more than thirty categories. New releases would be arranged alphabetically against the back wall of each store to make it easier for customers to make their selections.

Third, believing that many customers, particularly those with children, wanted to keep tapes for longer than a one-day period, he created the concept of a three-day rental period for $3. (In 1991, a two-evening rental program was implemented, making new releases only $2.50 for two evenings during the first three weeks after release; after this period, the usual $3 for three evenings would apply.)[7] If the tape was available, it would be behind the cover box. The customer would take the tape to the checkout line and hand the cassette and his or her membership card to the clerk, who would scan the bar codes on both the tape and the card. The customer would then be handed the tape and told that it was due back by midnight two days later. For example, if the tape were rented Thursday afternoon, it would be due back Saturday at midnight.

Fourth, Cook's superstores targeted the largest market segments, adults in the eighteen- to forty-nine-year-old group, and children in the six- to twelve-year-old group. Cook believed that if his stores could attract children, then the rest of the family would probably follow.[8] Blockbuster carries no X-rated movies, and its goal is to be "America's Family Video Store."[9] New releases are carefully chosen based on reviews and box-office success to maximize their appeal to families.

Finally, believing that customers want to choose a movie and get out of the store quickly, Cook decided that his superstores would offer customers the convenience of long operating hours and quick service. Hours are generally from 10 A.M. to midnight seven days a week. Members pay no initial fee but must show a credit card or leave a check for a security deposit. Members receive a plastic identification card that is read by the point-of-sale equipment, which was developed by the company. This system uses a laser bar code scanner to read important information from both the rental cassette and the ID card. The rental amount is computed by the system and due at the time of rental. Movie returns are scanned by laser and any late or rewind fees are recorded on the member's account and automatically recalled the next time the member rents a tape. This system reduces customers' checkout time and increases convenience. In addition, this system provides data on demographics, cassette rental patterns, and the number of times each cassette has been rented.[10]

These five elements of Blockbuster's approach were successful, and customers responded well. Wherever Blockbuster opened, the local mom-and-pop stores usually closed down, unable to compete with the number of titles and the quality of service that a Blockbuster store could provide. By 1986 Blockbuster owned eight stores and had franchised eleven more to interested investors who could see the potential of this new approach to video rental. Initially, the company opened stores in markets with a minimum population of 100,000. Franchises were located in Atlanta, Chicago, Detroit, Houston, San Antonio, and Phoenix. (The franchise agreements are discussed in greater detail later.)[11] New stores, costing an estimated $500,000 to $700,000 to equip, gross an average of $70,000 to $80,000 a month.[12] The present name of Blockbuster Entertainment Corporation was officially adopted by Cook's company in May 1986.[13]

EARLY GROWTH AND EXPANSION

John Melk, an executive at Waste Management Corp. who had invested in a Blockbuster franchise in Chicago, was to change the history of the company. He contacted H. Wayne Huizenga, a former Waste Management colleague, in February 1987 to tell him of the enormous revenue and profits his franchise was making.[14] Huizenga had experience in growing small companies in fragmented industries. In 1955 he had quit college to manage a three-truck trash-hauling operation; in 1962 he bought his own operation, Southern Sanitation. In 1968 Southern Sanitation merged with Ace Partnership, Acme Disposal, and Atlas Refuse Service to form Waste Management. In succeeding years, Huizenga borrowed against Waste Management's stock to buy more than 100 small companies that provided such services as auto-parts cleaning, dry cleaning, lawn care, and portable-toilet rentals. He used their cash flows to purchase yet more firms. By the time Huizenga, the vice chairperson, resigned in 1984, Waste Management was a $6 billion *Fortune* 500 company, and Huizenga was a very rich man.

Although Huizenga had a low opinion of video retailers, he agreed to visit a Blockbuster store. Expecting a dingy store renting X-rated films, he was pleasantly surprised to find a brightly lit family video supermarket. Detecting the opportunity to take Cook's superstore concept national, Huizenga, Melk, and Donald Flynn (another Waste Management executive) agreed

to purchase 35 percent of Blockbuster Entertainment Corporation.[15] The three investors formed an agreement with Cook and BEC to purchase 2,526,696 shares of common stock for $18.6 million in 1986. The three men became directors of BEC at this time.

In 1987 CEO David Cook decided to take his money and leave Blockbuster to pursue another venture at Amtech Corporation. With the departure of the founder, Huizenga took over as CEO in April 1987 with the goal of making Blockbuster a national company and the industry leader in the video-rental market.[16]

Recognizing his inexperience in retailing and franchising, Huizenga hired top managers experienced in developing and growing a retail chain. First, he hired Luigi Salvaneschi, a former McDonald's executive who had gained considerable expertise in facility location during his involvement in the rapid expansion of McDonald's.[17] He also hired Thomas Gruber, a former McDonald's marketing executive, as the chief marketing officer.[18] Through their experience at McDonald's, these men had the background to orchestrate Blockbuster's rapid growth.

BLOCKBUSTER'S EXPLOSIVE GROWTH

Together, Blockbuster's new top management team mapped out the company's growth strategy, the elements of which follow.

Location

Store location is a critical issue to a video-rental store, and Huizenga moved quickly with Salvaneschi to obtain the best store locations in each geographic area that Blockbuster expanded into.[19] They developed a cluster strategy, whereby they targeted a particular geographic market, such as Dallas, Boston, or Los Angeles, and then opened up new stores one at a time until they had saturated the market. Thus, within a few years, the local mom-and-pop stores found themselves surrounded; many, unable to compete with Blockbuster, closed down. Video superstores were always located near busy, well-traveled routes to establish a broad customer base. The cluster strategy eventually brought Blockbuster into 133 television markets (the geographic area that a television station reaches), where it reached 75 to 85 percent of the U.S. population.[20]

Marketing

On the marketing side, Blockbuster's chief marketing officer, Tom Gruber, applied his knowledge of McDonald's family-oriented advertising strategy to strengthen

Cook's original vision of the video retail business.[21] In 1988 he introduced Blockbuster Kids to strengthen the company's position as a family video store.[22] This promotion, aimed at the six- to twelve-year-old age group, introduced four characters and a dog to appeal to Blockbuster's young customers. The characters are Player, the leader of the gang; Stopper, who emphasizes safety; Rewind; Slo-Mo; and the dog, Pause. To further demonstrate its commitment to families, each store has forty titles recommended for children and a kids clubhouse with televisions and toys; thus, children can amuse themselves while their parents browse for videos.[23] In addition, Blockbuster allows its members to specify what rating category of tapes (such as PG or R) may be rented through their account.[24] A policy called youth-restricted viewing forbids R-rated tape rentals to children under the age of seventeen without written permission from parents.

Blockbuster also implemented a free program called Kidprint, through which a child's name, address, and height are recorded on a videotape that is given to parents and local police for identification purposes. In addition, Blockbuster has a program called America's Most Important Videos Are Free, which offers free rental of public-service tapes about topics such as fire safety and parenting.[25] As another community service, BEC donated videocassettes to the U.S. armed forces in the Middle East during the Gulf War.[26] Finally, to attract customers and to build brand recognition, Gruber initiated joint promotions between Blockbuster and companies such as Domino's Pizza, McDonald's, and PepsiCo.

Operations

Blockbuster also made great progress on the operations side of the business. As discussed earlier, the operation of a Blockbuster superstore is designed to provide fast checkout and effective inventory management. The company designed its point-of-sale computer system to make rental and return transactions easy. A laser bar code scanner reads important data from both the rental tape and the membership card to generate information on demographics and rental patterns as well as a summary report for financial control of each superstore. This system is available only to company-owned and franchised stores.[27]

Rapid expansion strains a company's operating systems. To support its stores, Blockbuster opened a 25,000-square-foot distribution center in 1986 in Dallas, Texas, giving the company effective distribution and inventory management critical for long-term success. The distribution center has the capacity to store 200,000 cassettes and is used not only to receive tapes and ship them to the stores but also to package cassettes in conformance with the company's standards. Each tape is removed from the original container, and a label with a security device is affixed to the cassette. Each videotape is then given a bar code and placed into a hard plastic rental case. The display carton is made by inserting foam and a security device into the original container and wrapping it. Initial inventory for a store is presorted by alphabet and by category. New releases are processed in the same way. The facility has the capacity to process the initial inventory requirement of about 10,000 tapes for up to three superstores per day. In addition, Blockbuster supplies the equipment and fixtures needed to operate a new store, such as computer software and hardware, shelving, signs, and cash registers.[28] In 1987 the physical facilities of the distribution center were expanded to double capacity to 400,000 videocassettes.[29]

The buying power of the company also gives it another operations advantage. It is the largest single purchaser of prerecorded videotapes in the U.S. market and, as a result, is able to negotiate large discounts off retail price.[30] Cassettes are bought at an average of $40 per tape and rented three nights for $3. Thus, the cash investment on hit videotapes is recovered in forty-five to sixty days, and the investment on nonhit titles is regained in two-and-a-half to three months. Blockbuster is also able to use its efficient distribution system to distribute extra copies of films that are declining in popularity to new stores where demand is increasing.[31] This ability to transfer tapes to where they are most demanded allows the company to use its inventory to the best advantage and to receive the maximum benefit from each videotape.

Management

For Blockbuster, as for any company, rapid growth poses the risk that control over daily operations will be lost. Recognizing this, Blockbuster established three divisions to manage the functional activities necessary to retain effective control over its operations as it grew. Blockbuster Distribution Corp. was created to handle the area licensing and franchising of new stores and to service their startup and operations. It offers both company-owned and franchised stores assistance with the selection; acquisition; assembling; packaging; inventorying; and distribution of videocassettes, supplies, and computer equipment. Blockbuster Management Corp. was established to assist with the training of new-store management, facility location and acquisition, and employee training. Finally, Blockbuster Computer Systems Inc. was formed to install, maintain, and support the software programs for the inventory and point-of-sale equipment.[32] Together these three divisions provide all the support services necessary to manage store expansion.

Blockbuster also oversees store operations through a regional- and district-level organizational structure.[33] In 1988 responsibility for store development and operations was decentralized to the regional level.[34] However, corporate headquarters is kept fully informed of developments in each regional area, and even in each store, through its computerized inventory and sales system. For example, Blockbuster's inventory and point-of-sale computer systems track sales and inventory in each store and each region.[35]

The organizational structure designed to manage its expansion is shown in Exhibit 2. As can be seen, these three functional divisions were set up so that they can quickly respond to the needs of new stores, facilitating Blockbuster's rapid growth and expansion. The role of regional management is to oversee the stores in their regions, providing advice and monitoring stores' performance to make sure that they keep up Blockbuster's high standards of operation as its chain of superstores grows.

New-Store Expansion

With Blockbuster's functional-level skills established, the next step for Huizenga was to begin a rapid program of growth and expansion. Huizenga believed that expanding rapidly to increase revenue and market share was crucial for success in the videocassette-rental industry. Under his control Blockbuster opened new stores quickly, developed a franchising program, and began to acquire competitors to increase the number of its stores.

Company-Owned Stores

To facilitate rapid expansion, Blockbuster began to use its skills in store location, distribution, and sales. At first, Blockbuster focused on large markets, preferring to enter a market with a potential capacity for 500 stores (normally a large city). Later, Blockbuster decided to enter smaller market segments, such as towns with a minimum of 20,000 people within driving distance.[36] All stores were built and operated using the superstore concept described earlier. Using the services of its three divisions, the company increased its number of new-store openings until by 1993 Blockbuster was opening one new store a day. By the end of 1993, it owned more thin 2,500 video stores. The growth in the number of company-owned stores over time is shown in Table 1.

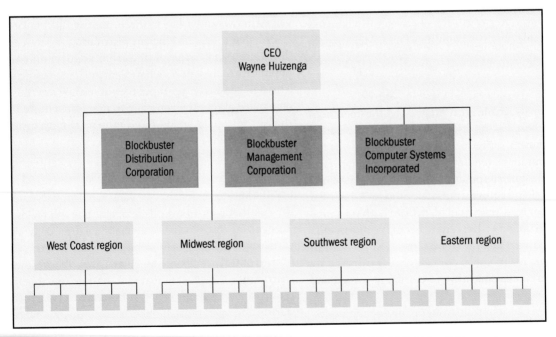

EXHIBIT 2   Blockbuster's Geographic Structure

TABLE 1

Blockbuster Video Stores by Region

Year	Company-Owned	Franchises	Total
1985	1	0	1
1986	8	11	19
1987	71	62	133
1988	341	248	589
1989	561	518	1,079
1990	787	795	1,582
1991	1.025	1,003	2,028
1992	2,002	1,125	3,127

Source: Blockbuster Annual Reports.

Acquisitions

Blockbuster's rapid growth is also attributable to Huizenga's skills in making acquisitions. Beginning in 1986 the company began to acquire many smaller video chains in order to gain a significant market presence in a city or region. In 1987, for example, the twenty-nine video stores of Movies to Go were acquired to expand Blockbuster's presence in the Midwest. Blockbuster then used this acquisition as a jumping-off point for opening many more stores in the region. Similarly, in 1989 it acquired 175 video stores from Major Video Corp. and Video Library to develop a presence in southern California. In 1991 it took over 209 Erol's Inc. stores to obtain the stronghold that Erol's previously held in the Middle-Atlantic States.

All acquired stores were made to conform to Blockbuster's standards, and any store that could not was closed. For example, forty substandard Erol's stores were closed.[37] Most acquisitions were financed by existing cash flow or by issuing new shares of stock rather than taking on new debt. These deals reflect Huizenga's reluctance to borrow a great deal of money.[38]

Licensing and Franchising

Recognizing the need to build market share rapidly and develop a national brand name, Huizenga also recruited top management to put in place an ambitious franchise program. Franchising, in which the franchisee is solely responsible for all financial commitments connected with opening a new store, allowed Blockbuster to expand rapidly without incurring debt. The downside of franchising is that Blockbuster had to share profits with the franchise owners. When franchising, it is important to maintain consistency in stores. Thus, the franchisees were required to operate their stores in the same way as company-owned stores and to follow the same store format for rental selection and the use of proprietary point-of-sale equipment.

Blockbuster's current method of franchising was established in January 1988. Under this plan, a franchisee is granted the right to open a store for twenty years with renewal rights of an additional five years if the store is in compliance with agreements. All franchise owners pay an initial fee of up to $55,000 for the privilege of using the Blockbuster Video trademark. The capital investment required to open a store generally ranges from $425,000 to $650,000. All licensed and franchised stores must meet Blockbuster's design criteria and use its standardized operating systems so customers have no problems in identifying and using the company's stores.[39] A charge of up to $30,000 is assessed for software, and the monthly software-maintenance fee varies from $500 to $650. Franchise owners pay royalty fees from 3 to 8 percent of gross revenue as determined by their agreement with Blockbuster, remit a certain percentage for marketing and promotions, and contribute 1 percent of gross receipts for national advertising. Contributions to national advertising began in 1989 when the five hundredth store was opened. All rental transactions must be recorded in the point-of-sale inventory control program, and any inventory must be approved by BEC. Moreover, franchise owners are required to buy from Blockbuster at least 5,000 videotapes of the required initial inventory of 7,000.[40] In addition, the franchise owner must complete Blockbuster's training program or hire a manager who has completed Blockbuster's training program to run the store. Assistance with activities such as site selection and employee training are available for a fee.[41]

Franchising facilitated the rapid expansion of Blockbuster Video. By 1992 the company had more than 1,000 franchised stores compared with 2,000 company-owned stores (see Table 1). However, recognizing the long-term profit advantages of owning its own stores, Blockbuster began to repurchase attractive territories from franchisees.[42] In 1993 the company spent $248 million to buy the 400 stores of its two largest franchisees and, with a

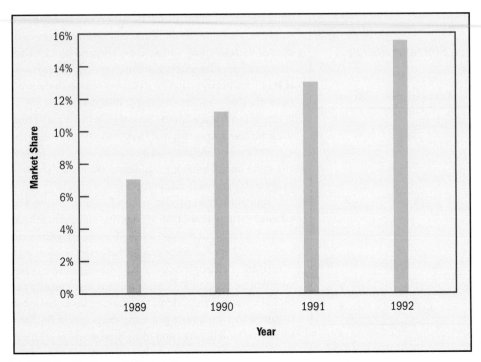

EXHIBIT 3   Blockbuster's Market Share

new store opening every day, by the end of 1993 it owned more than 2,500 stores.

However, by the end of 1992, despite its rapid growth, Blockbuster still only controlled about 15 percent of the market; its 27,000 smaller rivals shared the rest (see Exhibit 3). Consequently, in 1993 Blockbuster announced plans for a new round of store openings and acquisitions that would give it a 25 to 30 percent market share within two or three years.

THE HOME-VIDEO INDUSTRY

Revenues from video rentals now exceed the revenues obtained in movie theaters. For example, video-rental revenues rose to $11 billion in 1991 compared with movie theaters' revenue of $4.8 billion, cable movie channels such as HBO's revenue of $5.2 billion, and pay-per-view's $133 million.[43] Domestic video revenue in 1992 was nearly $12 billion.[44] The huge growth in industry revenues has led to increased competition for customers, and, as noted above, 28,000 video stores operate in the United States.

Blockbuster Video does not face a direct national competitor, and it is the only company operating beyond a regional level. The next largest competitor, West Coast Video, had only $120 million in 1991 revenues.[45] In contrast, Blockbuster Video had 1991 rental revenues of $868 million.[46] Blockbuster does, however, face many competitors at the local and regional levels. For example, various supermarket chains across the United States, such as Kroger and Winn Dixie, had aggregate video-rental revenues of $1.35 billion in 1991.[47] Similarly, video stores in the Pacific and Middle-Atlantic States have six competitors within 3 miles, and the competition between them has resulted in price wars in some areas. In the San Antonio market, for example, competition between video stores resulted in Blockbuster and its competitors reducing their prices to $2, but then HEB (a supermarket chain) responded by dropping its price to $1.50 and offering $.99 specials; this started a new price war. As a result, Blockbuster has been forced to give its stores some freedom in their pricing policies to meet local competitive conditions.

To handle increased competition from Blockbuster, some local competitors are emphasizing service. For example, salespeople at Video Factory in Buffalo, New York, wear tuxedos and use umbrellas to escort customers to their cars when it rains. Other competitors have introduced newer technology; California-based Tower Video, for example, rents 8-mm videos and laser disks, while Blockbuster concentrates on standard VHS videocassettes.[48] Stores can also compete by selling other products, such as prerecorded videotapes, blank videotapes, candy, and video games. Blockbuster has begun selling these items and is testing the sale of laser disks, which it will carry if there is a demand.[49]

Mature Market

As the video-rental market matures, the level of competition in the industry is changing. During the 1980s video rentals grew rapidly due to the proliferation of VCRs. By 1990, however, 70 percent of households had VCRs compared with 2 percent in 1980; industry growth dropped from the previous double digits to 7 percent.[50] Exibit 1 illustrates the changes in the percentage of people who owned VCRs for the period from 1980 to 1991. The current slow growth in VCR ownership and rentals will make competition more severe and put increased pressure on the weaker companies in the industry. Blockbuster, however, with its strong national base, is in a good position to compete in the poorer environment.

To a large degree, competition in the video-rental industry is so fierce because it is relatively easy for new competitors to enter the market; the only purchase necessary is videotapes (which movie studios will supply to any potential purchaser). This ease of start-up accounts for the existence of so many video stores, more than 28,000 nationwide.[51] Blockbuster, however, unlike small video-rental companies, is able to negotiate discounts with tape suppliers because it buys new releases in such huge volume.

Blockbuster's customers, who are principally individual families, do not pose a threat to the company. However, in an increasingly competitive situation, Blockbuster's three-day rental policy could be a disadvantage because of a sort of boomerang effect: all the highly demanded movies are checked out on Thursday so that they are not available until Sunday. Many of Blockbuster's customers come for the new releases. *Video Insider* magazine states that the twenty most popular movies at any one time account for 80 percent of tape rentals in the United States. Blockbuster, however, claims that the top fifty titles account for only 35 percent of its rental revenues, so its policy does not hurt sales; customers are not getting frustrated and going elsewhere when new releases are not available.[52]

New Technology

One growing problem facing Blockbuster is the variety of new ways in which customers can view movies and other kinds of entertainment. Blockbuster has always felt competition both from other sources of movies—such as cable TV and movie theaters—and from other forms of entertainment—such as bowling, baseball games, and outdoor activities. Technology is now giving customers more ways to watch movies. New technological threats include pay-per-view or video-on-demand systems through wired and wireless cable services (brought to the home via a small antenna), digital compression, and direct broadcast satellites.

By 1996 pay-per-view movies introduced directly into the home via satellite and wired and wireless cable service had become a major competitive threat to video-rental stores. Currently, with pay-per-view systems, cable customers can call their local cable company and pay a fee to have a scheduled movie, concert, or sporting event aired on their television set.[53]

Under test at the moment is a system in which cable customers can call up their local video company and choose any movie to be aired on their television for a fee; the cable company makes the movies available when the customer wants it. Increasingly, telephone companies are becoming interested in the potential for pay-per-view because this systems depends on an interactive network of fiber-optic cable that allows two-way communication between the customer and movie supplier. The fiber-optic cables that telephone companies are installing allow for two-way communication and can transmit movies as well. Furthermore, in 1995 Congress deregulated the cable industry and allowed telephone companies to compete with cable companies to supply customers with movies and cable television.

The threat of increased competition will become much stronger as the technology improves and as companies move to implement pay-per-view systems. Time Warner has already replaced coaxial cable with fiber optics to offer 150 cable channels in Queens, New York.[54] GTE Corporation is testing a system that transmits movies through fiber-optic cables. A bigger move comes from the largest U.S. cable operator, Tele-Communications, Inc. (TCI), which formed a strategic alliance with Carolco, a film producer, to release four movies for pay-per-view before they are released in the theater. Pay-per-view will be the foundation of TCI's plan to install technology and fiber-optic transmission systems capable of providing homes with 500 cable channels.

Video-on-demand takes the pay-per-view concept further. Bellcore, the research branch of the regional Bell companies, invented video-on-demand. With this system (still in the trial stage), a customer will use an interactive box to select a movie from a list of thousands, and the choice will be transmitted to an information warehouse that will store thousands of tapes in digital formats. The selected video will then be routed back to the customer's house through a series of switches, and a signal splitter will send the movie into the home through the phone lines. This essentially bypasses the local video-rental store because the movies are stored digitally on tape at the cable company's headquarters.

Movie companies or video stores such as Blockbuster could function as the information warehouse from which the video selections are made; Blockbuster is interested in acting as the warehouse so that it can control the video-on-demand market, which could become a direct threat to video rental as the technology is refined. Blockbuster began discussions with Bell Atlantic Corporation, which developed a video-on-demand system for customers in northern Virginia that went online in 1994. Blockbuster, which would provide the movies for the video-on-demand system, views this move as an expansion of its business rather than cannibalization of video rentals.

U.S. West, one of the Baby Bells, has also announced plans to build a video-on-demand network to serve 13 million homes in fourteen states; with its partner, Time Warner, it plans to eventually reach 25 percent of the viewing market. The linking of phone companies with other entertainment companies could become a direct threat to Blockbuster, but in 1994 Huizenga announced publicly that Blockbuster was not overly concerned about video-on-demand systems because only one-third of U.S. households have access to pay-per-view, and fiber optics is expensive.[55] Furthermore, Huizenga claimed that his company could make the local Blockbuster store the center of the video-on-demand network. Huizenga felt that phone companies would prefer to deal with Blockbuster rather than with companies such as Time Warner or Paramount, which lack both Blockbuster's skills in video retailing and its established customer base, the 50 million customers who made more than a billion trips to the local store in 1995.

Other new technologies include digital compression and direct broadcast satellites. Digital compression allows up to five television channels to be sent on the same bandwidth that used to be able to carry only one channel. This provides more space for movies to be sent to customers.[56] In 1995 local wireless cable service became widely available throughout the United States by installing a small antenna supplied free by wireless cable companies. In addition, Hughes Aircraft pioneered the development of direct broadcast satellites (DBS), in which customers buy a two-foot diameter satellite dish to receive programming. The dishes cost between $300 and $500 to purchase, and their price is falling as companies such as Hughes Aircraft and Sony mass-produce them. The huge increase in the number of television channels that customers can receive as a result of these developments and the large number of pay-per-view channels available could harm the video-rental industry because customers would no longer have to go to video-rental stores to get a movie.[57]

BLOCKBUSTER EXPANDS GLOBALLY

In 1994 Blockbuster, under Wayne Huizenga, exploited the skills and capabilities it has developed in the domestic video-rental market to expand globally. Its great size and secure financial position provided by the large growth in its domestic revenues allowed Blockbuster to diversify quickly into global markets and to exploit the possibilities offered by the new technological developments discussed earlier. Satellite systems, for example, are gaining importance in the European market.

The Global Marketplace

Seventy percent of the world's VCRs are in countries outside the United States, and foreign countries account for half of total world video-rental revenues. The United States is the largest video market, with 1991 revenues of $11 billion. Japan is second, with $2.6 billion, followed by the United Kingdom with $1.4 billion and Canada with $1.2 billion.[58] Blockbuster decided to seize this opportunity to increase its revenues by expanding abroad. Just as in the United States, Blockbuster had a program both to build new video superstores and to acquire foreign competitors abroad. Planning to be a leader in home entertainment around the world, Blockbuster's objective was to obtain a 25 percent share of international revenue by 1995 and to have 2,000 stores in international markets by 1996.[59] By the end of 1994, it had 1,333 international stores, and its expansion plans were on track.

Blockbuster began to expand into international markets in 1989, when it saw the opportunity to exploit its marketing expertise, superstore concept, operating knowledge, financial strength, and ability to attract franchisees abroad. In 1989 stores were opened in Canada and the United Kingdom.[60] In 1990 Blockbuster opened its first store in Puerto Rico. It continued its expansion into the United Kingdom, Canada, the Virgin Islands,

Venezuela, and Spain. Franchise agreements were also signed in Japan, Australia, and Mexico.[61] For example, an Australian franchisee agreed to open 150 outlets over a five-year period.[62] A similar agreement was attained in Mexico.[63] By the end of 1990, there were forty-seven franchises or joint ventures in Canada, twenty-five in the United Kingdom (six were company owned and nineteen were franchised), and one store each in Puerto Rico and Guam.[64]

In Japan, Blockbuster formed a joint venture in March 1991 with Den Fujita, who runs McDonald's Co. Japan and has a stake in ToysRUs Japan Ltd. This venture opened 15 stores in Japan in 1992 and planned to add 30 stores in 1993 and 1,000 stores within ten years. Due to fierce competition, the Japan stores are meeting only 90 percent of sales projections.[65] Under the terms of this 50/50 joint venture agreement with Fujita & Co., Ltd., Blockbuster can franchise more stores in Japan.[66] Blockbuster is exporting its video concepts to a market that is very interested in video rentals. By forming a joint venture, Blockbuster can benefit from the expertise of Japanese locals in running a business in Japan.

To expand in the United Kingdom, in February 1992 Blockbuster purchased Cityvision PLC, the United Kingdom's largest video retailer, for $81 million cash and 3.9 million shares of stock.[67] Under this arrangement, Blockbuster acquired around 97 percent of Cityvision's voting common stock and about 45 percent of its nonvoting preferred stock. At this time, Cityvision ran 875 stores in Britain and Austria under the name Ritz.[68] Blockbuster transformed the Ritz outlets into Blockbuster stores and used the chain as a start for further expansion into Europe, just as it had taken over large video chains in the United States on its way to becoming the national leader. joint ventures are also being negotiated in France, Germany, and Italy. Blockbuster is increasing the number of franchised stores in Mexico, Chile, Venezuela, and Spain. By the end of 1992, the company had 952 stores in nine foreign countries with plans to establish at least 1,200 more by 1995.[69] Eighty-six percent of its international stores are company owned and 14 percent are franchised.

Blockbuster created an international homevideo division to oversee and manage its expansion into foreign markets. Besides having expertise in international operations, marketing, merchandising, product purchasing, distribution, franchising, real estate, and field support, this division is proficient at dealing with differences in entertainment, language, and business culture between different countries and is successfully implementing Blockbuster's domestic strategy in its foreign operations.[70]

Diversification

Blockbuster became a national video-rental chain because of the way it positioned itself in the market as a family-oriented store with a wide selection of videos, convenient hours and locations, and fast checkout. In the 1990s Blockbuster began to expand its entertainment concept into several new areas of business.[71] The major areas of diversification were film entertainment programming and music retailing. In an effort to increase its revenue, Blockbuster also made deals to broaden its range of product offerings.

Film Entertainment Programming To enter the programming aspect of the filmed entertainment business, Blockbuster invested in both Spelling Entertainment Group, Inc., and Republic Pictures Corporation. Both of these companies have large film libraries, a source of inexpensive movies for Blockbuster's retail operations.[72] Blockbuster issued 7.6 million shares of common stock valued at $140 million to acquire a 48.2 percent interest in Spelling Entertainment from American Financial Corp., which is closely held by investor Carl Linder. Under the deal, Linder gains a 4 percent stake in Blockbuster; Blockbuster gains access to Spelling's library of 600 feature film and fifty-five television shows, including *Beverly Hills 90210*. Spelling will sell its programs in Blockbuster's video stores. This deal also provides Blockbuster with access to the broadcast and cable television markets. Spelling's proficiency in cable network programming could help Blockbuster, which might consider managing its own cable channel in the future.[73]

Blockbuster paid $25 million for a 35 percent stake in Republic Pictures, an independent film distributor and producer. Blockbuster has warrants to purchase an additional 810,000 shares.[74] Republic's programming library includes classics such as *High Noon, The Quiet Man,* and *The Bells of St. Mary's.* This investment also strengthens Blockbuster's hold in the programming side of the entertainment industry because Republic has ongoing deals with the television, home video, and theatrical markets.

Music Retailing Blockbuster also chose the music business as an area into which it could expand its entertainment concept. As in the video-store industry, many music stores are mom-and-pop businesses or parts of small chains. Moreover, music stores are increasingly selling videos such as the Walt Disney collection, musicals, and family movies. Blockbuster saw a fit between selling records, cassettes, and compact disks and renting or selling videos. Thus, it decided to employ the same strategy it had used in the video-rental market: opening new stores and acquiring chains of music stores using the revenues from its video superstores.

However, Blockbuster decided not to sell CDs and cassettes in its video stores. Instead, it decided to operate its music business independently, with separate stores, called Blockbuster Music stores, that will use the same superstore concept that was so successful in the video-rental business. The stores are very large (20,000 to 25,000 square feet) and offer a wide selection of music products such as recorded music, computer software, games, and books. Blockbuster developed a new design for its music stores to attract customers of all ages and musical tastes. Like its video stores, the music stores are clean and bright and offer a large selection of all types of music. The tapes are displayed by categories.

In addition, Blockbuster plans to build smaller outlets (10,000 to 15,000 square feet) and acquire existing chains. As part of its plan to diversify into the $8 billion record industry, in 1994 Blockbuster agreed to buy Sound Warehouse and Music Plus, two record-store chains, for $185 million, including assumption of debt, from Shamrock Holdings Inc. At the time, Sound Warehouse was the seventh largest music retailer and Music Plus was the twelfth largest. These two retail chains had a total of 236 stores in thirty-five states, primarily in California and the South. This acquisition made Blockbuster the seventh largest music chain in the United States.

With 50 million video customers, Blockbuster began to introduce joint promotions and advertising between its music and video stores, such as giving a customer a 15 percent discount on a CD for renting two videos.[75] In this way, it encourages customers who visited one of its stores to visit the other as well. Its ability to attract families and young people gives it a great advantage because more than 64 percent of record sales are to people aged fifteen to thirty-four, Blockbuster's main customer group.[76] Blockbuster also hopes that it will be able to apply aspects of its video business to the music business as well, such as its computer software and store-management skills.

At the end of 1995, Blockbuster had 516 music stores operating in the United States and more than 50 operating in Europe and Australia. In 1996 Blockbuster announced that it planned to open 500 new stores in the next five years to make it the dominant player in the music market.

Although part of the entertainment business, music retailing is significantly different from video retailing. For instance, the target market for music is generally not families, whereas the video stores are built around families. Blockbuster also faces strong competition in the U.S. music business. Because it is fifty years old, the record industry has more experienced competitors than the video industry. Some major competitors include the sixth largest retailer, Super Club, which owns Record Bar, Turtles, Tracks, Sam Goody's, and Tower Records, Tower, for example, plans to accelerate the development of its own 10,000- to 50,000-square-foot megastores.[77]

BLOCKBUSTER'S NEW STRUCTURE

In 1993, in an effort to manage the companies it acquired in its quest to become a full-service home entertainment retailer, Blockbuster reorganized and split into several divisions: domestic home videos, international home videos, music retailing, international music retailing, new-technology ventures, and other entertainment ventures (see Exhibit 4).[78]

THE MERGER WITH VIACOM

In 1994 Blockbuster was riding high with record revenues and profits and an ambitious plan to open thousands more video stores in the United States and abroad. Wayne Huizenga, however, despite his public claims that he thought Blockbuster could weather the threat of pay-per-view and video-on-demand cable systems and indeed become the movie warehouse at the center of such networks, was worried. It looked increasingly likely that technological breakthroughs would do to videotapes what the cassette-tape had done to 8-track tapes, and he began to think of Blockbuster's future.

Moreover, Huizenga was an entrepreneur who had previously built one empire by merging many small waste-management companies together to create WMX, a global waste-management company. Realizing that his investment in that industry had peaked, Huizenga had sold his holding at the right time and bought control of Blockbuster.

Given the threat of new technology and his feeling that growth at Blockbuster may be reaching its peak (especially in light of its incredibly fast rise), Huizenga had to decide what to do to protect his investment. An opportunity was handed to him when Sumner Redstone,

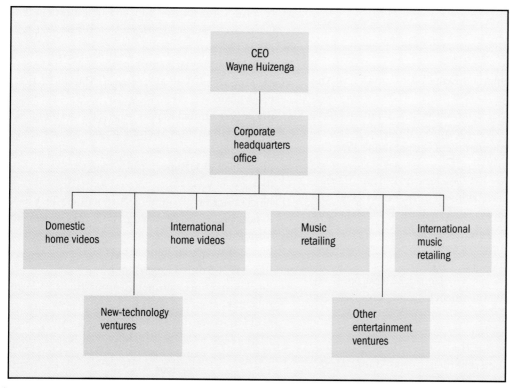

EXHIBIT 4 Blockbuster's New Structure

the CEO of Viacom, desperate to complete a takeover of Paramount, came to him to request cash in return for a stake in Viacom, a major provider of entertainment programming. The opportunity to give Blockbuster a bigger stake in the content or entertainment software side of the business was very appealing to Huizenga, and he agreed to provide $600 million out of Blockbuster's rich cash reserves. Redstone needed more money, however, and Huizenga, seeing an opportunity both to diversify Blockbuster's entertainment holdings and reduce the threat to Blockbuster from changes in technology, told Redstone that the price for financial assistance was a merger with Viacom. Huizenga proposed a stock swap in which Blockbuster's stockholders would receive stock in Viacom. In 1995 the merger went through, and Blockbuster became a wholly owned subsidiary of Viacom.

Huizenga agreed to assume the position of vice chairman of the board of directors under Redstone, but within a few months left the company to begin yet another empire, this time intending to build a nationwide chain of used-car dealerships, among other things.

After Huizenga's departure, the threat to Blockbuster's video rental business became clearer, as aggressive new video-rental chains sprung up that competed with Blockbuster by offering lower prices for two-day video rentals. Also, the rapid spread of pay-per-view movie systems on both wired and wireless cable television emerged as a major threat by 1996. Although the revenues Viacom receives from its Blockbuster video stores continued to increase because the number of its stores increased, sales at each store were flat as its customers turned to cheaper competitors and to pay-per-view.

Thus, in 1996, the prospects for Blockbuster in the future were unclear. Does Blockbuster have the core skills and capabilities to protect its position and develop its hold on the video-rental and music market to become the dominant company in the retail entertainment business? Alternatively, given new technological developments, will it lose hold on the video-rental market? In 1996 Viacom hired William Fields, formerly one of Wal-Mart's most senior managers, to craft a new strategy for both Blockbuster video and music to help them survive and prosper in the 1990s. Analysts are eagerly waiting to see whether he can revive both Blockbuster's and Viacom's fortunes or whether Viacom has bought a company whose revenues will fall as rapidly as they rose.

ENDNOTES

1. Blockbuster Entertainment Corp., *Value Line,* May 28, 1993.
2. Blockbuster Entertainment Corporation's 1990 Annual Report, p. 7.
3. Cook Data Services, Inc.'s 1984 10-K Report, pp. 2–3.
4. Cook Data Services, Inc.'s 1985 Annual Report, p. 1.
5. Blockbuster Entertainment Corporation's 1986 Annual Report, p. 9.
6. S. Sandomir, *New York Times,* June 19, 1991, pp. 522–525.
7. Blockbuster Entertainment Corporation's 1991 Annual Report, p. 24 (St. Petersburg, Fl.: QData Corporation Microfiche).
8. Greg Clarkin,"Fast Forward," *Marketing and Media Decisions,* March 1990, pp. 57–59.
9. G. DeGeorge, *Business Week,* January 22, 1990, pp. 47–48.
10. Blockbuster Entertainment Corporation's 1986 10-K Report, p. 7.
11. BEC's 1986 10-K Report, pp. 7–9.
12. Sandomir, *New York Times.*
13. "Blockbuster Entertainment Corporation," *Moody's Industrial Manual,* pp. 2667–2668.
14. Sandomir, *New York Times.*
15. Ibid.
16. Blockbuster Entertainment Corporation's 1987 Annual Report, pp. 4–5.
17. Sandomir, *New York Times.*
18. Ibid.
19. Ibid.
20. Clarkin, "Fast Forward."
21. Ibid.
22. Blockbuster Entertainment Corporation's 1988 Annual Report, p. 5 (St. Petersburg, Fl.: QData Corporation Microfiche).
23. Clarkin, "Fast Forward."
24. Blockbuster Entertainment Corporation's 1989 10-K Report, pp. 3–4 (St. Petersburg, Fl.: QData Corporation Microfiche).
25. Clarkin, "Fast Forward."
26. BEC's 1990 Annual Report, p. 7.
27. BEC's 1989 10-K Report, p. 3.
28. BEC's 1986 10-K Report, p. 8.
29. Blockbuster Entertainment Corporation's 1987 10-K Report, p. 11 (St. Petersburg, Fl.: QData Corporation Microfiche).
30. BEC's 1990 Annual Report, p. 15.
31. Eric Savitz, "An End to Fast Forward?" *Barron's,* December 11, 1989, pp. 13, 43–46.
32. Cook Data Services, Inc.'s 1985 Annual Report, p. 2.
33. "Global Notes: Focus—Blockbuster Entertainment Corp. (BV)," *Research Highlights,* October 26, 1990, p. 9.
34. BEC's 1988 Annual Report, pp. 4–5.
35. BEC's 1987 Annual Report, p. 15.
36. M. McCarthy, *Wall Street Journal,* March 22, 1991, pp. A1, A6.
37. BEC's 1991 Annual Report, p. 40 (St. Petersburg, Fl.: QData Corporation Microfiche).
38. Sandomir, *New York Times.*
39. BEC's 1989 10-K Report, p. 6.
40. Ibid., pp. 6–9.
41. Blockbuster Entertainment Corporation's 1991 10-K Report, pp. 7–9 (St. Petersburg, Fl.: QData Corporation Microfiche).
42. BEC's 1990 Annual Report, p. 21.
43. BEC's 1991 Annual Report, p. 10.
44. Blockbuster Entertainment Corporation's 1992 Annual Report, p. 5.
45. Gail DeGeorge, Jonathan Levine, and Robet Neff, "They Don't Call It Blockbuster for Nothing," *Business Week,* October 19, 1992, pp. 113–114.
46. *Value Line,* May 28, 1993.
47. Scott Hume, "Blockbuster Means More Than Video," *Advertising Age,* June 1, 1992, p. 4.
48. McCarthy, *Wall Street Journal.*
49. Blockbuster Entertainment Corporation's 1990 10-K Report, p. 6 (St. Petersburg, Fl.: QData Corporation Microfiche).
50. McCarthy, *Wall Street Journal.*
51. Ibid.
52. Savitz, "An End to Fast Forward?"
53. Shapiro, *New York Times,* February 21, 1992, p. D6.
54. Sandomir, *New York Times.*
55. Ibid.
56. Ibid.
57. "Global News."
58. BEC's 1991 Annual Report, p. 18.
59. QRP Merrill Lynch Extended Company Comment, November 16, 1990.
60. Blockbuster Entertainment Corporation's 1989 Annual Report, p. 27.
61. BEC's 1990 Annual Report, p. 19.
62. "Stock Highlight: Blockbuster Ent. (NYSE-14)," *Value Line: Selection & Opinion,* March 8, 1991, pp. 168–169.
63. BEC's 1990 Annual Report, p. 19.
64. QRP ML Extended Company Comment: Blockbuster ENTM (BV) (Merrill Lynch 1990),pp. 2–5.
65. DeGeorge, Levine, and Neff, "They Don't Call It Blockbuster for Nothing."

66. QRP ML Extended Company Comment: Block-buster ENTM (BV) (Merrill Lynch 1990), pp. 2–5.
67. DeGeorge, Levine, and Neff, "They Don't Call It Blockbuster for Nothing."
68. BEC's 1991 10-K Report, p. 4.
69. DeGeorge, Levine, and Neff, "They Don't Call It Blockbuster for Nothing."
70. BECs 1992 Annual Report, p. 17.
71. DeGeorge, Levine, and Neff, "They Don't Call It Blockbuster for Nothing."
72. *Value Line,* May 28, 1993.
73. Laurie Grossman and Gabriella Stern, "Blockbuster to Buy Controlling Stake in Spelling in Swap," *Wall Street Journal,* March 9, 1993, p. B9.
74. "Business Briefs: Blockbuster Entertainment Corporation," *Wall Street Journal,* February 12, 1993, P. B6.
75. Johnnie Roberts, "Blockbuster Officials Envision Superstores for Music Business," *Wall Street Journal,* October 28, 1992, p. B10.
76. Ibid.
77. Helene Cooper, "Blockbuster and Virgin Retail Group Plan a Chain of 'Megastores' in the U.S.," *Wall Street Journal,* November 17, 1992, p. B10.
78. Geraldine Fabrikant, "Blockbuster President Resigns: Video Chain Revamps to Adapt to New Units," *New York Times,* January 5, 1993, p. D6.

C A S E   1 5

The Evolution of Viacom Inc. ———— GARETH R. JONES

By 1995, under its billionaire chairman, Sumner Redstone, Viacom had grown to become one of the world's largest entertainment and publishing companies. Viacom is a leader in nearly every segment of the communications marketplace and controls some of the world's most valuable entertainment and publishing brand names such as MTV, Simon & Schuster, Paramount, and Blockbuster Video. Nevertheless, in early 1996 Viacom's stock price fell sharply after the company reported poor operating results, and Redstone fired Frank Biondi, Viacom's CEO, blaming him for its poor performance. Throughout the spring of 1996, Sumner and his new top lieutenants, Philippe Daumand and Tom Dooley, worked on a strategy to turn the company's fortunes around and obtain the value they believed was in Viacom's many different businesses. Wall Street analysts looked critically on, however, and wondered what success they would have. Was Viacom going to survive in its present form, or would major changes have to be made?

EARLY HISTORY

Viacom was established by CBS in the summer of 1970 to comply with regulations by the U.S. Federal Communications Commission barring television networks

This case is intended to be used as a basis for class discussion rather than as an illustration of either effective or ineffective handling of the situation. This case was prepared by Gareth R. Jones, Texas A & M University. Copyright © Gareth R, Jones, 1996, 1997.

from owning cable television systems or from syndicating their own programs in the United States. The increasing spread of cable television and the continuing possibility of conflicts of interest between television networks and cable television companies convinced CBS to spin off the company. Viacom separated formally from CBS in 1971, when CBS distributed Viacom's stock to its shareholders at the rate of one share for every seven shares of CBS stock.[1]

Viacom quickly became one of the largest cable operators in the United States, with more than 90,000 cable subscribers. It also owned the syndication rights to a large number of popular, previously run CBS television series that it made available for syndication to cable television stations. Revenue from these rights accounted for a sizable percentage of Viacom's income.

In 1976, to take advantage of Viacom's experience in syndicating programming to cable television stations, its managers decided to establish the Showtime movie network to compete directly with HBO, the leading outlet for films on cable television. In 1977 Viacom earned $5.5 million in sales of $58.5 million. Most of its earnings represented revenues from the syndication of its television series but also reflected growth of its own cable television systems, which at this time had grown to about 350,000 subscribers. Recognizing that greater profits could be earned by both producing and syndicating television programming, Viacom's managers decided to produce their own television programs in the late 1970s and early 1980s. Their efforts only produced mixed results, however; no hit series resulted from their work, and the Big Three television networks of ABC, NBC, and CBS continued to dominate the air waves at this time.

During the early 1980s, the push to expand the cable television side of its business became Viacom's managers' major priority. Cable television is a very capital-intensive business, and Viacom invested large amounts of money to build its cable infrastructure. Viacom spent $65 million on extending its customer base in 1981 alone, for example. By 1982 Viacom had added 450,000 subscribers to the 90,000 it inherited from CBS, making it the ninth largest cable operator in the United States. Also, by 1982 Viacom's sales had grown to $210 million, with about half its revenues coming from program syndication and about half from its cable operations.

Viacom's managers, however, continued to feel that its cable operations were not a strong enough engine for future growth. One reason was that cable television prices were regulated at this time, and cable companies were limited in how much they could charge customers. Viacom's managers continued to believe that the future lay in providing not just cable television service but also the content of cable programming—television programs. Given their previous failure in making their own programs, Viacom's managers sought to make acquisitions in the content side of the business, that is, in companies that made entertainment programs. In 1981 Viacom started in a small way by buying a minority stake in the Cable Health network, a new advertiser-supported television network. Then, in September 1985 it made the acquisition that would totally change the company's future. Viacom purchased the MTV networks from Warner Communications, a company that desperately needed cash because Warner's own cable television system was suffering from a lack of investment.

The MTV networks included MTV, a new popular music video channel geared toward the fourteen to twenty-four age group; Nickelodeon, a channel geared toward children; and VH-1, a music video channel geared toward an older twenty-five-to-forty-four-year-old audience. MTV was the most popular property in the MTV network. Its quick pace and flashy graphics were becoming popular and highly influential among young television viewers, and its young audience was a chief target of advertisers. Nickelodeon had been less successful, for it had not achieved any notable following among young viewers. Viacom moved quickly to revamp Nickelodeon, giving it the slick, flashy look of MTV and developing unique programming that appealed to children, programming that was very different from that offered by competitors such as the Disney Channel. In the next few years, Nickelodeon went from being the least popular channel on basic cable among children to the most popular. Viacom's managers were confident that they had in place the beginning of a new programming strategy to complement its cable television interests and guide the company to long-term success.

ENTER SUMNER REDSTONE

Viacom's managers' dreams were shattered when its Showtime channel lost about 300,000 customers between March 1985 and March 1986 because of intense competition from HBO. HBO, under its then CEO Frank Biondi, was making itself the dominant pay movie channel by producing its own innovative programming and by forming exclusive agreements with major movie studios such as Paramount to offer their movies to HBO first. As a result of the loss of customers, Viacom's cash flow dropped dramatically, and the company lost $9.9 million on sales of $919.2 million in 1986. Further weakened by the $2 billion debt load it had incurred to fund its cable expansion program and make its programming acquisitions, Viacom became a takeover target.

After a damaging six-month battle, Sumner M. Redstone, president of National Amusements Inc. (NAI), bought Viacom for about $3.4 billion in March 1986. Redstone was the owner of a closely held corporation that owned and operated 675 movie screens in fourteen states in the United States and England. Redstone, the controlling shareholder of NAI, became chairman of the board of Viacom and moved quickly to take full control of the company. Redstone had built NAI from fifty drive-in movie theaters to a modern theater chain. He is credited with pioneering the development of the multiplex movie theater concept that offers movie-goers a choice of a dozen or more screens to choose from. However, running a chain of movie theaters was very different from running a debt-laden media conglomerate as complicated as Viacom.

Many analysts felt that Redstone had overpaid for Viacom, but he saw a great potential for growth. Besides its cable television systems and syndication rights that now included the popular series *The Cosby Show,* Redstone recognized the potential of its MTV and Nickelodeon channels. Moreover, over the years Viacom had acquired five television and eight radio stations in major markets, which he saw as valuable investments.[2] Redstone moved quickly to solve Viacom's problems and with the hands-on directive management style for which he is well known he fired Viacom's top managers and began the search for capable managers who would be loyal and obedient to him.[3] To turn Showtime around, he immediately hired Frank Biondi, the chief executive who had made HBO the dominant movie channel, as CEO of Viacom.

Frank Biondi was just a few days away from moving to Hollywood to run Columbia Pictures when Redstone called and asked him to take over as CEO of Viacom. The forty-nine-year-old Biondi is known for his strong financial, deal-making, and strategic skills and for his expertise in managing a diverse group of young executives and building them into a cooperative unit. Unlike Redstone, who likes to be directly involved in the day-to-day operations of a business, Biondi felt that his job was to set challenging goals, find the resources—both capital and people—to achieve them, and then get out of the way to let his managers achieve them.[4] His approach is to decentralize control to his managers mid let them get the job done. Analysts felt the combination of Redstone's hands-on approach and Biondi's future-thinking style made them a very effective team to head the growing entertainment conglomerate.

THE NEW VIACOM

Redstone's takeover of Viacom was fueled by his belief that cable television programming would become the dominant means of providing consumers with their entertainment content in the future. With the acquisition of Viacom, Redstone now owned 76 percent of MTV and Nickelodeon, which together gave Viacom access to millions of viewers aged two to twenty-four. Redstone emerged as the foremost purveyor of pop culture to young America, something paradoxical since Redstone claimed that he didn't even like rock music.[5] Redstone believed Viacom's cable networks were its crown jewels because they provided half the company's revenues and profits, which came both from subscribers (the cable companies that bought the programming) and from advertisers (who advertised on these channels).[6] To strengthen the cable channel franchise and build its brand name, Redstone restructured MTV and installed a more aggressive advertising and sales staff.

Against the expectations of many industry analysts, MTV and Nickelodeon experienced continued growth and profitability. In 1989, for example, the MTV networks won 15 percent of all dollars spent on cable advertising. MTV was expanding throughout the world, broadcasting to Western Europe, Japan, Australia, and large portions of Latin America.[7]

Despite the success of the MTV channels, Redstone still faced the problem of paying off the debt that he had incurred to acquire Viacom, debt that amounted to $450 million in interest in the first two years following the takeover. Several fortuitous events aided him.[8] First, shortly after the buyout, Viacom began to earn millions of dollars from television stations wanting to show reruns of *The Cosby Show.* Second, in 1987 Congress deregulated cable television and allowed cable television companies to charge what they liked for their programming. The result was that the prices charged for cable television service soared and so did the price of cable television franchises. Redstone took full advantage of this situation and sold off some of Viacom's cable assets to help reduce debt. In February 1989, Viacom's Long Island and suburban Cleveland cable systems were sold to Cablevision Systems Corp. for $545 million, or about twenty times their annual cash flow. Cablevision also bought a 5 percent stake in Showtime for $25 million, giving it an interest in promoting the channel to Cablevision's customers, and this helped Showtime get back in competition with HBO. These events enabled Redstone to cut Viacom's debt significantly and negotiate more favorable terms on its loans. However, it was rough going, and Viacom lost $154.4 million in 1987, even though its sales increased to almost $1 billion.

With Viacom's finances on a firmer footing and with Showtime showing some renewed vigor, Redstone and Biondi began to plan how to make Viacom a leader in the production of creative entertainment content. In a strategic alliance with the Hearst Corp. and Capital Cities/ABC Inc., Viacom introduced Lifetime, a channel geared toward women. Viacom Pictures was started in 1989 so that the company could make its own movies. Viacom Pictures produced ten feature films in its first year at a cost of about $4 million a film, a very low cost compared with the money major studios such as Paramount and Universal spent. Under Biondi, Viacom's television production operations, which had only achieved mixed results, also achieved great success. Some successes were *Matlock* for NBC and *Jake and the Fatman* for CBS. To encourage the growth of the important Showtime channel further, in October 1989

Redstone sold 50 percent of Showtime to TCI, a major cable systems operator, for $225 million. TCI now had a major incentive to market Showtime to its millions of customers. In November of 1989, Viacom bought five more radio stations for $121 million to add to the nine it already owned.

Together with the five television stations and the fourteen cable systems it owned, all of Viacom's assets earned revenues of $1.4 billion in 1989 and generated profits of $131 million. However, while Viacom's sales continued to increase, in 1990 and 1991 Viacom had losses of $89 million and $49 million on sales of $1.6 billion and $1.7 billion, respectively.

VIACOM IN THE 1990S

With their new organization up and running, Redstone and Biondi faced the task of positioning Viacom for growth in the 1990s. Both executives felt that developing and expanding Viacom's strengths in programming—often referred to as entertainment software—was the key to its future success. They believed that the message, or content, that is sent is what really matters, not the medium or channels that carry it. As CEO Biondi put it, "In the end, a pipe is just a pipe. The customer won't give a danm how the information reaches him. All that matters is the message."

To build its programming strengths, Biondi went to work to build and expand on Viacom's MTV channels. His goal was to promote MTV networks as global brands that are perceived as having something unique to offer. Since MTV's viewers dominate the record-buying audience, Biondi sought to negotiate exclusive contracts that give MTV the first crack at playing most major record companies' music videos, thus making the channel unique. At the same time, under their control MTV went from being a purely music video channel as they championed new kinds of programming to appeal to a young audience. The result was innovative programming such as *Beavis and Butthead, Road Stories,* and other kinds of youth-oriented programming interspersed with music videos. In addition, Redstone and Biondi did not neglect the lucrative licensing market that accompanies hit television series. An example of this was when a slew of activity toys made by Mattel for new Nickelodeon characters hit the shelves in 1992. The Beavis and Butthead phenomenon also generated many lucrative spinoff products.[9]

In developing its programming strategy, however, Viacom's interest was not in promoting certain specific programs or stars (all of which may have short-lived popularity or fame) but in building its networks as unique brands. For example, on the MTV channel, the goal is to attract viewers because of what the channel as a whole personifies—an appeal to youth. Its success is based not on any particular person but because of what MTV stands for. Under its new management, MTV prospered and its franchise was extended into Europe, Asia, and Latin America. MTV now reaches 250 million households in seventy-four countries. Even Ted Turner's CNN is not as dominant overseas.[10] Viacom began to perform much better; in 1992 it made profits of $48 million on sales of $1.86 billion, and in 1993 it made profits of $70 million on sales of $2 billion.[11]

While the development of innovative new programming was one reason for Viacom's return to profitability, a second, very important reason was Redstone's emphasis on keeping costs under control. Redstone is well known for his frugal way of doing business. He runs Viacom in a cost-conscious manner, and this trend is evident throughout the organization, from the top executives to the lower levels of management. For example, Redstone has his office not in a prestigious Park Avenue, New York, location as the large networks do, but in a small unimposing building a couple of blocks from New York's red-light district. Despite his personal net worth of more than $2 billion, he still walks to work every morning and only on occasions takes a taxi.

Redstone tries to instill his cost-conscious attitude down the organization and on into its business ventures to its business projects. For example, costs have spiraled at many Hollywood studios and television networks because the producers are at the mercy of talent agencies who demanded high prices for their stars, high-priced writers, and expensive production companies. Not so with Viacom. Redstone demanded that all its own programming be produced by its own employees using low-cost, homegrown talent.[12] An example of this is the production of its MTV shows. All of its hosts are virtually unknown and are paid little relative to network hosts such as Dan Rather or Barbara Walters, who, are paid millions of dollars a year. When one of the series produced by Viacom became a hit, the agent for the star of the show demanded that the actor receive a big increase in pay. Redstone decided not to pay the price and hired a new actor at a much lower cost. In 1990 Viacom opened a state-of-the-art production facility in Orlando, Florida—Nickelodeon Studios Florida—to produce its own programming for its kids' network and thus keep its costs down.

TABLE 1			
Viacom Inc. and Subsidiaries Consolidated Statements of Operations ***(in millions, except per share amounts)***			

	Year Ended December 31		
	1995	**1994**	**1993**
Revenues	$11,688.7	$7,363.2	$2,004.9
Expenses:			
Operating	7,072.7	4,401.0	877.6
Selling, general and administrative	2,302.3	1,888.2	589.2
Depreciation and amortization	820.4	465.7	153.1
Total expenses	10,195.4	6,754.9	1,619.9
Operating income	1,493.3	608.3	385.0
Other income (expense):			
Interest expense, net	(821.4)	(494.1)	(145.0)
Other items, net	17.3	262.5	61.8
Earnings from continuing operations before income taxes	689.2	376.7	301.8
Provision for income taxes	(417.0)	(279.7)	(129.8)
Equity in earnings (loss) of affiliated companies, net of tax	(53.9)	18.6	(2.5)
Minority interest	(3.4)	14.9	—
Net earnings from continuing operations	214.9	130.5	169.5
Earnings (loss) from discontinued operations, net of tax	7.6	(20.5)	—
Earnings before extraordinary loss and cumulative effect of change in accounting principle,	222.5	110.0	169.5
Extraordinary loss, net of tax	—	(20.4)	(8.9)
Cumulative effect of change in accounting principle	—	—	10.4
Net earnings	222.5	89.6	171.0
Cumulative convertible preferred stock dividend requirement	60.0	75.0	12.8
Net earnings attributable to common stock	$ 162.5	$ 14.6	$ 158.2
Primary and fully diluted net earnings per common share:			
Net earnings from continuing operations	$ .41	$ .25	$ 1.30
Earnings (loss) from discontinued operations, net of tax	.02	(.09)	—
Extraordinary loss, net of tax	—	(.09)	(.07)
Cumulative effect of change in accounting principle	—	—	.08
Net earnings	$ .43	$ .07	$ 1.31
Weighted average number of common shares and common share equivalents:			
Primary	375.1	220.0	120.6
Fully diluted	375.5	220.4	120.6

MAJOR NEW DEVELOPMENTS

In their efforts to build their company's programming strengths, Redstone and Biondi realized that the environment around them was rapidly changing and that it was not at all clear how programming would be delivered to customers in the future. First, in the early 1990s the cable television industry was in a state of flux in the United States. Emerging technologies such as wireless microwave transmission threatened to bypass traditional cable systems, rendering Viacom's investment in wired cable much less valuable. Second, pressures were building to deregulate the telecommunications industry and to allow different kinds of companies, for example, cable companies and telephone companies, to enter each other's markets. A number of regional phone companies interested in supplying television programming to their phone customers through new fiber-optic phone lines contacted Redstone. These companies wanted to take advantage of Viacom's programming capabilities and transmit its channels through their phone lines.

Increasingly, Redstone and Biondi came to believe that during the coming decade, the most successful companies would not be those that offered customers a channel into the home—by cable, telephone wire, or wireless transmission. Instead, they believed that to prosper in this fast-changing environment an entertainment company should be the provider of the entertainment to all these channels. In other words, the most successful companies would be those that could offer the programming to go on the channels. With its MTV, Nickelodeon, Showtime, and Cinemax channels, as well as its syndicated programming and ability to make its own programming, Viacom was in a good position to form alliances with the companies that provided the channels into the home. Viacom would provide the software (the programming) to the companies that provided the hardware (the wired and wireless cable companies and telephone companies). However, Redstone and Biondi realized that to promote Viacom's strengths in programming would be both very difficult and very expensive; a large infusion of cash would be needed.

THE PARAMOUNT MERGER

Viacom now had a new mission to become a software-driven company and a goal to drive its entertainment software through every distribution system, to every Multimedia application, and to every region on earth.[13] To achieve Viacom's mission, Redstone began to search for a company that possessed the software strengths that could produce the programming content for worldwide distribution. In particular, he went looking for an entertainment company that had an already established film studio that would round out Viacom's programming portfolio by supplying feature films and television shows to its channels. Paramount provided Redstone with his opportunity.

Paramount's many businesses included both entertainment and publishing. Its entertainment businesses included the production, financing, and distribution of motion pictures, television programming, and prerecorded videocassettes. They included operation of motion picture theaters, independent television stations, regional theme parks, and Madison Square Garden. Paramount also owned a large library of movies. Paramount's publishing interests included the publication and distribution of hardcover and paperback books for the general public; textbooks for elementary schools, high schools, and colleges; and the provision of information services for businesses and professionals.[14]

Redstone and Biondi began to picture the extensive synergies that a merger with Paramount would provide Viacom in the future. As Redstone told reporters, "This merger is not about two plus two equaling four, but six, or eight, or ten."[15] Redstone believed that together Viacom and Paramount would be a much more efficient organization. He had a vision, for example, of Paramount's making films that featured MTV characters such as Beavis and Butthead and new cable television channels supported by Paramount's library of 1,800 films and 6,100 television programs. Both Redstone and Biondi believed that Paramount was a priceless asset for an entertainment company hoping to provide a broad range of programming content for future distribution to global customers. With its strengths not just in visual programming but also ill publishing books and magazines, Viacom would become a multimedia entertainment powerhouse that could redraw the competitive map in the entertainment industry.[16]

On September 12, 1993, after behind-the-scene talks between Redstone and Paramount executives, Paramount announced an $8.2 billion merger with Viacom. Soon, however, a bidding war for Paramount started. Barry Diller, the CEO of QVS Network Inc., another large entertainment company and the owner of the home-shopping network, recognized the logic behind Viacom's strategy and announced a hostile bid for Paramount. On September 20,1993, QVC announced an $80 per share, or $9.5 billion, bid for Paramount, and the battle between Viacom and QVC for ownership of Paramount Communications Inc. was on.

TABLE 2

Viacom Inc. and Subsidiaries Consolidated Balance Sheets (in millions)

	December 31, 1995	December 31, 1994
Assets		
Current Assets:		
Cash and cash equivalents	$ 464.1	$ 597.7
Receivables, less allowances of $126.0 (1995) and $75.8 (1994)	1,872.4	1,638.8
Inventory	903.1	830.9
Theatrical and television inventory	1,275.0	986.9
Other current assets	684.4	503.5
Net assets of discontinued operations	—	697.4
Total current assets	5,199.0	5.255.2
Property and Equipment		
Land	477.6	470.3
Buildings	1,161.7	798.8
Cable television systems	539.8	465.4
Equipment and other	1,795.6	1,365.1
	3,974.7	3,099.6
Less accumulated depreciation and amortization	756.8	516.5
Net property and equipment	3,217.9	2,583.1
Inventory	2,271.5	1,944.5
Intangibles, at amortized cost	16,153.2	16,111.7
Other assets	2,184.4	2,379.2
	$29,026.0	$28,273.7
Liabilities and Shareholders' Equity		
Current Liabilities:		
Accounts payable	$ 788.8	$ 770.9
Accrued interest	149.8	234.9
Deferred income	243.5	250.9
Merger consideration payable	167.4	261.7
Accrued compensation	449.4	340.6
Other accrued expenses	1,216.0	1,436.8
Participants' share, residuals and royalties payable	798.2	630.0
Program rights	240.4	184.4
Current portion of long-term debt	45.1	21.0
Total current liabilities	4,098.6	4,131.2
Long-term debt	10,712.1	10,402.4
Other liabilities	2,121.5	1,948.5
Commitments and contingencies		
Shareholders' Equity:		
Preferred Stock, par value $.01 per share; 200.0 shares authorized; 24.0 (1995) and 24.0 (1994) shares issued and outstanding	1.200.0	1,200.0
Class A Common Stock, par value $.01 per share; 200.0 shares authorized; 75.1 (1995) and 74.6 (1994) shares issued and outstanding	0.8	0.7
Class B Common Stock, par value $.01 per share; 1,000.0 shares authorized; 294.6 (1995) and 284.1 (1994) shares issued and outstanding	2.9	2.8
Additional paid-in capital	10,726.9	10,579.5
Retained earnings	173.1	10.6
Cumulative translation adjustments	(9.9)	(2.0)
Total shareholders' equity	12,093.8	11,791.6
	$29,026.0	$28.273.7

This unwelcome bid from QVS presented a significant problem for Redstone. He still had substantial debt that was the result of his original 1986 acquisition of Viacom and because of its rapid development of its own television programming, Redstone could not afford to counter QVS's bid unless he obtained other sources of financing, and he had to search around for partners to support his bid. After a career of financing deals with his own pocketbook, including the 1986 Viacom takeover, the 70-year-old tycoon was forced to turn to other companies to rescue the Paramount deal.[17] Redstone found two potential partners in NYNEX and Blockbuster.

NYNEX, one of the Baby Bell companies, anticipating that deregulation would allow it to enter the cable television market, wanted an alliance with a company that could supply it with programming content. Blockbuster Entertainment Corp., under its own energetic CEO, Wayne Huizenga, had grown to become the largest chain of video stores in the nation. Blockbuster was cash rich as a result of its recent rapid growth. Huizenga, recognizing the threat that the growth in electronic movie mediums (such as video pay-per-view, wireless cable, and videos through fiber-optic phone lines) could pose to the sale and rental of videocassettes, was on the lookout for a way to reduce this risk. He agreed to support Redstone's bid for Paramount as a way of diversifying Blockbuster's interests.

Redstone was not anxious to forge alliances with these companies, commenting that alliances are tricky: "No one who is not a hypocrite or a liar can guarantee how a relationship will look in the future." Moreover, Redstone also saw that Blockbuster's future was in doubt as a result of the growth in electronic means of providing home movie videos. However, his need for cash to outbid QVS for ownership of Paramount was stronger than his worries about forming the alliances. On October 21, 1993, after having aligned himself with these partners, Redstone obtained $600 million cash from Blockbuster and a $1.2 billion commitment from NYNEX Corp. Redstone then used this money to match QVC's offer of $80 per share for 51 percent of Paramount stock with the rest in Viacom stock. Furthermore, anticipating a higher offer by QVC, Viacom raised its bid to $85 a share for 51 percent of the stocks. Many analysts argued that this bidding war had become a personal battle between Redstone and QVC Chairman Barry Diller and that whoever was the winner was doomed to pay too much for Paramount.

On December 20 QVC raised its offer to $92 a share in cash for 50.1 percent, topping the offer of Viacom, which asked for more time to raise cash. Although Paramount signed a merger agreement with QVC on December 22, the bidding could continue with a deadline for final bids on February 1, 1994. Redstone, desperate for more cash, went to Blockbuster CEO Wayne Huizenga for more money. Huizenga, increasingly convinced that it was in the best interests of Blockbuster's shareholders to merge with Viacom, suggested that Viacom should take over Blockbuster for a hefty stock price. Redstone, recognizing the value of Blockbuster's cash reserves and huge cash flow from current operations, agreed. On January 7, 1994, Viacom announced an $8.4 billion merger with Blockbuster Entertainment. It also announced a new bid for Paramount for $105 a share in cash.

Diller hinted that he would sweeten his deal, but on February 13 he announced that QVC would not increase its bid. On February 15, 1995, Viacom won the takeover battle, claiming 75 percent of Paramount stock.[18] After a bruising nearly six-month battle with QVC, Viacom gained full ownership of Paramount on July 7, 1994. Redstone hailed the new Viacom as an "entertainment colossus" and "a massive global media company."[19]

THE NEW VIACOM

In a few short years, Redstone had gone from controlling several hundred movie theaters to controlling the properties and franchises of three major *Fortune* 500 companies—Viacom, Blockbuster Entertainment, and Paramount. Viacom had become one of the four largest entertainment companies in the world. (See Exhibit 1 for Viacom's revenue growth over time.) The value of the entertainment resources—both creative content and distribution—that Redstone and Biondi had to manage to create for aft of Viacom's new shareholders is described in the text that follows.

Creative Content

Viacom is one of the world leaders in the production of creative content and controls some of the most valuable entertainment and publishing brand names.

Motion Pictures   Viacom now controls Paramount Pictures, a world leader in the production of feature films such as *Mission Impossible, Braveheart, Forrest Gump, Clear and Present Danger,* and *Star Trek Generations.* Spelling Films International, a unit of Spelling Entertainment in which

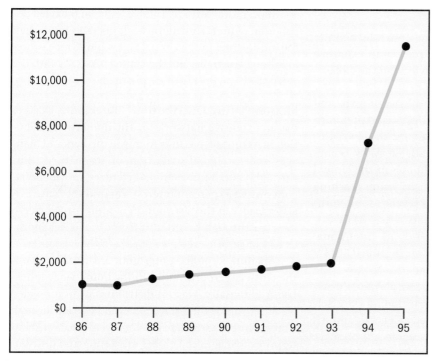

EXHIBIT 1   Viacom's Revenues, 1986–1995 (in millions of dollars).

Viacom holds a majority interest, coproduces up to ten films annually with major studios.

Television   Paramount Television is a large supplier of television programming for the broadcast, first-run syndication, and cable markets (for example, *Wings, Frazier, Matlock,* and *The Montel Williams Show*). Spelling Entertainment is a unit of Paramount that produces hit television series including *Beverly Hills 90210, Melrose Place,* and *Madman of the People.* Paramount Television, Viacom Productions, and Spelling Entertainment possess libraries of nearly 50,000 hours of network television programming, including half-hour and hour-long shows such as *Cheers, I Love Lucy,* and *Star Trek.*

Networks   Viacom controls the MTV networks (MTV, MTV Europe, MTV Latino, Nickelodeon, Nick at Nite, VH1, VH-1 U.K.). Innovative new programming from these networks includes *MTV Unplugged, The Real World,* Nickelodeon's animated programs such as *The Ren and Stimpy Show* and *Rugrats,* and VH1 (the premiere twenty-four-hour music network for twenty-five to forty-year-old music viewers). Showtime Networks Inc. includes Showtime, The Movie Channel, FLIX, the Sundance Channel, Set Pay per View, and Showtime en Español.

Publishing   Heading the list of publishers is Simon & Schuster, the largest educational book publisher in. the nation and a world-recognized publishing leader. In addition to its significant operations serving the consumer, business, and reference and professional markets, it is also the leading publisher of educational materials. Major imprints include Simon & Schuster, Pocket Books, Scribner, Silver Burdett Ginn, Prentice-Hall, Allyn & Bacon, The Free Press, and Macmillan Publishing USA.

Finally, Viacom is at the forefront in developing advanced technology and products for the expanding entertainment and educational interactive, multimedia marketplace. Viacom has a 90 percent interest in Viacom New Media and Viacom Interactive Entertainment, which develops, produces, publishes, markets, and distributes interactive software in the multimedia marketplace. These combined operations make Viacom one of the largest suppliers of multimedia software. Viacom New Media titles are Richard Scarry's *How Things Work in Busytown,* MTV's *Beavis and Butthead,* and Nickelodeon's *Director's Lab* and *Rocko's Modern Life.* Simon & Schuster Interactive also develops and markets entertainment, educational, and reference titles for the consumer market. In fact, it is the foremost and fastest-growing publisher of computer-based learning systems in the country.

Distribution

Viacom controls a vast and comprehensive distribution network that delivers its new programming, extensive libraries, and brands to consumers around the globe.

Cable and Broadcast Television Viacom owns and operates the largest group of basic cable and premium cable networks in the United States, and the global impact of these networks is unparalleled. MTV is currently in more than 58 million homes in the United States. It also has a worldwide distribution reaching more than 250 million homes in seventy-four countries through its international networks—MTV Europe and MTV Latino—as well as its intentional affiliates—MTV Brazil, MTV Internacional, MTV Japan, MTV Asia, and MTV Mandarin. Nickelodeon and VH1 also are international. Viacom also participates in several joint venture networks, including USA Network, the Sci-Fi Channel, Comedy Central, and All News Channel. It also maintains a significant presence in the premium cable and pay-per-view markets through its ownership of Showtime, The Movie Channel, FLIX, Showtime en Español, and SET Pay per View. Through Showtime Satellite Networks, Viacom is the largest distributor of basic cable programming to the home satellite dish market.

Viacom's television stations cover 15 percent of the United States and five of the top eleven markets. They are in the process of divesting and acquiring different stations to build a nationwide network of television stations to distribute Viacom's new UPN channel as well as its other channels. Viacom's Paramount division is spending millions to acquire new television networks to compete with the Big Three and Fox.

Viacom Radio is the sixth largest radio group in the United States ranked by market reach. The group owns and operates stations in seven of the top ten markets.

Viacom Cable owns and operates cable systems serving approximately 1. 1 million customers in the United States. Their systems are clustered in three regions of the country: the California region, the Puget Sound region, and the Midwest region.

Retail   Blockbuster Video is the largest retailer of home-video products in the world, operating more than 4,100 stores in fifty states in the United States and ten countries around the world. The company plans to enhance dramatically both its domestic and international presence over the next several years with many thousands of new stores planned.

Blockbuster Music is a global leader in the retail distribution of prerecorded music. It operates more than 550 music stores in the United States and 18 megastores in Europe, Australia, and the United States. As with the video stores, many more are planned.

Motion Picture Distribution   Paramount Pictures has an extensive network for the domestic distribution of its motion pictures to movie theaters and manages the foreign distribution of its feature films through United International Pictures, in which Viacom owns a 33 percent interest. Paramount Pictures is also a leader in the distribution of prerecorded videocassettes through Paramount Home Video, yet another way of getting creative content to the customer.

Spelling Republic Entertainment Home Video is the tenth largest distributor in the home-video industry. Additionally, Viacom distributes its home-video products outside the United States and Canada through Cinema International, B.V., a joint venture. World Enterprises manages the global marketing and distribution of Spelling's film and programming library to television, basic and premium cable, and home-video outlets.

Viacom plays a significant part in global film exhibition. It owns and operates Famous Players, a 465-screen theater chain in Canada; jointly owns the 349-screen Cinamerica circuit in the western United States; and jointly owns United Cinemas International, which operates 424 screens in nine countries.

Live Entertainment

Viacom has a strong and expanding presence in the burgeoning field of out-of-home entertainment.

Paramount Parks   A world leader in family entertainment, 12 million visitors annually visit five regional theme parks: Kings Island at Cincinnati, Ohio; Kings Dominion at Richmond, Virginia; Great America at Santa Clara, California; Carowinds at Charlotte, North Carolina; and Canada's Wonderland at Toronto, Canada. Parks have many rides and themed areas drawn from Paramount's various films and library titles, such as *Days of Thunder, Top Gun, Star Trek,* and *Wayne's World*. In 1995 Nickelodeon-themed areas were introduced.

Nickelodeon   As discussed earlier, Nickelodeon Studios in Orlando is the center of all production for the kids' network as well as the featured attraction of Universal Studios Florida. Since opening in 1990, Nickelodeon Studios has produced more than 1,200 programs and specials and has auditioned more than 24,500 hopeful participants for its shows. Nickelodeon Extreme Baseball at Shea, an action adventure arena for kids and families at Shea Stadium in New York, opened to the public in July 1994.

By engineering the three-way merger of Viacom, Paramount, and Blockbuster Entertainment, Redstone created one of the three largest media empires in the United States (the others being the Disney-Capital Cities/ABC and Time Warner-Turner, after the merger between Time Warner and Turner in 1996), with annual revenues in excess of $10 billion. This is a large jump from the $2 billion revenue that Viacom had just before these mergers. However, Redstone and Biondi faced several major challenges in managing Viacom's new entertainment empire.

ENGINEERING SYNERGIES

To justify the expensive purchase of Paramount and Blockbuster, it became essential that Redstone and Biondi engineer synergies between the different Viacom divisions just listed. Several efforts were immediately begun. Paramount's executives were instructed to evaluate the potential of new shows developed by MTV for sale to top television networks and stations. Viacom launched its new channel, the United Paramount Network (UPN), in January 1995 in conjunction with Paramount's partner, Chris-Craft Industries.[20] Executives of MTV Productions were instructed to begin quickly developing programming for the new network channel, which in 1996 was only on the air a few hours a day but through its 124 affiliates can reach 86.5 percent of all television households in the United States.

In another attempt to create synergies, Paramount's executives were instructed to make their moviemaking skills available to the MTV network and to help it make inexpensive movies that could be distributed through Paramount. One result of this was a Beavis and Butthead movie produced by Paramount and scheduled for late 1996. This was a first step in Redstone's strategy to boost the output of movies at the Paramount studio without having to finance a big increase in the studio's own movie budget.[21]

Redstone and Biondi also searched for synergies between Blockbuster and Viacom's other divisions. For example, they hoped that Blockbuster could link its retail stores with Viacom's cable networks and Paramount's extensive film library.[22] Perhaps Blockbuster could sell copies of Paramount's vast library of movies

to encourage people to create their own video collections. Also, the release of a new Paramount movie on video could be timed to coincide with a major advertising campaign in Blockbuster stores to promote the launch. In addition, Viacom's publishing division, Simon & Schuster, would be able to release paperback books to coincide with the release, and perhaps even a multimedia CD-ROM product could be introduced to boost sales. Finally, the launch of new movies could be timed to coincide with a major advertising blitz on the MTV channel, something which happened when Paramount released *Mission Impossible,* a youth-oriented movie, in the summer of 1996.

Viacom's top executives also planned to use Blockbuster's massive database of 50 million videorental customers to reverse engineer Paramount movies. The idea is to look at the entertainment tastes of consumers in this database and tailor Paramount's films to appeal to the customer, right down to the casting of actors. Viacom is also aggressively staking out the video-game market, in which Blockbuster is already an important player and Viacom is a latecomer. As Redstone said, "Viacom through its new combination of assets is poised to participate in, and in many ways define, the entertainment and information explosion about to engulf the globe.[23] Clearly, there is enormous potential for synergies to emerge between Viacom's various divisions. The contribution of each business unit to Viacom's revenues and profits is shown in Exhibits 2 and 3.

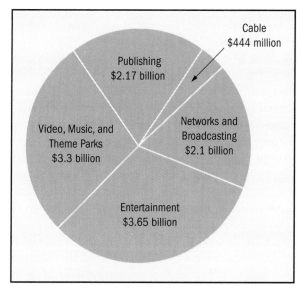

EXHIBIT 2 Breakdown of Viacom's Revenues by Business Segment, 1995

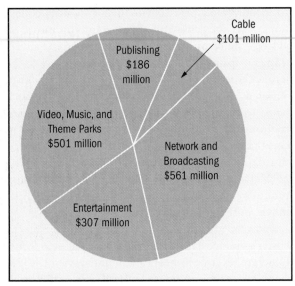

Cable
$101 million

Publishing
$186
million

Video, Music, and
Theme Parks
$501 million

Network and
Broadcasting
$561 million

Entertainment
$307 million

EXHIBIT 3   Breakdown of Viacom's Operating Profit by Business Segment, 1995

REDUCING DEBT

Obtaining synergies was one major challenge facing Viacom's top managers. Reducing debt was another. Because Viacom had nearly $12 billion in debt against just $4.8 billion in equity after the Paramount deal, Redstone realized the need to sell off some assets to reduce this debt. In keeping with Viacom's new strategy of being a provider of programming content, Redstone sought to protect his creative entertainment assets and decided to sell Viacom's distribution assets—some of Paramount's properties and its extensive cable system. The first asset to be put on the block was Madison Square Garden. There were many bids, but the best was by ITT and Cablevision, which bid $1.08 billion. The sale was finalized on March 10, 1995. Redstone also sold Viacom's 33 percent in the Lifetime cable network to its other partners, Capital Cities and Hearst, for about $318 million; television station VTXF-TV in Philadelphia to Fox for $200 million; and some television stations in San Antonio and Raleigh-Durham for undisclosed sums. Redstone had no intention of selling Paramount's seven television stations, however, which distributed the new United Paramount network to many major markets. Simon & Schuster, Viacom's publishing division, was also instructed to sell nonessential assets, and six professional book divisions were sold off because it was decided that they did not fit the publisher's strategy of focusing on consumer, education, business, reference, and international publishing.[24] Also, Viacom attempted to sell

Spelling Entertainment for $1 billion in late 1994 but then withdrew from the sale after it could not find a buyer at this price.

On January 20,1995, Viacom announced that it would sell its cable television systems division to a partnership of which Mitgo Corp., a company wholly owned by Frank Washington, a minority owner, was a part. The price was approximately $2.3 billion, subject to certain conditions. One of the main conditions of the sale was that Viacom receive a tax break for selling to a minority-controlled broadcasting partnership, which would allow Viacom to shelter $600 million in profits from taxes. However, Congress voted to repeal this tax loophole, and Viacom had to search for a new buyer. It found one in TCI Cable, one of the five biggest cable companies in the United States, which agreed to pay Viacom $1.6 billion for its cable interests. However, one of TCI's competitors filed a regulatory complaint to block the deal, and as of July 1996 the sales of its cable assets had not been finalized. Thus, Viacom is still saddled with a tremendous burden of debt at the same time that it is being forced to spend hundreds of millions of dollars to build a core strength in the production of creative programming and achieve synergies between its divisions.

MEDIA AND ENTERTAINMENT INDUSTRY CHALLENGES

The fast-changing entertainment and media industry also created many challenges for Redstone and Biondi. Currently, the major Hollywood players are changing rapidly. In the old Hollywood, seven major studios dominated film and television production, while the Big three networks—ABC, CBS, and NBC—delivered the programming to mass audiences. Now, the number of distribution channels is exploding, and the well-established relationship between producers and distributors is eroding.

Government regulations that bar broadcast networks from owning TV programs are also being phased out, which is the main reason why producers of major television programming such as Warner Bros. Inc. and Paramount started their own networks. The competitive dynamics of the industry are changing dramatically, and Viacom's strategy to develop a full line of entertainment programming fits well with the changes that are occurring in the industry. Also, as discussed previously, the regulations that prohibit telephone and cable companies from invading each other's turf are quickly being eliminated, prompting the Baby Bells to deliver video services. That is the main reason why many of these phone companies want to make a deal with

Viacom so that they are able to obtain access to Viacom's innovative programming and network channels. Emerging digital and wireless technology has vastly expanded the carrying capacity of cable and television networks. With hundreds of new channels to be offered, the search is on for high-impact programming to break through the clutter.[25] Also, in 1996 a new form of CD capable of holding one or several movies was introduced. Although this new CD requires a new kind of CD player, it is expected to replace the videotape within ten years.

The media and entertainment industry has also been growing because of rapid globalization. One of the key reasons for this globalization is the spread of U.S. movies, news, and television around the world. The U.S. market is the largest indigenous market for entertainment, so it has the advantage of being used as a test bed for American products. However, as the standard of living in many of the other countries increases, opportunities for expansion abroad are growing quickly. The key developments that ushered in a truly global entertainment market were the introduction of the VCR and the emergence of capitalism in communist-block countries. The VCRs created an environment that whet peoples' appetites with its introduction of new markets for feature films and television programming. A major challenge facing Viacom is to obtain access to the global marketplace, with a potential market of 900 million viewers in India and a billion-plus in China. Entertainment companies cannot ignore the global marketplace.[26] As an example of Viacom's global push, in March 1995 Viacom won a cable-television license to launch its Nickelodeon children's channel in Germany, Europe's biggest and potentially most lucrative media market. Also in 1995, Viacom got the green light to launch its VH-1 music channel in Germany to complement the MTV pop music network, which has operated in Europe since 1987.[27]

Finally, the growth of Viacom spurred the growing consolidation of the entertainment industry. In 1995 Time Warner announced that it would merge with Turner Broadcasting, and Disney announced that it would merge with Capital Cities/ABC. As a result, the industry is now composed of four major players: Viacom; Disney; Time Warner; and News Corp., headed by Rupert Murdoch, which owns the Fox channel.

STRUCTURE AND MANAGEMENT CHALLENGES

As discussed previously, 70-year-old Sumner Redstone is a manager who loves to take control and deal with the day-to-day running of the company. Redstone constantly gets involved in the problems facing the various divisions. He moved quickly to develop his own top management team across Viacom's new divisions and to install his cost-conscious frugal values in divisional managers. Paramount was run by an all-powerful boss, Martin S. Davis, and a group of executives who indulged in luxuries such as flying in corporate jets and spending company funds lavishly. Compare this with Redstone who flies on commercial airlines and walks or takes a cab to work. Redstone sold Paramount's two corporate jets and installed his own cost-conscious managers to change Paramount's free-spending habits. In 1994 Viacom dismissed Richard E. Snyder, the head-strong chairman of Simon & Schuster, also an executive known for his free-spending ways, and replaced him with Jonathan Newcomb, who has made his name as a competent administrator rather than a visionary publisher. Newcomb still plans to continue Snyder's strategy of overseas expansion and technological innovation, however.[28]

Through 1995, Viacom was run by a team of four managers: Redstone, Biondi, and two executive vice presidents, Thomas E. Dooley and Philippe P. Dauman, protégés of Redstone. Dooley and Dauman handle the nuts and bolts of the process of consolidating Viacom's assets to reduce costs and to create synergies. Viacom's organizational structure is illustrated in Exhibit 4.

THE CURRENT SITUATION

Soon after Redstone's expensive decision to buy Paramount, the Paramount movie, *Forrest Gump,* became a surprise hit generating more than $250 million for Viacom and silencing Redstone's critics who had argued that he spent too much to buy the movie company. Viacom's managers began to feel that as with Forrest Gump, with his philosophy that "life is like a box of chocolates: You never know what you're going to get," Redstone and Viacom had been in the right place at the right time and had made a very profitable acquisition. Just as Redstone had sensed the potential of MTV early, so too had he sensed the potential of Paramount and Blockbuster.[29]

By the summer of 1995, however, the selection of chocolates in Viacom's box did not seem as good as it did in 1994. Many of the hoped-for synergies had not been obtained or were taking longer to happen than Redstone and Biondi had hoped. For example, before the merger Redstone claimed that Blockbuster would be valuable to Viacom as a distributor of its creative

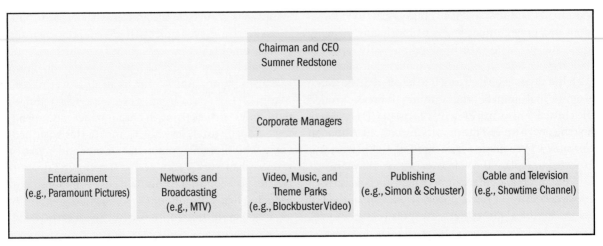

EXHIBIT 4   Viacom's Organizational Structure

programming; however, few benefits of this kind had been achieved. Similarly, analysts argued that Paramount must work much more closely with Viacom's cable television channels and with Blockbuster Video if synergies were to be forthcoming. Moreover, the performance of both the Paramount and Blockbuster divisions had been disappointing.

The Gump smash hit (which generated $300 million in movie theater revenues in 1994 and $200 million in 1995 from the sales of more than 16 million videocassettes) had been followed by a string of expensive failures. Redstone and Biondi had begun to realize that making movies is a very risky business and that past successes are no indication of future success. Paramount's share of the box office dropped from 14 percent in 1994 to 10 percent in 1995. Moreover, Redstone was annoyed about the high marketing and production costs of the movies that Paramount was making, and after a string of failures including *Jade, Sabrina,* and *Home for the Holidays,* wanted to know why the studio had spent $20 million advertising another flop, *Nick of Time,* which was clearly a loser.

Hit movies are vital to a movie studio because they provide the cash flow that pays for the flops and bankrolls the future. Paramount's poor performance was hurting Viacom's cash flow and ability to service its debt. Moreover, box-office hits are crucial because they drive the rest of a movie studio's profits from international markets to home video and television.[30]

To compound the Paramount problem, the Blockbuster division was also not doing well. Viacom had bought Blockbuster at the peak of its success, when its revenues were doubling every year. After the acquisi-

tion Blockbuster began to run into intense competition from two sources. First, a number of rival video chains had sprung up that were giving it intense competition. Second, pay-per-view television was spreading rapidly, especially in large urban markets, and the emergence of electronically transmitted video—which could then be taped (illegally) for future use—was taking away its customers. Blockbuster's revenues were flat, and the anticipated growth in cash flow to help service Viacom's debts had not occurred.

To make matters worse, Redstone had a failing out with the top management teams of Paramount and Blockbuster, which he thought were not doing a good job. Then, after forcing the resignations of many key executives, he had to search for new leadership talent. In January 1996 he stunned the entertainment world when he announced that he was firing his second in command, Frank Biondi, who was well respected throughout Hollywood, because he believed Biondi did not have the hands-on skills to manage the kinds of problems that Viacom was facing. Redstone felt that Biondi's decentralized management style was out of place in a company actively searching for synergies. In place of Biondi he promoted his two lieutenants, Phillipe Dauman and Tom Dooley, to orchestrate Viacom's strategy even though these executives had little direct experience of the entertainment business.

In March 1996 he hired William Fields to be the CEO and chairman of the Blockbuster division. Fields, formerly the next in line to be CEO of Wal-Mart, is a manager who has had extensive experience in running efficient retail operations, and his cost-cutting skills (developed at Wal-Mart, which is also another company known for its frugality) appealed to Redstone. Redstone hoped he could find a way to transform the Blockbuster Video stores into more broad-based entertainment-software stores, given that the video-rental business is likely to be swept away by the new wireless cable and direct broadcasting technologies. In February 1996 Blockbuster announced that it planned to open more than 3,000 new stores over the next three years.

Redstone, himself, became more involved in the day-to-day running of Paramount, spending more time with its marketing and production executives to understand the workings of the business.[31] Many analysts were stunned by his decision to fire Biondi because he was the person who understood all aspects of the entertainment business. Moreover, they wondered how well a job Redstone, who is after all seventy years old, or his inexperienced two protégés would do without the aid of a seasoned entertainment executive.

Analysts also point to another major hole in Viacom's armor—its lack of a strong global presence or any executives who are experienced globally. Analysts believe that in an age when most large consumer-oriented companies are often earning 50 percent of their revenues abroad, Blockbuster must have a strong presence in today's global entertainment industry. They also note that Redstone does not have any personal international experience.

In the spring of 1996 Viacom's stock price plunged from a high of $54.50 to $35 as investors fled the stock. In the summer of 1996, after a string of flops (with the exception of one movie, *Mission Impossible*), Redstone announced plans to cut back the number of movies Paramount would make and to reduce their cost as he searched for a new strategy. However, by 1996 there were signs that some potential synergies were emerging. For example, Simon & Schuster, Viacom's publishing division, announced plans to publish a new line of books to be called Nick Jr., based on Nickelodeon's television programs such as *Gullah Gullah Island* and *Allegra's Window*. Also, MTV, in an alliance between MTV and Simon & Schuster, brought out a successful line of Beavis and Butthead titles, and, as discussed previously, Paramount produced a Beavis and Butthead movie. In addition, to bolster Viacom's global presence, Redstone formed an alliance with the German media powerhouse, the Kirch group, to promote Viacom's European movies, television programs, and television channels. Finally, in June 1996, MTV announced that it was introducing a second MTV channel to be called MTV2, which would focus exclusively on music videos, as the regular MTV channel had become more involved in regular programming. As Redstone in his April 12 annual letter to shareholders said:

> Our mission is clear: to be the premier branded content provider, to deliver our products in every medium in every region of the planet, to work collaboratively throughout the corporation to extend each of our businesses and capitalize on our collective strengths—to be the ultimate global entertainment and publishing company.

As of July 1996, the jury is out. Will Redstone retain control of his company and restore its prosperity? Analysts are worried that Redstone has no succession plan in place in the event that he is not able to carry on at the helm of Viacom. Will another CEO be brought in to turn the company around, as the Disney Company brought in Michael Eisner? Alternatively, might the empire that Sumner Redstone built collapse and its various parts be sold off to other top management teams who can realize the synergies in Viacom's famous entertainment businesses?

ENDNOTES

1. *International Directory of Company Histories*, Vol. 7 (St. James Press, 1994), pp. 560–562.
2. Ibid.
3. Ibid.
4. "The Paramount Takeover: The Drama Ended, Two Stars Get New Scripts; Viacom's Biondi Has to Stretch to Fill Big Role," *Wall Street Journal*, February 16, 1994, p. B1.
5. "The MTV Tycoon—Sumner Redstone Is Turning Viacom into the Hottest Global TV Network," *Business Week*, September 21, 1992, pp. 56–62.
6. Ibid.
7. Ibid.
8. *International Directory of Company Histories*, pp. 560–562.
9. Matthew Schifrin, "I Can't Even Remember the Old Star's Name," *Forbes*, March 16, 1992, pp. 44–45.
10. Nancy Hass, "The Message Is the Medium," *Financial World*, June 8, 1993, pp. 24–25.
11. Viacom's 1991 and 1993 Annual Reports.
12. Schifrin, "I Can't Even Remember the Old Star's Name."
13. "Redstone in Motion," *Financial World*, December 6, 1994, pp. 36–38.
14. Viacom's Annual Report, 1993.
15. "Paramount: Do I Hear $11 Billion?" *Business Week*, November 8, 1993, p. 36.

16. "The Ending of Paramount's Script May Not Be Written Yet," *Business Week*, September 27, 1993, pp. 38–39.

17. "Sumner Redstone Gets a Little Help from His Friends," *Business Week*, October 11, 1993, p. 36.

18. "The Paramount Takeover. Wall Street's Final Analysis: Might Made Right," *Wall Street Journal*, February 16, 1994, P. B1.

19. "Viacom Now Is a Full Owner of Paramount After Vote," *Wall Street Journal*, July 8, 1994, p. B9.

20. "Viacom Inc.: Paramount Gets 'First look' at MTV Unit's TV Shows," *Wall Street Journal*, November 11, 1994.

21. "Viacom Firms Up Plans for Movie Produced by MTV," *Wall Street Journal*, June 14, 1994, p. B8.

22. "Sumner at the Summit," *Business Week*, February 28, 1994, p. 32.

23. "Deals Give Viacom Even More Muscle," *Wall Street Journal*, September 30, 1994, p. B1.

24. "Viacom Unit Continues Sell-off of Businesses That Don't Fit Strategy," *Wall Street Journal*, November 22, 1994, p. B4.

25. "Hollywood Scuffle," *Business Week*, December 12, 1994, p. 38.

26. "Frank Biondi—A Media Tycoon's Take on the 21st Century" *Business Week, 21st Century Capitalism*, 1996, p. 190.

27. "Viacom Inc. Wins German license for Nickelodeon," *Wall Street Journal*, March 1, 1995, p. B10.

28. "Remaindered at Simon & Schuster," *Business Week*, June 27, 1994, p. 32.

29. "Gump Happens—And Viacom Is Thanking Its Lucky Stars," *Business Week*, August 8, 1994, p. 29.

30. J. Lippman, "Paramount Feeling the Heat in the Wake of Biondi Firing," *Wall Street Journal*, January 22, 1996, p. B1.

31. M. Robichaux, "Redstone's One-Man Show Opens at Viacom," *Wall Street Journal*, January 19, 1996, p. B1.

C A S E   1 6

Philips NV ———————————————————— CHARLES W. L. HILL

INTRODUCTION

Established in 1891, the Dutch company Philips NV is one of the world's largest electronics enterprises. Its businesses are grouped into four main divisions: lighting, consumer electronics, professional products (computers, telecommunications, and medical equipment), and components (including chips). In each of these areas it ranks alongside the likes of Matsushita, General Electric, Sony, and Siemens as a global competitor. In the late 1980s, the company had several hundred subsidiaries in sixty countries, it operated manufacturing plants in more than forty countries, it employed approximately 300,000 people, and it manufactured thousands of different products. However, despite its global reach by 1990, Philips was a company in deep trouble. After a decade of deteriorating performance, in 1990 Philips lost $2.2 billion on revenues of $28 billion. A major reason seems to have been the inability of Philips to adapt to the changing competitive conditions in the global electronics industry during the 1970s and 1980s.

PHILIPS' TRADITIONAL ORGANIZATION

To trace the roots of Philips' current troubles, one has to go back to World War II. Until then, the foreign activities of Philips had been run out of its head office in Eindhoven. However, during World War II the Netherlands was occupied by Germany. Cut off from their home base, Philips' various national organizations began to operate independently. In essence, each major national organization developed into a self-contained company with its own manufacturing, marketing, and R&D functions.

Following the war, top management felt that the company could be most successfully rebuilt through its national organizations. There were several reasons for this belief. First, high trade barriers made it logical that self-contained national organizations be established in each major national market. Second, it was felt that strong national organizations would allow Philips to be responsive to local demands in each country in which it competed. And third, given the substantial autonomy that

Charles W. L. Hill, University of Washington. Reprinted with permission.

the various national organizations had gained during the war, top management felt that reestablishing centralized control might prove difficult and yield few benefits.

At the same time, top management felt the need for some centralized control over product policy and R&D in order to achieve some coordination between national organizations. Its response was to create a number of worldwide product divisions (of which there were fourteen by the mid-1980s). In theory, basic R&D and product development policy were the responsibilities of the product divisions, whereas the national organizations were responsible for day-to-day operations in a particular country. Product strategy in a given country was meant to be determined jointly by consultation between the responsible national organization and the product divisions. It was the national organizations that implemented strategy.

Another major feature of Philips' organization was the duumvirate form of management. In most national organizations, top-management responsibilities and authority were shared by two managers—one responsible for "commercial affairs" and another responsible for "technical activities." This form of management had its origins in the company's founders—Anton and Gerard Philips. Anton was a salesman and Gerard an engineer. Throughout the company there seemed to be a vigorous, informal competition between technical and sales managers, with each attempting to outperform the other. Anton once noted:

> The technical management and the sales management competed to outperform each other. Production tried to produce so much that sales would not be able to get rid of it; sales tried to sell so much that the factory would not be able to keep up. [Aguilar and Yoshino, 1987]

The top decision-making and policy-making body in the company was a ten-person board of management. While board members all shared general management responsibility, they typically maintained a special interest in one of the functional areas of the company (for example, R&D, manufacturing, marketing). Traditionally, most of the members of the management board were Dutch and had come up through the Eindhoven bureaucracy, although most had extensive foreign postings, often as a top manager in one of the company's national organizations.

ENVIRONMENTAL CHANGE

From the 1960s onward, a number of significant changes took place in Philips' competitive environment that were to profoundly affect the company. First, due to the efforts of the General Agreement on Tariffs and Trade (GATT), trade barriers fell worldwide. In addition, in Philips' home base, Europe, the emergence of the European Economic Community, of which the Netherlands was an early member, led to a further reduction in trade barriers between the countries of Western Europe.

Second, during the 1960s and 1970s a number of new competitors emerged in Japan. Taking advantage of the success of GATT in lowering trade barriers, the Japanese companies produced most of their output at home and then exported to the rest of the world. The resulting economies of scale allowed them to drive down unit costs below those achieved by Western competitors such as Philips that manufactured in multiple locations. This significantly increased competitive pressures in most of the business areas where Philips competed.

Third, due to technological changes, the cost of R&D and manufacturing increased rapidly. The introduction of transistors and then integrated circuits called for significant capital expenditures in production facilities—often running into hundreds of millions of dollars. To realize scale economies, substantial levels of output had to be achieved. Moreover, the pace of technological change was declining and product life cycles were shortening. This gave companies in the electronics industry less time to recoup their capital investments before new-generation products came along.

Finally, as the world moved from a series of fragmented national markets toward a single global market, uniform global standards for electronic equipment were beginning to emerge. This standardization showed itself most clearly in the videocassette recorder business, where three standards initially battled for dominance—the Betamax standard produced by Sony, the VHS standard produced by Matsushita, and the V2000 standard produced by Philips. The VHS standard was the one most widely accepted by consumers, and the others were eventually abandoned. For Philips and Sony, both of which had invested substantially in their own standard, this was a significant defeat. Philips's attempt to establish its V2000 format as an industry standard was effectively killed off by the decision of its own North American national organization, over the objections of Eindhoven, to manufacture according to the VHS standard.

ORGANIZATIONAL AND STRATEGIC CHANGE

By the early 1980s Philips realized that, if it was to survive, it would have to restructure its business radically. Its cost structure was high due to the amount of duplication across national organizations, particularly in the area of manufacturing. Moreover, as the V2000 incident demonstrated, the company's attempts to compete effectively were being hindered by the strength and autonomy of its national organizations.

The first attempt at change came in 1982 when Wisse Dekker was appointed CEO. Dekker quickly pushed for manufacturing rationalization, creating international production centers that served a number of national organizations and closing many small inefficient plants. He also pushed Philips to enter into more collaborative arrangements with other electronics firms in order to share the costs and risks of developing new products. In addition, Dekker accelerated a trend that had already begun within the company to move away from the dual leadership arrangement within national organizations (commercial and technical), replacing this arrangement with a single general manager. Furthermore, Dekker tried to "tilt" Philips' matrix away from national organizations by creating a corporate council where the heads of product divisions would join the heads of the national organizations to discuss issues of importance to both. At the same time, he gave the product divisions more responsibility to determine companywide research and manufacturing activities.

In 1986, Dekker was succeeded by Cor van de Klugt. One of van de Klugt's first actions was to specify that profitability was to be the central criterion for evaluating performance within Philips. The product divisions were given primary responsibility for achieving profits. This was followed in late 1986 by his termination of the U.S. Philips trust, which had been given control of Philips's North American operations during World War II and which still maintained control as of 1986. By terminating the trust, van de Klugt in theory reestablished Eindhoven's control over the North American subsidiary. Then, in May 1987, van de Klugt announced a major restructuring of Philips. He designated four product divisions—lighting, consumer electronics, components, and telecommunications and data systems—as "core divisions," the implication being that other activities would be sold off. At the same time he reduced the size of the management board. Its policy-making responsibility was devolved to a new group management committee, comprising the remaining board members plus the heads of the core product divisions. No heads of national organizations were appointed to this body, thereby further tilting power within Philips away from the national organizations toward the product divisions.

Despite these changes, Philips' competitive position continued to deteriorate. Many outside observers attributed this slide to the dead hand of the huge head office bureaucracy at Eindhoven (which comprised more than 3000 people in 1989). They argued that while van de Klugt had changed the organizational chart, much of this change was superficial. Real power, they argued, still lay with the Eindhoven bureaucracy and their allies in the national organizations. In support of this view, they pointed out that since 1986 Philips' work force had declined by less than 10 percent, instead of the 30 percent reduction that many analysts were calling for.

Alarmed by a 1989 loss of $1.06 billion, the board forced van de Klugt to resign in May 1990. He was replaced by Jan Timmer. Timmer quickly announced that he would cut Philips's worldwide work force by 10,000, to 283,000, and launch a $1.4 billion restructuring. Investors were unimpressed—most of them thought that the company needed to lose 40,000–50,000 jobs—and reacted by knocking the share price down by 7 percent. Since then, however, Timmer had made some progress. In mid-1991, he sold off Philips's minicomputer division—which at the time was losing $1 million per day—to Digital Equipment. He also announced plans to reduce costs by $1.2 billion by cutting the work force by 55,000. In addition, he entered into a strategic alliance with Matsushita, the Japanese electronic giant, to manufacture and market the Digital Compact Cassette (DCC). Developed by Philips and due to be introduced in late 1992, the DCC reproduces the sound of a compact disc on a tape. The DCC's great selling point is that buyers will be able to play their old analog tape cassettes on the new system. The DCC's chief rival is a portable compact disc system from Sony called Mini-Disk. Many observers see a replay of the classic battle between the VHS and Betamax video recorder standards in the coming battle between the DCC and the Mini-Disk. If the DCC wins, it could be the remaking of Philips.

REFERENCES

Aguilar, F. J., and M. Y. Yoshino. "The Philips Group: 1987." Harvard Business School, Case #388-050.

Anonymous. "Philips Fights the Flab." *The Economist,* April 7, 1992, pp. 73–74.

Bartlett, C. A., and S. Ghoshal. *Managing Across Borders: The Transnational Solution.* Boston, Mass.: Harvard Business School Press, 1989.

Kapstein, J., and J. Levine. "A Would-Be World Beater Takes a Beating." *Business Week,* July 16, 1990, pp. 41–42.

Levine, J. "Philips's Big Gamble." *Business Week,* August 5, 1991, pp. 34–36.

CASE 17

"Ramrod" Stockwell ——————————— CHARLES PERROW

The Benson Metal Company employs about 1500 people, is listed on the stock exchange, and has been in existence for many decades. It makes a variety of metals that are purchased by manufacturers or specialized metal firms. It is one of the five or six leading firms in the specialty steel industry. This industry produces steels in fairly small quantities with a variety of characteristics. Orders tend to be in terms of pounds rather than tons, although a 1000-pound order is not unusual. For some of the steels, 100 pounds is an average order.

The technology for producing specialty steels in the firm is fairly well established, but there is still a good deal of guesswork, skill, and even some "black magic" involved. Small changes are made in the ingredients going into the melting process, often amounting to the addition of a tiny bit of expensive alloying material in order to produce varieties of specialty steels. Competitors can analyze one another's products and generally produce the same product without too much difficulty, although there are some secrets. There are also important variations stemming from the type of equipment used to melt, cog, roll, and finish the steel.

In the period that we are considering, the Benson Company and some of its competitors were steadily moving into more sophisticated and technically more difficult steels, largely for the aerospace industry. The aerospace products were far more difficult to make, required more research skills and metallurgical analysis, and required more "delicate" handling in all stages of production, even though the same basic equipment was involved. Furthermore, they were marketed in a different fashion. They were produced to the specifications of government subcontractors, and government inspectors were often in the plant to watch all stages of production. One firm might be able to produce a particular kind of steel that another firm could not produce even though it had tried. These steels were considerably more expensive than the specialty steels, and failures to meet specifications resulted in more substantial losses for the company. At the time of the study about 20 percent of the cash value output was in aerospace metals.

The chairman, Fred Benson, had been president (managing director) of the company for two decades

Charles Perrow, Yale University. Reprinted with permission.

before moving up to this position. He is an elderly man but has a strong will and is much revered in the company for having built it up to its present size and influence. The president, Tom Hollis, has been in office for about four years; he was formerly the sales director and has worked closely with Fred Benson over many years. Hollis has three or four years to go before expected retirement. His assistant, Joe Craig, had been a sales manager in one of the smaller offices. It is the custom of this firm to pick promising people from middle-management and put them in the "assistant-to" position for perhaps a year to groom them for higher offices in their division. For some time these people had come from sales, and they generally went back as managers of large districts, from whence they might be promoted to a sales manager position in the main office.

Dick Benson, the executive vice president (roughly, general manager), is the son of Fred Benson. He is generally regarded as being willing, fairly competent, and decent, but weak and still much under his father's thumb. Traditionally, the executive vice president became president. Dick is not thought to be up to that job, but it is believed that he will get it anyway.

Ramsey Stockwell, vice president of production, had come into the organization as an experienced engineer about six years before. He rose rather rapidly to his present position. Rob Bronson, vice president of sales, succeeded Dick Benson after Benson had a rather short term as vice president of sales. Alan Carswell, the vice president of research, has a doctorate in metallurgy and some patents in his name, but he is not considered an aggressive researcher or an aggressive in-fighter in the company.

THE PROBLEM

When the research team studied Benson Metal, there were the usual problems of competition and price-cutting, the difficulties with the new aerospace metals, and inadequate plant facilities for a growing industry and company. However, the problem that particularly interests us here concerned the vice president of production, Ramsey Stockwell. He was regarded as a very competent production man. His loyalty to the company was unquestioned. He managed to keep outdated facilities operating and still had been able to push through the construction of quite modern facilities in the finishing phases of the production process. But he was in trouble with his own staff and with other divisions of the company, principally sales.

It was widely noted that Stockwell failed to delegate authority to his subordinates. A steady stream of people came into his office asking for permission for this and that or bringing questions to him. People who took some action on their own could be bawled out unmercifully at times. At other times they were left on their own because of the heavy demands on Stockwell's time, given his frequent attention to details in some matters, particularly those concerning schedules and priorities. He "contracted" the lines of authority by giving orders directly to a manager or even to a head foreman rather than by working through the intermediate levels. This violated the chain of command, left managers uninformed, and reduced their authority. It was sometimes noted that he had good men under him but did not always let them do their jobs.

The key group of production men rarely met in a group unless it was to be bawled out by Stockwell. Coordinating committees and the like existed mainly on paper.

More serious perhaps than this was the relationship to sales. Rob Bronson was widely regarded as an extremely bright, capable, likable, and up-and-coming manager. The sales division performed like a well-oiled machine but also had the enthusiasm and flashes of brilliance that indicated considerable adaptability. Morale was high, and identification with the company was complete. However, sales personnel found it quite difficult to get reliable information from production as to delivery dates or even what stage in the process a product was in.

Through long tradition, they were able to get special orders thrust into the work flow when they wanted to, but they often could not find out what this was going to do to normal orders, or even how disruptive this might be. The reason was that Stockwell would not allow production people to give any but the most routine information to sales personnel. In fact, because of the high centralization of authority and information in production, production personnel often did not know themselves. "Ramrod" Stockwell knew, and the only way to get information out of him was to go up the sales line to Rob Bronson. The vice president of sales could get the information from the vice president of production.

But Bronson had more troubles than just not wanting to waste his time by calling Stockwell about status reports. At the weekly top-management meeting, which involved all personnel from the vice presidential level and above, and frequently a few from below that level, Bronson would continually ask Stockwell whether something or other could be done. Stockwell always said that he thought it could be. He could not be pressed for any better estimations, and he rarely admitted that a job was, in fact, not possible. Even queries from President Tom Hollis could not evoke accurate forecasts from Stockwell. Consequently, planning on the part of sales and other divisions was difficult, and failures on the part of production were many because it always vaguely promised so much. Stockwell was willing to try anything, and worked his head off at it, but the rest of the group knew that many of these attempts would fail.

While the men under Stockwell resented the way he took over their jobs at times and the lack of information available to them about other aspects of production, they were loyal to him. They admired his ability and they knew that he fought off the continual pressure of sales to slip in special orders, change schedules, or blame production for rejects. "Sales gets all the glory here" said one. "At the semiannual company meeting last week, the chairman of the board and the managing director of the company couldn't compliment sales enough for their good work, but there was only the stock 'well done' for production; 'well done given the trying circumstances.' Hell, Sales is what is trying us." The annual reports over the years credited sales for the good years and referred to equipment failures, crowded or poor production facilities, and the like in bad years. But it was also true that problems still remained even after Stockwell finally managed to pry some new production facilities out of the board of directors.

Stockwell was also isolated socially from the right group of top personnel: He tended to work later than most, had rougher manners, was less concerned with cultural activities, and rarely played golf. He occasionally relaxed with the manager of aerospace sales, who, incidentally, was the only high-level sales person who tended to defend Stockwell. "Ramrod's a rough diamond; I don't know that we ought to try to polish him," he sometimes said.

But polishing was in the minds of many. "Great production man—amazing when he gets out of that mill. But he doesn't know how to handle people. He won't delegate; he won't tell us when he is in trouble with something; he builds a fence around his men, preventing easy exchange," said the president. "Bullheaded as hell—he was good a few years ago, but I would never give him the job again," said the chairman of the board. He disagreed with the president that Stockwell could change. "You can't change people's personalities, least of all production men." "He's in a tough position," said the vice president of sales, "and he has to be able to get his men to work with him, not against him, and we all have to work together in today's market. I just wish he would not be so uptight."

A year or so before, the president had approached Stockwell about taking a couple of weeks off and joining a leadership training session. Stockwell would have nothing to do with it and was offended. The president waited a few months, then announced that he had arranged for the personnel manager and each of the directors to attend successive four-day T-group sessions run by a well-known organization. This had been agreed on at one of the directors' meetings, though no one had taken it very seriously. One by one, the directors came back with marked enthusiasm for the program. "It's almost as if they had our company in mind when they designed it," said one. Some started having evening and weekend sessions with their staff, occasionally using the personnel manager, who had had more experience with this than the others. Stockwell was scheduled to be the last one to attend the four-day session, but he canceled at the last minute—there were too many crises in the plant, he said, to go off that time. In fact, several had developed over the previous few weeks.

That did it, as far as the other vice presidents were concerned. They got together themselves, then with the president and executive vice president, and said that they had to get to the bottom of the problem. A top-level group session should be held to discuss the tensions that were accumulating. The friction between production and sales was spilling over into other areas as well, and the morale of management in general was suffering. They acknowledged that they put a lot of pressure on production, and were probably at fault in this or that matter, and thus a session would do all the directors good, not just Stockwell. The president hesitated. Stockwell, he felt, would just ride it out. Besides, he added, the "Old Man" (chairman of the board) was skeptical of such techniques. The executive vice president was quite unenthusiastic. It was remarked later that Stockwell had never recognized his official authority, and thus young Dick feared any open confrontation.

But events overtook the plan of the vice president. A first-class crisis had developed involving a major order for their oldest and best customer, and an emergency top-management meeting was called, which included several of their subordinates. Three in particular were involved: Joe Craig, assistant to the president, who knows well the problems at the plant in his role as troubleshooter for the managing director; Sandy Falk, vice president of personnel, who is sophisticated about leadership training programs and in a position to watch a good bit of the bickering at the middle and lower levels between sales and production; Bill Bletchford, manager of finishing, who is loyal to Stockwell and who has the most modern-equipped phase of the production process and the most to do with sales. It was in his department that the jam had occurred, due to some massive scheduling changes at the rolling phase and to the failure of key equipment.

In the meeting, the ground is gone over thoroughly. With their backs to the wall, the two production men, behaving somewhat uncharacteristically in an open meeting, charge sales with devious tactics for introducing special orders and for acting on partial and misinterpreted information from a foreman. Joe Craig knows, and admits, that the specialty A sales manager made promises to the customer without checking with the vice president of sales, who could have checked with Stockwell. "He was right," says Vice President Bronson, "I can't spend all my time calling Ramsey about status reports; if Harrison can't find out from production on an official basis, he has to do the best he can." Ramsey Stockwell, after his forceful outburst about misleading information through devious tactics, falls into a hardened silence, answering only direct questions, and then briefly. The manager of finishing and the specialty A sales manager start working on each other. Sandy Falk, of personnel, knows they have been enemies for years, so he intervenes as best he can. The vice president of research, Carswell, a reflective man, often worried about elusive dimensions of company problems, then calls a halt with the following speech:

> You're all wrong and you're all right. I have heard bits and pieces of this fracas a hundred times over the last two or three years, and it gets worse each year. The facts of this damn case don't matter unless all you want is to score points with your opponents. What is wrong is something with the whole team here. I don't know what it is, but I know that we have to radically rethink our relations with one another. Three years ago this kind of thing rarely happened; now it is starting to happen all the time. And it is a time when we can't afford it. There is no more growth in our bread-and-butter line, specialty steels. The money, and the growth, is in aerospace; we all know that. Without aerospace we will just stand still. Maybe that's part of it. But maybe Ramsey's part of it too; this

crisis is over specialty steel, and more of them seem to concern that than aerospace, so it can't be the product shift or that only. Some part of it has to be people, and you're on the hot seat, Ramsey.

Carswell let that sink in, then went on.

Or maybe it's something more than even these .... It is not being pulled together at the top, or maybe, the old way of pulling it together won't work anymore. I'm talking about you, Tom [Hollis], as well as Fred [Benson, the chairman of the board, who did not attend these meetings] and Dick [the executive vice president, and heir apparent]. I don't know what it is, here are Ramsey and Rob at loggerheads; neither of them are fools, and both of them are working their heads off. Maybe the problem is above their level.

There is a long silence. Assume you break the silence with your own analysis. What would that be?

CASE 18

Rondell Data Corporation ———————— JOHN A. SEEGER

"God damn it, he's done it again?" Frank Forbus threw the stack of prints and specifications down on his desk in disgust. The Model 802 wide-band modulator, released for production the previous Thursday, had just come back to Frank's Engineering Services Department with a caustic note that began, "This one can't be produced either .... " It was the fourth time production had kicked the design back.

Frank Forbus, director of engineering for Rondell Data Corporation, was normally a quiet man. But the Model 802 was stretching his patience; it was beginning to look just like other new products that had hit delays and problems in the transition from design to production during the eight months Frank had worked for Rondell. These problems were nothing new at the sprawling old Rondell factory; Frank's predecessor in the engineering job had run afoul of them, too, and had finally been fired for protesting too vehemently about the other departments. But the Model 802 should have been different. Frank had met two months before (July 3, 1978) with the firm's president, Bill Hunt, and with factory superintendent Dave Schwab to smooth the way for the new modulator design. He thought back to the meeting....

"Now we all know there's a tight deadline on the 802," Bill Hunt Said, "and Frank's done well to ask us to talk about its introduction. I'm counting on both of you to find any snags in the system and to work together to get that first production run out by October second. Can you do it?"

"We can do it in production if we get a clean design two weeks from now, as scheduled," answered Dave

Schwab, the grizzled factory superintendent. "Frank and I have already talked about that, of course. I'm setting aside time in the card room and the machine shop, and we'll be ready. If the design goes over schedule, though, I'll have to fill in with other runs, and it will cost us a bundle to break in for the 802. How does it look in engineering, Frank?"

"I've just reviewed the design for the second time," Frank replied. "If Ron Porter can keep the salesmen out of our hair and avoid any more last-minute changes, we've got a shot. I've pulled the draftsmen off three other overdue jobs to get this one out. But, Dave, that means we can't spring engineers loose to confer with your production people on manufacturing problems."

"Well, Frank, most of those problems are caused by the engineers, and we need them to resolve the difficulties. We've all agreed that production bugs come from both of us bowing to sales pressure, and putting equipment into production before the designs are really ready. That's just what we're trying to avoid on the 802. But I can't have 500 people sitting on their hands waiting for an answer from your people. We'll have to have some engineering support.,

Bill Hunt broke in. "So long as you two can talk calmly about the problem I'm confident you can resolve it. What a relief it is, Frank, to hear the way you're approaching this. With Kilmann (the previous director of engineering) this conversation would have been a shouting match. Right, Dave?" Dave nodded and smiled.

"Now there's one other thing you should both be aware of," Hunt continued. "Doc Reeves and I talked last night about a new filtering technique, one that

John A. Seeger, Professor of Management, Bentley College. Reprinted with permission.

might improve the signal-to-noise ratio of the 802 by a factor of two. There's a chance Doc can come up with it before the 802 reaches production, and if it's possible, I'd like to use the new filters. That would give us a real jump on the competition."

Four days after that meeting, Frank found that two of his key people on the 802 design had been called to production for emergency consultation on a bug found in final assembly: two halves of a new data transmission interface wouldn't fit together because recent changes in the front end required a different chassis design for the back end.

Another week later, Doc Reeves walked into Frank's office, proud as a new parent, with the new filter design. "This won't affect the other modules of the 802 much," Doc had said. "Look, it takes three new cards, a few connectors, some changes in the wiring harness, and some new shielding, and that's all."

Frank had tried to resist the last-minute design changes, but Bill Hunt had stood firm. With a lot of overtime by the engineers and draftsmen, engineering services should still be able to finish the prints in time.

Two engineers and three draftsmen went onto twelve-hour days to get the 802 ready, but the prints were still five days late reaching Dave Schwab. Two days later, the prints came back to Frank, heavily annotated in red. Schwab had worked all day Saturday to review the job and had found more than a dozen discrepancies in the prints—most of them caused by the new filter design and insufficient checking time before release. Correction of those design faults had brought on a new generation of discrepancies; Schwab's cover note on the second return of the prints indicated he'd had to release the machine capacity he'd been holding for the 802. On the third iteration, Schwab committed his photo and plating capacity to another rush job. The 802 would be at least one month late getting into production. Ron Porter, vice president for sales, was furious. His customer needed 100 units NOW, he said. Rondell was the customer's only late supplier.

"Here we go again," thought Frank Forbus.

COMPANY HISTORY

Rondell Data Corporation traced its lineage through several generations of electronics technology. Its original founder, Bob Rondell, had set the firm up in 1920 as "Rondell Equipment Company" to manufacture several electrical testing devices he had invented as an engineering faculty member at a large university. The firm branched into radio broadcasting equipment in 1947 and

into data transmission equipment in the early 1960s. A well-established corps of direct salespeople, mostly engineers, called on industrial, scientific, and government accounts, but concentrated heavily on original equipment manufacturers. In this market, Rondell had a long-standing reputation as a source of high-quality, innovative designs. The firm's salespeople fed a continual stream of challenging problems into the Engineering Department, where the creative genius of Ed "Doc" Reeves and several dozen other engineers 11 converted problems to solutions" (as the sales brochure bragged). Product design formed the spearhead of Rondell's growth.

By 1978, Rondell offered a wide range of products in its two major lines. Broadcast equipment sales had benefitted from the growth of UHF TV and FM radio; it now accounted for 35 percent of company sales. Data transmission had blossomed, and in this field an increasing number of orders called for unique specifications, ranging from specialized display panels to entirely untried designs.

The company had grown from 100 employees in 1947 to over 800 in 1978. (Exhibit 1 shows the 1978 organization chart of key employees.) Bill Hunt, who had been a student of the company's founder, had presided over most of that growth and took great pride in preserving the "family spirit" of the old organization. Informal relationships between Rondell's veteran employees formed the backbone of the firm's day-to-day operations; all the managers relied on personal contact, and Hunt often insisted that the absence of bureaucratic red tape was a key factor in recruiting outstanding engineering talent. The personal management approach extended throughout the factory. All exempt employees were paid on a straight salary plus a share of the profits. Rondell boasted an extremely loyal group of senior employees and very low turnover in nearly all areas of the company.

The highest turnover job in the firm was Frank Forbus's. Frank had joined Rondell in January 1978, replacing Jim Kilmann, who had been director of engineering for only ten months. Kilmann, in turn, had replaced Tom MacLeod, a talented engineer who had made a promising start but had taken to drink after a year in the job. MacLeod's predecessor had been a genial old-timer who retired at 70 after thirty years in charge of engineering. (Doc Reeves had refused the directorship in each of the recent changes, saying, "Hell, that's no promotion for a bench man like me. I'm no administrator.")

For several years, the firm had experienced a steadily increasing number of disputes between research, engineering, sales, and production people—disputes

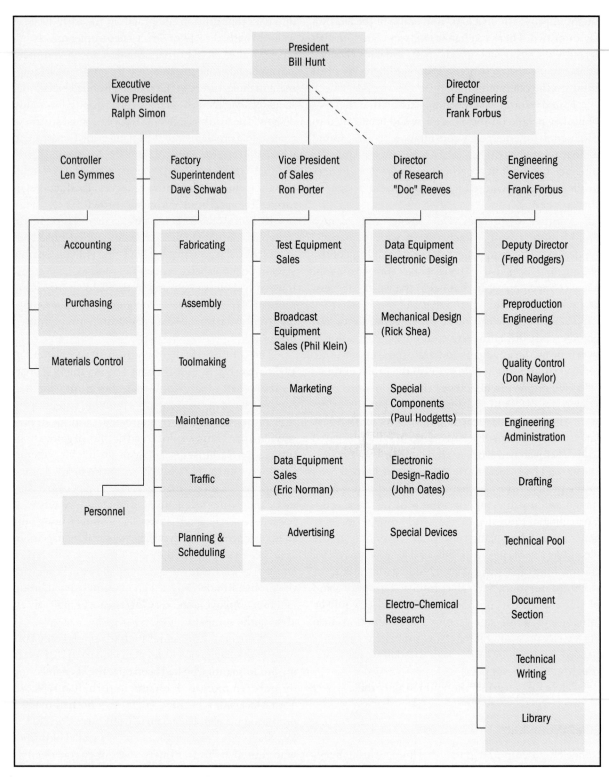

EXHIBIT 1   Rondell Data Corporation 1978 Organization Chart

generally centered on the problem of new product introduction. Quarrels between departments became more numerous under MacLeod, Kilmann, and Forbus. Some managers associated those disputes with the company's recent decline in profitability—a decline that, in spite of higher sales and gross revenues, was beginning to bother people in 1977. President Bill Hunt commented:

> Better cooperation, I'm sure, could increase our output by 5-10 percent. I'd hoped Kilmann could solve the problems, but pretty obviously he was too young, too arrogant. People like him—that conflict type of personality—bother me. I don't like strife, and with him it seemed I spent all my time smoothing out arguments. Kilmann tried to tell everyone else how to run their departments, without having his own house in order. That approach just wouldn't work here at Rondell. Frank Forbus, now, seems much more in tune with our style of organization. I'm really hopeful now.
>
> Still, we have just as many problems now as we did last year. Maybe even more. I hope Frank can get a handle on engineering services soon....

THE ENGINEERING DEPARTMENT: RESEARCH

According to the organization chart (see Exhibit 1), Frank Forbus was in charge of both research (really the product development function) and engineering services (which provided engineering support). To Forbus, however, the relationship with research was not so clear-cut:

> Doc Reeves is one of the world's unique people, and none of us would have it any other way. He's a creative genius. Sure, the chart says he works for me, but we all know Doc does his own thing. He's not the least bit interested in management routines, and I can't count on him to take any responsibility in scheduling projects, or checking budgets, or what-have-you. But as long as Doc is director of research, you can bet this company will keep on leading the field. He has more ideas per hour than most people have per year, and he keeps the whole engineering staff fired up. Everybody loves Doc—and you can count me in on that, too. In a way, he works for me, sure. But that's not what's important.

"Doc" Reeves—unhurried, contemplative, casual, and candid—tipped his stool back against the wall of his research cubicle and talked about what was important:

> Development engineering. That's where the company's future rests. Either we have it there, or we don't have it.
>
> There's no kidding ourselves that we're anything but a bunch of Rube Goldbergs here. But that's where the biggest kicks come from—from solving development problems, and dreaming up new ways of doing things. That's why I so look forward to the special contracts we get involved in. We accept them not for the revenue they represent, but because they subsidize the basic development work which goes into all our basic products.
>
> This is a fantastic place to work. I have a great crew and they can really deliver when the chips are down. Why, Bill Hunt and I (he gestured toward the neighboring cubicle, where the president's name hung over the door) are likely to find as many people here at work at 10:00 P.M. as at 3:00 in the afternoon. The important thing here is the relationships between people; they're based on mutual respect, not on policies and procedures. Administrative red tape is a pain. It takes away from development time.
>
> Problems? Sure, there are problems now and then. There are power interests in production, where they sometimes resist change. But I'm not a fighting man, you know. I suppose if I were, I might go in there and push my weight around a little. But I'm an engineer and can do more for Rondell sitting right here or working with my own people. That's what brings results.

Other members of the Research Department echoed Doc's views and added some additional sources of satisfaction with their work. They were proud of the personal contacts they built up with customers' technical staffs—contacts that increasingly involved travel to the customers' factories to serve as expert advisers in the preparation of overall system design specifications. The engineers were also delighted with the department's encouragement of their personal development, continuing education, and independence on the job.

But there were problems, too. Rick Shea, of the mechanical design section, noted:

> In the old days I really enjoyed the work—and the people I worked with. But now there's a lot of irritation. I don't like someone breathing down my neck. You can be hurried into jeopardizing the design.

John Oates, head of the radio electronic design section, was another designer with definite views:

> Production engineering is almost nonexistent in this company. Very little is done by the preproduction section in engineering services. Frank Forbus has been trying to get preproduction into the picture, but he won't succeed because you can't start from such an ambiguous position. There have been three directors of engineering in three years. Frank can't hold his own against the others in the company. Kilmann was too aggressive. Perhaps no amount of tact would have succeeded.

Paul Hodgetts was head of special components in the R & D department. Like the rest of the department, he valued bench work. But he complained of engineering services:

> The services don't do things we want them to do. Instead, they tell us what they're going to do. I should probably go to Frank, but I

don't get any decisions there. I know I should go through Frank, but this holds things up, so I often go direct.

THE ENGINEERING DEPARTMENT: ENGINEERING SERVICES

The Engineering Services Department provided ancillary services to R & D and served as liaison between engineering and the other Rondell departments. Among its main functions were drafting; management of the central technicians' pool; scheduling and expediting engineering products; documentation and publication of parts lists and engineering orders; preproduction engineering (consisting of the final integration of individual design components into mechanically compatible packages); and quality control (which included inspection of incoming parts and materials, and final inspection of subassemblies and finished equipment). Top management's description of the department included the line, "ESD is responsible for maintaining cooperation with other departments, providing services to the development engineers, and freeing more valuable people in R & D from essential activities that are diversions from and beneath their main competence."

Many of Frank Forbus's seventy-five employees were located in other departments. Quality control people were scattered through the manufacturing and receiving areas, and technicians worked primarily in the research area or the prototype fabrication room. The remaining ESD personnel were assigned to leftover nooks and crannies near production or engineering sections.

Frank Forbus described his position:

> My biggest problem is getting acceptance from the people I work with. I've moved slowly rather than risk antagonism. I saw what happened to Kilmann, and I want to avoid that. But although his precipitate action had won over a few of the younger R & D people, he certainly didn't have the department's backing. Of course, it was the resentment of other departments that eventually caused his discharge. People have been slow accepting me here. There's nothing really overt, but I get a negative reaction to my ideas.
>
> My role in the company has never been well defined really. It's complicated by Doc's unique position, of course, and also by the fact that ESD sort of grew by itself over the years, as the design engineers concentrated more and more on the creative parts of product development. I wish I could be more involved in the technical side. That's been my training, and it's a lot of fun. But in our setup, the technical side is the least necessary for me to be involved in.
>
> Schwab (production head) is hard to get along with. Before I came and after Kilmann left, there were six months intervening

when no one was really doing any scheduling. No work loads were figured, and unrealistic promises were made about releases. This puts us in an awkward position. We've been scheduling way beyond our capacity to manufacture or engineer.

Certain people within R & D—for instance, John Oates, head of the radio electronic design section—understand scheduling well and meet project deadlines, but this is not generally true of the rest of the R & D department, especially the mechanical engineers who won't commit themselves. Most of the complaints come from sales and production department heads because items—like the 802—are going to production before they are fully developed, under pressure from sales to get out the unit, and this snags the whole process. Somehow, engineering services should be able to intervene and resolve these complaints, but I haven't made much headway so far. I should be able to go to Hunt for help, but he's too busy most of the time, and his major interest is the design side of engineering, where he got his own start. Sometimes he talks as though he's the engineering director as well as president. I have to put my foot down; there are problems here that the front office just doesn't understand.

Salespeople were often observed taking their problems directly to designers, while production frequently threw designs back at R & D, claiming they could not be produced and demanding the prompt attention of particular design engineers. The latter were frequently observed in conference with production supervisors on the assembly floor. Frank went on:

> The designers seem to feel they're losing something when one of us tries to help. They feel it's a reflection on them to have someone take over what they've been doing. They seem to want to carry a project right through to the final stages, particularly the mechanical people. Consequently, engineering services people are used below their capacity to contribute and our department is denied functions it should be performing. There's not as much use made of engineering services as there should be.

Frank Forbus's technician supervisor added his comments:

> Production picks out the engineer who'll be the "bum of the month." They pick on every little detail instead of using their heads and making the minor changes that have to be made. The fifteen-to-twenty-year people shouldn't have to prove their ability any more, but they spend four hours defending themselves and four hours getting the job done. I have no one to go to when I need help. Frank Forbus is afraid. I'm trying to help him but he can't help me at this time. I'm responsible for fifty people and I've got to support them.

Fred Rodgers, whom Frank had brought with him to the company as an assistant, gave another view of the situation:

I try to get our people in preproduction to take responsibility, but they're not used to it and people in other departments don't usually see them as best qualified to solve the problem. There's a real barrier for a newcomer here. Gaining people's confidence is hard. More and more, I'm wondering whether there really is a job for me here.

(Rodgers left Rondell a month later.) Another of Forbus's subordinates gave his view:

If Doc gets a new product idea, you can't argue. But he's too optimistic. He judges that others can do what he does—but there's only one Doc Reeves. We've had 900 production change orders this year—they changed 2500 drawings. If I were in Frank's shoes I'd put my foot down on all this new development. I'd look at the reworking we're doing and get production set up the way I wanted it. Kilmann was fired when he was doing a good job. He was getting some system in the company's operations. Of course, it hurt some people. There is no denying that Doc is the most important person in the company. What gets overlooked is that Hunt is a close second, not just politically but in terms of what he contributes technically and in customer relations.

This subordinate explained that he sometimes went out into the production department but that Schwab, the production head, resented this. Personnel in production said that Kilmann had failed to show respect for old-timers and was always meddling in other departments' business. This was why he had been fired, they contended.

Don Taylor was in charge of quality control. He commented:

I am now much more concerned with administration and less with work. It is one of the evils you get into. There is tremendous detail in this job. I listen to everyone's opinion. Everybody is important. There shouldn't be distinctions—distinctions between people. I'm not sure whether Frank has to be a fireball like Kilmann. I think the real question is whether Frank is getting the job done. I know my job is essential. I want to supply service to the more talented people and give them information so they can do their jobs better.

THE SALES DEPARTMENT

Ron Porter was angry. His job was supposed to be selling, he said, but instead it had turned into settling disputes inside the plant and making excuses to waiting customers. He jabbed a finger toward his desk:

You see that telephone? I'm actually afraid nowadays to hear it ring. Three times out of five, it will be a customer who's hurting because we've failed to deliver on schedule. The other two calls will be from production or ESD, telling me some schedule has slipped again.

The Model 802 is typical. Absolutely typical. We padded the delivery date by six weeks, to allow for contingencies. Within two months, the slack had evaporated. Now it looks like we'll be lucky to ship it before Christmas. (It was now November 28.) We're ruining our reputation in the market. Why, just last week one of our best customers—people we've worked with for fifteen years—tried to hang a penalty clause on their latest order.

We shouldn't have to be after the engineers all the time. They should be able to see what problems they create without our telling them.

Phil Klein, head of broadcast sales under Porter, noted that many sales decisions were made by top management. Sales was understaffed, he thought, and had never really been able to get on top of the job.

We have grown further and further away from engineering. The director of engineering does not pass on the information that we give him. We need better relationships there. It is very difficult for us to talk to customers about development problems without technical help. We need each other. The whole of engineering is now too isolated from the outside world. The morale of ESD is very low. They're in a bad spot—they're not well organized.

People don't take much to outsiders here. Much of this is because the expectation is built up by top management that jobs will be filled from the bottom. So it's really tough when an outsider like Frank comes in.

Eric Norman, order and pricing coordinator for data equipment, talked about his own relationships with the Production Department:

Actually, I get along with them fairly well. Oh, things could be better of course, if they were more cooperative generally. They always seem to say, "It's my bat and ball, and we're playing by my rules." People are afraid to make production mad; there's a lot of power in there. But you've got to understand that production has its own set of problems. And nobody in Rondell is working any harder than Dave Schwab to try to straighten things out.

THE PRODUCTION DEPARTMENT

Dave Schwab had joined Rondell just after the Korean War, in which he had seen combat duty (at the Yalu River) and intelligence duty at Pyong Yang. Both experiences had been useful in his first year of civilian employment at Rondell: The wartime factory superintendent and several middle managers had been, apparently, indulging in highly questionable side deals with Rondell's suppliers. Dave Schwab had gathered evidence, revealed the situation to Bill Hunt, and stood by the president in the ensuing unsavory situation. Seven months after joining the company, Dave was named factory superintendent.

His first move had been to replace the fallen managers with a new team from outside. This group did not share the traditional Rondell emphasis on informality and friendly personal relationships and had worked long and hard to install systematic manufacturing methods and procedures. Before the reorganization, production had controlled purchasing, stock control, and final quality control (where final assembly of products in cabinets was accomplished). Because of the wartime events, management decided on a check- and-balance system of organization and removed these three departments from production jurisdiction. The new production managers felt they had been unjustly penalized by this organization, particularly since they had uncovered the behavior that was detrimental to the company in the first place.

By 1978, the production department had grown to 500 employees, 60 percent of whom worked in the assembly area—an unusually pleasant environment that had been commended by *Factory* magazine for its colorful decoration, cleanliness, and low noise level. An additional 30 percent of the work force, mostly skilled machinists, staffed the finishing and fabrication department. About sixty others performed scheduling, supervisory, and maintenance duties. Production workers were nonunion, hourly-paid, and participated in both the liberal profit-sharing program and the stock purchase plan. Morale in production was traditionally high, and turnover was extremely low.

Dave Schwab commented:

> To be efficient, production has to be a self-contained department. We have to control what comes into the department and what goes out. That's why purchasing, inventory control, and quality ought to run out of this office. We'd eliminate a lot of problems with better control there. Why, even Don Taylor in QC would rather work for me than for ESD; he's said so himself. We understand his problems better.
>
> The other departments should be self-contained too. That's why I always avoid the underlings and go straight to the department heads with any questions. I always go down the line.
>
> I have to protect my people from outside disturbances. Look what would happen if I let unfinished, half-baked designs in here—there'd be chaos. The bugs have to be found before the drawings go into the shop, and it seems I'm the one who has to find them. Look at the 802, for example. (Dave had spent most of Thanksgiving Day [it was now November 28] red-penciling the latest set

of prints.) ESD should have found every one of those discrepancies. They just don't check drawings properly. They change most of the things I flag, but then they fail to trace through the impact of those changes on the rest of the design. I shouldn't have to do that. And those engineers are tolerance crazy. They want everything to a millionth of an inch. I'm the only one in the company who's had any experience with actually machining things to a millionth of an inch. We make sure that the things that engineers say on their drawings actually have to be that way and whether they're obtainable from the kind of raw material we buy.

> That shouldn't be production's responsibility, but I have to do it. Accepting bad prints wouldn't let us ship the order any quicker. We'd only make a lot of junk that had to be reworked. And that would take even longer.
>
> This way, I get to be known as the bad guy, but I guess that's just part of the job. (He paused with a wry smile.) Of course, what really gets them is that I don't even have a degree.

Dave had fewer bones to pick with the Sales Department because, he said, they trusted him.

> When we give Ron Porter a shipping date, he knows the equipment will be shipped then.
>
> You've got to recognize, though, that all of our new-product problems stem from sales making absurd commitments on equipment that hasn't been fully developed. That always means trouble. Unfortunately, Hunt always backs sales up, even when they're wrong. He always favors them over us.

Ralph Simon, age 65, executive vice president of the company, had direct responsibility for Rondell's production department. He said:

> There shouldn't really be a dividing of departments among top management in the company. The president should be czar over all. The production people ask me to do something for them, and I really can't do it. It creates bad feelings between engineering and production, this special attention that they [R & D] get from Bill. But then Hunt likes to dabble in design. Schwab feels that production is treated like a poor relation.

THE EXECUTIVE COMMITTEE

At the executive committee meeting on December 6, it was duly recorded that Dave Schwab had accepted the prints and specifications for the Model 802 modulator, and had set Friday, December 29, as the shipping date for the first ten pieces. Bill Hunt, in the chairperson's role, shook his head and changed the subject quickly when Frank tried to open the agenda to a discussion of interdepartmental coordination.

The executive committee itself was a brainchild of Rondell's controller, Len Symmes, who was well aware of the disputes that plagued the company. Symmes had convinced Bill Hunt and Ralph Simon to meet every two weeks with their department heads, and the meetings were formalized with Hunt, Simon, Ron Porter, Dave Schwab, Frank Forbus, Doc Reeves, Symmes, and the personnel director attending. Symmes explained his intent and the results:

> Doing things collectively and informally just doesn't work as well as it used to. Things have been gradually getting worse for at least two years now. We had to start thinking in terms of formal organization relationships. I did the first organization chart, and the executive committee was my idea too—but neither idea is contributing much help, I'm afraid. It takes top management to make an organization click. The rest of us can't act much differently until the top people see the need for us to change.
>
> I had hoped the committee especially would help get the department managers into a constructive planning process. It hasn't worked out that way because Mr. Hunt really doesn't see the need for it. He uses the meetings as a place to pass on routine information.

MERRY CHRISTMAS

"Frank, I didn't know whether to tell you now, or after the holiday." It was Friday, December 22, and Frank Forbus was standing awkwardly in front of Bill Hunt's desk.

"But, I figured you'd work right through Christmas Day if we didn't have this talk, and that just wouldn't have been fair to you. I can't understand why we have such poor luck in the engineering director's job lately. And I don't think it's entirely your fault. But..."

Frank only heard half of Hunt's words, and said nothing in response. He'd be paid through February 28.... He should use the time for searching.... Hunt would help all he could.... Jim Kilmann was supposed to be doing well at his own new job, and might need more help....

Frank cleaned out his desk and numbly started home. The electronic carillon near his house was playing a Christmas carol. Frank thought again of Hunt's rationale: Conflict still plagued Rondell—and Frank had not made it go away. Maybe somebody else could do it.

"And what did Santa Claus bring you, Frankie?" he asked himself.

"The sack. Only the empty sack."

Company Index

Name Index

Subject Index